Internatior
the Sociology of Education

This collection brings together many of the world's leading sociologists of education to explore and address key issues and concerns within the discipline. The chapters draw upon theory and research to provide new accounts of contemporary educational processes, global trends, and changing and enduring forms of social conflict and social inequality.

The research, conducted by leading international scholars in the field, indicates that two complexly interrelated agendas are discernible in the heat and noise of educational change over the past 25 years. The first rests on a clear articulation by the state of its requirements of education. The second promotes at least the appearance of greater autonomy on the part of educational institutions in the delivery of those requirements. *The Routledge International Handbook of the Sociology of Education* examines the ways in which the sociology of education has responded to these two political agendas, addressing a range of issues which cover three key areas:

- perspectives and theories;
- social processes and practices;
- inequalities and resistances.

The book strongly communicates the vibrancy and diversity of the sociology of education and the nature of 'sociological work' in this field. It will be a primary resource for teachers, as well as a title of major interest to practising sociologists of education.

Michael W. Apple is John Bascom Professor of Curriculum and Instruction and Educational Policy Studies at the University of Wisconsin-Madison, USA.

Stephen J. Ball is Karl Mannheim Professor of Sociology of Education at the Institute of Education, University of London, UK.

Luis Armando Gandin is a Professor of Sociology of Education in the School of Education at the Federal University of Rio Grande do Sul in Porto Alegre, Brazil.

The Routledge International Handbook Series

The Routledge International Handbook of English, Language and Literacy Teaching
Edited by Dominic Wyse, Richard Andrews and James Hoffman

The Routledge International Handbook of the Sociology of Education
Edited by Michael W. Apple, Stephen J. Ball and Luis Armand Gandin

The Routledge International Handbook of Higher Education
Edited by Malcolm Tight, Ka Ho Mok, Jeroen Huisman and Christopher C. Morpew

The Routledge International Companion to Multicultural Education
Edited by James A. Banks

The Routledge International Handbook of Critical Education
Edited by Michael W. Apple, Wayne Au, and Luis Armando Gandin

The Routledge International Handbook of Lifelong Learning
Edited by Peter Jarvis

The Routledge International Handbook of the Sociology of Education

Edited by
Michael W. Apple, Stephen J. Ball
and Luis Armando Gandin

Routledge
Taylor & Francis Group

LONDON AND NEW YORK

First published 2010
by Routledge
2 Park Square, Milton Park, Abingdon, Oxon., OX14 4RN

Simultaneously published in the USA and Canada
by Routledge
711 Third Avenue, New York, NY 10017

Routledge is an imprint of the Taylor & Francis Group, an informa business

© 2010 Selection and editorial matter, Michael W. Apple, Stephen J. Ball and
Luis Armando Gandin; individual chapters, the contributors

Typeset in Bembo by
Florence Production Ltd, Stoodleigh, Devon
Printed and bound in Great Britain by
CPI Antony Rowe, Chippenham, Wiltshire

All rights reserved. No part of this book may be reprinted or
reproduced or utilised in any form or by any electronic, mechanical,
or other means, now known or hereafter invented, including photocopying
and recording, or in any information storage or retrieval system,
without permission in writing from the publishers.

Every effort has been made to contact copyright-holders. Please advise
the publisher of any errors or omissions, and these will be corrected in
subsequent editions.

British Library Cataloguing in Publication Data
A catalogue record for this book is available from the British Library

Library of Congress Cataloging in Publication Data
The Routledge international handbook of the sociology of education/
edited by Michael W. Apple, Stephen J. Ball and Luis Armando Gandin.
      p. cm.
   Includes bibliographical references.
   1. Educational sociology – Handbooks, manuals, etc.   I. Apple, Michael W.
   II. Ball, Stephen J.   III. Gandin, Luis Armando, 1967–.
   LC191.R684 2010
   306.43 – dc22   2009023567

ISBN10: 0–415–48663–7 (hbk)
ISBN10: 0–203–86370–4 (ebk)

ISBN13: 978–0–415–48663–7 (hbk)
ISBN13: 978–0–203–86370–1 (ebk)
ISBN13: 978–0–415–61996–7 (pbk)

Contents

CONTENTS

Contributors

Editors

Michael W. Apple is the John Bascom Professor of Curriculum and Instruction and Educational Policy Studies at the University of Wisconsin, Madison. Among his most recent books are *Educating the 'right' way: markets, standards, God, and inequality*, *The subaltern speak: curriculum, power, and educational struggles*, *Democratic schools: lessons in powerful education*, and *The Routledge international handbook of critical education*.

Stephen J. Ball is Karl Mannheim Professor of Sociology of Education at the Institute of Education, University of London, and Fellow of the British Academy. His work uses sociology in the analysis of education policy. Recent books include *Education plc* (Routledge, 2007) and *The education debate* (Policy Press, 2008).

Luis Armando Gandin is Professor of Sociology of Education at the Federal University of Rio Grande do Sul in Brazil. He is one of the editors of Currículo sem Fronteiras and Editor-in-Chief of *Educação & Realidade*. Professor Gandin has published several books in Brazil and Portugal and is one of the editors of *The Routledge international handbook of critical education*.

Contributors

Arshad Ali is a doctoral candidate at UCLA's Graduate School of Education and Information Studies. His current research explores the construction of the label 'Muslim' as an emerging racial and political marker in the United States. Arshad earned a Bachelor's degree in Sociology from UCLA, graduating *cum laude* with College Honors, and a Master's degree in Education from Harvard University, with a focus on pedagogy and educational policy. He has served as the founding director of MAPS, a UCLA-based outreach program working with students in south and west Los Angeles.

Jill Blackmore is a Professor of Education in the Faculty of Arts and Education, Deakin University, and Director of the Centre for Research in Educational Futures and Innovation. Recent publications include *Performing and reforming leaders: gender, educational restructuring and organizational change* (2007, SUNY Press).

Andrew Brantlinger is an Assistant Professor at the University of Maryland, College Park. His research interests are at the intersection of mathematics education, urban education and critical theory. He has trained and researched alternatively certified mathematics teachers in three urban school districts.

Ellen Brantlinger is Professor Emeritus from Indiana University-Bloomington. Her books include: *Politics of social class in secondary schools* (1993) and *Dividing classes: how the middle class negotiates and rationalizes school advantage* (2003). She directed the Undergraduate Special Education Teacher Education Programs at Indiana University for two decades and the Graduate Program in Curriculum Studies for five years.

Phillip Brown is Research Professor in the School of Social Sciences, Cardiff University. His forthcoming and recent books include: Brown, P., Lauder, H. and Ashton, D. (2009) *The global auction: the broken promises of opportunities, jobs and rewards*; Lauder, H., Brown, P., Dillabough J.-A. and Halsey, A.H. (eds) (2006) *Education, globalization and social change*, Oxford: Oxford University Press. Currently being translated into Japanese at Tokyo University: Brown, P. and Hesketh, A. (2004) *The mismanagement of talent*, Oxford: Oxford University Press; Brown, P., Green, A. and Lauder, H. (2001) *High skills: globalisation, competitiveness and skill formation*, Oxford: Oxford University Press. Brown, P. and Lauder, H. (2001) *Capitalism and social progress: the future of society in a global economy*, Basingstoke: Palgrave Press.

Laurel Cooley is an Associate Professor of Mathematics at Brooklyn College and studies urban mathematics education. She serves as co-PI for *MetroMath – mathematics for America's cities*. She teaches linear algebra to undergraduates and math content courses to secondary teachers.

Margaret Crean is a research assistant in Equality Studies in the UCD School of Social Justice, University College Dublin, and a community activist.

Brian Davies is Emeritus Professor of Education in the School of Social Sciences, Cardiff University, Wales, UK. Since his *Social control and education* (Methuen, 1976), he has taught and written widely on social theory and research, educational policy and pedagogic practice.

Greg Dimitriadis is Professor of Sociology of Education at the State University of New York at Buffalo.

Inés Dussel is a Researcher at the Latin American School for the Social Sciences (FLACSO)/ Argentina, and holds a Ph.D. from the University of Wisconsin-Madison. Her interests include the history and theory of pedagogy and schooling, and more recently the relationships between education and visual culture.

John Evans is Professor of Sociology of Education and Physical Education in the School of Sport and Exercise Sciences, Loughborough University, UK. He has written widely on the body, identity and equity in education, and is founding editor of the international journal *Sport, Education and Society*.

Johannah Fahey is a Research Fellow at Monash University, Australia. She has a Ph.D. in cultural studies from Macquarie University, Australia. Her latest co-edited book is called *Globalizing the research imagination*. Her latest co-authored book is *Haunting the knowledge economy*. Her earlier book is *David Noonan: before and now*.

Ramón Flecha is Professor of Sociology at the University of Barcelona and Doctor Honoris Causa by the University of Timisoara. He has made theoretical contributions in the fields of critical pedagogy, sociology and cultural studies: dialogic learning, dialogic societies, communicative methodology of research.

Adam Gamoran is Professor of Sociology and Educational Policy Studies and Director of the Wisconsin Center for Education Research at the University of Wisconsin-Madison. He recently edited, with Yossi Shavit and Richard Arum, *Stratification in higher education: a comparative study* (Stanford University Press, 2007).

David Gillborn is Professor of Education and Critical Race Studies in Education at the Institute of Education, University of London.

Kris D. Gutiérrez is Professor of Social Research Methodology, Graduate School of Education and Information Studies, at the University of California, Los Angeles. Her work examines the relationship between language/literacy, culture and learning. Specifically, her work focuses on the processes by which people negotiate meaning in culturally organized contexts, using language and literacies that are embedded within sociohistorical traditions. Issues of equity are central to her work.

Cecilia Henríquez is a doctoral student in the Division of Social Research Methodology at the University of California, Los Angeles Graduate School of Education & Information Studies. She received her B.S. degree in Mathematics from the Massachusetts Institute of Technology and her M.A. degree in Education from the University of California, Los Angeles. Her research interests include studying the everyday mathematical practices of non-dominant communities, including informal learning spaces, and the implication on educational practice.

Ursula Hoadley is a senior lecturer in curriculum theory in the School of Education at the University of Cape Town. She works in the areas of sociology of pedagogy, curriculum and teacher's work.

Jane Kenway is Professor of global education studies at Monash University and a Fellow of the Academy of the Social Sciences in Australia. Among her many books are *Consuming children* (with Bullen), *Masculinity beyond the metropolis* (with Kraack and Hickey-Moody) and *Haunting the knowledge economy* (with Bullen, Fahey and Robb).

Gloria Ladson-Billings is Kellner Family Professor in Urban Education, Professor of Curriculum and Instruction and Educational Policy Studies and H.I. Romnes Fellow at the University of Wisconsin, Madison.

Hugh Lauder is Professor of Education and Political Economy at the University of Bath His books include: Brown, P., Lauder, H. and Ashton, D. (2009) *The global auction: the broken promises of opportunities, jobs and rewards*; Lauder, H., Brown, P., Dillabough, J.-A. and Halsey, A.H. (eds) (2006) *Education, globalization and social change*, Oxford: Oxford University Press. Currently being translated into Japanese at Tokyo University: Brown, P., Green, A. and Lauder, H. (2001) *High skills: globalisation, competitiveness and skill formation*, Oxford: Oxford University Press. Brown, P. and Lauder, H. (2001) *Capitalism and social progress: the future of society in a global economy*, Basingstoke: Palgrave Press. He is the editor of the *Journal of Education and Work*.

Bob Lingard works in the School of Education at The University of Queensland. His research interests include school reform and education policy. He is the co-editor, with Jenny Ozga, of *The RoutledgeFalmer Reader in Education Policy and Politics* (2007) and co-author with Fazal Rizvi (2009) of *Globalizing Education Policy* (Routledge). He is an Editor of the journal *Discourse: Studies in the Cultural Politics of Education* and a former President of the Australian Association for Research in Education.

Pauline Lipman is Professor of Educational Policy Studies at the University of Illinois-Chicago. Her research focuses on race and class inequality in schools, globalization and the political economy of urban education, particularly in relation to neoliberal urban development.

Grace Livingston is Associate Professor and Director (2008–2009) of African American Studies at the University of Puget Sound, Tacoma, Washington, where she also works in its Race and Pedagogy Initiative. Her research investigates the structure of knowledge production relationships and the foundations of social theory, particularly in relation to matters of race and social class.

Kathleen Lynch is Professor of Equality Studies in the UCD School of Social Justice, University College Dublin.

Meg Maguire teaches and researches issues of policy and practice, teachers' lives and social justice in urban contexts. She is Professor of Sociology of Education in the Centre for Public Policy Studies at King's College London.

Marie Moran is assistant lecturer and doctoral candidate in Equality Studies, University College Dublin.

Louise Morley is a Professor of Education and Director of the Centre for Higher Education and Equity Research (CHEER) (www.sussex.ac.uk/education/cheer) at the University of Sussex, UK. She has a strong international profile in the field of sociology of higher education studies. Her research and publication interests focus on gender, equity, quality and power in higher education. She is currently directing an ESRC/DFID funded research project on Widening Participation in Higher Education in Ghana and Tanzania (www.sussex.ac.uk/education/wideningparticipation).

Johan Muller is Professor of Curriculum and Director of the Graduate School in the Faculty of Humanities at the University of Cape Town. He works and publishes in the area of the sociology of knowledge.

Geetha B. Nambissan is Professor of Sociology of Education at the Zakir Husain Centre for Educational Studies, Jawaharlal Nehru University, New Delhi, India. Her research has focussed on exclusion and inclusion in education, with a focus on marginal groups in India. Her publications include *Child Labour and the Right to Education in South Asia: Needs versus Rights?* (*co-ed.*) (Sage, 2003). She is on the advisory board of the *Journal of Education Policy*.

Maria Alice Nogueira is Professor of Sociology of Education at the Federal University of Minas Gerais (UFMG), Brazil. Her research has focused on the family–school relationships and social advantage in education. She has published many articles in Brazil and abroad. She has co-edited two books: *Família & Escola – trajetórias de escolarização em camadas médias e populares* (Vozes, 2000) and *A escolarização das elites – um panorama internacional da pesquisa* (Vozes, 2002).

António Nóvoa is Professor of Education. He earned a Ph.D. in History at Sorbonne University (Paris) and a Ph.D. in Educational Sciences at Geneva University (Switzerland). Since 2006, he has been the President of the University of Lisbon (Portugal).

Mark Olssen is Professor of Political Theory and Education Policy in the Department of Political, International and Policy Studies, University of Surrey. His most recent books are *Toward a global thin community: Nietzsche, Foucault, and the cosmopolitan commitment*, Paradigm Press, Boulder and London, published 2009; and *Michel Foucault: materialism and education*, Paradigm Press, Boulder and London, published in May 2006. He has published extensively in leading academic journals in Britain, America and in Australasia.

Diane Reay is a Professor of Education at the University of Cambridge, with particular interests in social justice issues in education, Pierre Bourdieu's social theory, and cultural analyses of social class. Her book on higher education choice and access degrees of choice (with Miriam David and Stephen Ball) was published in 2005 by Trentham Press.

Emma Rich is Senior Lecturer in 'The Body and Physical Culture' in the School of Sport and Exercise Sciences, Loughborough University, UK. She is co-author of *The medicalization of cyberspace* (2008) and *Education, disordered eating, and obesity discourse: fat fabrications* (2008), and the forthcoming edited text 'Expanding the obesity debate'. She is also founder of the Gender, Sport and Society Forum.

Susan L. Robertson is Professor of Sociology of Education and is located in the Centre for Globalisation, Societies and Education, University of Bristol. Her current research interests include understanding the dynamic relationship between knowledge production, circulation and consumption as it is mediated by scales of political and social action. Susan has been working particularly on developing a spatial analytic in the social analysis of education.

Neil Selwyn is a senior lecturer at the London Knowledge Lab, where his research and teaching address the sociology of technology use in educational settings.

Roger Slee holds a Chair in Inclusive Education at the Institute of Education, University of London. He is the Founding Editor of the *International Journal of Inclusive Education*.

Boaventura de Sousa Santos is Professor of Sociology at the School of Economics, University of Coimbra (Portugal), Distinguished Legal Scholar at the University of Wisconsin-Madison Law School and Global Legal Scholar at the University of Warwick. He is Director of the Center for Social Studies of the University of Coimbra and Director of the Center of

Documentation on the Revolution of 1974, at the same University. He has published widely on globalization, sociology of law and the state, epistemology, democracy and human rights, in Portuguese, Spanish, English, Italian, French and German.

Marília Pontes Sposito is full Professor in the area of Sociology of Education in the School of Education at the University of São Paulo, Brazil. Her research is in the fields of sociology of the youth, sociology of education and sociology of collective action.

Pat Thomson is Professor of Education and Director of Research in the School of Education, The University of Nottingham. Her recent publications include three Routledge books, *School leadership – heads on the block?*, *Doing visual research with children and young people* and *Helping doctoral students write: pedagogies for supervision.*

Agnès van Zanten is a sociologist and Senior Researcher at the Centre National de la Recherche Scientifique. She works at the *Observatoire Sociologique du Changement*, a research centre of Sciences-Po in Paris. She is also the Director of an international network on educational policy.

Carol Vincent is a Professor of Education at the Institute of Education, University of London. Her research interests include families' relationships with the education and childcare systems, social class, mothering and education policy. She is currently directing an ESRC-funded project exploring the educational strategies of the Black middle classes.

Lois Weis is State University of New York Distinguished Professor of Sociology of Education at the University at Buffalo, State University of New York. She is the author and/or editor of numerous books and articles relating to race, class, gender, education and the economy.

Philip A. Woods holds a Chair in Educational Leadership and Policy, University of Gloucestershire, UK. He has written and researched extensively on educational policy, leadership and governance, drawing on his sociological background, with a particular interest in democracy, alternative education, and entrepreneurialism and public values. He is co-editor of *Alternative education for the 21st century: philosophies, approaches, visions*, published by Palgrave in 2009.

Deborah Youdell is Professor of Education at the Institute of Education, University of London. Her work is located in the sociology of education and is concerned with educational inequalities and the way these are connected to student subjectivities and everyday life in schools.

Acknowledgements

Editing a Handbook is never easy. It seems like a good idea in theory but actually involves lots and lots of hard work and many frustrations and setbacks along the way. We were lucky to have Carolina Junemann, who acted as the book administrator and did a lot of that hard work and sorted out most of the frustrations and set backs – for which we are very, very grateful. We also wish to thank our contributors for keeping to time and to their word lengths; we were sorry to lose a couple of people along the way, through no fault of their own. And we are also grateful to Anna Clarkson for her encouragement and for making sure we crossed the road safely.

Abbreviations

AC	Alternative certification
ACU	Association of Commonwealth Universities
BITU	Bustamante Industrial Trade Union
CBOs	Community Based Organizations
CCC	Commercial Club of Chicago
CCS	Centre for Civil Society
CEC	Commission of the European Communities
CEU	Council of the European Union
CLS	Critical legal studies
CREATE	Campus for Research Excellence and Technological Enterprise
CRT	Critical Race Theory
EQUIP	Enabling Quality Improvement Programmes in Schools
EWI	Egalitarian World Initiative
FPR	Framework Programs of Research
GPA	Grade Point Average
HE	Higher education
HEC	Hautes Etudes Commerciales
HESA	Higher Education Statistics Agency
HLTA	Higher Level Teaching Assistant
IAS	Indian Administrative Service
IME	Intensive Mothering Expectations
IMF	International Monetary Fund
INSA	Institut National des Sciences Appliquées
IT	Information technology
JWL	Jamaica Welfare Limited
LSCs	local school councils
NCLB	No Child Left Behind
NGOs	Non-Government Organizations
NWU	National Workers Union
NYCTF	New York City Teaching Fellows

OP	Participatory Budget
PAP	People's Action Party
PNP	People's National Party
PR	Permanent Resident
PVOs	Private Voluntary Organizations
QSRLS	Queensland School Reform Longitudinal Study
SAT	Scholastic Aptitude Tests
SMED	Municipal Secretariat of Education
STEM	Science, technology, engineering and mathematics
TA	Teaching Assistant
TFA	Teach for America
TNC	Transnational Company
TNTP	The New Teachers Project
TPS	totally pedagogized societies
UCD	University College Dublin
UWI	University of the West Indies

Introduction

Mapping the sociology of education: social context, power and knowledge

Michael W. Apple, Stephen J. Ball and
Luis Armando Gandin

The sociology of education is a diverse, messy, dynamic, somewhat elusive and invariably disputatious field of work. Reflecting this Lather (1988) suggests that the names that sociologists use to represent themselves are best referred to in the plural – feminisms, phenomenologies, Marxisms, postmodernisms. The sociology of education is produced by a disparate and varied group of researchers, writers and teachers, who are variously invested in national traditions of study with different histories – although there is a marked convergence of topics, methods and perspectives in relation and in response to globalization (see below). The 'communications heavy, travel-based, market dependent' (Marginson and Considine, 2000: 48) world of higher education and the increased extent of co-mingling of scholars, as well as the global reach of multinational publishing houses, have established the conditions for ideas and theories to flow easily between sites of academic work, in the same way as in other fields – but also to flow in particular directions.

Nonetheless, the sociology of education continues to be marked by theoretical fissures, discontinuities and sometimes-acrimonious paradigm disputes. As one of us (Apple, 1996b: 125) put it in a review of sociology of education in the United States: 'what actually counts as the sociology of education is a construction'. That construction is an outcome of ideological and very practical struggles and is marked by differences in power and in resources. This collection is itself inevitably an act of construction: a drawing-up of boundaries, a marking-off of divisions, oppositions and positions, a 'carving up and carving out' (Edwards, 1996). It is not a 'policing action' (Apple 1996b), but, on the other hand, it is by no means an 'innocent' text. We did not set out deliberately to fashion a purist or definitive version of the field, quite the opposite, but the inclusions and exclusions and neglects announced by the collection will have something of that effect, and we discuss these later.

We can use sociological tools to think about the field of sociological practice. In Bernstein's terms, sociology, in common with other social sciences, has a 'horizontal knowledge structure', which consists of 'a series of specialized languages with specialized modes of interrogation and criteria for the construction and circulation of texts' (Bernstein, 1999: 162) which have no principles of integration. These specialized languages and their theoretical idiolects are 'not translatable' (p. 163) he argues, their speakers are exclusive, and their relations are serial. Thus, academic and social capital within the practice of sociology is bound up, as he sees it, with the 'defence of and the challenge of other languages' (p. 163). Development in such a 'horizontal discourse', as he termed it, is not greater generality or abstraction or integration but the development of a new language that 'offers the possibility of fresh perspective, a new set of questions, a new set of connections, and an apparently new problematic, and most importantly, a new set of speakers' (p. 163).

His point is that the discreteness of these languages and the competition between the narcissism of their dedicated speakers are fundamental barriers to incorporation. Within such a discursive regime, he suggests that the primary motivation lies in the 'marketing' of new languages. He goes on to describe what he calls the implicit 'conceptual syntax', or 'weak grammars' of horizontal knowledge structures, such as those of sociology of education, which present particular problems to acquirers, in terms of knowing whether they are 'really speaking or writing sociology' (p. 164). Acquisition is tacit and depends upon acquiring the appropriate 'gaze'; 'a particular mode of recognizing and realizing what counts as an "authentic" sociological reality' (p. 165). This gives rise then to 'segmental competences' and 'segmental literacies' that rest upon an 'obsession with language', but also, inasmuch that these knowledge structures are retrospective, they are also 'characterized by inherent obsolescence' (p. 167).

This collection offers some practical insights into what 'really speaking or writing sociology' means and to contribute to the development of sociological literacy. Bernstein goes on to say that the segmentalizing structures of sociology also 'shatters any sense of an underlying unity' (p. 170). Thus, in the past thirty years in particular, the sociology of education has been defined and redefined by a set of theoretical and methodological disputes, that is contending idiolects, and has also been subject to various breakaways and splits that have created new sub-fields, even distinct, new disciplines. These contending 'discourse communities' 'produce knowledge and establish the conditions for who speaks and who gets heard' (Brantlinger, 2000).

In all of this, sets of 'interests' are at stake. These are: the personal – related to the satisfactions, reputations and status of those in positions of power and patronage, and expressions of identity; those more conventionally referred to as 'vested' – including the material rewards from career, position and publication; and the ideological – matters of value, personal philosophy and political commitment. Such interests are at stake in the everyday life of academic practices. That is, in the decisions, appointments and influences that shape and change the field of sociology of education and its rewards. They have been reflected in the efforts of scholars of colour, women, gay and lesbian and disabled scholars to rework the boundaries, the analytic tools and theoretical bases of the sociology of education and, in doing so, get positions and grants, get published, assert control of key journals and/or create new ones. Struggles over interests take place, in an intellectual register, on the floor of conferences and in the pages of journals, but they are also played out, micro-politically, in editors' offices, in department meetings and in appointing committees. Such struggles are also embedded in 'the hidden curriculum in graduate sociology departments' (Margolis and Romero, 2000), taking two forms. A 'weak' version defines and attempts to control what it means 'to be a sociologist' as part of a professionalization process within which certain methods, topics, concerns and dispositions are validated as 'good sociology'.

This is described by Bourdieu (1988: 56) as the 'corporeal hexis', 'the visceral form of recognition of everything which constitutes the existence of the group, its identity, its truth, and which the group must reproduce in order to reproduce itself'. The 'strong' form works to reproduce stratified and unequal social relations, reinforcing, in particular, the control and influence of white, male scholars (see Bagilhole, 1993). In these terms, the sociology of education has its own sociology; its own 'collective scientific unconscious', in Bourdieu's words; and its own particular conditions of production, which at different points in time have set different limits upon thought through the deployment of specific sets of theories, problems and categories.

In its recent history, the boundaries between sociology and philosophy, political science, geography and social psychology have become fuzzy and loose. Consequently, it is sometimes difficult to say who is a sociologist of education and who is not, and where the field begins and ends. In particular, postmodernism 'has spread like a virus through the disciplines of the social sciences and humanities eating away at the boundaries between them' (MacLure, 2003: 4). The postmodern or linguistic turn can be seen, in typical paradoxical fashion, both as an invigoration of, and threat to, the sociology of education, or rather to modernist social science generally. It is 'the end' of social science and a new beginning. As Bloom (1987: 379) gloomily describes it, this is 'the last, predictable stage in the suppression of reason and the denial of the possibility of truth in the name of philosophy'. Postmodern theory does present a challenge to a whole raft of fundamental, often dearly cherished but sometimes un-examined, assumptions in sociological practice, most obviously and profoundly the deployment of totalizing 'grand narratives'. Large, all-encompassing and systemic 'explanations' of 'the social' are disrupted and eschewed by postmodernism, and indeed Lyotard defines the postmodern as an 'incredulity towards meta-narratives'. As Lather (1988: 7) explains: 'What is destroyed by the post-structuralist suspicion of the lust for authoritative accounts is not meaning, but claims to the unequivocal dominance of any one meaning'. As a result: 'Over the last two decades "postmodernism" has become a concept to be wrestled with, and such a battleground of conflicting opinions and political forces that it can no longer be ignored' (Harvey, 1989: 39). Various epistemological positions within this debate are taken up in the collection with both the deployment of grand narratives and some incredulity.

Of course, many sociologists do not take postmodernism seriously, in part perhaps because they regard postmodernism itself as lacking seriousness and condemn it as ironic, nihilistic and narcissistic and apolitical. Indeed, for some feminists, postmodernism is 'a problem', even just 'boys games', particularly in as much that postmodernism critiques the 'oppressions' embedded within the humanist tradition upon which 'women's liberation' draws. For others, postmodernism offers an extension to, and new possibilities for, critique and situated struggle. Kenway (1997: 132) goes as far as to argue that: 'In many senses feminist postmodernism has become "The New Way" to approach feminist research, pedagogy and politics'; but goes on to warn that: 'when one takes this new way, one confronts many confusions, difficulties, dilemmas and dangers'. This collection reflects the inroads of the postmodern, or perhaps more accurately the post-structural, into theorizing and research, but it also takes account of the continuing significance of various forms of modernist theory and modernist sociological research practice. In placing these multiple traditions side by side so to speak, we wish to argue that it is at the intersection of the varying positions within the sociology of education – each of which has its own overlapping critical impulses – that progress can be made in understanding the complex relations that connect education with the larger realities of our societies.

Bernstein's fundamental criticism of the sociology of education was that it is organized around commitments to 'languages of dedication' rather than to 'a problem and its vicissitudes' (1999: 170). This is true, to some extent, although Bernstein's account may be said to be unduly pessimistic and one-sided in terms of the overall balance between dedication and analytic rigour across contemporary sociology of education as a whole. But certainly, in different ways, the sociology of education rests on dedication and social commitment and is a redemptive practice. The papers in this collection share a commitment to social critique and social justice, and we

3

elaborate on this 'role' for the sociology of education below, but they also share and display a commitment to intellectual rigour – theoretical and/or empirical.

Despite its segmentalization and disputation, there is another version of the 'story' of the sociology of education, a set of continuities within difference. Rhoads (2000: 7), for example, notes that 'The work of postmodernists, feminists and critical theorists has been particularly attentive to issues of positionality and representation . . .' The recent history of the sociology of education demonstrates a set of common concerns, elisions and linkages. A good deal of contemporary work is eclectic (in the best sense) and integrationist – conciliatory even. Not that this is easily achieved in sociological work, Apple (1996b: 141) writes of 'the difficult problem of *simultaneously* thinking about both the specificity of different practices, and the forms of articulated unity they constitute . . .'. He goes on to argue, however, that:

> it is exactly this issue of simultaneity, of thinking neo [marxism] and post [modernism] together, of actively enabling the tensions within and among them to help form our research, that will solidify previous understandings, avoid the loss of collective memory of the gains that have been made, and generate new insights and new actions.

To a great extent, the vitality and purposefulness of the project of the sociology of education, and its attraction for students and practitioners, are underpinned by the continuing cross-play of tensions and disputes, not the least those tensions between, to borrow Moore's (1996: 159) formulation, critical research 'of' education and research 'for' education. However, this cross-play of positions, currents and influences is also a source of confusion and a major challenge for any newcomer seeking a sensible grasp of the field. This collection is aimed at making that grasp just a little easier.

In addition to its internecine struggles, the developments and discontinuities within sociology and the sociology of education both reflect and respond to changes in societies – national and global. However, there are neither inevitable nor simple relationships between social and political contexts and the preoccupations and dispositions of the academy. Over and against this, we must not forget that the social sciences act back on and in society through the recontextualization of the 'human sciences' within professional education or the work of *government*, although perhaps less directly now than in the past.

'Human science' knowledge functions politically and is intimately implicated in the practical management of social and political problems. The idea that human sciences such as sociology stand outside or above the political agenda concerning the management of the population or somehow have a neutral status embodied in a free-floating, progressive rationalism is a dangerous and debilitating conceit. 'Scientific' or theoretical vocabularies may distance researchers from the subjects of their activity but, at the same time, they also construct a 'gaze' that renders the 'landscape of the social' ever more visible and produce or contribute to discourses that create particular sorts of 'subject positions' for people to occupy.

However, governments are no longer content to wait for the harvest of research ideas that academics produce; they seek to engineer the crop through tenders and the funding of increasingly tightly focused research programmes. Policy desire increasingly shapes research offerings, and concomitantly increasing amounts of significant and sensitive research for 'government' is out-sourced to the commercial sector (see Ball, 2007) rather than entrusted to the university sector. University-based research is itself also increasingly subject to the 'authority and apparent objectivity of disciplines such as accountancy, economics and management' (MacKinnon, 2000: 297), through the incentives of academic capitalism and the operationalization of concepts such as 'quality' and 'policy-relevance' – a disciplining of the disciplines. The tension between 'making' and 'taking' problems in social research, noted by Young (1971), is being played out in new ways in the contemporary politics of research and university funding.

In taking seriously the issues surrounding the 'making' and 'taking' of social problems, in this Handbook we have chosen material that has a critical edge. A considerable number of the chapters included here are 'engaged', and one of the three sections has this as a particular focus. Many of the authors take a position that is similar to what Michael Burawoy has called 'organic public sociology'. In his words, but partly echoing Gramsci as well, the critical sociologist is an organic intellectual who:

> works in close connection with a visible, thick, active, local, and often counter-public. [She or he works] with a labor movement, neighborhood association, communities of faith, immigrant rights groups, human rights organizations. Between the public sociologist and a public is a dialogue, a process of mutual education . . . The project of such [organic] public sociologies is to make visible the invisible, to make the private public, to validate these organic connections as part of our sociological life.
>
> (Burawoy, 2005: 265)

This act of becoming (and this is a *project*, for one is *never* finished, *always* becoming) a critical scholar/activist is a complex one. Because of this, let us extend our earlier remarks about the role of critical research in education. Our points here are tentative and certainly not exhaustive. But they are meant to begin a dialogue over just what it is that 'we' should do.

In general, there are seven tasks in which critical analysis (and the critical analyst) in education must engage (Apple, 2006b).

1   It must 'bear witness to negativity'. That is, one of its primary functions is to illuminate the ways in which educational institutions, policies and practices are connected to the relations of exploitation and domination – and to struggles against such relations – in the larger society. We use the words exploitation and domination technically. They point to structures and processes that Nancy Fraser (1997) refers to as a politics of redistribution and a politics of recognition.

2   In engaging in such critical analysis, whenever possible it also must point to contradictions and to spaces of possible action. Thus, its aim is to critically examine current realities with a conceptual/political framework that also emphasizes the spaces in which counter-hegemonic actions can be or are now going on.

3   At times, this also requires an expansion of what counts as 'research'. Here, we mean acting as critical 'secretaries' to those groups of people and social movements who are now engaged in challenging existing relations of unequal power or in what elsewhere has been called 'non-reformist reforms'. This is exactly the task that was taken on in the thick descriptions of critically democratic school practices in *Democratic schools* (Apple and Beane, 2007) and in the critically supportive descriptions of the transformative reforms such as the Citizen School and participatory budgeting in Porto Alegre, Brazil (Gandin, 2006).

4   The ideal of the organic intellectual has particular salience in the sociology of curriculum, an area that has grown markedly within the sociology of education and in critical curriculum studies. When Gramsci (1971) argued that one of the tasks of a truly counter-hegemonic education was not to throw out 'elite knowledge' but to reconstruct its form and content so that it served genuinely progressive social needs, he provided a key to another

role 'organic intellectuals' might play (see also Gutstein, 2006; Apple, 1996a). Thus, we should not be engaged in a process of what might be called 'intellectual suicide'. That is, there are serious intellectual (and pedagogic) skills in dealing with the histories and debates surrounding the epistemological, political and educational issues involved in justifying what counts as important knowledge. These are not simple and inconsequential issues, and the practical and intellectual/political skills of dealing with them have been well developed. However, they can atrophy if they are not used. We can give back these skills by employing them to assist communities in thinking about this, learning from them and engaging in the mutually pedagogic dialogues that enable decisions to be made in terms of both the short-term and long-term interests of oppressed peoples.

5   In the process, critical work has the task of keeping traditions of radical work alive. In the face of organized attacks on the 'collective memories' of difference and struggle, attacks that make it increasingly difficult to retain academic and social legitimacy for multiple critical approaches that have proven so valuable in countering dominant narratives and relations, it is absolutely crucial that these traditions be kept alive, renewed, that new traditions be created and when necessary criticized for their conceptual, empirical, historical and political silences or limitations. This involves being cautious of reductionism and essentialism and asks us to pay attention to what we mentioned above, what Fraser has called both the politics of redistribution and the politics of recognition (Fraser, 1997). This includes not only keeping theoretical, empirical, historical and political traditions alive but also, very importantly, extending and (supportively) criticizing them. And it also involves keeping alive the dreams, utopian visions and 'non-reformist reforms' that are so much a part of these radical traditions (Jacoby, 2005; Apple, 1995; Teitelbaum, 1993).

6   Keeping traditions alive and also supportively criticizing them when they are not adequate to deal with current realities cannot be done unless we ask 'For whom are we keeping them alive?' and 'How and in what form are they to be made available?' All of the things we have mentioned before in this tentative taxonomy of tasks require the relearning or development and use of varied or new skills of working at many levels with multiple groups. Thus, journalistic and media skills, academic and popular skills, and the ability to speak to very different audiences are increasingly crucial. It also requires that we relearn and mobilize the technical skills of the most elegant statistical models available. For too long, such skills have been rejected by many critical sociologists as simply 'positivist'. This had meant that, in the public debates over policy means, ends and outcomes, statistics generated out of deeply problematic assumptions and ideologies dominate the discursive space and the media. Thus, as we engage in the spirited debates over what education does and should do, we need to be very cautious of not marginalizing valuable 'technical' skills and also need to find ways of making the data generated by such approaches visible and understandable to a wider public than those within the field of sociology of education (see Apple, 2006a).

7   Finally, critical sociologists of education must *act* in concert with the progressive social movements their work supports or in movements against the assumptions and policies they critically analyze (Gramsci, 1971). The role of the organic intellectual implies that one must participate in and give one's expertise to movements surrounding struggles over a politics of redistribution and a politics of recognition. It also implies learning from these social movements. This means that the role of the 'unattached intelligentsia' (Mannheim, 1936), someone who 'lives on the balcony' (Bakhtin, 1968), is not an appropriate model. As Bourdieu (2003: 11) reminds us, for example, our intellectual efforts are crucial, but

they 'cannot stand aside, neutral and indifferent, from the struggles in which the future of the world is at stake'.

The chapters included in this volume provide instances of authors taking up one or more of each of these tasks. These seven tasks are demanding, and no one person can engage equally well in all of them simultaneously. What we can do is honestly continue our attempt to come to grips with the complex intellectual, personal and political tensions and activities that respond to the demands of this role. Actually, although at times problematic, 'identity' may be a more useful concept here. It is a better way to conceptualize the interplay among these tensions and positions, since it speaks to the possible multiple positionings one may have and the contradictory ideological forms that may be at work both within oneself and in any specific context (see Youdell, in progress). And this requires a searching critical examination of one's own structural location, one's own overt and tacit political commitments, and one's own embodied actions.

Of course, not everyone who sees herself or himself as a critical sociologist of education will agree with all of what we have said above. This is to be expected. We outline the points above to document one of the major sets of goals – and the tensions that arise out of them – to establish a partial set of decision rules for judging the multiple senses of efficacy that might cohere with the chapters included here.

Even so, despite our best efforts, any selection of papers from the vast output of the sociology of education is bound to be both idiosyncratic and unsatisfactory. The point is, does it work, does it do a useful job for the intended readership, and is it the 'best' work for the purposes at hand? This is not a representative selection in any sense, whatever that might mean in terms of the sociology of education. But even now, as we write this, we can see ways in which we might have put the book together differently, made different choices, given space and emphases to different things. Clearly, not every sub-specialism, theoretical position or important figure is included. That would be impossible. Further, there is no systematic attempt directly to represent the founding 'fathers' of sociology, nor of the sociology of education. That sort of approach to the field is adequately dealt with in existing textbooks. This is not a collection of 'classic' papers; these can be accessed easily in other ways. Rather, the work included here is 'state of the art'; a set of newly written and previously unpublished papers by some of the leading scholars in the field. The emphasis is on theoretically informed and transposable work, work of international relevance and coverage that has a critical relevance.

On the whole, the papers operate at a level of generality and with a conceptual richness that make them readable in, and applicable to, a wide variety of national locations. They draw on literatures from a variety of different national settings and in many instances, of necessity, they take into account the overbearing and inescapable realities of globalizations, in all their forms, but not crudely or simplistically. Education itself is increasingly a traded good within international education service markets and global labour markets. The international trade in students has grown massively in the past ten years. It is already worth $400 billion worldwide; 2.7 million students are now studying outside their home countries, a 50 per cent increase since 2000, and this is estimated to rise to 8 million by 2025. Nonetheless, struggles over what it means to be educated, and against the commodification of education, and for and in defence of democratic and critical forms of education, involving students and teachers, occur in many locations. Thus, some of the papers address what Boaventura de Sousa Santos calls the 'sociology of absences' (Santos, 2004). That is, they aim to explain that what does not exist is, in fact, actively produced as non-existent, and thus to transform impossible into possible objects.

To be made present, these absences need to be constructed as alternatives to hegemonic experience, to have their credibility discussed and argued for and their relations taken as object of political dispute. The sociology of absences therefore creates the conditions to enlarge the field of credible experiences.

(The world social forum: toward a counter-hegemonic globalisation
(part 1): 239 www.choike.org/documentos/wsf_s318_sousa.pdf)

While localities and national systems inflect the processes of globalization differently and struggles ensue, convergences and homogenization of educational forms and modalities, driven by what Santos (2003) calls 'monocultural logics', are very clearly evident within and between settings. These logics are very evident in current education policies that privilege choice, competition, performance management and individual responsibility and risk management.

As editors, the three of us are more than a little aware of the necessity of avoiding such monocultural logics. Indeed, in trying to make this volume an international one, we are conscious of the power of a number of the arguments that have come out of the literature on both post-colonialism and globalization.

We are taken with the fact that post-colonial experience(s) (and the plural is important) and the theories of globalization that have been dialectically related to them are powerful ways of critically engaging with the politics of empire and with the ways in which culture, economy and politics all interact, globally and locally, in complex and overdetermined ways. Indeed, the very notions of post-colonialism and globalization 'can be thought of as a site of dialogic encounter that pushes us to examine center/periphery relations and conditions with specificity, wherever we may find them' (Dimitriadis and McCarthy, 2001: 10).

As they have influenced critical sociology of education, some of the core politics behind post-colonial positions are summarized well by Dimitriadis and McCarthy (2001) when they state that, 'The work of the postcolonial imagination subverts extant power relations, questions authority, and destabilizes received traditions of identity' (p. 10; see also Bhabha, 1994; Spivak, 1988).

Sociologists of education interested in globalization, in neo-liberal depredations and in post-colonial positions have largely taken them to mean the following. They imply a conscious process of repositioning, of 'turning the world upside down' (Young, 2003: 2). They mean that the world is seen relationally – as being made up of relations of dominance and subordination and of movements, cultures and identities that seek to interrupt these relations. They also mean that, if you are someone who has been excluded by the 'West's' dominant voices geographically, economically, politically and/or culturally, or you are inside the West but not really part of it, then 'postcolonialism offers you a way of seeing things differently, a language and a politics in which your interests come first, not last' (p. 2). Some of the best work in the field of sociology of education mirrors Robert Young's more general claim that post-colonialism and the global sensitivities that accompany it speak to a politics and a 'philosophy of activism' that involve contesting these disparities. It extends the anti-colonial struggles that have such a long history and asserts ways of acting that challenge 'Western' ways of interpreting the world (p. 4). This is best stated by Young (2003) in the following two quotes:

Above all, postcolonialism seeks to intervene, to force its alternative knowledges into the power structures of the west as well as the non-west. It seeks to change the way people think, the way they behave, to produce a more just and equitable relation between different people of the world.

(Young, 2003: 7)

and

> Postcolonialism . . . is a general name for those insurgent knowledges that come from the subaltern, the dispossessed, and seek to change the terms under which we all live.
>
> (Young, 2003: 20)

What Young says about post-colonialism is equally true about theories of globalization and about the entire tradition of critical sociological scholarship and activism in education. These reminders about insurgent knowledges, of course, have clear connections to the points we made earlier about the complex and multiple roles that critical sociologists of education in general need to consider. One of the important issues with which we will have to deal, a function implied in our listing of the tasks of the critical sociologist of education earlier, is to help to restore the collective memories of insurgent knowledges so that they can be used as resources, not only for critical research, but for people who seek to interrupt the relations of dominance and subordination that so deeply characterize so many nations and regions of this world. As you will see, this concern with the social production of, and conditions for, memory and forgetting will be brought up in this book.

Having said this, again we need to be aware of our own positioning within knowledge power structures. Given length limitations and the diversity of current tendencies and emerging traditions within the critical sociology of education, despite the international scope and range of the papers in the collection, there is a clear Western, Northern and Anglo-Saxon bias. Hence, another volume is necessary, one that would chart the progress, tensions and debates in a considerably larger range of nations and would counter the epistemological and ideological assumptions that may still underpin parts of this Handbook, even when we ourselves have tried to be conscious and critical of them. This would be an exceptionally worthwhile project, and we urge that it be taken up so that the debates within sociology of education can become even more international than they are now.

In editing this volume, we have tried to pay attention to the quality of the writing. While there is a wide variety of styles and forms of expression, again important in themselves, all the writers communicate their ideas effectively, although some papers are more 'difficult' than others. Some are more pedagogical, and some more writerly. Some report on research; others discuss and deploy theoretical analyses. Some are more influenced by cultural analysis; others by more structural concerns. In different ways, they show something of the social practices of sociology, that is, how sociological analysis is done and how sociological sensibilities are brought to bear upon significant contemporary issues. The make-up of the collection also reflects, to a degree, our own interests and prejudices, our own biographies in the sociology of education and our own sense of excitement about educational possibilities, or our frustrations with, anger at, and engagement with, injustices.

The papers are organized into three general but very porous sections: '*Perspectives and theories*', where the emphasis is on the application of theoretical ideas (e.g. psycho-social, feminism, Critical Race Theory) or the use of the work of particular writers (e.g. Foucault, Bernstein, Bourdieu, Butler) and the deployment of particular key concepts such as space, connectivity, pedagogy, globalization, governmentality, equality and disability; '*Social processes and practices*', where the focus is on various contemporary educational phenomena, which are subject to critical interrogation (families, home schooling, skills, tracking, integration, the middle class, university reform etc.); '*Inequalities and resistances*', where issues of class, race and gender and 'colonial mentalities' are critically addressed, and forms of social and political struggle and community involvement in education are examined and documented – what Santos calls the 'sociology of emergences' – 'to know better the conditions of the possibility of hope' (2004: 241).

The handbook is an odd, over-used and rather unwieldy literary form. We accept that; but nonetheless we hope you enjoy the book and find it useful, and we would like to know what you think about it – what you like and do not like, how you think it could be improved. With this in mind, we include here our email addresses so that the critical conversation can continue. We can be reached at: apple@education.wisc.edu (Michael W. Apple); s.ball@ioe.ac.uk (Stephen J. Ball); and gandin@edu.ufrgs.br (Luis Armando Gandin).

References

Apple, M.W. (1995) *Education and power*, 2nd edn, New York: Routledge.

Apple, M.W. (1996a) *Cultural politics and education*, New York: Teachers College Press.

Apple, M.W. (1996b) 'Power, meaning and identity: critical sociology of education in the United States', *British Journal of Sociology of Education* 17: 125–144.

Apple, M.W. (2006a) *Educating the 'right' way: markets, standards, God, and inequality*, 2nd edn, New York: Routledge.

Apple, M.W. (2006b) 'Rhetoric and reality in critical educational studies in the United States', *British Journal of Sociology of Education* 27: 679–687.

Apple, M.W. and Beane, J.A. (eds) (2007) *Democratic schools: lessons in powerful education*, Portsmouth, NH: Heinemann.

Bagilhole, B. (1993) 'How to keep a good woman down: an investigation of the role of institutional factors in the process of discrimination against women academics', *British Journal of Sociology of Education* 14: 261–274.

Bakhtin, M.M. (1968) *Rabelais and his world* (trans. H. Iswolsky), Cambridge, MA: MIT Press.

Ball, S.J. (2007) *Education plc: understanding private sector participation in public sector education*, London: Routledge.

Bernstein, B. (1999) 'Vertical and horizontal discourse: an essay', *British Journal of Sociology of Education* 20: 157–173.

Bhabha, H. (1994) *The location of culture*, New York: Routledge.

Bloom, A. (1987) *The closing of the American mind: how higher education has failed democracy and improverished the souls of today's students*, New York: Simon & Schuster.

Bourdieu, P. (1988) *Homo Academicus*, Cambridge: Polity Press.

Bourdieu, P. (2003) *Firing back: against the tyranny of the market 2*, New York: New Press.

Brantlinger, E. (2000) 'Using ideology: case of non-recognition of the politics of research and practice in special education', in S.J. Ball (ed.) *Sociology of education: major themes*, London: Routledge.

Burawoy, M. (2005) 'For public sociology', *British Journal of Sociology of Education* 56: 259–294.

Dimitriadis, G. and McCarthy, C. (2001) *Reading and teaching the postcolonial*, New York: Teachers College Press.

Edwards, D. (1996) *Discourse and recognition*, London: Sage.

Fraser, N. (1997) *Justice Interruptus*, New York: Routledge.

Gandin, L.A. (2006) 'Creating real alternatives to neoliberal policies in education: the citizen school project', in M.W. Apple and K.L. Buras (eds) *The subaltern speak: curriculum, power, and educational struggles*, New York: Routledge, pp. 217–241.

Gramsci, A. (1971) *Selections from the prison notebooks* (trans. Q. Hoare and G.N. Smith), New York: International Publishers.

Gutstein, E. (2006) *Reading and writing the world with mathematics*, New York: Routledge.

Harvey, D. (1989) *The condition of postmodernity*, Oxford: Basil Blackwell.

Jacoby, R. (2005) *Picture imperfect: Utopian thought for an anti-Utopian age*, New York: Columbia University Press.

Kenway, J. (1997) 'Having a postmodern turn or postmodernist angst: a disorder experienced by an author who is not yet dead or even close to it', in A.H. Halsey, H. Lauder, P. Brown and A. Stuart Wells (eds) *Education: culture, economy, society*, Oxford: Oxford University Press.

Lather, P. (1988) 'Ideology and methodological attitude', in *American Educational Research Association Annual Meeting*, New Orleans.

MacKinnon, D. (2000) 'Managerialism, governmentality and the state: a neo-Foucauldian approach to local economic governance', *Political Geography* 19: 293–314.

MacLure, M. (2003) *Discourse in educational and social research*, Buckingham: Open University Press.

Mannheim, K. (1936) *Ideology and Utopia*, New York: Harvest Books.

Marginson, S. and Considine, M. (2000) *The enterprise university*, Cambridge: Cambridge University Press.

Margolis, E. and Romero, M. (2000) ' "The department is very male, very white, very old, and very conservative": the functioning of the hidden curriculum in graduate sociology departments', in S.J. Ball (ed.) *Sociology of education: major themes*, London: Routledge.

Moore, R. (1996) 'Back to the future: the problems of change and possibilities of advance in the sociology of education', *British Journal of Sociology of Education* 17: 145–162.

Rhoads, R. (2000) 'Crossing sexual orientation borders: collaborative strategies for dealing with issues of positionality and representation, in S.J. Ball (ed.) *Sociology of education: major themes*, vol. 1, London: RoutledgeFalmer.

Santos, Boaventura S. (2003) 'Towards a counter-hegemonic globalisation', Paper presented at the XXIV International Congress of the Latin American Studies Association, Dallas, USA, March.

Santos, Boaventura S. (2004) 'The world social forum: toward a counter-hegemonic globalisation', in J. Sen, A. Anand, A. Escobar and P. Waterman (eds) *World social forum: challenging empires*, New Delhi: The Viveka Foundation, pp. 235–245. Available online at www.choike.org/nuevo_eng/informes/1557.html (accessed 20 April 2009).

Spivak, G. (1988) 'Can the subaltern speak?', in C. Nelson and L. Grossberg (eds) *Marxism and the interpretation of culture*, Urbana, IL: University of Illinois Press, pp. 271–313.

Teitelbaum, K. (1993) *Schooling for good rebels*, Philadelphia, PA: Temple University Press.

Youdell, D. (in progress) *After identity: power and politics in education*, London: Routledge.

Young, M.F.D. (ed.) (1971) *Knowledge and control*, London: Collier-Macmillan.

Young, R. (2003) *Postcolonialism*, New York: Oxford University Press.

Part 1
Perspectives and theories

1

'Spatializing' the sociology of education
Stand-points, entry-points, vantage-points[1]

Susan L. Robertson

Introduction

This chapter explores the implications of an absence of a critical spatial lens in the conceptual grammar of the field of the sociology of education. I argue that it is not sufficient to simply bring a spatial lexicon to our conceptual sentences (as in 'geographies' of classroom emotions; the school as a 'place'; communities of practice). This is to fetishize space, leaving a particular medium of power, projects and politics – space – to go unnoticed. Rather, to apply a critical spatial lens to the sociology of education means seeing the difference that space, along with time and sociality – the two privileged angles of view in modernity – makes to our understanding of contemporary knowledge formation, social reproduction and the constitution of subjectivities (Massey, 2005: 62; Soja, 1996: 71). By tracing out the ways in which space is deeply implicated in power, production and social relations, I hope to reveal the complex processes at work in constituting the social relations of 'education space' as a crucial site, object, instrument and outcome in this process. A 'critical' spatial lens in the sociology of education involves three moves: one, an outline of the ontological and epistemological premises of a critical theory of space; two, the specification of the central objects for enquiry to education and society; and three, bringing these theoretical and conceptual approaches together to open up an entry point for investigation, a vantage point from which to see education–society phenomena anew, and a standpoint from which to see how education space is produced and how it might be changed.

Move 1: a critical theory of space

Space is a highly contested concept in social science. Here, I will introduce the core vocabulary for a critical socio–spatial theory drawn from the leading theorists on space, including Lefebvre (1991), Soja (1996), Harvey (2006), Massey (1994), Smith (1992), Brenner (2003) and Jessop *et al.* (2008). This vocabulary, which has been developed over time and as a result of a series of spatial turns, offers us a set of theoretical and empirical concepts with which to work. The following assumptions are key: that, ontologically, space is social and real; that spaces are social relations stretched out; and that space is socially produced.

Epistemologically, space can be known through particular categories of ideas, as 'perceived', 'conceived' and 'lived' (Lefebvre, 1991), or as 'absolute', 'relative' and 'relational' (Harvey, 2006). These two framings will be developed in this chapter. Spaces are dynamic, overlapping and changing, in a shifting geometry of power (Massey, 1994). The organization of socio-spatial relations can take multiple forms and dimensions. This is reflected in a rich spatial lexicon that has been developed to make sense of the changing nature of production, (nation)state power, labour, knowledge, development and difference. Key concepts in this lexicon are 'territory', 'place', 'scale', 'network' and 'positionality'. These concepts are pertinent for the sociology of education, which has, as its central point of enquiry, on the one hand, the role of education in (re)producing modern societies, and on the other hand, an examination of transformations within contemporary societies and their consequences for education systems, education experiences, opportunities and outcomes.

An ontology of space

French philosopher Henri Lefebvre and British-born geographer David Harvey are both viewed as having transformed our understanding of space, from a largely geometrical/mathematical term denoting an empty area, to seeing space in more critical ways: as social, real, produced and socially constitutive. Lefebvre's intellectual project explicitly works with and beyond the binary of materialism and idealism. What marks out Lefebvre's meta-philosophical project is his concern with the possibilities for change by identifying 'third space' (Soja, 1996: 31), a space of radical openness. In other words, Lefebvre's approach is concerned, not only with the forces of production and the social relations that are organized around them, but *also moving beyond* to new, an-Other, unanticipated possibilities.

The introductory essay, 'The plan', in *The production of space* (1991) is regarded as containing Lefebvre's key ideas. Lefebvre begins by arguing that, through much of modernity, our understanding of space was profoundly shaped by mathematicians, who invented all kinds of space that could be represented through calculations and techniques (Lefebvre, 1991: 2), To Lefebvre, what was not clear was the relationship between these representations (mental space) and 'real space' – '. . . the space of people who deal with material things' (Lefebvre, 1991: 4).

However, Lefebvre was unhappy with pursuing an analytics of space centred on either continental philosophy or Marxism. He regarded this binary pairing as part of a conceptual dualism (conceived/idealism versus lived/materialism), closed to new, unanticipated outcomes. Lefebvre was particularly critical of the way continental philosophers, such as Foucault and Derrida, fetishized space, so that the mental realm, of ideas, representations, discourses and signs, enveloped and occluded social and physical spaces. To Lefebvre, semiology could not stand as a complete body of knowledge because it could not say much about space other than it was a text; a message to be read. Such thinking, he argued, was both political and ideological in that its science of space concealed the social relations of (capitalist) production and the role of that state in it (Lefebvre, 1991).

This did not mean Lefebvre embraced Marxism unproblematically. Though Lefebvre's project aimed to reveal the way the social relations of production projected themselves onto space (Lefebvre, 1991: 129), he was critical of the way Marxist theorists on the one hand fetishized temporality, and on the other hand reduced 'lived space' to labour and products, ignoring the complexities of all spheres of life (such as art, politics, the judiciary) and their attendant social relations. A more expansive idea of production was embraced to take account of the multiplicity of ways in which *ideas are produced, humans are created and labour, histories are constructed and minds are made* (Lefebvre, 1991: 70–72). For Lefebvre,

> social space subsumes things produced; and encompasses their relationships in their coexistence and simultaneity – their (relative) order and their/or their relative disorder. It is the outcome of a sequence or set of operations, and thus cannot be reduced to the rank of a simple object.
>
> (Lefebvre, 1991: 73)

Similarly mindful of the need to avoid fetishizing space over time and vice versa, theorists such as Harvey (1989) and Massey (1994: 2) refer to 'space–time' to emphasize the integral nature of space and time, while Massey (1994) and Rose (1993) have advanced theoretical projects around gender as a social relation that is also profoundly spatially organized.

The twin ideas of 'space' and 'production' are central to Lefebvre's analysis. Using an approach he calls 'analysis followed by exposition', Lefebvre's project is to make space's transparency and claim to innocence opaque, and therefore visible and interested. A 'truth of space', he argued, would enable us to see that capital and capitalism influence space in practical (buildings, investment and so on) *and* political ways (classes, hegemony via culture and knowledge). It is thus possible to demonstrate the role of space – as knowledge and action – in the existing capitalist mode of production (including its contradictions), to reveal the ways in which spaces are 'produced', and to show that each society had its own mode of production and produces its own space. Furthermore, if – as he argued was the case – the transition from one mode of production to another over time entailed the production of new spaces, then our analyses must also be directed by both the need to account for its temporality *and* also its spatiality.

Harvey, in an essay entitled 'Space as a keyword' (2006), draws upon a Marxist ontology of historical materialism and, like Lefebvre, seeks to understand processes of development under capitalism. However, Harvey's central focus has centred upon capitalist temporalities and spatialities, specifically the contradiction between capital's concern to annihilate space/time in the circuit of capital, and capital's dependence on embedded social relations to stabilize the conditions of production and reproduction (Harvey, 1982, 1989). Nevertheless, for both writers, the production of space, the making of history and the composition of social relations or society are welded together in a complex linkage of space, time and sociality, or what Soja has called the trialectics of spatiality (1996).

Epistemologies of space

If epistemology is concerned with how we know, then the question of how to know space is also complicated by the multiple ways in which we imagine, sense and experience space. We travel through space, albeit aided by different means. We also attach ourselves to particular spaces, such as places of belonging, giving such places psycho-social meaning. Lefebvre's theoretical approach is to unite these different epistemologies of space. In other words, in order to '. . . expose the actual production of space . . .' (Lefebvre, 1991: 16) '. . . we are concerned with logico-epistemological space, the space of social practice, the space occupied by sensory phenomena, including products of the imagination such as projects and projections, symbols and utopias' (Lefebvre, 1991: 11–12). These claims led Lefebvre to identify and develop three conceptualizations of space at work all of the time in relation to any event or social practice: spatial practice (the material, or *perceived space*); representations of space (or conceptualized space, or *conceived space*); and representational spaces (it overlays physical space and is directly lived through its associated images and symbols; or *lived space*) (Lefebvre, 1991: 38–39). Like his meta-philosophical embrace of idealism and materialism, Lefebvre's epistemology is never to privilege one spatial dimension over another, for instance conceived space over lived space. Rather, the three dimensions are part of a totality, a 'trialectics of being' (Soja, 1996: 71).

Harvey's epistemology of space is somewhat different. Though both agree upon the materiality of space, which Harvey calls 'absolute space', while Lefebvre refers to it as 'perceived space', Harvey offers two alternative concepts to make up a somewhat different tripartite division: that of 'relative space' and 'relational space'. Applied to social space, space is relative in the sense that there are multiple geometries from which to choose (or not), and that the spatial frame is dependent upon what is being relativized and by whom (Harvey, 2006: 272). So, for instance, we can create very different maps of relative locations depending on topological relations, the various frictions enabling movements through space are different, the different spatio-temporal logics at work, and so on. The idea of 'relational space' is intended to capture the notion that there are no such things as time and space outside the processes that define them. This leads to a very important and powerful claim by Harvey, of internal relations. In other words, 'an event or a thing at a point in space cannot be understood by appeal to what exists only at a particular point. It depends upon everything that is going on around it . . . the past, present and the future concentrate and congeal at a certain point' (Harvey, 2006: 274). This point is particularly pertinent for a critical theory of education and society, for it is to argue that it is critical to see 'events' in relation to wider sets of social, economic and political processes.

The spatiality and geometry of power

In the arguments advanced so far, the idea that space is a form of power is implicit. Doreen Massey (1994: 2005) makes this explicit. Not only is space social relations stretched out, but these social relations constitute a 'geometry of power' (Massey: 1994: 4). This is a dynamic and changing process. This implies a plurality (Lefebvre, 1991) or a '. . . lived world of a simultaneous multiplicity of spaces' (Massey, 1994: 3), of uncountable sets of social spatial practices made up of networks and pathways, bunches and clusters of relationships, all of which interpenetrate each and superimpose themselves on one another (Lefebvre, 1991: 86). This multiplicity of spaces is '. . . cross-cutting, intersecting, aligning with one-another, or existing in relations of paradox or antagonism' (Massey, 1994: 3). To insist on multiplicity and plurality, argues Massey, is not just to make an intellectual point. Rather, it is a way of thinking able to reveal the spatial as 'constructed out of the multiplicity of social relations across all spatial scales, from the global reach of finance and telecommunications through the geography of the tentacles of national political power, to the social relations within the town, the settlement, the household and the workplace' (Massey, 1994: 4).

Massey's (2005: 147) relational politics of space is also more in tune with Lefebvre's, of a framing imagination – like 'anOther' – that keeps things more open to negotiation, and that takes fuller account of the 'constant and conflictual process of the constitution of the social, both human and non-human' (2005: 147). In Massey's view (2005: 148), this is not to give ground to the modernist project, of no space and all time, or the postmodern project, of all space and no time, but to argue for configurations of multiple histories, multiple entanglements, multiple geographies, out of which difference is constituted, and where differences count.

The organization of spatial relations – a methodology

Jessop *et al.* (2008) take up the challenge of advancing a methodology for studying spatial relations. They propose a lexicon that includes key concepts such as 'territory', 'place', 'scale', 'network' and 'positionality'.

'Territory' refers to the boundaries that constitute space in particular ways, as differentiated, bordered areas of social relations and social infrastructures supporting particular kinds of economic and social activity, opportunity, investment and so on. Territories are arenas to be managed and governed, with the state and the boundaries of the nation state particularly important throughout the twentieth century (Harvey, 1982: 390, 404). Territories are filled with normative content, such as forms of identification. Interest in the idea of territory and processes of territorialization emerged when attention turned to the assumption that political power was established around national boundaries by nation states, and that these boundaries also served to define societies as 'nationally bounded'. The unbundling of the relationship between territory and sovereignty since the 1980s has resulted in changing spatialities of statehood (Brenner, 2003), the changing basis of citizenship claims (Robertson, 2009) and forms of subjectivity. Territory, as a spatial form of organization, can be read as absolute (a material thing, as in a human resource complex), as conceived (e.g. a map of a region) and as lived (e.g. attachment as a Canadian). It is relative in that the movement within and across territories, for instance, will be different, dependent upon where and how one is located. It is relational in that it is not possible to understand particular territories without placing them in their past, present or emergent futures.

'Scale' represents social life as structured in particular ways, in this case relationally, from the body to the local, national and global (Herod and Wright, 2002). This structuring of social life is viewed as operating at the level of the conceived and the material; in other words, that scales, such as the national or global are real enough; they are also powerful metaphors around which struggles take place to produce these social relations. Extending Lefebvre's insights into the social production of space, Smith (1990) has termed this the 'social production of scale'. Work on scales, their recalibration and re/production, have helped generate insights into the making of regions (scale-making), the global, the reworking of the local, and strategic bypassing of the scales (as in scale jumping) and so on. Scales themselves may shift in importance as a result of processes that include new regionalisms, globalization and decentralization. There have also been important critiques of scale advanced by writers such as Marston *et al.* (2005) for the conceptual elasticity of the concept and, more importantly, the privileging of vertical understandings of socio-spatial processes, rather than vertical and horizontal. Marston *et al.* (2005: 420) are at pains to point out that the power of naming (as in representations of space) should not be confused with either perceived or lived spaces. This is an important point and emphasizes the value of ensuring we keep these epistemologies distinct in our analysis.

'Place', on the other hand, is constituted of spatialized social relations and the narratives about these relations. Places, such as 'my home' or 'my school', only exist in relation to particular criteria (as in 'my school' draws upon criteria such as formal learning, teachers and so on), and, in that sense, they are material, they are social constructions or produced (Hudson, 2001: 257), and they are lived. Massey argues that place emerges out of the fixing of particular meanings on space; it is the outcome of efforts to contain, immobilize, to claim as one's own, to include and therefore exclude (1994: 5). 'All attempts to institute horizons, to establish boundaries, to secure the identity of places, can in this sense be seen as attempts to stabilize the meaning of particular envelopes of space-time' (Massey, 1994: 5). Amin puts this relational argument a little differently: that place is '. . . where the local brings together different scales of practice/social action' (2004: 38) and where meanings are constituted of dwelling, of affinity, of performativity (Amin, 2004: 34). From the perspective of production, places are '. . . complex entities; they are ensembles of material objects, workers and firms, and systems of social relations embodying distinct cultures and multiple meanings, identities and practices' (Hudson, 2001: 255). Importantly, places should not be seen as only whole, coherent, bounded or closed, though they may well be (Hudson, 2001: 258). Rather, we should *also* see places as potentially open, discontinuous, relational and as internally diverse, as they are materialized out of the networks, scales and overlapping territories that constitute this space–time envelope (Allen *et al.*, 1998: 55–56). For Hudson (2001: 258), the degree of 'closedness' or openness is an empirical question rather than an a priori assertion.

More recently scholars, influenced by the work of Castells (1996), have advanced a relational reading of space that '. . . works with the ontology of flow, connectivity and multiple expression' (Amin, 2004: 34). In this work, social relations stretch horizontally across space (implicitly questioning scale – as in local to global – as the main organizer of place). The metaphor representing this idea is the 'network'. The project is not to focus on spatial hierarchies, as is implied in the idea of scale, but on the transversal, the porous nature of knots and clusters of social relations. The idea of 'the network' has become particularly appealing and powerful in thinking about interspatial interconnectivity – for instance in governance systems, inter-firm dependencies, communities of participants and so on. And while this way of conceiving space has a materiality about it, as we can see with, for instance, communities of Internet game-players, the organization of a firm, or a network of experts, it is a way of representing spatial organization. Most importantly, however, the idea of the network is to press the temporality of spatial formations: as 'temporary placements of ever moving material and immanent geographies, as "hauntings" of things that have moved on but left their mark in situated moments in distanciated networks that cross a given place' (Amin, 2004: 34). The reason for pressing this way of reading (network versus scale and territory) is, for Amin, a question of politics: it relates, not only to the scope and reach of local political activity, but also what is taken to count as political. This is a particularly important point for understanding current developments in education, particularly higher education, as local entities, such as universities, stretch their institutional fabrics across space.

For Shepherd, 'positionality' is a corrective to the fascination with networked relations, which tend to overlook '. . . the asymmetric and path dependent ways in which futures of places depend on their interdependencies with other places' (2002: 308). Positionality within a network is dependent upon which network one participates in; it is emergent and contingent rather than pre-given; and it describes how different entities are positioned with regard to one another in space/time. Positionality is relational, it involves power relations, and it is enacted in ways that tend to reproduce and/or challenge existing configurations. For Shepherd (2002: 319), the idea of positionality is critical in calling attention to how connections between people and places – such as the World Bank in Washington and the African economies, or members of a household – play a role in the emergence of proximal and geographic inequalities. Similarly, drawing locales and their pre-capitalist forms of production into circuits of capitalist production (for instance, bringing pre-capitalist/pre-modern tribal relations in Samoa into capitalist colonial networks of relations) draws these actors into new social relations of power and inequality. Finally, the conditions for the possibility of place do not necessarily depend upon local initiative but, rather, with the interactions with distant places. For example, education provision in Cyprus is partly shaped by Cyprus's relations with the European Commission, while member states of the World

Trade Organization are differently positioned with regard to the centres of global power, so that negotiating education sectors will be differently experienced as a result.

The importance of Jessop *et al.*'s (2008) intervention is to advance an approach that overcomes the privileging of one spatial form of organization over another – e.g. scale over other spatialities: the result of what they argue are different turns that unfortunately display all of the signs of '. . . theoretical amnesia and exaggerated claims to conceptual innovation' (p. 389). For Jessop *et al.*, it is important to see that these processes and practices are closely linked and, in many cases, occurring simultaneously, and propose a way of reading these together. This is important and clearly offers sets of readings of events that are not limited to one spatial form of organization.

Move 2: the conceptual grammar of the sociology of education

The question of how to lay out the conceptual grammar of the field is a particularly challenging one. One way is to work at a particular level of abstraction so as to enable the possibility of translation across the different ontological and epistemological traditions that are bought to bear on the education and society relationship. Dale's (2006) work on 'the education questions' is particularly valuable here. There are three levels of questions. Level 1 focuses on the practice; level 2 on the politics of education; and level 3 on the outcomes of education. In opening up these three levels we can then begin to place key approaches, topics, issues and debates that have taken place over time and space and in relation to particular kinds of social relation and forms of social reproduction. These questions are specified in four ways:

1   *Who is taught what, how, by whom, where, when; for what stated purpose and with what justifications; under what (school/university classroom) circumstances and what conditions; and with what results?*
2   *How, by whom, and at what scale are these things problematized, determined, coordinated, governed, administered and managed?*
3   *In whose interests are these practices and politics carried out? What is the scope of 'education', and what are its relations with other sectors of the state, other scalar units and national society?*
4   *What are the individual, private, public, collective and community outcomes of education?*

In relation to *who is taught what, how, by whom, when and where*, we immediately can see that learning opportunities are differentially experienced, and different kinds of learning are acquired. This has been a major field of concern for sociologists such as Bourdieu (1986) and his argument that various forms of capital (cultural, economic and social) are differently mobilized and realized through learning experiences in the home, in schools and in the wider society. Similarly, Bernstein's (1990) work on pedagogic discourse and its relationship to class, codes and control links pedagogy to wider processes of social reproduction. There is a considerable literature on the ways in which social relations, such as gender, race, sexuality and old colonial relations (cf. Arnot and Reay, 2006; Gillborn and Youdell, 2006; Smith, 2006), are produced through what is taught to whom, and where.

Concerning the questions of '*how, by whom and at what scale are these things problematized, determined, coordinated, governed, administered and managed?*' and '*in whose interests are these practices and politics carried out?*', this is broadly the province of governance (cf. Dale, 1996). Sociological research around this question has concerned itself with the emergence of markets as a mechanism of coordination (cf. Gewirtz *et al.*, 1995; Ball, 2007; Ball *et al.*, 1996; Levin and Belfield, 2006);

the rise in importance of international organizations, such as the OECD, the World Bank and the World Trade Organization, in shaping education agendas within national states (Rizvi and Lingard, 2006; Robertson *et al.*, 2002); the emergence of private companies in providing education services (cf. Ball, 2007; Hatcher, 2006; Mahony *et al.*, 2004); and how new economic sectors are being produced, bringing education more tightly into the global economy (cf. Brown and Lauder, 2005; Guile, 2006; Kamat *et al.*, 2004).

Finally, in relation to the question about *outcomes* as a result of these projects and processes as they are mediated through education, we begin to see very clearly that particular identities are produced, families advantaged or excluded, classes constituted, genders reproduced, populations privileged and so on through education. Here, concepts such as social mobility, social inheritance, social stratification, social class, cultural consumption, citizenship, identity and community are facets of those wider social relations: the result of how knowledges, power and difference are also constituted through a multiplicity of differentiated education spaces.

Move 3: spatializing the sociology of education

In this final section, I want to reinforce the point I made in my introductory remarks: that the sociology of education is spatially rich in the metaphors used to name and understand social processes and relations, but analytically and theoretically weak in accounting for the difference that space makes. Adopting a critical spatial analytic, of the kind I have outlined above, means taking seriously the following propositions in relation to the sociology of education: that

1   social relations are *latent in space and* reproduced through systems such as education;
2   education spaces are a product;
3   education spaces are *produced;*
4   *education spaces are polymorphic;*
5   *education* spaces are dynamic geometries of power and social relations; and
6   education spaces and subjectivities are the outcome of a dialectical interaction.

There are any number of possible routes through, and reworkings of, the sociology of education in relation to space, time and sociality. It should also be noted that the different levels of education questions are likely to be worked out using particular combinations of concepts from the spatial lexicon outlined above.

For instance, absolute and perceived education spaces, such as a school, are simultaneously territorial (with boundaries that include and exclude) and networked (connected territories or nodes). We can use the two different epistemologies advanced by Lefebvre and Harvey above, together with the different forms of spatial organization outlined above, to generate a grid, as below with illustrative processes content.

Given the exigencies of length, I will only develop two examples from the education questions above to show what this might mean: first, 'tracking' students into different education groups, and second, processes of decentralization/marketization in education governance (see Tables 1.1 and 1.2). Typical organizational processes in which almost all schooling systems differentiate learners in some way in the education system are through spatial practices such as 'grouping', 'tracking' or 'streaming', or through the provision of different kinds of schooling experience, such as private versus public schools, or vocational schools versus comprehensive schools.

Table 1.1 'Tracking': spatial stratification

	Spatial practice [perceived space]	Representations of space [conceived]	Spaces of representation [lived]
Absolute space	particular knowledges/ lessons delivered to 'tracked' student; classroom	class groups/ability/ year levels/school types; school prospectus; school uniform;	aspiration; feelings of worth/ lessness; belonging; withdrawal; resistance and rebellion
Relative space	different levels of student development; local school ecology; school mix (of social classes; cultural backgrounds)	'ability' as innate intelligence/tracks and grades as reflecting capabilities; public– private school contrasts; inspection reports;	anxiety over resources need to produce competence; 'nothing here for us–we always fail; reject schooling as 'un-cool' failing/ successful school
Relational space	School as a system of reproduction over time; performance in the education system	Re/production of failure; 'meritocracy'; social stratification	being a competent learner; the working class ; class strategies such as voice, exit and choice; white flight

Table 1.2 Decentralisation/markets: spatial governance

	Spatial practice [perceived space]	Representations of space [conceived]	Spaces of representation [lived]
Absolute space	movement of responsibilities to new nodes outward and upward; downward; new sectors	local development plans; partnership plans; sub- contracting/outsourcing; school development plans; local visions; markets	anxieties over opportunities for choice; greater organisational responsibilities without power to affect necessary changes; surveillance; performativity
Relative space	Different geometries of governance relations that cut across scales; rescaling;	local development, social capital, community expertise, partnership; public/ private; third sector [networks]	differential choices; different inspection regimes; different feelings of involvement by wider community
Relational space	policy frameworks that operate at multiple nodes; competitiveness	global discourses of choice, markets, self management, entrepreneurialism; neo-liberal political project	desires of consumer; entrepreneur; flexible; anxiety about responsibility for one's future

Here, we can see particular geometries of power at work: the outcome of the way in which the social relations of production are projected onto education spaces, at the level of systems, schools, classrooms and groups. This system of spatial stratifying is a key mechanism of social reproduction. Space, as we can see in this example, is a medium and resource of power. This conception of education space – as thickened clusters of social relations legitimated by notions of ability/intelligence/learning capability – takes a material form. Children attend different classes and have different learning experiences. This spatial organization of education space is also regulated/governed through systems of assessment and self-management. It is a lived space, so that learners and teachers both feel, in palpable albeit different ways, the emotions that arise from discourses of aspiration, capability, achievement, responsibility, meritocracy and so on.

That lives to be lived in the future are shaped by this projected and deep penetration of the social relations of production onto education space, as workers in a system of capitalist social relations, illustrates the point Lefebvre and Harvey both make about the linkages between events and practices. In other words, the multiple epistemologies and modalities of space are deeply implicated in the making of pedagogic identities.

This second example focuses on the policy of 'decentralization' and the rolling out of education markets, a powerful, neo-liberal discourse that has resulted in the relocation of education activity away from previously fixed, institutionalized centres to new, reworked spaces of knowledge production with new geometries of social relations. In most cases, the centres of power in the Westphalian state, the national state, have rescaled selective functions to different nodes in the scalar architecture of the global order. These scales have, in turn, been reworked to include new sets of logics – around efficiency, choice, local partnership, self-management, responsibility. More importantly, unpicking institutionalized social relations has enabled new, non-state actors (particularly for-profit) into the reconstitution of education spaces. Much of the literature on decentralization has tended to view the movement of power in a downward direction – to the local organization/community. While this most certainly was the direction in which some education activity has flowed, viewing the movement only in this direction, and in terms of the official discourse – decentralization – would be to take at face value the spatial imaginary of the representation of space. The idea of scale – as opposed to decentralization – enables us to see quite what is at stake: the social production of scale and the reconstitution of social relations in a shifting spatial geometry of power and social relations. Using the concept of scale enables us to trace movements in multiple directions, as new nodes of power and rule are constructed or invigorated, struggled over and legitimated. In turn, we are able to see the emergence of a new functional and scalar division of the labour of education space. Positionality matters in this case, as the social relations arising from market-based relations are dependent upon who and what are included in the spatial organization of choice. So, too, do networks, which work as means of protection against exclusions as well as mechanisms to ensure inclusion – such as clubs. Spatializing state projects, such as 'decentralization' and 'markets', raise significant issues for the spatiality of the sociology of education – anchored as it has been in a deep, methodological nationalism and statism. This is despite the fact that the sites, scales, strategies and subjectivities for the re/constituting and governing of education have been highly dependent upon re/projecting and re/working education spatial and social relations.

Conclusion

This paper can only begin to set out the necessary parameters, and possibilities for insights that might be realized, in a project of reworking the sociology of education in spatial terms. At one level, the idea that space matters in the sociology of education might be to state something that is – for want of a better word – all too obvious. Those involved in education, whether as teachers, learners or researchers of these processes, are confronted with spatial metaphors all of the time. At another level, however, it continues to surprise me that the conceptual grammar in the sociology of education continues in a way that offers us a relatively banal reading of space, of the 'all too obvious' ways in which space matters – such as identifications with particular spaces and so on. While important, this is to understand only one of the spatial epistemologies through which we know and are constituted by the social. It is, therefore, to miss the very real, powerful and significant way in which the social relations within the multiplicity of overlapping education spaces are constantly being strategically, spatially recalibrated, reorganized and reconstituted to produce a very different geometry of power. Continuing with a conceptual grammar in the sociology of education that is oriented towards modernity's preoccupation with time and sociality, and not spatiality, means continuing with a set of concepts that are unable to grasp the full enormity of the changes that have been advanced under the rubric of globalization and the ways in which education space has been radically transformed. Clearly, one important implication of spatializing the sociology of education is the challenge that follows from this: the development of a set of methodological/organizational categories that are able to take full account of the concerns of sociologists of education. Finally, I would argue that, in spatializing the sociology of education, we, in turn, enhance the possibilities of what Lefebvre named 'anOther' space emerging: an alternative, differently constituted, social space, constructed out of ideas about being and becoming, that might in turn mediate the full onslaught of the social relations of global capitalism.

Note

1   I am extremely grateful to Peter Jones for his engagement and generative conversations on this project.

References

Allen, J., Cochrane, A. and Massey, D. (1998) *Re-thinking the region*, London: Routledge.

Amin, A. (2004) 'Spatialities of globalisation', *Environment and Planning A* 34: 385–399.

Arnot, M. and Reay, D. (2006) 'The framing of performance pedagogies: pupil perspectives on the control of school management and its acquisition', in H. Lauder, P. Brown, J. Dillabough and A.H. Halsey (eds) *Education, globalization and social change*, Oxford: Oxford University Press.

Ball, S. (2007) *Education plc: understanding private sector participation in public sector education*, Oxford and New York: Routledge.

—— Bowe, R. and Gewirtz, S. (1996) 'Circuits of schooling: a sociological exploration of parental choice of schooling in social class contexts', *Sociological Review* 43 (1): 52–78.

Bernstein, B. (1990) *The structuring of pedagogic discourse: class, codes and control*, London and New York: Routledge.

Bourdieu, P. (1986) 'The forms of capital', in J.G. Richardson (ed.) *Handbook of theory and research for the sociology of education*, Westport, CT: Greenwood.

Brenner, N. (2003) *New state spaces*, Oxford: Oxford University Press.

Brown, P. and Lauder, H. (2005) 'Globalisation, knowledge and the myth of the magnet economy', *Globalisation, Societies and Education*, 4(1): 25–57.

Castells, M. (1996) *The network society*, Oxford: Blackwell.

Dale, R. (1996) 'The state and the governance of education: an analysis of the restructuring of the state-education relation', in A.H. Halsey, H. Lauder, P. Brown and A. Stuart Wells (eds) *Education, culture, economy, society*, Oxford: Oxford University Press.

—— (2006) 'From comparison to translation: extending the research imagination', *Globalisation, Societies and Education* 4 (2): 179–192.

Gewirtz, S., Ball, S. and Bowe, R. (1995) *Markets, choice and equity in education*, Buckingham: Open University Press.

Gillborn, D. and Youdell, D. (2006) 'Educational triage and the D-to-C conversion: suitable cases for treatment', in H. Lauder, P. Brown, J. Dillabough and A.H. Halsey, (eds) *Education, globalization and social change*, Oxford: Oxford University Press.

Guile, D. (2006) 'What is distinctive about the knowledge economy? Implications for education', in H. Lauder, P. Brown, J. Dillabough and A.H. Halsey (eds) *Education, globalization and social change*, Oxford: Oxford University Press.

Harvey, D. (1982) *Limits to capital*, London and New York: Verso.

—— (1989) *The condition of postmodernity*, Oxford: Blackwell.

—— (2006) 'Space as a keyword', in N. Castree and D. Gregory, *David Harvey: a critical reader*, Oxford: Blackwell Publishing.

Hatcher, R. (2006) 'Privatization and sponsorship: the reagenting of the school system in England', *Journal of Education Policy* 21(5): 599–619.

Herod, A. and Wright, M. (eds) (2002) *Geographies of power: placing scale*, Oxford: Blackwell.

Hudson, (2001) *Producing place*, New York and London: The Guildford Press.

Jessop, B., Brenner, N. and Jones, M. (2008) 'Theorising sociospatial relations', *Environment and Planning D* 26: 389–401.

Kamat, S. Mir, A. and Mathew, M. (2004) 'Producing hi-tech: globalization, the state and migrant subjects', *Globalisation, Societies and Education* 2(1): 1–39.

Lefebvre, H. (1991) *The production of space* (trans. Donald Nicholson-Smith), Oxford: Blackwell.

Levin, H. and Belfield, C. (2006) 'The marketplace of education', in H. Lauder, P. Brown, J. Dillabough and A.H. Halsey (eds) *Education, globalization and social change*, Oxford: Oxford University Press.

Mahony, P., Hextall, I. and Menter, I. (2004) 'Building dams in Jordan, assessing teachers in England: a case study in edu-business', *Globalisation, Societies and Education* 2(2): 277–296.

Marston, S., Jones III, J.-P. and Woodward, K. (2005) 'Human geography without scale', *Transactions of the Institute of British Geographers* 30: 416–432.

Massey, D. (1994) *Space, place and gender*, Cambridge: Polity Press.

—— (2005) *For space*, London: Sage.

Rizvi, F. and Lingard, B. (2006) 'Globalisation and the changing nature of the OECD's educational work', in H. Lauder, P. Brown, J. Dillabough and A.H. Halsey (eds) *Education, globalization and social change*, Oxford: Oxford University Press.

—— (2009) 'Globalization, global governance and citizenship regimes: new democratic deficits and social inequalities', in W. Ayes, T. Quinn and D. Stovall (eds) *Social Justice in Education*, London and New York: Routledge.

—— Bonal, X. and Dale, R. (2002) 'GATS and the education service industry: the politics of scale and global reterritorialisation', *Comparative Education Review* 46(4): 472–496.

Rose, G. (1993) *Feminist theory and geography*, Cambridge: Polity Press.

Shepherd, E. (2002) 'The spaces and times of globalization: place, scale, networks and positionality', *Economic Geography* 78: 307–330.

Smith, L. (2006) 'Colonising knowledges', in H. Lauder, P. Brown, J. Dillabough and A.H. Halsey (eds) *Education, globalization and social change*, Oxford: Oxford University Press.

Smith, N. (1990) *Uneven development*, Cambridge, MA: Blackwell.

Smith, N. (1992) 'Geography, difference and the production of scale', in J. Doherty, E. Graham, and M. Malek, (eds) *Postmodernism and the social sciences*, New York: St. Martin's Press.

Soja, E. (1996) *Thirdspace: journeys to Los Angeles and other real and imagined spaces*, Oxford: Blackwell Publishing.

2

Foucault and education

Inés Dussel

It is somewhat paradoxical to devote a chapter to an author who insistently challenged the authority of proper names and who called for a dismantling of the "author function" as part of his critique of the essentialist view of the subject.[1] Yet, Foucault's name has become unavoidable for social theorists in the last thirty years, and his place within the sociology of education cannot be questioned—however problematic it remains, as will be discussed later. Not only was he a prolific writer, with fifteen books published during his lifetime (1926–1984), and several more, along with over 360 articles, chapters and interviews, collected and printed after his death,[2] but, in some respects, it could be argued that he continues to be so, as several of his courses at the Collège de France are still waiting to be edited and published, and new interviews and collections appear periodically. He has also been the subject of innumerable books and articles, with which whole libraries could be filled.

Although he did not consecrate an entire book, nor even a complete text, to the question of education, his impact on educational thought and particularly on the field of the sociology of education has been substantial. This fact is most remarkable considering that his philosophy is a bitter pill to swallow for educators, as it shakes most of the grounds on which modern schooling has been built: truth, knowledge, vocation, enlightenment, or salvation. Not surprisingly, his denunciation of the injustices committed by educational institutions has turned his work into a cornerstone for critical pedagogy since the mid 1970s.[3] For example, in the Anglo-speaking academic field, Stephen Ball (1990) edited a thoughtful compilation on the uses of Foucault's work for educational policy and sociology, and Tom Popkewitz (1991) produced a political reading of the rhetoric of educational reform and change, and of pedagogical discourse, based on Foucault's texts. These few examples show the extent to which Foucault's work has helped renew the topics and methodologies of educational thought.[4]

What is most important is that his political stances on education have extended in the educational field well beyond critical pedagogy. After Foucault, it is difficult to state undauntedly that education is concerned solely with doing good to people and promoting social progress. It is not unusual to listen to undergraduates or teachers speaking about the relationship between schools and the production of disciplined bodies, or to refer to histories of education in terms of genealogies. At least in continental Europe and Latin America, it has almost become commonplace to quote bits and pieces of *Discipline and punish* to denounce the fact that schools discipline (in the sense of repress) children (Foucault, 1995).

To become such a widely recognized author has not been without consequences. It could be said that the discomfort originally caused by Foucault's work has, more times than would be desirable, been domesticated and turned into a comfortable reading position (as was observed by McLeod, 2001). This chapter intends to argue against this taming of Foucault's work into a "safe knowledge strategy" and its conversion into a conceptual apparatus that already knows what it is going to find. Maybe it is about time to ask if the once-discomforting Foucaultian interventions can still be sharp and poignant, and if the knowledge they produce is useful for "cutting" our current ways of understanding education as a social action (Foucault, 2003b).

In the field of the sociology of education, this kind of domestication has led to Foucault's work being read as somewhat flat sociological descriptions. Let's take, for example, the book that has become part of the "vulgata" of educational sociology. Castro (2004b), author of an impressive book on Foucault's vocabulary, defies such a reading: "*Discipline and Punish* is not a book on sociology: it does not describe a society but an ideal." Something similar was asserted by Foucault in an interview conducted shortly after the publication of the book: "If I had wanted to describe 'real life' in the prisons, I indeed wouldn't have gone to Bentham." (Foucault, 2003a: 253) He immediately added that to assume that ideals are not part of reality is to hold a very poor notion of the real, but he certainly did not think that, when writing *Surveiller et punir*, he was producing the ultimate work on the sociology, or even the history, of the prison or of schooling.

This reading of Foucault's complex and multilayered work as plain sociological descriptions is one of the reasons why his inclusion within the field of the sociology of education remains problematic. Also, his texts refuse to comply with the classical rules of sociological work that prescribe detachment and neutrality, and renounce the possibility of finding "social" (namely, pre-discursive) truths and causes in a "real world" that is supposed to exist outside discursive practices (an assumption shared by critical sociological traditions).

On the other hand, many of his gestures have been welcomed by those seeking to renew sociological practices, especially when he looked for regularities and patterns of social discourses that simultaneously accounted for singularities, when he sought to problematize and historicize what we conceive of as "the social," and when he rejected prescriptive and judicial positions about social events. He intended to "address '*practices*' as a domain of analysis, approach the study from the angle of 'what was done'" (Foucault, 2003c: 4). Foucault's value for sociologists might well be the opposite of the flat descriptions we are currently offered: his work enables us to open up what we think the social is, and to interrogate the totalizing discourses of the social sciences.

Taking as its point of departure this problematic relationship between Foucault's work and the sociology of education, this chapter proposes an overall discussion of his texts around three concepts that can help unfold this tension in different directions. Those three concepts are power, body, and critique. In this piece, there is no intention to exhaust a far-too-vast *oeuvre*, not only because of its magnitude but also because it would be impossible to account for all the exegesis and critiques that have been raised about these main concepts. Another important point for this *International Handbook* is that the reading of Foucault is tied to national traditions and problematics, in many more ways than could be accounted for in these pages. Variations in the role of the state, of scientific discourses, and even the traditions of teaching produce disparate readings of Foucault that would need a closer scrutiny.[5] More humbly, the chapter aims at producing a few troubling effects on what we think we already know about Foucault and its value for a sociology of education, and will do so using less well-known texts that, hopefully, might still tell us something poignant about these highly navigated topics.

Power

Power has been a major theme in Foucault's work. Following Edgardo Castro's annotated vocabulary (2004a), "power" appears 7,276 times throughout all his French texts, while "knowledge" appears 4,025 times, and "body," 3,554. However, power is an elusive concept for the French philosopher. He stated that it should not be considered a substance but a relation; that it is microphysical and multiform, and operates in multiple games that have their own historicity (Foucault, 1983). There is no single power that can be located at a given place; it is some sort of an analytic grid or logbook that helps us understand how subjects relate to each other and how institutions are organized. It is a relationship that can be exercised from outside inside and from inside outside (Foucault, 1983). Power is not a zero-sum game: we all have some kind of power, not necessarily comparable to others. Another basic trait is that power is repressive as much as it is productive; power obliges, but also incites, mobilizes. It is embodied and enacted in our bodies and in our discourses:

> Governing people . . . is not a way to force people to do what the governor wants; it is always a versatile equilibrium, with complementarity and conflicts between techniques which impose coercion and processes through which the self is constructed or modified by himself.
>
> (Foucault, 1997b: 182)

At some point, Foucault (1997a: 51) provides a definition of power as "a whole series of particular mechanisms, definable and defined, which seem likely to induce behaviors or discourses." This capacity to "conduct the conduct," to influence others, is as marvelous as it is dangerous, and produces effects that have to be closely monitored. Foucault says, in a suggestive essay on the value of rebellion, that,

> The power that one man exercises over another is always perilous. I am not saying that power is evil by nature; I am saying that, owing to its mechanisms, power is infinite (which does not mean to say that it is all powerful; quite to the contrary).
>
> (Foucault, 1999: 134)

In this essay, he asserts that a proof that power is not totally oppressive is that there are human beings who revolt. And these revolts are the ones that allow history to become such, and not a determinist evolution. Foucault pictured those revolts as the anonymous rebellions of "abnormals," of outcasts, of those in the margins, but precisely because of that, the most heroic kinds of revolt. He considered that one should always have

> to be respectful when something singular arises, to be intransigent when power offends against the universal . . . It is always necessary to watch out for something, a little beneath history, that breaks it, that agitates it; it is necessary to look, a little behind politics, for that which ought to limit it, unconditionally.
>
> (Foucault, 1999: 134)

29

A little beneath history and a little behind politics: Foucault urges us to look *in other places*, and these other places are not defined *loci* (margins or centers) but are continuously redefined in terms of the game. The sociology of education, informed by a Foucaultian framework, should be thought of as a mobile and historical cartography, and not as a static picturing of an already defined topography.

How do these ideas resonate in the sociology of education? I would like to focus on the critique of teaching as an oppressive social power, an important part of the Foucault "vulgata" already mentioned. George Steiner, usually not very passionate about Foucault's thought, appraises the philosopher's contribution to thinking about pedagogical relationships, and especially about the figure of the Teacher.

> No matter how simplified it has become, Foucault's point of view is still relevant. Teaching could be considered as an exercise, open or hidden, of power relations. The Teacher has a psychological, social, and physical power. S/he can reward and punish, exclude and rise. Her authority is institutional, charismatic or both at the same time. She is helped by the promise or the threat.
>
> (Steiner, 2003: 13)

Steiner affirms unapologetically that Teachers (with a capital T) have a power that should be operated for good reasons. Yet similar statements about teachers always exercising some sort of power over their students, that exams are disciplinary institutions, and that authority always carries with it a risk have led some educators to incline themselves to a sort of pedagogical abstention, or to become wary of any type of education that has been equaled to imposition and authoritarianism.

Foucault's references on teaching reject this abstentionism and point to the need to understand, historically and sociologically, the discourses that have shaped teaching as a position of power.[6] In one of his last texts, he said that authority is not condemned to be useless or authoritarian:

> [the pedagogical institution] has often been rightly criticized . . . [Yet] I see nothing wrong in the practice of a person who, knowing more than others in a specific game of truth, tells those others what to do, teaches them and transmits knowledge and techniques to them. The problem in such practices where power—which is not in itself a bad thing— must inevitably come into play is knowing how to avoid the kind of domination effects where a kid is subjected to the arbitrary and unnecessary authority of a teacher, or a student put under the thumb of a professor who abuses his authority. I believe that this problem must be framed in terms of rules of law, rational techniques of government and ethos, practices of the self and of freedom.
>
> (Foucault 1996b: 447)

In this text, Foucault invites the reader to think about education as a social and historical practice that involves power relations but that can be none the less a training exercise in the paradoxes of freedom, and that seeks to expand its limits through new experiences. Sociology, then, is not reduced to what the social actually is, but includes how it turned to be that way, and also what it can be if different ways of thinking are introduced.

Body

The second concept that will be reviewed is the body. Foucault insists repeatedly, clearly in *Discipline and punish* but in many other texts as well, that power is exercised first and foremost on bodies, and that is precisely the source of its materiality. The body is the surface on which this game is played, on which power is produced and repressed. The body is the surface upon which the law is written, patterns of normality are shaped, and relations of subjection and obedience are founded (Nievas, 1998).

As with power, Foucault conceives of bodies, not as mere substances (although their materiality is never questioned), but as the effects of discourses of power that have their own historicity. His many writings on the topic intend to open up sociological and historical perspectives on the body, yet this movement does not reduce the body to being the effect of a transcendental and already determined context. For example, in *Discipline and punish*, he goes from the inside to the outside: from the discourses on disciplining bodies to the more general regularities for organizing space and time, individuals, or power grids. It is not because of a given context that the body is produced in particular ways, but it is through understanding the minutiae of everyday monastic rules or apprenticeship regulations that one can learn something about a given epoch.

Following Foucault, Brazilian historian Denise Bernuzzi Sant'Anna wrote that the body is a polysemic text in which biology, psychological expressions, cultural anxieties and phantoms, and history get mingled. The body is

a mutant memory of the laws and codes of each culture, a register for the solutions and for the technological and scientific constraints of each time . . . The body has not ceased to be fabricated throughout time.

(Bernuzzi de Sant'Anna, 1995: 12)

This idea of fabrication clearly speaks about social and educational processes. One of the great merits of Foucault's work has been to reframe the history and present of pedagogy as the history and present of an intervention on bodies. In the twentieth century, pedagogy and education were dominated by rational pedagogies, with echoes from Calvinist pedagogies—even in Catholic countries such as France or Spain—that conceived bodies as the site of sinful inclinations or, in the modern scientific version, pathologies and illnesses.

Foucault's work has rendered visible the phenomenal concern about bodies in educational institutions. As British sociologist Philip Corrigan (1988) said, one usually forgets what schools made "with, to, and for my body." Schools sought to produce a total transformation of students' bodily behavior, through rules and regulations that prescribed social performances, appearances, and moral scales and that established "normal" patterns as well as deviations. Notions of decency and decorum, cleanliness and filthiness were tied into political, economic, and moral categories, and constructed power relations that had pervasive effects (cf. Vigarello, 1988). This construction persisted for many decades. In her reflections on bodies and schools, a contemporary Brazilian educator, Guacira Lopes Louro (1999), recalls the struggle with the educational authorities over the regulation of attire, particularly over the donning of uniforms, which apparently expropriated the students of their bodies and turned them into an indivisible part of the school community. These struggles condensed issues of authority and knowledge in schools that were far from marginal to their educational aims.

Against this mode of subjectivation through rigid patterns, pedagogies of sexual freedom or the "express yourself" type flourished in the 1960s and 1970s (Vigarello, 1978). Foucault's work is very helpful also to counterbalance the influence of a certain naïf-romanticism on the natural qualities of bodies. Peter Cryle (2000), in an insightful essay on "The Kama Sutra as curriculum," provides good arguments to discuss the idea that the natural and the spontaneous are outside discourse, and that any teaching of bodily behaviors goes against the authenticity and freedom of one's own. Cryle points to the different modes of relationship to the body that are present in the Kama Sutra, whose sequence of exercises could even be conceived as a curriculum for erotic pleasure. Desire and pleasure, then, are never outside discourse; they are social practices that have been shaped by discourses that have their own historicity.

A sociological reading of Foucault's thought about bodies in schools could also point to the new discourses that are being stated on contemporary bodies. Studies on aesthetic patterns, diets, surgeries and medical treatments—including the increasing pharmacopedia which children's psychology is turning into—fashion, style, tattoing, piercings, are all important to understand how bodies are inscribed in and by power, and also where disruptions and revolts emerge.

Critique

The third point of this overview of Foucault's work and its value for the sociology of education will deal with the notion of "critique." Foucault was an acid critic of intellectuals' pretentious claims of detachment and objectivity. According to his view, all the building of modern social science had served for producing discourses of truth on human beings, knowledge, and society that had resulted in subjections and domestications. He was especially critical of leftist intellectuals who, in the name of socialism and revolution, never abandoned their claims to dictate what is good, just, and true for the rest of their human fellows, and were never self-critical about their complicity with institutional powers, be it the Party, the University or the State. He also attacked the idea of revolution, as he disbelieved in the synchrony of ruptures: there is no such limit as a revolution, but a series of transformations, and these transformations are not held together necessarily by any unifying principle or meaning (Castro, 2004a).

However distant he felt himself from the figure of the "critical intellectual," Foucault never gave up the role of critique and established, at least in some of his writings, a clear affiliation with what is usually known as the "progressive tradition" in social theory, particularly with Marxism and the Frankfurt School, although always escaping any re-introduction of the sovereign subject. In an entry on his own name that he prepared for a *Dictionnaire des philosophes* in the early 1980s, Foucault defined himself as heir to the critical tradition of Kant and decided to call his intellectual project "a critical history of thought" (in Rabinow and Rose, 2003: 1). In this respect, there are clear links between his project and the sociology of school knowledge and of educational discourses.

But there are other echoes of his view of "critique" that could point to different links and directions. In a conference delivered at the French Society for Philosophy in 1978, Foucault dealt with the notion of "critique" in a more consistent way. To the question of "what is critique?" he answered that it is an action, an instrument that "oversees a domain it would want to police and is unable to regulate" (Foucault, 1997a: 25). Rooted in the legacy of Enlightenment and in an attitude that has both come along with, and gone against, the political objectives of governing subjects, the art of critique has sought to be an act of defiance, of opposition; a way of changing the government, of seeking a form of escaping it or displacing it. Critique is

> A kind of cultural form, both a political and moral attitude, a way of thinking, etc. and which I would very simply call the art of not being governed or better, the art of not being governed like that and at that cost. I would therefore propose, as a very first definition of critique, this general characterization: the art of not being governed *quite so much.*
>
> (Foucault, 1997a: 29)

The locus of critique is not a neutral or safe space. There is no place that can be preserved from power/knowledge strategies, and, in these games, we are all participants, we all take sides and are complicit to one or another power play.

Also, the subject who criticizes and intervenes, the subject of politics, is not a sovereign subject that could be defined a priori. Once again, Foucault was a master of discontinuous thought and of a politics that continually has to recreate itself. In an interview performed around politics and problematization, he discussed his own participation in collective movements:

> "we" must not be previous to the question; it can only be the result—and the necessarily temporary result—of the question as it is posed in the new terms in which one formulates it . . . For example, I'm not sure that at the time when I wrote the history of madness, there was a preexisting and receptive "we" . . . Laing, Cooper, Basaglia[7] and I had no community, nor any relationship; but the problem posed itself to those who had read us, as it also posed itself to some of us, of seeing if it were possible to establish a "we" on the basis of the work that had been done, a "we" that would also be likely to form a community of action.
>
> (Foucault, 2003d: 21)

There is not a sovereign subject of revolt, nor is there one of critique, but communities of action. This comment also points to the fact that, as feminist and post-colonial critics have emphasized some years later building upon some of Foucault's insights,[8] critique is always a situated action that is to be localized in specific conditions and be engaged as a passionate activity, slanted and biased, that seeks to point out what the cost is of being governed in those ways, but also seeks to imagine which other forms would be possible so that we can reduce injustice and enlarge our margins of freedom.

To think around a situated critique implies a different relationship to temporality. In another interview conducted in 1978, Foucault manifested:

> one of the most destructive habits of modern thought . . . is that the moment of the present is considered in history as the break, the climax, the fulfillment, the return of the youth, etc. . . . . One must probably find the humility to admit that the time of one's own life is not the one-time, basic, revolutionary moment of history, from which every-thing begins and is completed. At the same time, humility is needed to say without solemnity that the present time is rather exciting and demands an analysis. We must ask ourselves the question, What is today? In relation to the Kantian question, "What is Enlightenment?" one can say that it is the task of philosophy to explain what today is and what we are today, but without breast-beating drama and theatricality and

maintaining that this moment is the greatest damnation or daybreak of the rising sun. No, it is a day like every other, or much more, a day which is never like another.

(Foucault, 1996a: 359)

Today is a day unlike any other day. One cannot sleep over one's own certainties, nor perform critical acts that repeat themselves and say nothing new. There is no definite or just solution to all social problems, but the important thing is that the question (of madness, of imprisonment, of power) remains open for a new strategy to emerge (Potte-Bonneville, 2007: 260). A just appraisal of Foucault within the sociology of education would be one that does not turn his work into a comfortable position, but one that keeps its vitality and poignancy. To think about schools and power after Foucault should imply daring to see what of his "art of impugnation" is helpful to think about this present, to grasp what it tells about ourselves as subjects of knowledge and as bodies, but also to see what discomforts us enough to build new communities of action in order to think and act differently about schools, knowledge, and power.

Notes

1   See, especially, "What is an author?" (Foucault, 1977). He was particularly wary of the kind of analysis that searches for a unifying principle within a certain *oeuvre* and that explains that principle in terms of the author's persona.
2   I have followed Bert (2004), who provides a thorough bibliography of Foucault.
3   Of course, Foucault's inscription in the field of critical pedagogy has not gone unchallenged. He has been labeled as a "young conservative" (Habermas, as quoted by Fraser, 1996), and it has been said that his work is characterized by an "absence of historicity, of individual agency, and of politics, in short" (Schrag, 1999). But also his work has been turned into a critical intervention against many of the assumptions stated by critical theories (see, for example, Popkewitz and Brennan, 1998; Tamboukou and Ball, 2003; Baker and Heyning, 2004). While it is important to understand these dissents and nuances, and this chapter clearly sides with the second type of intervention and not with the first type of reading, that path will not be pursued in these pages.
4   Among the earlier works can be noted Anne Querrien´s thought-provoking genealogy of elementary schooling, which was oriented by Foucault himself (Querrien, 1976), and Georges Vigarello's erudite history of the corrections (dressage) of the body as the genealogy of a pedagogical power, ranging from the sixteenth- to the twentieth centuries (Vigarello, 1978). Valerie Walkerdine (1988) used Foucault's critique of liberal rationality to put into question the primacy of educational psychologies to explain the acts of knowing. More recent scholarship includes Baker and Heyning (2004), Jardine (2005), Olssen (2006, first edition in 1999), and Peters and Besley (2007).
     It should be noted that the bibliography on Foucault/education is enormous and exceeds the few Anglo, Spanish, and French references I will be providing. Some other works are cited in the chapter, but I acknowledge that my selection is not fair to the numerous efforts made by many scholars to bring Foucault's work closer to the educational field. Apologies to all of them.
5   I thank Tom Popkewitz for pointing this out to me.
6   Popkewitz (1998) and McWilliam (1999) provide insightful Foucauldian readings of teaching.
7   All members of the anti-institutionalization movement in psychiatry in the 1960s.
8   This relationship has not been without tensions. Ann P. Stoler (1995) provides a good discussion on Foucault's silence on imperialism and colonialism. Spivak (2008) uses Foucault wisely to interrogate contemporary spectacles of punishment but also Middle East projects of modernization and westernization. Fraser (1996) and the collection in which it is included are but a few of the many examples that could be provided about these tensions.

References

Ball, S.J. (1990) *Foucault and education. Disciplines and knowledge*, London: Routledge.

Baker, B. and Heyning, K. (2004) *Dangerous coagulations. The uses of Foucault in the study of education*, New York and Bern: Peter Lang Publishing.

Bernuzzi de Sant'Anna, D. (1995) "Apresentaçao," in *Políticas do corpo. Elementos para uma história das práticas corporais*, São Paulo: Estaçao Liberdade.

Bert, J.-F. (2004) "Bibliographie générale," *Le Portique* 13–14 "Foucault: usages et actualités." Available online at http://leportique.revues.org/document643.html (accessed 6 January 2009).

Castro, E. (2004a) *El vocabulario de Michel Foucault. Un recorrido alfabético por sus temas, conceptos y autores*, Buenos Aires: Prometeo 3010/Universidad Nacional de Quilmes.

—— (2004b) "Descifrando a Foucault. Entrevista con Ivana Costa," *Diario Clarin* 19 June 2004. Available online at www.clarin.com/suplementos/cultura/2004/06/19/u-779060.htm (accessed 4 January 2009).

Corrigan, P. (1988) "The making of the boy: meditations on what grammar school did with, to, and for my body," *Journal of Education* 170(3).

Cryle, P. (2000) "The Kama Sutra as curriculum," in C. O'Farrel, D. Meadmore, E. McWilliam and C. Symes (eds) *Taught bodies*, New York and Bern: Peter Lang Publishing, pp. 17–26.

Foucault, M. (1977) "What is an author? (trans. Joshua Harari)," in D. Bouchard (ed.) *Language, knowledge, counter-memory: selected essays and interviews*, Ithaca, NY: Cornell University Press.

—— (1983) "The subject and power," in P. Rabinow and H. Dreyfus (eds) *Michel Foucault: beyond structuralism and hermeneutics*, Chicago, IL: Chicago University Press.

—— (1995) *Discipline and punish. The birth of the prison*, New York: Vintage Books.

—— (1996a) "How much does it cost for reason to tell the truth," in S. Lotringer (ed.) *Foucault live. Collected interviews, 1961–1984*, New York: Semiotext(e), pp. 348–362.

—— (1996b) "The ethics of the concern for self as a practice of freedom (interview with Raul Fornet-Betancourt, Helmut Becker, and Alfredo Gomez-Muller)," in S. Lotringer (ed.) *Foucault live. Collected interviews, 1961–1984*, New York: Semiotext(e), pp. 432–449.

—— (1997a) "What is critique?," in *The politics of truth*, New York: Semiotext(e).

—— (1997b) "Subjectivity and truth," in *The politics of truth*, New York: Semiotext(e).

—— (1999) "Is it useless to revolt?," in *Religion and culture. Michel Foucault*, New York: Routledge.

—— (2003a) "Questions of method," in P. Rabinow and N. Rose (eds) *The essential Foucault. Selections from the essential works of Foucault, 1954–1984*, New York: The New Press, pp. 246–258.

—— (2003b) "Nietzsche, genealogy, history," in P. Rabinow and N. Rose (eds) *The essential Foucault. Selections from the essential works of Foucault, 1954–1984*, New York: The New Press, pp. 351–369.

—— (2003c) "Michel Foucault. Maurice Florence," in P. Rabinow and N. Rose (eds) *The essential Foucault. Selections from the essential works of Foucault, 1954–1984*, New York: The New Press, pp. 1–5.

—— (2003d) "Polemics, politics, and problematizations: an interview with Michel Foucault," in P. Rabinow and N. Rose (eds) *The essential Foucault. Selections from the essential works of Foucault, 1954–1984*, New York: The New Press, pp. 18–24.

Fraser, N. (1996) "Michel Foucault: A 'Young Conservative'?" in S. Hekman (ed.) *Feminist interpretations of Michel Foucault*, University Park, PA: Penn State University Press, pp. 15–38.

Jardine, G. (2005) *Foucault and education*, New York: Peter Lang.

Lopes Louro, G. (ed.) (1999) *O corpo educado. Pedagogias da sexualidade*, Belo Horizonte: Autentica.

McLeod, J. (2001) "Foucault forever," *Discourse: studies in the cultural politics of education*, 22(1): 95–104.

McWilliam, E. (1999) *Pedagogical pleasures*, New York and Bern: Peter Lang Publishing.

Nievas, F. (1998) *El control social de los cuerpos*, Buenos Aires: Eudeba.

Olssen, M. (2006) *Michel Foucault: materialism and education*, Boulder, CO: Paradigm Publishers.

Peters, M. and Besley, T. (2007) *Subjectivity and truth: Foucault, education, and the culture of self*, New York: Peter Lang.

Popkewitz, T.S. (1991) *A political sociology of educational reform. Power/knowledge in teaching, teacher education, and research*, New York: Teachers' College Press.

—— (1998) *Struggling for the soul: the politics of education and the construction of the teacher*, New York: Teachers' College Press.

—— and M. Brennan (eds) (1998) *Foucault's challenge. Discourse, knowledge, and power in education*, New York: Teachers' College Press.

Potte-Bonneville, M. (2007) *Michel Foucault, la inquietud de la historia* (trans. Hilda García), Buenos Aires: Manantial.

Querrien, A. (1976) *L'Ensaignement. Travaux élementaires sur l'école primaire*, Fontenay-sous-Bois: Recherches.

Rabinow, P. and Rose, N. (2003) "Introduction. Foucault today," in *The essential Foucault. Selections from the essential works of Foucault, 1954–1984*, New York: The New Press.

Schrag, F. (1999) "Why Foucault now?," *Journal of Curriculum Studies*, Op-Ed paper. Available at http://faculty.ed.uiuc.edu/westbury/JCS/Vol31/Schrag.html.

Spivak, G. (2008) "1996: Foucault and Najibullah'," in *Other Asias*, Malden, MA: Blackwell Publishing.

Steiner, G. (2003) *Lecciones de maestros*, Madrid: Siruela.

Stoler, A. (1995) *Race and the education of desire. Foucault's history of sexuality and the colonial order of things*, Durham, NC, and London: Duke University Press.

Tamboukou, M. and Ball, S.J. (eds) (2003) *Dangerous encounters*, New York: Peter Lang.

Vigarello, G. (1978) *Le corps redressé. Histoire d'un pouvoir pédagogique*, Paris: J.P. Delarge.

—— (1988) *Concepts of cleanliness. Changing attitudes in France since the Middle Ages*, Cambridge/Paris: Cambridge University Press/Maison des Sciences de l'Homme.

Walkerdine, V. (1988) *The mastery of reason. Cognitive development and the production of rationality*, London and New York: Routledge.

3

Education and critical race theory

David Gillborn and Gloria Ladson-Billings

Introduction

> CRT's usefulness will be limited not by the weakness of its constructs but by the degree that many whites will not accept its assumptions; I anticipate critique from both left and right.
>
> (Taylor, 1998: 124)

One of us recently gave a keynote lecture that formed the centerpiece for a conference dedicated to new approaches to understanding race/racism[1] in education. The address focused on Critical Race Theory (CRT), a relatively new approach pioneered by scholars of color in US law schools in the 1970s and 1980s, which has grown quickly since its introduction into US educational studies in the mid 1990s (Ladson-Billings and Tate, 1995) and is now an increasingly popular approach that is building an international profile (see Hylton, 2008; Lynn and Parker, 2006; Taylor *et al.*, 2009). At the end of the lecture the chairperson invited questions, and a White professor, sitting on the front row, raised his hand. Once invited to speak, the man stood, turned his back on the chair and speaker, and addressed the audience for several minutes on the "danger" posed by CRT. It was, he explained, a retrograde step in the search for educational equity because it gave primacy to race and diverted attention from the "real" issue, which, he informed us, was social class inequality as diagnosed by his chosen version of Marxism. After a spirited exchange and several other questions, the session came to a close and, as the audience began to filter out, a Black woman practitioner approached the podium to ask the lecturer a question, explaining that she didn't like to ask it in front of the whole audience. Before she could pose the question, however, the White professor strode to the lectern and physically positioned himself between the questioner and the lecturer, keen to explain more about his view of the current state of social theory. The incident reminds us of similar episodes reported by Trina Grillo and Stephanie Wildman, who describe some of the "guerilla tactics" used by Whites to "steal back the center" (1991). By arguing that race/racism be placed at the forefront of social critique, CRT challenges the assumed right of White people to see *their* perspectives and *their* interests placed center stage, and, hence, CRT has not been universally welcomed as an addition to critical theory in education.

Despite its detractors, CRT has rapidly established itself as one of the most important strands in contemporary educational theory. It has done this partly by focusing on the vital link between social theory and social activism, as David Omotoso Stovall (2006: 257) notes:

> Arguing across conference tables is useless. For those of us who are concerned with the social justice project in education, our work will be done on the frontline with communities committed to change . . . neither race nor class exists as static phenomena.

Stovall is one of the leading writers in the new wave of critical race scholars who are taking forward CRT as both an academic discipline and a practice of resistance—praxis. The approach continues one of the basic assumptions of the foundational work in CRT, that is, that theory provides a set of *tools* to be applied and *ideas* to be used and refined. In this sense, social theory is always work in progress. But this does not mean that CRT is any less serious about the importance of theory—quite the contrary. From its very first iteration, critical race scholars have staked a claim to the conceptual importance of their work. The foundational critical race theorist, Kimberlé Williams Crenshaw, for example, recalls how she and colleagues identified a form of words that could be used to describe (and provide a rallying point for) the new ideas they were developing as they began to organize what was to become the first ever CRT workshop (held at the University of Wisconsin, Madison, in July 1989):

> Turning this question over, I began to scribble down words associated with our objectives, identities, and perspectives, drawing arrows and boxes around them to capture various aspects of who "we" were and what we were doing . . . we settled on what seemed to be the most telling marker for this peculiar subject. We would signify the specific political and intellectual location of the project through "critical," the substantive focus through "race," and the desire to develop a coherent account of race and law through the term "theory."
>
> (Crenshaw, 2002: 1360–1361)

This practical and strategic orientation reflects a perspective that Derrick Bell terms "racial realism": an approach that foregrounds an understanding of how the world really operates, rather than fetishizing some idealized notion that bears little resemblance to the lives and experiences of oppressed people (Bell, 1992). The real-world focus of CRT should not be seen as in any way lessening its claim to be taken seriously as a major innovation in social theory. As Crenshaw notes, from the very start CRT has encountered a patronizing attitude from academics who find its focus on race/racism distasteful and/or threatening. The foundational critical race scholars refused to be intimidated by such attacks:

> . . . interference dovetailed with criticisms that were beginning to emerge from Stanford quarters in the form of a counter-critique to our earlier work, characterizing it as essentialist. Whether intended or not, in that critique some of us heard a crude characterization of our work as theoretically unsophisticated and politically backward.
>
> (Crenshaw, 2002: 1357)

The roots of critical race theory

In many ways, CRT has its roots in the radical diasporic writings and resistances of previous centuries, including actions by enslaved African peoples (see Baszile, 2008; Bell 2004; Du Bois

1975, 1990; Mills, 1997, 2003). Contemporary CRT is a direct outgrowth from debates within US legal scholarship in the mid 1970s and 1980s. It began as a radical alternative to dominant perspectives, both the conservative "mainstream" and the ostensibly radical tradition of critical legal studies (CLS), which—in practice—treated race as a peripheral issue and foregrounded a concern with economic disadvantage (see Bell, 2005; Crenshaw, 2002; Crenshaw et al., 1995; Delgado and Stefancic, 2001; West, 1995).

Key foundational CRT scholars include Derrick Bell, Kimberlé Williams Crenshaw, Richard Delgado, Lani Guinier, Mari Matsuda, and Patricia Williams. Gloria Ladson-Billings and William Tate (1995) first introduced CRT into education in the mid 1990s, and since then a growing number of educators have begun working with these ideas (see Dixson and Rousseau, 2006; Lynn and Adams, 2002; Parker, 1998; Solórzano, 1997; Stovall, 2006; Yosso, 2006; Yosso et al., 2004). CRT now spans numerous disciplines, and the work often crosses epistemological boundaries (see Tate, 1997) and is also building an international presence, including work in the UK (Gillborn, 2005, 2008a; Hylton, 2008) and Australia (McDonald, 2003; Moreton-Robinson, 2004).

The tenets of critical race theory

From its earliest formulations, CRT has generally been united by a dual concern to understand and oppose race inequality. In an influential statement of the approach, Crenshaw and colleagues state:

> Although Critical Race scholarship differs in object, argument, accent, and emphasis, it is nevertheless unified by two common interests. The first is to understand how a regime of white supremacy and its subordination of people of color have been created and maintained . . . The second is a desire not merely to understand the vexed bond between law and racial power but to change it.
>
> (Crenshaw et al., 1995: xiii)

Within CRT, the term "White supremacy" is used in a particular way that differs from its usual understanding in mainstream writing: whereas the term commonly refers to individuals and groups who engage in the crudest, most obvious acts of race hatred (such as extreme nationalists and Neo-Nazis), in CRT the more important, hidden, and pervasive form of White supremacy lies in the operation of forces that saturate the everyday mundane actions and policies that shape the world in the interests of White people:

> [By] "white supremacy" I do not mean to allude only to the self-conscious racism of white supremacist hate groups. I refer instead to a political, economic, and cultural system in which whites overwhelmingly control power and material resources, conscious and unconscious ideas of white superiority and entitlement are widespread, and relations of white dominance and non-white subordination are daily reenacted across a broad array of institutions and social settings.
>
> (Ansley, 1997: 592)

Many critical race scholars view White supremacy, understood in this way, as central to CRT in the same way that the notion of capitalism is to Marxist theory and patriarchy to feminism

(Stovall, 2006). This perspective on the nature and extent of contemporary racism is one of the key defining elements of CRT.

The centrality of racism

> CRT begins with a number of basic insights. One is that racism is normal, not aberrant, in American society. Because racism is an ingrained feature of our landscape, it looks ordinary and natural to persons in the culture.
>
> (Delgado and Stefancic, 2000: xvi)

CRT views racism as more than just the most obvious and crude acts of race hatred; it focuses on the subtle and hidden processes that have the effect of discriminating, regardless of their stated intent. In the political mainstream, "racism" tends to be associated with acts of conscious and deliberate race hatred; discrimination is assumed to be an abnormal and relatively unusual facet of the education system. In contrast, CRT suggests that racism operates much more widely, often through the routine, mundane activities and assumptions that are unquestioned by most practitioners and policymakers, e.g. through the design of the curriculum, the operation of certain forms of assessment, and the selection and training of teachers who overwhelmingly replicate dominant cultural norms and assumptions about race and racial inequality (Ladson-Billings, 2004).

Critical race theorists do not view racism as a simple or unchanging aspect of society. CRT challenges ahistoricism by stressing the need to understand racism within its social, economic and historical context (Matsuda *et al.*, 1993: 6). The notion of "differential racialization" refers to the constantly changing and malleable nature of racist stereotypes. For example, a group once seen as conservative and conformist might be redefined as competitive and threatening at another time, e.g. Japanese workers in the US and "Asian" groups in the UK during the twentieth century.

The focus on racism in CRT does not operate to the exclusion of other forms of social inequality. Indeed, a key aspect of CRT is a concern with "intersectionality," that is, an attempt to analyze how racism operates within and across other axes of differentiation such as social class and gender (Crenshaw, 1995; Gillborn and Youdell, 2009; Tate, 1997).

A critique of liberalism

> CRT portrays dominant legal claims of neutrality, objectivity, color-blindness, and meritocracy as camouflages for the self-interest of powerful entities of society.
>
> (Tate, 1997: 235)

Another distinctive theme is CRT's critique of liberalism. In the education system, for example, racism is figured in the distribution of material and educational resources and even in teachers' notions of "ability" and motivation (Gillborn, 2008a). In this situation, the adoption of color-blind approaches (which refuse to acknowledge racial reality) and an emphasis on supposed "merit" (as measured by dominant assessments) may appear open and equitable, but the playing field is not level. Minoritized students are more likely to attend poorly funded schools with less highly qualified teachers and, because of socio-economic inequalities, they are less likely to enjoy additional educational resources at home (Ladson-Billings, 2006a). Under such unequal conditions, a color-blind insistence on a single "merit" standard will not only ensure that race inequalities continue but also present them as fair and just.

The call to context (experiential knowledge and storytelling)

CRT places a special importance on the experiential knowledge of people of color. There is *not* an assumption that minoritized groups have a singular or "true" reading of reality, rather there is recognition that, by experiencing racial domination, such groups perceive the system differently and are often uniquely placed to understand its workings.[2] Richard Delgado (1989) is one of the leading advocates of the need to "name one's own reality." Inspired by the scholarship of Derrick Bell and the centuries old traditions of storytelling in minoritized communities, Delgado argues forcefully for the use of narrative and counter-storytelling as a means of presenting a different reading of the world, one that questions taken-for-granted assumptions and destabilizes the framework that currently sustains, and masks, racial injustice. This approach makes CRT an easy target for those who are willing to oversimplify and seize the opportunity to accuse the approach of merely inventing its data, but such criticisms misunderstand the nature of counter-storytelling and ignore the fact that most CRT "chronicles" are tightly footnoted, so that detailed evidence is marshalled to back up each substantive part of the argument:

> CRT scholars are not making up stories—they are constructing narratives out of the historical, socio-cultural and political realities of their lives and those of people of color.
>
> (Ladson-Billings, 2006b: xi)

A revisionist critique of civil rights progress (the interest convergence principle)

Detractors have sought to present CRT as disrespectful of civil rights campaigns and their victories, but this misreads the approach. CRT is not critical of the campaigns or the people who sacrificed so much to advance race equality (Crenshaw *et al.*, 1995). Rather, CRT examines the limits to reform via law and policy making, and shows how even apparently radical changes are reclaimed and often turned back over time. A key element here is the concept of *interest convergence*. Put simply, this view argues that advances in race equality come about only when White elites see the changes as in their own interests. Derrick Bell (2004: 59), who coined the interest convergence principle, summarizes the idea like this:

Justice for blacks vs. racism = racism.
Racism vs. obvious perceptions of white self-interest = justice for blacks.

It is important to note that interest convergence does not envisage a rational negotiation between minoritized groups and White power holders, where change is achieved through the mere force of reason and logic. Rather, history suggests that advances in racial justice must be won, through protest and mobilization, so that taking action against racism becomes the lesser of two evils for White interests. For example, the moves to outlaw segregation in the 1960s are usually thought of as a sign of enlightenment and a landmark civil rights victory. But they must be understood within the context of the "cold war" and the US's need to recruit friendly African states (Dudziak, 1988):

> "No such decision would have been possible without the world pressure of communism" which made it "simply impossible for the United States to continue to lead a 'Free World' with race segregation kept legal over a third of its territory."
>
> (W.E.B. Du Bois, 1968, quoted in Bell, 2004: 67)

41

The moves to bring about desegregation would not have happened without the civil rights protests *and* a wider geo-political context that made continued violent suppression impractical. Furthermore, the gains themselves have rarely lived up to the politicians' rhetoric. The obvious signs of segregation—such as separate toilets and lunch counters—may have gone, but the reality of ingrained racism continues in economic, residential, and educational terms. It has been argued that more African Americans now attend segregated schools than they did in 1954 at the time of the Supreme Court decision in the *Brown v. Board of Education* case (Delgado and Stefancic, 2001: 33). Richard Delgado and Jean Stefancic (2001: 24) describe the process like this:

> after the celebration dies down, the great victory is quietly cut back by narrow interpretation, administrative obstruction, or delay. In the end, the minority group is left little better than it was before, if not worse. Its friends, the liberals, believing the problem has been solved, go on to something else . . . while its adversaries, the conservatives, furious that the Supreme Court has given way once again to undeserving minorities, step up their resistance.

Landmark victories may actually come to operate in ways that protect the racist status quo: these are sometimes known as "contradiction-closing cases," which operate like a safety valve to provide a solution when the gap grows too large between, on one hand, the liberal rhetoric of equal opportunities and, on the other hand, the reality of racism.

> [contradiction-closing cases] are a little like the thermostat in your home or office. They assure that there is just the right amount of racism. Too much would be destabilizing— the victims would rebel. Too little would forfeit important pecuniary and psychic advantages for those in power.
>
> (Delgado, 1995: 80)

Landmark cases such as the *Brown* desegregation case in the US and the *Stephen Lawrence Inquiry* in the UK (Macpherson, 1999) appear to have addressed blatant race inequalities, but in reality little or nothing changes.[3] Indeed, such cases are sometimes used as yet another weapon against further reform because they:

> allow business as usual to go on even more smoothly than before, because now we can point to the exceptional case and say, "See, our system is really fair and just. See what we just did for minorities or the poor."
>
> (Delgado, 1999: 445)

Myths and misunderstandings: beyond the stereotypes of CRT

Like any new perspective, CRT has been subject to a range of responses and critiques. Some of the engagement has been positive and constructive, pushing critical race scholars to clarify their arguments and develop further analyses. Other of the responses, however, have sought to reassert traditional assumptions (in the guise of "scientific rigor") or dismiss CRT as misguided or simplistic. As we have noted above, CRT offers a view of the world that is fundamentally at odds with mainstream assumptions, and so it is no surprise that the approach is often misunderstood. In this section we address three of the most common myths.

Myth 1: CRT assumes that race is the only thing that matters

Despite its central focus on racism, CRT does not insist that race is always the single most important factor in every situation. CRT argues that race/racism is always relevant to an understanding of wider social inequalities, but it is not the only element. Indeed, race inequity often cannot be fully understood in isolation from other axes of differentiation, such as class and gender. As Stovall (2006: 252) notes:

> Vital to this misinterpretation is the semantics of referencing CRT as a critique solely of "race." In no CRT literature is there a claim to the unanimity of race. The critique has and continues to be one of the functions of White supremacy and the complexities of race.

Myth 2: CRT sees all White people as a homogeneous mass of privileged racists

Detractors sometimes argue that, by identifying the underlying forces that legitimate and support White supremacy, CRT imagines all White people to be the same: in fact the criticism betrays a one-dimensional reading of CRT. Critical race scholars do not think that White people are uniformly privileged and racist, nor that all Whites benefit equally from White supremacy. Such a position is patently ludicrous, especially in view of the fact that foundational CRT writers have repeatedly noted how interest convergence usually operates to defend White elites at the expense of lower-class Whites (Bell, 2004). However, CRT *does* show how even working-class and poor Whites draw advantage from their Whiteness (Harris, 1993). Whites do not benefit *equally*, but they do all benefit from Whiteness to some degree (McIntosh, 1992). For example, when the attainment of the most economically disadvantaged White students in the UK dipped marginally below that of their Black peers, the media responded with stories blaming "the race relations industry" and claiming that neo-Nazi groups would gain an electoral advantage. The stories failed to mention that White students continued to out-perform virtually every minoritized group among the 86 per cent of the school population not counted as living in poverty (Gillborn, 2008b). Hence, even for the White students living in greatest poverty, their race means that the media perceive a national scandal if their achievement is not greater than similarly disadvantaged, minoritized peers.

Myth 3: CRT promotes hopelessness and despair by saying that things can never change

Derrick Bell (1992: ix) recalls an incident when he was challenged at a public reading of his work:

> "Professor Bell, you have achieved much despite racial discrimination. How dare you now deny our children the hope that they may enjoy a success like yours?"

The author responded that "it was the society and not me" that closes down opportunities for African Americans; he did not create the situation, he "simply chronicled what society had done and was likely to do" (Bell, 1992: ix). In fact, far from promoting a sense of hopelessness, CRT insists on the vital importance of active resistance against racism. Bell argues that a total victory over racism may prove elusive but sees a duty to combat injustice (against *all* oppressed groups) as a central component of what he calls "a life fulfilled" (Bell, 1992: xi). The history of racism and education in the UK, for example, clearly demonstrates that all meaningful advances in race equality have come about as a result of community action (Tomlinson, 2008). Antiracist activism may never entirely remove racism, but, in the absence of resistance, it is certain that racist inequity would worsen. As Frederick Douglass observed more than 150 years ago: "If there is no struggle, there is no progress . . . Power concedes nothing without a demand. It never did, and it never will" (quoted in Crenshaw, 2002: 1372).

Delgado and Stefancic respond to the accusation that CRT is a theory of despair by asking, "Is medicine pessimistic because it focuses on diseases and traumas?" (2001: 13). Indeed, Delgado turns the accusation on its head and identifies the lie at the heart of liberal perspectives that appear optimistic but disguise the true scale and nature of contemporary racism:

> Suppose I am sent to an inner city school to talk to the kids and serve as role model of the month. I am *expected* to tell the kids that if they study hard and stay out of trouble, they can become a law professor like me. That, however, is a very big lie: a whopper. When I started teaching law sixteen years ago, there were about thirty-five Hispanic law professors, approximately twenty-five of which were Chicano. Today, the numbers are only slightly improved . . . Despite this, I am expected to tell forty kids in a crowded, inner city classroom that if they work hard, they can each be among the chosen twenty-five.
>
> (Delgado, 1991: 1228, original emphasis)

Continuing debates and unresolved issues

CRT is gaining increasing attention but it is by no means a finished and settled set of approaches. CRT is a living and changing perspective, not a monolithic structure. There are, for example, many spin-off movements from traditional CRT, including critical race feminism and "LatCrit"—a version of CRT that focuses on the particular experiences and struggles of Latina/o communities (see Delgado and Stefancic, 1998; Dixson and Rouseau, 2006; Solórzano and Yosso, 2001; Wing, 1997). Although CRT in the US began with work that often focused on the position of African American communities, it is not the case that CRT adopts (or has ever supported) a simple racial binary perspective that views the world as divided between Whites and a unitary racial Other.

There are many important debates within CRT about the best way of conceiving its work and, in particular, the most effective means of moving things forward through a critical praxis, i.e. a combination of theoretical analysis and applied practical strategies of resistance (Lynn and Parker, 2006). Many of these debates raise issues that are relevant to a number of different perspectives and are by no means unique to CRT. For example, there is discussion about the level of group-identification/abstraction that is appropriate for different analytic and political purposes: sometimes it may be best to organize around a collective signifier that includes numerous minoritized groups, while at other times a more specific identity may be preferred (national, linguistic, or religious).

There is a continuing concern within CRT to understand the numerous, complex, and changing ways in which race/racism intersects with other axes of oppression, such as class, gender, disability, and sexuality. This concern with *intersectionality* is especially strong in critical race feminism (Wing, 1997; Youdell, 2006). Indeed, building on Crenshaw's work, UK scholars Avtar Brah and Ann Phoenix (2004) argue that intersectionality itself can provide a useful focus that offers numerous advances on current single-issue thinking. As Crenshaw (1995) argues, rather than viewing intersectionality as a kind of problem to be solved, the best way ahead may be to use intersectionality as a key means of understanding how White supremacy operates and how to mount effective resistance.

Notes

1   There is no consistent and meaningful biological basis for the group categories that human societies name "race." Although it masquerades as natural and fixed, "race" is a socially constructed category that changes from one society to another and even varies over time within the same society (see Mason, 2000; Mills, 1997; Omi and Winant, 1993). The social construction of "race" differences is *always* associated with raced inequities in some form (Leonardo, 2002); consequently, the notion of "race" inevitably carries racist consequences, and race/racism become categories that are mutually dependent and reinforcing.

2   This echoes Howard Becker's observation about the importance of "outsider" perspectives to critical sociological analyses (Becker, 1967).

3   For a detailed account of the Stephen Lawrence case, showing how apparently huge advances in equity law have been marginalized and ignored, see Gillborn (2008a: chapter 6).

References

Ansley, F.L. (1997) "White supremacy (and what we should do about it)," in R. Delgado and J. Stefancic (eds) (1997) *Critical white studies: looking behind the mirror*, Philadelphia, PA: Temple University Press, pp. 592–595.

Baszile, D.T. (2008) "Beyond all reason indeed: the pedagogical promise of critical race testimony," *Race Ethnicity & Education* 11: 251–265.

Becker, H.S. (1967) "Whose side are we on?" *Social Problems* 14: 239–247.

Bell, D. (1992) *Faces at the bottom of the well: the permanence of racism*, New York: Basic Books.

—— (2004) *Silent covenants* Oxford: Oxford University Press.

—— (2005) *The Derrick Bell reader*, R. Delgado and J. Stefancic (eds) New York: New York University Press.

Brah, A. and Phoenix, A. (2004) "Ain't I a woman? revisiting intersectionality," *Journal of International Women's Studies* 5: 75–86.

Crenshaw, K.W. (1995) "Mapping the margins: intersectionality, identity politics, and violence against women of color," in K. Crenshaw, N. Gotanda, G. Peller and K. Thomas (eds) *Critical race theory: the key writings that formed the movement*, New York: New Press, pp. 357–383.

—— (2002) "The first decade: critical reflections, or 'a foot in the closing door'," *UCLA Law Review* 49: 1343–72.

—— Gotanda, N., Peller, G. and Thomas, K. (eds) (1995) *Critical race theory: the key writings that formed the movement*, New York: New Press.

Delgado, R. (1989) "Storytelling for oppositionists and others: a plea for narrative," *Michigan Law Review* 87: 2411–2441.

—— (1991) "Affirmative action as a majoritarian device: or, do you really want to be a role model?" *Michigan Law Review* 89: 1222–1231.

—— (1995) *The Rodrigo chronicles: conversations about America and race*, New York: New York University Press.

—— (1999) "Rodrigo's committee assignment: a skeptical look at judicial independence," *Southern California Law Review* 72: 425–454.

—— and Stefancic, J. (eds) (1998) *The Latino/a condition: a critical reader*, New York: New York University Press.

—— and —— (2000) "Introduction," in R. Delgado and J. Stefancic (eds) *Critical race theory: the cutting edge*, 2nd edn, Philadelphia, PA: Temple University Press.

—— and —— (2001) *Critical race theory: an introduction*, New York: New York University Press.

Dixson, A.D. and Rousseau, C.K. (eds) (2006) *Critical race theory in education: all God's children got a song*, New York: Routledge.

Du Bois, W.E.B. (1968) *The autobiography of W.E.B. Du Bois: a soliloquy on viewing my life from the last decade of its first century*, New York: International Publishers.

—— (1975) *Dusk of dawn*, Millwood, NY: Kraus-Thomson Organization.

—— (1990) *The souls of Black folk*, 1st Vintage Books/Library of America edn, New York: Vintage Books/Library of America.

Dudziak, M.L. (1988) "Desegregation as a cold war imperative," *Stanford Law Review* 41: 61–120.

Gillborn, D. (2005) "Education policy as an act of white supremacy: whiteness, critical race theory and education reform," *Journal of Education Policy* 20: 485–505.

—— (2008a) *Racism and education: coincidence or conspiracy?*, London: Routledge.

—— (2008b) "Coincidence or conspiracy? Whiteness, policy and the persistence of the Black/White achievement gap," *Educational Review* 60(3): 229–248.

—— and Youdell, D. (2009) "Critical perspectives on race and schooling," in J.A. Banks (ed.) *The Routledge international companion to multicultural education*, New York: Routledge.

Grillo, T. and Wildman, S.M. (1991) "Obscuring the importance of race: the implication of making comparisons between racism and sexism (or other -isms)," in R. Delgado and J. Stefancic (eds) (2000) *Critical race theory: the cutting edge*, 2nd edn, Philadelphia, PA: Temple University Press, pp. 648–656.

Harris, C.I. (1993) "Whiteness as property," *Harvard Law Review* 106: 1707–1791.

Hylton, K. (2008) *"Race" and sport: critical race theory*, London: Routledge.

Ladson-Billings, G. (2004) "New directions in multicultural education: complexities, boundaries, and critical race theory," in J.A. Banks and C.A.M. Banks (eds) *Handbook of research on multicultural education*, 2nd edn, San Francisco, CA: Jossey-Bass, pp. 50–65.

—— (2006a) "From the achievement gap to the educational debt: understanding achievement in US schools," *Educational Researcher* 35: 3–12.

—— (2006b) "They're trying to wash us away: the adolescence of critical race theory in education," in A.D. Dixson and C.K. Rousseau (eds) (2006) *Critical race theory in education: all God's children got a song*, New York: Routledge, pp. v–xiii.

—— and Tate, W.F. (1995) "Toward a critical race theory of education," *Teachers College Record* 97: 47–68.

Leonardo, Z. (2002) "The souls of White folk: critical pedagogy, whiteness studies, and globalization discourse," *Race Ethnicity & Education* 5(1): 29–50.

Lynn, M. and Adams, M. (2002) "Critical race theory and education: recent developments in the field," *Equity & Excellence in Education* 35(2): 87–92.

—— and Parker, L. (2006) "Critical race studies in education: examining a decade of research on US schools," *The Urban Review* 38: 257–290.

McDonald, H. (2003) "Exploring possibilities through critical race theory: exemplary pedagogical practices for Indigenous students," paper prepared for NZARE/ AARE Joint conference. Available at http://eprints.jcu.edu.au/951/01/mcdonald_1.pdf (accessed 8 October 2008).

McIntosh, P. (1992) "White privilege and male privilege: a personal account of coming to see correspondences through work in Women's Studies," in R. Delgado and J. Stefancic (eds) (1997) *Critical white studies: looking behind the mirror*, Philadelphia, PA: Temple University Press, pp. 291–299.

Macpherson, W. (1999) *The Stephen Lawrence inquiry*, CM 4262-I, London: The Stationery Office. Available at www.archive.official-documents.co.uk/document/cm42/4262/4262.htm (accessed 2 May 2007).

Mason, D. (2000) *Race and ethnicity in modern Britain*, 2nd edn, Oxford: Oxford University Press.

Matsuda, M., Lawrence, C., Delgado, R. and Crenshaw, K. (1993) *Words that wound: critical race theory, assaultive speech, and the first amendment*, Boulder, CO: Westview.

Mills, C.W. (1997) *The racial contract*, London: Cornell University Press.

—— (2003) *From class to race: essays in white Marxism and black radicalism*, New York: Rowman & Littlefield.

Moreton-Robinson, A. (2004) "The possessive logic of patriarchal white sovereignty: the High Court and the Yorta Yorta decision," *Borderlands e-journal* 3. Available at http://eprints.qut.edu.au (accessed 10 October 2008).

Omi, M. and Winant, H. (1993) "On the theoretical status of the concept of race," in G. Ladson-Billings and D. Gillborn (eds) (2004) *The RoutledgeFalmer reader in multicultural education*, London: RoutledgeFalmer, pp. 7–15.

Parker, L. (1998) " 'Race is . . . race ain't': an exploration of the utility of critical race theory in qualitative research in education," *International Journal of Qualitative Studies in Education* 11(1): 43–55.

Solórzano, D. (1997) "Images and words that wound: critical race theory, racial stereotyping, and teacher education," *Teacher Education Quarterly* 24(3): 5–19.

—— and Yosso, T. (2001) "Critical race and LatCrit theory and method," *International Journal of Qualitative Studies in Education* 14: 471–495.

Stovall, D. (2006) "Forging community in race and class: critical race theory and the quest for social justice in education," *Race Ethnicity & Education* 9: 243–259.

Tate, W.F. (1997) "Critical race theory and education: history, theory, and implications," in M.W. Apple (ed.) *Review of research in education*, Washington DC: American Educational Research Association, pp. 195–247.

Taylor, E. (1998) "A primer on critical race theory: who are the critical race theorists and what are they saying?" *Journal of Blacks in Higher Education* 19: 122–124.

—— Gillborn, D. and Ladson-Billings, G. (eds) (2009) *Foundations of critical race theory in education*, New York: Routledge.

Tomlinson, S. (2008) *Race and education: policy and politics in Britain*, Maidenhead: Open University Press.

West, C. (1995) "Foreword," in K. Crenshaw, N. Gotanda, G. Peller and K. Thomas (eds) *Critical race theory: the key writings that formed the movement*, New York: New Press, pp. xi–xii.

Wing, A.K. (ed.) (1997) *Critical race feminism: a reader*, New York: New York University Press.

Yosso, T. (2006) *Critical race counterstories along the Chicana/Chicano education pipeline*, New York: Routledge.

—— Parker, L., Solórzano, D.G. and Lynn, M. (2004) "From Jim Crow to affirmative action and back again: a critical race discussion of racialized rationales and access to higher education," in R.E. Floden (ed.) *Review of research in education*, Washington DC: American Educational Research Association, pp. 1–25.

Youdell, D. (2006) *Impossible bodies, impossible selves: exclusions and student subjectivities*, Dordrecht, Netherlands: Springer.

4

The ethics of national hospitality and globally mobile researchers[1]

Johannah Fahey and Jane Kenway

Introduction

In a globalized world, talent is increasingly mobile, and therefore hospitality emerges as an important concept that can be used to consider the ethics involved when a nation-state welcomes privileged foreigners as guests. In this chapter, we seek to engage with the politics of foreignness and the ethics of national hospitality. We use such notions in our discussion of the Singaporean government's 'foreign talent' (highly skilled foreigners) policy rhetoric as a means to problematize the relationship between the host nation, its citizens and guests. More specifically, we draw on Derrida's ideas about conditional and unconditional hospitality to examine the hospitality ideal and the ideal figure of the foreigner articulated within such discourse. This inquiry is situated more broadly in our ongoing political, epistemological, ontological and ethical analysis of both moving policies on researcher mobility and of mobile researchers themselves (Fahey and Kenway, 2008; Kenway and Fahey, 2008).

The knowledge economy

The idea of the knowledge economy has come to dominate the policy lexicon of transnational organizations and governments in many places around the world (Kenway *et al.*, 2006). Knowledge economies are 'directly based on the production, distribution and use of knowledge and information' (OECD, 1996: 7). Concerns about their economic power and status in the global knowledge economy have led most nations and regions into an intensifying competition for highly accomplished 'knowledge workers', now often called 'talent'. The increasing international mobility of talent has resulted in fears about 'brain drain' and about how to harness the expertise of 'highly mobile' talent. Brain drain/gain/mobility policy discourse is concerned with the implications of such mobility for the nation-state's or region's techno-scientific knowledge and innovation and creative capacity and thus ultimately the implications for its position in the global economy.

The extent to which a nation-state or region is negatively affected by the global movement of talent depends largely on its position within global geographies of power and knowledge.

There is a well-documented 'brain drain' from many 'developing to developed' nations, with little compensating 'regain' in terms of people and knowledge for the so-called 'sending' country (Lowell and Findlay, 2002). However, such nation-states are not the only ones expressing concern and seeking to attract and retain mobile, highly skilled talent. Many places are assessing their geopolitical situation and developing strategies both to prevent the loss of talent and to harness the talents of the globally mobile.

We seek to enhance the debates about the ethics of globally mobile policies on high-skills mobility and of mobile people themselves. Ethical questions are not usually high on the policy agenda, except when associated with the drain of highly skilled individuals from developing countries to developed countries and the disastrous consequences of such asymmetrical mobility for developing countries. While these debates are crucial and deserve much more attention, it is also the case that other ethical issues arise with regard to different geopolitical locations and the place-specific manner in which they participate in this global domain.

We focus here on Singapore and its state-led policy initiative to recruit and retain highly skilled 'foreign talent'.[2] Given the scope of our interests in this paper, we will talk generally about debates in Singapore on foreign talent (high-skills knowledge workers) and more specifically about how such discussions apply to university researchers (who are a significant sector of the knowledge economy).

Singapore

Singapore is the smallest nation (a city-state) in South East Asia, has no natural resources and therefore relies on people or 'human capital' as a key economic resource. However, owing to its small population of approximately 4.59 million (Singapore Department of Statistics, 2008), it has a limited pool of 'local talent'. Therefore, Singapore's success in the knowledge economy is dependent on its being able to recruit talent from elsewhere to develop a globally competitive work force. In 2006, Singapore's intake of foreign talent represented 13.4 per cent (about 90,000 people) of Singapore's total non-resident population (Yeoh, 2007a). In global terms, it is uniquely positioned as a tiny nation, with a highly competitive economy (the sixth wealthiest country in the world in terms of GDP per capita), contending with other, much larger nations within the region, including China, India and Australia. More than this, it is precisely because of Singapore's geographical location, as an intersection point between these larger nations, that it is emerging as a significant knowledge hub within this region.

Now an independent republic, Singapore was once a British colony and, upon achieving independence from Britain, it became a part of Malaysia (1963–1965) before being expelled from the federation. The ruling People's Action Party (PAP) has been in power since Singapore's first compulsory elections in 1959, and many commentators have suggested that Singapore is a procedural rather than a true democracy (Mauzy and Milne, 2002; Mutalib, 2003): 'the development of Singapore as a nation-state through government decisions tends to be conflated with the party's directives' (Ho, 2006: 388).

As Singapore relies on the recruitment of foreign talent, there is much emphasis within its state-initiated policy discourse on the country and its citizens being 'open', 'accommodating', 'big-hearted' and 'welcoming' towards talented foreigners (Singapore Government, 1997; Lee, 2006). It is important to acknowledge, however, that Singapore's purported policy 'openness' towards foreigners stands in marked contrast to its rigid political system. In this respect, Singapore's state-initiated foreign talent policy can be viewed as paternalistic (Mauzy and Milne, 2002), where the state as 'host' represents its citizens.

Hospitable nations

In a world where the highly skilled are increasingly on the move, countries such as Singapore must position themselves as 'hospitable' nations if they are to attract (and retain) globally mobile talent and thus compete in the global knowledge economy. When someone is hospitable, the ethics of such an act tend to remain unquestioned. However, given the nature of Singapore's highly paternalistic political system, the government's policy-initiated hospitality does invite a consideration of ethical issues.

Within brain drain/gain/mobility debates, we advance thinking by entering from a different ethical perspective. We offer a new conceptual apparatus that may help to broaden the debate so as to ensure that ethics is not quarantined as an issue that relates to poor countries alone. We move from considering brain mobility to thinking about hospitality. Rather than considering the ethics of loss and gain, we are interested in the ethics of the host and the guest. As opposed to thinking about such debates in terms of competition between more or less developed nation-states, we are interested in the ways in which policy-sanctioned hospitality is mobilized within a nation-state, particularly in terms of the kinds of politics, values and judgements that underpin such governmental generosity.

Furthermore, when considering the status of the foreigner, we also mobilize an alternative perspective to frame ethical questions. Debates concerning foreigners are often informed by either a negative view of the foreigner as a threat (i.e. terrorists, refugees) or a positive view of the foreign as a supplement (i.e. founders, immigrants) to the receiving nation-state (Honig, 2003). Discussions about the politics of foreignness largely emerge from within the field of political theory, where issues of immigration, citizenship, democracy and national identity are framed in terms of the ways in which nation-states can either secure their borders against, or more generously accommodate, such foreigners within the boundaries of the host nation-state (Guiraudon and Joppke, 2001; Ngai, 2004). In these discussions, the legal status of foreigners is a key subject, particularly in relation to issues of civil and political rights (e.g. the rights to asylum) (Benhabib, 2004). Overall, many ethical issues arise around identity, difference and belonging when considering the relationship between states, citizens and foreigners.

One way to conceptualize this relationship is in terms of hospitality, particularly in terms of the ways the host nation-state makes the foreigner feel welcome and the responsibilities that the nation-state as host has to the foreigner as guest. Clearly, these issues become particularly pressing in relation to vulnerable foreigners who have been forcibly displaced.

Kant first posed the question of hospitality in the context of international relations in *A project for a perpetual peace* (1796). Derrida's theory of hospitality (1995, 1999, 2000, 2001; and see Borradori, 2003), which informs our expanded discussion below, is a reworking of *Perpetual peace*. And in his recent work he discusses a hospitality of laws and nations and focuses on France and its hospitality to foreigners (i.e. illegal refugees). Through his notion of 'unconditional' hospitality, he conceptualizes a form of hospitality that operates outside all rules and laws.

While Derrida's argument focuses on the most disempowered of all globally mobile people, our argument operates from the opposite end of the spectrum and considers the ethics of hospitality in relation to globally mobile talent or privileged guests. Examining Singapore's recruitment and retention policy strategies involves investigating the relationship between the nation-state and foreign talent and entails considering the ethical nuances of 'the invitation' and its acceptance.

The Singaporean government is seeking to do its best by those at home by bringing foreign talent to Singapore and therefore building the economy. And, in its role as host, the Singaporean government offers an encouraging welcome to foreign talent. Notably in policy discourse, foreign talent is represented as a supplement to the nation-state, and there is much emphasis on getting away from the 'foreigners–them, locals–us' attitude (Singapore Government, 1997: 13). There is no doubt that the Singaporean government fulfils its role as host, but a complicated ethical regime governs hospitality when it is being offered to a privileged population such as foreign talent. In this context, the onus is not placed solely on the host (as it is in the case of vulnerable foreigners); rather there is also an onus on the guest to fulfil certain responsibilities.

Hospitality

In broad terms, hospitality refers to the relationship between a guest and a host. It also refers to the act or practice of being hospitable, of welcoming guests, visitors or strangers, with liberality and goodwill. We focus on Derrida's theory in particular, as his foundation for understanding this concept is based on the interchangeable and intertwined relationships between ethics and hospitality (1999). His notion of hospitality allows us to interpret Singapore's foreign talent policy discourse not simply in terms of a general idea of hospitality, but in terms of the connection between hospitality, the politics of foreignness and the limits of an ethical engagement with the foreigner.

Unconditional and conditional hospitality

When trying to conceptualize 'hospitality', Derrida acknowledges a fundamental paradox that turns on 'conditional' and 'unconditional' hospitality (2000; Borradori, 2003). When the host of the house, country or nation extends an invitation to a guest, it is through this invitation that they also demonstrate to the guest that they are in control of the property or territory. In other words, in order to be hospitable one must have the power to host. But the host must also have some control over the people who are being hosted. Hospitality fails when the guests take control of the house. If the host is no longer in control, they are not being hospitable to their guests (Derrida, 2000). According to Derrida, this kind of hospitality is 'conditional', as it is dependent on imposing certain limits on guests. And as hospitality always involves placing limitations on guests, hospitality is inherently inhospitable.

Alternatively, 'unconditional' hospitality involves no limitations and an abandonment of control. It requires extending a welcome to all in need of hospitality, instead of making judgements about who will and who will not receive that hospitality (Borradori, 2003; Derrida, 2000). Paradoxically, it is through such 'unconditional' hospitality that the very possibility of hospitality is defeated: it becomes impossible to host anyone at all, precisely because there is no ownership or control. 'Unconditional' hospitality is not possible, but for Derrida the very notion of hospitality relies upon this concept and is inconceivable without it. We will now use this paradoxical framework to examine Singapore's hospitality.

Singapore's hospitality

'Singapore Vision 21' is Singapore's key policy strategy focused on attracting foreign talent. Prime Minister Goh Chok Tong launched it in 1997 (Singapore Government, 1997), but it is still operational today, as evidenced by recent references to the initiative in ministerial speeches (Lee, 2006). When discussing Singapore's foreign talent policy discourse, we draw primarily on the 'Attracting talent vs looking after Singaporeans' section of the 1997 Singapore 21 report (S21), but also on more recent ministerial speeches.

Derrida maintains that 'tolerance is actually the opposite of hospitality' (in Borradori, 2003: 127), because merely tolerating someone means limiting one's welcome by retaining control over one's home or territory. Significantly, in the S21, the policy discourse operates according to Derrida's distinction between hospitality and tolerance. And given the emphasis on welcoming as opposed to merely tolerating foreigners, when taken at face value the S21 (Singapore Government, 1997: 22) could be read as offering a kind of unconditional hospitality:

> Ultimately it is not enough to 'tolerate' foreigners because they are of use to Singapore. We must welcome them, make them feel at home and that they belong here. To be welcoming to foreigners requires an open mind and a big heart . . . Singapore must retain an open and hospitable attitude.

However, the motivations for such overt hospitality in policy discourse may be based on the fact that, while the government sees foreign talent as a welcome addition to the nation-state, Singaporean local talent and citizens more broadly are more ambivalent about such foreigners. As such, this policy rhetoric could be viewed as a kind of propaganda, promoting the figure of the idealized foreigner as a means to convince citizens that foreign talent is not a threat to their livelihood.

Despite the rhetoric, we are therefore not suggesting that the S21 is an example of unconditional hospitality. For, as Derrida maintains, unconditional hospitality is in fact impossible: 'no state can write it into its laws' (in Borradori, 2003: 129). Rather, we are interested in the conditional hospitality that arises from the 'hospitality ideal' articulated in Singapore's foreign talent policy rhetoric. Examining the ways in which this policy rhetoric is played out in practice may enable a more complex understanding of the ethical and political responsibility the Singaporean government shows towards foreign talent and its own talented citizens.

Foreign talent

'Foreign talent' is the term used in Singaporean policy discourse to describe highly skilled, globally mobile individuals: 'people who have certain internationally marketable experiences and skills' (Singapore Government, 1997). The profile of foreign talent in Singapore shows that they come primarily from Malaysia, China and India, but also Australia, New Zealand, Japan, Britain, Europe, South Africa, Canada and the US (Brooks, 2002). Of the over half a million (600,000) foreign workers employed in Singapore, around 90,000 of these are highly skilled foreigners with degrees, professional qualifications or specialist skills, who hold employment passes (and can therefore apply for permanent residence) (Eng Fong, 2006). It is these skilled foreigners with university degrees who are our focus.

In terms of Singapore attracting 'research talent', as a small nation-state that is seeking to create a global presence, it scales up its policy by focusing on institutions rather than individuals. Recognizing that it is a relatively insignificant nation on a global scale, Singaporean research institutions seek to collaborate with globally significant international research institutions and faculty members to build up the nation-state's global status and networks and to become more attractive to globally mobile researchers.

By 2010, the facilities for the Campus for Research Excellence and Technological Enterprise (CREATE) will consist of a number of world-class research centres that will have intensive research collaboration with Singapore-based research institutions. For example, an existing initiative is the Singapore–MIT Alliance for Research and Technology. In policy discourse, international research institutions such as MIT are thought of as 'talent magnets' (Singapore Government, 2008 online), drawing talent to Singapore from all over the world.

This 'geo-institutional realignment' (Olds and Thrift, 2005: 280) of predominantly US elite research institutions in Singapore has geospatial implications. It is by amassing foreign research institutions within Singapore that the nation-state seeks to compete with other great attractors in Asia, namely India and China. By seeking to become a significant knowledge hub within the region, Singapore is trying to position itself at the centre, rather than on the edge, of Asia. According to government policy discourse, 'CREATE offers a multi-national, multi-disciplinary research enterprise unlike anything known till now, strategically located in the heart of Asia, at the nexus of East and West' (National Research Foundation, 2008).

But just as Singapore tries to engage Asia, it also tries to transcend Asia (Koh, 2005), motivated by its small-nation aspirations to insert itself, via CREATE, into a *global*, networked environment. The Singaporean government is savvy about the geopolitical position of countries and regions and Singapore's own location within the globe and the region. It understands that 'many US and European universities are eager to establish a presence in Asia in a way never contemplated before because of the keen awareness of the rise of Asia and the increasing shift of global dominance towards Asia' (National Research Foundation, 2008). It is this formidable foreign institutional presence that the Singaporean government uses to consolidate Singapore's geopolitical standing, in a bid to become a global knowledge hub attracting and retaining world-class research talent and thereby curbing their global circulation.

Foreign and local talent

Policy discourse suggests that 'besides bringing valued skills, knowledge and ideas, the foreign talent's vigour provides powerful motivation for us [i.e. Singapore] to continually strive for higher standards . . . Their example can make us aware of the dangers of being complacent' (Singapore Government, 1997: 2). Ong maintains that foreign talent 'are increasingly coded as exemplars of intellectual capital and risk-taking behaviours' (2005: 339). Therefore, on the basis of the subtle contrast between driven foreign talent and 'complacent' citizens in the statement above, we suggest that this 'coding' is reinforced through an implicit suggestion that local talent do not have sufficiently entrepreneurial skills to compete in the knowledge economy.[3] In other words, in policy discourse, receptiveness is extended towards foreign talent, not simply to supplement a small population, but also because they are seen as being vital in providing the skills and know-how Singaporeans lack (Yeoh and Huang, 2004).

Hospitality at home

How then do we begin to think about the ways in which such discourse constructs the relationship between foreign and local talent in terms of hospitality? Let us suppose that hospitality dictates that, when one welcomes guests, these guests are not received at the expense of those who are in residence. The lack of generosity the Singaporean government shows towards local talent in such discourse, with the implication that local talent is in some way deficient, becomes an issue of ethical import, particularly when considering the reasons why local talent might favour complacency and conformity over risk-taking.

James Gomez is one of the 6,000 Singaporean citizens that the Singapore government consulted for its S21 report. In terms of critical thinking, creativity and business, he believes that it is the interventionist policies of the PAP government over the last few decades that have created 'an apathetic and non-risk taking culture' because 'people were criminalized and persecuted for voicing alternative political points of view and as a result conformity has become ingrained as a consequence of coercion' (Gomez, 1999). Therefore, while policy discourse draws attention to the 'dangers of being complacent', it does not highlight the reasons why such complacency among its citizens may exist.

Sen (1999) describes 'the Lee Thesis' (after Lee Kuan Yew, the former prime minister of Singapore, who formulated it succinctly) as the idea that 'basic civil and political freedoms . . . hamper economic growth and development' (1999: 148). However, he disputes such claims, arguing that there is no empirical evidence to support them. Gomez's statement draws attention to the trade-offs that have been made in Singapore between national economic development and citizen compliance. He demonstrates how the restriction of citizens' basic civil and political freedoms in Singapore have impacted on their critical and creative thinking, and this is particularly pertinent as this lack of 'risk-taking' or entrepreneurial skill has become one justification for inviting foreign talent to Singapore.

Derrida states 'the host remains master of . . . the nation' (1999: 67). Indeed, Derrida argues that it is on this proviso that the nation is able to offer hospitality. In Singapore, the rigid political system curtails dissenting political views; therefore there is no doubt that the Singaporean government is the master of the nation, particularly when it comes to maintaining control of its citizens. But, if the ways in which the host nation controls its citizens are ethically questionable, then is it in a position to offer hospitality to guests – particularly as the Singaporean government denies its citizens some of the liberties that guests are allowed?

As suggested, we do not seek to imply that the hospitality that Singapore extends to its guests is unconditional, but at the same time there are nuances to conditions within conditional hospitality. In this context, the host does not impose 'his' mastery by insisting that the guest follow the practices and laws of the territory. Foreign talent does not have to abide by the same laws, rules and conventions as Singaporean citizens. In fact, the S21 says attracting foreign talent 'involves removing obstacles to the entry of talent. Regulatory mechanisms can be loosened. Rules should be simplified' (Singapore Government, 1997: 16). Foreign talent are also offered fast-tracked employment passes, subsidized housing, education and healthcare and tax incentives (Singapore Government, 1997). Not surprisingly, offering this kind of hospitality to privileged guests impacts on those at home.

Citizens at 'home'

Among Singaporean citizens, 'there is significant resentment regarding the privileges [offered] to attract foreign talent' (Ho, 2006: 393). In terms of considering the nuances of the invitation to foreign talent, the Singaporean government extends its generosity to foreign talent, but such generosity is offered at the expense of local talent. The favouritism that the Singaporean government shows to foreign talent, where the government is more accommodating of its guests than of its citizens, makes its own citizens feel neglected. Therefore, the fundamental ethics of this hospitality, where citizens may benefit economically, but at the same time feel sacrificed for the sake of foreigners, and make sacrifices politically, must be questioned.

The S21 states that 'above all, citizenship is about belonging to a place, having a sense of ownership and calling it home' (Singapore Government, 1997: 13) And yet, as a consequence of feeling like 'second-class citizens' (Singapore Government, 1997: 12), some residents feel displaced in Singapore (Ho, 2006). According to Ho, 'the mobility of foreigners into Singapore can have a detrimental impact on whether citizens feel that Singapore is home' (2006: 397). A further corollary of destabilizing citizens' feelings of belonging to the nation-state is that they feel more inclined to migrate to other countries. In fact 'the higher the education among Singaporeans, the more they appear disenchanted with Singapore being a caring society or a good place to make a living and raise a family' (Ooi *et al.*, 2003: 6). And yet, local talent migrating permanently to other countries is exactly what the Singaporean government is seeking to avoid, and in its policy rhetoric there is an emphasis on local talent developing 'a deep-seated sense of belonging – or rootedness – to Singapore' (Singapore Government, 1997: 1).

Foreigners at 'home'

At the same time, the Singaporean government seeks not only to attract, but also to 'root' foreign talent to Singapore. And yet those guests that do choose to linger do not necessarily mingle with their hosts. Foreign talent often reside in 'expat-enclaves', and this not only creates a sense of isolation for them but also prevents them from becoming fully immersed in the Singaporean community (Brooks, 2002).

Of course, despite the fact that many talented foreigners do call Singapore home, for the most part, foreign talent's long-term commitment to the nation remains in doubt. Even when Permanent Resident (PR) status and Singaporean citizenship are offered as enticements, they do not guarantee that foreign talent will stay (Yeoh, 2007b). As they are 'flexible citizens' (Ong, 1999) who have the credentials to remain globally mobile in the knowledge economy, foreign talent are free to enjoy the privileges that Singapore affords them and then leave the country. 'In fact, attaining Singaporean citizenship or Permanent Resident status may confer a higher degree of potential mobility on them, enabling them to gain entry more easily as tourists and immigrants in other gateways around the world' (Yeoh, 2007b: 55).

In terms of the ethics of hospitality, this draws attention to the obligations, if any, that constantly mobile foreign talent have to a host nation such as Singapore. It is precisely because foreign talent are guests, because Singapore is not their home, that particular liberties are bestowed upon them. And by accepting the Singaporean government's hospitality, foreign talent are able to accumulate educational credentials and experiences that further enhance their educational and class privileges in a global labour market. Ironically, offering PR status or citizenship to foreign talent does not necessarily make foreign talent stay in Singapore; rather it enables them to be mobile. And this leads us to think about the obligations involved when accepting an invitation. Clearly, constant mobility does not necessarily serve to cultivate territorial responsibilities. But, in terms of the guest's ethical responsibilities, is this precisely what the host nation and its citizens require?

Broader implications

Our analysis has implications for the ways in which the sociology of education and of knowledge develops a global research imagination (Kenway and Fahey, 2009). Ethical issues must be at the forefront. In this context, the concept of hospitality has considerable potential.

55

What, for example, might 'hospitality' mean in different places? And what might the ethical implications of such hospitality be? It directs us to think about whether a host nation has to have a demonstrated record of generosity towards those at home, and at the very least fulfil its moral obligations to its citizens, in order to be in a position to welcome privileged guests from abroad. Are there certain ethical responsibilities placed on privileged guests if they accept a host's invitation? In terms of brain mobility debate more broadly, in a globally mobile world, host nations need to ascertain the kinds of territorial loyalty that can be expected from constantly mobile guests. Does the host nation have any ethical expectations with regard to privileged guests? Do the constantly mobile and constantly hosted develop any territorial responsibilities? Or do they just float free of these? In other words, what is an ethics of mobility? And what is an ethics of place?

Notes

1   This paper arises from an Australian Research Council grant for the project *Moving ideas: mobile policies, researchers and connections in the social sciences and humanities – Australia in the global context (2006–2009)*.

2   In terms of ethical issues, related research literature on foreign talent tends to focus on the inequalities between unskilled and skilled foreigners (Eng Fong, 2006; Ong, 2004; Yeoh and Huang, 2004). We focus solely on skilled foreigners or foreign talent.

3   We acknowledge that the Singaporean government's Internationalization Strategy (1997) encourages Singaporeans to work overseas as a means to enable them and the Singaporean nation to become more globally competitive. Here we are referring particularly to local talent that stays in Singapore.

References

Benhabib, S. (2004) *The rights of others: aliens, residents and citizens*, Cambridge, UK: Cambridge University Press.

Borradori, G. (2003) *Philosophy in a time of terror: dialogues with Jürgen Habermas and Jacques Derrida*, Chicago, IL and London: University of Chicago Press.

Brooks, A. (2002) *A question of belonging – global talent and issues of settlement in Singapore*, Report prepared for the Remaking Singapore Committee on 'Beyond Condo – Sense of ownership and belonging to Singapore', Singapore: Institute of Policy Studies.

Derrida, J. (1995) *The gift of death* (trans. D. Wills), Chicago, IL: University of Chicago Press.

—— (1999) *Adieu to Emmanuel Lévinas* (trans. P.A. Brault and M. Naas), Stanford, CA: Stanford University Press.

—— (2000) *Of hospitality* (trans. R. Bowlby), Stanford, CA: Stanford University Press.

—— (2001) *On cosmopolitanism and forgiveness*, London: Routledge.

Fahey, J. and Kenway, J. (2008) *Brain drain or mind-shift: reconsidering policies on researcher mobility*, Melbourne: Monash Institute for the Study of Global Movements.

Eng Fong, P. (2006) 'Foreign talent and development in Singapore', in C. Kuptsch and P. Eng Fong (eds) *Competing for global talent*, Geneva: International Labour Office.

Gomez, J. (1999) *The Singapore 21 report: a political response*. Available online at www.singapore-window.org/sw99/90521jgz.htm (accessed 10 October 2008).

Guirandon, V. and Joppke, C. (2001) *Controlling migration*, London: Routledge.

Ho, E.L.-E. (2006) 'Negotiating belonging and perceptions of citizenship in a transnational world: Singapore, a cosmopolis?', *Social & Cultural Geographies* 7(3) (June): 385–401.

Honig, B. (2003) *Democracy and the foreigner*, Princeton, NJ: Princeton University Press.

Kant, E. (1796) *A project for a perpetual peace: a philosophical essay*, London: Couchman.

Kenway, J., Bullen, E., Fahey, J. with Robb, S. (2006) *Haunting the knowledge economy*, London: Routledge.

—— and Fahey, J. (2009) (eds) *Globalizing the research imagination*, London: Routledge.

—— and —— (2008) 'Policy incitements to mobility: some speculations and provocations', in R. Boden, R. Dean, D. Epstein, F. Rizvi and S. Wright (eds) *World yearbook of education 2008: geographies of knowledge, geometries of power: higher education in the 21st century*, London: Routledge.

Koh, T. (2005) 'Singapore and Asia: engaging and transcending the region', Speech at Raffles Asia Programme Opening Ceremony Cum Seminar, Raffles Junior College, 22 April. Available online at www.ips.org.sg/staff/tommykoh/index1.htm (accessed 10 October 2008).

Lee, Hsien Loong (2006) 'Prime Minister's National Day rally speech', 20 August, University Cultural Centre. Available online at www.pmo.gov.sg/News/Speeches/Prime+Minister/ (accessed 10 October 2008).

Lowell, B.L. and Findlay, A. (2002) 'Migration of highly skilled persons from developing countries: impact and policy responses – synthesis report', *International Migration Papers 44*, Geneva: International Labour Office.

Mauzy, D.K. and Milne, R.S. (2002) *Singapore politics under the People's Action Party*, London: Routledge.

Mutalib, H. (2003) *Parties and politics: a study of opposition parties and the PAP in Singapore*, Singapore: Eastern Universities Press.

National Research Foundation (2008) *Campus for research excellence and technological enterprise*. Available at www.nrf.gov.sg/NRF/otherProgrammes.aspx?id=188 (accessed 10 October 2008).

Ngai, M.M. (2004) *Impossible subjects: illegal aliens and the making of modern America*, Princeton, NJ: Princeton University Press.

Olds, K. and Thrift, N. (2005) 'Cultures on the brink: reengineering the soul of capitalism – on a global scale', in A. Ong and S. Collier *Global assemblages: technology, politics and ethics as anthropological problems*, Malden, MA and Oxford: Blackwell Publishing.

Ong, A. (1999) *Flexible citizenship: the cultural logics of transnationality*, Durham, NC and London: Duke University Press.

—— (2004) 'Intelligent island, baroque ecology', in R. Bishop, J. Phillips and W.W. Yeo (eds) *Beyond description: Singapore space historicity*, London and New York: Routledge.

—— (2005) 'Ecologies of expertise: assembling flows, managing citizenship', in A. Ong and S. Collier *Global assemblages: technology, politics and ethics as anthropological problems*, Malden, MA and Oxford: Blackwell Publishing.

Ooi, G.L., Tan, E.S. and Soh, K.C. (2003) *The study of ethnicity, national identity and sense of rootedness in Singapore*, Singapore: Institute of Policy Studies.

Organization for Economic Co-operation and Development (OECD) (1996) *The knowledge-based economy*, Paris: OECD.

Sen, A. (1999) *Development as freedom*, Oxford: Oxford University Press.

Singapore Department of Statistics (2008) *Latest population data*. Available online at www.singstat.gov.sg/stats/latestdata.html#12 (accessed 10 October 2008).

Singapore Government (1997) *Singapore 21 subject committee reports: attracting talent vs looking after Singaporeans*. Available online at www.singapore21.org.sg/menu_resources.html (accessed 10 October 2008).

—— (2008) *Campus for Research Excellence and Technological Enterprise (CREATE)*. Available online at www.nrf.gov.sg/NRF/otherProgrammes.aspx?id=188 (accessed 10 October 2008).

Yeoh, B.S.A. (2007a) *Singapore: hungry for foreign workers at all skill levels*. Available online at www.migrationinformation.org/Profiles/display.cfm?ID=570 (accessed 10 October 2008).

—— (2007b) 'Migration and social diversity in Singapore', in T.T. How (ed.) *Singapore perspectives 2007: a new Singapore*, Singapore: Institute of Policy Studies.

—— and Huang, S. (2004) '"Foreign talent" in our midst: new challenges to "sense of community" and ethnic relations in Singapore', in Lai Ah Eng (ed.) *Beyond rituals and riots: ethnic pluralism and social cohesion in Singapore*, Singapore: Institute of Policy Studies, Eastern Universities Press.

5

Towards a sociology of the global teacher

Meg Maguire

Introduction

> Education will always be a cause for concern, a focus for debate, a problem to be resolved, because it is one of the basic mechanisms through which human life is reproduced.
>
> (Scott and Freeman-Moir, 2000: 8)

> The teacher is the key actor in the process of educational transformation.
>
> (Tedesco, 1997: 23)

In an internationally competitive marketplace, education plays a critical role in helping each nation to create and maintain a competitive edge – or so the argument goes. Thus, in response to aspects of the globalisation discourse, attempts have been made to conform educational provision to the 'needs' of capital in many international settings. Many nations, aware of international comparisons such as TIMSS and PISA, have been spurred on to reform their educational provision and raise their measurable levels of attainment. What has emerged is a new set of public policy demands for efficiency, accountability, effectiveness and flexibility – what Ball (2008: 41) has described as a 'generic global policy ensemble' – aimed at reforming public sector education provision.

In this chapter, I will explore what these demands mean in relation to the (re)construction of the teacher and of teachers' work. The chapter starts with a brief discussion of globalisation and its influence on education policy. It then explores some of the ways in which attempts have been made to reconstruct the teacher and the work of the teacher in the light of these policies. Nonetheless, drawing on some examples of teacher education reforms, I argue that the construction of the teacher is always context-dependent – the teacher is produced out of local histories, cultures and politics. These 'differences' play out in the ways in which relationships between globalisation and education policy continue to evolve.

Contextualising the global teacher

Many of the claims currently being made about the need for educational reform rest on the assertion of there being a 'new world order': the globalisation thesis (Green *et al.*, 2007; Held *et al.*, 1999; Waters, 1995). What is meant by globalisation is contested: there are 'strong' versions that are based on the premise of the emergence of an almost inevitable world market that displaces the role and influence of the nation-state in decision-making (Ohmae, 1990, 1996); there are other versions that suggest that globalisation can produce 'new pressures for local autonomy' (Giddens, 1999: 13). At its most general, however, globalisation implies a world where time/space compression reduces the 'constraints of geography' (Waters, 1995: 3) and where economic, cultural and political changes have become interwoven and inter-dependent, fuelled and sustained by communication and technological developments (Olssen *et al.*, 2004).

Globalisation is a discursive as well as a material set of practices. That is, discourses of globalisation make possible certain ways of thinking, acting and being, and they displace or conceal alternatives. The world watches the Olympic games 'as it happens'; the international community experiences the fall-out from the melt-down in the sub-prime US housing markets; the wide-spread circulation of blockbuster Hollywood (and increasingly Bollywood) movies – all these material outcomes demonstrate the interconnectedness and convergence of the contemporary world. These 'events' are amplified and circulated as illustrations of the reach of globalisation. In the UK, the impact of globalisation discourses, specifically in terms of economic theories and imperatives, has been profound (Barber and Sebba, 1999). For example, the (then) UK Prime Minister Tony Blair put it like this:

> We are going to live in a market of global finance and there will be investors that decide to move their money in and out of countries. Even though we're living with a very serious economic problem . . . we have also derived enormous benefit from greater international trade, from the absence of protectionism and the absence of control exchange.
>
> (Blair, 1998)

The iteration and reiteration of the globalisation thesis and its ubiquitous claims appear to have influenced education policy and provision across the world. While Ball (2008: 25) warns that 'the idea of globalisation has to be treated with care', a point that cannot be fully dealt with in this chapter (but see Ball (2008) and Gewirtz (2001) for further discussion), the impulse of globalisation in terms of education policy is evident virtually everywhere. In many nation states, education policy is being articulated and constructed in response to the apparently irresistible discourses of globalisation that assert the 'need' for infrastructural and economic reforms to support and enhance international competitiveness.

Education has been repositioned as a vital tool for creating and maintaining economic prosperity and for retaining a competitive edge in world markets. According to Olssen *et al.* (2004: 13), 'it is imposed policies of neoliberal governmentality, rather than globalization as such, that is the key force affecting (and undermining) nation-states today' (see also Colclough, 1996). As Ball (2008: 53) asserts, 'Education policy is increasingly subordinated to and articulated in terms of economic policy and the necessities of international competition'.

Whatever one's explanation of what is propelling international educational reform-making (globalisation and/or neo-liberalism), dominant discourses emphasising the economic aims of education currently seem to have displaced alternative discourses (Winch and Gingell, 2004).

59

The outcomes can be seen in current international preoccupations with raising standards and measured attainment, making state education more accountable in relation to internationally derived targets and ensuring that curriculum and pedagogy are managed in order to 'deliver' these demands. What is being given primacy is the production of a labour force that, at least in the West, 'matches' the demands of a de-industrialising, post-industrial world, although the relationship between globalisation and education reform is currently articulated in the policy statements of virtually all governments around the world.

While the impact of a 'new world order' has undoubtedly influenced educational reforms, economic globalisation has not been experienced as a homogenous phenomenon. Within the unfolding changes of late capitalism, it is evident that changes in capitalist relations and policy production are tempered by the specificities of local histories and cultures (economic, political and social) and are recalibrated over time. To take the English context as a case, in the wake of the international oil crisis of the 1970s, the neo-liberal policy response emphasised the need for market forces (competition and school autonomy) to counter the educational 'crisis' of 'under-achievement' and 'poor' teaching that had allegedly contributed towards an economic downturn. By the 1990s, policy now included deregulation and 'choice' as part of government attempts to raise school standards and make schools more accountable and business-like, although, paradoxically, some forms of teacher preparation became tightly prescribed and highly centralised (Furlong et al., 2000). Currently, there is a focus on a 'for-profit' element in state education (Ball, 2007) and an approach towards individualising and personalising provision (Clarke et al., 2007). To some extent, these moves have also been reflected in a series of changes in teacher 'training'. All these different policy shifts are still firmly set within the regulating discourses of economic necessity and of the need for international competitiveness.

Reconstructing the global teacher

Contemporary teacher education reform, and concomitantly the construction of a 'new' teacher for the 'new world order', is predicated on a range of suppositions: that schools have failed in the past, owing, in some part, to inefficient and incompetent teachers, and that policymakers and governments are best placed to determine what makes an 'effective' teacher and a 'good' school (Fischman, 2000). In consequence, teacher reforms have been enacted that set out precisely what it is that teachers are to do, as well as how they are to be assessed (Maguire, 2002). There is some separation in the literature between work that considers policy developments in pre-service, initial teacher education (for example, see Acedo, 2007; Bales, 2006; Phelan and Sumsion, 2008) and research into the construction of the teacher via reforms that have attempted to reconstruct schools (Ball, 2003). In this chapter, I will deal with both literatures – for they offer a set of overlapping and integrated arguments that work towards new narratives of the teacher. In what follows, I want to explore this matter in terms of three aspects: these are regulation and control, standards and, finally, performance and accountability.

One way of ensuring teacher quality is to reform teaching at source by regulating and controlling pre-service teacher education. Many nations, including the US, UK, New Zealand, Australia, Canada and countries in Europe and in the Asia–Pacific region, now seek to manage recruitment and pre-service training through the generation of lists of competencies that have to be met before the teacher can be licensed to practice in schools (Fitzsimons and Fenwick, 1997). And many of these competencies include prescriptions about what constitutes 'best practice' that intending teachers are expected to adopt and perform in the practicum element of their course. The emphasis in these restructured courses is arguably on 'teacher-proofing' classroom practice. Thus, the emphasis, more and more, is on successful in-school experience, technical skills such as teaching literacy through centrally prescribed methods, behaviour management, familiarity with testing regimes etc. Other matters, for example, those of commitment, values and judgement are frequently sidelined, made optional or simply omitted; teacher education is constructed as a skill, and any political complexity is bleached out of the agenda (Cochrane-Smith, 2004). Put simply, the teacher is reconstructed as a state technician, trained to deliver a national curriculum, in the nation's schools. Alongside this competency-based model of the technical skills-based teacher is a market model of the 'flexiblisation' of teaching work, a move towards individual contracts and pay negotiations, including the use of non-qualified teachers and teaching assistants – where the teacher is positioned as part of the contracted labour force rather than as a professional partner in the process of education.

In many ways, the English case is the most acute example of this reforming movement (McPhee *et al.*, 2003). Regulation is managed through the production of a curriculum for teacher education, the generation of criteria against which teacher 'competence' is measured and frequent inspections of the teaching courses and providers. Controls are built into the initial training and are carried into the early years of teaching in order to maintain a culture of high expectations, attention to national targets, and a concentration on the basic skills of literacy and numeracy. In this way, a very particular version of the 'teacher' is made up. The emphasis is on compliance with competencies rather than with thinking critically about practice; focusing on teaching rather than learning; doing rather than thinking; skills rather than values. This regime is maintained (and justified) by the regular production of local, national and international league tables that exert pressure to raise the stakes and raise the game at every opportunity (Barber, 2001; Barber and Sebba, 1999). In this way, the pressures of regulation and control in producing the teacher are inserted into, and circulated through, the state school system.

These systems of regulation and control are glued together by the production of sets of data about the achievements of children and young people all around the world. Nation-states (and their various ministries of education) regularly compare themselves with one another (Shorrocks-Taylor *et al.*, 2000). Economists assess international profiles of educational attainment in their attempts to review the capacity of 'human capital stocks' (Barro and Lee, 2001). The preoccupations with standards and raising standards are powerful, internationalised discourses that are realised in target setting. The capacity to meet (or not) these targets in turn becomes the measure of success and a lever in assessing and raising the performance of the individual child, the teacher, the school and thus the nation-state's educational achievements.

At the heart of this, in the everyday world of practice, teachers may well face a personal and professional set of tensions. In meeting the targets, they may sometimes have to 'teach to the test' and sideline any other pedagogical concerns, such as aesthetic, moral, social or any wider cognitive goals. In this reorienting and reworking of the 'teacher', alternative identities such as those based on a commitment to the common good or to different sets of values and dispositions (for example, developmentally and culturally sensitive curricula) are displaced. In working to 'mediate' complex and sometimes contradictory values in their practice, teachers may find themselves caught up in struggles around professional judgements and a new way of being. Ball (2003: 218) writes of teachers being caught up in a new 'culture of competitive performativity', where there is the potential to be graded as 'successful' and 'outstanding'. But 'being' and 'doing' this new type of entrepreneurial teacher, whose targets and 'aspirations' are governed by national testing schemes, can produce feelings of what Ball (2003) calls 'inauthenticity'. This new teacher, measured and evaluated through techniques such as monitoring, the production of documentary 'evidence' of effective planning for teaching, performance reviews, appraisals, inspections and the like, may become professionally conflicted: 'commitment, judgement and authenticity within practice are sacrificed' at the altar of measurable outcomes (Ball, 2003: 221).

Education policy making has been driven by the need to ensure that young people are being equipped with the means to contribute to, and compete in, a world without borders. At their most simple, calls for teacher accountability are demands for teachers to be answerable for making demonstrable improvements in their students' learning. 'Each teacher assumes responsibility for creating a classroom where students can master school knowledge at an appropriate pace and with a high degree of challenge' (Lieberman and Miller, 1999: 22). Thus, a battery of accountability techniques has been developed to monitor, assess and evaluate the degree to which teachers meet these responsibilities, mainly through testing the children and students that they teach. There are inevitable tensions: teachers may concentrate on testing rather than comprehension; teachers may feel pressured to attend to targets that they may construe as being inappropriate (Ball's 'inauthentic' teacher); teachers may offer what they believe to be a limited and diluted curriculum. Teachers may simply become overwhelmed by accelerating demands and additions to their work roles (Bartlett, 2004) and may leave the job altogether. All these pressures have been well documented (Fuhrman and Elmore, 2004; Lambert and McCarthy, 2006). Nonetheless, 'holding schools to account' (Wilcox and Gray, 1996) is a key policy strategy in reforming the teacher and the work of the teacher.

There is a wealth of evidence that charts an international reforming tendency towards reconstructing the teacher to 'fit' the needs of a globalising economy, the 'world-class' teacher. This signals a form of policy convergence, a move towards making up a global teacher who is at once a 'professional classroom manager, an expert providing "high quality" client services in "more for less" times' (McWilliams, 2008: 35). The reconstructed teacher is produced out of sets of recipes for action, systemic rules, technologies of performance and routine classroom actions that are designed (by others) to 'deliver' quality and 'assure' high standards. The teacher is reconstituted as a technical 'risk manager' who, in McWilliam's terms (2008: 36), makes 'learning outcomes more visible, calculable and thus more accountable' in a context where, to some extent, any competing versions of the teacher have been erased.

Recontextualising the global teacher

While there may be a set of overarching principles and conditions that influence policy production – globalisation and neo-liberalism, for instance – these 'rarely, if ever, translate into policy texts or practice in a direct or pristine form' (Ball, 1998: 126). In terms of the reconstructed global teacher who, so far, has been cast as an entrepreneurial manager rather than an organic intellectual, we need to ask, is this everywhere the case? To what degree has education been conformed to the needs of the international/national marketplace? To what extent has this chapter presented an altogether pessimistic and determinist view of the global teacher? In recontextualising the global teacher, I now want to consider some points of difference that are interwoven into the making up of the teacher, which are context dependent and are produced out of the specificities of local histories, cultures and politics, in particular issues of supply and demand, 'flexibility' in teacher production, and geopolitical distinctions.

One of the most intractable differences relates to the complexities and local distinctions that shape the supply and demand of teachers. In parts of the US, areas such as Michigan, Louisiana, and in cities such as New York, it is increasingly difficult to recruit and retain teachers (Steadman and Simmons, 2007). In Mississippi, although there are calls for 'quality' teachers, the shortage is so acute that the state has been forced to introduce emergency licensing. In part, this shortfall of teachers is to do with the relatively low salaries and status of teachers in the state. Mississippi has responded by introducing emergency one-year licences to teach for individuals whose school district will vouch for them. New York City has created the Teaching Fellows programme to recruit those interested in a career change into teaching in challenging schools. Both of these approaches place the intending teachers in classrooms in high-need schools while they are learning to become teachers. In terms of the Mississippi experience, one problem lies in the way in which the licence can be easily extended, without much support for professional development or interventions from teaching colleges. In NYC, the Teaching Fellows programme offers college accreditation and in-school mentoring, but the retention rates are low. Both schemes place would-be teachers in challenging classrooms with, in the main, 'disadvantaged' children. In the UK, there are similar teacher training programmes that aim to fill the same sorts of gap (Ross and Hutchings, 2003).

Although some aspects of some of these 'alternative route' schemes have been positively rated – for instance the NYC route and Teach First in the UK – they all report problems with teacher retention rates. There are also issues for 'challenging schools' that have to manage with higher than average levels of teacher turnover and inexperienced and less well-qualified teachers. There are additional issues of social justice related to 'high-need' students being taught by teachers (however well intentioned and however good their first degree) who are learning on the job and not staying long. In terms of the construction of the global teacher, these emergency schemes signal a degree of flexibility and perhaps disposability that surrounds the recruitment of the teacher; it also highlights a 'crisis' in the supply side of teaching – at least in certain parts of the world. One outcome of these shortages has been the creation of a 'global market' in teacher recruitment (Menter, 2008).

The production of these 'emergency' flexible teachers speaks to the tensions involved in the (northern-hemisphere) public sector labour market, as well as in some of the normalising discourses that surround the production of the teacher – perhaps that anyone can do this work. In terms of the labour market, less competitive salaries and poorer work conditions have limited recruitment to teaching. Another factor that compounds teacher shortages in some countries is that, in many nations, until relatively recently, teaching provided an early opportunity for women to undertake professional work (Anker, 1998). Currently, 'the teaching profession has to compete with many other attractive and prestigious job options' now open to women (Tedesco, 1997: 29). Working in the public sector may be less attractive – although, in periods of economic downturn, recruitment to jobs that look secure frequently goes up. Simultaneously, in the public sector there is an awareness that the new educational professional is an entrepreneurial individual, someone who seeks performance-related rewards, who is compared with and compares him/herself against his/her 'colleagues'. Many of the dominant and normalising discourses that currently surround 'being a teacher' speak of being open to change and the 'developing professional' as a lifelong project – even where, paradoxically, a view of teaching as a career for life has been eroded. The 'enduring' sense behind this lifelong project of constant improvement may not be something that new graduates feel particularly drawn towards.

Teaching as a profession has been repositioned as a responsibility towards producing the requirements for the labour markets of the future and, inevitably, what McWilliam (2008: 41) calls the culture of 'enterprise [that] has come to replace a more long-term culture of public service'. Yet, for more and more emergent graduates in northern-hemisphere nation-states, teaching is becoming a short-term occupation, perhaps a first step beyond university. Thus, while there are discourses of lifelong processes of learning to teach, the reality is frequently one of high teacher turn-over. In the UK, for example, what fuels this movement out of teaching are high levels of stress and burn-out, as well as emotional dissatisfaction with some of the policy demands to which teachers have to demonstrate compliance (Smithers and Robinson, 2005).

In other parts of the world, supply and demand issues are differently experienced. In less/differently economically developed countries and transitional countries, there are problems in recruiting teachers for state-funded schools. This is less so in some fee-paying private schools, where teacher salaries and working conditions may be better – although it depends on the school itself (Kitaev, 2007; Thakur, 2008). There can also be difficulties in staffing schools in rural and less accessible areas within northern-hemisphere settings, as well as in less economically privileged locales, some of which may be populated by minoritised communities (Whatman, 2002). There may be difficulties in getting and holding on to teachers for particular phases of schooling. For instance, in some parts of the world, a basic school-leaving certificate may enable someone to become a primary teacher; however, the subject knowledge demands of the secondary curriculum make it more complicated to prepare and retain secondary school teachers (Mulkeen *et al.*, 2007).

In neo-liberal times, one consequence of deregulation and national shortages has been the emergence of the 'migrating' teacher – the teacher who can move to a place where his/her skills are in short supply. This can sometimes mean that the West 'imports' teachers from countries where teachers are in short supply, even when, as in the UK, there are protocols in place to limit this process (Morgan *et al.*, 2005). However, the cultural norms of his/her initial training and his/her own schooling may not sit easily with those of the new setting; in Menter's words (2008: 224), 'when a teacher migrates . . . it is likely that significant processes will ensue that affect her professional identity'. Professional identities that are formed largely from a 'service ethic', for example (Menter, 2008: 224), may be less compatible with a teacher identity dominated by the need for compliance with lists of competences, skills and outcomes. A teacher identity that is formed in the expectation of having to teach through a rote-based pedagogy may experience disruptions in an inner-city, 'hard to teach' school setting. Yet, the international movement of people (such as teachers and international students) produces new spaces in which to construct identities that are 'intercultural with multiple cultural defining points' (Rizvi, 2000: 223) – what Rizvi calls a 'new global generation'.

In the reconstruction work that is taking place in the making up of the teacher, there are other points at issue. In a setting that is characterised by shortages in teacher supply, who is and what is a teacher is being called into question. For instance, in England, the production of the teaching assistant (TA) and the higher-level teaching assistant (HLTA) means that teachers are supported by other adults who, in the case of the HLTA, will act as a specialist assistant for certain areas of the curriculum and who will sometimes lead classes, supervise in the teacher's absence and 'assess, record and report on the progress of children' (see http://careersadvice. direct.gov.uk/helpwithyourcareer/jobprofiles/profile). The production of these assistants (Kamen, 2008) may well add to the richness of the classroom for children and students; however, at a maximum salary of £16,000 for a TA and £18,000 for a HLTA, these people will sometimes be acting as teacher-substitutes on a much lower salary, an exploitative situation. Their education and training may concentrate on policy directives and compliance rather than a capacity to make informed pedagogical judgements. However, while the UK/English government argues that a 'more flexible workforce will help to reduce the bureaucratic load on teachers', freeing them up to teach, the UK teacher unions have been 'deeply suspicious of these developments, suspecting that these less well-paid staff' may be used to replace teachers (Menter, 2008: 223).

And what then of the organised teacher? What role do teacher unions play in this making up or contesting of the neo-liberal, globalising teacher? Although concerns are being expressed about the intensification of teachers' workloads and the 'unjust criticism by politicians' of teachers (OECD, 2004: 39, cited in Jones, 2008: 54), the capacity of teachers to assert control over their working lives has been eroded in many parts of the world (but see Compton and Weiner, 2008). In a neo-liberal world, teachers experience a 'loss of capacity for self-definition, both in the workplace and in the political sphere' (Jones, 2008: 56). In terms of some European trends, Jones notes the ways in which Greek, Catalan and French teachers have been able to mobilise public support in defence of public education. In contrast, he details the way in which the English unions' focus on teacher salary was less able to engender popular support and paved the way for more overt control of teachers.

One of the best-known examples of challenges to neo-liberalism in education is the Citizen School movement in Porto Alegre, Brazil, where the intention is to 'build support for more progressive and democratic policies there in the face of the growing power of neo-liberal movements at a national level' (Gandin and Apple, 2002: 260). These schools are grounded in an approach that requires and enables the full participation of the school staff, parents, administrators and students in decision-making. Teachers make up half of the membership of the school council; the other half is made up of parents and students. The school council makes decisions about the curriculum and resource allocation and elects the principal. In these schools, teachers, parents and students are working together to build a different school and a more democratic society where the curriculum is negotiated and starts from the histories, cultures and politics of the local community. What this demonstrates is a different way of 'doing school' and of being a teacher.

Reshaping the teacher – complexities and costs

In this chapter, I have argued that neo-liberal and globalising impulses are having discernable outcomes in reshaping the work of the teacher in many parts of the world. In this final section, I want briefly to discuss some points that are raised by this work. In speaking of 'the world' or 'international change', there is sometimes a tendency for northern-hemisphere researchers to concentrate on northern-hemisphere cases, frequently the UK, the US and Australia, that then stand as a proxy for the 'global world'. Here, I have tried to draw on a wider range of work on teachers in an attempt to avoid this problem, but there is always a danger of superficiality when speaking of distinctive contexts in a short piece. Teaching is a complex, diffuse and differentiated occupation. Internationally, there are wide variations in entry qualifications, the duration of pre-service education and in the status and salaries of different 'types' of teacher. For example, the teacher of elite groups may bear very little resemblance to the teacher of the poor within the same national setting. The preparation, status and salary of the early-years teacher and the specialist secondary school teacher might be very different. Teachers in a national state sector might differ from those in the fee-paying sector in the same setting. Thus, there can be dangers of essentialising and homogenising what it is to be a teacher.

While global neo-liberalism is influencing what it means to teach and be a teacher, 'the future has not been written and no one can ever claim a definitive understanding of the current relationships between globalization, the state, education, and social change' (Morrow and Torres, 2000: 53). Markets and states are prone to failure (Jessop and Sum, 2006). There are differences in outcomes, as well as some 'big and small struggles and victories' (Robertson, 2007). One way towards 'coping' with the ways in which neo-liberal policies differently inflect the construction of teacher in different contexts is suggested by Lingard (2000), who argues for an approach that simultaneously recognises global changes in terms of their 'vernaculars'; that is, the localised and sometimes distinctive ways in which these changes are configured and rewritten into national settings.

Nevertheless, the encroaching privatisations that are being inserted into education policy more widely (Ball, 2007), as well as into the reconstruction of the teacher and the work of the teacher, seem set to continue. It may well be the teachers of the poor and the disenfranchised, wherever they are located (in the global cities of the northern hemisphere, in the favellas and shanty towns of the southern hemisphere), who are most immediately subjected to the imperatives of neo-liberal reforms that are forced upon them by international agencies. More generally, the cost of being made up as the new global teacher, wherever this is taking place, may be the 'existential redundancy' (Rutherford, 2008: 16) of the professional, ethical and decision-making teacher.

References

Acedo, C. (2007) 'Teacher education and accountability policies for improving teaching effectiveness in the Philippines', in M.T. Tatto (ed.) *Reforming teaching globally*, Oxford: Symposium Books.

Anker, R. (1998) *Gender and jobs: sex segregation of occupations in the world*, Geneva: International Labour Office.

Bales, B. (2006) 'Teacher education policies in the United States: the accountability shift since 1980', *Teaching and Teacher Education* 22: 395–407.

Ball, S.J. (1998) 'Big policies/small world: an introduction to international perspectives in education policy', *Comparative Education* 34(2): 119–130.

—— (2003) 'The Teachers' soul and the terrors of performativity', *Journal of Education Policy* 18(2): 215–228.

—— (2007) *Education plc: understanding private sector participation in public sector education*, London: Routledge.

—— (2008) *The education debate*, Bristol: Policy Press.

Barber, M. (2001) 'The very big picture', *School Effectiveness and School Improvement* 12(2): 213–228.

—— and Sebba, J. (1999) 'Reflections on progress towards a world class education system', *Cambridge Journal of Education* 29(2): 183–193.

Barro, R.J. and Lee, J.W. (2001) 'International data on educational attainment: updates and implications', *Oxford Economic Papers* 53: 541–563.

Bartlett, L. (2004) 'Expanding teacher work roles: a resource for retention or a recipe for overwork?', *Journal of Education Policy* 18(5): 565–582.

Blair, T. (1998) The *Today* programme, BBC Radio 4, 30 September 1998, cited in D. Held, 'Globalisation, the timid tendency', *Marxism Today* Nov/Dec: 24–28.

Clarke, J., Newman, J., Smith, N., Vidler, E. and Westmarland, L. (2007) *Creating citizen-consumers: changing publics and changing public services*, London: Sage Publications.

Cochrane-Smith, M. (2004) *Walking the road: race, diversity, and social justice in teacher education*, New York: Teachers College Press.

Colclough, C. (1996) 'Education and the market: which parts of the neo-liberal solution are correct?', *World Development* 24(4): 589–610.

Compton, M. and Weiner, L. (eds) (2008) *The global assault on teaching, teachers and their unions. Stories for resistance*, New York and Basingstoke: Palgrave Macmillan.

Fischman, G. (2000) *Imagining teachers: rethinking gender dynamics in teacher education*, London/New York: Rowman & Littlefield.

Fitzsimons, P. and Fenwick, P. (1997) *Teacher competencies and teacher education: a descriptive literature review: a report*, Wellington, NZ: New Zealand Council for Educational Research, New Zealand Ministry of Education.

Fuhrman, S. and Elmore, R.F. (2004) *Redesigning accountability systems for education*, New York: Teachers College Press.

Furlong, J., Barton, L., Miles, S., Whiting, C. and Whitty, G. (2000) *Teacher education in transition*, Buckingham: Open University Press.

Gandin, L.A. and Apple, M.W. (2002) 'Challenging neo-liberalism, building democracy: creating the Citizen School in Porto Alegre, Brazil', *Journal of Education Policy* 17(2): 259–280.

Gewirtz, S. (2001) 'Interactions of the global and the local: a framework for comparative analysis of the relationship between 'globalisation' and education', Paper presented at the Conference on Travelling policy/local spaces: globalisation, identities and education policy in Europe, University of Keele, 27–29 June.

Giddens, A. (1999) 'Globalization', Lecture 1 of the BBC Reith Lectures, BBC News Online Network Homepage, 1–6.

Green, A., Little, A.W., Ketch, M.O. and Vickers, E. (2007) *Education and development in a global era: strategies for 'successful globalisation*, London: Department for International Development (DFID).

Held, D., McGrew, A. and Goldblatt, D. (1999) *Global transformations: politics, economics and culture*, Cambridge: Polity Press.

Jessop, B. and Sum, N.L. (2006) Beyond the regulation approach: putting capitalist economies in their place, Cheltenham: Edward Elgar Publishing.

Jones, K. (2008) 'An English vernacular. Teacher trade unionism and educational politics', in S. Gewirtz, P. Mahony, I. Hextall and A. Cribb (eds) *Changing teacher professionalism. International trends, challenges and ways forward*, London and New York: Routledge, pp. 54–64.

Kamen, T. (2008) *Teaching assistant's handbook*, 2nd edn, London: Hodder Arnold.

Kitaev, I. (2007) 'Education for all and private education in developing and transitional countries', in P. Srivastava and G. Walford (eds) *Private schooling in less economically developed countries. Asian and African perspectives*, Oxford: Symposium Books, pp. 89–110.

Lambert, R.G. and McCarthy, C.J. (2006) *Understanding teacher stress in an age of accountability*, Charlotte NC: Information Age Publications.

Lieberman, A. and Miller, L. (1999) *Teachers – transforming their world and their work*, New York and London: Teachers College, Columbia University.

Lingard, B. (2000) 'It is and it isn't: vernacular globalization, educational policy and restructuring', in N.C. Burbules and C.A. Torres (eds) *Globalization and education: critical perspectives*, New York: Routledge, pp. 79–108.

McPhee, A., Forde, C. and Skelton, F. (2003) 'Teacher education in the UK in an era of performance management', *Asia Pacific Journal of Teacher Education and Development* 6(2): 37–56.

McWilliam, E. (2008) 'Making excellent teachers', in A. Phelan and J. Sumsion (eds) (2008) *Critical readings in teacher education. Provoking absences*, Rotterdam/Taipei: Sense Publishers, pp. 33–44.

Maguire, M. (2002) 'Globalisation, education policy and the teacher', *International Studies in Sociology of Education* 12(3): 261–276.

Menter, I. (2008) 'Teachers for the future. What have we got and what do we need?', in S. Gewirtz, P. Mahony, I. Hextall and A. Cribb (eds) *Changing teacher professionalism. International trends, challenges and ways forward*, London and New York: Routledge, pp. 217–228.

Morgan, J.W., Sives, A. and Appleton, S. (2005) 'Managing the international recruitment of health workers and teachers: do the Commonwealth agreements provide an answer?', *The Round Table* 94(379): 225–238.

Morrow, R.A. and Torres, C.A. (2000) 'The state, globalization and education policy', in N.C. Burbules and C.A. Torres (eds) *Globalization and education: critical perspectives*, New York: Routledge, pp. 27–56.

Mulkeen, A., Chapman, D., DeJaeghere, J. and Leuet, E. (2007) *Recruiting, retaining, and retraining secondary school teachers and principals in Sub-Saharan Africa*, Washington, DC: Africa Region Human Development Department, The World Bank.

Ohmae, K. (1990) *The borderless world: power, and strategy in the interlinked economy*, New York: Harper Perennial.

—— (1996) *The end of the nation state: the rise of regional economics*, New York: Free Press.

Olssen, M., Codd, J. and O'Neil, A.M. (2004) *Education policy. Globalization, citizenship and democracy*, London: Sage Publications.

Phelan, A. and Sumsion, J. (eds) (2008) *Critical readings in teacher education. Provoking absences*, Rotterdam/Taipei: Sense Publishers.

Rizvi, F. (2000) 'The production of the global imagination', in N.C. Burbules and C.A. Torres (eds) *Globalization and education: critical perspectives*, New York: Routledge, pp. 205–225.

Robertson, S.L. (2007) *"Remaking the world": neo-liberalism and the transformation of education and teachers' labor*, published by the Centre for Globalisation, Education and Societies, University of Bristol, UK. Available online at www.bris.ac.uk/education/people/academicstaff/edslr/publications/17slr/.

Ross, A. and Hutchings, M. (2003) *Attracting, developing and retaining effective teachers in the United Kingdom of Great Britain and Northern Ireland*, OECD Country Background Report. Available online at www.oecd.org/dataoecd/62/25/2635748.pdf (accessed 20 August 2008).

Rutherford, J. (2008) 'The culture of capitalism', *Soundings* 38: 8–18.

Scott, A. and Freeman-Moir, J. (2000) *Tomorrow's teachers. International and critical perspectives on teacher education*, Christchurch NZ: Canterbury University Press.

Shorrocks-Taylor, D., Jenkins, E.W. and Angell, C. (2000) *Learning from others: international comparisons in education*, Dordrecht, Netherlands, and London: Kluwer Academic.

Smithers, A. and Robinson, P. (2005) *Teacher turnover, wastage and movements between schools*, Nottingham: DfES.

Steadman, S. and Simmons, J. (2007) 'Teachers not certified by universities burden our best teachers', *Education Digest* 72(7): 19–24.

Tedesco, J.C. (1997) 'Enhancing the role of teachers', in C. Day, D. van Veen and W.-K. Sim (eds) *Teachers and teaching: international perspectives on school reform and teacher education*, Leuven/Apeldoorn: Garant Publishers, pp. 23–36.

Thakur, A.S. (2008) *Development of educational system in India: a source book for teacher educators and teachers-in-training*, Delhi: Shipra Publications.

Waters, M. (1995) *Globalization*, London and New York, Routledge.

Whatman, S.L. (2002) 'Teacher preparation in a remote indigenous school: a human rights issue?', *Journal of Australian Indigenous Issues* 4(2): 16–24.

Wilcox, B. and Gray, J. (1996) *Inspecting schools: holding schools to account and helping schools to improve*, Buckingham: Open University Press.

Winch, C. and Gingell, J. (2004) *Philosophy and educational policy*, London and New York: RoutledgeFalmer.

6

Codes, pedagogy and knowledge
Advances in Bernsteinian sociology of education

Ursula Hoadley and Johan Muller

Introduction

The intractability of working-class failure has remained an unresolved issue for the sociology of education over the last forty years. Although some inroads have been made in understanding *how* inequality is engendered through schooling (and through pedagogy in particular), in ongoing developments in curriculum policy globally, knowledge, or 'the what' of schooling, is perennially left out, even as global achievement comparisons such as TIMSS and PIRLS (Progress in International Reading and Literacy Study) highlight its salience. The policy trend towards expressing the objects of learning in generic, outcomes or skills-based terms in curricula systematically avoids an engagement with knowledge. Curriculum studies and sociology of education in the twenty-first century cannot continue to avoid interrogating what children know and don't know. Thus far, it has been silent on the issue. In what follows, we offer a broad outline of the development of the sociological theory of Basil Bernstein, explaining how the development of his ideas across a period of forty years has progressively generated theoretical resources to explore not just how students learn, but what they learn. This theory has brought the question of the what and the how of teaching and learning to the forefront. In this way, Bernstein's theory offers a theoretically informed approach to the awkward question of the intractability of unequal schooling outcomes.

Code theory

Pedagogy is a formal, state-controlled medium for specializing the consciousness of young people. Code theory provides a grammar for an analysis of how consciousness is differentially specialized. For Bernstein, this grammar was necessary to explain the difference between middle-class and working-class success in schooling.

'Code' refers to an orientation to organizing experience and making meaning. The initial work on codes examined the relation between social class, maternal modes of control and communicative outcomes (Bernstein and Brandis, 1970; Bernstein and Henderson, 1969;

Henderson, 1970). Through this early work, Bernstein sought to investigate how different forms of socialization acted differentially upon the speech forms acquired and used by different social classes. These different kinds of language were hypothesized to have differential potential for learning at school. In order to analyse speech patterns, a linguistic theory had to be selected. Bernstein (1973: 73) describes how he deliberately decided not to use Chomsky's transformational grammar, which was dominant at the time, as this theory divorced linguistics from semantics and it was thus not appropriate to a study where the major point of the enquiry was about the relationship between the social structuring of relevant meanings and the form of their linguistic expression. Halliday's linguistic theory, on the other hand, satisfied the requirements created by the sociological aspects of the thesis, as it put forward a set of interrelated linguistic contexts in which the child is socialized into language. Bernstein selected four of these contexts: regulative, instructional, imaginative and interpersonal, and related them to Hasan's (1968) theory of cohesion, whether speech stands apart from its context so that the meanings are made explicit, or whether speech is a part of the context, so that it is necessary for the speaker to refer to the context of the speech or to the speaker's situation to understand the speech. This led to the working out of his concepts of elaborated and restricted codes.

In their original 'sociolinguistic' form, restricted codes are associated with particular grammatical and syntactical forms (generally simple, incomplete), as well as with more implicit meanings; elaborated codes are associated with the accurate grammatical and syntactical regulation of what is said, and with explicit meanings (Lee, 1973). The elaborated code allowed thus, by definition, the generation of context-independent meanings; the restricted code, contextual meanings. Further experiments consolidated the concepts. Hawkins (1969), for example, used a series of four pictures of boys playing with a ball, kicking the ball through a window and being scolded by an adult. He asked middle-class and working-class children to describe the pictures. He found that, for the middle-class children, verbal communication was explicit and could be understood without heavily depending on the context. For the working-class children, on the other hand, meaning was implicit and context-dependent, and relied largely on the listener's prior knowledge of the narrative content.

The theory showed that elaborated and restricted codes were realizations of particular control relations in the homes of children. The work of Cook-Gumperz (1973), in particular, gave empirical support to Bernstein's distinction between three modes of control: personal, positional and imperative. In middle-class homes, personal forms of control were largely found; in working-class settings, imperative modes predominated; and positional control was found in mixed-class families. Crucially, the personal and positional modes could overlap linguistically (Halliday, 1978: 82–83).

The concept of code underwent change and refinement. Whereas code, in the work discussed above, was used to refer to features of language only, in later work it was refined to refer to the principles of solidarity and communication regulating social life, what Diaz (2001) called the 'meaning matrices'. It is through these matrices that we select what is relevant to us in any given context, and with them that we organize experience. In this way, codes become the grids by which consciousness is specialized.

By this redefinition, elaborated codes refer to the prioritizing and deployment (or recognition and realization) of context-independent meanings, and restricted codes refer to the recognition and realization of context-dependent meanings; here, language is the *linguistic realization* of the code, rather than the code itself. One of the main studies exemplifying this shift was an experiment reported by Holland (1981). In this experiment, seven-year-old working-class and middle-class learners were shown pictures of different foodstuffs and were asked to group them however they wanted. They were asked the reasons for their groupings. They were then asked to group the food a second time and to again provide criteria for the grouping. The experiment showed that working-class children mostly used context-dependent principles for their sorting, in that their groupings referred to personal and particularistic meanings (e.g. 'I like those things'; 'That is what mother cooks for breakfast.'), which generally referred to everyday use. They did not change their principles for sorting the second time, demonstrating a single (restricted) coding orientation. Middle-class children were found to respond to the task first by referring to general, non-context-dependent principles (e.g. a food category), and, in a second grouping, to more personalized, local meanings. They thus demonstrated two coding orientations, elaborated and restricted, where context-independent meanings were privileged for the school context. Thus different social class groupings were shown to display different coding orientations. It was argued that the focus of the child's selections were not a function of the child's IQ or cognitive power, but rather a difference in the recognition and realization rules used by the children to read the particular context (the school), make selections (around what is appropriate given the context) and realize a particular text (their groupings of the food).

Bernstein's work was criticized for describing the restricted code, and, hence, working-class language, as deficient. Bernstein (1996: 182) rejected this interpretation, explaining that '[c]odes arise out of different modes of social solidarity, oppositionally positioned in the process of production, and differentially acquired in the process of formal education'. Restricted codes are necessary in convivial modes of everyday life, but the school requires an elaborated code for success. This means that working-class children have a double hurdle to clear, namely acquiring both the specialized knowledge of school, as well as the coding orientation with which to realize this acquisition.

Pedagogy – sociological studies of the classroom

Bernstein developed a conceptual language to describe the elaborated code of the school, based on the core notions of classification and framing. Classification refers to the organizational aspects of pedagogy, the way in which *power* activates certain categories – of school subjects, agents, discourse and space. Framing, on the other hand, refers to the interactional aspects of pedagogy, the way in which knowledge is selected, sequenced, paced and evaluated in the classroom, regulating the moral order of the classroom and who has *control* over it. The distinction between power and control, unique in the discipline of sociology (but see Douglas, 1966), allows for the description of the making (power) and the potential unmaking (control) of the social reproduction of inequality.

The early Bernsteinian studies of classrooms used the concepts of personal and positional relations and elaborated and restricted codes to describe the structure of pedagogy. Cooper (1976) and Edwards (1981) attempted to show differences between different types of classroom in terms of the social relations of control and the associated codes. The focus was on comparisons between different social class groupings of students. This work lead Bernstein to clarify the particular meanings attributed to codes. He maintained that codes vary across universalistic/particularistic, context-independent/context-dependent and embedded/disembedded meanings continua (1996: 162). He also pointed out that, although there is a relation between forms of control and orientations to meanings, an elaborated code may be realized under either positional or personal modes of control. This has recently been given empirical support in work identifying optimal pedagogies for working-class student success (Lubienski, 2004; Hoadley and Ensor, 2009).

Through these studies, the distinction between the moral order and the instructional order of the school and classroom was clarified. Bernstein's work had originally distinguished between an instructional dimension to pedagogy and a moral dimension, in the early terms 'expressive' and 'instrumental orders'. These aspects were brought back in the theorizing of classification and framing. In particular through the work of Pedro (1981), 'instructional' and 'regulative' *discourse* came to describe the transmission of specific instructional knowledge and skills, embedded in the normative moral order, or regulative discourse of the school. Pedagogic discourse was thus defined as an instructional discourse consisting of a number of dimensions, embedded in a regulative discourse.

At the level of the classroom, the instructional discourse was operationalized through describing strong or weak framing relations over selection, sequence, pace and evaluative criteria. The regulative discourse was examined by describing hierarchical control relations between transmitter and acquirer as operationalized through modes of personal and positional control. Strong framing relations were deemed to display modes of imperative/positional (that is, teacher) control, while weak framing was deemed to display personal (that is, learner) control. The hierarchical rules focused on the verbal elaboration between teachers and students. Bernstein in this way brought classroom processes to the fore in the sociology of education. In a key paper, Bernstein (1981) sketched a model for understanding pedagogic discourse and reproduction. This broad theoretical work continues to inform and has been developed by the work of a number of researchers concerned with explaining pedagogy in different contexts.

Most notably, the ongoing work of the Sociological Studies of the Classroom at the University of Lisbon (ESSA) (for example, Morais and Neves, 2001; Morais *et al.*, 2004) has focused on the micro processes in the classroom to explore the 'relations present in the context of reproduction of the pedagogic discourse' (Neves *et al.*, 2004: 280). The various authors show that specific aspects of pedagogic practice favour the development of the elaborated coding orientation required for learning context-independent school knowledge. Pedagogic modalities, designed in terms of success demonstrated in experimental studies, were then tested by trained teachers with learners from different social class backgrounds.

Key to this successful modality is 'explicating the evaluative criteria as the most crucial aspect of a pedagogic practice to promote higher levels of learning of all students' (Morais, 2002: 568). Making the evaluative criteria explicit consists of

> clearly telling children what is expected of them, of identifying what is missing from their textual production, of clarifying the concepts, of leading them to make synthesis and broaden concepts and considering the importance attributed to language as a mediator of the development of higher mental processes.
>
> (Morais *et al.*, 2004: 8)

The authors show how schooling *can* make a difference, and specify in what ways. Here is the crux of their argument, and the impetus for theirs and others' work:

> When family codes and practices are in continuity with school pedagogic codes and practices, acquisition of the recognition and realisation rules appropriate to school contexts is facilitated by the elaborated orientation brought in by children. Similar power and control relations in the family and the school permit more efficient access to recognition and realisation rules in school contexts. This immediately gives an advantage to children whose processes of primary socialisation are regulated by pedagogic codes similar to school codes. In general, these children tend to come from higher social or

dominant ethnic groups. However, this situation can be altered by school pedagogic practices whose characteristics permit access to the school coding orientation.

(Morais and Neves, 2001: 213–214)

In addition to explication of the evaluative criteria, weak framing over pacing is identified as being crucial for facilitating access to school knowledge for working-class learners, creating the opportunity to individualize the rate of acquisition. In research into literacy pedagogy for 'indigenous learners', Rose (2004) likewise specifies the dimensions facilitating a weakening of the negative relation between social class and educational achievement: a weakening of the framing of pacing and sequencing rules, and a weakening of 'the framing regulating the flow of communication between the school classroom and the community the school draws on' (p. 106).

These findings have been confirmed elsewhere in studies that draw on the fine-grained and rigorous methodologies for coding and analysis of data developed by the ESSA group. What Davies and Fitz (forthcoming) have called the 'anatomising of pedagogy' has led to a clear statement of what is important in the 'how' of pedagogy. In beginning mathematics, 'explicit evaluation criteria improve achievement gain for the sample, particularly teachers' use of error to provide explicit feedback on incorrect answers' (Reeves, 2005) and also for pedagogic disciplines where the criteria are traditionally tacit, such as cabinet making – 'criterial rules are very strongly framed throughout' (Gamble, forthcoming) – and in high school art – 'criteria need to be agreed upon, specified and made explicit' (Bolton, 2006: 73). Bernstein had said it clearly prior to this crop of empirical outcomes: 'We can see that the key to pedagogic practice is continuous evaluation' (Bernstein, 1996: 50). What allowed for comparability across a range of contexts was a common theoretical language, sufficiently developed for its empirical application and operating at a level of abstraction that allowed for commonalities to be discovered across the diverse settings of its application.

The differential pedagogic modalities that are deployed for different learners are an enduring concern across a broad range of contexts. Dooley (2001) examined the adaptation of pedagogy for Taiwanese migrant students in a state secondary school in Australia. She is particularly interested in the teacher–student relations realized in particular forms of classroom interaction. The main finding of the study was that differential pedagogic types were made available to Taiwanese, Chinese and other Asian students, compared with local students.

Singh (2002) examined the structuring of English curricular knowledge and forms of teacher–student interaction in secondary school classrooms in Queensland, Australia. Arnot and Reay (2004) focus on framing in the analysis of pupils' participation in their learning and on the consequences of contemporary pedagogic practice in a middle-class and working-class school in the United Kingdom. Hoadley (2008) shows how the gap between the school and the home for working-class learners is detrimentally closed by working-class teachers, who deploy a pedagogic modality akin to the restricted code orientation that students enter the school with. All these studies not only give empirical support to the theoretical account of the inner logic of pedagogy, thereby revealing the structuring of inequality, but also suggest how that inequality might be pedagogically reversed.

The weight of the empirical evidence underlines the futility of current curriculum policy debates, most notably in the USA, South Africa and Australia, between 'learner-centred' approaches and the 'back to basics' lobbies. What works instead is a mixed pedagogy, especially for working-class students. The studies show what the mix should look like, and in all cases explicit evaluation is critical. We show below, in the subsequent development of the theory and the empirical work that has been generated by the framework, the issue of evaluation remains central to the theory.

73

The pedagogic device

In 1996, Bernstein published a terse and somewhat enigmatic statement of his theory in terms of what he called the 'pedagogic device'. This was an ambitious attempt to capture the role of education in the sociological big picture, reaching from social structure to individual consciousness. The pedagogic device consists of a hierarchical relation between three sets of rules – distributive, recontextualizing and evaluative – that together describe the process of the transformation of knowledge from the field of production of knowledge, to the field of recontextualization, to the field of reproduction in the classroom. In short, it is a description of the structure by which knowledge is transformed into pedagogic communication. The introduction of the device highlighted a number of important conceptual relationships in its attempt to offer a more abstract and general unified theory. It also introduced a number of important issues that had been somewhat neglected in the development of the theory.

Two issues are singled out here. The first is the issue of knowledge, which is elaborated further below. The distributive rules distribute different types of knowledge to different social agents. Knowledge types or structures, the 'what' of education in the field of production (the university), had as yet been insufficiently adumbrated. How these knowledge structures related to curriculum structures, or the recontextualized knowledge found in schooling, had also so far received limited attention. A second issue raised in the pedagogic device concerned the third level of rules – the evaluative rules. Bernstein talks about the device being 'condensed' in the evaluative rules. By condensation he means that, at this level (of the classroom, and through acquisition) it is possible to see what the work of the device has been – in other words, in terms of the distribution of what knowledge to which social groups. The 'what' of the distributive rules and the control over the process of transmission through the recontextualizing rules result in differential specialization of consciousness through acquisition. It is at the moment of evaluation that we see the extent to which the distributive rules (both in terms of instructional knowledge and social norms) have been realized. The evaluative rules bring the 'what' (classification) and the 'how' (framing) into a final relation to each other. They condense the device. It is only at the point of evaluation that we can see the mutual operation of the distributive rules and the recontextualizing rules. But what of the knowledge to be distributed? The theory had yet to describe how it differed in form, and its curriculum and pedagogical implications.

It is these two aspects of the pedagogic device – the question of knowledge structure introduced through the distributive rules and the acquisition dimension that inheres in the evaluative rules – that offer fruitful directions for future research. We discuss the first issue briefly below.

Knowledge and the curriculum

The notion of the evaluative rules raises the question: evaluations of what? The answer – of the knowledge to be acquired – has mostly been avoided. Muller (2007) has argued that in any discipline there are a specifiable, necessary minimum set of incremental steps that must be pedagogically traversed, and each requires the necessary explicit evaluation. How to think about the *'what'* of education entails turning to how this specification might be accomplished.

It was only late in his career that Bernstein turned to the question of what knowledge was, its structure and its social base. He draws a strong distinction between two basic classes of knowledge: mundane or everyday knowledge, and esoteric or universal, principled knowledge. These two classes of knowledge are intrinsic to language, and they exist in all societies, even though their content may vary historically and culturally. A direct relation between meanings and a specific material base is termed horizontal discourse. In horizontal discourse, meanings cannot transcend their immediate context and so always refer to everyday or mundane contexts. Vertical discourse, by contrast, requires systematic ordering principles for the generation of meaning. The knowledge 'bits' fit together in a time and space not given by a specific context.

There are two forms of vertical discourse. They differ, first, by their form of conceptual advance (by their 'verticality') and, second, by their form of objectivity (their 'grammaticality'). As to the first: some knowledges tend towards robust, conceptually justifiable advances. Their knowledge structure is determined by their ever-advancing conceptual spine, which tends towards unity (which does not mean that there is only one conceptual spine in the knowledge structure: see Wignell, 2007). The curriculum implication of this type of conceptual advance is that these disciplines in their mature form develop long 'hierarchies of abstraction', which are best learnt in sequence under the guidance of specialists (mathematics and science are the most obvious examples). We may say that these disciplines are, in a specific sense, concept-rich. It is not that they necessarily involve large numbers of concepts. It is that they have long sequences of hierarchically related concepts. Getting stuck at any rung of the hierarchy usually means that conceptual learning stops. Other knowledges tend towards advance through variation or diversification of concepts; this, however, is less about concepts than it is about different contents or content-clusters, although there is usually a macro-conceptual organizing principle (the 'past' (or more abstractly time) for history and 'space' for geography, for example) involved. Still others develop practically, by developing new skills. Practical development may refer to new practices within traditional manual crafts such as cabinet making or to new forms of conceptual practice such as software development or website design. Concepts, content and skills are embedded in each knowledge structure, but their relative salience is what differentiates them.

There has been a range of exploratory empirical work in relation to different knowledge structures and their pedagogical and distributional implications. Reeves and Muller (2005), for example, consider what a knowledge structure of mathematics looks like when translated into the South African school curriculum. Christie and Macken-Horarick (2007) reconstruct 'verticality' in subject English in the Australian curriculum. More broadly, Young and Gamble (2006) and Wheelahan (2007) examine issues of skills and their orderings in vocational education curricula, and Maton (2005) has been concerned with sociology and its weak grammar knowledge structure. Moore (2007) and Young and Muller (2007) consider the humanities and the question of knowledge growth in horizontal disciplines. This work has opened up the question of the relations between knowledge structures and their corresponding curriculum structures. School mathematics is not the same as the knowledge structure of the discipline of mathematics. What kinds of limit to recontextualization do the latter place on how the curriculum structure of mathematics is constituted? Two recent, edited volumes (Christie, 1999; Christie and Martin, 2007) show the substantial work and theoretical resources that the work of the systemic functional linguists has to offer in this regard. Interestingly, this returns the theory to its former strong links to the sociolinguists during the development of code theory. Again, based on the initial work of Halliday's functional grammar, the work offers fruitful ways in which specialist forms of knowledge can be identified and explored, connecting the linguistic object of study with the Bernsteinian sociological focus on social structure.

The verticality of a particular knowledge structure places limits on its progression, sequencing and pace. This is the link to pedagogy: the more hierarchical a particular discipline, the more restriction on these dimensions of framing. Perhaps future research could involve a greater exploration of knowledge structure in relation to pedagogy. This might include both its moral and instructional content.

In conclusion: there have been significant methodological advances in this tradition, especially with regard to developing external languages of description to describe *transmission*. Perhaps a next stage of research might be to shift the focus to the evaluative rules, in order to develop similar methodologies for describing acquisition. It is at this level that an expanded notion of both instructional and regulative discourse can be considered, one that can take proper account of the distributive rules for different knowledge structures.

References

Arnot, M. and Reay, D. (2004) 'The framing of pedagogic encounters: regulating the social order in classroom learning', in J. Muller, B. Davies and A. Morais (eds) *Reading Bernstein, researching Bernstein*, London: RoutledgeFalmer.

Bernstein, B. (1973) *Class, codes and control, volume 2: Applied studies towards a sociology of language*, London: Routledge & Kegan Paul.

—— (1981) 'Codes, modalities and the process of cultural reproduction – a model', *Language in Society* 10(3): 327–363.

—— (1996) *Pedagogy, symbolic control and identity: theory, research, critique*, London: Taylor & Francis.

—— and Henderson, D. (1969) 'Social class differences in the relevance of language to socialization', *Sociology* 3(1): 1–20.

—— and Brandis, W. (1970) 'Social class differences in communication and control', in W. Barndis and D. Henderson (eds) *Social class, language and communication*, London: Routledge & Kegan Paul.

Bolton, H. (2006) 'Pedagogy, subjectivity and mapping judgement in art, a weakly structured field of knowledge', *Journal of Education* 40: 59–78.

Christie, F. (1999) *Pedagogy and the shaping of consciousness: linguistic and social processes*, London: Continuum.

—— and Macken-Horarik, M. (2007) 'Building verticality in subject English', in F. Christie and J.R. Martin (eds) *Language, knowledge and pedagogy: functional linguistic and sociological perspectives*, London: Continuum.

—— and Martin, J.R. (eds) (2007) *Language, knowledge and pedagogy: functional linguistic and sociological perspectives*, London: Continuum.

Cook-Gumperz, J. (1973) *Social control and socialization: a study of class differences in the language of maternal control*, London: Boston Routledge & Kegan Paul.

Cooper, B. (1976) *Bernstein's codes: a classroom study*, University of Sussex, Education Area, Occasional Paper, 6.

Davies, B. and Fitz, J. (forthcoming) 'Educational policy and social reproduction', in P. Singh and A. Sadovnik (eds) *Knowledge, knowers and pedagogic modes: building on the sociology of Basil Bernstein*, Peter Lang.

Diaz, M. (2001) 'Subject, power and pedagogic discourse', in A. Morais, I. Neves, B. Davies and H. Daniels (eds) *Towards a sociology of pedagogy: the contribution of Basil Bernstein to research*, New York: Peter Lang.

Dooley, K.T. (2001) 'Adapting to diversity: pedagogy for Taiwanese students in mainstream Australian secondary school classes', unpublished Ph.D. thesis, Brisbane, Griffith University. Available online at: www4.gu.edu.au:8080/adt-root/uploads/approved/adt-GU20030102.105906/public/02Whole.pdf.

Douglas, M. (1966) *Purity and danger: an analysis of concepts of pollution and taboo*, London: Routledge.

Edwards, A.D. (1981) 'Analysing classroom talk', in P. French and M. Maclure (eds) *Adult–child conversation*, London: Croom Helm.

Gamble, J. (forthcoming) 'The relation between tacit knowledge and moral order in the vocational curriculum', in P. Singh and A. Sadovnik (eds) *Knowledge, knowers and pedagogic modes: building on the sociology of Basil Bernstein*, Peter Lang.

Halliday, M.A.K. (1978) *Language as social semiotic*, London: Edward Arnold.

Hasan, R. (1968) 'Grammatical cohesion in spoken and written English, part one', Paper 7 of *Programme in Linguistics and English Teaching*, London: Longmans Green.

Hawkins, P.R. (1969) 'Social class, the nominal group and reference', *Language and Speech* 12(2): 125–135.

Henderson, D. (1970) 'Contextual specificity, discretion and cognitive socialization: with special reference to language', *Sociology* 4(3): 311–317.

Hoadley, U. (2008) 'Pedagogy and social class: a model for the analysis of pedagogic variation', *British Journal of Sociology of Education* 29(1): 63–78.

—— and Ensor, P. (2009) 'Teachers' social class, professional dispositions and pedagogic practice', *Teaching and Teacher Education* 25: 876–886.

Holland, J. (1981) 'Social class and changes in orientations to meaning', *Sociology* 15: 1–18.

Lee, V. (1973) 'Social relationships and language: some aspects of the work of Basil Bernstein', in *Language and learning, block 3*, Milton Keynes: The Open University.

Lubienski, S. (2004) 'Decoding mathematics instruction: a critical examination of an invisible pedagogy', in J. Muller, B. Davies and A. Morais (eds) *Reading Bernstein, researching Bernstein*, London: RoutledgeFalmer.

Maton, K. (2005) 'The sacred and the profane: the arbitrary legacy of Pierre Bourdieu', *European Journal of Cultural Studies* 8(1): 121–132.

Moore, R. (2007) 'Hierarchical knowledge structures and the canon: a preference for judgements', in F. Christie and J.R. Martin (eds) *Language, knowledge and pedagogy: functional linguistic and sociological perspectives*, London: Continuum.

Morais, A. (2002) 'Basil Bernstein at the micro level of the classroom', *British Journal of Sociology of Education* 23(4): 559–569.

—— and Neves, I. (2001) 'Pedagogical social contexts: studies for a sociology of learning', in I. Neves, B. Davies, and H. Daniels, (eds) *Towards a sociology of pedagogy: the contribution of Basil Bernstein to research*, New York: Peter Lang.

——, —— and Pires, D. (2004) 'The *what* and the *how* of teaching and learning', in J. Muller, B. Davies and A. Morais (eds) *Reading Bernstein, researching Bernstein*, London: RoutledgeFalmer.

Muller, J. (2007) 'On splitting hairs: hierarchy, knowledge and the school curriculum', in F. Christie and J.R. Martin (eds) *Language, knowledge and pedagogy: functional linguistic and sociological perspectives*, London: Continuum.

Neves, I., Morais, A. and Afonso, M. (2004) 'Teacher training contexts: study of specific sociological characteristics', in J. Muller, B. Davies and A. Morais (eds) *Reading Bernstein, researching Bernstein*, London: RoutledgeFalmer.

Pedro, E.R. (1981) *Social stratification and classroom discourse: a sociolinguistic analysis of classroom practice*, Stockholm: Stockholm Institute of Education, Department of Educational Research.

Reeves, C. (2005) 'The effect of opportunity-to-learn and classroom pedagogy on mathematics achievement in schools serving low socio-economic status communities in the Cape Peninsula', unpublished Ph.D. thesis, University of Cape Town.

—— and Muller, J. (2005) 'Picking up the pace: variation in the structure and organization of learning school mathematics', *Journal of Education* 37: 103–130.

Rose, D. (2004) 'Sequencing and pacing of the hidden curriculum: how indigenous children are left out of the chain', in J. Muller, B. Davies and A. Morais (eds) *Reading Bernstein, researching Bernstein*, London: RoutledgeFalmer.

Singh, P. (2002) 'Pedagogic discourses and student resistance in Australian secondary schools', in A. Morais, I. Neves, B. Davies and H. Daniels (eds) *Towards a sociology of pedagogy: the contribution of Basil Bernstein to research*, New York: Peter Lang.

Wheelahan, L. (2007) 'How competency-based training locks the working class out of powerful knowledge: a modified Bernsteinian analysis', *British Journal of Sociology of Education* 28(5): 637–651.

Wignell, P. (2007) 'Vertical and horizontal discourses and the social sciences', in F. Christie and J.R. Martin (eds) *Language, knowledge and pedagogy: functional linguistic and sociological perspectives*, London: Continuum.

Young, M. and Gamble, J. (eds) (2006) *Knowledge, curriculum and qualifications for South African further education*, Pretoria: HSRC Press.

—— and Muller, J. (2007) 'Truth and truthfulness in the sociology of educational knowledge', *Theory & Research in Education* 5(2): 173–201.

7

Social democracy, complexity and education

Sociological perspectives from welfare liberalism

Mark Olssen

In the second half of the nineteenth century, in the period after John Stuart Mill, and into and including the first third of the twentieth century, a group of philosophers, sociologists, economists and journalists systematically adapted classical liberal arguments to make them relevant to the appalling social conditions generated by the development of capitalism in the eighteenth and nineteenth centuries. Their writings contained distinctive models of society, of human nature and of change that are relevant to sociologists studying education in the twenty-first century. My aim throughout this chapter will be to work through the arguments of the new liberals, accepting those that meet the tests of a critical interrogation as being relevant to twenty-first century global capitalism, and adapting or rejecting them as is appropriate. Although some of their arguments will be found wanting, I will argue that their original ideas in defence of social democracy can be restated in terms of developments in science and philosophy over the century since they wrote. Developments in post-quantum complexity theory, within both the physical and social sciences, will enable us to reground social democratic arguments and state them in a more plausible way for the twenty-first century.

The sociology of John Atkinson Hobson

In the last decades of the nineteenth and first decade of the twentieth century, the economist John Atkinson Hobson advanced a justification for the welfare state complementing the contributions of T.H. Green and L.T. Hobhouse. In a way similar to Hobhouse's 'harmonic principle', Hobson's analysis of individual and society was facilitated methodologically by the organic model of social structure. The organic model was analogical in that it likened society to a 'social organism'. In utilizing such an analogy, Hobson invoked comparisons with the Hegel and German Idealism, which created alarm among classical liberals. In developing his conception of the organic view, Hobson was influenced by John S. Mackenzie, whose book *An introduction to social philosophy* (2006), originally published in 1890, developed a coherent conception of the organic to challenge both the monadistic view (of classical liberalism and Leibniz) and the monistic view, which asserted the priority of the whole over the parts (Idealism). The organic view sees the individual as determined by social conditions. In this sense, the relation of individual to society is an 'intrinsic one' (p. 150). Society is not a mere aggregate of separate individuals, nor is it a mechanist (dualist) or chemical combination of them. The evidence that it is not a monistic system is that, if that were the case, as society changed, so the parts would change almost simultaneously. This is not to say that there is not an aspect of the monadic and an aspect of the monistic, which operate at different times and places, in different contexts, for there are mixed modes; just as complexity does not completely displace mechanism, but rather should be seen as supplementing or extending it. Further, although we are all penetrated and constituted by our surroundings, this does not mean that we are all the same. As MacKenzie put it, there is no contradiction between social determinism and the independence of the individual:

> That there is no contradiction between the independence which is now claimed for the individual and the fact of his social determination, becomes evident when we consider the nature of that determination and of that independence. That the individual is determined by his society, means merely that his life is an expression of the general spirit of the social atmosphere in which he lives. And that the individual is independent, means merely that the spirit which finds expression in him is a living force that may develop by degrees into something different.
>
> (2006, p. 158)

Hobson's use of the organic metaphor is compatible with Mackenzie's and, like Mackenzie's, it has received stringent criticism. As R.N. Berki (1981: 193–194) notes, Hobson was frequently characterized as an idealist, and his idealism was 'born of the endeavour to comprehend political reality in *unitary* terms'. Although Hobson claimed to reject the monistic doctrine of Idealism, in that he rejected prioritizing the force of the whole over the parts, he was idealist in the weaker sense that he still saw society as a unified whole. Such a whole, in his sense, was merely a system of interactions, and unity was represented as not incompatible with difference. Besides, Hobson did not see unity itself as of value, but recognized specific normative criteria drawing on Ruskin's concept of *life* as determining the conditions for inclusion and exclusion from the whole. The common good is thus represented by Hobson as a unified development of the whole society, which contrasts with those aspects that are dysfunctional, evil, or represent what he termed, following Ruskin, *illth*. This is the sense in which David Long detects idealism in Hobson's approach, for he 'idealistically condemned present arrangements for failing to come up to the standards of his rational ideal' (Long, 1996: 16).

Although not problem-free, Long concludes that 'the organic analogy remains a useful start for a holistic analysis of society and Hobson's use of the analogy was certainly progressive for his time' (1996: 16). One must not expect too much from an analogical method of course. It must be seen, as is true for all analogies, as comprising both likenesses and unlikenesses. Human societies are in some ways like living things but in others not. For classical liberals, the analogy does not do justice to the issue of the claimed independence of individual consciousness. One can also criticize the analogical weighting given to uneven influence of the central organs over other parts of the body. Yet, in that it differentiates a particular form of unity from those types characteristic of monism, monadism, chemical integration or mechanical solidarity, it presents a certain viability, even given its analogical limitations.

One possible sense in which the organic model can be criticized was its implications for conservativism. Although Hobson wrote against the politics of conservativism, John Allett (1990:

74) argues that 'there is a significant conservative aspect to Hobson's thought'. In Allett's view, 'Hobson's conservativism is centred in his sociology' (p. 76). As he puts it:

> Hobson's interest in conservativism is limited primarily to its usefulness as a corrective (not an alternative) to liberal individualism. There are occasions, however, when he engages in a kind of high moralizing about supra-individual forces of restraint that threatens to propel him beyond liberalism and its ultimate commitment to the self-directing personality.

The entailment of conservatism cannot simply derive from the axiom of interdependence, or from the recognition of society as structure separate from its parts, but must reside in privileging unity or harmony above what is normatively required by life. While Hobson would have disputed any such charge, appealing to the independent normativity of his notions of *life* and *illth*, it may be that the model of organicism exerts, as Allett sees it, an independent pressure for unity and the status quo at the expense of justice or equality implied by a model of democratic socialism.

To the extent that the organic analogy coerces undue support for unity, I want to suggest that complexity theory can offer a more nuanced model in order to theorize the relations between individuals and social structures, as well as to theorize conception of causality, change or evolution, creativity, originality, agency and much else besides. Indeed, I will claim, it provides a revised model for social science and especially for educational research. Although Hobson recognized certain complexity formulations, in most senses the organic analogy still conforms to the prevailing notions of Enlightenment science in its focus on closed, deterministic and integrable systems. In contrast, complexity theory represents a shift from matter-based to an energy-based physics, and offers a non-reductionist conception of the relationship between parts and whole that stresses the open nature of systems and where difference and unity are paired in a new and novel manner.

Complexity theories thus provide better models that enable an avoidance of conservative priority on unity or the status quo, do not prioritize the whole over the parts, or the spiritual over the material, and are compatible with recent post-quantum traditions in science as they have developed in the twentieth century. Although having roots in ancient Chinese and Greek thought, versions of complexity theory are a relatively new field of scientific enquiry, and are perhaps one of the most notable new developments since the advent of quantum theory in the early 1900s. Such theories are not only compatible with materialism, but are systemic, or holist, in that they account for diversity and unity in the context of a systemic field of complex interactional changes.

In his book *Complexity and postmodernism*, Paul Cilliers (1998: viii) defines complexity in the following way:

> In a complex system . . . the interaction constituents of the system, and the interaction between the system and its environment, are of such a nature that the system as a whole cannot be fully understood simply by analysing its components. Moreover, these relationships are not fixed, but shift and change, often as a result of self-organisation. This can result in novel features, usually referred to in terms of emergent properties. The brain, natural language and social systems are complex.

Cilliers presents a useful contemporary summary and update of complexity research. Complex systems interact dynamically in a non-linear and asymmetrical manner. Interactions take place in open systems through 'self-organisation' by adapting dynamically to changes in both the environment and the system. Self-organisation is an *emergent* property of the system as a whole. An emergent property is a property that is constituted owing to the combination of elements in the system as a whole. As such, it is a property possessed by the system but not by its components.[1] Cilliers (1998: 90) defines 'self-organisation' as 'the capacity of complex systems which enables them to develop or change internal structure spontaneously and adaptively in order to cope with or manipulate the environment'. Such systems are not in equilibrium because they are constantly changing as a consequence of interaction between system and environment, and as well as being influenced by external factors are influenced by the history of the system (1998: 66). Cilliers identifies social systems, the economy, the human brain and language as complex systems.[2]

In the recent history of science, the work of Ilya Prigogine (1980, 1994, 1997, 2003; Prigogine and Stengers, 1984; Prigogine and Nicolis, 1989) has advanced the field of post-quantum complexity analysis at the macroscopic and microscopic levels, based in non-equilibrium physics, linked to the significant work of the Solvay Institutes for Physics and Chemistry. Prigogine received a Nobel Prize in 1977. Like Nietzsche and others before him, he translated the effects of a theory of becoming, based on a Heraclitean idea of ceaseless change, providing a post-quantum understanding of the universe in terms of dimensions of chance, self-organization, unpredictability, uncertainty, chaos, non-equilibrium systems, bifurcation and change. Prigogine's central contribution was to non-equilibrium statistical mechanics and thermodynamics and the probabilistic analysis of dissipative structures (2003: 45, 82). His main ideas (expressed non-mathematically) were that 'nature leads to unexpected complexity' (2003: 8); that 'self-organization appears in nature far from equilibrium' (p. vii); that 'the universe is evolving' (p. 9); that the messages of Parmenides (that nothing changes) must be replaced by those of Heraclitus (that everything always changes) (pp. 9, 56); that 'time is our existential dimension' (p. 9); that 'the direction of time is the most fundamental property of the universe' (p. 64); that nothing is predetermined (p. 9); that non-equilibrium, time-irreversibility, feedback, non-integration and bifurcation are features of all systems, including evolution, which is to say that our universe is full of non-linear, irreversible non-determined processes (p. 59); that life creates evolution (pp. 61, 65); and that everything is historical (p. 64). [3] Writing over the same period as Michel Foucault,[4] he was concerned to analyse *irreversible processes* that generate successively higher levels of organizational complexity, where the complex phenomena are not reducible to the initial states from which they emerged. His work has been especially important for understanding changes within open systems,[5] for theorizing time as a real dimension,[6] and for theorizing interconnectedness as a 'characteristic feature of nature' (2003: 54).[7] Of especial relevance, his work theorizes the possibilities of chance as the outcome of system contingencies.[8]

Prigogine speaks highly about Henri Bergson. Although, in his famous debate with Einstein, Bergson clearly misunderstood relativity theory, he was right about the issue of time, says Prigogine (2003: 61). For Bergson (1998), time was a real dimension, and, contrary to classical views, he saw it as irreversible: 'We do not *think* real time. But we *live* it, because *life* transcends intellect' (p. 46). The irreversibility of time dictates the impossibility of turning back, as well as the irreversibility of decisions and actions. The broader view is one of life and the universe as changing, where time means creation and elaboration of novel and original patterns. It enables an understanding of how each individual is shaped by his/her society and yet unique. In such a conception, where duration represents the real dimension of time:

consciousness cannot go through the same state twice. The circumstances may still be the same, but they will act no longer on the same person, since they find him at a new moment in his history. Our personality, which is being built up each instant with its accumulated experience, changes without ceasing. By changing, it prevents any state, although superficially identical with another, from ever repeating it in its very depth. That is why our duration is irreversible.

(Bergson, 1998: 5–6)

New actions will take place at new times. Life changes constantly, and new states are never precisely repeated in identical form. In drawing from Bergson, Prigogine (2003: 20) notes how such a thermodynamic vision once again makes individual agency pivotal. Independence develops, not apart from the system, but in and through the system.

Such a complex analysis, which retains a conception of individual agency within system parameters, was also centrally important for Hobson. In order to give his theory normative anchorage, though, Hobson utilizes a philosophy of life. It was certainly Hobson's normative vision to promote enhanced well-being and human welfare as central. In accord with life philosophy, it was Ruskin who gave Hobson his concept of social welfare. This involved redefining the concept of wealth away from a concern with exchange, to a concern with its intrinsic worth, or, as Allett (1981: 18) puts it, for its 'life sustaining properties'. In representing individuals as social beings, Hobson echoed the insights of Mackenzie who had written that '[i]t is only through the development of the whole human race that any one man can develop' (Mackenzie, 2006: 180). This is a crucial theoretical axiom from the standpoint of educational analysis, for it formulates the social democratic idea that it is the way we organize the society at large and its institutional structures that is so crucial for the development of each and every person. In such a view, the entire social democratic structure of society is a prerequisite for the application of liberal principles, for uneven development and social inequality negate the significance of liberal ideals such as freedom.

It was because of the inadequacy of representing individuals as solitary atoms that Hobson derived the central importance of social and institutional organization. What frequently went unacknowledged was the assistance that individuals utilized in achieving their plans. To embark on a business initiative, for instance, presupposes sufficient acumen, skills, knowledge, resources, capital and infrastructures, which presuppose their availability in institutional form. Production thus has a 'social element' underpinning it. So, too, does individual development, for each human being could only develop with various familial, educational and community assistance. Once one acknowledges this, one sees that the development of adequate social structures is a *prerequisite* for individual development.

Progress for Hobson was concerned with enhancing well-being, which exalted human welfare as the end or good to be sought after. For Hobson, welfare was a necessary social good. It is through his focus on welfare that he develops his economic philosophy concerned to develop the well-being of all of the international community and all humanity. Work was the medium through which individuals and societies would invest creative energy for production and progress. It was work that generated 'the power to sustain life'. [9]

Hobson recognized that society was more than the separate individuals who comprised it, and that classical liberalism could not adequately theorize the organic relations of individuals within society. It was based on such a view that he advanced his theory of surplus. [10] He theorized surplus as arising through organized cooperation, which was essential to social and economic production. It is through cooperation that individuals produce more than is possible simply as a function of each individual contribution.[11] Cooperation is thus a productive power in Hobson's theory, both productivity and well-being being increased by it.

It was from his theory of cooperation that Hobson developed his theory of under-consumption, which has been his chief contribution to economic theory and was to have a major influence on Keynes. In his classic book, co-authored with A.F. Mummery, *The industrial system*, underconsumption is represented as the manifestation of dysfunctional economic development, which distorts the system of the distribution of wealth and income by creating waste and inequality. Capitalism inherently supports a system of distorted development. The very process by which unproductive surplus was obtained, by business cunning and other strategies of deception, meant that the overall distribution and investment lacked any correlation with what the future of humanity required. Hobson proposed that a rational law of distribution would be in accord with human needs and capacities, thus affirming an affinity with democratic socialism of a distinctively social democratic variety.

Underconsumption was a surplus of production and too little consumption. It was an economy with not enough spending. In Hobson's view, underconsumption results from three principal causes: overproduction, over-saving and unequal distribution of surplus. It was the over-savings aspect that Keynes responded to. For Keynes, Hobson failed to distinguish *savings* from *investment*. In Keynes's theory, it was the distinction between savings and investment that became central to his break from neoclassical economics. Too much saving, in his view, resulted in too little investment, and, hence, the classical adage concerning the virtues of thrift were incorrect from the point of view of benefit to the community. It was for this reason that Keynes favoured public spending and government direction of investment to restore demand in aggregate spending, whereas Hobson advocated a more moral and political argument against unregulated capitalism.

Keynes can, in this sense, be seen as part of a tradition of social democratic thinking that developed from the 1870s to the 1930s. In his later life, he acknowleged a great respect for Hobson's influence. His great contribution to social democracy was his appreciation of complexity dynamics as effecting outcomes that rendered traditional neoclassical conceptions of equilibrium effectively redundant. In this sense, he took Hobson's organic analogy and rendered it more fittingly as a complexity model.

His conception of uncertainty was not seen as something that could be overcome, or that only operated in certain situations, but that arose as a consequence of the complexity created by real time. Because individuals' actions in time created unique patterns, it was theoretically impossible to predict or foretell future events. As he states:

> We have, as a rule, only the vaguest idea of any but the most direct consequences of our acts ... Thus the fact that our knowledge of the future is fluctuating, vague and uncertain, renders wealth a peculiarly unsuitable topic for the methods of classical economic theory ... [A]bout these matters there is no scientific basis on which to form any calculable probability whatsoever. We simply do not know.
>
> (Keynes, 1937: 213–214)

Keynes proposed, in *The general theory* (1953: 152), that in such a situation the only recourse is reliance on rules or conventions as to how the economy ought to work in order to produce stability through institutional coordination. He thus incorporates post-quantum complexity themes *avant la lettre*. This is especially important in relation to his conception of real time, which underpins his views on ignorance, uncertainty and human agency. His conception of real time replaces the traditional Newtonian conception, which characterized neoclassical economics as well as standard models of science. As O'Driscoll and Rizzo (1985) explain it, Newtonian time is spatialized, represented as a succession of points (continuous time) or line segments (discrete time) (p. 53), and is characterized by homogeneity, mathematical continuity and causal inertness (p. 54). For Bergson (1998: 338), change, or succession, is not real in the Newtonian theory. When it is conceived as a real addititive dimension, no matter how much action reproduces the patterns of the past, any future actions will be unique, for the context of repetition will always vary.

It is this reconfiguration of time through the recognition of complexity that results in the emphasis on uncertainty in Keynes's work. Uncertainty also incorporates novelty, non-repeatability and unpredictability, and also entails indeterminism in decisions. It thus asserts a thesis of creative human agency and imperfect foresight and knowledge. While creative decision-making is possible, it is in relation to a world that is not only unknown but unknowable. Hence, the importance of ignorance means: '[t]he (perceived) unlistability of all possible outcomes' (O'Driscoll and Rizzo, 1985: 62). For Keynes, institutions, although not eliminating uncertainty, attempt to control it. To see Keynes as a complexity management theorist broadens the scope and relevance of his insights from economics to politics, and from politics to education. For all institutions play a crucial role in sustaining life and achieving equilibrium of forces.

Complexity and education

Keynes's arguments for the economy, regarding uncertainty, risk and ignorance as the outcome of complex determinations, are applicable outside the economy narrowly defined, and can be seen to apply to other areas: welfare, various forms of assistance for disability and critical need; matters of urgency or crisis (floods, tornados, tsunamis, hurricanes etc.); health, or education or training.

In this quest for complexity reduction, education is a central institution, as was recognized by John Dewey, who explored the role and function of education in adapting to, and coping with, uncertainty in the environment. For Dewey, education was conceptualized, not as a discipline-based mode of instruction in 'the basics', but according to an interdisciplinary, discovery-based curriculum defined according to problems in the existing environment. As Dewey says in *Experience and nature*, 'The world must actually be such as to generate ignorance and inquiry: doubt and hypothesis, trial and temporal conclusions . . .' (1929: 41). The rules of living and habits of mind represent a 'quest for certainty' in an unpredictable, uncertain and dangerous world (p. 41). For Dewey, the ability to organize experience proceeded functionally in terms of problems encountered that needed to be overcome in order to construct and navigate a future. In terms of learning theory, Dewey used the concept of 'continuity' in order to theorize the link between existing experience and the future based upon the 'interdependence of all organic structures and processes with one another' (1929: 295). Learning, for Dewey, thus represented a cooperative and collaborative activity centred upon experiential, creative responses to contingent sets of relations to cope with uncertainty. As such, Dewey's approach conceptualizes part and whole in a dynamic interaction, posits the learner as interdependent with the environment, as always in a state of becoming, giving rise to a dynamic and forward-looking notion of agency as experiential and collaborative. In such a model, learning is situational in the sense of always being concerned with contingent and unique events in time.

Central to such a complexity approach is that learning must deal with the uncertainty of contingently assembled actions and states of affairs, and by so doing it transforms itself from an undertaking by discrete individuals into one that is shared and collective activity. In terms of navigating a future in relation to economics, politics or social decisions, it places the educational emphasis upon the arts of coordination. It is through plan or pattern coordination that institutions function and that a future is embarked upon. Because in planning one must assume incomplete information due to the dispersal of knowledge across social systems, such coordination can be more or less exact or loosely stochastic and probabilistic in terms of overcoming uncertainty. Because learning is time-dependent, and individuals and communities are always experiencing unique features of their worlds, uncertainty cannot be eliminated. Hence, all that is possible is pattern coordination in open-ended systems, where planning is formed around 'typical' rather than 'actual' features. Such plan or pattern coordination can only be a constructed order. Constructing plans becomes the agenda for education for life in Dewey's sense. Dewey ultimately held to the faith, as Keynes did, that, despite unpredictability and uncertainty, the macro-societal (or macro-economic) coordination of core social problems was possible.

Such a complexity approach is also pertinent for new research in the sociology of education, for such approaches can contribute to the study of non-linear dynamics in order better to understand schooling. Rather than view the social system in the image of traditional social science, inspired by Newtonian mechanics, as a linear system of predictable interactions, the approach of both Hobson and Keynes highlights the emergent character of social systems as self-organizing, non-linear and evolving systems, characterized by uncertainty and unpredictability and emphasizing both determinism and chance in the nature of events. What characterizes an emergent phenomenon is that it cannot be characterized reductively solely in terms of an aggregative product of the entities or parts of a system, understood through linear, mechanistic, causal analysis, in terms of the already-known behaviours and natures of the parts, which are themselves ontologically represented as constants, but must be seen non-reductively in relation to their contingent self-organization in terms of non-linear dynamics, as well as a theory of real time and of emergent phenomena. Schooling in such a view is characterized as a dynamic system whose states change with time through iteration, non-linearity and self-organization. Such an approach does not displace traditional mechanistic linear analyses, such as those that assert correlations between social class and educational attainment, but supplements them. It enables a more nuanced consideration of their variabilities. For the sociology of education, this has the advantage of forging a new reconciliation of the micro–macro issues, enabling a theory of social life where levels of analysis between individual and group, as well as determinism and human agency, can be more accurately assessed. Its mission becomes that of describing and explaining the complexity of systems and their changes, starting from a conception of the whole, while avoiding an exclusive emphasis on atoms or sensations that characterized the old Newtonian paradigm. It offers the scope of supplementing linear mathematical analyses with non-linear mathematical or qualitative analyses for addressing issues of future concern. Theoretically, too, it enables a new approach to the modelling of social systems where the parts of a system interact, combine and modify or change in novel and unpredictable ways, and where the parts themselves may change in the process. In this, it enables us better to understand the role of individuals and of human agency in relation to systems, institutions and cultural patterns; how decisions of the will may introduce into the course of events a new, unexpected and changeable force; how the moral qualities of individuals can alter the course of history; and why, as some older sociological and philosophical approaches tended to maintain, such phenomena as the qualities of individuals or actions in life cannot be explained solely by general sociological laws of development, social class attributes or cultural patterns. Although individuals are constituted by external social forces, given that time and space individuate those forces, the products of social evolution are inevitably unique and, in addition, through the exercise of imagination, choice operates to forge a conception of freedom quite compatible with the social production of selves. Such an account thus makes possible more historical forms of method, where contingency (both dependent causality, mutability and uncertainty) and novelty, free choice, creativity and unpredictability become integral elements of the research approach, and where top-down forms of deductive reasoning must be balanced by bottom-up analyses of individual or group agency and social interaction.

Finally, to conclude, we can also note that contemporary sociological approaches, such as that of Michel Foucault, contain complexity accounts of change of relevance for extending work in the sociology of education. Foucault's notion of *dispositif*, or *apparatus*, as a 'strategic assemblage' enables a conceptualization of the school within a new pluralist reconciliation of part and whole simultaneously balancing the poles, as he calls them, of 'individualization' and 'totalization'. For Foucault, the *dispositif* was defined as

> a resolutely heterogeneous grouping comprising discourses, institutions, architectural arrangements, policy decisions, laws, administrative measures, scientific statements, philosophic, moral and philanthropic propositions, in sum, the said and the not-said, these are elements of apparatus. The apparatus is itself the network that can be established between these elements.
>
> (Foucault, 1980: 194)

In this conception, Foucault makes it clear that the apparatus permits a duality of articulation between discourse and material forms that varies contingently and operates in non-linear ways, resisting linear, mechanical, causal explanations of the traditional Newtonian sort. It is in this sense that every form is a contingently expressed compound of relations between forces. Such multiple articulations are indeed essential to his idea of how an entity or construct constitutes its being in time, as well as to his conception of historical change, as well as to his conception of *strategy* as a non-subjective intentionality; that is, as an order that cannot be reduced to a single strategist or underlying cause or actor, but which nevertheless has intelligibility at the level of the society or institutions that emerges from an assemblage of heterogeneous elements, operating contingently and unpredictably within time and space. For Foucault, phenomena such as sexuality, security and normalization constitute such strategic assemblages. In such a model, as for Dewey, the school functions as a stabilizing mechanism that reduces or manages complexity, constituting it as a variably and contingently constituted disciplinary strategy within life itself. Issues such as 'early school leaving', 'employability' or 'the curricula' define the school as such a stabilizing institution, concerned to adapt education to labour market requirements and citizens to society. In such a model, the school is an institution that enables the navigation of an uncertain future.

Notes

1   For other forms of emergentist materialism in Western thought, see Bunge (1977), Haken (1977, 1990) and Eve *et al.* (1997).
2   For another view of complexity theory, see Kauffman (1993, 1995). Kauffman suggests that, although events can be seen as having antecedent conditions that explain them, in open environments the

possible combinations are unpredictable. Other characteristics of complex systems are that they do not operate near equilibrium; the relationships between components are non-linear and dynamic; elements do not have fixed positions; the relationships between elements are not stable; and there are always more possibilities than can be actualized.

3   Prigogine mostly applies these ideas to physical systems, but does sometimes demonstrate their applicability to the social and human world. Discussing his theories of time and irreversibility, he notes how every event (e.g. a marriage) 'is an irreversible event' (2003: 67). The consequence of irreversibility is that 'it leads to probabilistic descriptions, which cannot be reduced to individual trajectories or wave functions corresponding to Newtonian or Quantum mechanics' (p. 75).

4   Prigogine's publications date from 1964 until shortly before his death in 2003.

5   This involves a different description at the level of physics of elementary processes and a reversal of classical physics which saw systems as integrable, leading to determinism, and premised on time reversibility and equilibrium (as from Newton to Poincaré). Prigogine's approach replaces classical and quantum mechanics in a concern for thermodynamics and probability and emphasizes variables such as noise, stochasticity, irreversibility. Such an approach suggests distinct limits to reductionism.

6   In this, he differs from Einstein, who saw time as an illusion, as well as from classical mechanics. He acknowledges debts to Bergson (Prigogine, 2003: 19–20), to Heidegger (2003: 9) and to Heraclitus (2003: 9, 10).

7   Interconnectedness means that 'individualities emerge from the global', and counters the idea that 'evolution is independent of environment' (2003: 54).

8   Pomian (1990) discusses issues such as determinism and chance in relation to Prigogine's work. Also see Prigogine (1997).

9   Hobson adopted a number of Ruskin's phrases, and this is one of them. I cite from Long (1996: 18).

10 Surplus was either productive, through labour and cooperation, or unproductive, through rents, interests or profit.

11 Hobson gives the example of three persons building a boat to illustrate how, through cooperation, each can contribute to something that individually they could not have produced (see Hobson, 1996: 146–147).

References

Allett, J. (1981) *New liberalism: the political economy of J.A. Hobson*, Toronto: Toronto University Press.
—— (1990) 'The conservative aspect of Hobson's new liberalism', in M. Freeden (ed.) *Reappraising J.A. Hobson: humanism and welfare*, London: Unwin Hyman, pp. 74–99.
Bergson, H. (1998, originally 1911) *Creative evolution* (trans. Arthur Mitchell), New York: Dover Publications.
Berki, R.N. (1981) *On political realism*, London: Dent.
Bunge, M. (1977) 'Emergence and the mind: commentary', *Neuroscience* 2: 501–509.
Cilliers, P. (1998) Complexity and postmodernism: understanding complex systems, London: Routledge.
Dewey, J. (1929) *Experience and nature*, New York: Dover Publications.
Eve, R.A., Horsfall, S. and Lee, M.E. (1997) *Chaos, complexity and sociology: myths, models and theories*, Thousand Oaks, CA: Sage Publications.
Foucault, M. (1980) 'The confession of the flesh', in C. Gordon (ed.) *Power/knowledge: selected interviews and other writings, 1972–1977*, New York: Pantheon, pp. 194–228.
Haken, H. (1977) *Synergetics – an introduction*, Springer Series of Synergetics, 1, Berlin: Springer.
—— (1990) 'Synergetics as a tool for the conceptualization and mathematization of cognition and behaviour – how far can we go?', in H. Haken and M. Stadler (eds) *Synergetics of cognition*, Berlin: Springer, pp. 2–31.

Hobson, J.A. (1996, reprint of the 1902 edition) *The social problem* (Introduction by James Meadowcroft), Bristol: Thoemmes Press.

Kauffman, S.A. (1993) *The origins of order: self-organisation and selection in evolution*, New York: Oxford University Press.

—— (1995) *At home in the universe; the search for laws of complexity*, London: Viking Press.

Keynes, J.M. (1937) 'The general theory of employment', *Quarterly Journal of Economics* 51(2) February.

—— (1953, originally 1936) *The general theory of employment, interest and money*, San Diego, CA: Harcourt, Brace Javanovich Publishers.

Long, D. (1996) *Towards a new liberal internationalism: the international theory of J.A. Hobson*, Cambridge: Cambridge University Press.

Mackenzie, J.S. (2006, originally 1890) *An introduction to social philosophy*, New York: Elibron Classics.

O'Driscoll, G.P. and Rizzo, M.J. (1985) *The economics of time and ignorance*, Oxford: Basil Blackwell.

Pomian, K. (ed.) (1990) *La querelle du determinisme. Philosophie de la science aujourd'hui*, Paris: Gallimard/Le Debat.

Prigogine, I. (1980) *From being to becoming*, San Francisco, CA: W.H. Freeman & Company.

—— (1994) *Time, chaos and the laws of chaos*, Moscow: Ed. Progress.

—— (1997) *The end of certainty: time, chaos and the new laws of nature*, New York: The Free Press.

—— (2003) *Is future given?*, River Edge, NJ: World Scientific.

—— and Nicolis, G. (1989) *Exploring complexity*, New York: W.H. Freeman.

—— and Stengers, I. (1984) *Order out of chaos*, New York: Bantam.

8

The 'new' connectivities
of digital education

Neil Selwyn

The social significance of connectivity

The notion of (dis)connection underpins the organization of all aspects of human life, from the biological and social, to the economic and technological. As such, connectivity has been a central element of societal change throughout history. Key developments in corporeal travel and communications technology, for example, underpinned a steady intensification of the connectedness of everyday life throughout the nineteenth and twentieth centuries. Innovations such as the telegraph, railway engine and airplane were associated with fundamental shifts in the connections between people, places, institutions and information. Yet it could be argued that the past thirty years have been subject to a set of especially accelerated and intense shifts in connectivity. A distinct 'imperative to connect' is acknowledged to underpin recent geopolitical, economic and technological shifts of globalization, deriving in no small part from rapid advances in connectivity fostered by information and telecommunications technologies (Green *et al.*, 2005). In particular, the connectivities afforded by the Internet have been foregrounded in popular and academic accounts of late-modern societal change in terms of the 'network society', 'shrinking world', 'digital age' and so on. With these recent articulations of connectivity in mind, the present chapter examines the bearing of Internet connectivity on the processes and practices of contemporary education.[1]

This chapter argues that technology-enhanced connectivity merits close consideration from sociologists hoping to make sense of the apparently fast-changing nature of education in the (late-) modern age. In particular, it argues that careful thought needs to be paid to the *networked* connectivities that digital technologies such as the Internet now afford – i.e. the interconnection of people, objects, organizations and information, regardless of space, place or time. As Kevin Kelly (1995: 201) noted at the beginning of the Internet's rise to mainstream prominence, 'the central act of the coming era is to connect everything to everything . . . all matter, big and small, will be linked into vast webs of networks at many levels.' The subsequent integration of Internet connectivity into many aspects of everyday life has prompted popular and political commentators to proclaim networked 'connectedness' as an 'essential feature' of contemporary society (Rifkin, 2000). Even within the relatively sober terms of academic sociology, the notion of networked connectivity is now being touted as an 'organizing framework in which all institutions, knowledge and relationships are ordered' (Cavanagh, 2007: 24). So, if these claims are to be believed, what are the implications for education in the early twenty-first century? The remainder of this chapter considers how digital technologies such as the Internet are shaping the connectivities of education and learning, and in so doing attempts to unpack the various discourses of novelty and transformation that often pervade discussions of education and technology. In particular, the chapter seeks to challenge the dominant orthodoxy within the education community that Internet connectivity is somehow leading to new and improved forms of education. Having laid out the basis for a critique of connectivity, I conclude by offering some suggestions for future sociological investigations of education and learning in an era of ever-increasing Internet use.

The technologies and conditions of networked connectivity

While the concept of connection has long been a central element of computer science and information systems thinking, the proliferation of the World Wide Web during the 1990s and 2000s has placed networked connectivity at the heart of contemporary technology design, development and use. Using the World Wide Web via the Internet is now part of the fabric of everyday life for many citizens in developed countries – with a present global population of around 1.3 billion users soon set to treble once the capacity for wireless Internet access is extended to the world's 3.6 billion mobile telephone users (Castells, 2008). The Internet (*inter*national *net*work) was designed to be a global network of connected computerized devices that can communicate with each other and exchange data via a series of software protocols. Unlike previous forms of networked computing, the architectural logic of the Internet was predicated upon 'the interconnectedness of all elements' (Dreyfus, 2001: 10), a condition described by technologists as a 'rhizomatic' connectivity akin to the underground stem systems of plants whose roots and stems are both separate *and* collective. As with these rhizomatic plants, every point on the Internet has the potential to be a recipient *and* provider of information. Perhaps more than any other aspect of its design, it is this interconnected logic that is the defining technical feature of the Internet.

The Internet-based applications of the 1990s, such as email and downloading information resources from web pages, marked a significant step-change in computer users' sense of connection. The subsequent wave of 'web 2.0' tools during the 2000s then led to what many technologists describe as a 'mass socialization' of Internet connectivity (see O'Reilly, 2005; Shirky, 2008). Unlike the 'broadcast' mode of information exchange that characterized Internet use in the 1990s, web 2.0 applications such as Wikipedia, Facebook and YouTube were predicated upon connectivity to openly shared digital content that was authored, critiqued, used and reconfigured by a mass of users – what is termed a condition of 'many-to-many' connectivity as opposed to a 'one-to-many' mode of transmission. Most recently, interest is growing in the development of 'semantic web' technologies that seek to augment individuals' interactions with the Internet via machine-provided artificial reasoning, therefore fostering and supporting 'intelligent' forms of connectivity (see Ohler, 2008). While differing in terms of technical design, all these forms of Internet use share a common sense of individual users being connected to any*thing* and any*one* else on the Internet. In this sense, the individual Internet user can be seen as subject potentially to an 'always-on' state of connectivity.

Of particular sociological interest is how these technical capabilities have informed a range of claims concerning the social nature of Internet connectivity. This is perhaps most evident in the widely held belief in the Internet somehow being able to 'liberate' the user from social structure and hierarchy, boosting individual freedoms and reducing centralized controls over what can and what cannot be done. For many commentators, the various forms of Internet connectivity described above imply a fundamental reconfiguration of the social. At a macro level of analysis, for example, the 'flattening out' of hierarchies and the introduction of 'networking logic' to the organization of social relations is seen to support the open (re)configuration of society and corresponding underdetermination of organizational structure (e.g. Castells, 1996; Friedman, 2007). Conversely, a micro level 'sense' of connectivity is seen to boost the individualization of meaning-making and action. Here, it is argued that the contemporary condition of enhanced connectivity between individuals, places, products and services has prompted a resurgence of more 'primitive', pre-industrial ways of life. For instance, the Internet has long been portrayed as rekindling a sense of tribalism, nomadism and communitarianism (D'Andrea, 2006; Rheingold, 1994). A range of claims have also been made regarding the role of the Internet in providing new opportunities for informal exchanges of knowledge, expertise and folk-wisdom (Sproull and Kiesler, 1991), supplementing an individual's social capital (Haythornthwaite 2005; Wellman *et al.*, 2001) and even 'breaking down the barriers and separate identities that have been the main cause of human suffering and war' (Mulgan, 1998, cited in Robins and Webster, 2002: 247). Even if we discount the more fanciful and idealistic aspects of such accounts, the majority of popular and academic commentary concurs that Internet connectivity has recast social arrangements and relations along more open, democratic and ultimately empowering lines. As Charles Leadbeater concluded recently:

> the web's extreme openness, its capacity to allow anyone to connect to virtually anyone else, generates untold possibilities for collaboration . . . the more connected we are, the richer we should be, because we should be able to connect with other people far and wide, to combine their ideas, talents and resources in ways that should expand everyone's property.
>
> (2008: 3)

The educational seductions of Internet connectivity

Amid this broad consensus, the specific *educational* merits of networked connectivity have tended to be expressed through a set of articulations concerning the empowerment of individual learners within networks of connected learning opportunities. Perhaps most prominent is a perception that the Internet offers a ready basis for learning to take place as a socially situated and communal activity. In particular, Internet-based learning is often seen to embody sociocultural and constructivist views of learning being 'situated' within networks of objects, artifacts, technologies and people. The centrality of Internet connectivity to current articulations of sociocultural theories of learning is reflected most explicitly in an emerging theory of 'connectivism' that frames learning as the ability to access and use distributed information on a 'just-in-time' basis (see Siemens, 2004). From this perspective, learning is seen as an individual's ability to connect to specialized nodes or information sources as and when required, and the attendant ability to nurture and maintain these connections. As Siemans (2004) puts it, learning is therefore conceived in terms of the 'capacity to know more' via the Internet, rather than reliance on the accumulation of prior knowledge in terms of 'what is currently known'.

Aside from a prominent role within accounts of the cognitive 'science' of learning, notions of networked connectivity are increasingly prevalent within popular, political and academic understandings of the social processes and practices of 'doing education'. In particular, the Internet is often described as underpinning the capacity of individual learners to build and maintain connections with various components of the education system – what is presented in policy terms as the 'personalization' of learning. This notion of personalization reverses the logic of education provision, 'so that it is the system that conforms to the learners, rather than the learner to the system' (Green *et al.*, 2006: 3), with learners therefore (re)positioned at the centre of networks of learning opportunities. Within these accounts of personalization, any such repositioning of the individual learner is assumed usually to be contingent on the use of the Internet and other digital technologies. For example, the Internet-connected learner is often celebrated as being no longer the passive recipient of learning instruction but cast instead into an active role of (re)constructing the nature, place, pace and timing of the learning event. As Nunes (2006: 130) concludes, contemporary forms of technology-supported education now:

> conflate access and control; transmission in other words is figured as a performative event in the hands of the student, thereby repositioning the student in relation to institutional networks. To this extent, the [student] is anything but marginal; as both the operator that enacts the class and the target that receives course content, the student occupies a metaphorical and experiential centre for the performance of the course.

The perceived capacity of the Internet to enhance the 'goodness of fit' between education provision and individual circumstance has also been promoted as increasing the democratization of education opportunities and outcomes. In this sense, learning with the Internet is portrayed as more egalitarian and less compromised than would otherwise be the case. Through Internet connections, for example, it is argued that learners can enjoy access to a more diverse range of formal and informal learning opportunities, regardless of geography or socio-economic circumstance. Much has also been written about the Internet's capacity to stimulate episodes of informal learning through access to vast quantities of information – what has been described in some quarters as a realization of 'the dream of the universal library' (Kruk, 1999: 138). This democratizing of formal and informal opportunities to learn has prompted much enthusiasm among politicians and policymakers, who see increased connectivity to information, people and resources as a significant means of 'empower[ing] people with new opportunities for the future' (Gordon Brown, 2008), regardless of circumstance or social background. As such, the notion of boundless Internet connectivity corresponds with a number of social as well as educational agendas, not least the enhancement of social justice and reduction of social inequalities.

Towards a critical perspective of Internet connectivity and education

These preceding arguments – and others like them – underpin an established orthodoxy in the minds of many educationalists and policymakers. Here, connectivity via the Internet is seen to offer the basis for a 'transformation' of contemporary education, centred on the actions of the empowered individual learner. Of course, education is not the only domain of social activity where such transformatory expectations are expressed. Indeed, much discussion of the Internet and society centres on assumptions of personalization and improvement where 'the connection between the individual and the social whole becomes increasingly personalized according to the use of commodities and devices which facilitate this connection' (Holmes, 1997: 38). Against this background, the tendency of educationalists to celebrate individuals' self-determination of their learning via the Internet is perhaps best seen as a constituent element of a wider societal turn towards the networked individualism of everyday life (see Beck and Beck-Gernsheim, 2002).

While remaining mindful of these wider discursive contexts, I would argue that the transformatory rhetoric currently found within prevailing accounts of education 'in the digital age' is worthy of specific attention from sociologists of education. In particular, there is a need to counter the uneasy and often unconvincing amalgam of theoretical agendas that currently propel much educational thinking about the Internet towards an unwarranted valorization of the individual 'rational' learner operating within an efficient technological network. While the tendency to approach technology-based processes as a closed 'black box' is not unique to education, I would contend that there is a need for educationalists to give due consideration to the socio-technical nature of educational technology use and, it follows, acknowledge the perpetuation of rather more 'messy' social relations and structures. In particular, more thought needs to be given to the apparent continuities, as well as the potential discontinuities, of education in the Internet age, therefore considering 'whether technology-based action simply *adds on* to existing social relationships or in fact, transforms them' (Gane, 2005: 475). Thus, it is in relation to challenging prevailing expectations of transformation and novelty that sociology of education has a clear and important role to play.

Perhaps the most obvious corrective that sociologists can offer is a refocusing of debate towards the present realities rather than future potentials of Internet-based education. The 'dearly held commitment to the here and now' that characterizes most sociological enquiry (Cavanagh, 2007: 7) allows for further questions to be raised concerning the disappointments, silences and contradictions of educational Internet use. In this sense, issues of inequality and exclusion are perhaps in most need of being (re)introduced into current discussion. Despite an ongoing concern with digital exclusion in disciplines such as communication studies and information science (see Yu, 2006), discussions of the Internet among educationalists have tended to pay little attention to the exclusionary potentials of networked learning. Of course, most educationalists would concur that the notion of *all* learners benefitting from unfettered and equitable connectivity to the same resources is, at best, ambitious. Even as levels of Internet connectivity appear to approach 'universal' levels in some developed countries, inequalities between groups of 'information-haves' and 'information-have-less' remain. These inequalities range from basic abilities to self-include oneself into networks, to subsequent abilities to benefit from these connections once they are established. We are also reminded by sociological studies of Internet use throughout the general population that connectivity should not be seen as a constant state – one is not 'connected for life' once having used the Internet. Instead, individuals often 'dip' in and out of Internet use as life-stage and circumstances dictate (see Anderson, 2005). Thus issues of *dis*connectivity certainly require more foregrounding in current education debate.

The promise of online connectivity to (m)any places and people should also not obscure what sociologists would identify as the continued importance of immediate 'local' contexts in framing learning processes and practices. In this sense, it is erroneous to perceive technology-based learning as somehow 'detached from the spatial condition of common locality' (Thompson, 1995: 32). One particular shortcoming within current descriptions of the Internet and education is the often context-free and abstracted reading of connections between learners, institutions and information. Instead, any instance of online learning is better understood as being situated within local contexts such as the school, university, home and/or workplace and, it follows, the social interests, relationships and restrictions that are associated with them. This contextualized perspective on the Internet and education allows for recognition of the many compromises of Internet connectivity for the individual learner that are not often acknowledged within education debate. For instance, within schools and universities, the 'official' establishment of Internet connectivities is often centred on concerns and interests of the institution rather than the interests of the individual. This can be seen, for example, in education institutions' implementation of digital technologies to support bureaucratic and administrative concerns, not least significant ongoing investments in student information systems, payroll software and managed learning environments. It could be argued that these priorities leave educational use of the Internet often shaped by 'new managerial' concerns of efficiency, modernization and rationalization of spending costs, rather than specific concerns of learning and learners. Against this background, the shaping of connectivity around the interests of the institution rather than the interests of the individual merits more consideration in analyses of contemporary education.

A further issue highlighted by a sociological reading of connectivity is the enrolment of individuals into bureaucratic networks of surveillance. It has often been argued that the information society is perhaps more accurately seen as a 'surveillance society', with innumerable electronic networks accumulating and aggregating information on individuals' everyday activities and transactions (see Lyon, 2006). Much has been written of the digital extension of Foucault's notion of the Panopticon as disciplinary technology, with electronic networks seen to act as ready means of surveillance, observation and regulation (e.g. Poster, 1995). In an educational sense, therefore, the Internet can be seen as contributing to the internal surveillance of learners within education institutions, alongside the external surveillance of education institutions through the management of performance information. As Hope (2005: 360) concludes, while the practices and processes of education are predicated upon observation and knowledge-gathering about learners, 'technological developments have meant that both the capacity to carry out surveillance and the potential for resistance have grown'. These opportunities to resist and test authority range from the relatively playful ability for students to conceal their informal online activities, to the rather more challenging instances of 'sousveillance', where students (and others) can seek access to proscribed online information through 'hacking' into otherwise restricted administrative systems and databases.

A sociological perspective also raises questions of how digital technologies are shaping connections between education systems and the interests of state, economy, industry and other stakeholders. Perhaps the most prominent manifestation of this element of education technology has been the political use of the Internet as a policy device to align education systems more closely with global economic concerns of national competiveness and the up-skilling of workforces. Yet, aside from these concerns of economy and nation, the Internet should also be seen as one of the many 'privatizations' of contemporary education (see Ball, 2007). This is evident, for example, in terms of the privatization of Internet use within educational institutions, with school and university use of online content and services becoming a core element of the fast-growing education services industry in most developed countries. Similarly, in many developing countries, information technology networks are now well established as a focus for philanthropic activity and quasi-developmental aid from organizations in the US and elsewhere in the developed world. This is perhaps most apparent at present in initiatives such as 'One laptop per child', where developing nations are encouraged to invest in US-produced laptop computers to 'create educational opportunities for the world's poorest children by providing each child with a rugged, low-cost, low-power, connected laptop with content and software designed for collaborative, joyful, self-empowered learning' (OLPC, 2008). This use of Internet connectivity prompts obvious comparison with what Ball (2007: 125) terms the 'Victorian, colonial philanthropic tradition [of] outsiders behaving as if they were missionaries'. In short, instances such as these highlight the fact that the Internet serves to connect education systems – as well as individuals and institutions – to a wide range of interests and agendas that they may have previously been less directly connected with (see also Michael W. Apple's (2004) discussion of the use of Internet-based tuition by neo-conservative and fundamentalist religious groups in the US to support alternative forms of home schooling outside state control).

Conclusion

This brief discussion hopefully illustrates the contribution that sociology may make in providing a counterpoint to the orthodoxy of optimism that otherwise surrounds the Internet and education. In particular, this chapter has sought to highlight a number of key issues and tensions worthy of further investigation by anyone seeking to make sense of contemporary education. Above all, any discussion of the Internet and education should include consideration of issues such as *dis*connection, *dis*empowerment, *in*equality, commercialization, bureaucracy, power, control and regulation. In providing a 'way in' to unpacking these issues, a sociological perspective on education and connectivity is able to help refocus debate towards the similarities and continuities between the present, ostensibly 'new era' of digital education and education in preceding times. Indeed, many of the issues and tensions highlighted in this chapter lend support to Holmes' (1997: 28) contention that 'computerization and its connectivity are continuations of the social contract by other – if more efficient – means'. With this thought in mind, I would argue that the study of education would benefit from richer understandings of the deep embedding of technology-based practices within the realities of social relations. In this sense, sociologists of education are well placed to re-politicize the debate over technology and education, and refocus discussion away from the presumed transformation of social relations and towards more realistic readings of the technological.

The need remains, therefore, for careful reconsideration of the ways in which educationalists approach the 'promise' of Internet connectivity. In particular, it would seem clear that important discussions of difference need to take place, asking *who* benefits in *what* ways from the connectivities supported by the Internet and other digital technologies. For instance, does the Internet amplify rather than disrupt existing social patterns and relations? Is the Internet acting merely as an instrument of empowerment for the already empowered and therefore furthering the reciprocal relationship between online and offline? Moreover, what are the differences between an individual having connectivity 'done to them', as opposed to being able to 'do' connectivity themselves? What advantages and pleasures (if any) are to be had by being disconnected rather than connected? It is likely that such questions will grow in significance as the twenty-first century progresses and education becomes framed increasingly within a 'register of connectivity' (Wittel *et al.*, 2002: 208). Redressing these tensions through sustained empirical and theoretical analyses should now constitute a next step in a rigorous, sociologically informed rethinking of the connectivities of contemporary education. The prevailing 'imperative to connect' within contemporary education should be accompanied by an attendant imperative to critique as well as celebrate.

Note

1   While I remain mindful of the political-economic significance of *non*-technology based connectivity, this chapter focuses primarily on the educational implications of connections afforded by digital technologies – in particular the Internet. Broader considerations of globalization and the 'disembedding' of social systems of late/postmodern society provide the focus for other chapters in this book, such as the contributions from Susan L. Robertson, Roger Dale, Jane Kenway, Hugh Lauder and others.

References

Anderson, B. (2005) 'The value of mixed-method longitudinal panel studies in ICT research', *Information Communication & Society* 8(3): 343–367.

Apple, M.W. (2004) 'Are we wasting money on computers in schools?', *Educational Policy* 18(3): 513–522.

Ball, S. (2007) *Education plc: understanding private sector participation in public sector education*, London: Routledge.

Beck, U. and Beck-Gernsheim, E. (2002) *Individualization*, London: Sage.

Brown, G. (2008) Speech given at the Google Zeitgeist Conference, London, 19 May.

Castells, M. (1996) *The rise of the network society*, Oxford: Blackwell.

—— (2008) 'Internet beyond myths: the record of scholarly research', Presentation to London School of Economics, 24 October.

Cavanagh, A. (2007) *Sociology in the age of the Internet*, Buckingham: Open University Press.

D'Andrea, A. (2006) 'Neo-nomadism: a theory of post-identitarian mobility in the global age', *Mobilities* 1(1): 95–119.

Dreyfus, H. (2001) *On the Internet*, London: Routledge.

Friedman, T. (2007) *The world is flat*, Release 3.0, New York: Farrar, Straus and Giroux.

Gane, N. (2005) 'An information age without technology', *Information, Communication and Society* 8(4): 471–476.

Green, H., Facer, K., Rudd, T., Dillon, P. and Humphreys, P. (2006) *Personalization and digital technologies*, Bristol: Futurelab.

Green, S., Harvey, P. and Knox, H. (2005) 'Scales of place and networks: an ethnography of the imperative to connect through information and communications technologies', *Current Anthropology* 46(5): 805–826.

Haythornthwaite, C. (2005) 'Social networks and Internet connectivity effects', *Information, Communication and Society* 8(2): 125–147.

Holmes, D. (1997) *Virtual politics*, London: Sage.

Hope, A. (2005) 'Panopticism, play and the resistance of surveillance: case studies of the observation of student Internet use in UK schools', *British Journal of Sociology of Education* 26(3): 359–373.

Kelly, K. (1995) *Out of control: the new biology of machines, social systems, and the economic world*, New York: Basic.

Kruk, M. (1999) 'The internet and the revival of the myth of the universal library', *The Australian Library Journal* 48(2): 137–147.

Leadbeater, C. (2008) *We-think*, London: Profile.

Lyon, D. (2006) *Theorizing surveillance: the panopticon and beyond*, Uffculme: Willan.

Nunes, M. (2006) *Cyberspaces of everyday life*, Minneapolis: University of Minneapolis Press.

Ohler, J. (2008) 'The semantic web in education', *Educause Quarterly* 31(4): 7–9.

OLPC (One Laptop Per Child) (2008) *One laptop per child – mission statement*. Available online at www.laptop.org/vision (accessed 30 November 2008).

O'Reilly, T. (2005) *What is web 2.0? Design patterns and business models for the next generation of software*. Available at www.oreillynet.com/pub/a/oreilly/tim/news/2005/09/30/what-is-web-20.html (accessed 30 November 2008).

Poster, M. (1995) *The second media age*, Cambridge: Polity.

Rheingold, H. (1994) *The virtual community*, London: Secker and Warburg.

Rifkin, J. (2000) *The age of access*, Harmondsworth: Penguin.

Robins K. and Webster, F. (2002) 'Prospects of a virtual culture', *Science as Culture* 11(2): 235–256.

Shirky, C. (2008) *Here comes everybody: the power of organizing without organizations*, London: Allen Lane.

Siemens, G. (2004) *Connectivism: a learning theory for the digital age*. Available at www.elearnspace.org/Articles/connectivism.htm (accessed 30 November 2008).

Sproull, L. and Kiesler, S. (1991) *Connections: new ways of working in the networked organization*, Cambridge, MA: MIT Press.

Thompson, J. (1995) *The media and modernity*, Palo Alto, CA: Stanford University Press.

Wellman, B., Haase, A., Witte, J. and Hampton, K. (2001) 'Does the Internet increase, decrease, or supplement social capital?', *American Behavioral Scientist* 45(3): 436–455.

Wittel, A., Lury, C. and Lash, S. (2002) 'Real and virtual connectivity', in S. Woolgar (ed.) *The virtual society*, Oxford: Oxford University Press.

Yu, L. (2006) 'Understanding information inequality', *Journal of Librarianship and Information Science* 38(4): 229–252.

9

A cheese-slicer by any other name? Shredding the sociology of inclusion

Roger Slee

At the age of 82, Mikhail Kalashnikov, the inventor of the AK–47 rifle, first produced in 1947, declared: 'I wish I'd made a lawnmower.' He lamented the destructive deployment of his invention (gasp) and wished that he'd made '. . . something that would help farmers with their work' (Connolly, 2002). While it is not altogether convincing that a former Russian military officer is taken aback by the malevolent application of his weapon, there have been many instances where well-meaning projects have generated perverse effects. Connolly (2002) instances Einstein. Distraught at his contribution to the development of the atom bomb, he reflected that he should have been a watchmaker rather than a physicist. Grunenthal, the German pharmaceutical company, developed thalidomide as an anti-emetic to assist pregnant women with morning sickness, apparently oblivious to side effects. History is littered with such unintended outcomes.

Surveying the field of inclusive education, we are confronted by the unintended consequences that diminish its record of reform. This chapter is a brief reminder of the importance of the sociology of education to the emergence of inclusive education as an explanatory framework, as well as educational aspirations and practices. I will consider how the appropriation and popularization (Said, 2000) of inclusive education by traditional special education and educational management have resulted in escalating levels of exclusion and increased educational vulnerability. My aim is to expand the objective of inclusive education from the diagnosis of individual student deficits, to be ameliorated through specialist interventions and the fabrication of individual education plans, to a more expansive interrogation of the political economy of schooling as a platform for reconstruction congruent with the challenges of new times in education.

Understanding exclusion?

Exclusion is ubiquitous (Harvey, 1996; Bauman, 1997, 2004, 2008). Educational disadvantage and exclusion may reveal themselves in confronting and obvious forms. Alternatively, they may lurk in, and operate through, the shadowy world of what I loosely call school cultures: an agglomeration of pedagogic practices, curriculum choices, assessment regimes and the demographic and policy context of schooling (Apple, 2006; Ball, 2008a; Bernstein, 1971, 1996; Unterhalter, 2007). An obvious global manifestation of disadvantage and exclusion is shaped by the economic gulf that divides the so-called *developed and developing* nation-states. The extremes between wealth and poverty reveal educational and social marginalization at a level that is overwhelming. 'Eight million people', writes Jeffrey Sachs, 'around the world die each year because they are too poor to stay alive' (2005: 1). The United Nations Secretary-General's Special Envoy for HIV/AIDS in Africa, Stephen Lewis, is driven to 'perpetual rage' (2005: 4) when speaking of the extent, depth and causes of the degradation of Africa in the face of the pandemic. He cites the International Monetary Fund and the World Bank as architects of continuing immiseration through their insistence on 'conditionality' in the structural adjustment programme that governs loans.

> The conditions ranged from the sale of public sector corporations, to the imposition of 'cost-sharing' (the euphemism for user fees imposed on health and education), to savage cutbacks in employment levels in the public service, mostly in the social sectors. To this day, the cutbacks haunt Africa: the IFIS continue to impose 'macroeconomic' limits on the numbers of people (think nurses and teachers) who can be hired, and if that doesn't do the trick, there are financial limits placed on the amount of money that can be spent on the social sectors as a percentage of a country's gross national product (GNP). The damage is dreadful. One of the critical reasons for Africa's inability to respond adequately to the pandemic can be explained by user fees in health care . . . at the heart of structural adjustment policies there lay two absolutes: Curtail and decimate the public sector; enhance, at any cost, the private sector.
>
> (Lewis, 2005: 5–6)

The complicity of the so-called developed world in the continuing plundering of the colonized and marginalized world has been meticulously chronicled (Ball and Youdell, 2008; Emmett and Green, 2006; Jones, 2006). My point here is that there is an obvious and shameful process of educational and social exclusion of staggering proportion. A '. . . recent recalculation', suggests that, 'there are about 77 million children not enrolled in school and an estimated 781 million adults who have not yet had the opportunity to learn to read and write – two-thirds of them women' (UNESCO, 2007). While such phenomena seem remote, only reaching us intermittently through the light touch of headlines and celebrity causes, there are local 'geographies of exclusion', 'geographies of injustice' (Harvey, 1996; Sibley, 1995).

Harvey (1996) draws our attention to the plight of the twenty-five workers who died and fifty-six others who were seriously injured in the 1991 fire in the Imperial Foods chicken processing plant in the US town of Hamlet, North Carolina, to suggest that poverty and oppression are a part of our local geographies. He draws comparison with the Triangle Shirtwaist Company fire of 1911, when 146 employees perished. The 1911 incident led to protests, with over 100,000 people marching through Broadway, and was a precursor to the health and safety laws and regulations. The 1991 incident hardly rated as news, despite the fact that 'the Imperial workers died as the women in New York had: pounding desperately on locked or blocked fire doors' (Harvey, 1996: 336). For Harvey, this incident ought to draw our attention to the conditions in which 150,000 workers in over 250 plants across the 'Broiler Belt' find themselves. They are paid below minimum wages in towns that rely on, and are at the mercy of, this industry. Exploitation is sustained by chronic unemployment, little urban or social infrastructure, impoverished educational provision and the abandonment of hope.

In that same self-described 'developed' country of the West, Kozol (1991,1995, 2000; Kozol and Ebrary, 2005) has repeatedly diarized pictures of a poverty-enforced apartheid, where African American children are condemned to inferior housing, attenuated education and severely reduced opportunities. In the UK, the Fabian Commission on Life Chances and Child Poverty (Fabian Society, 2006) reported that one in every five children in Britain grows up in poverty, some 3.5 million children (2006: 115). Disaggregating their data, they reveal the disproportionate concentration of poverty on particular groupings within the population. For a child living in a household where there is a disabled parent, the risk of poverty increases from 19 per cent to 30 per cent (p. 119). Forty-nine per cent of disabled people of working age in Britain were employed, whereas, for non-disabled people of working age, the statistic was 81 per cent. Sixty-one per cent of children of Pakistani or Bangladeshi origin in Britain are living in poverty (Fabian Society, 2006: 136).

The link between poverty and school failure, disengagement and exclusion has been well documented (Connell, 1993). The complicity of schools in the production of inequality and exclusion, she argues, is longstanding:

> Education is not . . . a mirror of social or cultural inequalities. That is all too still an image. Education systems are busy institutions. They are vibrantly involved in the production of social hierarchies. They select and exclude their own clients; they expand credentialed labour markets; they produce and disseminate particular kinds of knowledge to particular users.
>
> (Connell, 1993: 27)

The persistence of unequal educational outcomes contingent on class continues, according to Australian researchers Teese and Polesel (2003: 7): 'The fact that more young people rely on school for jobs or further training does not mean that school is an equally effective path for all.' They go on to say:

> Economic marginalization through school is experienced more often by children of manual workers and the unemployed. School has become a link in the re-creation of poverty. This is because, while dependence on completed secondary school has grown, achievement in programmes offered by schools is closely linked with socio-economic status.
>
> (Teese and Polesel, 2003: 9)

Ball (2008b) considers the impact of relentless policy reforms in education in England and Wales through the late twentieth and early twenty-first centuries. Class, he argues, remains a constant feature throughout periods of great policy, demographic and infrastructural changes in education. The neo-conservative policy reform agenda from Thatcher through to New Labour has not resulted in an equalization of 'educational outcomes in terms of labour market access or income', he asserts, '. . . by many indicators they are more unequal' (Ball, 2008b: 1). Like Bernstein before him, Ball argues that, if we want to intervene in 'the persistence of educational inequality', then the school in isolation from the complex matrix of social relations is not the sole source for effecting positive and enduring reforms. He returns to Bernstein, Bourdieu and to his extensive empirical work to demonstrate how privilege, advantage and disadvantage assert themselves through the mixed markets of schooling (Ball, 2007).

'In effect class and policy and class and educational practices are being realigned' (Ball, 2003: 170). Accordingly, in the now 'ambiguous nature of class reproduction' (Ball, 2003: 178), his research examines a cohort of English middle-class parents who, displaying a mix of confidence and fear, assert their capitals to secure a purchase on their children's futures in and through the education marketplace. A contemporary and pervasive ideology of 'good parenting' (Vincent, 2006) places strain on the family to bring additional resources to assist, first, in the selection of better schools and, second, in the purchase of educational accoutrements such as tutors, technology, after-school programmes, cramming schools (Ball, 2008a). If necessary, they may secure the diagnosis of syndromes and defects to attract additional support or leverage (Slee, 2008). And, 'most families on low incomes or living in poverty are by definition excluded from these possibilities' (Ball, 2003: 177).

Schools, as Connell (1993) observed, are not passive agents in the education marketplace: there exists a perverse reciprocity, a juggling of positional disadvantage and advantage. They reflect and refract social inequalities. Choice is not only the prerogative of some parents; schools too attempt to exert choices. The instruments of testing, inspection and league tables interplay with the intervention of private entrepreneurial interest and divisions between types of school (e.g. city academies, pupil referral units) to form a hierarchy of schools and students.

As schools attempt to improve their profile to attract a suitable clientele, students with poor educational prognoses present a serious risk of failure at inspection (Slee *et al.*, 1998; Gillborn and Youdell, 2000). This is illustrated in an interview with Dave Gillborn and Deborah Youdell, who:

> discovered the extent of the reach of the standards agenda, and the way in which schools were focussing on the 'D' students and trying to convert them into Cs. They realized the significance of their 'D to C conversion' and its link with the process of 'educational triage' which was going on, a means of apportioning scarce resources to greatest areas of need: 'it was naming what lots of people were living' and it was clear to them that the strategies for triage being operated in schools were producing exclusion for those deemed 'hopeless cases' by concentrating on candidates who could be targeted for upward conversion.
>
> (Allan and Slee, 2008: 38)

Gillborn and Mirza (Gillborn, 2008; Gillborn and Mirza, 2000; Mirza, 2008) demonstrate that there is little chance involved in the failure of black pupils in England. In the US, Parrish (2002) has chronicled the racialization of special education. Put simply, there is an over-representation of African American students in special education. This is particularly distressing when put into the context of Crawford's (2004) review of labour market statistics. His review of data indicates that children who attend segregated special education are less likely to find employment in the paid labour market.

The causes of exclusion run deep in the architecture of schooling. A priority for researchers in the field of inclusive education is the identification, interrogation and interruption of these patterns of exclusion. To this end, allies must be sought across fields of social research, as the diminution of exclusion and disadvantage cannot be achieved by the classroom teacher alone, the introduction of a new phonics programme to increase functional literacy or the addition of new ways of monitoring the performance of individual schools or local authorities. I am arguing that we ought to resist the reduction of inclusive education to a narrow concern to secure mainstream schooling for disabled pupils. All too often, in the minds of education policymakers, researchers and teachers, inclusive education becomes a default vocabulary for 'the education of (so-called) Special Educational Needs pupils' (Slee, 1996). The exclusion of disabled pupils, however, remains a key item in the broad agenda of inclusive education research. In the next section of this chapter I want to trace the emergence of inclusive education as a field for research and policy activism, identify the unintended consequences of its popularization and then suggest areas for further research to restore integrity to the field.

Misunderstanding inclusion?

As the authors state in the opening pages of *Doing inclusive education research* (Allan and Slee, 2008: 1), inclusive education has become a *catchall* term describing divergent research genres and education practices. 'A troubled and troubling field', it is riven by contest and contradiction, and claims and counterclaims of theoretical authenticity. Instances of this that have attracted attention internationally are seen in Ellen Brantlinger's (1997) considered response to the trenchant critique of inclusion as unscientific and educationally dangerous mounted in Kauffman and Hallahan's (1995) collection of essays, *The illusion of full inclusion*. She draws on Dunkin's (1996) depiction of the types of error common to the synthesizing of education research to demonstrate flaws in Kauffman and Hallahan (1995) and their colleagues' work according to their own criteria for valid research. Their dismissal of inclusive education as ideological and therefore unscientific, she argues, illustrates their incapacity to recognize their own presuppositions and predispositions. In this respect, the debate was not dissimilar to protracted debates through the journals between Martyn Hammersley and Barry Troyna, the former suggesting that *partisan research* (Troyna, 1995) was undermined by its political intent. More recently, Kauffman and Sasso (2006) targeted Deborah Gallagher (2004, 2006) as an object for intellectual derision, once more charging that critical theory and postmodernism, which they use as a blended derogation, attenuates the progress of scientific research.

These debates are not tidy skirmishes over methodology. They represent tactical engagements between different understandings of disability and disablement and correspondingly of the form and objectives of education for disabled students. The emergence of inclusive education as a field of interest within the sociology of education is traceable to the work of scholars and activists such as Sally Tomlinson (1981, 1982), Len Barton (1987), Gillian Fulcher (1989) and Mike Oliver (1990), who between them enlisted Weberian, Marxist and post-structural analyses to explain the oppressive origins and deleterious impacts of traditional segregated education. Applying a sociological lens, it was suggested that disabled people had their vulnerability exacerbated and their marginal social status entrenched by dominant discourses of disability that:

- positioned disabled people as objects of pity and charity;
- romanticized them in tales of triumph over personal tragedy;
- framed them within medical discourses of pathological defectiveness;
- reduced disabled people with fixations with their impairment requiring policy solutions.

Disability studies became simultaneously an alternative explanatory frame and a platform for activism and social reform (Oliver, 1990, 1996).

This work encouraged the new sociology of education to broaden its consideration of educational disadvantage and exclusion to include disabled students. Special educational needs, argued Barton, was a euphemism for the failure of schools to educate all students. As both a field of research in its own right and an extension of critical sociologies of education, inclusive education sought to advance the rights of all those rendered vulnerable or excluded by cultures and processes of schooling. As Tomlinson (1981), Gillborn (1995) and Gillborn and Youdell (2000) had demonstrated, the convergence between ethnicity, race and disability demanded a more sophisticated analysis of schools as elements of a pathology of educational failure.

Hard-fought-for legislative reform and the expansion of the disability movement and parent groups lobbying for rights of passage for their children insinuated themselves more generally through social discourse. Globally, governments and education jurisdictions modified their language and delivered policy statements about the importance of inclusive education consistent with The Salamanca Statement and Framework for Action on Special Needs Education, adopted by the World Conference on Special Needs Education: Access and Quality (UNESCO, 1994). Those whom Brantlinger (1997) and Allan and Slee (2008) describe as traditional special educators found themselves in the often awkward position of showing a commitment to inclusive education while not letting go of the paradigmatic foundations for special education knowledge and practices. Following Said's (2000) treatise on the 'taming and domestication' of radical theory in his essay, 'Travelling theory', I will offer two brief points to explain unintended outcomes of inclusive education's newfound popularity.

First is the emergence of more complicated discursive fractures and fault-lines, between and within those described as working either in the field of special education or inclusive education, that generate confusion about the nature and objectives of the research and reform. One of the first sources of confusion is the existence of those who claim to be special and inclusive educators. There has been an uncomfortable elision that has not been sufficiently challenged. The discourse of inclusive education has unwittingly offered a new vocabulary for the practice of traditional special education (Slee, 1993). Indeed, the expensive and glossy (Brantlinger, 2004) special education primers developed for teacher training programmes and special education courses have inserted the words *inclusive education* into their titles and now offer readers a chapter on inclusion and special educational needs. Remarkably, there is no sense of the conceptual irony carried by the linking of inclusive education and special education needs. It is only when pressed to delineate the vagaries of their inclusive language that the caveats and conditions emerge (Slee, 1996). Colin Low (2007: 3) is indicative in his implausible call for 'the banishment of ideology from the field of special education once and for all' and the replacement of the radical calls for full inclusion by 'moderate inclusion'.

A recent example of the dizzying expanse of interpretive latitude is provided in Ruth Cigman's (2007) collection of essays entitled *Included or excluded? The challenge of the mainstream for some SEN children*. The collection was prompted by Baroness Warnock's (2005) *New look* controversial pamphlet for the Philosophy of Education Society of Great Britain. In this publication, Warnock pronounced inclusion to be 'the most disastrous legacy of the 1978 Committee of Enquiry into the Education of Handicapped, Special Education Needs Report' (Warnock, 2005: 22). The leader of the British Conservative Party and a supporter of separate special schooling, David Cameron declared in the House of Commons that this was a 'stunning recantation' (Hansard, 22 June 2005, Col. 825). In his essay in Cigman's text, Ainscow suggests that Warnock's pamphlet was helpful as it moved the issue of inclusion closer to the centre of education debates, but that it had the negative impact of 'encouraging some in the field to retreat into traditional stances' (Cigman, 2007: 128). Indeed, the Warnock pamphlet has resuscitated stalwarts of unreconstructed special schooling, such as Michael Farrell (2008a,b), to speak out against inclusive education as a failed reform initiative, a form of flawed 'politically correct' educational thinking.

Returning to Said (2000), this surge in inclusive education as the Trojan horse for special education is of concern, as special education remains a functionalist imperative. In other words, in its well-meaning interventions to support individual children inside and outside the mainstream of schooling, it provides a sheer veneer to hide the deep cracks in the edifice of mass schooling in the twenty-first century. This observation is not offered as an apology for dogmatism, for adherence to a decontextualized catechism of inclusive education. As Said (2000), Williams (1965) and Giddens (1994) have observed, effective critique is contingent and dynamic. The project of inclusive education therefore may not be best served by pressing for intellectual foreclosure on its definition. Preferable may be a commitment to the ongoing exposure and dismantling of exclusions. This chapter does not resolve the tensions between and within special education and inclusive education; it argues for the necessity of acknowledging the tensions as a source for devising better research questions and policy work. Herein lies a challenge for sociologies of education.

The second major subversion of the inclusive education project is in the development of models for supporting the targets of inclusion. The funding of inclusive education is widely restricted to the establishment of models for allocating 'additional' resources for disabled pupils. Effectively, this has meant devising algorithms that first establish the extent of defect or impairment and then calculate the level of additional resources to be applied to support the education of the child in the regular classroom. The gravity of such models presses diagnosticians to register more serious levels of impairment to extricate more resources. Research has documented escalating levels of diagnosis, particularly in the normative areas of behaviour and attention disorders (Graham and Slee, 2008), together with regional variations (Daniels, 2006) and, as I have mentioned, the racialization of disability (Parrish, 2002).

The most frequent allocation of funds is to provide an adult helper or aide. Recent research registers a growing disquiet with an apparent retreat of teachers from educational responsibility and reliance on the 'aide' to be the *de facto* teacher of the disabled pupil. Notwithstanding the allocation of additional financial support to schools claiming inclusion support, there is little evidence to suggest an increasing capacity of schools to come to terms with the different populations who seek an education. In fact, systemic mechanisms have been established to enable schools to divert students who threaten their examination results profiles to alternative placements (Slee, 1998). Inclusive education policy has thereby generated policies and procedures that jeopardize access, participation and success for increasing numbers of students. Here I return to the beginning of the chapter and to the discussion of the complex structures and pervasive patterns of exclusions. No single site of intervention for reform that targets a particular student identity will of or in itself achieve inclusive schooling. Inclusive education research ought to host a more comprehensive research programme.

Let me suggest that sociology of education may be a platform for the next generation of inclusive education researchers and activists. I offer two reasons here for this. First, the longstanding preoccupation with the structural and cultural formation of disadvantage and privilege provides an opportunity for us to step to the side of the entanglements and vagaries of competing conceptions of inclusion, to approach reform through the analysis and decon-struction of exclusion. It tackles the broader antecedents of educational disadvantage and failure to build a potential beyond functionalist entrapment in individual pathologies. Second, the sociology of education has broad theoretical shoulders, thereby providing the range of analytic tools to engage with the complexity of exclusion. An *ecumenical* posture, where the intersections rather than the constituencies of exclusion become the source of alliance and analysis, assists in the task of revealing layers of identity and the production of vulnerability.

Taking exclusion seriously?

Just as the English satirist Denis Norden suggested that a harp is nothing more than an over-sized cheese-slicer with cultural pretensions, a rebadged special education approximates neither a convincing theory of social and educational inclusion, nor a blueprint for inclusive curriculum and pedagogy. The aim is not to demonize special education as the poor relation of the regular school. The two are conjoined and share vital theoretical and structural organs. Inclusive education that proceeds from a willingness first to understand the nature and forms of educational exclusion demands a more careful reading of social theory and critique and a commitment to extensive reform.

References

Allan, J. and Slee, R. (2008) *Doing inclusive education research*, Rotterdam: Sense Publishers.

Apple, M.W. (2006) *Educating the 'right' way: markets, standards, god, and inequality*, 2nd edn, New York and London: Routledge.

Ball, S.J. (2003) Class strategies and the education market: the middle classes and social advantage, London: Routledge/Falmer.

—— (2007) *Education plc: understanding private sector participation in public sector education*, Abingdon: Routledge.

—— (2008a) *The education debate*, Bristol: Policy Press.

—— (2008b) Annual Education Lecture, Strathclyde University, unpublished draft.

—— and Youdell, D. (2008) *Hidden privatisation in public education. Report for Institute of Education*, London: University of London.

Barton, L. (ed.) (1987) *The politics of special educational needs*, Lewes: Falmer Press.

Bauman, Z. (1997) *Postmodernity and its discontents*, Cambridge, Polity.

—— (2004) *Wasted lives: modernity and its outcasts*, Oxford: Polity.

—— (2008) *Does ethics have a chance in a world of consumers?*, Cambridge, MA, London: Harvard University Press.

Bernstein, B. (1971) *Class, codes and control*, London: Routledge & Kegan Paul.

—— (1996) *Pedagogy, symbolic control and identity: theory, research, critique*, London: Taylor & Francis.

Brantlinger, E. (1997) 'Using ideology: cases of non-recognition of the politics of research and practice in special education', *Review of Educational Research* 67(4): 425–459.

Brantlinger, E. (2004) 'The big glossies: how textbooks structure (special) education', in D. Biklen (ed.) *Common solutions: inclusion and diversity at the centre*, New York: Syracuse University Press.

Cigman, R. (2007) *Included or excluded? The challenge of the mainstream for some SEN children*, London: Routledge.

Committee of Enquiry into the Education of Handicapped (1978) *Special educational needs: report of the Committee of Enquiry into the Education of Handicapped Children and Young People*, (The Warnock Report), London: HMSO.

Connell, R. (1993) *Schools and social justice*, Philadelphia, PA: Temple University Press.

Connolly, K. (2002) 'Kalashnikov: "I wish I'd made a lawnmower"', *The Guardian*, 30 July. Available online at www.guardian.co.uk/world/2002/jul/30/russia.kateconnolly (accessed 5 December 2008).

Crawford, C. (2004) 'Fulfilling the social contract in public education', Paper presented at the National Summit on Inclusive Education, Toronto City.

Daniels, H. (2006) 'The dangers of corruption in special needs education', *British Journal of Special Education* 33(1): 4–10.

Dunkin, M. (1996) 'Types of errors in synthesizing research in education', *Review of Educational Research* 66(2): 87–97.

Emmett, B. and Green, D. (2006) *In the public interest: health, education, and water and sanitation for all*, Oxford: Oxfam International.

Fabian Society, Commission on Life Chances & Child Poverty (2006) *Narrowing the gap: the final report of the Fabian Commission on Life Chances and Child Poverty*, London: Fabian Society.

Farrell, M. (2008a) *Educating special children: an introduction to provision for pupils with disabilities and disorders*, New York, London: Routledge.

—— (2008b) *The special school's handbook: key issues for all*, London: Routledge.

Fulcher, G. (1989) *Disabling policies? A comparative approach to education policy and disability*, London: Falmer.

Gallagher, D. (ed.) (2004) *Challenging orthodoxy in special education: dissenting voices*, Denver: Love Publishing.

—— (2006) 'If not absolute objectivity, then what? A reply to Kauffman and Sasso', *Exceptionality* 14(2): 91–107.

Giddens, A. (1994) *Beyond left and right: the future of radical politics*, Cambridge: Polity Press.

Gillborn, D. (1995) *Racism and antiracism in real schools: theory, policy, practice*, Buckingham, UK, Philadelphia, PA: Open University Press.

—— (2008) *Racism and education coincidence or conspiracy?* London: Routledge.

—— and Mirza, H.S. (2000) *Educational inequality: mapping race, class and gender; a synthesis of research evidence*, Great Britain: Office for Standards in Education.

—— and Youdell, D. (2000) *Rationing education: policy, practice, reform, and equity*, Buckingham, UK, Philadelphia, PA: Open University Press.

Graham, L. and Slee, R. (2008) 'An illusory interiority: interrogating the discourse/s of inclusion', *Educational Philosophy and Theory* 40(2): 277–293.

Harvey, D. (1996) *Justice, nature, and the geography of difference*, Oxford: Blackwell Publishers.

Jones, P.W. (2006) *Education, poverty and the World Bank*, Rotterdam: Sense Publishers.

Kauffman, J.M. and Hallahan, D.P. (1995) *The illusion of full inclusion: a comprehensive critique of a current special education bandwagon*, 2nd edn, Austin, TX: Pro-Ed.

—— and Sasso, G. (2006) 'Toward ending cultural and cognitive relativism in special education', *Exceptionality* 14(2): 65–90.

Kozol, J. (1991) *Savage inequalities: children in America's schools*, New York: Crown Pub.

—— (1995) *Amazing grace: the lives of children and the conscience of a nation*, New York: Crown.

—— (2000) *Ordinary resurrections: children in the years of hope*, New York: Crown Publishers.

—— and Ebrary, I. (2005) *The shame of the nation: the restoration of apartheid schooling in America*, New York: Crown Publishers.

Lewis, S. (2005) *Race against time*, Toronto: House of Anansi Press.

Low, C. (2007) 'A defence of moderate inclusion and the end of ideology', in R. Cigman (ed.) *Included or excluded? The challenge of the mainstream for some SEN children*, Abingdon: Routledge.

Mirza, H.S. (2008) *Race, gender and educational desire: why black women succeed and fail*, London: Routledge.

Oliver, M. (1990) *The politics of disablement*, London: Macmillan Education.

—— (1996) *Understanding disability: from theory to practice*, Basingstoke: Macmillan.

Parrish, T. (2002) 'Racial disparities in the identification, funding and provision of special education', in D. Losen and G. Orfield (eds) *Racial inequality in special education*, Cambridge, MA: Harvard Education Press.

Sachs, J. (2005) *The end of poverty: economic possibilities for our time*, New York: Penguin Press.

Said, E.W. (2001) *Reflections on exile and other literary and cultural essays*, London: Granta.

Sibley, D. (1995) *Geographies of exclusion: society and difference in the west*, London: Routledge.

Slee, R. (1993) 'New sites for old practice?', *Disability, Handicap & Society*, 8.

—— (1996) 'Clauses of conditionality', in L. Barton (ed.) *Disability and society: emerging issues and insights*, London: Longman.

—— (1998) 'High reliability organisations and liability students – the politics of recognition', in R. Slee, G. Weiner and S. Tomlinson (eds) *School effectiveness for whom? Challenges to the school effectiveness and school improvement movements*, London: Falmer Press, pp. 101–114.

—— (2008) 'Beyond special and regular schooling? An inclusive education reform agenda', *International Studies in Sociology of Education* 18(2): 99–116.

—— Weiner, G. and Tomlinson, S. (eds) (1998) *School effectiveness for whom*, London: Falmer.

Teese, R. and Polesel, J. (2003) *Undemocratic schooling: equity and quality in mass secondary education in Australia*, Carlton, Vic.: Melbourne University Publishing.

Tomlinson, S. (1981) *Educational subnormality: a study in decision-making*, London: Routledge & Kegan Paul.

—— (1982) *A sociology of special education*, London: Routledge & Kegan Paul.

Troyna, B. (1995) 'Beyond reasonable doubt? Researching "race" in educational settings', *Oxford Review of Education* 21(4): 395–408.

UNESCO (1994) *The Salamanca Statement and Framework for Action on Special Needs Education*, adopted by the World Conference on Special Needs Education: Access and Quality, Geneva. Available online at http://portal.unesco.org/education/en/ev.php-URL_ID=8412&URL_DO=DO_TOPIC& URL_SECTION=201.html (accessed 7 December 2008).

—— (2007) *Education for all – international coordination*, Geneva. Available online at http://portal. unesco.org/education/en/ev.php-URL_ID=52210&URL_DO=DO_TOPIC&URL_ SECTION=201.html (accessed 6 December 2008).

Unterhalter, E. (2007) *Gender, schooling and global social justice*, London: RoutledgeFalmer.

Vincent, C. (2006) *Childcare, choice and class practices: middle-class parents and their children*. Abingdon: Routledge.

Warnock, M. (2005) *Special educational needs: a new look*, Keele: Philosophy of Education Society of Great Britain.

Williams, R. (1965) 'The British left', *New Left Review*. Reprinted in R. Williams (1989) *Resources of Hope*, London: Verso, pp. 131–140.

10

The sociology of mothering

Carol Vincent

The new momism: the insistence that no woman is ever truly complete or fulfilled unless she has kids, that women remain the best primary caretakers of children, and that to be a remotely decent mother, a woman has to devote her entire physical, psychological, emotional and intellectual being, 24/7 to her children . . . The 'new momism' is a set of ideals, norms and practices most frequently and powerfully represented in the media, that seem on the surface to celebrate motherhood, but which in reality promulgate standards of perfection which are beyond your reach.

(Douglas and Michaels, 2004: 4–5)

If we are to understand the significance of class we need to take lay normativity, especially morality, much more seriously than sociology has tended to do.

(Sayer, 2005: 948)

Introduction

Against a background of increased attention being given to mothering roles and responsibilities by policymakers and by the media, this chapter explores the outlines and contours of normative mothering in the affluent Western countries, particularly the USA and the UK, at the beginning of the twenty-first century. I will discuss the discursive power of Intensive Mothering Expectations (IME) (Johnston and Swanson, 2006), and the way in which this particular set of practices and outlook has become universalised as standard. I argue that, far from being a shared experience common to all women with children, mothering practices, including consumer behaviour, are infused by class. I finish with a brief portrayal of two women, who live close together in London, but have strongly divergent understandings and experiences of mothering.

First, a note on the scope and terminology of this chapter. Its focus is social class, but this is only one aspect (albeit a key one) of a mother's identity, and in order to fully understand experiences of mothering it is necessary to also consider how these are gendered and raced. This, however, is a larger project than space allows for here. On terminology: in order to include fathers, policy documents in the UK use the term 'parents' and 'parenting' (e.g. DCSF, 2007). However, I am going to focus on mothers and mothering. This is not to belittle or ignore the role of fathers, nor the ways in which many men are more actively involved with their children than were their own fathers (see e.g. Dermott, 2008; O'Brien, 2005; Williams, 2008). Rather, my choice of focus is a simple assertion that it is mothers who are generally positioned as retaining the ultimate responsibility for child-rearing in popular discourses and moral understandings, as will be further examined below. Indeed, debates about maternal responsibilities and actions have a long history, as do directives aimed at mothers conveying counsels of perfection. Hardyment, for example, quotes a sixteenth-century didactic poem written in Latin that chides mothers for their laziness and selfishness in using wet nurses (2007: 4).

Intensive mothering

Sharon Hays' (1996) well-known phrase describes the current normative understanding of 'good mothering': an approach that is child-focused, with the mother having the responsibility to care, both intensively and extensively, for all aspects of the child's physical, moral, social, emotional and intellectual development. Intensive mothering, according to Hays (1996: 46), is an 'expert-guided and child-centered', 'emotionally absorbing, labor intensive, financially expensive' ideology in which mothers are primarily responsible for the nurture and development of the 'sacred' child, and in which children's needs take precedence over the individual needs of their mothers. Mother–child interaction is expected to be 'sensitive', whereby mothers talk to their children in a way that features an explicit pedagogy, explained in a reasoning and rational style (Walkerdine and Lucey, 1989).

By privileging mothers over other adults, especially fathers, intensive mothering contributes to a situation of unequal parenting, where men's primary contribution to the family remains that of breadwinner, and the adoption of an identity as 'involved father' is virtuous, but optional. Women with children are discursively positioned as mothers first, and then, if they are in paid work, the identity of worker is additional to that. Not necessarily optional – as many women have little or no option but to work – but an addendum (Himmelweit and Sigala, 2002; Vincent and Ball, 2006).

Intensive mothering is an approach (regime might be a better word) that has become reified and normalised as what all mothers should aspire to. Hays points to several contradictions here as mothers in paid employment try to meet the differing demands – the 'cultural contradictions' – of the workplace and home, but always prioritise the moral narrative of 'doing the best for the children' (Hays, 1996: 149). 'Perhaps the strongest indication of the opposition between the logic of intensive mothering and the logic of a self-interested, competitive, rationalized market society is mothers' persistent pre-occupation with the theme of the good mother's lack of selfishness' (Hays, 1996: 168).

In some ways, intensive mothering can be understood as a response to the relative formality of earlier child-rearing styles, such as that promulgated in the 1920s and 1930s and advocated by, for instance, Truby King, where the requirement for routine and order demanded the compliance of the baby and young child to regulation. In response to this formality, the 1950s and 1960s witnessed the rise of psychological, cognitive and popular conceptualisations that stressed the importance of maternal attention and focus on the child (Hattery, 2001). Intensive mothering also seeks to regulate the behaviour of the mother, in her interactions with the child. Daniel Miller claims that White, middle-class women approaching first-time motherhood commonly adopt an intensive approach. He argues that the result for these women, who have been educated to have a career and have had the experience of exercising a considerable degree of autonomy in their lives, is 'the complete negation of their own previous life project' as 'the infant's constant demands are accepted as essential priorities and at no point should the mother's own desires prevent them from being attended to' (Miller, 2004: 37).

The important point to make here is not to criticise a woman's desire to care for her children, but to draw attention to the power of IME (Johnston and Swanson, 2006). Thus, women in paid work go to considerable lengths to continue mothering intensively (Hays, 1996). For example, Johnston and Swanson cite Garey's (1995) comment that mothers 'weave' an identity that reflects their commitment to employment with their commitment to intensive mothering. Garey studied nurses who chose to work the night shift in order to maintain the image of full-time domestic motherhood during the day. Hattery's (2001) research also included those she refers to as 'pragmatists' and 'innovators', who seek to conform to dominant motherhood ideologies while also being in paid work. Another strategy is that adopted by affluent working mothers who employ at-home care givers such as nannies. Macdonald suggests they are acting out of

the belief that their children deserve and require a consistently present, focused and attentive caregiver at all times. In an effort to emulate the intensive mothering ideal, these mothers hired nannies so that their children could have non-stop quality time in rotating shifts.

(Macdonald, 1998: 41)

Johnston and Swanson (2006), in their own study of mothers with different paid employment commitments and their accompanying orientations to intensive mothering, suggest that mothers construct the meaning of accessibility, maternal happiness and separate spheres differently, on the basis of employment status. That is, they construct and adapt career commitments and mothering ideologies to ensure broadly consistent narratives about good mothering and their own performance of it. It is not the case, therefore, that women offer no resistance to such demanding expectations of motherhood, nor that they do not actively engage with ideas about appropriateness and necessity, but rather, as Tina Miller points out, 'Ideologies of intensive mothering are both drawn upon and resisted, but their dominance and power remains resolute, shaping both engagement *and* resistance' (Miller, 2005: 85).

May (2008) offers another example of IME shaping respondents' self-presentations in her study of Finnish women who were inhabiting the apparently 'spoiled identity' of lone mother-hood.

What unites these women [lone mothers] is the dialogue they hold with social norms relating to 'proper' family life . . . The narrators . . . do not refute social norms around the two parent family but attempt to show how, despite at face value appearing to be 'unsuccessful', their families have in fact been 'successful' ones.

(May, 2008: 481)

May asks why 'individuals whose lives are in some way non-normative simply do not discard unhelpful social norms' [which] 'risk exposing them as immoral?' Similarly, Hays questions why, since mothering intensively places such demands on employed women, middle-class professional mothers with much to gain from the workplace, in terms of money, satisfaction and status, do not simply reconstruct ideas about appropriate child-rearing (1996: 151). Both authors conclude that putting the children first and labouring to ensure their well-being are imperatives for all mothers 'in order to claim a moral self' (May, 2008: 481). Sayer's (2005) discussion of the moral aspects of class is helpful here, as he argues that the avoidance of shame and the pursuit of self-respect either drive us to conform, or to resist and refuse normative values. The latter is particularly hard to do in relation to mothering, owing to fundamental societal expectations about the primacy of a mother's care.[1]

Performances of mothering: class biases and professional mothers

Clearly, access to particular cultural and economic resources (e.g. time, money, confidence, an acceptance of a mother's primary and total responsibility for the child, and a particular set of child-rearing goals), all of which are unequally distributed through the population, makes intensive mothering more or less possible.

Studies of child-rearing advice over the twentieth century (Hardyment, 2007; Apple, 2006) illustrate the presumed inability of working-class families to bring up children 'properly', and therefore the urgency of providing them with instruction. This concern remains today, with parenting classes and advisers being a favoured government response within the UK (e.g. DCSF, 2007). Poor working-class women in the US and the UK are also encouraged and coerced into entering the workforce (DWP, 2007; Hays, 2003; Korteweg, 2002). Their capacity to mother their children is devalued when set against their lack of waged income. Indeed, such is the deficit view of 'welfare mothers' that the implicit assumption of policymakers appears to be that children are better off in childcare while their mother works. Although the extent to which mothers from different ethnic and social class groups do recognise and try and live by the tenets of intensive mothering remains an empirical question, what can be asserted is that the 'material and cultural circumstances in which women live their lives' (Miller, 2005) are still overlooked in the moral and practical simplicities of policy and public discourses around mothering. As Kehily notes in her study of UK pregnancy and parenting magazines,

> the widely held assumption running through all these magazines is that pregnant women and new mums are between 20 and 45, in heterosexual couples, in stable, long term relationships. The regular features, articles and interactive parts of the magazine conjure up a readership of women with social resources and the ability to exercise choice in their lives . . . There was little discussion of teenage motherhood, single motherhood, parenting in poverty, or women who did not have choice in their lives.
>
> (Kehily, 2008: 4)

Within all of this, mothering is frequently decontextualised and reduced to a series of correct behaviours or tasks (Suissa, 2006). For example, a recent UK policy document, *Every parent matters*, claims,

> it's what parents do, not who they are, that makes the difference . . . The evidence that good parenting plays a huge role in educational attainment is too compelling to ignore. It outstrips every single other factor – including social class, ethnicity or disability – in its impact on attainment.
>
> (DCSF, 2007: unnumbered Foreword)

Thus, policies on parenting and the family trade upon unexamined assumptions that normalise the moral possibilities of middle-class living, while the realities of mothering for many working-class families are displaced by easy stereotypes and careless, patronising and damaging generalisations (also Gewirtz, 2001).

Mothering as a personal, intensive and intuitive experience is infused with classed behaviours, values, actions and dispositions. Class is ubiquitous, if less frequently overtly named: what Savage calls the 'everywhere and nowhere quality of class discourse' (Savage, 2005, in Dicks, 2008: 440). The language of class in the UK is composed of largely moral judgements that elicit highly emotional responses from social actors (Dicks, 2008: 440; Savage 2005; Sayer, 2005). This same process also accurately describes the way in which classed behaviour infuses mothering practices. In our preferences, our consumer behaviour, our actions, our values around our children we reveal distinctions and divisions based on social class. One example of this is the food we give our children. Rebecca O'Connell's (2008) study of London childminders illustrates the way in which control of the child through the food that he/she eats is negotiated between mother and childminder. Noting the adherence of some middle-class mothers to organic food, O'Connell cites Goodman and Du Puis's (2002: 17) description of organic food as a 'middle class privilege', a 'class diet'. The (working-class) childminder's resistance to what they perceived as over-priced and over-rated food and their awareness that it was not eaten by 'people like us' were made manifest in their use of the term 'organics' 'as a local working class pejorative term to describe a certain sort of "arty" middle class "incomer"' (O'Connell, 2008: 185). Organic food has come to symbolise a particular facet of good mothering for the affluent middle classes. It is one example of a 'morality tale' told and performed by middle-class mothers (Liechty, 2003: 69), and part of a production of a 'class-cultural space' (Liechty, 2003: 256). Liechty notes such a production is 'accomplished through two conceptually distinct forms of cultural practice: discursive, narrative or linguistic practice on the one hand and embodied, physical or material practice (including the use of goods) on the other' (Liechty, 2003). This class cultural space of mothering has become homogenised and universalised – the practices and discourses becoming not those associated with one social group, but what all mothers *should* do.

An example of this universalisation is the promulgation of what could be called 'professional mothering', a particular approach to meeting IME. Intensive mothering is infused with a discourse of 'expertee-ism'. This is not to say that the advice of apparent experts – in medicine, psychology or child-rearing – is to be slavishly followed, but the responsibility of the mother is to search out such forms of advice and then evaluate their appropriateness to her and her children. This is 'professional mothering', a style adopted by middle-class mothers, who have or have had professional careers and now seek to use their personal and professional skills and resources in bringing up their children. Brooks and Wee (2008), writing about middle-class professional mothers in Singapore, cite middle-class mothers talking about mothering as a 'career', with an evaluative 'end product' of successful and happy children.

One facet of professional mothering is the concern to create the circumstances in which the child's intellectual, physical and creative skills are fully and extensively developed. Bourdieu (1986) argues that, in order fully to understand the distribution of academic capital, we must look at the work done inside the family in the transmission of cultural capital, as this form of capital increases the efficiency of the cultural transmission by the school. I have written elsewhere (with Stephen Ball: Vincent and Ball, 2007) on the volume of activities available to children and their parents: from dance, drama and art, through sport, music and cooking, to more esoteric options such as yoga, life coaching and pottery. These activities are part of an attempt at 'concerted cultivation', as identified by Annette Lareau.

Lareau's recent US study into class-related differences in the 'cultural logics of childrearing' (2002: 772) illustrates the way in which social class informs the 'rhythms of family life'. She identifies the 'cultural logic of middle class parents' as emphasising 'concerted cultivation' of their children. 'They enrol their children in numerous age-specific, organised activities that dominate family life and create enormous labour, particularly for mothers. The parents view these activities as transmitting life skills to children' (2002: 748). Lareau argues that the child-rearing strategies of the working-class and poor parents in her study emphasise, by contrast, the 'accomplishment of natural growth'. 'These parents believe that, as long as they provide love, food and safety, their children will grow and thrive. They do not focus on developing their children's special talents' (2002: 748–749). Lareau is at pains to argue that interacting with children in this fashion is not to be seen as negative, as it gives the children opportunities for unsupervised, unstructured play. Similarly, Gillies (2007) draws on her study of working-class mothers to argue that 'the mothers viewed their role in terms of caring, protecting and loving their children, rather than teaching or cultivating them' (p. 154).

Concerted cultivation involves the buying in of goods and services. Indeed, parental consumption on behalf of their children is another site of class-infused performance of mothering. In a study that looked at the preparation made for babies, including the decorating of a nursery, by pregnant women living in North London, Clarke argues that, 'Pregnancy forms the beginning of a sustained relationship between activities of provisioning, their objects and values, and the construction of "mothering" and "the child"' (Clarke, 2004: 56). She continues,

> provisioning an unborn infant requires choices and expertise in an unfamiliar arena where the stakes could not be higher – for every object and every style has attached to it some notion of a type of mothering or a expression of a desired mother/infant relationship.
>
> (Clarke, 2004: 61; see also Kehily, 2008).

Such provisioning[2] involves the purchase and use of products associated with differently classed lifestyles: particular brands of baby buggies and equipment, clothes retailers (independent shops, chain stores, supermarkets), foods (organic or not), toys (wooden or plastic) Williams' (2006) study of US toy stores gives her plentiful material to discern the status hierarchies of class and race that are being marked out through consumers' decisions over where to shop). This is not simply an individual activity but one through which social networks of similar others can be identified and marked out, a process of deploying loose-fitting but practical signifiers to help us 'place' people in the social world. As Bourdieu argues,

> Taste classifies and it classifies the classifier. Social subjects classified by the classification distinguish themselves by the distinctions they make, between the beautiful and the ugly, the distinguished and the vulgar.
>
> (1986: 6)

Having noted the dominance of intensive mothering as a normative construction of mothering style and scope, and looked at the way in which class inflects performances of mothering, I now turn to two brief portrayals taken from recent research projects that feature two mothers who live approximately half a mile apart in London, but within very different material contexts of mothering.

Jill and Mary

Jill and Mary were mothers whom we interviewed for our consecutive research projects exploring middle-class and working-class families' engagement with childcare provision. Their lives and words illustrate the class-related differences in normative presentations of good mothering. They are not at extreme ends of our samples in any sense, either in terms of their financial income, or the ease with which they manage their lives on a day-to-day basis, or their approaches to child-rearing. The differences between them are often small and nuanced – this is not a simple case of rich and poor, although income differentials play a key role (see Vincent *et al.*, 2008, for more detail)

Jill is a Black, Caribbean-origin woman with three children.[3] Her oldest two are in their teens, and her youngest started school during the course of the research (4/5 years old). Jill now manages a betting shop, where she has worked for over a decade. She lives in a housing association flat on a small, smart estate and drives a car. She left school at 16 with few qualifications. Mary has two children under 6. She is married to Gary, who is a recruitment consultant. She is educated to degree level, although Gary did not complete his degree. Mary is an artist and lecturer, but was not working at the time of the first interview. By the time of the second, she was running a children's art club. Mary and Mike own their own house and both drive. The family were planning to leave London for the countryside. Despite evidence of changing family structures in the UK (Office for National Statistics, 2001) and elsewhere, the two-parent household, with the woman at home or working part-time, retains considerable discursive power. Jill is clearly aware that her household differs from the 'norm' and appears to regret this 'deviance', saying,

> I would like to stay at home, but that's if I had a husband, to stay at home and play that proper role model, I suppose, but it's not . . . it's not real. Not for me.

Friendship networks

One of the differences we found between the working-class and middle-class mothers in our research concerned their friendship networks. In many cases, working-class women derived their primary social support from family, while the middle-class mothers were much less likely to have local family members and had instead, through antenatal groups and other child-focused activity, established networks of similar mothers (see Vincent *et al.*, 2008). Illustrating this division, Mary's networks generated considerable social capital through 'weak ties' (Granovetter, 1973). This is 'bridging' social capital, although within a socially homogenous group, which provides Mary with a site of information-sharing about schools and nurseries, alerts her to the job she takes, the nanny she shares and then the existence of the small crèche her children attend. The interconnected nature of local middle-class mothers' networks is clear from her comment on looking round primary schools. 'In looking at a state school and you think, I know all these mothers, that's good. I suppose you feel a bit like it is going to be OK. You know, this big step.'

Jill has a much looser network of friends. Working full-time, her main sources of adult support and companionship outside the workplace appear to be her sister and her mother. In the narratives of the working-class women in our research, female relatives play a key role in offering practical support and information.

Approaches to childcare

Jill's youngest daughter attended a state-funded day-care nursery full time since she was 9 months old, and then a state school. Jill has a sense of security that derives from her faith in the state. It is important to her to know that her daughter is with qualified staff, and the staff in state nurseries seem to her to be more regulated than those in private nurseries (which are in any case too expensive) or childminders. This faith in the state has survived despite her two older children being let down, as she sees it, by schools. She is in search of a childcare environment that is safe and reliable and will prepare her youngest daughter for success at school.

Mary does not mention state nurseries, despite the developed network in the area. She uses a nanny-share, a small, parent-run, cooperative crèche for both children, a community nursery for her younger child and a non-selective independent primary school for her elder. She states clearly that she is in search of a childcare environment that is nurturing, intimate and creative. The nanny who looks after both children is not qualified but is seen as having the right personal characteristics to look after babies. Toddlers are understood to need more creative activities, hence the switch to nursery.

Mary's and Jill's 'choices' were again replicated in the wider sample, where working-class mothers spoke mostly of their fear of physical harm and neglect from a carer, which influenced their choice of nurseries as safe, public spaces, open to scrutiny and in which the workers can police each other. The middle-class parents were more likely to emphasise the importance of small, intimate care spaces for the under-threes.

Paid work

Jill's long hours of retail work, including regular weekend work, mean that she relies on her teenage daughter to collect her youngest daughter from after-school club and prepare her tea. She feels strongly that she is absent from home for too long.

> Nothing's positive [about work], it is just financial solely. I think the government should have more control on these companies . . . because I think people are forced to work such long hours and they don't get no support from the government and your family completely misses out . . . It's all negative working when you've got young children, because I do have lots of guilty feelings that I'm not there. And you're constantly battling.

Jill is proud of her youngest daughter, who is getting on well at school. This success lessens her anxiety somewhat. 'I used to feel guilty with [older children] because I think I should have been there more because they needed that because of their dyslexia. But what could I do? Nothing much.'

Mary accepted IME by giving up her job, after her second child was born. In compliance with IME, she emphasises her part-time job is carefully arranged so that 'there aren't any downsides', especially not for the children.

> [After my second child] I just felt completely overwhelmed by the whole thing and I knew that I was going to be staying at home. And I was happy to do that. But then, you see them becoming more independent and you realise that you'd like some of that independence too. And they need to go off and socialise and be at nursery. Just a little bit. Not full time or anything . . . Neither of them would know whether I am working or not.

During the course of the research, Mary's partner also moved to working at home in order to spend more time with children, although he also had work-related reasons for making the change. Both women see their jobs as a source of income necessary to maintain the family's viability and their own independence, by which they both set great store. Jill aspires to become a midwife, an occupation about which she is intensely enthusiastic ('my passion'). Similarly, Mary's sense of self is not invested in her current paid work, but in her case derives from her own art work.

School choice

Choosing a primary school is a much more nuanced, lengthy and anxiety-inducing process for Mary than for Jill. Mary rejects a nearby school on the basis of its too-basic facilities, lack of friendliness from teachers and an implied concern that the peer group may be too 'rough' for her child. Matching individual children with particular institutions is commonly alluded to by middle-class parents as a mechanism of choice (Ball, 2003; Gewirtz et al., 1995). So she keeps her daughter at the small, alternative, independent school until the family plan to move. 'I've heard from people I know, they hint at [rejected school] being maybe just a little rough around the edges . . . And I looked at my daughter's personality and I looked at the school and I couldn't see them matching.'

As Jill works such long hours, her choice of school is driven by the availability of an after-school club and ease of location for other family members to collect her daughter. Jill sees few differences between schools and generally maintains a hands-off approach, except in times of crisis, commenting, 'I don't go up the school'. Again, this distance is often mentioned by working-class mothers and has been extensively discussed and analysed elsewhere (Gillies, 2006; Lareau, 1989; Reay, 1998; Vincent, 1996).

My point in highlighting these differences between Jill and Mary is not to suggest that one woman is a 'better' mother than the other. Clearly, differences in financial resources underpin many of the distinctions mentioned here, but there are differential resources of social and cultural capital in play as well. As a result, Mary is in a position to live by IME, whereas Jill cannot and, in some ways (e.g. interaction with school), does not wish to. As both nurturer and provider, Jill displays considerable resilience, yet still experiences considerable anxiety over the effect of her absences on her children. This anxiety was heightened by one teenager recently being convicted of illegal activity, and we suggest that, despite her identity as 'good' worker and provider, Jill is aware that the time she spends away from her children means that she is at risk of being positioned as a 'bad' mother, revealing a tension between being in paid employment and being with the children that she cannot resolve.

Conclusion

Lawler describes class as

> dynamic; as a system of inequality which is continually being re-made in the large and small-scale processes of social life: through the workings of global capital and the search for new markets, but also through claims for entitlement (and of non-entitlement), through symbols and representations, *and in the emotional and affective dimensions of life*.
>
> (2005: 797, emphasis added)

My argument here is that mothering is one example of a site in which class is realised and reproduced, with those who do not conform to the normative ideal at risk of being exposed as morally insufficient.

The experience of mothering is often presented as a common bond between women, despite the other differences and distinctions in their lives. Yet the expectations established by a normative discourse of intensive mothering are divisive. IME demands from the mother an unremitting focus on the child that many women are unable or unwilling to maintain. It is, of course, easier to work with and around IME if you are affluent and, perhaps, if you have a partner. Explanations focusing on those who do not live by its precepts often slip from structural poverty into cultural poverty, and resistance to IME becomes 'bad' mothering. Although absent fathers are condemned, a particular ferocity informs moral judgement of 'bad' mothers. Middle-class performances of mothering map out and inhabit a class cultural space determined by an 'intensive' approach, one that is both 'sensitive' in terms of the mother's interaction with the child, and 'professional' in her approach to the task of moulding her child. Here is the 'implicit ought' (Lawler, 2005: 801) of mothering, the 'moral boundary drawing' (Sayer, 2005), which lays open non-normative performances of mothering to charges of inadequacy and also, potentially, to a refusal to recognise the mother as a moral self.

Notes

1   It is frequently noted that mothers whose care and protection of their children are inadequate are quickly demonised, and to a greater extent than fathers who hurt their children. Recent UK cases include that of Fiona MacKeown (whose daughter was murdered while she was away from home).

2   The emphasis on parental consumption on behalf of the child is one aspect of a commodification of childhood, increasingly apparent over the last century. The other aspect is direct marketing to children (Cook, 2000; Kenway and Bullen, 2001).

3   Reynolds' (2005) discusses the experiences and understandings of Black Caribbean mothers.

References

Apple, R. (2006) *Perfect motherhood: science and childrearing in America*, New Brunswick: Rutgers University Press.

Ball, S. (2003) *Class strategies and the education market*, London: Routledge.

Bourdieu, P. (1986) *Distinction: a social critique of the judgment of taste*, London: Routledge.

Brooks, A. and Wee, L. (2008) 'Reflexivity and the transformation of gender identity: reviewing the potential for change in a cosmopolitan city', *Sociology* 42(3): 503–521.

Clarke, A. (2004) 'Maternity and materiality: becoming mother in consumer culture', in J. Taylor, L. Layne and D. Wozniak (eds) *Consuming motherhood*, New Brunswick, NJ: Rutgers University Press.

Cook, D. (2000) 'The rise of "the toddler" as subject and as merchandising category in the 1930s', in M. Gottdiener (ed.) *New forms of consumption: consumers, culture and commodification*, Oxford: Rowman & Littlefield.

Department for Children Schools and Families (DCFS) (2007) *Guidance on education-related parenting contracts, parenting orders and penalty notices*, revised edn, London: DCSF.

Department for Work and Pensions (DFWP) (2007) *Green paper: in work, better off*, London: DFWP.

Dermott, E. (2008) *Intimate fatherhood*, London: Routledge.

Dicks, B. (2008) 'Performing the hidden injuries of class in coal-mining heritage', *Sociology* 42(3): 436–452.

Douglas, S. and Michaels, M. (2005) *The mommy myth*, New York: Free Press.

Garey, A. (1995) 'Constructing motherhood on the night shift: "working mothers" as "stay-at-home" moms', *Qualitative Sociology* 18: 415–437.

Gewirtz, S. (2001) Cloning the Blairs, *Journal of Education Policy* 16(4): 365–378.

—— Ball, S. and Bowe, R. (1995) *Markets, choice and equity*, Buckingham: Open University Press.

Gillies, V. (2006) 'Working class mothers and school life: exploring the role of emotional capital', *Gender and Education*, 18 (3), 281–293.

—— (2007) *Marginalized mothers*, London: Routledge.

Goodman, D. and Du Puis, E.M. (2002) 'Knowing food and growing food: beyond the production–consumption debate in sociology of agriculture', *Sociologia Ruralis* 42, 1, 5–21.

Granovetter, M. (1973) 'The strength of weak ties', *American Journal of Sociology*, 78, 1360–1380.

Hardyment, C. (2007) *Dream babies*, London: Frances Lincoln.

Hattery, A. (2001) Women, work and family: balancing and weaving, London: Sage.

Hays, S. (1996) *The cultural contradictions of motherhood*, New Haven, CT: Yale University Press.

—— (2003) *Flat broke with children*, Oxford: Oxford University Press.

Himmelweit, S. and Sigala, M. (2002) *The welfare implications of mothers' decisions about work and childcare*, Working paper 20, ESRC Future of Work Programme.

Johnston, A. and Swanson, D. (2006) 'Constructing the "good mother": the experience of mothering ideologies by work status', *Sex Roles: A Journal of Research* 54(7/8).

Kehily, M.J. (2008) 'Pregnant with meaning: pregnancy magazines and the encoding of the maternal subject', Draft paper.

Kenway, J. and Bullen E. (2001) *Consuming children: education-entertainment-advertising*, Buckingham: Open University Press.

Korteweg, A. (2002) *Ideologies of class, motherhood and work: the subject of the working mother viewed though the lens of welfare reform*, Berkeley Occasional Papers no. 38. Available online at http://escholarship. bc.edu/wfn_bwpaper/36/ (accessed October 2008).

Lareau, A. (1989) *Home advantage*, London: Falmer Press.

—— (2002) 'Invisible inequality: social class and childrearing in Black and White families', *American Sociological Review* 67: 747–776.

Lawler, S. (2005) 'Introduction: class, culture and identity', *Sociology* 39(5): 797–806.

Liechty, M. (2003) *Suitably modern: making middle class culture in a new consumer society*, Princeton, NJ: Princeton University Press.

Macdonald, C. (1998) 'Manufacturing motherhood: the shadow work of nannies and au pairs', *Qualitative Sociology* 21(1): 25–53.

May, V. (2008) 'On being a "good" mother: the moral presentation of self in written life stories', *Sociology* 42(3): 470–486.

Miller, D. (2004) 'How infants grow mothers in North London', in J. Taylor, L. Layne and D. Wozniak (eds) *Consuming motherhood*, New Brunswick, NJ: Rutgers University Press.

Miller, T. (2005) *Making sense of motherhood*, Cambridge: Cambridge University Press.

O'Brien, M. (2005) *Shared caring: bringing fathers into the frame*, London: EOC.

O'Connell, R. (2008) 'The meaning of home-based childcare in an era of quality: childminding in an inner London borough and the encounter with professionalisation', unpublished doctoral thesis, UCL.

Office for National Statistics (2001) *Ethnicity, marriage and families*, National Statistics. Available online at www.statistics.gov.uk.

Reay, D. (1998) *Class work*, London: UCL Press.

Reynolds, T. (2005) *Caribbean mothers: identity and experience in the UK*, Stoke: Trentham Press.

Savage, M. (2005) 'Working class identities in the 1960s: revisiting the affluent worker studies', *Sociology* 39(5), 929–946.

Sayer, A. (2005) 'Class, moral worth and recognition', *Sociology* 39(5): 947–964.

Suissa, J. (2006) 'Untangling the mother knot: some thoughts on parents, children and philosophers of education', *Ethics and Education* 1(1): 65–77.

Vincent, C. (1996) *Parents and teachers: power and participation*, London: Falmer.

—— and Ball, S. (2006), *Childcare, choice and class practices*, London: Routledge.

—— and —— (2007) '"Making up" the middle class child: families, activities and class dispositions', *Sociology* 41(6): 1061–1077.

—— Braun, A. and Ball, S. (2008) 'Caring for young children in the UK', *Critical Social Policy* 28(1): 5–26.

Walkerdine, V. and Lucey, H. (1989) *Democracy in the kitchen*, London: Virago.

Williams, C. (2006) *Inside toyland*, Berkley, CA: University of California Press.

Williams, S. (2008) 'What is fatherhood: searching for the reflexive father', *Sociology* 42(3): 487–502.

11

Rationalisation, disenchantment and re-enchantment
Engaging with Weber's sociology of modernity

Philip A. Woods

Introduction

Max Weber is seen as one of the founders of sociology, making up a triumvirate of 'founding fathers' with Marx and Durkheim. However, this does not capture the scope and ambition, nor the emotional engagement of Weber's scholarly work. What drove him was a demand to address the 'cultural crisis' that was represented by the creation of the modern world (Kettler *et al.*, 2008). Undertaking his research and writing from the late nineteenth century to his relatively early death in 1920, Weber saw at first hand in detailed empirical studies the replacement of traditional agricultural society in Germany by 'a new "employment regime" based on capitalistic wage labour' (Whimster, 2007: 16). The intensity with which he approached his studies led to a number of breakdowns in his health. A large part of that intensity arose from an unclouded recognition of what was being lost with the expansion of modernity, namely a sense of meaning that was embedded in the everyday relationships and activities of human life. This was, however, not a recognition of loss characterised by soft nostalgia. In his immensely varied and historically focused breadth of studies – from Chinese society to the development of capitalism in the West – Weber understood the pervasiveness of issues such as power, and identified how they were differently manifested in different kinds of social order. His was a determination to understand the new, modern society from within the perspective of that society, utilising the rational, scientific approach to increasing knowledge. Crucially, this scientific approach to knowledge of the cultural world had to be appropriate to that world. Hence, Weber emphasised, not only the formulation of concepts, ideal types and detailed empirical analysis of the development of social orders, but also the need for the cultural analyst to exercise *verstehen* (an empathetic understanding of what it is or was to be of and in a certain social order and cultural context) and the necessity of choice in deciding from what angle or point of view to select the focus of study.

This chapter concentrates on his characterisation of modernity through the interrelated conceptualisations of rationalisation and disenchantment, the key challenge it generates (concerning the possibility of freedom in a rationalised social order), and ways in which this challenge may be engaged with.

Rationalisation and disenchantment

Weber is best known for his development of the concept of *rationalisation* as a means of understanding the distinct character of the modern world. Modernity raises instrumental rationality to be the most valued mode of social action, one that pervades social life. The modern social order, according to Weber, is characterised by bureaucratic organisation and procedures, which he analysed by means of the construction of ideal types. Thus, the ideal typical bureaucracy possessed the characteristics of rule-driven behaviour, responsibilities and powers defined by the office of the person and an ordered hierarchy of posts and positions, with authority dependent on where a post-holder fitted into that hierarchy and underpinned by legal-rational authority – that is, 'the legitimacy of the power-holder to give commands [resting] upon rules that are rationally established by enactment, by agreement, or by imposition' (Weber, 1948c: 294).

Weber's analysis was, however, much more than a description of the dominant organisational form of modern society. His compelling interest was in the question of what type of human being is encouraged by different social orders (Hennis, 1988). In what ways do different types of society and culture shape the type of person who lives within them? Modernity is a historically unique social order that gives rise to a distinctive conduct of life which is lived by and continually shaped by a particular person type. The driving question for Weber's work is an exploration of the 'inner effect' on personality (Hennis, 1988: 57).

One of the most famous concepts to emerge from that work is that of the 'iron cage'. This encapsulates the idea that modern people are trapped in a rationalistic, bureaucratised organisation prison that deprives them of freedom and creativity. In fact, this idea is better rendered in English as the 'steel shell' (Wells, 2001). What confines people is not an external 'cage', but something much more sinister: a characteristic that has become *part of* the person (as a shell is an organic part of an animal), a characteristic moreover that is forged (like steel) by human beings in modern society and is not a natural or organic product. The implication is that it is alien matter that is insidiously introduced within the human frame for living.

Sociologically speaking, instrumentally rational action is privileged. At the level of personal relationships, 'traditional and charismatic-style social relations are replaced by technical-rational ones, meaning that relationships with colleagues and students are more impersonal, calculative and formalised, increasingly governed by detailed codes of conduct' – with staff in universities, for example, becoming employees subject to performance evaluations instead of members of an academic community (Samier, 2005: 87). In terms of Weber's typology of social action, *zweckrational* (instrumentally rational action) predominates over the other action types: namely, *wertrational* (value-rational action), which involves an overriding commitment to values as a result of prior conscious reasoning or, as Weber puts it, 'self-conscious formulation of the ultimate values governing' the action; affectual action – '(especially emotional) . . . determined by the actor's specific affects and feeling states'; and traditional action 'determined by ingrained habituation' (1978: 24–25). Samier's analysis of universities, from a perspective of Weberian public administration, highlights the procedural, performative bureaucratisation trend, which involves the forging of an academic staff as an 'entrepreneurial and managerially orientated cadre who adopt obedience to bureaucratic authority and performance management' (Samier, 2005: 81) and the creation of a 'new entrepreneurial professor' (p. 82).

Weber's analysis was weighted with both analytical and normative understandings. That is, he sought to analyse the world of human beings as clearly and in an as unbiased way as possible, undertaking enormous amounts of cultural and historical analyses over his lifetime; at the same time he recognised that where the social scientist applied his energies and the driving research questions he pursued were the result of choices that are value-laden. He had a *feeling* for his work, as well as the sharp eye of the analyst. Understanding modernity was a pressing challenge because of the fundamental change it wrought in the people who are embedded in its conduct and social structures. Weber was pessimistic about the fate of the individual within the tightening parameters of the instrumental, means–end rationality of bureau-capitalism and the disciplines emanating from the forces of rationalisation, all tending towards 'a universal phenomenon [which] will make irresistible headway in every sphere of human life' (Weber, 1978: 1150).

Why it is a crisis and why it should evoke pessimism are only understandable if there is a sense of something of great value being lost in the conduct and the person type of modernity. Thus, the full meaning of the concept of rationalisation is understandable only in relation to another concept pivotal in Weber's work, namely *disenchantment*. Influenced by Nietzsche, Weber's view was that, in the modern world, God is dead, and all objective order of value is gone (Hennis, 1988: 158–159). The bearing of the modern person in the rationalised world 'has been disenchanted and denuded of its mystical but inwardly genuine plasticity' (Weber, 1948a: 148). The inner capacity for a sense of spirituality and profound meaning has not disappeared, but an understanding and a belief system that pervade the social structures and social conduct life have withdrawn.

> Precisely the ultimate and most sublime values have retreated from public life either into the transcendental realm of mystic life or into the brotherliness of direct and human relations. It is not accidental that . . . today only within the smallest and intimate circles, in personal human situations, in *pianissimo*, that something is pulsating that corresponds to the prophetic *pneuma*, which in former times swept through the great communities like a firebrand, welding them together.
>
> (Weber, 1948a: 155)

In contemporary times, we know that personal spirituality in many countries, as well as persisting individually, is articulated and shaped through an industry of mind, body and spirit publications, diverse kinds of groups and activities and New Age movements, and the growth of corporate and academic interest in the relevance of spirituality and values to organisational life and work relationships. In one sense, this can be understood as a rationalisation of a human impulse to seek and create meaning, an impulse that the forces of bureaucratic capitalism are able to take advantage of, as with any other actual or potential human demand (commodification). (Another perspective is to see in it a potential for countering the dominance of instrumental rationality, which will be discussed further below.) This rationalisation is manifest, for example, in the systematic (instrumentally rational) attention that business and other organisations are willing to give to the connection between spirituality on the one hand and organisational leadership, management, staff development policies and organisational performance on the other (Casey, 2002; Reave, 2005).

The idea of spiritual intelligence as a capability for problem-solving is an example. Spirituality here is formulated as:

> the intelligence with which we address and solve problems of meaning and value, the intelligence with which we can place our actions and our lives in a wider, richer, meaning-giving context, the intelligence with which we can assess that one course of action or one life-path is more meaningful than another.
>
> (Zohar and Marshall, 2000: 3–4)

123

The point here is not to suggest that rational approaches to meaning are inadmissible. Systematic approaches – both intellectual and practical (through the exercise of meditative techniques for example) – have long been characteristic of religious views of the world, and Weber certainly recognised this. The point is that the most personal and demanding questions of meaning are, in modern society, capable of being embedded in, and dominated and appropriated by, the single-minded focus of bureaucratic capitalism on marshalling the best means to serve the ends of organisational performance and maximisation of income.

This is evident in education. The interest in values and the meaning that educational leaders and staff espouse and live by can be understood as a move from simple instrumentalism to subtle instrumentalism (Woods, 2005): from the former, which treats people as subjects who can be moulded and manoeuvred through direction and sanctions, as means to organisational and economistic ends, and as organisational members whose worth and progress is to be measured through tests; to the more finely tuned approach of subtle instrumentalism, which retains the fundamental perspective of people as means to ends, but recognises that moulding, manoeuvring and assessing them requires a great deal more sensitivity to their emotions and motivations. Hartley (2004) sums up this new form of instrumentality in education and sees in this a further unfolding of Weber's rationalisation thesis:

> This new 'emotional' discourse has the attraction of appealing subliminally to those who have become disenchanted with consumerism's promise that its goods and services will serve, at last, to render the self at ease and to give life meaning. Put another way: if meaning and emotional satisfaction in life is not being derived from consumerism *outside* of work, then perhaps it can be derived from 'consumerism' *within* work. It is the emphasis on the emotional and on the spiritual that arguably renders the new *emotional leadership* discourse so persuasive . . . At root, as Weber predicted, emotional management seems to be a technical endeavour, born of modernity, set for standardization, to be rendered as objective and measurable, and made ready for audit.
>
> (Hartley, 2004: 592; emphases in original)

The diagnosis of modernity that Weber offers is a conceptualisation characterised by rationalisation *and* disenchantment as mutually sustaining concepts. Too often the latter (the integral significance of disenchantment) is marginalised or given only implicit or cursory recognition in the application of Weber's formulation of rationalisation. However, to do that is to lose the depth of the demand of modernity. That demand arises from the dominance of science – the rational, systematic investigation of the world – as the source of understanding and knowledge. Self-clarification and knowledge, therefore, are 'not the gift of grace of seers and prophets dispensing sacred values and revelations', and this is 'the inescapable condition of our historical situation', one which we cannot evade 'so long as we remain true to ourselves' (Weber, 1948a: 152). As Koshul (2005: 14), in his discussion of Weber's postmodern significance, succinctly puts it:

> Plain intellectual honesty and integrity require that we, as moderns, reject all claims of special gifts and grace claiming to provide access to, and possession of, sacred values and revelation because such claims cannot be justified on rational, scientific grounds.

The demand of modernity, unabated as it unfolds and expands globally into what some call postmodern society, is to understand, accept and bear the meaninglessness of the world. What values and meaning and spiritual significances the moderns embrace cannot have the force and legitimacy of universal, objectively grounded truths. We – in ourselves, our families, social groups and networks – are left to define for ourselves what values and meanings we take to be ultimate (if any at all). Meaning is arbitrary and partial. As a basis for studies of the social construction of knowledge and values, this is liberating. However, as a basis for life, it is unnerving and roots the everyday conduct of living in an existential angst.

Freedom in a rationalised social order?

The challenge put into sharp relief by Weberian analysis is whether some degree of genuine freedom is possible within the rationalising social order of the modern world. Is there a possibility for moderns to be anything more than 'cheerful robots' (Mills, 1970) C. Wright Mills' phrase – cheerful robots – captures perfectly the denuded conception of the human being where the understanding of what is fundamentally to be valued is confined within the scope of rationalised and marketised society alone. In ideal-typical terms, the modern social actor is defined by the 'steel shell', which comes to be a very part of their being. In this section I will consider three responses: the entrepreneurial turn in modern bureaucracy; the individualistic response that is represented by Weber's idea of 'inner distance'; and possibilities for counter-rationality based on explorations of meaning. (Space precludes specific discussion of the postmodern response. See Gane (2002).)

The entrepreneurial turn

The emphasis on entrepreneurs and entrepreneurialism in education and other areas of the public sector (Woods *et al.*, 2007) introduces a complexity to bureaucratic organisation. It is seen as a feature of bureaucratisation and an extension of contractual relations, as in Samier's (2005) analysis for example; but it also launches into bureaucratic organisation an impetus to innovation, change and lateral thinking that is in tension with the certainties and order of rational procedures. Entrepreneurial and bureaucratic rationalities vie with each other – another example of practice being characterised by multiple models, as Weber emphasised, rather than pure ideal types. The imperative for the entrepreneur is to challenge the traditional and bureaucratically honoured ways of doing things and, therefore, to be motivated by their own initiative, conviction and sense of values and purpose. Entrepreneurial activity is characterised by enthusiasm and excitement, which contrasts with the dominance in bureaucracy of 'a spirit of formalistic impersonality: "*Sine ire et studio*," without hatred or passion, and hence without affection or enthusiasm' (Weber, 1978: 225). Weber recognised this subversive, potentially liberating character of the entrepreneur. The capitalist entrepreneur 'is the only type who has been able to maintain at least relative immunity from subjection to the control of rational bureaucratic knowledge' (Weber, 1978: 225).

A more entrepreneurial character is exactly what is being introduced into modernised bureaucracies in education and the rest of the public sector, intensifying pressure on organisational members to commit their *person* to work and the office. The bureaucratic principle that separates the office from the person and calls for an absence of 'personal enthusiasm' is the antithesis of modern leadership discourse in which 'the person is integral to, and a key resource in, the office itself . . . its very material and spiritual embodiment' (Newman, 2005: 720). In education, the idea of a 'new enterprise logic' is having a compelling influence, with schooling

125

being seen as 'an undertaking that is difficult, complicated and at times risky, often calling for daring activity . . . and is thrilling in its execution . . .' (Caldwell, 2006: 76). A key aim is constant improvement (Ofsted, 2002), by 'constantly generating and increasing knowledge inside and outside the organization' (Fullan, 2001: 8). A more entrepreneurial culture is seen as overcoming the alleged stiffness, lethargy and unresponsiveness of traditional bureaucracy (du Gay, 2000), and the desire to create a more enterprising approach to education underpins the creation of a new kind of school organisation in England – academies – sponsored by businesses and other private people and organisations (Woods *et al.*, 2007). Academies in England are intended to be hybrid (public–private) organisations, where the entrepreneurial spirit can flourish, and which, arguably, bring into organisational form a bureau-enterprise culture that combines the dynamism of that spirit with the values of public bureaucracy (Woods, P.A., 2007).

In this change to a more innovative, entrepreneurial organisational regime, is there a growth of freedom – scope for dilution of the 'steel shell' of rationality? The entrepreneurial maverick has the potential to utilise the relative immunity of the entrepreneur. However, the parameters within which entrepreneurial creativity and difference are encouraged can act to constrain and construct a person type that functions in and for the organisational goals and priorities. This is the burden of the critique of new public management and managerialism – that the freedom it invokes is accompanied by forging an inner disposition, a soul, that defines its values and spirit in terms of gains in measurable performance and enthusiasm for the idea of innovation and change as abstract goods. System and organisational mechanisms and strategies seek 'to reshape the ways in which each individual . . . will conduct him- or herself in a space of regulated freedom' (Rose, 1999: 22) The promised benefits of managerialist culture are founded in an instrumental orientation that values processes, techniques and change, which serve this goal of constant improvement. Entrepreneurialism in this regard is ultimately subservient to the dominant rationalised culture.

The individualistic response of 'inner distance'

Weber insisted that, despite the rationalisation of the modern social order and its disenchantment of the world, an individual could hold on to and express ultimate values. In particular, this is the demand that the true political leader must face up to. In his lecture, 'Politics as a vocation', Weber addresses the normative question of what kind of person one must be to be allowed to wield political power, and what differentiates different power-holders who all claim noble, lofty intentions (Weber, 1948b: 115, 119). His answer is that it is one who is guided by an ethic of responsibility, one who carefully attends to the consequences of policy and to the irreconcilable tensions it involves and who also complements this and who recognises that, at a certain point, the ethic of absolute ends comes into its own. There is a point to hold to the ultimate principle and declare 'Here I stand! I can do no other'.

The capacity that Weber is highlighting here is that of inner distance – that is, a self-conscious adherence to certain ethical values, in the face of the immense daily pressures to conform to a rationalised and disenchanted world, a capability to resist loss of 'personality' under the relentless pressure of the demands of routine. There is, as Schroeder (1991: 62) explains, the possibility for:

> an unfettered self which tries to assert its individuality by affirming certain constant values in the face of the impersonal forces which increasingly dominate the modern world.

However, this conception of inner distance is individualistic and dependent solely on the personal resources of the individual. In addition, Weber does not give it any systematic or substantive content to the concept (Schroeder, 1991). As a result, the choice of values, or how we might arrive at that choice, is arbitrary. We can make the 'decisive choice of a leading drive or value' that inner distance demands and that gives direction (Owen, 1991: 84). However, we do not, from Weber's work, have the resources to discriminate between less and more valid choices.

The possibility of counter-rationalities of veridical meaning

As noted above, Weber's construction of ideal types, such as those of bureaucracy and instrumental rationality, were not intended to reduce the real world to one-dimensional concepts. In the practice of social life, people are likely to be moved by multiple cultural conceptions of, and dispositions towards, social relationships. In particular, different types of social or organisational authority are likely to be apparent in practice, rather than pure forms of bureaucratic (legal-rational), traditional or charismatic authority.

> In general, it should be kept clearly in mind that the basis of every authority, and correspondingly of every kind of willingness to obey, is a *belief* . . .
>
> The composition of this belief is seldom altogether simple. In the case of 'legal authority', it is never purely legal . . . it is partly traditional. Furthermore, it has a charismatic element, at least in the negative sense that persistent and striking lack of success may be sufficient to ruin in any government.
>
> (Weber, 1978: 263; emphasis in original)

There is an inner activity that helps to shape that animating belief to which Weber refers. An interesting insight into modern organisations is given by Casey's (2002) international study. This found, in organisations across the world, 'various new forms of self-expressiveness, meaning-making and spirituality' (p. 152), opportunities for time in 'quiet rooms' and the 'gentle arts' of 'spirit-seeking, magic and divination' (p. 155). Casey suggests that organisational members, through this kind of activity and perspective, bring a 'potentially disruptive counterposition to bureaucratic and neo-rationalist organizational management' (p. 75) and that the

> current of spiritual and self-expressivist explorations and demands among bureaucratic organizational employees, reveals . . . signs of persons striving for subjectivation – for the accomplishment of becoming an acting subject . . . [and] are efforts toward a freedom not reduced to an instrumental rationality of economic choice.
>
> (Casey, 2004)

There is evidence, too, of the importance of spiritual and deeper meaning making for educationalists – among both religious believers and non-believers – within school organisations (Woods, G.J., 2007).

The possibility for counter-rationalities rests on the potential for inner distance, not simply as an individual phenomenon, but as something that can be developed and nurtured collectively – namely, the idea of *shared inner distance*. People have both inner and social resources for this through multiple sources of identity orientation, which include forms both of social identity and of exogenous points of orientation that represent ideals and values that supersede more

127

mundane needs and interests (Woods, 2003). One expression of this is through art – and from a postmodernist perspective, radical artistic practices (Gane, 2002) – which subverts instrumental rationality. The capacity for inner distance is not, therefore, simply a withdrawal, but an expansion of the symbolic resources that are allowed to enable social action. Moreover, it is integral to the idea of a rich conception of democracy that infuses society and organisations. Seeking and shaping alternatives to rationalisation are shared, collective activities to which everyone is capable of contributing.

The possibility for counter-rationalities that embrace veridical meaning rests on finding, as other social theorists such as Marx have tried to do, 'some centre in man-as-man which would enable them to believe that in the end he cannot be made into, that he cannot finally become, such an alien creature [the cheerful robot] – alien to nature, to society, to self' (Mills, 1970: 190).

I have argued, engaging with Weber (in Woods (2001), on which this paragraph is based), that there needs to be, underlying sociological study, an appreciation that 'there is a human faculty, however frequently clouded by emotions, social interests and the like, that can on occasions provide social action with that *foundation* that allows us to characterize it as something other than relativism or emotivism' (Woods, 2001: 694), a faculty for intuiting the good and values that have transcendent and universal force. The idea of such a human faculty is the necessary foundation for it to make sense for Weber to express an ethical passion in 'Politics as a vocation' (1948b). That lecture, as Tester (1999) argues, is not 'emotivist' – that is, it does not presuppose that all moral judgements and criteria collapse into expressions of preference and feeling. But there is, nevertheless, a contradiction between Weber's sociological project and his fundamental ethical stance that is not acknowledged in Tester's analysis. Weber's sociology exists in a framework that eschews a foundationalist social analysis allowing for, or specifying, ultimate values or goods for humanity. The only way meaning and values are possible in Weber's philosophical anthropology is through human choice: to this extent, Weber is an existentialist. Although this is consistent with emotivism, it is not emotivism per se. 'Politics as a vocation' is non-emotivist and implies the existence of the kind of human faculty referred to above. But, crucially, Weber did not incorporate this faculty to discern or glimpse truths that are more than feelings or preferences or contingent social constructions into the framework of social action studied by sociology. The failure to incorporate such a faculty diminishes the sensitivity of sociology to the human-ness of its subject of study and to the potential to move beyond the constraints of rationalisation.

Re-enchanting education

The Weberian theme of rationalisation and disenchantment allows us to set up a simple dichotomy for education: two ideal types of formal education. In the first, education acts to form people who fit into a world dominated by instrumental rationality and who carry with them, as part of their essential defining identity, the 'steel shell' that imbues them with the standards of a rationalising and disenchanting society. This takes as the overriding priority of education a need to prepare students for the activities and demands of organisational life driven by calculation and performance. Endres (2006), for example, uses Weber's theory to explain the role of functional activity in modern schooling.

The second ideal type places priority on re-enchantment. Enchantment here is the unfolding of human capabilities to sense that which is true and right, to develop sensibilities to nature and affective human communication (through art), and to share and enjoy a sense of connectedness with other people, the world and the phenomena and experiences that often attract the label spiritual – in other words, the capacity to sense and create veridical meaning. If the basic Weberian question is what type of person is forged by different social orders, the fundamental educational question that arises from the specific Weberian analysis of modernity is: Which person type is education for? The second ideal type takes seriously the demand to respond to the dominant rationalising context by creating an educational environment that nurtures a different person type. It answers that education is not about creating cheerful robots, but that its aim is to foster persons who are capable of enchantment and of challenging domination by rationalising forces.

Examples of the second ideal type (not necessarily in pure form) are discernible within conventional forms of education. For example, the critical events that Peter E. Woods (1993) found in primary and secondary education – school projects such as plays, concerts, film-making etc., in which adults and students work together – have the features of educational processes that are not reducible to rationalised procedures and outcomes. This is his description of critical events, based on his experience of them through sustained empirical research. Critical events:

> have something of the spirit of what Turner calls 'communitas'. The essential characteristic of this according to Musgrove is 'a relationship between concrete, idiosyncratic individuals, stripped of both status and role'. It contrasts with social structure and therefore is sometimes called social antistructure . . . The antistructure is a state of undifferentiated, homogeneous human kindness. 'Communitas' has something magical about it. Outside, above and beyond structure, it has a quality that is both intensely real and intensely unreal. Latent or suppressed feelings, abilities, thoughts, aspirations are suddenly set free. New persons are born and, almost in celebration, a new collective spirit. Uncommon excitement and expectations are generated. All this is something special, though exactly why is difficult to explain. Something is always lost in the attempt. After all, the more successful the magic, the more impenetrable the solution.
>
> (Woods, P.E., 1993: 7)

In this, one can see some of the elements of the three possibilities discussed in the previous section – for example, educational entrepreneurialism (enterprising initiatives by teachers that bring about and make a reality successful, ambitious projects that engage numbers of students and adults); the passion of individuals that critical events attract and that goes beyond (is distanced from) the confines of work aimed at achieving just measurable achievement; the immediacy of artistic expression, enjoyed and appreciated for its intrinsic value, and the social solidarity and collective working that create a kind of democracy of learning in which all contribute and share. Other examples of the second ideal type occur in alternative educational settings (Woods and Woods, 2009).

Concluding remarks

The sociological question is to what extent, in what forms and under what conditions the second ideal type of education occurs in contemporary society. The work of Weber sensitises the sociologist to the complexity of addressing such a question. As Whimster (2007: 189) observes, in 'Weber's historical sociology, outcomes happen for reasons – motivational states and the

129

pattern of external determination. But how they interact and combine is hard to predict.' In this spirit, it is possible to observe that alternatives and challenges are more likely to be found where there is a condition of relative immunity (from the dominance of rationalisation) arising from an amalgam of structural and subjective factors. The latter include a degree of freedom (as with entrepreneurial actors) to mobilise ideas and resources; awareness of the importance of inner distance from dominant presumptions; a valuing of intrinsic experience and value-rationality; opportunities to engage with others collegially in the task of creating alternatives to the subservience to rationalising forces; and ideational resources, to be engaged with rather than simply ingested, that provide an alternative view of society and human progress.

There are many dimensions to Weber's work, which continue to stimulate and engage sociologists. The significance of his work that this chapter has highlighted is his characterisation of modernity through the interrelated conceptualisations of rationalisation and disenchantment. This analysis of modernity throws into sharp relief the full import and vulnerability of the challenges to rationalisation and disenchantment discussed above, and marks them out as enormously important subjects for study because they (consciously or unconsciously) challenge what Weber (1948a: 155) describes as the 'fate of our age, with its characteristic rationalization and intellectualization and, above all, the "disenchantment of the world"'.

References

Caldwell, B.J. (2006) *Re-imagining educational leadership*, London: Sage.

Casey, C. (2002) *Critical analysis of organizations: theory, practice, revitalization*, London: Sage.

—— (2004) 'Bureaucracy re-enchanted? Spirit, experts and authority in organizations', *Organization* 11(1): 59–79.

du Gay, P. (2000) *In praise of bureaucracy*, London: Sage.

Endres, B. (2006) 'Education for economic life: the role of communicative action', *Teachers' College Record* 108(10): 2001–2020.

Fullan, M. (2001) *Leading in a culture of change*, San Francisco, CA: Jossey-Bass.

Gane, N. (2002) *Max Weber and postmodern theory: rationalization versus re-enchantment*, New York and Basingstoke: Palgrave.

Hartley, D. (2004) 'Management, leadership and the emotional order of the school', *Journal of Education Policy* 19(5): 583–594.

Hennis, B. (1988) *Weber: essays in reconstruction*, London: Allen & Unwin.

Kettler, D., Loader, C. and Meja, V. (2008) *Karl Mannheim and the legacy of Max Weber*, Aldershot: Ashgate.

Koshul, B.B. (2005) *The postmodern significance of Max Weber's legacy*, New York and Basingstoke: Palgrave.

Mills, C.W. (1970) *The sociological imagination*, Harmondsworth: Penguin.

Newman, J. (2005) 'Enter the transformational leader: network governance and the micro-politics of modernization', *Sociology* 39(4): 717–734.

Ofsted (2002) *Local education authorities and school improvement 1996–2001*, London: Ofsted.

Owen, D. (1991) 'Autonomy and "inner distance": a trace of Nietzsche in Weber', *History of the Human Sciences* 4(1): 79–91.

Reave, L. (2005) 'Spiritual values and practices related to leadership effectiveness', *The Leadership Quarterly* 16: 655–687.

Rose, N. (1999) *Powers of freedom: reframing political thought*, Cambridge: Cambridge University Press.

Samier, E. (2005) 'Toward a Weberian public administration: the infinite web of history, values, and authority in administrative mentalities', *Halduskultuur* 6: 60–94.

Schroeder, R. (1991) '"Personality" and "inner distance": the conception of the individual in Max Weber's sociology', *History of the Human Sciences* 4(1): 62–78.

Tester, K. (1999) 'Weber's alleged emotivism', *British Journal of Sociology* 50(4): 563–573.

Weber, M. (1948a) 'Science as a vocation', in H.H. Gerth and C. Wright Mills, *From Max Weber*, London: Routledge & Kegan Paul.

—— (1948b) 'Politics as a vocation', in H.H. Gerth and C. Wright Mills, *From Max Weber*, London: Routledge & Kegan Paul.

—— (1948c) 'The social psychology of the world religions', in H.H. Gerth and C. Wright Mills, *From Max Weber*, London: Routledge & Kegan Paul.

—— (1978, originally 1956) *Economy and society*, vols. I & II, Berkeley, CA: University of California Press.

Wells, G.C. (2001) Issues of language and translation in Max Weber's protestant ethic writings, *Max Weber Studies* 2(1): 33–40.

Whimster, S. (2007) *Understanding Weber*, London: Routledge.

Woods, G.J. (2007) 'The "bigger feeling": the importance of spiritual experience in educational leadership', *Educational Management Administration and Leadership* 35(1): 135–155.

Woods, P.A. (2001) 'Values-intuitive rational action: the dynamic relationship of instrumental rationality and values insights as a form of social action', *British Journal of Sociology* 52(4): 687–706.

—— (2003) 'Building on Weber to understand governance: exploring the links between identity, democracy and "inner distance"', *Sociology* 37(1): 143–163.

—— (2005) *Democratic leadership in education*, London: Sage.

—— (2007) 'Authenticity in the bureau-enterprise culture: the struggle for authentic meaning', *Educational Management, Administration, and Leadership* 35(2): 297–322.

—— and Woods, G.J. (eds) (2009) *Alternative education for the 21st century philosophies, approaches, visions*, New York: Palgrave.

——, —— and Gunter, H. (2007) 'Academy schools and entrepreneurialism in education', *Journal of Education Policy* 22(2): 263–285.

Woods, P.E. (1993) *Critical events in teaching and learning*, London: Taylor & Francis.

Zohar, D. and I. Marshall (2000) *Spiritual intelligence: the ultimate intelligence*, London: Bloomsbury.

12

Recognizing the subjects of education
Engagements with Judith Butler

Deborah Youdell

Introduction

Among scholars in education sociology and allied areas such as cultural studies, Judith Butler is now a well-known and well-used theorist. Her theoretical work invites us to consider discomforting matters of gender and sexuality, of sexed and raced bodies, of being human. Throughout, she is concerned with forms of power and what is speakable and what is silenced. While not a part of the education mainstream, this work is a significant influence on and resource for post-structural, queer, feminist, and anti-racist strands in sociology of education, where these ideas invite us to consider "who" gets to be recognized as a person, or subject, in education and how these processes of recognition and refusal take place. In offering these conceptual tools, Judith Butler's work opens up exciting possibilities for *thinking differently about education and for imagining education and its subjects in new ways*. In this sense, her work offers a set of new lenses through which sociologists of education can make the familiar world of education "strange" (Delamont, 1995).

In this chapter, I offer accounts of Butler's central ideas concerning the subject, how s/he is constituted and constrained, and how s/he might engage in forms of resistance and politics. I begin by setting these in the context of Butler's own intellectual and political location and concerns, and go on to show how these have been made use of in sociology of education. In doing this, I illustrate how work in sociology of education has made use of Judith Butler's ideas to extend the insights offered by Foucault and education scholars influenced by him, and articulated these with feminist, anti-racist, and post-colonial analyses and concerns. Finally, I consider the potential future contributions that Butler's work might make to the sociology of education.

I first read Judith Butler, in the early 1990s, having been given a photocopy of her chapter, "Imitation and gender insubordination," from Diane Fuss's early Queer Studies collection *Inside/out* and, later, a copy of her book *Gender trouble*, both gifts from the same friend. These texts excited and overwhelmed me with the density of their ideas, the further reading in new fields that they demanded, and the conceptual tools they offered. Importantly, these texts promised to help me move past what I felt were the limitations of existing thinking about identity and politics in sociology of education at the time. Fifteen years later, Judith Butler's ongoing work continues to offer me significant tools for thinking about educational institutions, the subjects who populate them and the ways in which these might be reconfigured. It is in the spirit of this early labor and ongoing intellectual investment, and pleasure at the purchase that these tools continue to provide in my own work and in the work of others, that I write this chapter.

Who is Judith Butler?

An interrogation of the acceptance in Western thought and societies of a person who is complete and self-knowing and who exists outside relations of power, ideas, language or meaning runs throughout Butler's work. Her project, or at least one of them, has been to trouble the taken-for-grantedness of this pre-existing, self-contained, rational person, or subject. She does this to expose the constraints that are brought into play through this acceptance of the unitary subject and the political possibilities opened up by this troubling. Offering an account of who Judith Butler is, then, a rather contradictory activity.

I have heard Judith Butler tell a story about an occasion when a speaker at a meeting of activists and scholars concluded with the rebuke "Fuck You Judith Butler!" "Who," Judith wondered, was this "Judith Butler" to whom "Fuck you" was addressed, and what had "she" got to do with "her"? In her writing, she considers the place of herself in her work, in an intellectual space of ideas and in the world. What does it mean, she wonders, to speak as the "lesbian" in "imitation and gender insubordination," what are the effects of taking up and speaking under this sign? (Butler, 1991) And "who," she asks, is the "I" who considers the limits and possibilities of politics and agency in "Contingent foundations" (Butler, 1992)? As Butler herself observes, who she is, her ideas, and the writing she produces are not synonymous, but nor are they wholly devisable. Her writing and her ideas take on new meanings as they circulate, are taken up, are engaged and reworked, they exceed her and are beyond her control. And at the same time, in the call "Fuck you Judith Butler!" a particular reading of the meaning of her work is asserted, and she is constituted as the author of this reading, a constitution that might injure and might be difficult to resist.

That said, the attachment to the illusion of the unitary subject that is one of Butler's (and my own) objects of study compels me to say something solid. Judith Butler is Maxine Elliot Professor in the Departments of Rhetoric and Comparative Literature in the University of California, Berkeley. Her location across these two departments is indicative of the inter-disciplinarity of her work, which crosses the boundaries of continental philosophy, literary theory, politics, feminist theory, queer theory, and psychoanalysis. She is also engaged with political movements: for instance, she has been involved in political debates over hate speech legislation and lesbian pornography, as well as transgender activism and the political and psychic meanings of gender reassignment (see Butler, 2004a). These locations begin to demonstrate how Butler's work is situated in wider intellectual milieux and socio-political movements.

When the book that brought Butler to wide attention, *Gender trouble*, was published in 1990, she was one of a number of scholars working in the US, the UK, and Australia who were developing new analyses of gender and sexuality in these English-speaking contexts by engaging ideas from contemporary French philosophy, psychoanalysis, and feminism, by writers such as Michel Foucault, Jacques Derrida, Luce Irigaray, and Julia Kristeva. These engagements can be found in the work of authors such as Deborah Britzman, Bronwyn Davies, Michelle Fine, Elizabeth Grosz, and Valerie Walkerdine. In this sense, Butler's work can be seen as being part of an intellectual *zeitgeist*, temporally and contextually situated ideas and politics emerging in response to a particular set of concerns and in the light of a particular set of conceptual resources with which to engage these, and through interrelated but potentially separate endeavors rather than through the work of a given writer. It might be argued, then, that we would have found ourselves somewhere like "here" without Judith Butler, but the conceptual tools her work develops have undoubtedly been profoundly useful for getting us "here."

Conceptual tools—making subjects

The nature of the person, or subject; the limits of "who" this subject might be; the constraints and disavowals that are intrinsic to particular subject positions; the reasons why we might be attached to forms of subjectivity that appear to injure us; and the potential for subject positions to be resisted or mean something else are all concerns at the heart of Judith Butler's work. These concerns are connected to feminist, queer, anti-racist, and disability politics that aim to move beyond claims for "recognition" of their group identity and "equality" for their members to a politics concerned to trouble and unsettle notions of fixed identities and the privileges and exclusions that work through these. This is because these "identity politics" are seen as working to constrain group members, at the same time as offering them recognition, and also acting further to exclude others who do not fit the group identity. I say more about these politics later; first I turn to this understanding of the subject.

The work of Foucault provides an important point of departure for Butler and for many education scholars who engage with her work. Foucault's ideas about power, knowledge, and discourse are key. Foucault (1991) sets the idea of power that is *disciplinary* or *productive* alongside the more usual conception of power as something that is held by the powerful and wielded over the powerless, in Foucault's terms *sovereign power*. Foucault (1991) sees this disciplinary power as being produced and having its effects in the micro-circuits of ideas and practice, focusing in particular on the way that institutionalized practices, or technologies, make the person visible and knowable to others as well as to her/himself. Allied to this idea of power as productive is the idea of knowledge as located and partial (Foucault, 2002). For Foucault, knowledge is inseparable from the circulation of power—he posits the notion of power/knowledge to express this and suggests that this is evident and effected in discourse (Foucault, 1990, 1991). In a Foucauldian sense, discourses are multiple and shifting systems of knowledge with varied and potentially porous statuses ranging from what is taken as self-evident and valorized—a "regime of truth"—through to what is unspeakable or ridiculed—"disavowed" or "subjugated" knowledges (Foucault, 1990). Discourse, then, refers to much more than talk: discourses are cited by and circulate in speech and writing, as well as visual representations, bodily movements and gestures, and social and institutional practices.

This understanding of power as productive and implicated in the making of and surveillance of subjects, who are in turn self-surveillant, and the idea that this productive power is itself produced in discourses that make claims to knowledge and so frame what is knowable, are taken up and developed in Butler's thinking about the subject.

Performativity, subjectivation, and intelligibility

Notions of performativity, subjectivation, and intelligibility all play a significant part in Butler's work for understanding the contemporary subject and have been drawn on heavily in sociological engagements with empirical accounts of education.

Performativity

A useful starting point for understanding performativity is Butler's engagement with a debate between Austin and Derrida (see Derrida, 1988). In Austin, performatives are things that are said that *make something happen*, and while illocutionary performatives always have the effect they speak, perlocutionary performatives may not have an immediate effect, may have no effect at all, or may have a different effect than the one expected (Austin, 1962). Austin sees these as failures or "infelicities." In contrast, Derrida suggests an inherent "contextual break" between the intentions of a speaker and the meaning and effect of a performative; instead of thinking about "infelicities," he conceives of a space of performative "misfire," a space where the meaning and the effects of communication might change (see Derrida, 1988). Butler's use of the idea is guided by Derrida's reading of the inherent break between performative and effect and the risk and promise of misfire, and situated in a Foucauldian understanding of discourse and relations of productive power. She defines the performative as:

> [T]hat discursive practice that enacts or produces that which it names.
>
> (Butler, 1993: 13)

And:

> Discursive performativity appears to produce that which it names, to enact its own referent, to name and to do, to name and to make . . . [g]enerally speaking, a performative functions to produce that which it declares.
>
> (Butler, 1993: 107)

Such performatives make subjects through their deployment in the classificatory systems, categories, and names that are used to designate, differentiate, and sort people. According to Butler (1990, 1993, 1997a, 2004a), designations such as "boy" and "girl," "man" and "woman" are performative—they *create* the gendered subject that they name. Furthermore, these performatives do this while appearing to be just *descriptive*. By appearing to be descriptive, they create the *illusion* of genders' *prior* existence. So, while it appears that the subject *expresses* a gender, this is actually a performative *effect* of gender categorizations and their use. Suturing this idea to Bourdieu's notion of habitus, Butler also offers an account of the performative force of forms of embodiment and bodily practice, suggesting that: "the bodily *habitus* constitutes a tacit form of performativity, a citational chain lived and believed at the level of the body" (Butler 1997a: 155).

Butler's understanding of the performative has been taken up in a range of work in the sociology of education to make sense of how the discourses of gender, sexuality, race, ethnicity, religion, social class, ability, and disability circulating in schools and other education spaces might operate as performatives. Reflecting the critique of identity politics concerned with recognition that I indicated earlier, this take-up has been most evident among education scholars whose concern with inequalities leads them to focus on the ways that subject positions marked by gender, class, and so on are constituted and regulated through the everyday practices of teachers, students, and educational institutions. For this reason, the notion of the performative has been particularly useful to those researching practices at the micro level: using detailed ethnographic observations and interviews, as well as readings of popular and cultural artefacts such as films, television, media representations, websites, fashion, and so on to explore how discursive performatives constitute and regulate education's subjects.

For instance, in a paper in *Gender and education* (Youdell, 2005) I show how the names that students call each other, whether in friendship or judgment, are not simply descriptors with various degrees of accuracy, but are performatives with various degrees of force and with significant implications:

Virgin girls, slapper girls, and other girls

DY (the researcher, mid/late twenties, woman, White)
Molly, Nicola, Diane, Annie, Milli (year 11 students, girls, White)

Sitting in a group around a table in the year base while the rest of the tutor group are in a PSE lesson. The group is debating whether or not particular boys are virgins.

DY: How do you know if people are virgins or not?
Molly: I dunno, because people don't give a shit.
Diane: (*indicating Nicola*) she ain't.
Nicola: (*shouting, high pitch*) I am Diane!
Molly: (*laughing*) she ain't.
DY: How do you know?
Molly: It's just the way she goes round.
DY: What about . . .?
Molly: (*interrupting*) Puts herself across to boys.
DY: What does she do?
Molly: She goes running up to them and cuddling them and (*impersonating Nicola*) "Oooh."
Nicola: (*screeching*) No I don't!
DY: She flirts a little bit?
Molly: Yes, and she goes, "Ah, I'll have sex with you later if you open the door."
Nicola: (*laughing*) I do not say things like that!
[. . .]
Molly: And [boy] goes "Ok come on then, lets go" and she actually walks up to him and goes "Come on."
Nicola: (*more serious, agitated*) But I'm still joking around, I'm just having a laugh Molly!
Molly: Yeah but people like [boy] and [boy], they'll take it differently and think "Ah, she's a right little slapper" and that. Think about what happened to [girl].
Nicola: Sorry, I ain't gonna spend the night shagging someone if I don't love them and trust them, I ain't gonna shag anyone that I ain't going out with.

(Interview, Youdell, 2005: 260–261)

In the paper, I suggest that this scene illustrates not a contest over the "fact" of virgin/not-virgin, but the very processes of being constituted in these ways. Through the girls' dialogue, it becomes evident that what "counts" here is the meaning that boys will make of Nicola's practices; how they will "take it." And the risk asserted is that certain boys, whose performative namings are understood as having particular authority and force, will constitute Nicola as a "right little slapper." That is, if these boys constitute Nicola as slapper this is likely to have effects, and Nicola will *be* slapper. Molly presents a virgin/whore dichotomy established by boys, yet, in "warning" Nicola of the risks she runs, Molly exposes the role that girls play in policing the boundaries of this dichotomy and implicates girls in the performative constitution of themselves and other girls within its terms. The threat of "slapper" implicit in Molly"s "warning" leads Nicola to concede ultimately that she is not a virgin but that she only has sex with boys if "I love them and trust them," that is, if she is in a relationship. This "admission" may be Nicola's attempt to constitute herself in terms of acceptable heterosexual feminine desire and so differentiate herself from slapper and pre-empt this performative.

This analysis demonstrates how normative hetero-feminine subjects are constituted and regulated in school spaces through the everyday, mundane performative practices of young people and, by extension, exposes the failure of liberal approaches to gender equity to account for either everyday processes or young people's investments in such subjectivities. Readings such as this have been offered by a number of scholars in sociology of education, deepening understandings of how students recognized through particular intersecting categories of gender, race, and so on come to be performatively constituted as such and offering insights into how these performative constitutions are connected to educational inequalities. For instance, Mary Lou Rasmussen's (2006) book *Becoming subjects* draws on Butler's notion of the performative to analyze empirical accounts and cultural artefacts and offer an extensive analysis of the constitution of sexualities in secondary schools. Emma Renold's (2005) book *Junior sexualities* draws on ethnographic data generated in primary school to offer an analysis of the performative constitution of younger children's subjectivities, arguing that gender constitutions are simultaneously constitutions of young sexualities. Ringrose and Renold (2009) use the performative to interrogate the gendered constitution of violence in schools. I have used the notion of race performativity to understand processes of racialization and how particular raced subject positions are tied to particular performative judgments of students by schools (Youdell, 2003). And Sue Saltmarsh and myself (Saltmarsh and Youdell, 2004) and Linda Graham (2007) have developed analyses of the performative constitution of students as "special" and "problematic" in education policy and institutional and teacher practices.

An important development in understanding the performative constitution of students in schools has been in work that unravels the performative constitution, not of single classificatory systems, e.g. gender, or single categorizations, e.g. girl, or obviously entangled subjectivities, such as sex-gender, but of *multiple and intersecting performatives* that make multifaceted subjects and subjectivities. For instance, Mary Lou Rasmussen and Valerie Harwood (2003) explore a range of interconnecting performatives, including race, gender, sexuality, size, and ability, whose injurious effects work together to make schooling untenable for one girl. In a similar vein, my book *Impossible bodies, impossible selves* (Youdell, 2006) examines the ways that constellations of performative categorizations come together in students' and teachers' discursive practices, sometimes colliding and sometimes cohering.

Subjectivation

Butler (1997a, 1997b, 2004a) also makes use of the idea of "subjectivation," sometimes also referred to as "subjectivization" or "subjectification"; an idea that Butler draws from Foucault (1982) and that in turn connects to Althusser's (1971) idea of subjection. According to Foucault, the person is *subjectivated*—s/he is at once rendered a subject and subjected to relations of power through discourse. That is, productive power constitutes and constrains, but does not determine, the subjects with whom it is concerned. In engaging with Foucault's account of the relationship between the subject and power, Butler asserts that:

> "subjectivation" . . . denotes both the becoming of the subject and the process of
> subjection—one inhabits the figure of autonomy only by becoming subjected to a power,

a subjection which implies a radical dependency. . . . Subjection is, literally, the *making* of a subject, the principle of regulation according to which a subject is formulated or produced. Such subjection is a kind of power that not only unilaterally *acts on* a given individual as a form of domination, but also *activates* or forms the subject. Hence, subjection is neither simply the domination of a subject nor its production, but designates a certain kind of restriction *in* production.

(Butler, 1997b: 83–84, original emphases)

Subjectivation, in some sense, can be seen as an extension and elaboration of the idea of performativity, and one that foregrounds the relationship between these constitutive processes and productive power. Indeed, we might understand the discursive performative as being an aspect of, or culpable in, processes of subjectivation. Butler's engagement with the idea of subjectivation has been a more recent turn, and current work in the sociology of education is making increasing use of this notion. In a 2006 special edition of the *British Journal of Sociology of Education*, dedicated to the usefulness of Butler's work in the field, Bronwyn Davies demonstrates how Butler has developed the Foucauldian notion of subjectivation and shows how the notion can be used to interrogate encounters between teachers and students (Davies, 2006). Likewise, in my contribution to the issue, I use subjectivation to analyze how young people named as "Arabic" are constituted within the terms of prevailing anti-Islamic discourses through the practices of teachers and the teachers' incorporation of the young people's own practices (Youdell, 2006b).

Intelligibility

Notions of intelligibility, recognizability, and speakability are useful for thinking about how performative constitutions are constrained and why they are necessarily embroiled in processes of subjectivation. Discursive processes of subjectivation and the discursive performatives involved in these processes have to make sense to work—they have to be *"recognizable"* (Butler, 1997a: 5, original emphasis) in the discourses that are circulating in the settings and moments in which they are deployed.

In my book *Impossible bodies, impossible selves* (Youdell, 2006a), I stress that, in school contexts, being a schoolgirl or boy, being gifted, having emotional or behaviour difficulties "makes sense"—these subjects are intelligible because they cite enduring institutional discourses about who students are and what schools are about. Performatives that do not make sense in the discourses that frame schooling, or that are counter to prevailing institutional discourses, may fail or may act to constitute a subject outside the bounds of acceptability as a student. As I highlighted above, these processes of subjectivation are processes of "restriction *in* production" (Butler 1997b: 83–84, original emphasis). This understanding of the ongoing subjectivation of subjects through discursive performativity enables us to see how schools come to be suffused with exclusions, with what the student-subject cannot be, with who cannot be the student-subject—the "impossible students" and "impossible learners" (Youdell, 2006a). As Bronwyn Davies notes: "[s]ubjects, and this includes school students, who are constituted as lying outside intelligibility are faced with the constitutive force of a language that grants them no intelligible space" (Davies, 2006: 434). These ideas demonstrate that subjecthood—and studenthood—comes with costs. This emphasis on intelligibility intersects with notions of recognition and mis-recognition from psychoanalysis, bringing into play the subject's unconscious desire to be recognized and, indeed, the necessity of this recognition for being a subject. This extends a Foucauldian notion of subjectivation by offering us tools for understanding further why subjects might take up, and be attached to, subject positions that may appear to injure, disadvantage, or constrain them.

Conceptual tools—political subjects

Understanding students as subjectivated through ongoing performative constitution has at times been interpreted as a pessimistic or even fatalistic move that leaves no space for action or change. Yet spaces for action and change are evident in the work of Foucault and Butler, both of whom emphasize that subjectivation involves subjection to power *and* recognition as a subject— a recognition that includes the subject's capacity to act. In the remainder of this chapter, I detail Butler's conception of *discursive agency* and the *performative politics* this suggests, demonstrating these in work in sociology of education that maps how performatives can be intercepted in order to constitute students differently.

Discursive agency and performative politics

Building on Derrida's assertion that any performative is open to misfire and Foucault's insistence that no discourse is guaranteed, Butler suggests that discourse and its performative effects offer political potential. Returning to processes of subjectivation, Butler stresses that:

> the one who names, who works within language to find a name for another, is presumed to be already named, positioned within language as one who is already subject to the founding or inaugurating address. This suggests that such a subject in language is positioned as both addressed and addressing, and that the very possibility of naming another requires that one first be named. The subject of speech who is named becomes, potentially, one who might well name another in time.
>
> (Butler, 1997a: 29)

Butler calls the subjectivated subject's capacity to act within discourse and to subjectivate another "discursive agency." This is not the agency of a sovereign subject who exerts its will. Rather, this agency is derivative, an effect of discursive power:

> Because the agency of the subject is not a property of the subject, an inherent will or freedom, but an effect of power, it is *constrained but not determined* in advance . . . As the agency of a postsovereign subject, its discursive operation is delimited in advance but also open to a further unexpected delimitation.
>
> (Butler, 1997a: 139–140, my emphasis)

Agency is, therefore, simultaneously enabled and constrained through discourse. This subject retains intention and can seek to realize this intent through the deployment of discursive practices; however, the effects of this deployment cannot be guaranteed. By thinking of agency as discursive we are able to conceive of a political subject who might challenge prevailing constitutions as part of a set of self-conscious discursive practices, without assuming a rational, self-knowing subject who exists outside subjectivation.

This understanding of discursive agency allows Butler to imagine insurrectionary practices that would involve:

> decontextualizing and recontextualizing . . . terms through radical acts of public mis-appropriation such that the conventional relation between [naming and meaning] might become tenuous and even broken over time.
>
> (Butler, 1997a: 100)

The sedimented meanings of enduring discourses might be unsettled and *re*signified or *re*inscribed. And subjugated or silenced discourses might be deployed in, and made meaningful in, contexts from which they have been barred. This does not mean that a performative politics is simply a matter of asserting a new meaning, but nor does it render such a politics hopeless: normative meanings are resistant to *re*inscription but they are never immune from it. As Butler writes:

> contexts inhere in certain speech acts in ways that are very difficult to shake . . . [but] contexts are never fully determined in advance . . . the possibility for the speech act to take on a non-ordinary meaning, to function in contexts where it has not belonged, is precisely the political promise of the performative.
>
> (Butler, 1997a: 161)

In thinking about education, this suggests that the enduring inequalities that are produced through the performative practices of institutions, teachers, and students might be unsettled. In various ways, my work has been concerned to show how young people in schools are already engaged in practices that can be understood in these terms: everyday practices that resist the normative meanings and ascribed subjectivities of the institution and instead assert and enact meanings and subjectivities of their own. In particular, in relation to students subjectivated in ways that act to wound or exclude—gay students, Black students, Arabic students, disabled or special students—I have detailed not just processes of subjectivation but also practice of resistance, performative politics in action (see Saltmarsh and Youdell, 2004; Youdell 2004a,b, 2006a,b). Yet young people's everyday practices of self do not resemble the organized action of the traditional left or newer movements in identity politics or global coalitions, such as anti-capitalist or eco-activism.

What is pressing to explore in sociology of education at this juncture, then, is whether these performative practices can, need, or should be multiplied and/or corralled in ways that make them more recognizable as political practices; whether we might better reconfigure our understanding of what "counts" as the political; and whether we need more than a performative politics if we are to shift sedimented meanings and enduring inequalities in education and, if so, what understandings of power and political tactics we might take up. These are questions that are currently being explored by education scholars such as Valerie Hey (2006); Emma Renold and Debbie Epstein (2008); Jessica Ringrose (2008); Elizabeth Atkinson and Renee DePalma (2009); and myself (Youdell 2006c, 2010 forthcoming).

References

Althusser, L. (1971) "Ideology and ideological state apparatuses" (trans. B. Brewster), in *Lenin and philosophy*, London: Monthly Review Press, pp. 170–186.

Atkinson, E. and DePalma, R. (2009) "Un-believing the matrix: queering consensual heteronormativity," *Gender and Education*, 21(1): 17–29.

Austin, J.L. (1962) *How to do things with words*, Cambridge, MA: Harvard University Press.

Butler, J. (1990) *Gender trouble: feminism and the subversion of identity*, London: Routledge.

—— (1991) "Imitation and gender insubordination," in D. Fuss (ed.) *Inside/out: lesbian theories, gay theories*, London: Routledge.

—— (1992) "Contingent foundations: feminism and the question 'postmodernism'," in J. Butler and J.W. Scott (eds) *Feminists theorise the political*, London: Routledge, pp. 3–21.

—— (1993) *Bodies that matter: on the discursive limits of "sex,"* New York: Routledge.

—— (1997a) *Excitable speech: a politics of the performative*, London: Routledge.

—— (1997b) *The psychic life of power: theories in subjection*, Stanford, CA: Stanford University Press.

—— (2004a) *Undoing gender*, London: Routledge.

Davies, B. (2006) "Subjectification: the relevance of Butler's analysis for education," *British Journal of Sociology of Education* 27(4): 425–438.

Delamont, S. and Atkinson, P. (1995) *Fighting familiarity: essays on education and ethnography*, Cresskill, NJ: Hampton Press.

Derrida, J. (1988) "Signature event context," in J. Derrida (ed.) *Limited Inc.*, Elvanston, IL: Northwestern University Press, pp. 1–23.

Foucault, M. (1982) "The subject and power" in H.L. Dreyfus and P. Rabinow *Michel Foucault: beyond hermenutics and structuralism*, Brighton: Harvester, pp. 208–226.

—— (1990) *The history of sexuality: an introduction*, vol. 1, London: Penguin.

—— (1991) *Discipline and punish: the birth of the prison*, London: Penguin.

—— (2002) *The order of things*, London: Routledge.

Graham, L.J. (2007) "Speaking of 'disorderly' objects: a poetics of pedagogical discourse," *Discourse* 28(1): 1–20.

Hey, V. (2006) "The politics of performative resignification: translating Judith Butler's theoretical discourse and its potential for a sociology of education," *British Journal of Sociology of Education* 27(4): 439–457.

Rasmussen, M. (2006) *Becoming subjects*, London: Routledge.

Rasmussen, M.L. and Harwood, V. (2003) "Performativity, youth and injurious speech," *Teaching Education* 14(1): 25–36.

Renold, E. (2005) *Girls, boys and junior sexualities: exploring childrens' gender and sexual relations in the primary school*, London: RoutledgeFalmer.

Renold, E. and Epstein, D. (2008) "Sexualities, schooling and schizoid agendas," Negotiating Difference and Sameness: Sexualities, Schooling and Schizoid Agendas Conference, London.

Ringrose, J. (2008) "Intensifying affect: sex, gender and conflict in young people's negotiations of online social networking sites," The Emotional Geographies of Education Conference, London.

—— and Renold, E. (2009 forthcoming) "Boys and girls performing normative violence in schools: a gendered critique of bully discourses," in C. Barter and D. Berridge (eds) *Children behaving badly? Exploring peer violence between children and young people*, John Wiley & Sons.

Saltmarsh, S. and Youdell, D. (2004) "'Special sport' for misfits and losers: educational triage and the constitution of schooled subjectivities," *International Journal of Inclusive Education* 8(4): 353–371.

Youdell, D. (2003) "Identity traps or how black students fail: the interactions between biographical, sub-cultural, and learner identities," *British Journal of Sociology of Education* 24(1): 3–20.

—— (2004a) "Wounds and reinscriptions: schools, sexualities and performative subjects," *Discourse* 25(4): 477–493.

—— (2004b) "Bent as a ballet dancer: the possibilities and limits for a legitimate homosexuality in school," in M.L. Rasmussen, E. Rofes and S. Talburt (eds) *Youth and sexualities: pleasure, subversion and insubordination in and out of schools*, Basingstoke: Palgrave Macmillan.

—— (2005) "Sex-gender-sexuality: how sex, gender and sexuality constellations are constituted in secondary schools," *Gender and Education*, 17(3): 149–170.

—— (2006a) *Impossible bodies, impossible selves: exclusions and student subjectivities*, Dordrecht: Springer.

—— (2006b) "Subjectivation and performative politics—Butler thinking Althusser and Foucault: intelligibility, agency and the raced-nationed-religioned subjects of education," *British Journal of Sociology of Education* 27(4): 511–528.

—— (2006c) "Diversity, inequality, and a post-structural politics for education," *Discourse* 27(1): 33–42.

—— (2010 forthcoming) *School trouble: identity, power and politics in education*, London: Routledge.

Part 2
Social processes and practices

13

Doing the work of God
Home schooling and gendered labor

Michael W. Apple

Introduction

In *Educating the "right" way* (Apple, 2006; see also Apple *et al.*, 2003), I spend a good deal of time detailing the world as seen through the eyes of "authoritarian populists." These are conservative groups of religious fundamentalists and evangelicals whose voices in the debates over social and educational policies are now increasingly powerful. I critically analyzed the ways in which they construct themselves as the "new oppressed," as people whose identities and cultures are ignored by, or attacked in, schools and the media. They have taken on subaltern identities and have (very selectively) re-appropriated the discourses and practices of figures such as Dr. Martin Luther King to lay claim to the fact that they are the last truly dispossessed groups. A considerable number of authoritarian populist families have made the choice to home school their children.

Home schooling is growing rapidly. Although I shall focus on the United States in this chapter, it is witnessing increasingly large rates of growth in many nations in Europe, in Australia, in Canada, and elsewhere (see Beck, 2008, 2006). However, it is not simply an atomistic phenomenon in which, one by one, isolated parents decide to reject organized public schools and teach their children at home. Home schooling is a *social movement*. It is a collective project, one with a history and a set of organizational and material supports (Stevens, 2001: 4).

While many educators devote a good deal of their attention to reforms such as charter schools, and such schools have received a good deal of positive press, there are far fewer children in charter schools than there are being home schooled. In 1996, home school advocates estimated that there are approximately 1.3 million children being home schooled in the United States. More recent estimates put the figure even higher. Given the almost reverential and rather romantic coverage in national and local media of home schooling, the numbers may in fact be much higher than this, and the growth curve undoubtedly is increasing. At the very least, more than 2.2 percent of school-age children in the United States are home schooled (Sampson, 2005).

The home schooling movement is not homogeneous. It includes people of a wide spectrum of political/ideological, religious, and educational beliefs. It cuts across racial and class lines

(Sampson, 2005). As Stevens notes, there are in essence two general groupings within the home school movement, "Christian" and "inclusive." There are some things that are shared across these fault lines, however: a sense that the standardized education offered by mainstream schooling interferes with their children's potential; that there is a serious danger when the state intrudes into the life of the family; that experts and bureaucracies are apt to impose their beliefs and are unable to meet the needs of families and children (Stevens, 2001: 4–7). These worries tap currents that are widespread within American culture and they too cut across particular social and cultural divides.

Demographic information on home schoolers is limited, but in general home schoolers seem to be somewhat better educated, slightly more affluent, and considerably more likely to be White than the population in the state in which they reside (Stevens, 2001: 11). Although it is important to recognize the diversity of the movement, it is just as crucial to understand that the largest group of people who home school have conservative religious and/or ideological commitments (Apple, 2006). Given the large number of conservative Christians in the home schooling movement, this picture matches the overall demographic patterns of evangelical Christians in general (Smith, 1998).

Based on a belief that schooling itself is a very troubled institution (but often with widely divergent interpretations of what has caused these troubles), home schoolers have created mechanisms where "horror stories" about schools are shared, as are stories of successful home schooling practices. The metaphors that describe what goes on in public schools and the dangers associated with them, especially those used by many conservative evangelical home schoolers, are telling. Stevens puts it in the following way:

> Invoking the rhetoric of illness ("cancer," "contagion") to describe the dangers of uncontrolled peer interaction, believers frame the child-world of school as a kind of jungle where parents send their kids only at risk of infection. The solution: keep them at home, away from that environment altogether.
>
> (2001: 53)

Given these perceived dangers, through groups that have been formed at both regional and national levels, home schooling advocates press departments of education and legislatures to guarantee their rights to home school their children. They have established communicative networks—newsletters, magazines, and increasingly the Internet—to build and maintain a community of fellow believers, a community that is often supported by ministries that reinforce the "wisdom" (and very often godliness) of their choice. And as we shall see, increasingly as well the business community has begun to realize that this can be a lucrative market (Stevens, 2001: 4). Religious publishers, for-profit publishing houses large and small, conservative colleges and universities, Internet entrepreneurs, and others have understood that a market in cultural goods—classroom materials, lesson plans, textbooks, religious material, CDs, and so forth—has been created. They have rushed both to respond to the expressed needs and to stimulate needs that are not yet recognized as needs themselves. But the market would not be there unless what created the opportunity for such a market—the successful identity work of the evangelical movement itself—had not provided the space in which such a market could operate.

Conservative Christian home schoolers are part of a larger evangelical movement that has been increasingly influential in education, in politics, and in cultural institutions such as the media (Apple, 2006; Binder, 2002). Nationally, White evangelicals constitute approximately

25 percent of the adult population in the United States (Green, 2000: 2). The evangelical population is growing steadily (Smith, 1998), as it actively provides subject positions and new identities for people who feel unmoored in a world where, for them, "all that is sacred is profaned" and where the tensions and structures of feeling of advanced capitalism do not provide either a satisfying emotional or spiritual life. The search for a "return"—in the face of major threats to what they see as accepted relations of gender/sex, of authority and tradition, of nation and family—is the guiding impulse behind the growth of this increasingly powerful social movement (Apple, 2006).

Home schooling and compromising with the state

A large portion of social movement activity targets the state (Amenta and Young, 1999: 30), and this is especially the case with the home schooling movement. Yet, although there is often a fundamental mistrust of the state among many religiously conservative home schoolers, there are a considerable number of such people who are willing to compromise with the state. They employ state programs and funds for their own tactical advantage. One of the clearest examples of this is the growing home schooling charter school movement in states such as California. Even though many of the parents involved in such programs believe that they do not want their children to be "brainwashed by a group of educators" and do not want to "leave [their] children off somewhere like a classroom and have them influenced and taught by someone that I am not familiar with" (Huerta, 2000: 177), a growing number of Christian conservative parents have become quite adept at taking advantage of government resources for their own benefit. By taking advantage of home school charter programs that connect independent families through the use of the Web, they are able to use public funding to support schooling that they had previously had to pay for privately (pp. 179–180). This is also one of the reasons that the figures on the number of parents who home school their children are unreliable.

But it is not only the conservative evangelical parents who are using the home schooling charter possibilities for their own benefit. School districts themselves are actively strategizing, employing such technological connections to enhance their revenue flow but maintaining existing enrolments or by actively recruiting home school parents to join a home school charter. This can be expected to increase given the economic crisis currently being experienced by so many nations. By creating a home school charter, one financially pressed small California school district was able to solve a good deal of its economic problems. Over the first two years of its operation, the charter school grew from 80 students to 750 (Huerta, 2000: 180). Since there are only very minimal reporting requirements, conservative Christian parents are able to act on their desire to keep government and secular influences at a distance, and, at the very same time, school districts are able to maintain that the children of these families are enrolled in public schooling and meeting the requirements of secular schooling.

Yet, we should be cautious of using the word "secular" here. It is clear from the learning records that the parents submit that there is a widespread use of religious materials in all of the content. Bible readings, devotional lessons, moral teachings directly from online vendors, and so on were widely integrated by the parents within the "secular" resources provided by the school.

Such content, and the lack of accountability for it, raises serious question about the use of public funding for overtly conservative religious purposes. It documents the power of Huerta's claim that "In an attempt to recast its authority in an era of fewer bureaucratic controls over schools, the state largely drops its pursuit of the common good as public authority is devolved to local families" (Huerta, 2000: 192). In the process, technologically linked homes are reconstituted as a "public" school, but a school in which the very meaning of public has been radically transformed so that it mirrors the needs of conservative religious form and content.

Home schooling as gendered labor

Even with the strategic use of state resources to assist efforts, home schooling takes hard work. But to go further we need to ask an important question: *Who* does the labor? Much of this labor is hidden from view. Finding and organizing materials, teaching, charting progress, establishing and maintaining a "proper" environment, the emotional labor of caring for, as well as instructing, children—and the list goes on—all of this requires considerable effort. And most of this effort is made by *women* (Stevens, 2001: 15).

Because home schooling is largely women's work, it combines an extraordinary amount of physical, cultural, and emotional labor. This should not surprise us. As Stambach and David (2005) have powerfully argued, and as Andre-Bechely (2005) and Griffith and Smith (2005) have empirically demonstrated, assumptions about gender and about the ways in which mothers as "caretakers" are asked to take on such issues as educational choice, planning, and, in the case we are discussing here, actually doing the education itself underpin most of the realities surrounding education. But home schooling heightens this. It constitutes an intensification of women's work in the home, since it is added on to the already extensive responsibilities that women have within the home and especially within conservative religious homes, with their division of labor in which men may be active, but are seen as "helpers" of their wives, who carry the primary responsibility within the domestic sphere. The demands of such intensified labor have consistently led women to engage in quite creative ways of dealing with their lives.

This labor and the meanings attached to it by women themselves need to be situated into a much longer history and a much larger context. A number of people have argued that many women see rightist religious and social positions and the groups that support them as providing a non-threatening, familiar framework of discourse and practice that centers directly upon what they perceive to be issues of vital and personal concern: immorality, social disorder, crime, the family, and schools. Yet, the feelings of personal connection are not sufficient. Rightist action in both the "public" and the "private" spheres (see Fraser (1989) regarding how these concepts themselves are fully implicated in the history of gendered realities, differential power, and struggles) empowers them as women. Depending on the context, they are positioned as "respectable, selfless agents of change deemed necessary, or as independent rebels" (Bacchetta and Power, 2002: 6).

Usually, fundamentalist and evangelical women are depicted as essentially dedicated to acting on and furthering the goals of religiously conservative men (Brasher, 1998: 3). This is much too simplistic. Rather, the message is more complex and compelling—and connected to a very clear understanding of the realities of many women's lives. Women are to have not a passive but a very active engagement in their family life and the world that impinges on it. They can and must "shape their husband's actions and alter disruptive family behaviors." Further, only a strong woman could mediate the pressures and the often intensely competitive norms and values that men brought home with them from the "world of work." Capitalism may be "God's economy" (see Apple, 2006), but allowing its norms to dominate the home could be truly destructive. Women, in concert with "responsible" men, could provide the alternative but complementary assemblage of values so necessary to keep the world at bay and to use the family as the foundation for both protecting core religious values and sending forth children armed against the dangers of a secular and profane world.

Divine creation has ordained that women and men are different types of being. Although they complement each other, each has distinctly different tasks to perform. Such sacred gender walls are experienced, not as barriers, but as providing and legitimating a space for women's independent action and power. Interfering with such action and power in this sphere is also interfering in God's plan (Brasher, 1998: 12–13).

This vision of independence and of what might be called "counter-hegemonic thinking" is crucial. Bringing conservative evangelical religion back to the core of schooling positions secular schooling as hegemonic. It enables rightist women to interpret their own actions as independent and free thinking—but always in the service of God. Let me say more about this here.

Solving contradictions

One of the elements that keeps the Christian Right such a vital and growing social movement is the distinctive internal structure of evangelical Protestantism. Evangelicalism combines orthodox Christian beliefs with an intense individualism (Green, 2000: 2).

This is a key to understanding the ways in which what looks like never-ending and intensified domestic labor from the outside is interpreted in very different ways from the point of view of conservative religious women, who willingly take on the labor of home schooling and add it to their already considerable responsibilities in the domestic sphere. Such conservative ideological forms see women as subservient to men and as having the primary responsibility of building and defending a vibrant, godly "fortress-home" as part of "God's plan" (Apple, 2006). Yet, it would be wrong to see women in rightist religious or ideological movements as only being called upon to submit to authority per se. Such "obedience" is also grounded in a call to act on their duty as women (Enders, 2002: 89). This is what might best be seen as *activist selflessness*, one in which the supposedly submerged self reemerges in the activist role of defender of one's home, family, children, and God's plan. Lives are made meaningful and satisfying—and identities supported—in the now reconstituted private and public sphere in this way.

Protecting and educating one's children, caring for the intimate and increasingly fragile bonds of community and family life, worries about personal safety, and all of this in an exploitative and often disrespectful society—these themes are not only the province of the Right and should not be only the province of women. Yet, we have to ask how identifiable people are mobilized around and by these themes, and by whom.

The use of a kind of "maternalist" discourse and a focus on women's role as "mother" and as someone whose primary responsibility is in the home and the domestic sphere does not necessarily prevent women from exercising power in the public sphere. In fact, it can serve as a powerful justification for such action and actually *reconstitutes* the public sphere. Educating one's children at home so that they are given armor to equip them to transform their and others' lives outside the home establishes the home as a perfect model for religiously motivated ethical conduct for all sets of social institutions (see Apple, 2006). This tradition, what has been called "social housekeeping," can then claim responsibility for non-familial social spaces and can extend the idealized mothering role of women well beyond the home. In Marijke du Toit's words, it was and can still be used to forge "a new, more inclusive definition of the political" (2002: 67).

All of this helps us make sense of why many of the most visible home school advocates devote a good deal of their attention to "making sense of the social category of motherhood." As a key part of "a larger script of idealized family relations, motherhood is a lead role in God's plan" for authoritarian populist religious conservatives (Stevens, 2001: 76). Again in Stevens' words, "One of the things that home schooling offers, then, is a renovated domesticity—a full-time motherhood made richer by the tasks of teaching, and [by] some of the status that goes along with those tasks" (p. 83).

Yet it is not only the work internal to the home that is important here. Home schooling is outward looking as well in terms of women's tasks. In many instances, home schooling is a collective project. It requires organizational skills to coordinate connections and cooperative activities (support groups, field trips, play groups, time off from the responsibilities that mothers have, etc.) and to keep the movement itself vibrant at local and regional levels. Here too, women do the largest amount of the work. This has led to other opportunities for women as advocates and entrepreneurs. Thus, the development and marketing of some of the most popular curriculum packages, management guides, self-help and devotional materials, and so on has been done by women. Indeed, the materials reflect the fact that home schooling is women's work, with a considerable number of the pictures in the texts and promotional material showing mothers and children together (Stevens, 2001: 83–96). A considerable number of the national advocates for evangelically based home schooling are activist women as well.

Marketing God

Advocacy is one thing, being able to put the advocated policy into practice is quite another. In order to actually *do* home schooling, a large array of plans, materials, advice, and even solace must be made available. "Godly schooling" creates a market. Even with the burgeoning market for all kinds of home schooling, it is clear that conservative evangelicals and fundamentalists have the most to choose from in terms of educational and religious (the separation is often fictional) curricula, lessons, books, and inspirational material (Stevens, 2001: 54). Such materials not only augment the lessons that home schooling parents develop, but increasingly they become *the* lessons in mathematics, literacy, science, social studies, and all of the other subjects that are taught. This kind of material also usually includes homework assignments and tests, as well as all of the actual instructional material. Thus, a complete "package" can be assembled or purchased whole in a way that enables committed parents to create an entire universe of educational experiences that is both rigorously sequenced and tightly controlled—and prevents unwanted "pollution" from the outside world. Much of this material is easily ordered on the Web and is based in an inerrantist approach to the Bible and a literalist reading of Genesis and creation, one in which, for example, evolution is dismissed (Apple, 2006; Numbers, 2006). The difference between right and wrong is seen as answerable only through reference to biblical teachings (Stevens, 2001: 55).

While there are pedagogic differences among these sets of materials, all of them are deeply committed to integrating biblical messages, values, and training throughout the entire curriculum. Most not only reproduce the particular biblically based worldviews of the parents, but they also create an educational environment that relies on a particular vision of "appropriate" schooling, one that is organized around highly sequenced formal lessons that have an expressly moral aim. Technological resources such as videos are marketed that both provide the home schooler with a model of how education should be done and the resources for actually carrying it out (Stevens, 2001: 56).

The *organizational form* that is produced here is very important. As I have argued elsewhere (Apple, 2006), since much of the religiously conservative home schooling movement has a sense of purity and danger in which all elements of the world have a set place, such an organization of both knowledge and pedagogy embodies the ideological structure underlying the evangelical universe. As Bernstein (1977) reminds us, it is often in the form of the curriculum that the social cement that organizes our consciousness at its most basic level is reproduced.

Importance is given to structured educational experiences that are infused with strong moral messages. This is not surprising given the view of a secular world filled with possible sins, temptations, and dangers. The emphasis then on equipping children with an armor of strong belief supports a pedagogical belief that *training* is a crucial pedagogic act. Although children's interests have to be considered, these are less important than preparing children for living in a world where God's word rules. This commitment to giving an armor of "right beliefs" "nourishes demands for school material" (Stevens, 2001: 60). A market for curriculum materials, workbooks, lesson plans, rewards for doing fine work such as merit badges, videotapes and CDs, and so many other things that make home schooling seem more doable is not only created out of a strategy of aggressive marketing and of using the Web as a major mechanism for such marketing, but it is also created and stimulated because of the ideological and emotional elements that underpin the structures of feeling that help organize the conservative evangelical home schooler's world (see Apple, 2006).

Technology and the realities of daily life

Of course, parents are not puppets. Although the parent may purchase or download material that is highly structured and at times inflexible, by the very nature of home schooling parents are constantly faced with the realities of their children's lives, their boredom, their changing interests. Here, chat rooms and Internet resources become even more important. Advice manuals, prayers, suggestions for how one should deal with recalcitrant children, and biblically inspired inspirational messages about how important the hard work of parenting is and how one can develop the patience to keep doing it—all of this provides ways of dealing with the immense amount of educational and especially *emotional* labor that home schooling requires.

The technology enables women, who may be rather isolated in the home owing to the intense responsibilities of home schooling, to have virtual but still intimate emotional connections. It also requires skill, something that ratifies the vision of self that often accompanies home schooling parents. We don't need "experts." With hard work and creative searching, we can engage in a serious and disciplined education by ourselves. Thus, the technology provides for solace, acknowledging and praying for each other's psychic wounds and tensions—and at the same time enhances one's identity as someone who is intellectually worthy, who can wisely choose appropriate knowledge and values. What, hence, may seem like a form of anti-intellectualism is in many ways exactly the opposite. Its rejection of the secular expertise of the school and the state is instead based on a vision of knowledgeable parents, and especially mothers, who have a kind of knowledge taken from the ultimate source—God.

Higher education and an expanded mission field

So far I have focused on elementary and secondary level education. But home schooling's reach has extended to higher education as well. A prime example is Patrick Henry College. Patrick

151

Henry is a college largely for religiously conservative, home schooled students. With its motto of "For Christ and for liberty," it has two major emphases—religion *and* government. The principles that animate its educational activities are quite clear in the following description:

> The Vision of Patrick Henry College is to aid in the transformation of American society by training Christian students to serve God and mankind with a passion for righteousness, justice and mercy, through careers of public service and cultural influence.
>
> The Distinctives of Patrick Henry College include practical apprenticeship methodology; a deliberate outreach to home schooled students; financial independence; a general education core based on the classical liberal arts; a dedication to mentoring and disciplining Christian students; and a community life that promotes virtue, leadership, and strong, life-long commitments to God, family and society.
>
> The Mission of the Department of Government is to promote practical application of biblical principles and the original intent of the founding documents of the American republic, while preparing students for lives of public service, advocacy and citizen leadership.
>
> (www.phc.edu/about/FundamentalStatements.asp)

These aims are both laudable and yet worrisome. Create an environment where students learn to play active roles in reconstructing both their lives and the larger society. But make certain that the society they wish to build is based wholly on principles that themselves are not open to social criticism by non-believers. Only those anointed by their particular version of God and only a society built upon the vision held by the anointed are legitimate. All else is sinful.

Thus, for all of its creative uses of technology, its understanding of "market needs" and how to fill them, its personal sacrifices, the immense labor of the mostly women who are engaged in the work of actually doing it, and its rapid growth fostered by good press and creative mobilizing strategies, a good deal of home schooling speaks the language of authoritarian populism. There's an inside and an outside. And for many authoritarian populists, the only way to protect the inside is to change the outside so that it mirrors the religious impulses and commitments of the inside. Doing this is hard political, educational, and emotional work. And new technologies clearly are playing a growing role in such personal and social labor.

Conclusion

In this chapter, I have examined a number of the complexities involved in the cultural and political efforts within a rapidly growing movement that has claimed subaltern status. I have argued that we need to examine the social movement that provides the context for home schooling and the identities that are being constructed within that social movement. I have also argued that we need to analyze critically the kind of labor that is required in home schooling, *who* is engaged in such labor, and how such labor is interpreted by the actors who perform it. Only in this way can we understand the lived problems that home schoolers actually face and the solutions that seem sensible to them. And I have pointed to how the space for production of such "solutions" is increasingly occupied by ideological and/or commercial interests who have responded to and enlarged a market to "fill the needs" of religiously conservative home schoolers.

A good deal of my focus has been on the work of mothers, of "Godly women," who have actively created new identities for themselves (and their children and husbands) and have found in such things as new technologies solutions to a huge array of difficult personal and political problems in their daily lives. Such Godly women are not that much different from any of us. But they are "dedicated to securing for themselves and their families a thoroughly religious and conservative life" (Brasher, 1998: 29). And they do this with uncommon sacrifice and creativity.

The picture I have presented is complicated, but then so too is reality. On the one hand, one of the dynamics we are seeing is social disintegration, that is, the loss of legitimacy of a dominant institution that supposedly bound us together—the common school. Yet, and very importantly, what we are also witnessing is the use of things such as the Internet, not to "de-traditionalize" society but, in the cases I have examined here, to *re-traditionalize* parts of it. However, to call this phenomenon simply re-traditionalization is to miss the ways in which such technologies are also embedded, not only in traditional values and structures of feeling. They are also participating in a more "modern" project, one in which self-actualized individualism intersects with the history of social maternalism, which itself intersects with the reconstitution of masculinities as well.

But such maternalism needs to be seen as both positive and negative, and not only in its partial revivification of elements of patriarchal relations—although obviously this set of issues must not be ignored in any way. We need to respect the labor and the significant sacrifices of home schooling mothers (and the fathers as well, since the question of altered masculinities in home schooling families is an important topic that needs to be focused upon in a way that complements what I have done here). This sensitivity to the complexities and contradictions that are so deeply involved in what these religiously motivated parents are attempting is perhaps best seen in the words of Jean Hardisty when she reflects on populist rightist movements in general:

> I continue to believe that, within that movement, there are people who are decent and capable of great caring, who are creating community and finding coping strategies that are enabling them to lead functional lives in a cruel and uncaring late capitalist environment.
>
> (Hardisty, 1999: 2–3)

However, recognizing such caring, labor, and sacrifice—and the creative uses of technologies that accompany them—should not make us lose sight of what this labor and these sacrifices also produce. Godly technologies, godly schooling, and godly identities can be personally satisfying and make life personally meaningful in a world in which traditions are either destroyed or commodified. But at what cost to those who don't share the ideological vision that seems so certain in the minds of those who produce it?

References

Amenta, E. and Young, M.P. (1999) "Making an impact: conceptual and methodological implications of the collective goods criterion," in M. Guigni, D. McAdam and C. Tilly (eds) *How social movements matter*, Minneapolis, MN: University of Minnesota Press, pp. 22–41.

Andre-Bechely, L. (2005) *Could it be otherwise? Parents and the inequalities of public school choice*, New York: Routledge.

153

Apple, M.W. (2006) *Educating the "right" way: markets, standards, God, and inequality*, 2nd edn, New York: Routledge.

—— , Aasen, P., Gandin, L. A., Oliver, A., Sung, Y. K., Tavares, H. and Wong, T. H. (2003) *The state and the politics of knowledge*, New York: RoutledgeFalmer.

Bacchetta, P. and Power, M. (2002) "Introduction," in P. Bacchetta and M. Power (eds) *Right-wing women*, New York: Routledge, pp. 1–15.

Beck, C. (2006) "Parents view on school," unpublished paper, University of Oslo, Institute of Educational Research, Oslo.

—— (2008) "Home education and social integration," unpublished paper, University of Oslo, Institute of Educational Research, Oslo.

Bernstein, B. (1977) *Class, codes, and control*, Vol. 3, 2nd edn, London: Routledge & Kegan Paul.

Binder, A. (2002) *Contentious curricula*, Princeton, NJ: Princeton University Press.

Brasher, B. (1998) *Godly women*, New Brunswick, NJ: Rutgers University Press.

du Toit, M. (2002) "Framing volksmoeders," in P. Bacchetta and M. Power (eds) *Right-wing women*, New York: Routledge, pp. 57–70.

Enders, V. (2002) "And we ate up the world," in P. Bacchetta and M. Power (eds) *Right-wing women*, New York: Routledge, pp. 85–98.

Fraser, N. (1989) *Unruly practices*, Minneapolis, MN: University of Minnesota Press.

Green, J. (2000) "The Christian right and 1998 elections," in J. Green, M. Rozell and C. Wilcox (eds) *Prayers in the precincts*, Washington, DC: Georgetown University Press, pp. 1–19.

Griffith, A. and Smith, D. (2005) *Mothering for schooling*, New York: Routledge.

Hardisty, J. (1999) *Mobilizing resentment*, Boston, MA: Beacon Press.

Huerta, L. (2000) "Losing public accountability: a home schooling charter," in B. Fuller (ed.) *Inside charter schools*, Cambridge, MA: Harvard University Press, pp. 177–202.

Numbers, R. (2006) *The creationists*, 2nd edn, Cambridge, MA: Harvard University Press.

Sampson, Z.C. (2005) "Home schools are becoming more popular among blacks," *The New York Times*, December 11: A34.

Smith, C. (1998) *American evangelicalism*, Chicago, IL: University of Chicago Press.

Stambach, A. and David, M. (2005) "Feminist theory and educational policy: How gender has been 'involved' in family school choice debates," *Signs* 30: 1633–58.

Stevens, M. (2001) *Kingdom of children*, Princeton, NJ: Princeton University Press.

14

New states, new governance and new education policy

Stephen J. Ball

In national settings of various kinds across the world, there is underway a set of general and highly significant experimental and evolutionary 'moves' that involve the modernisation of public services, state apparatuses, the overall institutional architecture of the state and its scales of operation.

The most basic and general of these moves is what Jessop (2002) calls 'destatization', which 'involves redrawing the public–private divide, reallocating tasks, and rearticulating the relationship between organisations and tasks across this divide' (p. 199). This redrawing and reallocation has various aspects – some older, some new – such as the creation of executive agencies, the establishing of private–public partnerships (of many different kinds), contracting out state services to private providers (see Burch, 2006), the use of think tanks, consultants and knowledge companies for policy research and evaluation, philanthropic activity and sponsorship to fund educational programmes and innovations, the involvement of the voluntary sector (charities, NGOs, trust and foundations etc.) in service provision, and the use of social entrepreneurs to address intractable social problems – sometimes in complex combinations. In other words, tasks and services previously undertaken by the state are now being done by various 'others', in various kinds of relationship among themselves and to the state and to the remaining more traditional organisations of the public sector, although in many cases the working methods of these public sector organisations have also been fundamentally reworked, typically by the deployment of market forms (competition, choice and performance-related funding). Thus, new voices and interests are represented in the policy process, and new nodes of power and influence are constructed or invigorated. All of this involves an increased reliance on subsidiarity and 'regulated self-regulation', or what Stoker (2004: 166) calls 'constrained discretion', but typically involves deconcentration rather than devolution. It drastically blurs the already fuzzy divides between the public/state, the private and the third sectors and produces a new mix of hierarchies, markets and *heterarchies*. That is, it replaces or combines bureaucracy and administrative structures and relationships with a system of organisation replete with overlap, multiplicity, mixed ascendancy and/or divergent-but-coexistent patterns of relation. Heterarchy is an organisational form, somewhere between hierarchy and network, that draws upon diverse horizontal links that permit different elements of the policy process to cooperate (and/or complete) while individually optimising different success criteria. Embedded in this shift, as indicated above, and in many ways fundamental to it are processes of privatisation – endogenous and exogenous. The first making state organisations more business-like and like businesses. The second replacing state organisations with private providers (public service businesses) or voluntary organisations or social enterprises. As put by Tony Blair, 'market mechanisms are critical to meeting social objectives, entrepreneurial zeal can promote social justice' (1998: 4).

There are now various manifestations of policy heterarchies in education, in many different settings (different parts of the public sector, sectors of education, regions and localities, nation states – some are transnational, as in the examples below), working on and changing the policy process and policy relations, each of which combines elements of destatization, and which involve a limited range of new players, stakeholders and interests in state education, education planning and decision-making and education policy conversations.

This chapter will discuss and examine some of these changes in the state and the policy process as they are evident in relation to education particularly, but by no means exclusively, and later give some examples.

Violence and bio-politics

These changes need to be situated in relation to a broader set of social and political changes in the techniques and modalities of government, which have the aim and effect of producing new kinds of 'active' and responsible, entrepreneurial and consenting citizens and workers – an explosion in modes of governing. However, this is only a partial description of contemporary government. In thinking about these changes while I shall be focusing on those new strategies and technologies that are involved, I do not in anyway want to suggest that older, more direct methods of government and governing have been totally displaced. The 'methods' and relations of heterarchy do not totally displace other forms of policy formation and policy action, but rather take their place in 'the judicious mixing of market, hierarchy and networks to achieve the best possible outcomes' (Jessop, 2002: 242) – 'best' that is from the point of view of the state. Sovereignty and violence are very much with us. Indeed, rather, 'there is a contemporary proliferation of the techniques of arrest, incarceration, punishment, expulsion, disqualification and more broadly coercion' (Dean, 2008: 104). These are what Jessop (2002: 201) calls 'countertrends in the state', drawing on Poulantzas's notion of 'conservation-dissolution' effects. Such effects 'exist insofar as past forms and functions of the state are conserved and/or dissolved as the state is transformed' (Jessop, 2002: 201). Thus, alongside the use of new techniques of governing that rely upon the 'conduct of conduct', existing methods based upon the sovereign and biopolitical powers of life and death remain firmly in place, and new ones are being invented. Indeed, Dean and others argue that forms of sovereign power are increasingly exercised through 'states of exception' – the use of decisive authority beyond the limits of the law and the state itself – Guantanamo is the paradigm case. Broadly speaking, alongside what Foucault called 'the government of souls and consciences . . . or of oneself' (Foucault, 1997), that is an emphasis upon the use of freedom and choice in relation to those deemed responsible and productive, there is a continuing or indeed increased discriminate use of violent power, forms of 'micro-violence', in relation to particular social groups such as asylum seekers and welfare recipients, unemployed or troublesome youth, who are seen as a threat to social order, together with, generally, more intrusive forms of surveillance and scrutiny. While economic competitiveness and the production of certain forms of entrepreneurial citizenship have become primary 'necessities' of contemporary government, 'the diagnoses of disorder and pathology require the reimposition of authority and the reinscription of not only the poor but all groups and classes with a hierarchy' (Dean, 2008: 105). Dean refers to this new form of hybrid rule as 'authoritarian liberalism'. Furthermore, and relatedly, 'countering the denationalization of statehood are attempts of national states to retain control of the articulation of different spatial scales' (Jessop, 2002: 201). That encompasses both a 'defence' of national borders through immigration controls, and 'tougher' refugee regulations and the imprisonment of suspected terrorists, and the use of military power to counter 'threats' to national security. The point is that we should not expect nor look for a consistency between sovereign forms of government and governmentality, nor should we be surprised by failures of government and that the mixes involved are sometimes unstable. The particular form of hybridity of government in any setting requires empirical mapping. It is also important to bear in mind that the state has always been a site of struggle, in which resources and 'voice' have been differentially distributed across genders, ethnicities and classes.

From government to governance

The concern here is with one particular dimension of what is a whole set of wide-ranging and fundamental 'moves' across the terrain of government – that is education policy and the delivery of public education services – which are particularly but not exclusively ongoing in the West. Only some aspects of the range of new techniques of governing are directly relevant here. Dean (2008: 101) sums up these 'moves' as a whole, the changing mix of modalities of governing and the shift of emphasis from sovereignty to governmentality, in the form of a 'thought experiment' – see Table 14.1.

The various dimensions of the shift from government to governance (Rhodes, 1995, 1997; Rhodes and Marsh, 1992; Marinetto, 2005), which are outlined in Dean's table, are achieved in the government of unitary states (and increasingly regions) in and by heterarchies. That is, a new form of 'experimental' and 'strategic' governance that is based upon network relations within and across new policy communities, designed to generate new governing capacity and enhance legitimacy. These new policy networks bring some new kinds of actor into the policy process, validate new policy discourses – discourses flow through them – and enable new forms of policy influence and enactment and in some respects disable or disenfranchise or circumvent some of the established policy actors and agencies. These new forces are able to colonise, to an extent, the spaces opened up by the critique of existing state organisations, actions and

Table 14.1 Contemporary governing in liberal democracies

Governing through freedom ⟷	Powers of life and death
Shaping of choice ⟷	Sovereign decision
Techniques of contract ⟷	Deployment of violence
Management of risk ⟷	Securitisation of threats
Multiple communities ⟷	Society as a realm of defence and source of obligation
Global economy and reform ⟷	Imposition of authority
New forms of citizenship ⟷	Obligation and techniques of subjection
Dissolution of the territorial state ⟷	Protection of borders and assertion of sovereignty

actors (Apple, 2006). This is a means of governing through governance, or the exercise of metagovernance. That is, the management of 'the complexity, plurality and tangled hierarchies found in prevailing modes of coordination' (Jessop, 2002: 243). However, in deploying and discussing such changes, I need to be clear that I am not suggesting that this involves a giving up by the state of its capacity to steer policy, this is not a 'hollowing out' of the state; rather, it is a new modality of state power, agency and social action and indeed a new form of state. That is, the achievement of political ends by different means: 'States play a major and increasing role in metagovernance' (Jessop, 2002: 242). It also needs to be pointed out that governance networks, or heterarchies, as indicated above, do not tell us everything we need to know about policy and the policy process.

As noted already, these heterarchies 'enlarge the range of actors involved in shaping and delivering policy' (Newman, 2001). Governance involves a 'catalyzing of all sectors – public, private and voluntary – into action to solve their community problems' (Osborne and Gaebler, 1992: 20); it is achieved on 'the changing boundary between state and civil society' (Bevir and Rhodes, 2003: 42) – and between state and the economy. In general terms, this is the move towards a 'polycentric state' and 'a shift in the centre of gravity around which policy cycles move' (Jessop, 1998: 32) – the deoncentration and dispersal of policy locations. All of this suggests that both the form and modalities of the state are changing. 'The state, although not impotent, is now dependent upon a vast [or perhaps vaster, SJB] array of state and non-state policy actors' (Marinetto, 2005).

In the UK, these heterarchies form 'new kinds of educational alliance' (Jones, 2003: 160), which 'New Labour seeks to create' around 'its project of transformation' (p. 160) and which in turn provide support and legitimation for reform. They are examples of what Kickert et al. (1997) refer to as 'loosely-coupled weakly-tied multi-organisational sets'. They are a policy device, a way of trying things out, getting things done, changing things and avoiding established public sector lobbies and interests. They are a means of interjecting practical innovations and new sensibilities into areas of education policy that are seen as change-resistant and risk-averse, and in general terms they 'pilot' moves towards a form of service provision that increasingly the state contracts and monitors, rather than directly delivering services, using the mundane practices of 'performance' measurement, benchmarking and targeting to manage a diversity of providers and forms of provision. New forms of power, authority and subjectivity are brought to bear in shaping governable domains and governable persons.

While heterarchies are justified in terms of innovation, risk-taking and creativity, they are also often selective and exclusive, both in terms of memberships and discourses. They serve to 'short-circuit' existing policy blockages. Some potential or previous participants in policy are specifically excluded – trades unions for example – and challenges from outside the shared basis of discourse 'may be easily deflected or incorporated' (Newman, 2001: 172). Heterarchies also work to disperse and re-spatialise policy, creating new sites of influence, decision-making and policy action. That is, the 'territory of influence' (Mackenzie and Lucio, 2005) over policy is expanded, and at the same time the spaces of policy are diversified and dissociated. As a result, as these new sites within the contexts of influence and text production (Ball, 2002) proliferate, there is a concomitant increase in the opacity of policy making. Within their functioning, it is unclear what may have been said to whom, where, with what effect and in exchange for what (see Cohen, 2004). Heterarchies are in part defined by commercial interest in particular policy outcomes, and some of the relationships within them are specifically contractual and financial, but they also encompass social commitments by volunteers and philanthropists. Sometimes the two are blurred.

These policy networks give space within policy for new kinds of talk. New narratives about what counts as a 'good' education are articulated and validated (see Ball, 2007); in particular, the network members enact, embody and disseminate narratives of enterprise and enterprising solutions to social and educational problems (see below). New linkage devices and lead organisations are being created over and against existing ones, excluding or circumventing but not always obliterating more traditional sites and voices. The public sector generally is worked on and in by these new policy actors, from the outside in and the inside out. Linkages and alliances around policy concerns and new policy narratives cross between the public and the private sector. New values and modes of action are thus instantiated and legitimated, and new forms of moral authority are established, and again others are diminished or derided.

Partnerships

Partnerships are a key policy trope within emerging heterarchies. Partnerships are what Jessop calls a 'linkage device' and they encourage 'a relative coherence among diverse objectives' (2002: 242). They can bring about a form of values and organisational convergence and they reshape the context wintin which public sector organisations work. Davies and Hentschke (2005: 11) describe partnerships as 'a third form of organizational activity' that have 'elements of both hierarchies and markets as well as unique features'. Sullivan and Skelcher (2002) were about to document 5,500 local level service delivery partnerships in Britain. In practice, they vary enormously in form and in terms of their power relations and contractual conditions (Cardini, 2006). Some forms of partnership and consortia bring 'the private' into the public sector in the form of joint ventures and profit sharing, without wresting 'ownership' entirely from public sector hands. Nonetheless, the relations of power within partnerships vary quite markedly. Although within these relationships there may be ambiguities and 'differences in language, culture and perceptions of strategic interests' (Newman 2001: 121), partnerships can work to colonise local government and public bodies and re-interpolate public sector actors as entrepreneurs. In some versions, they imply 'a process of incorporation into the values of the dominant partner' (Newman, 2001: 125–126), but they may also be fragile and short-lived.

Two examples

I want to put some flesh onto this account with two examples of heterarchies, in two very different locations, chosen from a wide variety on which I am currently working, to highlight different features of heterarchy. To a great extent, the details, the substance of these examples do not matter; it is the form, the changes in the architecture of governance that they illustrate and display and forms of relationships and flows of narrative that they contain that are important. More in-depth discussion and analysis of each can be found in Ball (2008) and Nambissan and Ball (2009). In both cases, the representations of the relationships involved are of necessity simplified.

The first example is drawn from one small part of research I am currently undertaking in the UK on the role of philanthropy in education policy (Ball, 2008); specifically, it is a set of links and exchanges between Scottish business philanthropists and the government of Scotland (see Figure 14.1).

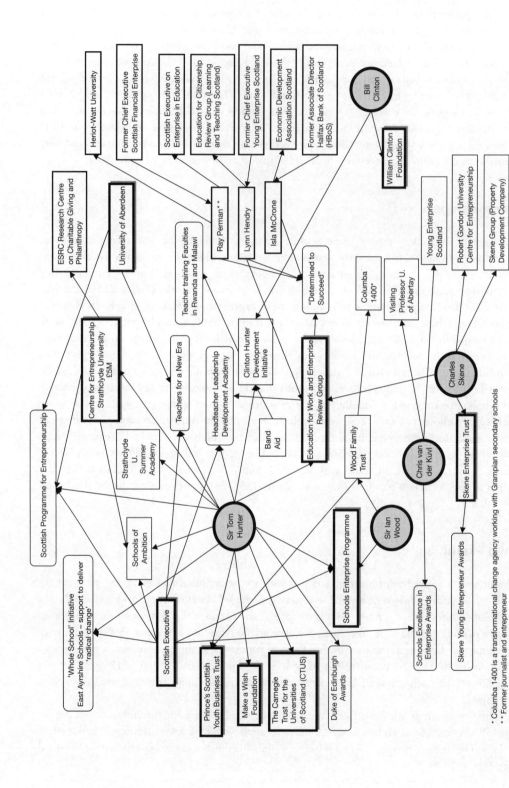

Figure 14.1 Philanthropy, business and education policy in Scotland

* Columba 1400 is a transformational change agency working with Grampian secondary schools

** Former journalist and entrepreneur

There are many different sorts of relationship involved here, focused on the involvement of Sir Tom Hunter, a Scottish businessman and philanthropist, whose money was made from a chain of sportswear shops, who has pledged to give away £1 billion before he dies and become 'one of the greatest philanthropists of his time' (Scotsman.com). His activities have generated a number of partnerships between his charitable foundation and the Scottish government, local government, schools, universities and various parastatal organisations. Several of the programmes represented in Figure 14.1 are based upon 'matched funding' from the Scottish Executive. Sir Tom himself sits on various groups and committees. In a very straightforward way, money buys voice and influence within the policy process and can also be used to attempt to change the culture and priorities of organisations in descisive ways. There are two primary themes that run through these relationships and interventions – they are change and the narrative of enterprise. That is, various attempts to 'modernise' public sector schooling (Schools of Ambition, 'radical change in East Ayrshire', Leadership Development, Teachers for a New Era) and, related to this, the insertion of forms of enterprise and enterprise education into schools and universities. These insertions carry with them a set of values values that are 'fundamentally premised on the construction of moral agency as the necessary ontological condition for ensuring an entrepreneurial disposition in the case of individuals and socio-moral authority in the case of institutions' (Shamir, 2008: 7). That is, the enterprising self and business-like organisations that display creativity, risk-taking, flexibility, innovation and adaptation.

Compared with England, there is very little direct privatisation or involvement of education businesses in this heterarchy, but 'the private' is indirectly represented through the actors themselves (virtually all White and male) and their 'interests' and the forms of discourse that they articulate. Other successful entrepreneurs and philanthropists such as Sir Ian Wood, Charles Skene and Chris van der Kuvl are also drawn into the construction of this narrative and serve to embody it and its virtues. Indeed, the discourse of enterprise and entrepreneurship has many points of articulation and many institutional sites and powerful agents and organisations in this heterarchy to provide for its reiteration and legitimation.

This heterarchy, through the work of the Clinton–Hunter Development Initiative, also illustrates the international flow of philanthropy and its influence through international policy networks in late developing countries. Clearly, the governments of such countries, and crisis states in particular, can be particularly susceptible to external, non-governmental influence, and the work of 'destatization' and public sector transformation is an international phenomenon (see Larbi, 1999). As Larbi points out in relation to developing societies and 'crisis' states, the

> large international management consultants, accountancy firms and international financial institutions . . . have been instrumental in the increasing 'importation' of new management techniques into the public sector. They have played an important role in packaging, selling and implementing NPM techniques, as state agencies contemplating institutional change or strengthening often enlist the services of expert consultants to clarify available options – and recommend courses of action.
>
> (Larbi, 1999: 5)

In many late-developing countries and crisis states, 'NGOism' is now an important factor in policy formation and the delivery of government services – such as education (e.g. see 'From NGOism to creating a movement', a talk of Nooria Haqnigar delivered on 26 April in Kabul during the seminar *Strengthening Women's Movements: National and Transnational Experiences*. Available online at www.mazefilm.de/dokupdf/haqnigar.pdf (accessed 17 April 2009)).

The second example comes from work done with Geetha Nambissan (also a chapter author in this collection). This shows the relationships between a group of international (US- and UK-based), pro-market, pro-choice, policy think tanks and a set of local Indian think tanks and businesses, which together are seeking to change the policy architecture of schooling in India by introducing the possibility of private schooling to supplement or replace state schooling. One of the ways pro-market, pro-choice advocacy works is through the circulation and recirculation of ideas and joining up of points of articulation. Foundations and think tanks and the media are important in the take-up and dissemination of ideas and their establishment within policy thinking.

The Indian choice policy network is linked by a complex of funding, exchange, cross-referencing, dissemination and sponsorship (see Figure 14.2). The Centre for Civil Society, the Educare Trust and the Liberty Institute (India) are key points of the local articulation and inward flow of choice policy ideas, but are also engaged in a bigger enterprise of neo-liberal state reform. The majority of studies of policy borrowing and policy transfer tend to pay little attention to the role of advocacy and philanthropy networks (apart from NGOs) in the flow of and influence of policy ideas, but these groups and individuals often have very specific and very effective points of entry into political systems. Stone (2000: 216) points out, quite rightly, that: 'The authority and legitimacy for think tank involvement in global affairs is not naturally given but has been cultivated and groomed through various management practices and intellectual activities'. She goes on to note that, 'In some cases, however, the think tank scholarly "aura" and independence may be misleading . . . in reality ideas become harnessed to political and economic interests'.

The Indian pro-choice think tanks are linked to a number of other co-belief organisations in other countries. They are members of a global network of neo-liberal organisations run by the Atlas Economic Research Foundation, which has its headquarters in Arlington, Virginia, and has launched or nurtured 275 such think tanks in seventy nations around the world. Atlas believes that 'the prospects for free societies all over the world depend upon "intellectual entrepreneurs" in civil society, who wish to improve public policy debates through sound research' (http://atlasnetwork.org/). Its mission is 'To discover, develop and support "intellectual entrepreneurs" worldwide who can advance the Atlas vision of a society of free and responsible individuals.' This is a formidable network of power, influence, ideas and money, which presents a simple message easily understood by politicians and policymakers in diverse locations.

The Indian pro-choice think tanks are involved in sponsoring choice campaigns, introducing school-voucher schemes and lobbying at the state and city level for the legalisation of 'for-profit' private schooling. The 'School choice campaign', launched in January 2007 by the Centre for Civil Society (CCS), awards school vouchers to poor children across seven states in India. In Delhi, applications were invited from parents in poor settlements (through local NGOs active in these areas), and around 400 children were chosen through a lottery. The vouchers were awarded at a venue frequented by the cultural elite of the city, and this was duly reported by the media. Significantly, the chief minister of Delhi state was present to give away the vouchers. The CCS website appeals to prospective donors in India, UK and US to contribute to the voucher fund and also has forms for donations posted on its website. The website says:

> Each voucher worth up to INR 6000 will fund one child's education in the school of their choice for a year. The voucher will be given until they complete their primary education from their preferred school . . . You can support this pioneering effort by sponsoring one or more vouchers. You will thus brighten a child's future by giving her the power to choose her school. You had a choice, give her a choice.

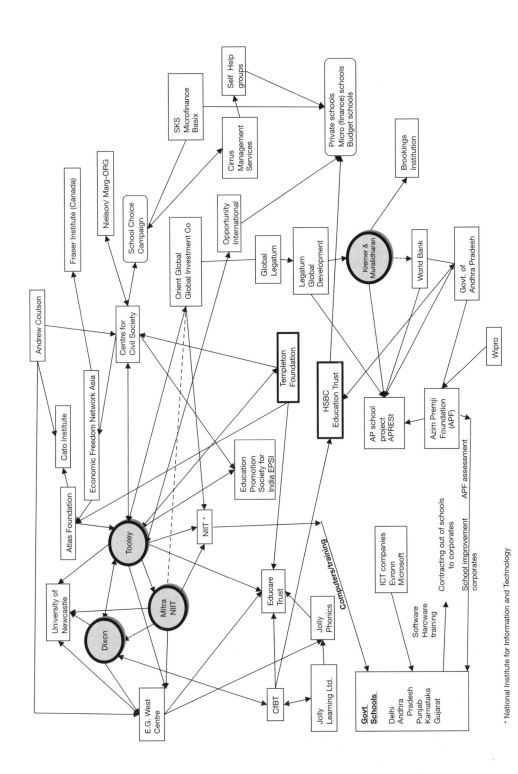

Figure 14.2 Advocacy networks, choice and schooling of the poor in India

* National Institute for Information and Technology

Alongside such local efforts to invigorate choice and private schooling, multinational banks such as HSBC, Standard Chartered and Citicorp are providing micro-finance loans for private school 'start-ups', in the case of HSBC, through a programme called EQUIP (Enabling Quality Improvement Programmes in Schools). *Business Line* (19 July 2004) reported that 'about 30 private schools [in Hyderabad] have shown interest in joining the initiative. Of them, 16 will be given loans in the first phase'. The minister for school education of the Andhra Pradesh government was quoted as asking HSBC 'to expand the scheme to government schools that form more than 80 per cent of the 91,000 schools in the State'.

Further to all this, there are a range of corporate efforts in school education in India, especially at the elementary stage, and private participation in government-run schools in the provision of infrastructure and facilities, the supply of meals, as well as involvement in the development of curriculum, pedagogy and assessment. Information technology (IT) in schools is also a key area of entry for the corporate sector – in the provision of computers and software, as well as technical support and training in state schools. In 2007, the Ministry of Human Resource Development launched a policy initiative on 'ICT in school education', with significant participation by private companies and 'facilitated' by two private organisations, Gesso and CSDMS, which have associations with technology vendors.

In addition, charitable Foundations established by corporations such as the APF (Wipro) and Pratham (ICICI) are an increasingly visible presence in the arenas of education policy making and in initiatives aimed at quality improvement in government schools in some states. A more recent phenomenon is the contracting out of 'under-performing' schools by state governments to corporate foundations. Among other examples, *Akshara*, an NGO established by the wife of the CEO of Infosys (a leading corporate organisation), now runs schools for the poor in Bangalore.

Within all of this there is a newly emerging set of 'policy' relationships between the state, philanthropy (local and international), think tanks and businesses (local and multinational), which are increasingly complex – a newly emerging heterarchy within which philanthropy and business are tightly intertwined. A variety of direct and indirect, commercial, financial and ideological interests are now able to 'voice' their concerns in contexts of policy influence and in contexts of practice. Set over and against the 'failure' of the Indian state to provide schooling for all children and the poor quality of many state schools, this is beginning to change the landscape of state schooling in India, bringing in increasing numbers of private providers (sole-traders and chains) and creating opportunities for business in all sectors of education. In a recent interview, Krishna Kumar sketches out a set of relations between liberalisation, privatisation and modernisation in the government of India and suggests that education has become 'a significant arena to study liberalisation' (LaDousa, 2007: 139) and that 'privatisation has become a major force' (p. 139).

Discussion

Two sorts of related change are going on here. One is in forms of government, and the other in the identity and interests of the participants in processes of governance. These new forms constitute, in the language of political science, 'network governance' – that is 'webs of stable and ongoing relationships which mobilise dispersed resources towards the solution of policy problems' (Pal, 1997); of course, these relationships do not completely overturn conventional policy instruments, as argued above, but they are placed within the context of new interests and sensibilities. Increasingly, policymaking occurs 'in spaces parallel to and across state institutions and their jurisdictional boundaries' (Skelcher et al., 2004: 3), and, in the process, parts of *the state and some of its activities are privatised.*

Heterarchies are indicative of a new 'architecture of regulation', based on interlocking relationships between disparate sites in and beyond the state, and display many of the characteristics of what Richards and Smith (2002) call a 'postmodern state', which is dependent, flexible, reflexive and diffuse, but centrally steered. Policy is being 'done' in a multiplicity of new sites 'tied together on the basis of alliance and the pursuit of economic and social outcomes' (MacKenzie and Lucio, 2005: 500); although the strength of such alliances should not be overstated.

Although steering may have become more complicated across the 'tangled web' of policy networks, as Marinetto (2005) and Holliday (2000) argue the 'core executive' retains substantial authoritative presence over policy, and in some respects (certainly in education) the central state has achieved an enhancement of capacity through its monopoly and deployment of very particular powers and resources. The paradox is that, at the heart of contemporary politics, there is actually a 'filling in' rather than a 'hollowing out' (Taylor, 2000) of the state, exercised through a studied manipulation of the conditions and possibilities under which networks operate and the careful, strategic use of financial controls and allocation of resources. Relations here are complex but clearly asymmetric. There is an important shift of *emphasis* involved, but it is not an absolute break or rupture; bureaucracies continue to be the vehicle for a great deal of state activity, and the state does not hestitate to regulate or intervene when its interests or objectives are not served. The process of governance through heterarchies is increasingly significant but always contingent.[1]

Note

1   I am grateful to Meg Maguire, Carolina Junemann and Michael Apple for their helpful comments on earlier drafts of this chapter.

References

Apple, M.W. (2006) *Educating the right way: markets, standards, God and inequality*, New York: Routledge.

Ball, S.J. (2002) 'Textos, discursos y trayectorias de la politica: la teoria estrategica', *Paginas* 2: 19–33.

—— (2007) *Education plc: understanding private sector participation in public sector education*, London: Routledge.

—— (2008) 'New philanthropy, new networks and new governance in education', *Political Studies* 56(4): 747–765.

Bevir, M. and Rhodes, R.A.W. (2003) 'Searching for civil society: changing patterns of governance in Britain', *Public Administration* 81: 41–62.

Blair, T. (1998) *The third way: new politics for the new century*, London: Fabian Society.

Burch, P.E. (2006) 'The new educational privatization: educational contracting and high stakes accountability', *Teachers College Record* 108: 2582–2610.

Cardini, A. (2006) 'An analysis of the rhetoic and practice of educational partnerships: complexities, tensions and power', *Journal of Education Policy* 21: 393–415.

Cohen, N. (2004) *Pretty straight guys*, London: Faber & Faber.

Davies, B. and Hentschke, G. (2005) *Public/private partnerships in education*, Nottingham: National College for School Leadership.

Dean, M. (2008) *Governing societies*, Maidenhead: Open University Press.

Foucault, M. (1997) *Ethics: subjectivity and truth. Essential works of Michel Foucault 1954–84*, Vol. 1, New York: New Press.

Holliday, I. (2000) 'Is the British state hollowing out?', *Political Quarterly* 71(2): 167–176.

Jessop, B. (1998) 'The narrative of enterprise and the enterprise of narrative: place marketing and the entrepreneurial city', in T. Hall and P. Hubbard (eds) *The entrepreneurial city: geographies of politics, regime and representation*, Chichester: John Wiley.

—— (2002) *The future of the capitalist state*, Cambridge: Polity.

Jones, K. (2003) *Education in Britain: 1944 to the present*, Cambridge: Polity Press.

Kickert, W.J.M., Klijn, E.H. and Koppenjan, J.F.M. (1997) 'Managing networks in the public sector: findings and reflections', in W.J.M. Kickert, E.H.Klijn and J.F.M. Koppenjan (eds) *Managing complex networks: strategies for the public sector*, Thousand Oaks, CA: Sage.

LaDousa, C. (2007) 'Liberalisation, privatisation, modernisation and schooling in India: an interview with Krishna Kumar', *Globalisation, Societies and Education* 5: 137–152.

Larbi, G. (1999) *The new public management approach and crisis states*, UNRISD Discussion Paper No. 112.

Mackenzie, R. and Lucio, M.M. (2005) 'The realities of regulatory change: beyond the fetish of deregulation', *British Journal of Sociology* 39: 499–517.

Marinetto, M. (2003) 'Governing beyond the centre: a critique of the Anglo-governance school', *Political Studies* 51(4): 592–608.

Nambissan, G. and Ball, S.J. (forthcoming) 'Advocacy networks, choice and schooling of the poor in India', *Global Networks*.

Newman, J. (2001) *Modernising governance: New Labour, policy and society*, London: Sage.

Osborne, D. and Gaebler, T. (1992) *Re-inventing government*, Reading, MA: Addison-Wesley.

Pal, L.A. (1997) 'Virtual policy networks: the Internet as a model of contemporary governance?', in *Proceedings of ISOC*. Available online at www.isoc.org/inet97/proceedings/G7/G7_1 (accessed 25 September 2009).

Rhodes, R. (1995) 'The new governance: governing without government', in *State of Britain ESRC/RSA Seminar Series*, Swindon: ESRC.

—— (1997) *Understanding governance: policy networks, governance, reflexivity and accountability*, Buckingham: Open University Press.

—— and Marsh, D. (eds) (1992) *Policy networks in British government*, Oxford: Clarendon Press.

Richards, D. and Smith, M.J. (2002) *Governance and public policy in the United Kingdom*, Oxford: Oxford University Press.

Shamir, R. (2008) 'The age of responsibilitization: on market-embedded morality', *Economy and Society* 37: 1–19.

Skelcher, C., Mathur, N. and Smith, M. (2004) 'Negotiating the institutional void: discursive alignments, collaborative institutions and democratic governance', paper presented at the Political Studies Association Annual Conference, INLOGOV, University of Birmingham, April 2004.

Stoker, G. (2004) *Transforming local governance*, Basingstoke: Palgrave Macmillan.

Stone, D. (2000) 'Think tanks across nations: the new networks of knowledge', *NIRA Review*: 34–39.

Sullivan, H. and Skelcher, C. (2002) *Working across the boundaries: collaboration in public services*, Basingstoke: Macmillan.

Taylor, A. (2000) 'Hollowing out or filling in? Taskforces and the management of cross-cutting issues in British government', *Journal of Politics and International Relations* 2: 46–71.

15

Towards a sociology of pedagogies[1]

Bob Lingard

Introduction

Some years ago, it might have been unusual to find a chapter on pedagogy in a handbook on the sociology of education. In the past, within the sociology of education, pedagogical concerns would have focused largely on critical pedagogy. This is a tradition that can be traced to Paulo Freire's (1973) *Pedagogy of the oppressed*, linked to actual pedagogical practices in literacy, which sought 'conscientization' as a goal and rejected a banking conception of pedagogy. This pedagogy of the oppressed has had real impact in literacy programmes around the world, particularly, but not exclusively, in post-colonial countries. A literature on feminist pedagogy also emerged from the 1980s (e.g. Luke and Gore, 1992; Weiner, 1994), the political intentions of which were similar to those of Freire's pedagogy of the oppressed, but focused on women's liberation.

As the theory framing critical pedagogy became more arcane, its connections to actual pedagogy in actual classrooms became somewhat attenuated. Giroux (2003: 83), a leading theorist of critical pedagogy, stated: 'I use pedagogy as a referent for analyzing how knowledge, values, desire, and social relations are constructed, taken up and implicated in relations of power in the interaction among cultural texts, institutional forms, authorities, and audiences.' This definition of critical pedagogy indicates the need for a sociological approach and the distance of the genre from teachers in classrooms. Indeed, much of the critical pedagogy literature in the sociology of education involved largely exhortatory calls for teachers to work against the grain and resist dominant constructions of knowledge and produce critical citizens. This work was based much more theoretically and politically, rather than empirically and practically. There were some challenges in the sociology of education to its effectiveness and critique of its masculine orientation (Ellsworth, 1989).

There have been, however, more recent reconsiderations of critical pedagogies that have widened their purview to take account of new social movements and that also seek to document some actual practices of critical pedagogy. For example, Trifonas's (2003) edited collection, *Pedagogies of difference*, works with the 'identity construction' element of pedagogies, while also acknowledging their knowledge construction aspect. At the same time, it wants to create a community of difference across feminist, antiracist, post-colonial and gay and lesbian critical pedagogues. This collection articulates pedagogies of difference, which aim to 'create an openness toward the horizons of the other' (p. 4). Writing about educational develop-ments in the USA, Dimitriadis and McCarthy (2001) note how, in a time of multiplicity and difference, most pedagogies seek to tame and regulate as a response – pedagogies of the same, rather than pedagogies of difference. Peter McLaren and Joe Kincheloe's edited collection (2007), *Critical pedagogy: where are we now?*, deals with the theoretical, pedagogical and political aspects of critical pedagogy, demonstrating its eclectic character and illustrating some actually existing critical pedagogies.

This chapter argues that a sociology of pedagogies demands a more empirically grounded approach, yet one that works with the political aspirations of critical and feminist pedagogy. This stance recognizes the veracity of Michael W. Apple's position that critical pedagogies ought not simply be about 'academic theorizing'. Rather, he notes, 'Critical approaches are best developed in close contact with the object of one's analysis' (Apple, 2006: 210).

In what follows, the renewed interest in pedagogy within the sociology of education is considered, as is some of the emerging literature. The chapter then turns to definitions of pedagogy and the emergence of issues of public pedagogy. Next, the research that developed the concept of 'productive pedagogies' is outlined. This is done to exemplify a possible way forward for sociological research about pedagogy that is empirically based, theoretically and politically informed, and of potential use to teachers. Such a sociological account of pedagogy recognizes that pedagogies can make a difference in an opportunity sense, but not all the difference (Apple, 2000, 2006; Hayes *et al.*, 2006), and thus need to be accompanied by broader redistributive policies. The productive pedagogies research fits within what has been called 'new pedagogy studies' (Green, 2003), which recognize that pedagogical change is at the heart of effective school improvement.

Renewed interest in sociology of pedagogy

Pedagogy is endemic to schooling – it is through pedagogy that schooling gets done – and thus understanding pedagogy is central to the sociology of education. Some contemporary factors have also sparked a renewed interest in pedagogies within the sociology of education. These include policy developments over the last two decades in Anglo-American countries, which have introduced tight accountabilities into schooling systems that have affected teachers' pedagogical work. High stakes testing has become a central policy for steering schools' and teachers' practices, with negative effects on pedagogic possibilities. These policy-driven changes to pedagogies have provoked a renewed sociological interest.

These policy developments have seen greater usage of outcomes testing, both nationally and internationally, as a way of framing education policy and of steering schools. This has been about making teachers and their work more accountable and auditable (Mahony and Hextall, 2000) as part of the audit culture (Power, 1997), which suffuses state practices under the new public management and which has been very evident in schooling systems. In an influential study of teachers' work, published more than two decades ago, Connell (1985) argued that teaching was a labour process without a product. In the context of the introduction of new outcomes accountabilities, this observation does not hold true today, at least in Anglo-American models of school reform. Smyth (1998: 193) observed, in respect of such outcome accountability: 'A crucial element of this educational commodity approach to teachers' work is the attention to calculable and measurable aspects of the work, especially educational outputs.' This has had reductive effects on pedagogy, as McNeil (2000) has demonstrated in respect of the US, where test-driven schooling has led to what she calls 'defensive pedagogies'. Hursh (2008) similarly has demonstrated the reductive effects on pedagogies, what he calls the decline of teaching and learning, of George Bush's No Child Left Behind reform and associated testing regime.

This accountability development has been accompanied by reductionist accounts within policy of teachers as the most significant school-based factor for 'determining' student learning outcomes. These policies see teachers as decontextualized practitioners and as both the 'cause' of, and 'solution' to, any problems with learning outcomes, often reduced to student performance on high stakes testing. School effectiveness research in its earlier iterations gave some intellectual or 'evidence base' to this framing of education policy. These accounts decontextualized the factors involved in school performance, particularly for disadvantaged young people, and failed to recognize or acknowledge that it is those societies with low Gini coefficients of social and economic inequality that achieve high quality and high equity in schooling outcomes (Green et al., 2006).

In this policy context, pedagogy has also come to the attention of policymakers and teacher registration agencies. Thus, for example, in New South Wales, Australia, there is a quality pedagogy policy endorsed by the state department. In England, for example, with the literacy hour, there is almost a state- or nationally sanctioned, technicist form of pedagogy (Marsh, 2007).

These policy developments have brought pedagogy under the purview of sociologists of education again. Thus, we have seen a range of sociological studies of pedagogy (e.g. Alexander, 2008; Comber and Nixon, 2009; Hayes et al., 2006; Munns, 2007; Sellar, 2009; Yates, 2009; Zipin, 2009), special issues of journals on pedagogies (e.g. International Journal of Inclusive Education 11(3), 2007; Discourse 30(3), 2009; Pedagogy, Culture & Society 17(1), 2009) and a new Taylor & Francis journal entitled Pedagogies: An international journal.

The renewed focus on pedagogy by sociologists of education has also been linked to some influential research. There is Robin Alexander's monumental (2000) study of pedagogy in relation to culture in five countries, Culture and pedagogy, which is also distinctive within its field of comparative education in its focus on classroom practices and their embeddedness in broader culture. Alexander acknowledged the relationships between pedagogy and social control and recognized the 'truth' of Bernstein's (1971: 47) well-known observation that: 'How a society selects, classifies, distributes, transmits and evaluates the educational knowledge it considers to be public, reflects both the distribution of power and principles of social control.' Alexander assumed and documented the linkages between pedagogies and different cultural and historically bound 'ideas and values, habits and customs, institutions and world views' (2000: 5). His research worked with a very broad and culturally based definition of pedagogy, extending its meaning well beyond teaching or instruction.

Alexander's account follows Bernstein in its conceptualization of pedagogy as 'cultural relay'. Bernstein (2004: 196) observed that 'pedagogic practice can be understood as relay, a cultural relay: a uniquely human device for both the production and reproduction of culture'. Alexander's comparative research clearly demonstrated the veracity of this observation. Elsewhere, Alexander (2008) has provided stinging attacks on the negative effects of New Labour school reform, particularly consequential accountability, on pedagogy in England, reducing its meaning and neglecting its connections to culture. Alexander's work also insinuated the necessity of a sociological approach to pedagogy.

This reference to Bernstein also makes us aware that there is another tradition of pedagogical work in the sociology of education, that of Bernstein (1990, 1996) and his deeply theoretical constructions of the message systems of schooling, curriculum, pedagogy and evaluation.

Bernstein argued that changes in one message system effected changes symbiotically in the other, a reality obvious in the effects of new testing and accountability arrangements on pedagogy in England. In his later work, Bernstein was also concerned with the relations internal to schooling systems of the message systems and 'the recontextualising field of pedagogic discourse'. Such a pedagogic discourse recontextualizes knowledge into curricula, syllabuses and pedagogical knowledge and practices.

Within a similar intellectual field and related to considerations of social and cultural reproduction, Bourdieu saw pedagogies as necessarily involving power relations and as also central to the reproductive mechanisms, in social structural terms, of schooling systems. This was particularly so for those pedagogies that assumed a cultural homology between the capitals of schooling and pedagogy and those of the home. These are pedagogical practices that regarded school performance as a function of individual capacity, rather than cultural experience and the possession of particular school-relevant cultural capitals, and thus misrecognized a '*social* gift treated as a *natural* one' (Bourdieu, 1976: 110).

As Bernstein (2004: 205) has noted, academic success at school demands two complementary sites of pedagogic acquisition, that of the home and that of the school. Bernstein also suggests that the pacing of curricula and the amount of material to be covered in a finite period of time mean that school success demands complementary 'official pedagogic time at home'. And, of course, the capacity to offer this pedagogic time is social class based.

Working within a different intellectual tradition, that of US school reform, Newmann *et al.*'s work (1996) on authentic pedagogy has also been influential in the US and Australia and was the background to the large Queensland School Reform Longitudinal Study, which developed the concept of productive pedagogies. This concept was taken up by the Queensland government and used as the basis for professional development for teachers, while it also formed the basis of the development of a quality pedagogy model framing schooling in New South Wales, as well as being influential elsewhere. Contemporary research in Singapore, for example, has built on productive pedagogies to consider more closely the pedagogies–knowledges relationship (Luke and Hogan, 2006). The Teaching and Learning Research Programme in the UK, funded by the Economic and Social Research Council, has also provoked a renewed research interest in pedagogy.

The policy-driven construction of pedagogy presents a thinned out version that eschews these broader definitions and that rejects the notion of theory attached to teaching. It is this effect that has attracted sociological attention. From within a theoretical and research frame, some have also recognized the difficulty of making pedagogy a stable object of theory and research (e.g. Sellar, 2009). In the next section, definitions of pedagogy and the changing contexts of pedagogy will be considered.

Definitions of pedagogy

Here, I will make an attempt at definitions and, given the width and complexity of these, briefly consider the different literatures that considerations of pedagogy are located within. Alexander makes a very clear distinction between teaching and pedagogy. Put succinctly, he asserts that pedagogy is the art of teaching *plus* its associated discourses to do with learning, teaching, curriculum and much else. For Alexander (2000: 540), pedagogy is both an act (teaching) *and* a discourse. This is pedagogy as cultural relay and its multiple and associated discourses. As Alexander (2000: 540) states: 'Pedagogy connects the apparently self-contained act of teaching with culture, structure and mechanisms of social control.' While noting that the field is quite muddled concerning a definition, Alexander (2008: 3) suggests the complex field of pedagogy includes 'culture and classroom, policy and practice, teacher and learner, knowledge both public and personal'. Pedagogy is thus more than what is usually implied by the use of instruction to refer to teaching in US teacher professional discourses and is also more than teaching, the more common term used in the UK, Australia and New Zealand. Pedagogy could be seen also to link closely to the other message systems of schooling, curriculum and evaluation and through them to culture. This broader definition of pedagogy suggests the need for a sociological account. However, the use of pedagogy in this way is also culture bound, as Alexander (2000) demonstrates. In much of Europe, especially in the Nordic countries, and in Russia, pedagogy refers to both the act and idea of teaching framed by a very broad knowledge base (Alexander, 2000: 542).

While this chapter is concerned with pedagogy as linked to schooling and teacher practices, pedagogies have seeped out of educational institutions to other social institutions and workplaces. This is part of the de-differentiation associated with the knowledge economy and the pedagogizing of many aspects of work and public policy. Bernstein (2001a,b) has spoken of the 'totally pedagogised society' to refer to the ways in which social policy and professional practice today have become pedagogized. What we have is 'pedagogic inflation' (Bernstein, 2001a: 367), where 'the State is moving to ensure that there's no space or time which is not pedagogised' (Bernstein, 2001b: 377). This is why Bernstein suggests that a sociology of the transmission of knowledge is now required, which is focused on the broader changes towards the totally pedagogized society; this is an enterprise that would subsume the narrower sociology of pedagogy.

In terms of the features of the totally pedagogized society, think for example of public health policies of a preventative kind. Think of mandatory courses for single parents and welfare recipients. Think of policies that require all young people to be in education, training or work or a combination of these, rather than being welfare beneficiaries. Think of the pedagogic functions of art galleries and museums, of the Web and the Internet.

This broadened conception of pedagogy is also linked to the effects of the new technologies and the potential globalization of pedagogies (Edwards and Usher, 2008). The older technologies of pedagogy were bounded by classrooms and the technology of the book, while new technologies have seriously challenged these pedagogies of enclosure. These challenges link more broadly to social theory as well, with a conception of public pedagogy linked to social theory and a politics of change. It is almost as if, today, social theory needs a public pedagogy as a bearer of change (Lingard et al., 2008).

The remainder of this chapter will deal, however, with a narrower conception of pedagogy, namely that associated with schooling, while being aware of insights that can be gained for a sociology of pedagogy from broader considerations of public pedagogy in social theory. I turn now to a consideration of the productive pedagogies research, which worked across the critical and empirical traditions in the sociology of pedagogy.

Productive pedagogies

The Queensland School Reform Longitudinal Study (QSRLS) (Lingard et al., 2001), from which the concept of productive pedagogies was derived, was commissioned by the state government in 1997. The QSRLS developed out of Newmann and Associates' (1996) US research on 'authentic pedagogy' and backward mapped from classroom practices to structures, with priority given in the research design to classroom practices. As Rose has noted: 'The vantage point from which you consider schools – your location physically and experientially – will affect what you see and what you can imagine' (1995: 230). The model of productive pedagogies was derived from long periods of observation in actual classrooms across Queensland government primary and secondary schools. The model derived from maps of teacher pedagogies developed from a classroom observation tool, in turn developed out of the relevant research literature and from an interrogation of the classroom data. The point to stress here is that the model has come from observing *actual* teachers at work in *actual* classrooms.

Although the QSRLS was developed out of Newmann and Associates' (1996) research on 'authentic pedagogy', it was recontextualized to take account of the Queensland context. The Newmann research identified the concept of 'authentic pedagogy' to refer to teacher classroom practices that promoted high-quality learning and boosted achievement for all students. Newmann found that authentic pedagogy boosted the achievement of students from disadvantaged backgrounds, closing to some extent the equity gap in performance.

In the Newmann research, authentic pedagogy incorporated the concepts of authentic instruction and authentic assessment.[2] The QSRLS research differentiated between pedagogies and assessment, while at the same time recognizing the importance of aligning the two. Authentic instruction requires higher-order thinking, deep knowledge, substantive conversations and connections to the world beyond the classroom. Authentic assessment involves students being expected to organize information, consider alternatives, demonstrate knowledge of disciplinary content and processes, perform elaborate communication, solve problems that are connected to the world beyond the classroom and present to an audience beyond the school.

The QSRLS augmented the concepts of authentic pedagogy and assessment so as to take account of social as well as academic student outcomes. Consequently, the elements of authentic instruction were expanded into a broader grid consisting of twenty items for productive pedagogies (and authentic assessment into seventeen items for productive assessment), each mapped on a five-point scale.

There were twenty-four carefully selected research schools, selected because of their reputations for reform; half were primary and half secondary. Eight schools were studied in each year of the research, with each being visited twice, for a week at a time. Classes observed in these schools were Year 6 (penultimate primary year), Year 8 and Year 11 (penultimate secondary year), in the subject areas of English, maths, science and social science.

The expanded elements of productive pedagogies were derived from a literature review and included work from the sociology of education, critical readings of school effectiveness and school improvement research, socio-linguistic studies of classrooms, social psychology including sociocultural approaches, social cognition, learning communities and constructivism, critical literacy, critical pedagogies, along with Freirean, indigenous, post-colonial and feminist pedagogies.

It was in the construction of the twenty-element model of productive pedagogies from the literature, which also formed the basis of the classroom observation manual, that the attempt was made to construct a progressive pedagogy for contemporary times. This was evident in the emphasis upon the constructed nature of knowledge and multiple perspectives on things and also in the constructivist and collectivist approach to learning. It was also evident in the connectedness of the pedagogies, to biographies, to previous knowledge, to the world in which students currently learn and play, and to students' everyday/everynight practices. Derived from Bourdieu (1990), the contemporary and progressive characters of productive pedagogies were also evident in the required explicitness of criteria and in the substantive conversations, which were conceived as being central to the distribution of multiple capitals to all students.

The emphasis upon working with and valuing difference attempted to construct a pedagogy of difference (ethnic, indigenous, gender, disability, sexuality), in terms of representation in texts and examples utilized in classroom pedagogies, and also in student inclusion in classroom activities, and in the creation of activist citizens who saw the global space as that for contemporary politics, but who would also work on the local and national. Thus, productive pedagogies sought to work with, not against, multiplicity (Dimitriadis and McCarthy, 2001) and 'with a culture of respect for the history, the language and culture of the peoples represented in the classroom' (Rose, 1995: 414). Stuart Hall (2000: 216) has insightfully captured the stance taken on difference in the research: 'This is not the binary form of difference between what is absolutely the same, and what is absolutely 'Other'. It is a 'weave' of similarities and differences that refuse to separate into fixed binary oppositions'. Despite the strong theoretical underpinnings of the difference dimension of productive pedagogies, it was difficult to operationalize the concept for the classroom mapping exercise.

On the basis of about 1,000 classroom observations in twenty-four case study schools, over three years (1998–2000) (about 250 teachers, each observed four times), statistical analysis

Table 15.1 Relationships between productive pedagogies and productive assessment

Dimensions	Productive pedagogies	Productive assessment
Intellectual Quality	Problematic knowledge Higher order thinking Depth of knowledge Depth of students' understanding Substantive conversation Metalanguage	Problematic knowledge: construction of knowledge Problematic knowledge: consideration of alternatives Higher-order thinking Depth of knowledge: disciplinary content Depth of knowledge: disciplinary processes Elaborated written communication Metalanguage
Connectedness	Connectedness to the world beyond the classroom Knowledge integration Background knowledge Problem-based curriculum	Connectedness: problem connected to the world beyond the classroom Knowledge integration Link to background knowledge Problem-based curriculum Connectedness: audience beyond school
Supportiveness	Students' direction Explicit quality performance criteria Social support Academic engagement Student self regulation	Students' direction Explicit quality performance criteria
Engagement with and valuing of difference	Cultural knowledges Active citizenship Narrative Group identities in learning communities Representation	Cultural knowledges Active citizenship Group identities in learning communities

supported a multidimensional model of pedagogy – what we called 'productive pedagogies'. The twenty elements of productive pedagogies fitted into four dimensions, as shown in Table 15.1, which the research team named: intellectual quality, connectedness, social support and working with and valuing of difference. Table 15.1 outlines the four dimensions, including the way the twenty elements fall under each of the dimensions, as well as the reconceptualization of authentic into productive assessment.

Pedagogies of indifference

Each of the elements that made up the dimensions of productive pedagogies was measured on a five-point scale, with a score of five representing high presence and quality of an element. The 'findings' in relation to productive pedagogies suggest that, across the entire sample, there was a high degree of support for students (although very few opportunities for them to affect the direction of activities in the classroom), but not enough intellectual demandingness, connectedness to the world or engagement with, and valuing of, difference (see Table 15.2). In relation to intellectual quality and connectedness, there was a high standard deviation, indicating that these dimensions were present in some classrooms. In contrast, there was a high mean and a low standard deviation for supportiveness (see Table 15.2). What we saw were very supportive and caring teachers, teachers practising an almost social-worker version of teachers' work.

In the context of growing inequality, we believe that teachers should be congratulated for the levels of social support and care they offered to students. This care was particularly evident in schools located in disadvantaged communities. Schools do contribute to what contemporary public policy likes to call 'social capital', that is, the creation of social trust, networks and community – the collective (but also dangerous) 'we' of local communities (Sennett, 1998). However, the research would suggest that such support is a necessary, but not sufficient requirement for enhancing student outcomes, both social and academic, and for achieving more equality of educational opportunity. Following Bourdieu and the research findings, socially just pedagogies must work with a more equitable distribution of cultural capital through explicitness.

Table 15.2 Mean ratings of dimensions of productive pedagogies from 1998 to 2000

	1998 (n=302)		1999 (n=343)		2000 (n=330)		TOTAL (n=975)	
	Mean	Std dev.	Mean	Std dev.	Mean	Std dev.	Mean	Std dev.
Intellectual quality	2.16	.77	2.17	.73	2.47	.91	2.27	.82
Connectedness	1.84	.77	1.97	.79	2.39	.97	2.07	.88
Supportive classroom environment	2.75	.63	3.05	.67	3.26	.67	3.03	.69
Engagement with difference	1.79	.51	1.89	.50	2.13	.54	1.94	.54

The actual pedagogies mapped, then, could be classified as pedagogies of indifference, in their non-connectedness, their lack of intellectual demand and their absence of working with and valuing difference. They were pedagogies of indifference in failing to make *a* difference, particularly for students from families not possessing the requisite cultural capital. However, it should be stressed that the teachers who were observed were not indifferent in terms of their care, concern and indeed support for students.

There are structural reasons for these findings, including class sizes, contemporary policy pressures (earlier social justice policies, which perhaps emphasized care *over* intellectual demand) and contemporary testing policies, which reduced intellectual demand, a crowded curriculum, time demands of curriculum coverage, pacing, pressures on teachers, a focus on structural change and so on. Allan Luke (2006), a member of the QSRLS research team, observed that interviews with teachers supported an explanation that 'the testing, basic skills, and accountability push had encouraged narrowing of the curriculum' and was affiliated with the finding of 'a shaving off of higher order and critical thinking and a lowering of cognitive demand and intellectual depth' (p. 123).

The lack of intellectual demand (particularly in schools serving disadvantaged communities and particularly in secondary schools) had serious social justice implications. Indeed, this absence of intellectual demand works in the way in which Bourdieu suggests schools reproduce inequality, that is, by demanding of all that which they do not give, those with the requisite cultural capital are advantaged in schooling. Such a lack probably reflects the substantial amount of curriculum content teachers felt they had to cover in a finite period of time; thus coverage became more important than the pursuit of higher-order thinking, citizenship goals and so on. This pedagogy for success requires a complementary pedagogy at home, thus reproducing class-based inequalities around familial cultural capital.

The lack – indeed absence – of engagement with difference perhaps reflected teacher doubt about what the appropriate responses were and a serious lack of effective professional development on such matters. In our view, this did not reflect so much a failure to recognize that something had to be done, but rather not knowing what to do in an increasingly xenophobic political environment. From its election in 1996 through until its defeat in 2007, the Howard government in Australia shifted 'the public gaze and preoccupation to global events such as the War on Terror, the potential avian flu epidemic and, at the micro level, encourages its population to be wary of strangers, to be conscious of the vulnerability of Australia and Australian shores to illegal immigrants' (Crowley and Matthews, 2006: 6), provoking a fear of difference, rather than robust multiculturalism and robust reconciliation with Indigenous Australians. We also found (apart from the Aboriginal community school) an inverse relationship between the extent of engagement and valuing of difference in pedagogical practices and the ethnic diversity of the school's population, a counter-intuitive finding.

Conclusion

This development towards a sociology of pedagogies has suggested that there have been two traditions within the sociology of education in respect of pedagogies. The first was that of critical and feminist pedagogy, largely political approaches, which has also continued to develop in parallel to the diversification of social theory across a range of social differences. Gaby Weiner (2007), in a review of feminist pedagogies, suggested that they remain an aspiration rather than a set of actual practices. The second is that associated with the work of Bernstein and Bourdieu, located within considerations of social and cultural reproduction.

I have also suggested that contemporary education policy developments have again brought sociological considerations of pedagogy to the fore. These policy developments around accountability and high stakes testing have ushered in enhanced sociological interest in pedagogies and what has been called new pedagogy studies. At the same time, some research, particularly that of Alexander, has contributed to a revitalization of the sociological study of pedagogies.

The Queensland productive pedagogies research was dealt with because it sought to cut across the critical pedagogy tradition, including feminist pedagogy, and more empiricist accounts such as that of Newmann and Associates (1996). Jennifer Gore (1993), in *The struggle for pedagogies*, established another binary in her account of critical and feminist pedagogies: between the social vision of these approaches and the more explicit instructional focus of empiricist accounts. Rejecting this opposition, she argued that 'instruction and vision are analytical components of pedagogy, insofar as the concept implies both, each requires attention' (1993: 5). Productive pedagogies,[3] politically aware and empirically based – working with both vision and instructional concerns – would appear to offer potential for future pedagogical research from a sociological perspective.

Notes

1   Although pedagogy is both singular and plural, I have used pedagogies in this chapter to pick up on multiple approaches to pedagogy both in its narrower construction in relation to schooling and broader conceptions in contemporary social theory.
2   The concept of 'authentic' was rejected in the QSRLS because of its modernist overtones. Pedagogy was pluralized to indicate that many pedagogical styles could be aligned with productive pedagogies, while acknowledging that pedagogy, like sheep, is pedantically both singular and plural. Productive resonated with the idea of teachers actually producing something in a positive sense.
3   There has been critique of the productive pedagogies model and research design (see Ladwig, 2007; Mills *et al.*, 2008).

References

Alexander, R. (2000) *Culture and pedagogy international comparisons in primary education*, London: Blackwell.
—— (2008) *Essays on pedagogy*, London: Routledge.
Apple, M.W. (2000) 'The shock of the real: critical pedagogies and rightist reconstructions', in P. Trifonas (ed.) *Revoluntary pedagogies*, New York: Routledge.
—— (2006) 'Critical education, politics and the real world', in L.Weis, C.McCarthy and G. Dimitriades (eds) *Ideology, curriculum, and the new sociology of education: revisiting the work of Michael Apple*, New York: Routledge.
Bernstein, B. (1971) 'On the classification and framing of educational knowledge', in M.F.D. Young (ed.) *Knowledge and control*, London: Collier-Macmillan.
—— (1990) The structuring of pedagogic discourse, London: Routledge.
—— (1996) *Pedagogy, symbolic control and identity*, Bristol: Taylor & Francis.
—— (2001a) 'From pedagogies to knowledge', in A. Marais, I. Neves, B. Davies and H. Daniels (eds) *Towards a sociology of pedagogy: the contribution of Basil Bernstein to research*, New York: Peter Lang.
—— (2001b) 'Video conference with Basil Bernstein', in A.Marais, I.Neves, B.Davies and H.Daniels (eds) *Towards a sociology of pedagogy: the contribution of Basil Bernstein to research*, New York: Peter Lang.

—— (2004) 'Social class and pedagogic practice', in S.J. Ball (ed.) *The RoutledgeFalmer reader in sociology of education*, London: Routledge.

Bourdieu, P. (1976) 'The school as a conservative force: scholastic and cultural inequalities', in R. Dale, G. Esland and M. MacDonald (eds) *Schooling and capitalism: a sociological reader*, London: Routledge & Kegan Paul.

—— (1990) 'Principles for reflecting on the curriculum', *Curriculum Journal* 1(3): 307–314.

Comber, B. and Nixon, H. (2009) 'Teachers' work and pedagogy in an era of accountability', *Discourse: Studies in the Cultural Politics of Education* 30(3): 333–345.

Connell, R.W. (1985) *Teachers' work*, Sydney: Allen & Unwin.

Crowley, V. and Matthews, J. (2006) 'Museum, memorial and mall: postcolonialism, pedagogies, racism and reconciliation', *Pedagogy, Culture & Society* 14(3): 263–277.

Dimitriadis, G. and McCarthy, C. (2001) *Reading and teaching the postcolonial: from Baldwin to Basquiat and beyond*, New York: Teachers' College Press.

Edwards, R. and Usher, R. (2008) *Globalisation and pedagogy space, place and identity*, 2nd edn, London: Routledge.

Ellsworth, E. (1989) 'Why doesn't this feel empowering? Working through the repressive myths of critical pedagogy', *Harvard Educational Review* 59: 297–324.

Freire, P. (1973) *Pedagogy of the oppressed*, Harmondsworth: Penguin.

Giroux, H. (2003) *Public spaces private lives: democracy beyond 9/11*, New York: Rowman & Littlefield.

Gore, J. (1993) *The struggle for pedagogies critical and feminist discourse as regimes of truth*, New York: Routledge.

Green, A., Preston, J. and Janmaat, J.G. (2006) *Education, equality and social cohesion: a comparative analysis*, London: Palgrave.

Green, B. (2003) 'An unfinished project? Garth Boomer and the pedagogical imagination', *Opinion: Journal of the South Australian Teachers' Association* 47(2): 13–24.

Hall, S. (2000) 'Conclusion: the multi-cultural question', in B. Hesse (ed.) *Un/settled multiculturalism*, London: Zed Books.

Hayes, D., Mills, M., Christie, P. and Lingard, B. (2006) *Schools and teachers making a difference? Productive pedagogies and assessment*, Sydney: Allen & Unwin.

Hursh, D. (2008) *High-stakes testing and the decline of teaching and learning*, New York: Rowman & Littlefield.

Ladwig, J. (2007) 'Modelling pedagogy in Australian school reform', *Pedagogies: An International Journal* 2(2): 57–76.

Lingard, B., Ladwig, J., Mills, M., Bahr, M., Chant, D., Warry, M., Ailwood, J., Capeness, R., Christie, P., Gore, J., Hayes, D. and Luke, A. (2001) *The Queensland School Reform Longitudinal Study*, vols. 1 and 2, Brisbane: Education Queensland.

—— Nixon, J. and Ranson, S. (2008) 'Remaking education for a globalized world: policy and pedagogic possibilities', in B. Lingard, J. Nixon and S. Ranson (eds) *Transforming learning in schools and communities*, London: Continuum.

Luke, A. (2006) 'Teaching after the market: from commodity to cosmopolitan', in L.Weis, C.McCarthy and G. Dimitriades (eds) *Ideology, curriculum, and the new sociology of education revisiting the work of Michael Apple*, New York: Routledge.

—— and Hogan, D. (2006) 'Redesigning what counts as evidence in educational policy: the Singapore model', in J. Ozga, T. Seddon and T. Popkewitz (eds) *Education research and policy steering the knowledge-based economy*, London: Routledge.

Luke, C. and Gore, J. (eds) (1992) *Feminisms and critical pedagogy*, New York: Routledge.

Mahony, P. and Hextall, I. (2000) *Reconstructing teaching standards, performance and accountability*, London: Routledge.

Marsh, J. (2007) 'New literacies and old pedagogies: recontextualising rules and practices', *International Journal of Inclusive Education* 11(3): 267–281.

McLaren, P. and Kincheloe, J. (eds) (2007) *Critical pedagogy: where are we now?*, New York: Peter Lang.

McNeil, L. (2000) *Contradictions of school reform: educational costs of standardized testing*, New York: Routledge.

Mills, M., Goos, M., Keddie, A., Gilbert, R., Honan, E., Khan, E., Nichols, K., Pendergast, D., Renshaw, P. and Wright, T. (2008) *Longitudinal study of teaching and learning in Queensland state schools*, Brisbane: Department of Education, Training and the Arts.

Munns, G. (2007) 'A sense of wonder: pedagogies to engage students who live in poverty', *International Journal of Inclusive Education* 11(3): 301–315.

Newmann, F. and Associates (1996) *Authentic achievement: restructuring schools for intellectual quality*, San Francisco, CA: Jossey-Bass.

Power, M. (1997) *The audit culture rituals of verification*, Oxford: Oxford University Press.

Rose, M. (1995) *Possible lives: the promise of public education in America*, New York: Penguin.

Sellar, S. (2009) 'The responsible uncertainty of pedagogy', *Discourse: Studies in the Cultural Politics of Education*, 30(3): 347–360.

Sennett, R. (1998) *The corrosion of character: the personal consequences of work in the new capitalism*, New York: Norton.

Smyth, J. (1998) 'Finding the 'enunciative space' for teacher leadership and teacher learning in schools', *Asia-Pacific Journal of Teacher Education* 26(3): 191–202.

Trifonas, P. (2003) 'Introduction. Pedagogies of difference: locating otherness', in P. Trifonas (ed.) *Pedagogies of difference rethinking education for social change*, New York: Routledge.

Weiner, G. (1994) *Feminisms in education an introduction*, Buckingham: Open University Press.

—— (2007) 'Out of the ruins: feminist pedagogy in recovery', in B. Francis and C. Skelton (eds) *Handbook for gender and education*, London: Sage.

Yates, L. (2009) 'From curriculum to pedagogy and back again: knowledge, the person and the changing world', *Pedagogy, Culture & Society* 17(1): 17–28.

Zipin, L. (2009) 'Dark funds of knowledge, deep funds of pedagogy: exploring boundaries between lifeworlds and schools', *Discourse: Studies in the Cultural Politics of Education* 30(3): 317–331.

16

Families, values, and class relations
The politics of alternative certification

Andrew Brantlinger, Laurel Cooley and Ellen Brantlinger

Social organizations play a powerful role in the reproduction of social inequality. According to critical sociologists Perrucci and Wysong (2003), the perpetuation of class inequalities is linked closely to scripts of organizations controlled by the privileged (pp. 32–33). While often espousing democratic ideals, these organizations advantage children, friends, and associates of privileged classes who have the orientations, credentials, and social ties to "fit" such organizations. Although he includes micro-level analyses, theories of deep-rooted inequality scripts are consistent with Ball's (2003) critical, post-structural analysis of policy and class power relations.

Reassured of their own strengths, the privileged class focuses on subordinated class deficits (Ryan, 1971). Privileged people do not acknowledge or recognize how their control of institutions structures the advantages that lead to the superior outcomes of their class (Brantlinger, 2003). They claim that playing fields are level, or can be made level, and opportunity is available to those who put forth an effort. Privileged people are confident that their advancement and the school circumstances that facilitate it result from their own efforts and merits. Higher status and achievement are attributed to family values rather than family privilege. Because superiority myths are reified through the supposed objectivity of science, subordinate classes are persuaded about the others' superiority, or they are silenced; hence, inequality is perpetuated.

Critical sociologists and scholars of color have turned explanations about distinctive school outcomes from the personal and cultural deficits of the poor to structural bias. A number of ethnographies refute claims to lower-income people's intellectual inferiority, lack of effort, and not valuing education (e.g. Brantlinger, 2003; Carter, 2005). Other studies illustrate the absence of opportunity in low-income US schools on a national level (Kozol, 2005). Theories about the reproduction of social status through class-distinctive K-12 institutional arrangements are well known (Bowles and Gintis, 1976). However, this phenomenon is rarely addressed in teacher development programs and broader education policy.

Privileged class organizations define social problems narrowly and offer narrow solutions to these problems. Because they are far more palatable than direct solutions (e.g. the redistribution of wealth), elites have long promoted educational solutions to poverty and other social ills (Tyack, 1974). President Johnson's War on Poverty featured massive federal expenditures on

179

such educational programs as Title 1 and Head Start, yet economic inequality is greater today than it was in the 1960s (Perrucci and Wysong, 2003). Rather than reducing disparities, governmental and philanthropic interventions mostly maintain and intensify them (McDermott, 2007).

In this chapter, we explore how class dominance permeates new organizations and innovations in teacher recruitment and training. Alternative certification (AC) is at the heart of current education reforms designed to uplift the poor. Young AC teachers from privileged families are seen as "change agents" who will reform troubled schools and ameliorate social inequality. Yet, while there is little evidence that AC has benefited the poor, there is clear evidence that it benefits the wealthy. In this chapter, we focus on non-profit AC organizations that have garnered lucrative relationships with urban districts. While using democratic rhetoric in describing their mission, organizational leaders provide elites like themselves unobstructed access to jobs in urban education.

Our assertions are based on research on the New York City Teaching Fellows (NYCTF) conducted by MetroMath at the City University of New York. This research includes hundreds of surveys, classroom observations, and several dozen interviews. We also include an analysis of print media and Internet information on NYCTF, The New Teachers Project (TNTP), and Teach for America (TFA). The impact of privileged class dominance on these organizations, their teacher recruitment policies, and the effectiveness of graduates are addressed in this chapter.

Organizations created to improve the quality of the teaching force

In spring of 2000, Harold Levy became NYC schools chancellor. A former corporate lawyer, Levy was the first non-educator to hold this position (Goodnough, 2004). As with most urban areas, poor neighborhoods in New York City (NYC) were, and still are, plagued by various educational woes, including the persistent scarcity of a stable, qualified teaching force (Boyd *et al.*, 2005). State pressure compelled Levy to replace uncertified teachers with certified ones in the city's "lowest performing" schools. Though it would not become law until 2001, No Child Left Behind (NCLB) legislation heightened concerns about teacher quality in NYC and other urban areas (No Child Left Behind, 2001).

Shortly after Levy began, state education commissioner Mills threatened to sue NYC leadership for their reliance on uncertified teachers. In response, Levy petitioned the state to approve an alternative route to teaching:

> Levy told Vicki Bernstein [at the NYC Board] to do whatever it took to get a career-changer program up and running by September [of 2000] . . . Levy was confident that he could persuade Mills to recognize his recruits as certified if he could prove they were well-educated and committed.
>
> (Goodnough, 2004: 34)

Mills and the state complied, creating a "transitional" license that allowed "career changers" and recent college graduates to be paid as teachers of record after they completed a short preservice program.

Working with Bernstein and TNTP, Levy fashioned the NYCTF program in his own image. NYCTF attracted privileged class outsiders to a school system that Levy and others believed was badly mismanaged by educationist insiders. While verbalizing interest in minorities,

NYCTF primarily sought upper-class candidates with elite credentials. In a *New York Times* opinion piece titled "Why the Best Don't Teach," Levy (2000) complained,

> a quarter of those teaching in [NYC] public schools earned their bachelor's degrees from institutions that "Barron's Rankings of Colleges and Universities" describes as "less competitive or noncompetitive" . . . Our children need teachers with outstanding abilities and rigorous academic training.

Social class was a subtext of Levy's push for AC teachers. Levy assumed schools would be better run by elites and corporate-types. Levy saw Fellows as "change agents" who would reform a troubled school system from the bottom-up (Goodnough, 2004: 197).

NYCTF was good public relations. New AC policy allowed the Fellows to be counted as "certified" after they completed only 200 hours of preservice training. While they were less prepared to teach than many of the uncertified teachers they replaced, the Fellows were also considered "highly qualified" under NCLB guidelines. NYCTF was selective, with some 2300 applicants applying for 320 positions in the first year. Large percentages of Fellows graduated from top-tier universities, had professional experience, and passed state certification exams. Further, the term "Fellow" sounded exclusive and attracted elites who would not consider teaching without special recognition and other privileges (Goodnough, 2004).

Despite a lack of evidence, NYCTF was readily heralded as a success and it expanded ten-fold in the next two years. TNTP began to partner with districts and states around the country to replicate the Fellows program. Founded in 1997 by former TFA "core members," TNTP was created to "eliminate school inequality" (TNTP website, 2008). TNTP reports the following on their website:

> [TNTP] is a national nonprofit dedicated to closing the achievement gap by ensuring that high-need students get outstanding teachers . . . Since its inception, TNTP has trained or hired approximately 33,000 teachers, benefiting an estimated 4.8 million students nationwide. It has established more than 70 programs and initiatives in 28 states and published three seminal studies on urban teacher hiring and school staffing.

TNTP assumes that AC recruits have superior educational backgrounds and, hence, need little, if any, preparation to teach. This is an assumption shared by many AC advocates. For example, Raymond, Fletcher and Luque (2001) assert that TFA teachers are a: "select group of college graduates, culled from the finest universities [and that it's] possible that traditional certification programs and pedagogical training are less necessary for them than they are for the typical teacher" (p. 68). Contradicting such arguments, Darling-Hammond (1994) provides strong evidence that TFA training leaves its privileged class recruits woefully unprepared for their first year of urban teaching.

Both TFA and TNTP cloak class-biased recruitment and training strategies in language of scientific neutrality and objectivity. The TNTP website advertizes:

> [TNTP helps] select outstanding teachers by using: A proven set of selection criteria based on achievement, character, leadership and other fundamental qualities and personality traits. Trained selectors use a continually refined, research-based selection model. A highly professional, rigorous and competitive application process maximizes our ability to assess candidates' qualifications and inspires candidates to teach. Carefully-structured and

normed rating tools promote consistent assessment of candidates. Rigorous training and quality control ensure that the selection process is implemented effectively and fairly.

As Perrucci and Wysong (2003) note, such supposedly "rigorous, neutral, scientific methods to determine merit" present a facade that disguises privilege (p. 76). TFA uses a similar "objective" formula for selecting their AC teachers (Foote, 2008). Pretensions to science and technical expertise allow elites and "experts" to quash democratic impulses and monopolize control of educational decision-making (Tyack, 1974).

TNTP, TFA, other non-profit educational organizations (e.g. New Leaders for New Schools), and think tanks (e.g. the Education Trust) are closely linked. They serve on one another's executive boards and share a similar philosophy of reform that narrowly focuses on "reducing the achievement gap." Leaders of these organizations attended Ivy League universities and generally came from privilege. As such, they have close ties to powerful people (e.g. wealthy philanthropists, politicians, lawyers) who lend financial and political support. TNTP and TFA board members also transition easily into leadership positions in other educational and governmental organizations. The best-known example is Michelle Rhee, the first president of TNTP, who became DC Schools Chancellor in 2007, in spite of the fact that she only taught for two years.

Lesser-known TFA members have garnered prestigious jobs, often in education, after similar short stints as teachers. Because they have greater cultural, social, and financial capital, Fellows and TFA teachers are able to profit off of short experiences as teachers in ways that others cannot. Fellows are paid a stipend to attend preservice training, receive a publically subsidized Masters degree, and become paid teachers of record after fulfilling minimal preservice requirements. Foote (2008) describes how TFA partners new recruits with wealthy donors who serve as future connections for employment.

The privileged class increasingly identifies with private rather than public interests (Reich, 2007). While not private, TFA and TNTP are non-profit organizations that conform to neo-liberal trends in education (Apple, 2006). Funded with both philanthropic and public monies, leadership teams make corporate-level salaries ($120,000–250,000) and earn additional income through outside consulting. However, rather than being seen as welfare programs for the privileged, TFA and TNTP are advertised and generally perceived as benevolent ventures that serve the needs of underprivileged students.

Facts about NYCTF

Despite being the biggest AC program in the country, research on NYCTF is scarce. However, the extant research is troubling. Stein (2002) finds close to 90 percent of the first-year Fellows she surveyed were already considering leaving their initial placements in high-needs schools. She concludes that NYCTF "is an unqualified success at producing certified teachers; however, it is unlikely that it will reduce the problem of teacher turnover and lack of certified teachers at [failing] schools" (p. 1). Others observe that Fellows are thrust into the classroom with minimal formal training and struggle to teach effectively (Costigan, 2004; Goodnough, 2004; Meagher and Brantlinger, under review). While many have the potential to become effective and committed teachers, novice Fellows focus on daily survival and often teach in a control-centered fashion.

In an analysis of pupil achievement data from NYC, Boyd *et al.* (2006) find that Grades 4–8 students of Fellows have lower achievement gains on mathematics tests than do comparable students of traditionally certified teachers. They also find that less experienced teachers—and Fellows are disproportionally inexperienced—are far less effective than mathematics teachers with three or more years' experience. Further, NYCTF teachers have considerably lower rates of retention than college-recommended or temporary-license teachers at similar NYC schools. Attrition of Fellows is particularly acute in the highest-poverty schools. Boyd *et al.* (2005) find that, in NYC, "highly qualified teachers are more likely to quit or transfer than less-qualified teachers, especially if they teach in low-achieving schools" (p. 167). It should be noted that these researchers equated "highly qualified" with a score in the upper quartile of those who took state certification exams (i.e. many Fellows). In sum, NYCTF has not been shown to improve the academic and life chances of lower SES urban students. This is important given the links between teacher quality and student achievement (Sanders and Rivers, 1996).

Preliminary MetroMath research results

In the summer of 2007, MetroMath surveyed 269 of approximately 300 mathematics Fellows in the newest "cohort." Closed items asked respondents to report both demographic and school background information. Open-response items asked about their perceptions of urban teaching, relationships to students in high-needs urban schools, and reasons for becoming an AC mathematics teacher.

The demographic data reveal little experiential or contextual commonalities between Fellows and students in the high-needs schools in which they teach. Only about 20 percent of survey respondents reported attending such schools themselves. Five in six report attending a selective school (both private or public) or being placed in a selective program within a non-selective school. Less than 15 percent of survey respondents reported growing up lower income or working class. Approximately one third of the math Fellows were black or Latino. However, the racial composition of the mathematics Fellows does not come close to reflecting the ethnic composition of children in high-needs NYC schools.

Fellows' lack of connection to high-needs urban districts is problematic. Qualified teachers should be able to relate constructively to pupils and their guardians (O'Connor and McCartney, 2007). Yet, the MetroMath survey indicates that many preservice mathematics Fellows appear unable to do so. One open-ended survey item asked respondents to report similarities and differences between students in high-needs urban schools and the students they went to school with. Respondents named more than twice as many differences than similarities (Table 16.1). The three most common themes were the following: (1) outside distractions and difficult home lives that interfere with students' academic success; (2) students' academic skills, engagement, and behavior; and (3) school resources (e.g. financial and human capital) and educational access.

The approximately fifty-five hours of fieldwork the mathematics Fellows completed in their summer prior to teaching appeared to solidify the dominant view that youth in high-needs schools have more outside distractions, less supportive families, and were less academically able and engaged than students with whom the Fellows had attended school themselves. Many survey respondents, though certainly not all, openly articulated deficit views blaming urban communities, guardians, and youths for lesser educational outcomes, while generally failing to name school context distinctions. One Fellow elaborated: "I went to school with kids who knew they were there to study and who seemed self-motivated to do their best. In high needs

Table 16.1 Fellows as students and students in high-needs urban schools

	Outside distractions or difficult home life	Academic skills or engagement	School resources or access
Similar	16	35	4
Different	101	95	82

schools, even if the kids are able to do better, the culture doesn't seem to motivate excellence." Another wrote that at his childhood schools: "Parents were more involved and paid tuition! Students wore uniforms. There was more discipline!" Criticism of urban families included: "dysfunctional," "lack of attention from guardians/parents," "education not a high priority," and "clash between home and school expectations." Despite limited contact with urban communities, many Fellows wrote that students had no one: "pushing them," "stressing the importance of education," or "involved in their lives." In contrast, when in secondary school they experienced: "white peers with structured lives," "fear of disappointing parents," and "more self-motivation." Academic differences were generally attributed to students' drive, (mathematics) ability, intelligence, engagement, interest, values, tastes, attention span, emotional stability, and respect for others and school.

Discussions of socioeconomic inequality, systemic institutional failure, racism, and class bias generally were muted or absent in these responses. However, as Table 16.1 also indicates, slightly more than one third of respondents brought up issues of equity and access when comparing high-needs urban schools with schools of their own youth. One said: "I went to school with no diversity. My classrooms were equipped with everything above and beyond what was needed." Another remarked: "We had more technology, more sports, more programs to keep us interested in education." Another concluded: "I went to a very good school in Brooklyn, but those in the high needs schools are usually given the short end of the stick. They are not given the tools they need to succeed in this society." Yet, even those who identified gaps between resources in high-needs urban schools and the schools of their own formative years (i.e. contextual lacks) as reasons for distinctive student outcomes generally did not espouse theories of generalized structural inequalities.

Some of the above results are attributable to a survey methodology that limits opportunities for extended responses. However, interviews with twenty-seven mathematics Fellows conducted by MetroMath provide further evidence that mathematics Fellows generally hold meritocratic views of educational achievement. Though privilege was a subtext, interviewees give versions of hard work, motivation, and intelligence as reasons for superior school outcomes. Many verbalize that their goal in entering NYCTF is to impart the ethic of "hard work pays off" to low-income minority students—a principal goal of TFA and TNTP.

MetroMath data indicate that their meritocratic idealism is generally shaken once they began as teachers of record. In particular, surveys with 167 and interviews with 18 mathematics Fellows with one or two years of teaching experience show that experience makes mathematics Fellows fatalistic about their inability to change school conditions or students' fates. Many of these Fellows planned to move to a "better" school as soon as they could. Of the fraction who wished to remain in teaching, the majority planned to apply to suburban, private, or selective public schools within the next five years. Other Fellows aspired to higher-paying and more prestigious leadership positions within their schools, districts, universities, or governmental or non-profit organizations.

Large numbers of younger mathematics Fellows—and over two thirds are between the ages of 21 and 27 when they begin—see urban teaching as temporary. When asked why they became a Fellow, twelve such Fellows candidly admitted to a lack of decent wage alternatives and a need for employment. Others confessed they knew from the beginning that their commitment would be short term: one "needed a break before graduate school," eight "wanted to live in NYC." A few reported that the experience would look good on their résumé.

Downward mobility and an intensification of opportunity hoarding

Teaching has rarely been considered high status or lucrative enough to attract privileged classes. Individuals who are first in their family to attend college understand teaching as a secure, respectable, and fairly well-paid career (Brantlinger, 2003). With the exception of middle-class women, who see teaching as a reasonable way to accommodate child rearing and supplement a husband's salary, public school teaching has been eschewed as below the capability of children from professional families. Societal instability, however, has caused a downward trajectory for the middle class (Reich, 2007). Objective measures and subjective impressions indicate that young workers today find it difficult to match the living standards achieved by previous generations (Lasch, 1995; Perrucci and Wysong, 2003). The number and type of applicants to NYCTF suggest that unemployment and underemployment among the educated class has lead to aspiration reduction.

We contend that the privilege-class response to occupation scarcity is to create new post-baccalaureate opportunities, such as NYCTF and TFA, for their children (Devine, 2004). Even Fellows with no intention of staying in the teaching profession still earn an income on the short run, a publicly subsidized Masters degree, and experience that enhances their résumé. This teaching experience, however brief, enables them to compete for higher-status and lucrative jobs in a credentialed society. Of course, there has also been an even greater decline in reasonable employment opportunities for subordinated groups—even college graduates from less privileged backgrounds (Smiley, 2008). Yet, the types of non-profit organization discussed here do not represent them or their interests. African Americans, Latinos, and the working class do not control the messages or organizations that respond to such downward trends—that is the domain of the privileged. Despite the dominant class's protest against affirmative action, obviously such programs as NYCTF selectively privilege the dominant class.

Who designs alternative routes? And why?

Traditional teacher education programs face a barrage of criticism for insufficiently preparing teachers and allowing the wrong people into the field. Rumblings that teacher education is unnecessary because good teachers are born, raised by good (affluent) parents, or educated at elite universities periodically surface. In response to the perceived lacks in undergraduate programs, the Holmes Group tried to establish teacher education as a post-baccalaureate degree. This approach was rejected by some university officials, who argued that, given the expense of higher education, adding a fifth year would eliminate potential candidates, particularly minorities, children of the working class, and first-generation college attenders.

The current neo-liberal approach has been to bypass teacher education and concentrate on recruiting teachers from tier one colleges. Proponents have convincingly argued that tuition waivers and stipends are needed to attract these qualified individuals and high-quality minority candidates. Candidates in mathematics, science, and special education are of particular interest. Urban schools are targeted because of their persistent teacher shortages. Because they are funded by property taxes, schools in low-income districts lack equivalent human and physical resources (Kozol, 2005). Hence, teacher shortage in urban areas is largely due to class discrimination. Attrition is not only the result of resource gaps, but repressive demands at "failing schools." Teachers at these schools are often subjected to draconian scrutiny from administrators and are required to enact scripted curriculum aimed at high-stakes tests (Goodnough, 2004). Diminished conditions lead to a dearth of applications from qualified candidates and high faculty turnover (Boyd *et al.*, 2005). The continuation of deep school inequalities leads the authors to be skeptical that, without redressing the ubiquitous and pernicious economic and social inequities, recruiting teachers from any teacher education program will solve the problem of lack of qualified teachers in impoverished urban schools.

The impact of the new teacher education programs

While privileged-class members do work hard, they are not self-made. Unlike less-privileged classes, they have the capital and clout to facilitate aspirations for status maintenance and upward mobility. Instead of recognizing how organizations are biased toward them, they see schools and society as fair and just. As the epitome of super-class advantage, the policies and practices of NYCTF and TFA that privilege the elite must be changed to allow access by residents of poor urban neighborhoods and the types of candidate who traditionally have made a longtime career of effective teaching in high-needs urban schools. Our evidence and a review of the literature reveal that the better-known and most selective alternative programs we studied result in the following:

Social class displacement

Teaching Fellows take the place of uncertified or temporary licensed teachers who have staffed high-needs schools since the early 1980s or before. Some of these teachers had backgrounds in the fields that they taught. Many had more teaching experience and educational training than first-year Fellows. Most had strong ties to the schools and communities where they worked. As noted earlier, novice uncertified teachers appear to be about as effective in mathematics as Fellows (Boyd *et al.*, 2006).

Middle-class welfare

NYCTF spends approximately $25,000 per Fellow for training for a Master's degree (Goodnough, 2004). Given that there are 2500–3500 new Fellows annually, this translates into tens of millions of taxpayer dollars going to Master's coursework and other professional support for new Fellows. Less-privileged candidates who hold temporary licenses must pay for their own training and Master's degree. Prior to 2004, new teachers in NYC did not receive mentoring unless they came through an AC route. Although most are needier than NYCTF recruits, once again the career building of middle-class people has become a priority. Granted this phenomenon resulted from social and economic conditions in which privileged students have been unable to find acceptable jobs in the areas of their earned degrees. It is no surprise that NYCTF applications would increase substantially in lean times. Levy has called NYCTF "an opportunity for people to make good on their altruistic desires," without identifying the "people" to whom he referred. Lower SES people are likely to see teaching as a long-term career, an attitude that is healthier than the missionary-savior complex that our evidence shows will soon be thwarted.

Absence of high qualifications

Our data suggest that the claim that the mathematics Fellows are more "highly qualified" and especially "talented" does not hold true. Contradicting NYCTF rhetoric about recruiting the "best and the brightest," well over three quarters of mathematics Fellows do not have adequate backgrounds in mathematics (Donoghue *et al.*, 2008). If rapport with, and respect for, students are judged, then Fellows also fall short.

Negative side effects and lack of improvement

The NYCTF program claims to "tap professional class idealism" (Keller, 2000: 1). Levy saw NYCTF recruits as a vanguard that would work against the status quo culture in schooling. Our research and that of others (e.g. Boyd *et al.*, 2005; Costigan, 2004) document that Fellow optimism and idealism are short lived, that teachers rarely identify with their urban students, rarely understand the actual constraints on their lives, and do not remain in high-needs schools.

Alternative certification as a business solution to complex social problems

Writing from a liberal perspective, Robert Reich (2007) sees members of the privileged class as increasingly identifying with private rather than public interests and producing "secessionist ideas and consequences" (cited in Perrucci and Wysong, 2003: 65). Workers involved in production have declined from 33.1 percent in 1970 to a projected 11.6 percent in 2008 (Perrucci and Wysong, 2003). This decline is accompanied by a corresponding rise in moderate- to low-paid service-sector jobs at firms with a small number of highly paid "core" workers, such as "managers and symbolic analysts," and a large group of moderate- to low-paid "peripheral" workers who are viewed as less central to organizational needs and goals.

Temporary agencies and contract or contingent laborers

Viewed increasingly as peripheral and contingent, "temp workers" fill in as teachers (Perrucci and Wysong, 2003 p. 73). These interlocked organizational networks are directed by privileged, credentialed-class leaders who use them to pursue strategies and objectives that reinforce the shared economic, political, and cultural interests of their class. The super-class shares values, worldviews, and a commitment to maintaining the status quo. From where privileged-class leaders stand, life is good, and the corporate market model of the magic of the market works (p. 76).

Despite consolidating considerable amounts of philanthropic and government funds, TFA, TNTP, and NYCTF have done little, if anything, to eliminate educational inequality, even in schools they directly serve (Boyd *et al.*, 2006; Darling-Hammond, 1994). The rhetoric is about serving the poor, yet it is the privileged class that benefits most directly from these new teacher education organizations and the policies and practices that enable them. It is appropriate to conclude that the values of the super-class are aimed at preserving class advantage, and, hence, are self-centered, self-serving, and exclusive as they prevent subordinates' access to a level playing field and social mobility.

References

Apple, M.W. (2006) *Educating the "right" way: markets, standards, God, and inequality*, 2nd edn, New York: Routledge.

Ball, S.J. (2003) *Class strategies and the educational market: the middle class and social advantage*, New York: RoutledgeFalmer.

Bowles, S. and Gintis, H. (1976) *Schooling in capitalist America*, London: Routledge & Kegan Paul.

Boyd, D., Lankford, H., Loeb, S. and Wyckoff, J. (2005) "Explaining the short careers of high-achieving teachers in schools with low-performing students," *American Economic Review Proceedings* 95(2): 166–171.

——— Grossman, P., Lankford, H., Loeb, S. and Wyckoff, J. (2006) "How changes in entry requirements alter the teacher workforce and affect student achievement," *Education Finance and Policy* 1(2): 176–216.

Brantlinger, E. (2003) *Dividing classes: how the middle class negotiates and rationalizes school advantage*, New York: Routledge.

Carter, P. (2005) *Keepin' it real: School success beyond Black and White*, New York: Oxford University Press.

Costigan, A. (2004) "Finding a name for what they want: a study of New York City's Teaching Fellows," *Teaching and Teacher Education: An International Journal* 20(2): 129–143.

Darling-Hammond, L. (1994) "Who will speak for the children? How 'Teach for America' hurts urban schools and students," *Phi Delta Kappan* 76: 21–34.

Devine, F. (2004) *Class practices: how parents help their children get good jobs*, New York: Cambridge University Press.

Donoghue, E., Brantlinger, A., Meagher, M. and Cooley, L. (2008) "Teaching mathematics in urban schools: the New York City Teaching Fellows Program," (Roundtable) Paper presented at the Annual Meeting of the American Educational Research Association, New York, March 2008.

Foote, D. (2008) *Relentless pursuit: A year in the trenches with Teach for America*, New York: Knopf.

Goodnough, A. (2004) *Ms. Moffett's first year: becoming a teacher in America*, New York: Public Affairs.

Keller, B. (2000) "States move to improve teacher pool," *Education Week* June 14: 1, 20.

Kozol, J. (2005) *The shame of the nation: the restoration of apartheid schooling in America*, New York: Crown Publishers.

Lasch, C. (1995) *The revolt of the elites and the betrayal of democracy*, New York: W.W. Norton.

Levy, H. (2000) "Why the best don't teach," *New York Times* (September 9, 2000).

McDermott, K. (2007) "'Expanding the moral community' or 'blaming the victim'? The politics of state education accountability policy," *American Educational Research Journal* 44(1): 77–111.

Meagher, M. and Brantlinger, A. (under review) "When am I going to learn to be a mathematics teacher? A case study of a New York City Teaching Fellow."

No Child Left Behind Act (2001), Pub. L. No. 107–110 (2001).

O'Connor, E. and McCartney, K. (2007) "Examining teacher-child relationships and achievement as part of an ecological model of development," *American Educational Research Journal* 44(2): 340–369.

Perrucci, R. and Wysong, E. (2003) *The new class society: goodbye American Dream?*, 2nd edn, Oxford: Rowman & Littlefield.

Raymond, M., Fletcher, S.H. and Luque, J. (2001) *Teach for America: an evaluation of teacher differences and student outcomes in Houston, Texas*, Stanford, CA: The Hoover Institution, Center for Research on Education Outcomes.

Reich, R. (2007) *Supercapitalism: the transformation of business, democracy, and everyday life*, New York: Vintage.

Ryan, W. (1971) *Blaming the victim*, New York: Random House.

Sanders, W. and Rivers, J. (1996) *Cumulative and residual effects of teachers on future student academic achievement. Research progress report*, Knoxville, TN: University of Tennessee Value-Added Research and Assessment Center.

Smiley, T. (2008) "Entering the workforce after college," *My America*, August 21. Available online at www.pri.org/business/economic-security/workforce-after-college.html.

Stein, J. (2002) *Evaluation of the NYCTF Program as an alternative certification program*, New York: New York City Board of Education.

The New Teacher Project Website (2008, November 24). Available online at www.tntp.org/ (accessed November 24, 2008).

Tyack, D. (1974) *The one best system: a history of American urban education*, Cambridge, MA: Harvard University Press.

17

Popular culture and the sociology of education

Greg Dimitriadis

Understanding the connections between school life and broader social structures today necessitates understanding the worldwide prevalence of popular culture and media forms and their increasingly pronounced role in the lives of youth.[1] Contemporary cultural shifts and dislocations raise new kinds of questions for education, including how the everyday cultural practices of youth intersect with the imperatives of school life today. As is well known by now, the technocratic imperatives of No Child Left Behind and other high stakes testing mechanisms have narrowed the curricula today in ways that have squeezed out much beyond the basic "skill and drill" types of pedagogy. The disjuncture between in-school and out-of-school culture has become increasingly pronounced—prompting many to take on questions of popular culture in new ways. Yet, it is important to note that these dislocations and disjunctures between everyday cultural practices and school life have been a longstanding concern for many in sociology and related disciplines—racing back over seventy-five years. While our moment is specific in many ways, then, several generations of scholars have taken on these questions. In particular, many have acknowledged the ways young people gravitate towards popular culture in the absence of compelling or legitimate school knowledges and structures. In this chapter, I will trace three traditions and bodies of work—the Chicago School of Sociology, the Birmingham School of Cultural Studies, and the new sociology of education. Each of these traditions evolved in distinct though overlapping ways. Taken together, they offer a productive set of resources for understanding the intersections between popular culture and the sociology of education.

Chicago School of Sociology

In many respects, the first efforts to understand popular culture were undertaken by scholars of the Chicago School of Sociology. The Chicago School of Sociology rose to prominence in the early part of the twentieth century. Like many cities, Chicago at the turn of the last century was marked by unprecedented expansion. Urban life meant new divisions of labor, as well as new modes of association, new kinds of human connection around a wide range of tastes, dispositions, and lifestyles. Under the direction of Robert Park, early sociologists at the University of Chicago looked to understand many of the new forms of association first-generation immigrant youth created. This work was an early manifestation of what came to be known as "subculture" theory. Perhaps most notably, Thrasher's *The gang: a study of 1,313 gangs in Chicago* (1927) looked to understand how young people formed "gangs" in the "in-between" or "interstitial" spaces newly emerging in Chicago. Other notable books are Nel Anderson's *The hobo: the sociology of the homelesss man*; Paul Cressey's *The taxi-dance hall: a sociological study in commercialized recreation and city life*; Louis Wirth's *The ghetto*; and Harvey Zorbaugh's *Gold Coast and slum: a sociological study of the near north side*.

Thrasher famously studied many aspects of youths' lives, including their reading and viewing habits—what we would call today "popular culture." Movies, in particular, were a new and unexplored medium around this time and were the source of keen attention by Thrasher and others. Here, Thrasher notes that film is "a cheap and easy escape from reality" and that gang boys consumed films voraciously (p. 102). Thrasher acknowledged the fact that boys picked up certain "patterns" of behavior from these films, often providing fodder for their fantasy lives. Yet, he does not claim that these films "influenced" these boys in simple, direct ways. Thrasher resists the "hypodermic needle" theory of media influence so prevalent at the time. According to this hypothesis, there is a one-to-one correlation between media representation and individual actions. Around this time, moral panics around the effects of film, books, and comics proliferated, causing many to postulate a simple relationship between these media and juvenile delinquency. While Thrasher argued that films do, in fact, have effects in young people's lives, he resists this one-to-one correlation. Towards the end of the chapter, Thrasher argues against the idea of censorship, as he would do elsewhere. He argues here that "new" media such as the movies always have the potential to "disturb social routine and break up the old habits upon which the superstructure of social organization rests" (p. 114). Yet, abolishing film would be akin to banning automobiles. While boys in gangs are perhaps more "susceptible" to media influence, these forces can only be understood against a social backdrop. Thrasher would become the first professor to hold a position in the sociology of education in the US, at NYU.

While at NYU, Thrasher was commissioned to conduct a larger study of the Boys' Club in New York City. The goal was to situate this club and its effects in radical community context. Thrasher built an important piece of this study around the question of movies and their effects. It was funded, in part, by the Payne Fund, an initiative taken up and funded by William Short, as detailed in the book *Children and the movies* (Jowett et al., 1996). Thrasher would soon bring fellow sociologist Paul Cressey (author of *Taxi-dance hall: a sociological study in commercialized recreation and city life*) to help with this study. Their resulting manuscript, "Movies, delinquency, and crime," has never materialized. However, some portions of Cressey's text have turned up. Arguing against dominant logic of the time, he sums up much: "Social causation [of movie effects] is entirely too complex a problem to be explained by any . . . simplistic interpretation of incomplete data" (Jowett et al., 1996: 126). He also acknowledged, importantly, the pedagogical value of popular culture—including the ways it eclipsed traditional such institutions. Popular culture "should not be linked to boys' delinquency, but must instead be viewed as a powerful source of 'informal education' that served boys in a far more direct and practical way than did schools or the Boys' Club" (p. 350).

Importantly, this work was girded by normative, functionalist underpinnings—ones perhaps best described as "Durkheimean." That is, scholars were interested in the ways groups came to the US and undertook the process of assimilation. While Thrasher painted rich, sympathetic portraits of young "gang boys," he ultimately saw such gangs as a functional reaction to living in so-called "in-between" city spaces—what he called interstitial spaces. The goal was to figure out ways to more efficiently integrate these young men into what he perceived as a dominant American culture. This would be a theme picked up by others in the Chicago School, including William Whyte in his classic *Street corner society*. Although these theoretical underpinnings would come to be challenged in some fundamental ways, the Chicago School of Sociology prefigured how popular culture would be taken up by sociologists in years to come. In particular, we see an effort to understand the cultural dimensions of young people's lives in times of social and technological upheaval. We see a stress on the educative function of popular culture—the ways popular culture steps into the void of traditional school life for many. We see, finally, an effort to look at popular culture in the context of young people's lives. Perhaps most importantly, we see the impulse to apply the insights of sociology—an emerging, empirical discipline—to the lives of youth. Popular culture was one part of situating these lives in broader social and economic context.

Cultural studies

Emerging from the UK in the 1960s and 1970s, work in cultural studies took up such questions around youth culture, though in specific and somewhat distinct ways. Drawing more explicitly on the work of Gramsci, cultural studies saw culture and ideology as a site of struggle, with young people both actively resisting and reproducing the class positions in which they found themselves. Scholars such as EP Thompson, Stuart Hall, Raymond Williams, Richard Hoggart, all opened up important questions about the role of "culture" in the lives of young people—work extended by Paul Willis, Dick Hebdige, Angela McRobbie, and others. This work drew upon an explicitly critical and theoretical tradition to help explain the role of popular culture in reproducing and resisting dominant ideology and hegemony, especially around class. If work in the Chicago School was concerned with questions of assimilation in a plural society, work in cultural studies would come to offer a more fundamental critique of capitalism.

Stuart Hall's *The popular arts* (1964) (co-authored with Paddy Whannel) is an early and important text out of this Birmingham School of Cultural Studies. Importantly, this book was rooted in Hall's experience as a teacher attempting to understand the range of cultural resources and influences young people bring to the classroom. For Hall and Whannel, popular culture is an important site for the young—in many ways, a more important site than traditional school settings. They write, "Their symbols and fantasies have a strong hold upon the emotional commitment of the young at this stage in their development, and operate more powerfully in a situation where young people are tending to learn less from established institutions, such as the family, the school, the church and the immediate adult community, and more from one another" (Hall and Whannel, 1964: 276). We see, of course, echoes of Cressey and other Chicago School sociologists here. However, like much of the work that would follow, this book was concerned with popular culture as "text," and brought a traditional literary lens to the subject. Much of this text was concerned with understanding a question that would haunt scholars for generations to come—how to understand "popular culture" and its continuities and discontinuities with so-called folk culture and emerging mass culture. This would be taken up by others, including, most notably, Raymond Williams. In a series of influential texts, Williams talked about the complex distinctions at work in the term—from everyday folk culture to mass mediated culture. All laid claim to the term "popular culture." While Thrasher was not concerned with drawing conceptual distinctions between the stories and songs young people told each other and the mediated culture produced in more centralized spaces, such conceptual concerns were central to Williams and others. Williams, Hall and others came to see "popular culture" not as a transcendent category—it could not be—but as a "terrain of struggle" over which young people contested. If work in the Chicago School was influenced by Durkheim, work in cultural studies was influenced by Marx and Gramsci—in particular, the latter's notion of popular culture as a terrain of struggle. In sum, work in the Chicago School was concerned with how young people carved identities out of the instabilities of immigrant identities, while work out of the Birmingham School was concerned with the ways young people lived out the instabilities of class across generations.

Resistance through rituals: youth subcultures in post-war Britain, edited by Stuart Hall and Tony Jefferson (1976), was in many ways a watershed book of the movement and moment. Drawing together many of the figures who would be central to these debates in following years (Hall, Hebdige, McRobbie, and Willis, among them), the editors and authors focused on youth subcultures—groups, as Clarke *et al.* write, "which have reasonably tight boundaries, distinctive shapes, [and] have cohered around particular activities, focal concerns and territorial spaces" (Hall and Jefferson, 1976: 13). These include those of the mods, skinheads, Rastafarians, punks, and teddy boys. As the authors demonstrate, such subcultures are a way for youth to carve out symbolic space between the "parent" or working-class culture and the dominant culture. "For our purposes," they write, "sub-cultures represent a necessary, 'relatively autonomous', but inter-mediary level of analysis" (Hall and Jefferson, 1976: 14). Through these symbolic, subculture forms, youth try to solve (or "magically resolve") the problems of their class position. They are a way for youth both to resist against the dominant order—and also to be incorporated into it.

Subculture: the meaning of style (Hebdige, 1979) was another key text here. In particular, *Subculture* took the everyday cultural lives of young people seriously, looking at everyday "style" as a site of resistance to dominant culture and its logics. Hebdige's study was closely focused on the "semiotics" of youth culture. That is, he was interested in how young people took the symbols and signs available in everyday life and used them in new and different ways to carve out their own, distinctive subcultural identities. Hebdige gave us a language of "appropriation" and "re-appropriation." In this study, Hebdige focused on the range of "spectacular" subcultures that emerged in London after World War II—skinheads, punks, mods, teddy boys, Rastafarians, and others. For Hebdige, as with others noted above, these cultural forms were a response to instability around how "class" was lived in England in a post-war context. In the absence of firm foundations, young people developed a set of subcultures to help "resolve" the contradictions around class. He writes

> The persistence of class as a meaningful category within youth culture was not . . .
> generally acknowledged until fairly recently and, as we shall see, the seemingly spontaneous
> eruption of spectacular youth styles has encouraged some writers to talk of youth as the
> new class.
>
> (Hebdige, 1979: 75)

This raises the question of style as bricolage and style as homology—two central concerns of Hebdige. For Hebdige, youth subcultures are key sites where different cultural signs and symbols can be "mixed and matched" in new and creative ways. This is bricolage. Drawing on Levi-Strauss, he argues that young people can draw "implicitly coherent, though explicitly bewildering, systems of connection between things which perfectly equip their users to 'think' their own world." He continues, "These magical systems of connection have a common feature: they are capable of infinite extension because basic elements can be used in a variety of improvised combinations to generate new meanings within them" (p. 103). For Hebdige, young people are like artists, drawing together distinct signs and symbols and creating a coherent meaning system among them. Recall the punk use of the safety pin, the spiked haircut, the dramatic collages—all helped form a coherent meaning system.

Work in cultural studies helped open up critical questions about the cultural dimensions of young people's lives—questions that would be taken up around the world in important ways throughout the 1980s and 1990s (Grossberg *et al.*, 1992). Much of this work was concerned with understanding the ways young people's everyday lives were saturated with social and political meanings, often expressed as "style." This work was useful in opening a new conversation about how politics works in the lives of youth. In particular, this work helped open up a space to think about how popular culture and everyday life were a terrain upon which young people struggled over the politics of meanings—in ways often unrecognized or ignored. Popular culture itself became a pedagogical site—one that both helped reproduce and resist hegemonic norms (Giroux, 1996, 2000).

New sociology of education

Coming out of the UK, beginning in the 1970s, work in the "new sociology of education," looked more specifically at all the ways in which curricula worked to effect social and economic reproduction. This work shares much with the work noted above—in particular, the ways distinctions between "elite" and "everyday" knowledge served to reproduce distinctions that marginalized working-class youth. Much of this work was drawn together in the highly influential volume, *Knowledge and control: new directions for the sociology of education* (1971), edited by M.F.D. Young. This collection included contributions by (among others) Young, Basil Bernstein, and Pierre Bourdieu—all of whom would be critical for the field. All of this work was concerned with similar such questions as those in cultural studies—most specifically, the ways in which different knowledges are stratified. Such scholars were concerned with the ways in which working-class youth's culture was marginalized in school—pushing them out in unfair ways (Bernstein, 1973, 1977). In many respects, this work can be seen as one of the earliest iterations of the "popular culture and education" question, which would come to mark the field in years to come.

Like many neo-Marxist curriculum scholars, M.F.D. Young was interested in the connections between social stratification and knowledge stratification. In particular, he was interested in the ways schools marginalized working-class youth by producing arbitrary and unfair distinctions between "high" and "low" status knowledge. The former is so-called "pure," not applied, knowledge. Such knowledge operates at the level of broad generalities, not specificities. This distinction helps explain why vocational education is typically marginalized in school settings. Often attractive to working-class youth, this kind of education is often marked as low status. For M.F.D. Young, these distinctions between high- and low-status knowledge help explain why schools do not serve the needs and interests of working-class youth.

In arguing for this, Young underscores a point that would be critical to the new sociologists of education—that knowledge itself was a social construction. This insight opened up a critical space to think about the curricula as a politically contested construct. Curricular knowledge is not simply "given" but a function of power. This raised a series of questions, including:

Who controls curricular knowledge? And whose interest does it serve? For Young and others, this is not only a question of curricula content. It is a question of how knowledge itself was organized. More specifically, Young was interested in the question of how knowledge becomes specialized, and how this specialized knowledge falls under the purview of the elite. Indeed, the separation of knowledge into discrete disciplines was itself a function of power. All of this worked to create specific kinds of knowledge stratification that helped to maintain broader kinds of social stratification. For Young and others, the pressing question was one of social class.

Another key thinker in the new sociology of education is the French sociologist Pierre Bourdieu. Beginning in the 1970s, including in the volume, *Knowledge and control*, Bourdieu raised a series of questions and issues that would prove central to neo-Marxist curriculum studies. In 1977, he published, with Jean-Claude Passeron, the seminal *Reproduction in education, society, and culture* (Bourdieu and Passeron, 1977). This volume brought together and crystallized many of his most central insights for the field. Like others in neo-Marxist curriculum studies, Bourdieu was centrally concerned with showing how school curricula served the interests of the elite, even as they appeared neutral and disinterested. More than anyone, Bourdieu opened up important questions about the nature of "elite" cultural activities and the process by which they become legitimated. As Bourdieu argued, so-called "high art" forms enter a certain intellectual field that is controlled by and serves the interests of the elite (Bourdieu, 1984). This intellectual field—and its associated critics, teachers, other artists, etc.—works to confer a particular kind of legitimacy upon these forms. These elite art forms are often quite different from those privileged by the working classes. So, for example, classical music is privileged over and above interior design or cookery. The particular power of these distinctions, of course, is that they do appear as "elite." Their power is made to appear natural and immutable. Schools play a particular role in this process. For Bourdieu (and Passeron), schools reward the cultural dispositions of the elite, translating them into different kinds of success and achievement. In particular, schools translate the "cultural capital" that elites typically grow up with into "economic capital." In turn, schools marginalize working class youth—committing a kind of "symbolic violence" upon them. For Bourdieu, this violence is arbitrary, as are these cultural distinctions. They work only to reproduce the power of elites—here, through school knowledge.

As this work traveled to the US—in particular, with the work of Michael Apple (2006)— these questions began to look beyond class as the only stable reference point. Questions of race and gender moved to the fore, as did other ideological predispositions that helped form school life and curricular knowledge in the US. Perhaps most notably, Apple has focused on how the Right has produced a certain kind of "common sense" that has drawn together various factions —those of Christian evangelicals, the new middle classes, cultural conservatives, and neo-liberals—under a common umbrella. There has been an "accord" between these groups that has produced a certain kind of common sense about the role of education in the world. In particular, a set of business logics have deeply lodged themselves in the popular imagination around education—one of vouchers, high stakes testing, as well as related interventions. All of these have drawn on and mobilized a popular knowledge and common sense in specific ways.

Curriculum scholars today face several new challenges. As M.F.D. Young (2007) argued in a recent retrospective, the field has never developed a viable, alternative curriculum to the one offered in school settings. For Young, the work has remained largely critical, often assuming the primacy of a de facto "common curriculum" of the people. That is, if schools offered a largely "pure" and disconnected curriculum that did not draw on the lives of the working-classes, the solution would be an applied, vocational curriculum that drew on the strengths of these groups.

As Young argued, this was largely a fruitless effort to "flip the binary," and did not answer more fundamental questions about which knowledge is most worth teaching. This remains a central question for those in popular culture in education—how does one draw distinctions in what is most valuable to teach? How does one decide what is better or worse curricular knowledge? While Young's concerns resonate (at least partially) in the UK context, Apple and others have worked hard to develop responses to this challenge on a global stage. With nearly 500,000 copies in print, the two editions of *Democratic schools* (Apple and Beane, 1995, 2007) are perhaps the best examples of popular, curricular alternatives developed from within the new sociology of education tradition.

Future directions

The methods and theories discussed above are brought to bear on much work on popular culture and education today. But many of its defining constructs are proving insufficient to address the specificities of our moment—in particular, around the complexities of globalization and new technologies (Huq, 2006). Many of the projects described above rely upon fairly stable notions of the nation-state and the political projects and theories that gird them—whether functionalist or Marxist. Yet, many wrestle with constructs that have remained stable over time.

The question of "sub-cultures" is key. Anita Harris (2008) sums this up nicely in her collection *Next wave cultures: feminism, subcultures, activism*:

> Nowadays, subcultures are not perceived simply as singular, fixed categories that youth are affiliated to in order to work out their class identities or to resist dominant culture. Instead, theorists talk about neotribes, youth lifestyles, scenes, new communities and so on as momentary and changeable expressions of identity.
>
> (Harris, 2008: 3)

Subculture theory assumed that groups had seemingly stable boundaries that could be explained both in terms of their resistance to, and incorporation in, an industrial economy. With the rise of post-industrial, neo-liberal economic regimes and the destabilizing cultural effects of globalization, however, much more is "up for grabs" today, as evidenced by this and related work (Dolby and Rizvi, 2008). Indeed, the shifts and dislocations associated with globalization are registering for young people in often disorientating and paradoxical ways. Young people are growing up in a world increasingly marked by new, massive disparities in wealth, the worldwide circulation of (often rigidly fundamentalist) ideologies and belief systems, a dizzying array of signs and symbolic resources dislodged from their traditional moorings, as well as a veritable explosion of new technologies. Youth are now trying to find their "place(s)" in this world, "moving" across this terrain in ways we are only beginning to understand and appreciate. As recent work is making clear, young people are crafting new identities and social networks using a range of globally generated and proliferating resources. Young people are "moving," both literally and figuratively, crossing national borders with their bodies as well as imaginations, crafting new and unexpected kinds of identity.

Key ethnographic work continues to open up interesting questions about the worldwide circulation of popular texts. These studies highlight the ways in which "urban" cultural texts are circulating around the world, landing in particular ways in particular contexts, in ways that allow youth to articulate their own contemporary circumstances (see Condry, 2006; Dimitriadis,

2001; Dolby 2001; Mitchell, 2001; Tempelton, 2006). I recall here the work of Brett Lashua (2005). For several years, Lashua worked with First Nations youth in the city of Edmonton, Alberta, helping to construct a studio for these youth to record their own rap songs. As Lasuha demonstrated, these young people both drew on the dominant tropes and themes in rap music while linking them to specificity of life on "the rez." Like others, Lashua shows how these young people address their contemporary concerns through contemporary "urban" art forms such as hip hop. Linked closely to notions of place, these texts have traveled the world, allowing young people to carve out their own senses of self in often hostile sets of social circumstances. Lashua's study throws these issues into sharp relief—highlighting the ways First Nations youth bring their concerns into the urban present through hip hop, challenging often debilitating stereotypes about indigenous youth.

Other studies take on more traditional questions about youth "learning" through popular culture, though in new ways (see, for example, Buckingham, 1996, 1998, 2000; Buckingham and Sefton-Green, 1995; Goodman, 2003; Mahiri, 1998; Morrell, 2004, 2008; Sefton-Green, 1998, 1999). For example, Leif Gustavson's (2007) important book *Youth learning on their own terms* carefully traces the out-of-school creative practices of three youth in the US around the urban East—Ian, Miguel, and Gil—immersing himself in their complex and multifaceted life-worlds, teasing out how they understand the particulars of their crafts. In looking at these creative practices through three very specific biographies, Gustavson highlights their deep and often ignored cognitive components and dimensions. In each of these cases—Ian's 'zine writing and slam poetry, Miguel's graffiti writing, and Gil's turntable work—we see creative minds at work, making choices and decisions as they work through the intricacies of their media. We see, as well, the particular, productive intersections between these practices and their specific raced and classed backgrounds—not as determining but as constitutive of their material and aesthetic lives.

This underscores the importance of new modes of distribution and circulation of popular culture. This is a debate taken up, among other places, in "fandom" studies but it is one education would do well to explore (Gray *et al.*, 2007). Indeed, the global proliferation of contemporary media forms has allowed young people around the world to tailor their own leisure practices in very specific and particular ways. If the dominant media model used to be "broadcasting," today's world of inexpensive cable and widespread Internet penetration is perhaps one of "narrowcasting." Young people around the world are carving out new, unpredictable, and in some ways rhizomatic, forms of cultural identification in ways often invisible (and typically inexplicable) to adults. Sometimes these are defined by taste. Sometimes these are defined by race or ethnic identity. Sometimes—often—they are marked by both. Inextricably intertwined with this are new articulations of technology, including the emergence of what Henry Jenkins calls "convergence culture." Here, Jenkins refers to

> the flow of content across multiple media platforms, the cooperation between multiple media industries, the search for new media financing that fall at the interstices between old and new media, and the migratory behavior of media audiences who would go almost anywhere in search of the kind of entertainment experiences they want.
>
> (Jenkins, 2006: 282)

If the media landscape used to be divided fairly clearly between the "producers" and "consumers" of popular culture, young people today occupy a new, middle ground. Using largely inexpensive forms of technology, young people are creating their own self-styled cultural texts across multiple platforms—as evidenced by the explosion of MySpace, YouTube, Facebook, Blogger, and other such sites. These texts are both proliferating in their own specific communities as well as "speaking back" to corporate culture in ways that can have constitutive effects on the material production of culture.

Benefiting from the theoretical and methodological advances of the last decade, work on contemporary youth culture is moving in several directions at once, opening up multiple and complex notions of identity as it is lived in the everyday. In particular, this work looks towards the ways in which young people are navigating their everyday lives using popular cultural texts in complex and unpredictable ways. None of this work reduces the lives and experiences of these youth to tight, subcultural boundaries. At its best, such work can force us closer and closer to the lives of young people, showing us unexpected vistas for thought and reflection. Indeed, much of the best work in popular culture and education has done exactly this—de-centering the presumed and presumptive authority of the researcher and educator. Such work allows us to see the affective investments young people have in the texts and practices most salient in their lives. Such work can destabilize the ways in which educators choose to organize and control knowledge.

Note

1   This chapter explores issues further elaborated upon in my book *Studying urban youth culture* (2008, Peter Lang).

References

Apple, M.W. (2006) *Educating the "right" way*, 2nd edn, New York: Routledge.
—— and Beane, J. (eds) (1995, 2007) *Democratic schools*, Alexandria, VA: Association for Supervision and Curriculum Development.
Bernstein, B. (1973) *Class, codes and control*, Vol. 1, London: Routledge.
—— (1977) *Class, codes and control*, Vol. 3, London: Routledge.
Bourdieu, P. (1984) *Distinction: A social critique of the judgment of taste* (trans. R. Nice), Cambridge, MA: Harvard University Press.
—— and Passeron, J. (1977) *Reproduction in education, society, and culture*, Thousand Oaks, CA: Sage.
—— (1996) *Moving images: understanding children's emotional responses to television*, Manchester: Manchester University Press.
—— (ed.) (1998) *Teaching popular culture: beyond radical pedagogy*, London: UCL Press.
—— (2000) *The making of citizens*, London: Routledge.
—— and Sefton-Green, J. (1995) *Cultural studies goes to school: reading and teaching popular media*, London: Taylor & Francis.
Condry, I. (2006) *Hip-hop Japan: rap and the paths of cultural globalization*, Durham, NC: Duke University Press.
Dimitriadis, G. (2001) *Performing identity/performing culture: hip hop as text, pedagogy, and lived practice*, New York: Peter Lang.
Dolby, N. (2001) *Constructing race: youth, identity, and popular culture in South Africa*, Albany, NY: SUNY Press.
—— and Rizvi, F. (eds) (2008) *Youth moves*, New York: Routledge.
Giroux, H. (1996) *Fugitive cultures: race, violence, and youth*, New York: Routledge.
—— (2000) *Impure acts: the practical politics of cultural studies*, New York: Routledge.

Goodman, S. (2003) *Teaching youth media: a critical guide to literacy, video production and social change*, New York: Teachers College Press.

Gray, J., Sandvoss, C. and Harrington, L. (eds) (2007) *Fandom*, New York: NYU Press.

Grossberg, L., Nelson, C. and Treichler, P. (1992) *Cultural studies*, New York: Routledge.

Gustavson, L. (2007) *Youth learning on their own terms*, New York: Routledge.

Hall, S. and Jefferson, T. (eds) (1976) *Resistance through rituals: youth subcultures in post-war Britain*, Birmingham, UK: Open University Press.

—— and Whannel, P. (1964) *The popular arts*, New York: Pantheon.

Harris, A. (ed.) (2008) *Next wave cultures: feminisms, subcultures, activism*, New York: Routledge.

Hebdige, D. (1979) *Subculture: the meaning of style*, London: Routledge.

Huq, R. (2006) *Beyond subculture: pop, youth and identity in a postcolonial world*, New York: Routledge.

Jenkins, H. (2006) *Convergence culture: where old and new media collide*, New York: NYU Press.

Jowett, G., Jarvie, I. and Fuller, K. (eds) (1996) *Children and the movies: media influence and the Payne Fund studies*, Cambridge: Cambridge University Press.

Lashua, B. (2005) "Making music, re-making leisure in The Beat of Boyle Street," unpublished Ph.D. dissertation, University of Alberta, Canada.

Mahiri, J. (1998) *Shooting for excellence: African American and youth culture in new century schools*, Urbana, IL: National Counsel of Teachers of Education.

Mitchell, T. (eds) (2001) *Global noise: rap and hip-hop outside the USA*, Middletown, CT: Wesleyan University Press.

Morrell, E. (2004) *Becoming critical researchers: literacy and empowerment for urban youth*, New York: Peter Lang.

—— (2008) *Critical literacy and urban youth: pedagogies of access, dissent, and liberation*, New York: Routledge.

Sefton-Green, J. (ed.) (1998) *Digital diversions: youth culture in the age of multimedia*, New York: Routledge.

—— (ed.) (1999) *Young people, creativity and new technologies*, New York: Routledge.

Tempelton, I. (2006) "What's so German about it?: Race and cultural identity in Berlin's hip hop community," unpublished Ph.D. dissertation, University of Stirling.

Thrasher, F. (1927) *The gang: a study of 1,316 gangs in Chicago*, Chicago, IL: University of Chicago Press.

Young, M. (1971) *Knowledge and control: new directions for the sociology of education*, New York: Macmillian.

—— (2007) *Bringing knowledge back in*, New York: Routledge.

18

Schooling the body in a performative culture

John Evans, Brian Davies and Emma Rich

The body is a great intelligence, a plurality with one mind, a war and a peace, a flock and a shepherd.

And thy little intelligence, my brother, which thou callest 'spirit' – is a tool of the body, a little tool and a plaything of thy great intelligence.

I thou sayest, and art proud of the word. But a greater matter – which thy wilst not believe – is thy body and its great intelligence. It saith not I, but it doeth I.

(Nietzsche, *Thus Spake Zarathustra*, Bozman, 1957)

I have always written with my whole body: I do not know what purely intellectual problems are.

(Nietzsche, *Thus Spake Zarathustra*, Pascal, 1952)

In many respects, the sociology of education is quintessentially 'of the body', though it has not always articulated its mission as such. Historically, it has sought to document how individuals are fashioned and inscribed with social meaning, status and value through organizational and pedagogical practices reflecting particular cultural and class interests and ideals. Much less frequently, it has sought to understand how material flesh and blood, thinking, feeling, sentient beings are written on to social and cultural landscapes utilizing attributes variously defined as habits, aptitudes, abilities or intelligences, which may be recognized as of value in and outside schools. But either we understand the social world as the intersection of embodied agency and structure, critically as a dialectic of biology and culture (Evans *et al.*, 2009; Grosz, 1995; Shilling, 2008a,b) or we fail to understand human existence and its reproduction at all.

The founding figures of sociology were, as Chris Shilling (2008a,b) has pointed out, keenly interested in how 'corporeal processes could be interpreted as actual indicators of social reproduction and change'. He noted, for example, that both Durkheim (1995, originally 1912) and Weber (1991, originally 1904–1905) sought explication of the social importance of what he termed 'the cultural *body pedagogics* characteristic of a society' based on recognition that culture is 'not just a matter of cognitive or symbolic knowledge, but entails an education into socially sanctioned bodily techniques, dispositions and sensory orientations to the world (Mauss, 1973, originally 1934)' (Shilling, 2008a: viii). They explored those forms of 'body pedagogics' central either to the inception and development of *industrial* society, or those minimal forms that could be associated with the consolidation of *any* social group. However, as Shilling pointed out, it was Heidegger (1993, originally 1954: 320, 329, 333) who provided the most relevant and disturbing vision of 'body pedagogics' associated with the culture of advanced, technological society in the West, the defining property of which was that '*people* themselves are regarded as a standing-reserve for the demands of a system that prioritizes production over all else' (Shilling, 2008a). Such a situation could go unrecognized by the majority of those subject to it, used to regarding the world through the prism of rational instrumentalism, 'failing to see that they have become the object of this logic' (Shilling, 2008a: x). In such a culture, our bodily selves are increasingly subject to, not only the performative expectations of the labour market, but those of consumer culture centred around visions of physical perfection, usually articulated as slender body ideals (Evans *et al.*, 2008b; Gordon, 2000; Grogan, 1999; Shilling, 2008a; Shilling and Mellor, 2007; Wright and Harwood, 2009). The characteristic experience associated with this instrumental orientation towards life is that:

> the body becomes *objectified* as an absent-present raw material that we are responsible for controlling in line with external standards (rather than as the vehicle of our sensuous and creative being-in-the-world) . . . the embodied subject is either positioned as a '*standing reserve*' for the demands of productivity or is stigmatised and viewed as morally suspect.
>
> (Shilling, 2008a: xi)

The precise manner in which this 'enframing' of the body proceeds varies across institutions and is clearly exemplified in contemporary approaches to health.

Sociological interest in 'the body' is, then, nothing new, although most sociologists of education have been less than universally eager to embrace it directly in their analyses. Yet, long before the likes of Foucault, Bernstein, Elias, Bourdieu, Derrida, Douglas, Grosz, Butler or their contemporary, school-focused apostles depicted it rather prosaically as a shadowy, ghostly, disembodied figure in the educational machine, Wallard (1932) had already pointed out in seminal detail that schools were complex social organizations comprising people in roles and motion, living 'an organismic interdependence' (p. 6). It was not possible to affect them in part without altering the shape of the whole; schools were manifestly social bodies, whose inherently relational and contingent elements had ripple effects on others within and beyond them. Within them, those in authority were set to work on others' bodies, essentially to socialize, skill, organize and differentiate them by age, ability, sex and potential occupational status. Patently, they sorted 'able' from 'less able', boys from girls, one religious affiliation from another, or none, and even black from white. Such corporeal categories were regularly writ large in school names and signage above many a school door. Manipulating classrooms, corridors, playgrounds and time-tabled time, schools variously sifted and sorted, segregated and differentiated, ordered and classified, imposing geographies of the body, nurturing social relations that celebrated either a sense of '*similarity to*' or '*difference from*', depending on the philosophy, ideology and nature of the privileging educational code (Evans and Davies, 2004). The body, then, has always been writ large in the organization of schooling, via its classifications and framing of pedagogy, curriculum and assessment techniques, by virtue of their mission to allocate position and privilege and distribute success, failure, status and value. In simultaneously disciplining, punishing or privileging in terms of myriad rules and evaluations, schools inevitably either affirm, damage or enhance individuals' corporeality in place, space and time.

Against a backdrop of near global economic, medical and technological change, of a kind alluded to by Shilling, *pace* Heidegger, governments across affluent Western and westernized societies have sought, not only to alter surface features of education so as to ensure the electoral allegiance of the already privileged and aspirant, but also to reach into and manipulate its deeper structures. In recent decades, there has been a significant step change in attention paid to the body by purveyors of popular culture and burgeoning body/health industries, and central governments have been increasingly tempted to claim control of its underlying ethics, codes and principles, which regulate communication and embodied consciousness and their location. Such inclinations have often been sanctified as being necessary in order to control and better 'educate' potentially volatile and, purportedly, increasingly unhealthy (overweight and obese) populations. A new and pervasive form of 'surveillance education' has emerged in which 'perfection codes' (Evans and Davies, 2004) (which centre attention on one's *'relationship to one's embodied self'*) and 'surveillance medicine and health' (Armstrong, 1995), reaching way beyond schools, feature prominently. Its narratives are neither arbitrary nor socially innocent. Although couched in good intent, they serve, nonetheless, to fashion and alter individuals' consciousness and relationships to their bodies in such a way that existing social hierarchies and westernized, affluent, white, middle-class cultural values are celebrated within a particularly narrow version of 'being healthy' (Azzarito and Solomon, 2006). In the process, the lifestyles, cultures and embodied characteristics of many are 'abjectified' (Kenway *et al.*, 2006), while those of relatively few (slim, active, independent individuals) are privileged and portrayed as corporeal exemplars of desirable aspirational ideals. It is hardly surprising, then, that we find in countries across such societies a ubiquitous fear, especially among the middle classes, of being defined as 'overweight', inactive and manifestly insufficiently thin.

'Body pedagogics' and the medicalization of our lives

In what some refer to as the *medicalization* of people's lives (Furedi, 2005), the reclassification of populations globally as 'at risk', in perpetual states of being 'potentially unwell', has no more been accident than conspiracy on the part of science or health educators' malicious intent. It has owed as much to changing approaches in medicine to 'health' over the last forty years as to the way in which nation-states have increasingly sought to exercise authority and control over potentially recalcitrant populations, while simultaneously serving global capitalism's interests. Generating surplus value rests on increasing consumption, even when dieting. In late twentieth-century medicine, the quest for *cures* for ill health gave way to a search for its *causes* (see Le Fanu, 1999). This shift was driven by two very different specialties: 'new genetics' opened up possibilities of identifying abnormal genes in social diseases; and 'epidemiology' insisted that most common diseases, such as cancer, heart disease and diabetes, are caused by social factors connected to unhealthy lifestyles and are preventable by changing behaviour, such as switching diets, taking more exercise and reducing exposure to risk factors. Together, these approaches, especially when recontextualized through the ideologies of neo-liberalism and free market economics, generated policies that provided the basis for a radical shift from solving health problems through therapeutic measures to *intervention* – the earlier the better – making the lives of children and young people and their families and schools primary targets of health and education policies. Though driven by genuinely altruistic desire to improve the health of individuals and populations, when framed within an ideology of 'liberal individualism' and 'performativity' (see Ball, 2003, 2004) 'health' has taken on particularly narrow connotations around weight loss and slenderness, serving the interests not of education but surveillance and new forms of social control.

At the same time, in Western (and westernized) societies, coercive means of manipulating populations using explicit force and oppressive rule of law have given way to more subtle and less certain means of control involving a combination of mass surveillance and self-regulation, which Foucault (1978, 1979, 1980) called 'disciplinary power'. Here, individuals and populations are ascribed responsibility for regulating and looking after themselves, though often according to criteria over which they have very little say or control, while, at the same time, being more or less relentlessly monitored in their capacity to do so, in some respects from cradle to grave (see Foresight Commission, 2007: 63). As nation-states have become 'more concerned about the management of life (biopower) and the governing of populations' (Howson, 2004: 125), particularly in relation to health, disease, sexuality, welfare and education, individuals and communities become objects of 'surveillance, analysis, intervention and correction across space and time' (Nettleton, 1992, quoted in Howson, 2004). Biopower, however: 'depends on technologies through which the state and its agencies can manage "the politics of life to shape the social to accord with the tasks and exigencies faced by the state"' (Hewitt, 1983: 225, quoted in Howson, 2004). Foucault's reference 'to the knowledges, practices and norms that have been developed to regulate the quality of life of the population as bio-politics' indicates that the body becomes 'the raw material for this undertaking'. Distinct physical spaces become locations in which people are monitored by those in authority who may observe them with minimum effort: 'Relations within such spaces are based on the observation of the many by the watchful eyes of the few, or on the "gaze" which judges as it observes and decides what fits – what is normal – and what does not' (Howson, 2004: 126).

One unfortunate legacy of the Foucauldian moment in the sociology of education, health and physical education, however, is the tendency (not altogether mitigated in the concept of biopower) to characterize the aforementioned processes dichotomously and somewhat misleadingly as either external or internal forms of regulation of the body politic and the body's corporeality, rather than as the intersection of two mutually reinforcing modes of achieving order and control. Societies are depicted as having shifted from exercising imposed, disciplinary power to 'technologies of the self', whereby individuals or populations are 'encouraged' to regulate and continually work on their own bodies and 'self regulate'. Calling on a variety of government-provided expertise enjoined 'to shape, guide, direct the conduct of others' and 'bridle the individual's passions', individuals are induced to control their own instincts; they 'govern themselves' (Rose, 1999: 3). This rather caricatures the way in which order and control are pursued in advanced technological societies, obfuscating how different forms of embodiment may be nurtured when external and internal forms of regulation work conjointly on the body to 'enframe' subjectivity and embodied action, a process in which some bodies may achieve 'authenticity' and are compliant, while others are 'abjectified' and alienated and offer dissent.

But exercise of biopower neither assumes nor guarantees acceptance or internalization of its normalizing roles, rules and codes, not least because it cannot foresee or regulate the unintended consequence of policies, for example, with respect of individual or population failure to adopt 'correct' behaviours relating to weight, exercise and food. Pursuit of 'self induced' order always occurs within frameworks of disciplinary control. Moreover, given that disciplinary power and surveillance may vary across settings, individuals may experience corporeal 'authenticity' or 'abjection' across different sites of practice, depending on the proximity of their cultural values to prevailing social (corporeal) norms and/or their willingness to 'self regulate' within given or perceived zones of influence: psycho-social locations (communities of encoded practice) that are experienced somatically by individuals to have various levels of meaning, significance and/or control over their behaviour and development (Walkerdine, 2009). For example, some young people may experience 'the family' (or particular relations within it) or websites as having greater influence than schools on their understanding of health, food and body issues. Others may experience their peers as having greater influence on their developing corporeality than, say, teachers (De Pian, 2008; McLeod and Yates, 2006).

How governments or other institutions respond to weaknesses or invoke changes in their chosen or inherited modes of control should, therefore, reside high among the concerns of an embodied sociology of education (Gard and Kirk, 2007). In 'totally pedagogized societies' (TPS) (Bernstein, 2001) and totally pedagogized schools,[1] there is contingent intersection rather than shift or dislocation of external and internal forms of control in the interests of ensuring that populations are both orderly and controlled. Hence, where the pursuit of internal regulation fails (as surely it must if the majority population has little or no control over, or say in, the normalized, corporeal states they are expected to achieve), levels of surveillance and intervention can be activated and intensified to ensure conformity to stated ideals. Indeed, in plural, secular societies, such as the UK, where 'inner regulation' drawn either from theological or ethical codes is sometime depicted as either weak, dissonant or absent, the failure of certain populations to embrace state-manufactured, alternative ideologies, such as those of 'liberal individualism' and its guiding rules (e.g. around diet, exercise and weight), has been accompanied by increasing levels of coercive intervention and heightened levels of surveillance of populations in and outside schools.

It is in such contexts of heightened surveillance that new forms of normalizing practices emerge and prevail in many sites of social practice through the exercise of *body pedagogics* (Shilling, 2005, 2007), *bio-pedagogies* (Wright and Harwood, 2008) and *body pedagogies* (Evans and Davies, 2004; Evans *et al.*, 2008b), and their specific variants in schools. Such practices work as part of the bio-politics of contemporary Western cultures, steeped in body centric (e.g. obesity) discourse (see Campos, 2004; Gard and Wright, 2001, 2005; Halse *et al.*, 2007; Rich and Evans, 2005). Bio-pedagogies shape and form the body pedagogies of popular culture and schools and are infused with performance and perfection codes. How individuals interpret and recontextualize the inherent meanings and principles of such discourse determine how the body is schooled. We need ask: what forms of corporeality emerge, or rather, are induced and enacted in such contexts? Are some bodies privileged (authenticated), while others are abjectified, damaged or defiled (see Figure 18.1)? How are the possibilities for experiencing health and other forms of fulfilment governed by different levels of surveillance and one's value position in relation to preferred social norms? How is the *corporeal device* (see below) enacted within various zones of influence or 'networks of intimacy' (e.g. including relationships between parents and siblings, friends and partners (Heath and Cleaver, 2003: 47; Heath and Johnson, 2006; Paton, 2007a,b; De Pian, 2008)), mediating somatically their signs, meanings and message systems and how is 'proximal development' (Vygotsky, 1978) embodied in such contexts? Again, sociology of education, properly 'embodied', would begin to throw light on these concerns.

Where does work on the body occur?

Pedagogical activity thus occurs not only in formal education and schooling but in other socio-political and cultural sites, such as families, schools, churches, mosques and doctors' surgeries, in which work on the body occurs, and in emerging socio-technological landscapes of new media such as the Internet. Lupton (1999), for example, has argued that, for many lay people,

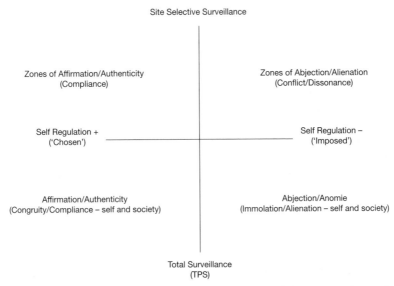

Figure 18.1 Zones of proximal influence – psych-social locations (of encoded meanings, signs and symbols) in which individuals somatically experience 'authenticity' or 'abjection' depending on the proximity of their cultural values (and other relevant dispositions) to those prevailing and valued within the particular social setting. Where the value systems are ubiquitous and inescapable such as in TPS, some individuals or populations may experience a profound and potentially destructive sense of anomie or alienation from their embodied selves as resentment or disaffection is turned inward toward the embodied self.

mass media now constitute *the* most important sources of information about health and medicine. As Lyons (2000: 350) contends: 'previously, medical practitioners dominated coverage of health and illness information, whereas today there are a variety of voices to be heard, including dissident doctors, alternative therapists, journalists, campaigners, academics and so on'. Miah and Rich (2008) have shown that many young people access health information not just from traditional medical sources but from newspapers, magazines, television and other electronic media. Research continues to highlight the importance of 'media representations of health and illness in shaping people's health beliefs and behaviors' (Giles, 2003: 318), critiquing many for their 'ability to mislead and misinform the public about health issues' (Giles, 2003: 217). Furthermore, Miah and Rich (2008) argue that, with the advent of a range of digital platforms that merge entertainment with the regulation of the body, such as Internet-based nutrition games and the use of games consoles such as the Nintendo Wii Fit, cyberspace may be providing a forum for new forms of regulative practices concerning health. (Armstrong, 1995). Environments, for example the Wii Fit, provide contexts that allow the individual to 'virtualize' his or her identity, leading to a 'prostheticisation of the body within cyberspace', through which it is projected. Cyberspace has thus extended the means through which body pedagogies and mechanisms of self-surveillance of the body can be articulated. In so doing, these contexts invoke a particular ontology of the body as materiality and flesh, but also as a prosthetic that represents itself in some fixed capacity within cyberspaces (Rich and Miah, 2009).

Body-centred discourses (e.g. around obesity) do not, then, reach straightforwardly into the lives of young people and certainly not only through formal educational practices, but circulate globally through the media and websites as forms of 'popular pedagogy' before finding their way into schools, both through official policies and initiatives (Evans *et al.*, 2008b). Health discourse as popular pedagogy is formed as part of a relentless cycle of policy and spin, generating initiatives that reach way beyond the school setting. In this context, formal education constitutes a relatively small, yet extremely significant, element in the configuration of processes by which the body is now schooled. It both refracts and helps forge global 'healthscapes', the 'symbolic universes' and meaning systems that reconfigure people's lives. As others have pointed out, such scapes know no physical nor geographical boundaries, are almost always hierarchical and linked to 'global ideoscapes and mediscapes of abjection', now commonly 'associated with food, waste and sexual difference' (Kenway *et al.*, 2006: 129, citing Kristeva, 1982). They also note that, in popular culture, 'the abject' has 'come to be associated with those bodily fluids, people, objects and places that are depicted as unclean, impure, and even immoral':

> The 'abject' disturbs 'identity, system, order' (Kristeva, 1982: 4) and provokes the desire to expel the unclean to an outside, to create boundaries in order to establish the certainty of the self. It involves the erection of social taboos and individual defences. Insofar as the abject challenges notions of identity it must be cast out. Abjection involves the processes whereby that or those named unclean are reviled, repelled, and resisted.
>
> (Kenway *et al.*, 2006: 120)

Increasingly, 'the abject' in affluent cultures are those who either cannot or will not ascribe to health discourse and its 'slender body' ideals, more often than not the working-class poor, or those who, because of their ethnicity, culture or lifestyles (e.g. single-parent families), are blamed and shamed for purportedly prohibiting their offspring to exercise regularly and eat the correct foods at the correct time. Whether inadvertently or intentionally, such 'scapes of abjection' 'justify injustice, draw attention away from social suffering and thus deny the social reality of the marginalized . . . while constructing the poor as "the source of pollution and moral danger" (Sibley, 1995: 55)' (Kenway *et al.*, 2006: 120–121). Transmitted uncritically through the informal and formal practices of communities and schools, contemporary health discourse may serve such social functions, reproducing social hierarchies while damaging the identities of the most vulnerable.

The complexity of embodied social reproduction

Given that complex processes of socio-cultural reproduction involve multiple sites of practice, multiple agencies and meaning systems and the need to avoid overdetermination in accounts of how health discourse is reproduced as pedagogy, any sociology of education interested in the body would need to explore how obesity and wider body-centred discourse are translated into principles of communication. How are they recontextualized within particular social settings, afforded different levels of influence, and how are prevailing meaning systems, rules and resources within them either adopted, adapted, resisted or reshaped through individual 'knower structures' (Maton, 2006) given by culture and social class? In the flow and recontextualization of discourse within and between sites of practice, such as translation of government policies into school policy/initiatives, gaps open up, creating a space in which 'ideology can play' (Bernstein, 1996: 47). Individuals can read, interpret and recontextualize received wisdom or 'sacred' health knowledge that schools and other sites of practice convey through the cognitive filters of their culture and class. Research has persistently emphasized that young people are neither cultural dopes nor dupes, recontextualizing health knowledge critically through their own 'knower structures', their personal, culturally encoded, affective understandings of their own and others' bodies and health, within the framework of the imperatives of health education policy and the performative cultures of their schools.

The corporeal device

Used insensitively, a Foucauldian perspective may foster the notion that our individual subjectivity is merely an epiphenomenon, a discursive production of multiple knowledge(s) brought into play on the body by various 'technologies of truth'. This is not altogether unhelpful, enabling us to register differences between knowledge and ideology and to see that some ('health') knowledge(s) may be considered 'sacred' (objective, detached, unambiguous, predictive and reliable), others profane (contaminated by the subjectivities and immediacies and values systems and ideologies of everyday life) and of little value in formal education. All such discourses, however, are always, inevitably, mediated for individuals through their material, flesh and blood, sentient, thinking and feeling bodies, their actions and those of their peers, parents/guardians and other adults, usually within complex networks of relative intimacy that exercise various levels of influence over them. As a way of articulating the materiality of the *lived experiences* typically associated with acquiring the attributes required by obesity discourse and 'the actual embodied changes resulting form this process' (Shilling, 2005: 13), we have been inclined, *pace* Bernstein, to talk of the '*corporeal device*', to focus on the body as not just a discursive representation and relay of messages and power relations external '*to itself*' but as a voice '*of itself*' (Evans *et al.*, 2009). As a material/physical conduit it has an internal grammar and syntax given by the intersection of biology, culture and the predilections of class, which regulate embodied action and consciousness, including the ways in which discursive messages (and all other social relations) are read and received. This concept, we suggest, privileges neither biology nor culture and endorses Frank's (2006: 433) view that neither 'the experience of embodied health nor the observation of signs of health circulating outside bodies has to trump the other as being the real point of origin, rather, each is understood as "*making the other possible*"'. Others have rediscovered *Pragmatism* (Shilling, 2008b) and the works of John Dewey (1997) (Quennerstedt, Öhman and Ohman, 2010, forthcoming) to articulate similar concerns. How the corporeal device finds expression as conscious and subconscious embodied action and is subjectified (given shape, form and definition as 'personality') in and outside schools should be an enduring concern. At one level, it signals a concern with how body-centric health knowledge(s) produced in the primary field of knowledge production in science communities comes to be considered 'the thinkable' and 'sacred'; that is to say, 'official truth' as to what we ought to believe about the body and its capacity for health, fit to be purveyed in schools. At another level, it involves an exploration of embodied subjectivity, tracing how health knowledge(s), recontextualized within popular culture (through TV, websites and other media imagery), translate into education/health policies directed at schools. Mediated by teachers' and pupils' class and cultures, official health knowledge may become separated or dislocated from everyday health knowledge, which may become reclassified and read as unhealthy or 'profane'.

Conclusion

Across affluent Western and westernized worlds, young people are being both privileged and marginalized by popular cultural practices and their education and schooling. Increasingly, they have to deal with the normalizing expectations and requirements of performative culture and body-centred health (e.g. obesity) discourse. Understanding how they evade, accommodate or recontextualize relentless and penetrating surveillance of their bodies in school time and space requires us to press beyond analyses of the intrinsic content of body-centred health 'messages' to consider 'the voice' of education itself and how it is shaped by the *pedagogic device*.[2] Contemporary health discourse nurtures a language, grammar and syntax with regulative and instructional principles and codes that define thought and embodied action, a 'meaning potential' for 'health', largely in terms of weight, size and shape, where the solution to 'problems' is a matter of weight loss through taking more exercise and eating less food. Its language relates to global trends in policy and pedagogies on education and health that inadvertently endorse actions which both sustain social hierarchies and may be damaging for some young people's education and health.

Globally, an increasing number of educational issues, conversations, programmes and curricula are organized and operationalized on the basis of body-centred concerns with weight. As a consequence, certain problems are arising in relation to the well-being of young people. As Shilling (2008a) and others (e.g. Campos, 2004; Evans *et al.*, 2008b; Grogan, 1999; Halse *et al.*, 2008) have noted, the first is that the emphasis on shape, weight and 'fitness' concerns in school overlooks or marginalizes a whole series of other considerations that are important to young people, which are not provided with a place in this schema. Second, the effects of focusing on body and weight issues in school environments, already saturated by particular expectations regarding educational achievement, can be potentially devastating. It is hardly surprising that research is documenting young people increasingly constructing their identities and subjectivities, health and illness, through the language of performativity and health discourses that dominate contemporary culture in and outside schools. But they are not simply duped, nor are their problems merely discursive reflections of pressures endemic in society and schools. Young people neither simply read nor internalize these body-centric messages uncritically or merely 'cognitively' through disembodied 'knower structures'. They are mediated somatically and within their sub-cultural location in a specific time and space. Research evidence attests that young people tend to locate their difficulties viscerally and relationally in antecedent experiences of their fast-changing, sometimes awkward, less than 'perfect' bodies, among their families, teachers and peers. Within these networks of relative intimacy, their changing bodies are inescapably subjected to their own and others' evaluative gazes. For some, engaging in 'deviant' actions, for example, radical body modification involving excessive exercise and eating little or no food, experiencing the joy of achieving the distinction of 'thin' beyond the slender ideal, becomes a perfectly rational, morally acceptable goal that avoids the pain of being 'othered', made to feel different, less worthy and excluded. The sociology of education has barely begun to investigate and understand how these processes enter the lived experiences of children and young people through popular and formal pedagogies that feature in and outside school.

The growing pressure wrought through contemporary body-centric policies and their associated pedagogies to obtain 'the right' body size/shape is not, then, simply about being healthy, but carries moral characterizations where the 'obese' or 'overweight' become lazy, self-indulgent and greedy. Body-centric narratives, infused with performance and perfection codes, sieve, separate, celebrate and vilify manifest body shape and form. They simultaneously celebrate and abjectify particular lifestyles, people, positions and actions. Such a performative culture, for example, induces individuals from a disturbingly young age to learn to fear and loathe bodies that are not the correct shape or weight; control, virtue and goodness (hence, 'acceptance', employability and trainability) are to be found in slenderness and processes of becoming excessively thin. Responsibility falls upon individuals to accept that correct diet, involvement in physical activity and the pursuit of 'perfection' academically are moral as well as corporeal obligations. Given the social sanctions that accompany this discourse, including bullying, stigma and labelling, particularly reported by young people defined by their peers as 'fat', it is hardly surprising that some not only take drastic action to lose weight but became seriously depressed, as well as physically ill.

The sociology of education needs to engage with changing worlds in which health and other body-centred discourses are configured. Further theoretical and empirical work on such issues is badly needed, to engage with the paradox of rejecting the performative values that are driving social change and current conceptions of health while accepting that there are immediate problems to deal with in the form of poor diets, too few opportunities for play and exercise, and ill health, having origins in the impoverished and inequitable social conditions of people's lives in a context of global capitalism. In Apple's (2006) terms, unless we honestly confront and think tactically about neo-liberal-inspired market proposals and neo-liberal purposes, we will fail to create counter-hegemonic common sense about health or build counter-hegemonic alliances. As Apple implores, our analyses have to be sufficiently connected to ways in which conservative modernization has altered common sense and transformed material and ideological conditions surrounding schooling, including those relating to the body and health. They also have to be aware of, and draw on, alternative belief systems and conceptions of 'health' and embodiment and strategies for disseminating them when contesting current health policy orthodoxies and pedagogic modalities. Doing so would locate 'the body' and embodied learning as central to sociology of education's concerns.

Notes

1   In such contexts, concern for the shape and 'health' of 'the body' is no longer the preserve only of those areas of the curriculum historically concerned with body issues, such as physical education, health education or personal and social education, but is regarded as everyone's concern in classrooms, playgrounds, dining halls and corridors. No one and 'no body' escapes the evaluative gaze. These changes, then, concern internal and external forms of regulation and the range and reach of authority and control into the lives of individuals and populations (Evans et al., 2008b).

2   Bernstein (1990: 190) refers to the voice of pedagogy that is constituted by the *pedagogic device*: 'a grammar for producing specialized messages (and) realizations, a grammar which regulates what it processes: a grammar which orders and positions and yet contains the potential of its own transformation'. Body-centred discourses constructed *outside* schools help form pedagogic discourse, foregrounding its instructional and regulative dimensions whose understanding needs to precede our attempts to understand how body pedagogies nurtured *inside* schools are infused with *competence, performance and perfection codes*, whose principles regulate but cannot 'determine' the embodied actions and positions of individuals. The discursive intersection of instructional and moral imperatives forms pedagogic discourse and provides principles that configure body pedagogies and implicit pedagogic positions and identities that circulate in popular culture and schools' health curricula and young people's responses to them.

References

Apple, M.W. (2006) 'Producing inequalities: neo-liberalism, neo-conservativism, and the politics of educational reform', in H. Lauder, P. Brown, J.-A. Dillabough and A.H. Halsey (eds) *Education, globalisation and social change*, Oxford: Oxford University Press.

Armstrong, D. (1995) 'The rise of surveillance medicine', *Sociology of Health and Medicine* 17: 393–404.

Azzarito, L. and Solomon, M.A. (2006) 'A post-structural analysis of high school students' gender and racialized bodily meanings', *Journal of Teaching in Physical Education* 25: 75–98.

Ball, S.J. (2003) 'The teacher's soul and the terrors of performativity', *Journal of Education Policy* 18(2): 215–228.

—— (2004) 'Performativities and fabrications in the education economy: toward the performative society', in S.J. Ball (ed.) *The RoutledgeFalmer reader in sociology of education*, London: RoutledgeFalmer.

Bernstein, B. (1990) *The structuring of pedagogic discourse*, Vol. 4, *Class, codes and control*, London: Routledge.

—— (1996) *Pedagogy, symbolic control and identity*, London: Taylor & Francis.

—— (2001) 'From pedagogies to knowledges', in A. Morias, I. Neves, B. Davies and H. Daniels (eds) *Towards a sociology of pedagogy: the contribution of Basil Bernstein to research*, New York: Peter Lang.

Bozman, M.M. (1957) *Nietzsche, thus spake Zarathustra* (trans. A. Tille, revised M.M. Bozman), London: Heron Books.

Campos, P. (2004) *The obesity myth*, New York: Gotham Books.

De Pian, L. (2008) 'Young people's decision making about health as an embodied social process', Ph.D. in progress, Loughborough University.

Dewey, J. (1997, originally 1938) *Experience and education*, New York: Simon & Schuster.

Durkheim, E. (1995, orginally 1912) *The elementary forms of religious life*, New York: Free Press.

Evans, J. and Davies, B. (2004) 'The embodiment of consciousness: Bernstein, health and schooling', in J. Evans, B. Davies and J. Wright (eds) *Body knowledge and control*, London: Routledge.

—— , —— and Rich, E. (2008a) 'The class and cultural functions of obesity discourse: our latter day child saving movement', *International Studies in Sociology of Education* 18(2): 117–132.

—— , —— and —— (2009) 'The body made flesh: embodied learning and the corporeal device', *British Journal of Sociology of Education* 30(4): 391–407.

—— Rich, E., Allwood, R. and Davies, B. (2008b) 'Body pedagogies, P/policy, health and gender', *British Educational Research Journal* 34(4): 387–403.

Foresight Commission (2007) *Tackling obesities: future choices – project report*, London: Government Office for Science.

Foucault, M. (1978) 'The means of correct training', in H. Lauder, P. Brown, J.-A. Dillabough and A.H.Halsey (2006) *Education, globalization & social change*, Oxford: Oxford University Press.

—— (1979) *Discipline and punish*, London: Peregrine.

—— (1980) *Power/knowledge: selected interviews and other writings 1972–1977*, Colin Gordon (ed.), New York: Pantheon.

Frank, A.W. (2006) 'Health stories as connectors and subjectifiers', *Health: An Interdisciplinary Journal for the Social Study of Health, Illness and Medicine* 10: 421, 440.

Furedi, F. (2005) 'Our unhealthy obsession with sickness', *Spiked Health*. Available online at www.spiked-online.com/Articles/0000000CA958.htm (accessed20 August 2008).

Gard, M. and Kirk, D. (2007) 'Obesity discourse and the crisis of faith in disciplinary technology', *Utbildning & Demorrati*, 16(2): 17–36.

—— and Wright, J. (2001) 'Managing uncertainty: obesity discourse and physical education in a risk society', *Studies in Philosophy and Education* 20: 535–549.

—— and —— (2005) *The obesity epidemic: science, morality and ideology*, London: Routledge.

Giles, D.C. (2003) 'Narratives of obesity as presented in the context of a television talk show', *Journal of Health Psychology* 8(3): 317–326.

Gordon, R.A. (2000) *Eating disorders: anatomy of an epidemic*, Oxford: Blackwell.

Grogan, S. (1999) *Body image: understanding body dissatisfaction in men, women and children*, London: Routledge.

Grosz, E. (1995) *Space, time and perversion: the politics of bodies*. Sydney: Allen & Unwin.

Halse, C., Honey, A. and Boughtwood, D. (2007) 'The paradox of virtue: (re) thinking deviance, anorexia and schooling', *Gender and Education* 19(2): 210–235.

—— , —— and —— (2008) *Inside anorexia. The experience of girls and their families*, London: Jessica Kingsley Publishers.

Heath, S. and Cleaver, E. (2003) *Young, free and single? Twenty-somethings and household change*, Basingstoke, UK: Palgrave.

—— and Johnson, B. (2006) 'Decision making about employment and educational pathways as embedded social practice: methodological considerations', Paper presented at SRHE Annual Conference, Brighton, 12–14 December 2006.

Heidegger, M. (1993) 'The question concerning technology', in D. Krell (ed.) *Martin Heidegger: basic writings*, London: Routledge.

Hewitt, M. (1983) 'Biopolitics and social policy: Foucault's account of welfare', *Theory, Culture and Society* 2: 67–84.

Howson, A. (2004) *The body in society: an introduction*, Oxford: Polity.

Kenway, J., Kraak, A. and Hickey-Moody, A. (2006) *Masculinity beyond the metropolis*, Basingstoke: Palgrave Macmillan.

Kristeva, J. (1982) *Powers of horror*, New York: Columbia University Press.

Le Fanu, J. (1999) *The rise and fall of modern medicine*, London: Abacus.

Lupton, D. (ed.) (1999) *Risk and socio-cultural theory: new directions and perspective*, Cambridge: Cambridge University Press.

Lyons, S. (2000) 'Examining media representations: benefits for health psychology', *Journal of Health Psychology* 5: 349–358.

Maton, K. (2006) 'On knowledge structures and knower structures', in R. Moore, M. Arnot, J. Beck and H. Daniels (eds) *Knowledge, power and educational reform*, London: Routledge.

Mauss, M. (1973, originally 1934) 'Techniques of the body', *Economy and Society* 2: 70–88.

McLeod, J. and Yates, L. (2006) *Making modern lives*, Albany: State University of New York Press.

Miah, A. and Rich, E. (2008) *The medicalisation of cyberspace*, London and New York: Routledge.

Nettleton, S. (1992) *Power, pain and dentistry*, Buckingham: Open University Press.

Pascal, R. (1957) 'Introduction', in Neitzsche, (1952) *Thus spake Zarathustra* (trans. A. Tille, revised M.M. Bozman), London: Heron Books.

Paton, K. (2007a) *Conceptualising choice: a review of the theoretical literature*, Working Paper for the ESRC-funded project 'Non-participation in higher education: decision-making as an embedded social practice', School of Education, University of Southampton.

—— (2007b) *Models of educational decision-making*, Working Paper for the ESRC-funded project 'Non-participation in Higher Education: Decision-making as an embedded social practice', School of Education, University of Southampton.

Quennerstedt, M., Öhman, J. and Ohman, M. (2010 forthcoming) 'Investigating learning in physical education' in *Sport, education and society*, 15.

Rich, E. and Evans, J. (2005) 'Making sense of eating disorders in schools', *Discourse: Studies in the Cultural Politics of Education* 26(2): 247–262.

—— and Miah, A. (2009) 'Prosthetic surveillance: the medical governance of healthy bodies in cyberspace', *Surveillance and Society: Special edition on Medical Surveillance*, 20 February 2009.

Rose, N. (1999) *Powers of freedom: reframing political thought*, Cambridge: Cambridge University Press.

—— (2005) 'Body pedagogics: a programme and paradigm for research', Paper presented to the School of Sport and Exercise Sciences, University of Loughborough.

—— (2007) *Embodying sociology: retrospect, progress and prospects*, London: Blackwell.

—— (2008a) 'Foreword: body pedagogics, society and schooling', in J. Evans, E. Rich, B. Davies and R. Allwood *Education, disordered eating and obesity discourse*, London: Routledge.

—— (2008b) *Changing bodies: habit, crisis and creativity*, London: Sage/TCS.

—— and Mellor, P.A. (2007) 'Cultures of embodiment: technology, religion and body pedagogics', *Sociological Review* 55(3): 531–549.

Sibley, D. (1995) *Geographies of exclusion, society and difference in the West*, London: Routledge.

Vygotsky, L.S. (1978) *Mind in society: the development of higher psychological processes*, M. Cole, S. John-Steiner, S. Scribner and E.S. Souberman (eds and trans.) Cambridge, MA: Harvard University Press.

Walkerdine, V. (2009) 'Biopedagogies and beyond', in J. Wright and V. Harwood (eds) *Biopolitics and the 'obesity epidemic': Governing bodies*, London: Routledge.

Wallard, W. (1932) *The sociology of teaching*, New York: John Wiley & Sons.

Weber, M. (1991, originally 1904–1905) *The protestant ethic and the spirit of capitalism*, London: HarperCollins.

Wright, J. and Harwood, V. (eds) (2009) *Biopolitics and the 'obesity epidemic': Governing bodies*, London: Routledge.

19

Tracking and inequality
New directions for research and practice

Adam Gamoran[1]

For more than a century, educators and researchers have debated the merits of separating students for instruction into different tracks, classes, and groups, according to their purported interests and abilities (for historical perspectives, see Loveless, 1998, 1999; Oakes, 2005; Oakes *et al.*, 1992; Powell *et al.*, 1985). The practice, known as "tracking" and "ability grouping" in the US and "streaming" and "setting" in the UK, is intended to create conditions in which teachers can efficiently target instruction to students' needs.[2] Despite this intended benefit, tracking has been widely criticized as inegalitarian, because students in high tracks tend to widen their achievement advantages over their low-track peers, and because measures of school performance commonly used to assign students to tracks typically coincide with the broader bases of social disadvantage such as race/ethnicity and social class, leading to economically and/or ethnically segregated classrooms. Yet tracking has been highly resistant to lasting change and remains in wide use in various forms in the US, the UK, and in school systems around the world.

Although struggles over tracking involve instructional and political challenges that play out in schools and classrooms, the persisting debate reflects not only local concerns but also broader tensions inherent in education systems (Oakes *et al.*, 1992). On the one hand, schools are charged with providing all students with a common framework of cognitive and social skills essential for full participation in the civic and economic activities of adult society. On the other hand, schools are structured to sort and select students for different trajectories aligned with their varied orientations and capacities. This ongoing tension between commonality and differentiation is at the heart of the tracking debate: Is the purpose of schooling to provide all students with a common socialization? Or is it to differentiate students for varied futures? The former aim is consistent with mixed–ability teaching, whereas the latter is consistent with tracking, and the debate has no simple resolution because school systems embody both goals.

Building on past research, recent work on tracking has advanced in three areas that indicate promising new directions for research and practice. First, new international scholarship has extended knowledge about the consequences of tracking for student achievement to contexts beyond the US and UK, where most prior research had been conducted. Second, recent studies of attempts to reduce or eliminate tracking and ability grouping have yielded important insights about why tracking is resistant to change and how some of the obstacles to detracking may be surmounted. Third, a new wave of research on classroom assignment and instruction has pointed towards approaches that, while not resolving the tension between commonality and differentiation, may capture the benefits of differentiation for meeting students' varied needs without giving rise to the consequences for inequality that commonly accompany tracking and ability grouping. These findings in turn call for new research and experimentation in practice.

Before turning to these latest findings, I summarize the earlier literature on the effects of grouping and tracking on student achievement. This research has been well covered in prior reviews (e.g. Gamoran, 2004; Gamoran and Berends, 1987; Hallam, 2002; Harlen and Malcolm, 1997; Kulik and Kulik, 1982; Oakes *et al.*, 1992; Slavin, 1987, 1990), but I begin with it here because it sets the stage for the promising work of the present and the new directions for the future. Thus, the remainder of this chapter is divided into four sections: a review of findings about tracking and achievement that links work from the 1970s, 1980s, and 1990s to updated studies in the same vein; a discussion of recent international research on tracking, both between and within schools; an analysis of new studies of efforts to reduce or eliminate tracking; and a conclusion calling for new research and practice based on the latest findings.

Tracking and achievement: increased inequality without benefits to productivity

Following Gamoran and Mare (1989), one may distinguish between two possible consequences of tracking for achievement: it may affect *productivity*, that is, the overall level of achievement in the school or class; and it may affect *inequality*, that is, the distribution of achievement across the different tracks, classes, or groups. Although not all studies have reached the same conclusions about these outcomes, the weight of the evidence indicates that tracking tends to exacerbate inequality with little or no contribution to overall productivity. This occurs because gains for high achievers are offset by losses for low achievers. A compelling example of this pattern comes from Kerckhoff's (1986) study of ability grouping between and within schools in England and Wales. Kerckhoff used data from the National Child Development Study, which followed for more than thirty years all children born in the UK in the first week of March in 1958. He examined secondary school achievement in reading and mathematics among students enrolled in schools for high achievers (grammar schools), low achievers (secondary modern schools) and those of widely varying achievement levels (comprehensive schools). He also compared students assigned to high, middle, low, and mixed-ability classes within the different types of school. Comparisons between and within schools told a consistent story: There were no overall benefits to average achievement in contexts that differentiated students for instruction as compared with mixed-ability contexts. However, sorting students into selective schools and classes was associated with increasing gaps between high and low achievers over time (see also Kerckhoff, 1993). The comparison of tracking to mixed-ability teaching has received less attention in the US because tracking has been nearly universal at the secondary level (Loveless, 1998), but comparisons of ability-grouped with mixed-ability classes in middle school mathematics and science (Hoffer, 1992) and English (Gamoran and Nystrand, 1994) have yielded the same pattern. National survey analyses in the US also demonstrated that, over the course of high school, students assigned to high and low tracks grow farther and farther apart in achievement (e.g. Heyns, 1974; Alexander, Cook and McDill, 1978; Gamoran, 1987a, 1992; Gamoran and Mare, 1989; Lucas and Gamoran, 2002).

Because track location is correlated with traditional bases of socio-economic disadvantage, tracking not only widens achievement gaps but also reinforces social inequality (Lucas and Berends, 2002; Oakes *et al.*, 1992). In contrast to socio-economic status, which has direct effects on track assignment, race and ethnicity affect track assignment indirectly: Minority students whose test scores and socio-economic background match those of Whites are no less likely to be placed in high tracks (Gamoran and Mare, 1989; Lucas and Gamoran, 2002; Tach and Farkas, 2006). However, because minority students tend to reach high school with lower test scores and less advantaged socio-economic circumstances, tracking works to the disadvantage of minority students and contributes to achievement gaps.

As the demographic make-up of US schools has changed, new patterns of inequality associated with tracking have become more salient. With regard to language minority students, Callahan (2005) argued that schools often conflate limited proficiency in English with limited ability to master academic content. As a result, English language learners are tracked into classes with modified curricula that are less rigorous than those of regular classes, which prevents these students from gaining access to advanced instruction even as their language skills develop. While Callahan supported these assertions with a study of a rural California school, Paul (2005) reached a similar conclusion based on her study of five diverse urban schools. Paul noted that enrollment in algebra 1, the gateway to the college-preparatory curriculum, was stratified by race and ethnicity, with Asian American and White students enrolled in higher proportions, and African American and Hispanic students enrolled in lower proportions. When English language learners enrolled in the same levels of algebra as fluent English speakers, they had similar rates of college-preparatory course work. Foreshadowing this work, Padilla and Gonzales (2001) argued that one reason recent immigrants to the US from Mexico outperform second-generation students is that the immigrants have spent less time in low tracks in US schools.

New forms of tracking in the US have exhibited patterns of inequality comparable with those of earlier forms. Using high-school transcripts from a national sample of students, Lucas (1999) showed that students were grouped on a subject-by-subject basis rather than by broad curricular programs. Nevertheless, students' course levels tended to correlate across subject areas, and this more subtle version of tracking still resulted in achievement inequality. Mitchell and Mitchell (2005) demonstrated that multi-track, year-round schools also tended to stratify students by social origins. Both Lewis and Cheng (2006) and Mickelson and Everett (2008) found that the transformation of vocational education into career and technical education, though accompanied by greater emphasis on academic work within technical courses of study, still resulted in stratified class enrollments.

Generally, elementary and middle schools have witnessed a pattern of increasing inequality similar to that observed at the high school level (e.g. Gamoran *et al.*, 1995; Hoffer, 1992; Rowan and Miracle, 1983). Until recently, national data have been available only at the secondary level, so it was not possible to examine the generalizability of patterns of inequality associated with elementary school ability grouping. However, recent analyses of data from a national sample of children who entered kindergarten in 1998 have confirmed the pattern of widening gaps for within-class reading groups in kindergarten (Tach and Farkas, 2006). Using later waves of the same data, Lleras and Rangel (2009) reported similar findings for between-class ability grouping in Grades 1 and 3. Taking exception to the general pattern, Slavin (1987) reported, based on a synthesis of research on elementary school grouping, that within-class grouping for mathematics had positive effects for students in low-ranked as well as those in high-ranked groups. Slavin also noted that, when students were regrouped for specific subjects, rather than being tracked for the entire school day, ability grouping had positive effects for students at all achievement levels. On the basis of these findings, Slavin proposed that elementary school ability grouping can have positive effects when assignment is based on criteria relevant to the subject, when students can be moved from one group to another as appropriate to their progress, and when curriculum and instruction are differentiated to meet the needs of students assigned to the different groups.

Slavin's conclusions have recently been reaffirmed by Connor and her colleagues (Connor et al., 2007; Connor et al., 2009). Connor's work shows that small reading groups can be used effectively to tailor reading instruction to students' needs. In a randomized comparison, Connor et al. (2007) reported that students taught by teachers who arranged students into reading groups according to carefully assessed student performance levels, and who aimed instruction at students' specific needs, performed much better by the end of first grade than those taught by teachers who did not have access to the systematic approach to assigning students and differentiating instruction. Though based on less precise evidence, Tomlinson et al. (2003) advanced similar claims about the value of within-class differentiation of instruction as a strategy for effective teaching of students with varied interests and skills.

Challenges in measuring track effects

Two methodological challenges have confronted researchers studying the impact of tracking and ability grouping on student achievement. One challenge has been to measure accurately students' group and track locations. At the secondary level, research from the 1970s and 1980s often relied on students to report whether their curricular programs could best be described as academic/college-preparatory, vocational, or general. This *social-psychological* measure of tracking was useful as an indicator of students' perceptions, but did not necessarily represent students' actual learning opportunities. Lucas (1999) developed a *structural* measure of track location by using students' transcripts to identify tracks based on the courses students had taken. Lucas and Gamoran (2002) showed that structural and social-psychological dimensions of tracking had independent effects on student achievement, and both contributed to achievement gaps. Other researchers have used network analysis techniques to identify tracks through the configuration of courses in which students enroll (Friedkin and Thomas, 1997; Heck et al., 2004), reaching similar conclusions about tracking and inequality. More recent studies have also uncovered inequality using teacher reports to distinguish among ability groups at high, middle, and low levels (Carbonaro, 2005; Tach and Farkas, 2006).

The second methodological challenge has been to distinguish the effects of track assignment from the effects of pre-existing differences among students assigned to different tracks. Obviously, students in high and low tracks are on different achievement trajectories to begin with; that is how they came to be located in different tracks. All the analyses discussed here have controlled for prior achievement and social background, but owing to unreliability and measurement error, not all pre-existing conditions may have been captured by the controls, and the potential for selectivity bias remains. Researchers have endeavored to respond to this challenge in two ways. First, a few studies, mainly prior to 1970, used random assignment to tracked or untracked settings to rule out selectivity bias (Slavin, 1987, 1990). These studies yielded widely varying estimates of track effects that centered around zero. Because they provided little information on what was going on inside the tracks, it is difficult to assess the generalizability of these small and long-ago experiments. In at least some cases of zero effects, teachers designed instruction and curriculum to be the same across tracks, in contrast to the real world where tracking is typically accompanied by curricular and instructional differentiation. These findings led Gamoran (1987b) to argue that the effects of tracking depend on how it is implemented, a conclusion later supported by both case study (Gamoran, 1993) and survey analyses (Gamoran, 1992).

Second, researchers have used econometric techniques to mitigate selectivity bias. Gamoran and Mare (1989) estimated endogenous switching regressions that model track assignment and track effects simultaneously, allowing for correlated errors among unobserved predictors of assignment and outcomes. Their results, which focused on mathematics achievement and high school completion for the high school class of 1982, indicated that the pattern of increasing inequality observed in standard regression analyses with rich controls was upheld in the more complex technique. Lucas and Gamoran (2002) replicated these results for the high school class of 1992, as well as the class of 1982, and with course-based as well as self-reported indicators of track location. Again, the main findings were upheld. However, Betts and Shkolnik (2000), who estimated both propensity models and two-stage least squares regression models of track effects on mathematics achievement, concluded that the differential effects of tracking for students in high and low tracks were much smaller than reported in earlier studies that relied on simple regressions. Figlio and Page (2002) similarly called into question the inequality consequences of tracking on secondary school math achievement, on the basis of two-stage least squares regression models.[3] While it is premature to conclude that tracking is not harmful to low achievers, these studies, combined with the early experimental research, suggest the effects may be smaller than is typically assumed. Since Gamoran and Mare focused on broad curricular tracking, while Betts and Shkolnik and Figlio and Page examined between-class ability grouping, the findings may also indicate that the latter are less consequential for inequality than the former.

Mechanisms of track effects on achievement

With few exceptions, the evidence indicates that tracking tends to magnify inequality. Why is that the case? Conceptually, researchers have identified mechanisms of social comparison as well as differentiated instruction, but empirically it appears that instructional variation across tracks and groups at different levels is the more prominent reason for increases in achievement gaps between tracks. A number of studies have concluded that students in high tracks encounter more challenging curricula, move at a faster pace, and are taught by more experienced teachers with better reputations, while students in low tracks encounter more fragmented, worksheet-oriented, and slower-paced instruction provided by teachers with less experience or clout (for reviews, see Gamoran, 2004; Oakes *et al.*, 1992). These findings have emerged at the elementary, middle, and high school levels. Instructional differences reflect not only what teachers do in classrooms, but also how students respond. A recent finding along these lines comes from the work of Carbonaro (2005), who demonstrated that achievement diverges in part because high-track students put forth more effort on their schoolwork than low-track students. While this finding reflected, in part, low-track students' responses to instruction that was less intellectually stimulating than the instruction given to high-track classes, it also stemmed from differences that students brought with them to class.

Other new examples of instructional mediation of track effects come from both hypothesis-testing and interpretive research. In a study of sixty-four middle and high school English classes, Applebee *et al.* (2003) reported greater use of discussion-based approaches to literature instruction in high-ability than in low-ability classes, and this difference accounted for just over one third of the effect of ability group assignment on writing performance. Discussion-based approaches included authentic questions and uptake (questions with no prespecified answer and those that build on prior statements), open discussion, drawing in multiple perspectives (envisionment-building), and conversations that connected different curricular topics. Watanabe (2008) reported parallel instructional differences based on in-depth analyses of 68 hours of classroom observation in two teachers' language arts classes. In high-ability classes, she found more engagement with challenging and meaningful curricula, more writing assignments in more diverse genres, and more feedback from teachers, as contrasted with more emphasis on test preparation in low tracks.

Findings that instructional differentiation accounts for much of the effect of tracking have led some observers to conclude that tracking per se does not generate inequality, but rather inequality has emerged because of the way in which tracking has been implemented (e.g., Hallinan, 1994). If instruction in low tracks could be effectively geared towards students' needs, this argument states, then tracking might mitigate rather than exacerbate inequality. While reasonable in principle, this goal has proven difficult to accomplish in practice, and there are few examples of effective instruction in low-track classes (for exceptions, see Gamoran, 1993, and Gamoran & Weinstein, 1998). At the same time, it is important to acknowledge that most studies of ability grouping and curriculum tracking have found that high-achieving students tend to perform better when assigned to high-level groups than when taught in mixed-ability settings. Proponents of tracking tend to emphasize the benefits of high-level classes for high-achieving students, with little attention to implications for inequality, while critics tend to focus on inequality without acknowledging the effects for high achievers. As a result, proponents and critics are apt to talk past one another with little chance for resolution, and student-assignment policies often lurch from one system to another, without recognition of the strengths and shortcomings of each (Boaler et al., 2000; Gamoran, 2002; Tsuneyoshi, 2004).

New international research on tracking and achievement

An emerging body of international work is largely consistent with the findings from the US and the UK. Perhaps the most revealing results come from new cross-national studies of international achievement data. Analyses from PISA 1999 (Program on International Student Assessment), a study conducted in twenty-eight OECD countries, indicated that countries with more differentiated school systems are characterized by greater inequality by social origins in reading achievement (OECD, 2002). Hanushek and Woessmann (2006) reinforced this conclusion by comparing twenty countries that participated in both PISA and PIRLS (Progress in International Reading Literacy Study), showing that achievement inequality tends to increase more between the primary and secondary grades in countries that practice early tracking than in countries that do not. Similarly, research on twenty-four countries that participated in TIMSS 2003 (Trends in International Mathematics and Science Survey) at Grades 4 and 8 showed that countries that rely on between-class ability grouping for mathematics exhibit more growth in achievement inequality from Grades 4 to 8 than countries that make less use of ability grouping (Huang, in press). These findings are consistent with numerous single-nation studies showing that tracking tends to reinforce inequality.

A recurring theme in the international work is that grouping and tracking come in many forms, a point that is easily missed when one focuses on a single nation. For example, countries differ on whether tracking occurs largely between schools (e.g. Japan, Germany), within schools (Australia, Belgium, Israel, US), or both (Taiwan, UK). In these different tracking systems, the scope of tracking may be wide (covering many subjects) or narrow (implemented on a subject-by-subject basis). Countries also differ on whether differentiation is introduced early or late, and whether or not the system is flexible enough to allow mobility between tracks. These structural differences were anticipated by Sørensen (1970), but have been greatly elaborated as international differences have become evident (LeTendre *et al.*, 2003). What is striking about the variation in the *forms* of tracking, however, is that the *results* are broadly similar: where tracking systems are present, achievement tends to diverge, and to reinforce initial differences by social class. New studies from Japan (Ono, 2001), Korea (Park, 2009), South Africa (Hoadley, 2008), Israel (Ayalon, 2006), Germany (Cheng *et al.*, 2007), Belgium (Van de Gaer *et al.*, 2006; Van Houtte, 2004), and the UK (Boaler *et al.*, 2000; Ivinson and Duveen, 2005; Ireson *et al.*, 2002) all identify aspects of increasing inequality associated with grouping between or within schools. Moreover, as ethnic minority groups increase in size, and ethnic inequality is increasingly recognized in nations that were formerly relatively homogeneous (such as European countries with new populations of guest workers), researchers are finding that tracking reinforces ethnic inequalities (Cheng *et al.*, 2007). Ivinson and Duveen (2005) in the UK and Ayalon (2006) in Israel also demonstrated that horizontal differentiation (i.e. divisions between subjects) tend to stratify students by social origins, just as does vertical differentiation (divisions between levels). Finally, Van Houtte (2004) presented findings from Belgium that supported the conclusion from US research that track effects are driven by instructional differences to an important degree.

Within this common framework, interesting differences also emerge. For example, in countries with well-articulated standards tied to curriculum and assessment, the harmful effects of tracking may be mitigated by incentives for success in lower level classes. Broaded (1997) reported that high-stakes exams targeted at different achievement levels in Taiwan led all students, including those in low tracks, to work hard at their studies, and, as a result, tracking contributed to *smaller* achievement inequalities. Similarly in the case of Israel, Ayalon and Gamoran (2000) found that schools with multiple ability levels within college-preparatory mathematics programs tended to have *less* inequality by social origin than schools with only a single level. They attributed this result to meaningful incentives attached to lower level mathematics courses that, like higher level courses, led to high stakes assessments at the end of high school. Likewise, a secondary curriculum reform in Scotland that raised standards for lower level students resulted in declining inequality of achievement over time (Gamoran, 1996), and in Australia, a reform in secondary English that reduced the number of tracks and simultaneously raised standards in low tracks may have boosted test scores overall (Stanley and McCann, 2005). In the US, a parallel finding is that Catholic schools, which place more academic demands on students in lower tracks than public schools, tend to exhibit less achievement inequality between tracks than public schools (Gamoran, 1992). These findings reinforce Broaded's (1997) conclusion that the impact of tracking is context-dependent and suggest that, in principle, tracking's pernicious effects on low achievers can be reduced or eliminated. Thus far, however, attempts to use ability grouping to raise achievement in the context of high standards in US public schools have met with limited success (Lewis and Cheng, 2006; Mickelson and Everett, 2008; Sandholtz *et al.*, 2004).

New insights from US research on detracking

More than fifteen years ago, Oakes (1992) insightfully identified three challenges to detracking: normative challenges, based on long-standing beliefs that young persons differ by ability and that schools should be structured to meet those differences; political challenges, reflecting the difficulty of overcoming vested interests in tracking such as those held by parents of high-achieving students and by teachers who enjoy teaching honors classes; and technical challenges, reflecting the difficulty of instructing students of widely varying levels of performance, a task for which few teachers are prepared. Most of the emphasis in Oakes' subsequent work (see especially the 2005 edition of her classic book, *Keeping track*) and that of her colleagues and students (e.g. Oakes and Wells, 1998; Wells and Serna, 1996; Welner, 2001; Yonezawa *et al.*, 2002) has been on the normative and political challenges, reasoning that if these challenges could be met, the technical difficulties could be overcome. Recent evidence, however, suggests the opposite: failure to solve the technical problems of mixed-ability teaching is a major impediment to addressing the normative and political challenges. While the technical challenges have defied easy solution, recent work has identified conditions under which effective teaching in mixed-ability contexts may be more successful than in the past.

Challenges of detracking

Loveless's (1999) analysis of detracking reforms in California and Massachusetts revealed substantial resistance from teachers who believed that they were not equipped to succeed in instructing students at widely varying performance levels within the same classrooms. Teachers' attitudes towards detracking tended to differ by subject matter, with mathematics and foreign language teachers more resistant than teachers in other subjects, owing to beliefs about the sequential nature of knowledge in these disciplines (see also Ball, 1987; Gamoran and Weinstein, 1998). Even in social studies, however, a subject area that might be viewed as particularly conducive to mixed-ability teaching because of the potential for discussion of topics from diverse viewpoints, detracking efforts have run into technical difficulties. One case study found that teachers struggled to engage students in classes with widely varying achievement levels: low-achieving students had difficulty with assignments, while high-achieving students were bored (Rosenbaum, 1999). In another study, Rubin (2008) found that detracking in social studies seemed to work well in a middle-class suburban school with a relatively homogeneous population, as teachers emphasized active learning and differentiated assignments for students at different performance levels. However, detracked social studies classes appeared less effective in a more diverse school, where teachers aimed more for relevance than for high standards; and in an inner-city school with a low-income population, detracking resulted in a highly routinized curriculum with little challenge for students. Rubin's observations in the inner-city school mirrored earlier findings by Gamoran and Weinstein (1998) from an urban school in which tracking in mathematics was eliminated by diluting the curriculum in mixed-ability classes to a level that all students could follow, with the result that teachers complained students were not being prepared to move to more advanced mathematics.

Ironically, findings from all three of these case studies (Gamoran and Weinstein, 1998; Rosenbaum, 1999; Rubin, 2008) suggest that high-achieving minority students may have the most to lose when detracking is unsuccessful. These students are often found in urban schools where detracking has not resulted in challenging instruction in mixed-ability classes, and they may lack the support outside of school to succeed in the absence of a challenging curriculum. Rubin (2003) brought this problem to life based on interviews and observations of a high-achieving minority student in a detracked school, who socialized with a small group consisting of less academically oriented peers, to the detriment of her academic work.

Some schools have attempted to reduce the use of tracking by allowing students to select their own track assignments. Recent case studies suggest, however, that student choice is not an effective detracking mechanism, because students tend to sort themselves into classes in much the same way as a traditional tracking system, and with the corresponding results for social class and race/ethnic divisions (Watanabe, 2007). Yonezawa *et al.* (2002) proposed that differential access to information and varied aspirations among students contributed to this pattern. In addition, they noted that minority students preferred classes in which they were not racially isolated and in which their cultural backgrounds were valued. These findings reflect the familiar tension between commonality and differentiation: while there may be benefits to students' academic performance from pursuing a common curriculum, students are motivated by their interests and social concerns, which may result in ethnic as well as academic divisions among students.

Boaler and Staples (2008) uncovered mixed success in another detracking case study. Initially, achievement gains appeared in one detracked school compared with two others that did not detrack. However, the gains were not sustained over the three years of the study. Moreover, the achievement benefits were not evident on the high stakes state standardized test, and it is difficult at any rate to attribute achievement trends to any single reform in a sample of three schools. Nonetheless, the study is enticing in its call for further examination of instruction in detracked schools.

Addressing the technical challenge: differentiated instruction in mixed-ability classes

Not all cases of mixed-ability teaching have met with frustration. In the same research project that uncovered a case of diluted curriculum in a detracked school (discussed in the last section), Gamoran and Weinstein (1998) also identified a successful instance of detracking in secondary school mathematics. In this urban, east-coast high school, in which half the students were eligible to receive free or reduced-price lunch, student performance on authentic assessments was the highest of all the twenty-five highly restructured schools from which this case was drawn. In this school, mathematics and science instruction were integrated in the same class, and student work was project-oriented; for example, researchers observed students applying principles of mathematics and physics in completing an assignment to design rides in an amusement park. Students were assessed based on portfolios of work in a variety of subjects, and expectations for students took into account their progress as well as the levels of excellence they had attained. Moreover, students were expected to have mastered elementary mathematics, and, if they had not, a Saturday tutoring program was available to help them along. Key elements that supported a rigorous curriculum in a mixed-ability setting in this school were small classes (limited to fifteen students), the supplemental tutoring program, a visionary leader who had selected a staff with congruent attitudes, and the opportunity to interview students prior to students' admission to the school.

More recently, Burris and her colleagues (Burris *et al.*, 2006, 2008) also identified cases of high achievement in mathematics that resulted from a move to mixed-ability teaching. The authors used an interrupted time series design to assess the impact of the reform, comparing the achievement trajectories of schools before the reform with their trajectories afterwards, as well as with the trajectories of other schools that did not undergo the reform over the same time period. At the middle school level in this New York school district (Burris *et al.*, 2006), teachers implemented an accelerated curriculum for all students paired with a supplemental workshop to support students who had trouble keeping up. They also introduced common preparation time for teachers and increased the use of calculators in class. At the high school level, the low-track non-Regents class was eliminated, and all students were placed in mathematics classes that led to the Regents diploma. Students who struggled with this class had available to them a supplementary class that met three times each week. At both levels, student achievement rose following the introduction of the reform. Achievement gaps narrowed as low achievers gained more than high achievers, but there was no evidence that high achievers suffered in their performance as a result of the reform. Achievement gains did not reflect increasing high-school dropout rates; on the contrary, dropout rates declined over the period of the reform. It should be noted that this case involved an economically advantaged school district with relatively few high-needs students compared with other New York school districts. The supplemental class also provided about 50 percent more mathematics instruction to low-achieving students.

The new research by Burris and colleagues is extremely important because it demonstrates that detracking *can* result in gains for low achievers *without* the losses for high achievers observed in earlier attempts. As in the case study reported by Gamoran and Weinstein (1998), however, success was based in part on favorable circumstances, particularly the resources that enabled the school to offer extra mathematics instruction for struggling students. This accomplishment calls for replication in other contexts to assess its broader viability.

Conclusion: new directions for research and practice

While definitive solutions remain elusive, the present time is witness to exciting new prospects for balancing the aims of commonality and differentiation in arranging students for instruction. Recent findings lend support to two approaches that merit further experimentation in research and practice: raising standards for low achievers in differentiated classrooms; and providing differentiated learning opportunities in mixed-ability classrooms. The key to evaluating both approaches will be careful monitoring of the nature and quality of instruction and the relation between instruction and achievement, however students are arranged for class.

Raising standards for low-achieving students

The practical conclusion from years of tracking research that low-level, dead-end courses should be eliminated is no longer seriously debated. High-school courses such as general math and business English do not prepare students for post-secondary opportunities and are less effective than regular courses such as algebra and college-preparatory English, even for students with low skill levels in these areas. This conclusion still leaves open the possibility, however, that meaningful instruction at all skill levels could make differentiated classes an effective way to organize students for learning.

Critics of tracking such as Oakes (2005) argue that, because tracking is inherently stratifying, it is just not possible to offer effective instruction to low-achieving students in ability-grouped classes. Indeed, examples of high-quality instruction in low-ability classes are rare. Yet recent international research shows that differentiated class settings for low achievers can be effective when they are tied to meaningful outcomes, such as assessments that are aligned to the curriculum, and provide access to jobs and further education. Studies from Taiwan (Broaded, 1997) and Israel (Ayalon and Gamoran, 2000) demonstrated that differentiation within academic

222

programs in which meaningful instruction and valued incentives are present at all ability levels can result in less inequality than systems of fewer levels in which low-achieving students lack access to meaningful incentives. Other research from Scotland (Gamoran, 1996) and Australia (Stanley and McCann, 2005) observed that the negative effects of tracking for low achievers diminished when the degree of tracking was reduced and when academic standards in the lower level classes were elevated. The common ingredient in all four cases was a meaningful assessment that had value for students in lower-level as well as higher-level classes.

Do these findings have any bearing on the US, where classes for low achievers typically lack meaningful incentives for effort or performance? The finding that Catholic schools obtain smaller achievement gaps between tracks than public schools by providing more rigorous instruction in low tracks, and cases of successful low-track instruction in Catholic schools (Gamoran, 1993) and restructured public schools (Gamoran and Weinstein, 1998) merely show that exceptions are possible, not that making low-track instruction more effective by raising standards overall is a viable reform strategy for the US. The current emphasis on test-based accountability in the US might, in principle, lead schools to create effective low-ability classes in order to meet accountability requirements. However, the evidence so far suggests that accountability-driven tracking is no more effective for low achievers than other forms of tracking (Sandholtz et al., 2004). Based on insights from the international work, one can identify at least three elements that would need to change to make low-track classes more effective: First, the assessments towards which students were striving would need to be tied to futures that were more visibly meaningful to students than is currently the case. At present, students are prodded to perform on multiple-choice tests whose underlying standards are not evident to students and which demand fragmented knowledge rather than coherent mastery of subject matter that has relevance beyond the test itself. Second, the assessments would need to offer incentives for students as well as schools; at present, schools are held accountable for student performance, but the students themselves are not. Positive incentives such as access to jobs and/or post-secondary education would need to be offered, not merely negative sanctions such as denial of a high school diploma. Third, the alignment between the course curriculum and the assessment would need to be tighter than has typically been the case in the US.

Differentiating instruction in mixed-ability settings

Although detracking remains a challenging solution, with more examples of failure than success, the findings of recent studies are positive enough to warrant further efforts. An examination of reports of effective instruction in mixed-ability classes yields several common ingredients. First, the success stories all recognize that students differ in the skills and interests they bring with them to class. Successful cases reported by Burris, Gamoran, and Connor and their colleagues are not instances in which teachers acted as if students were all alike. Instead, teachers responded to variation among students in their teaching. Second, and correspondingly, all the successful cases involved differentiated instruction within the mixed-ability setting. In the secondary school cases reported by Burris, Gamoran, and their colleagues, differentiation involved supplemental instruction that was available for students who struggled with class materials. In Connor's elementary school research, differentiation meant carefully analyzing students' skill levels, matching skills to particular instructional strategies, and arranging students for instruction within classes in such a way as to match the skill levels with instructional approaches. Third, teachers in each of these cases had access to important resources that allowed them to supplement instruction and tailor it to students' needs. Future efforts would do well to keep these elements in mind.

Combining research on tracking with research on teaching

After a century of research on tracking and ability grouping, one might expect to see a definitive answer to the question of how best to organize students for instruction. Yet the dilemma persists, because the goals of commonality and differentiation lie in uneasy proximity to one another, because every approach has disadvantages as well as advantages, and because the consequences of different solutions vary by context. Research in the last decade has made important progress, however, by focusing on the instruction provided to students assigned to class in different ways. Ultimately, how students are arranged matters less than the instruction they encounter, so bringing together research on tracking with research on teaching offers the most useful way to continue to shed light on this topic of continuing interest.

Notes

1   The author is grateful for helpful research assistance from Michelle Robinson and exceptional editing from Cathy Loeb.
2   US writers often use the terms "tracking" and "ability grouping" interchangeably. For brevity I use the single term "tracking" to capture all the various forms of structural differentiation for instruction. When distinguishing among different forms, I use the term "tracking" to refer to the practice of dividing students into separate classes (or clusters of classes) for all of their academic subjects, and the term "ability grouping" to mean the division of students into classes on a subject-by-subject basis. This use parallels the different meanings of the terms "streaming" and "setting" used in the UK. I use the terms "within-class ability grouping" to refer to the use of instructional groups within class for a particular subject, and "between-school grouping" to refer to systems in which students are assigned to separate schools targeted to different futures on the basis of varied academic performance.
3   Models estimated by Betts and Shkolnik (2000) and Figlio and Page (2002) rely on very strong assumptions, so their results should be interpreted with particular caution. Betts and Shkolnik's conclusions rest on comparisons of classes at similar ability levels as reported by teachers but located in schools that differed on whether the principal reported that tracking was used for mathematics. Yet teacher reports of class ability levels may reflect between-class ability grouping irrespective of the principal's report. Figlio and Page (2002) used as instruments for track assignment indicators that, on the face of it, seem far-fetched: two- and three-way interactions between the number of courses required for graduation, the number of schools in the county, and the fraction of voters in the county who voted for President Reagan in 1984. Weak instruments would undermine the estimates of track effects and could bias them towards zero.

References

Alexander, K.L., Cook, M.A. and McDill, E.L. (1978) "Curriculum tracking and educational stratification," *American Sociological Review* 43: 47–66.

Applebee, A.N., Langer, J., Nystrand, M. and Gamoran, A. (2003) "Discussion-based approaches to developing understanding: classroom instruction and student performance in middle and high school English," *American Educational Research Journal* 40: 685–730.

Ayalon, H. (2006) "Nonhierarchical curriculum differentiation and inequality in achievement: a different story or more of the same?" *Teachers College Record* 108: 1186–1213.

——— and Gamoran, A. (2000) "Stratification in academic secondary programs and educational inequality: comparison of Israel and the United States," *Comparative Education Review* 44: 54–80.

Ball, S.J. (1987) *The micro-politics of the school: Towards a theory of school organization*, London: Methuen.

Betts, J.R. and Shkolnik, J.L. (2000) "The effects of ability grouping on student achievement and resource allocation in secondary schools," *Economics of Education Review* 19: 1–15.

Boaler, J. and Staples, M. (2008) "Creating mathematical futures through an equitable teaching approach: the case of Railside School," *Teachers College Record* 110: 608–645.

—— Wiliam, D. and Brown, M. (2000) "Students' experiences of ability grouping: disaffection, polarisation, and the construction of failure," *British Educational Research Journal* 26: 631–648.

Broaded, C.M. (1997) "The limits and possibilities of tracking: some evidence from Taiwan," *Sociology of Education* 70: 36–53.

Burris, C.C., Heubert, J.P. and Levin, H.M. (2006) "Accelerating mathematics achievement using heterogeneous grouping," *American Educational Research Journal* 43: 105–136.

—— Wiley, E., Welner, K. and Murphy, J. (2008) "Accountability, rigor, and detracking: achievement effects of embracing a challenging curriculum as a universal good for all students," *Teachers College Record* 110: 571–607.

Callahan, R. (2005) "Tracking and high school English learners: limiting opportunity to learn," *American Educational Research Journal* 42: 305–328.

Carbonaro, W. (2005) "Tracking, students' effort, and academic achievement," *Sociology of Education* 78: 27–49.

Cheng, S., Martin, L. and Werum, R.E. (2007) "Adult social capital and track placement of ethnic groups in Germany," *American Journal of Education* 114: 41–74.

Connor, C.M., Morrison, F.J., Fishman, B.J., Schatschneider, C. and Underwood, P. (2007) "The early years: algorithm-guided individualized reading instruction," *Science* 315: 464–465.

—— Piasta, S.B., Fishman, B., Glasney, S., Schatschneider, C., Crowe, E., Underwood, P. and Morrison, F.J. (2009) "Individualizing student instruction precisely: effects of child by instruction interactions on first graders' literacy development," *Child Development* 80: 77–100.

Figlio, D.N. and Page, M.E. (2002) "School choice and the distributional effects of ability tracking: does separation increase inequality?" *Journal of Urban Economics* 51: 497–514.

Friedkin, N.E. and Thomas, S.L. (1997) "Social positions in schooling," *Sociology of Education* 70: 239–255.

Gamoran, A. (1987a) "The stratification of high school learning opportunities," *Sociology of Education* 60: 135–155.

—— (1987b) "Organization, instruction, and the effects of ability grouping: comment on Slavin's 'best-evidence synthesis'," *Review of Educational Research* 57: 341–345.

—— (1992) "The variable effects of high school tracking," *American Sociological Review* 57: 812–828.

—— (1993) "Alternative uses of ability grouping in secondary schools: can we bring high-quality instruction to low-ability classes?" *American Journal of Education* 101: 1–22.

—— (1996) "Curriculum standardization and equality of opportunity in Scottish secondary education, 1984–1990," *Sociology of Education* 29: 1–21.

—— (2002) *CES briefing: Standards, inequality, and ability grouping*, Edinburgh, Scotland: Centre for Educational Sociology.

—— (2004) "Classroom organization and instructional quality," in M.C. Wang and H.J. Walberg (eds) *Can unlike students learn together? Grade retention, tracking, and grouping*, Greenwich, CT: Information Age Publishing, pp. 141–155.

—— and Berends, M. (1987) "The effects of stratification in secondary schools: synthesis of survey and ethnographic research," *Review of Educational Research* 57: 415–435.

—— and Mare, R.D. (1989) "Secondary school tracking and educational inequality: compensation, reinforcement, or neutrality?" *American Journal of Sociology* 94: 1146–1183.

—— and Nystrand, M. (1994) "Tracking, instruction, and achievement," *International Journal of Educational Research* 21: 217–231.

—— , ——, Berends, M. and LePore, P.C. (1995) "An organizational analysis of the effects of ability grouping," *American Educational Research Journal* 32: 687–715.

—— and Weinstein, M. (1998) "Differentiation and opportunity in restructured schools," *American Journal of Education* 106: 385–415.

Hallam, S. (2002) *Ability grouping in schools*, London: University of London Institute of Education.

Hallinan, M.T. (1994) "Tracking: from theory to practice," *Sociology of Education* 67: 79–84.

Hanushek, E.A. and Woessmann, L. (2006) "Does educational tracking affect performance and inequality? Differences-in-differences evidence across countries," *The Economic Journal* 116: C63-C76.

Harlen, W. and Malcolm, H. (1997) *Setting and streaming: a research review*, Edinburgh: Scottish Council for Research in Education.

Heck, R.H., Price, C. and Thomas, S.L. (2004) "Tracks as emergent structures: a network analysis of student differentiation in a high school," *American Journal of Education* 110: 321–353.

Heyns, B. (1974) "Selection and stratification within schools," *American Journal of Sociology* 79: 1434–1451.

Hoadley, U. (2008) "Social class and pedagogy: a model for the investigation of pedagogic variation," *British Journal of Sociology of Education* 29: 63–78.

Hoffer, T.B. (1992) "Middle school ability grouping and student achievement in science and mathematics," *Educational Evaluation and Policy Analysis* 14: 205–227.

Huang, M.-H. (in press) "Classroom homogeneity and the distribution of student math performance: a country-level fixed-effects analysis," *Social Science Research*.

Ireson, J., Hallam, S., Hack, S., Clark, H. and Plewis, I. (2002) "Ability grouping in English secondary schools: effects on attainment in English, mathematics, and science," *Educational Research and Evaluation* 8: 299–318.

Ivinson, G. and Duveen, G. (2005) "Classroom structuration and the development of social representations of the curriculum," *British Journal of Sociology of Education* 26: 627–642.

Kerckhoff, A. (1986) "Effects of ability grouping in British secondary schools," *American Sociological Review* 51: 842–858.

—— (1993) *Diverging pathways: social structure and career deflections*, Cambridge, England: Cambridge University Press.

Kulik, C.-L. and Kulik, J.A. (1982) "Effects of ability grouping on secondary school students: a meta-analysis of evaluation findings," *American Educational Research Journal* 19: 415–428.

LeTendre, G.K., Hofer, B.K. and Shimizu, H. (2003) "What is tracking? Cultural expectations in the United States, Germany, and Japan," *American Educational Research Journal* 40: 43–89.

Lewis, T. and Cheng, S.-Y. (2006) "Tracking, expectations, and the transformation of vocational education," *American Journal of Education* 113: 67–99.

Lleras, C. and Rangel, C. (2009) "Ability grouping practices in elementary school and African American/Hispanic achievement," *American Journal of Education* 115: 279–304.

Loveless, T. (1998) *The tracking and ability grouping debate*, Washington, DC: Fordham Institute.

—— (1999) *The tracking wars: state reform meets school policy*, Washington, DC: Brookings Institution Press.

Lucas, S.R. (1999) *Tracking inequality*, New York: Teachers College Press.

—— and Berends, M. (2002) "Sociodemographic diversity, correlated achievement, and de facto tracking," *Sociology of Education* 75: 328–348.

—— and Gamoran, A. (2002) "Track assignment and the black-white test score gap: divergent and convergent evidence from 1980 and 1990 sophomores," in T. Loveless (ed.) *Closing the gap: promising strategies for reducing the achievement gap*, Washington, DC: Brookings, pp. 171–198.

Mickelson, R.A. and Everett, B.J. (2008) "Neotracking in North Carolina: how high school courses of study reproduce race and class-based stratification," *Teachers College Record* 110: 535–570.

Mitchell, R.E. and Mitchell, D.E. (2005) "Student segregation and achievement tracking in year-round schools," *Teachers College Record* 107: 529–562.

Oakes, J. (1992) "Can tracking research inform practice? Technical, normative, and political considerations," *Educational Researcher* 21(4): 12–22.

—— (2005) *Keeping track: how schools structure inequality*, 2nd edn, New Haven, CT: Yale University Press.

—— Gamoran, A. and Page, R.N. (1992) "Curriculum differentiation: opportunities, outcomes, and meanings," in P.W. Jackson (ed.) *Handbook of research on curriculum*, New York: Macmillan, pp. 570–608.

—— and Wells, A.S. (1998) "Detracking for high student achievement," *Educational Leadership* 55(6): 38–41.

OECD (Organization for Economic Cooperation and Development) (2002) *Education policy analysis*, Paris: OECD.

Ono, H. (2001) "Who goes to college? Features of institutional tracking in Japanese higher education," *American Journal of Education* 109: 161–195.

Padilla, A.M. and Gonzales, R. (2001) "Academic performance of immigrant and U.S.-born Mexican heritage students: effects of schooling in Mexico and bilingual/English language instruction," *American Educational Research Journal* 38: 727–742.

Park, H. (2009) "Growing curriculum differentiation and its implications for inequality in Korea," Paper presented at the Annual Meeting of the Association of Asian Studies, Chicago, March.

Paul, F.G. (2005) "Grouping within Algebra I: a structural sieve with powerful effects for low-income, minority, and immigrant students," *Educational Policy* 19: 262–282.

Powell, A.G., Farrar, E. and Cohen, D.K. (1985) *The shopping mall high school*, Boston, MA: Houghton Mifflin.

Rosenbaum, J.E. (1999) "If tracking is bad, is detracking better?" *American Educator* 47: 24–29.

Rowan, B. and Miracle, A.W. Jr. (1983) "Systems of ability grouping and the stratification of achievement in elementary schools," *Sociology of Education* 56: 133–144.

Rubin, B.C. (2003) "Unpacking detracking: when progressive pedagogy meets students' social worlds," *American Educational Research Journal* 40: 539–573.

—— (2008) "Detracking in context: how local constructions of ability complicate equity-geared reform," *Teachers College Record* 110: 646–699.

Sandholtz, J.H., Ogawa, R.T. and Scribner, S.P. (2004) "Standards gap: unintended consequences of local standards-based reform," *Teachers College Record* 106: 1177–1202.

Slavin, R.E. (1987) "Ability grouping and achievement in elementary schools: a best-evidence synthesis," *Review of Educational Research* 57: 293–336.

—— (1990) "Achievement effects of ability grouping in secondary schools: a best-evidence synthesis," *Review of Educational Research* 60: 471–499.

Sørensen, A.B. (1970) "Organizational differentiation of students and educational opportunity," *Sociology of Education* 43: 355–376.

Stanley, G. and MacCann, R.G. (2005) "Removing incentives for 'dumbing down' through curriculum re-structure and additional study time," *Educational Policy Analysis Archives* 13: 1–10.

Tach, L.M. and Farkas, G. (2006) "Learning-related behaviors, cognitive skills, and ability grouping when school begins," *Social Science Research* 35: 1048–1079.

Tomlinson, C.A., Brighton, C., Hertberg, H., Callahan, C.M., Moon, T.R., Brimijoin, K., Conover, L.A. and Reynolds, T. (2003) "Differentiating instruction in response to student readiness, interest, and learning profile in academically diverse classrooms: a review of literature," *Journal for the Education of the Gifted* 27: 119–145.

Tsuneyoshi, R. (2004) "The new Japanese educational reforms and the achievement 'crisis' debates," *Educational Policy* 18; 364–394.

Van de gaer, E., Pustjens, H., Van Damme, J. and De Munter, A. (2006) "Tracking and the effects of school-related attitudes on the language achievement of boys and girls," *British Journal of Sociology of Education* 27: 293–309.

Van Houtte, M. (2004) "Tracking effects on school achievement: a quantitative explanation in terms of the academic culture of school staff," *American Journal of Education* 110: 354–388.

Watanabe, M. (2007) "Lessons from a teacher inquiry group about tracking: perceived student choice in course-taking and its implications for detracking reform," *Teachers College Record* 109: 2136–2170.

—— (2008) "Tracking in the era of high-stakes state accountability reform: case studies of classroom instruction in North Carolina," *Teachers College Record* 110: 489–533.

Wells, A.S. and Serna, I. (1996) "The politics of culture: understanding local political resistance to detracking in racially mixed schools," *Harvard Educational Review* 66: 93–118.

Welner, K.G. (2001) *Legal rights, local wrongs: when community control collides with educational equality*, New York: SUNY Press.

Yonezawa, S., Wells, A.S. and Serna, I. (2002) "Choosing tracks: 'Freedom of choice' in detracked schools," *American Educational Research Journal* 39: 37–67.

20

Economic globalisation, skill formation and the consequences for higher education

Phillip Brown and Hugh Lauder

Introduction

There are striking parallels between the stories that were told to justify economic policy over the past decade in Britain and America and the stories that have been told about the benefits of globalisation and the knowledge economy. Just as we have been told that the business cycle could be abolished – the end to boom and bust – so the advent of the 'knowledge' economy was accompanied by claims that, for those who invested in education, the rewards would be great. The management guru Peter Drucker (1993) argued that we were in a new stage of capitalist development that would lead to a fundamental shift in power from the owners and managers of capital to knowledge workers. Not only would they assume power, but with it would come greater autonomy, creativity and rewards.

This is a story that politicians and policy makers have sold to the public and it has placed education at the centre of questions of economic competitiveness and social justice. In this scenario, Drucker's thinking echoes the pioneering work of Bell (1973), who predicted that the growing importance of 'knowledge' work, reflected in the historical shift from blue-collar to white-collar work, would significantly raise the demand for educated workers and give them greater autonomy in paid work.

The fundamental problem with this beguiling vision is that it does not take into account the power relations and imperatives of capitalist economies. There is little doubt that there have been significant changes in the division of labour and the nature of work in developed capitalist economies, in which issues relating to the control of knowledge work have been linked to economic globalisation. But rather than these changes leading to greater creativity and autonomy for the majority of knowledge workers, only a minority has benefitted, while the majority is being confronted by routinisation created by intense global competitive pressures and a resulting labour market for high-skilled, low-waged work. Routinisation has been developed through the process of *digital Taylorism*, which we describe below, while the labour market for high-skilled, low-waged work has created a *global auction* in which high-skilled work goes to those who offer the lowest price. These processes challenge existing theories of the education–economy relationship. In turn, a fundamental recasting of existing theories is required. However, the argument made here is particularly relevant to the West, while, in the economies of India and China, the picture is different, as these same trends have resulted in a growing middle class alongside a new class of the super rich.

Education and capitalism

We can identify two theoretical approaches to the education–economy relationship, those of consensus and conflict. Drucker's (1993) view is representative of the consensus approach, which assumes that the knowledge economy represents the pinnacle of a historical process in which, as new technologies have been developed, so education has played an increasingly central role in economic development and social justice. This is because it is assumed that, as technologies become more complex, so a more highly educated workforce is required. In turn, this leads to greater opportunities for upward social mobility and a reduction in poverty as more people gain the education required for higher paid work. For Drucker, the advent of what he considers to be the knowledge economy also changes the power relationships between the highly educated and capital, since the latter now depends on the expertise of the former. The consensus approach has a long pedigree, dating back at least to the work of Kerr et al. (1973), and has been embraced by policy makers because it represents a 'win–win' approach to economic development and social justice. Underlying these views is the theory of human capital and its contemporary variant, skill bias theory.

Human capital theory makes the claim that if individuals invest in education they will be suitably rewarded in the labour market, because their education will reflect their enhanced capacity for productivity, and it is on this basis that they will earn high wages (Baker, 2009; Becker, 2006).

Skill bias theory (Acemoglu, 2002) can be seen as a more sophisticated variant of human capital theory. It has become popular because it sees new technology as the driver of the demand for educated labour: it recognises that some uses of technology can be skill-replacing, that is, workers are deskilled, either as technologies make their jobs simpler through routinisation, or as they are simply replaced by machines. However, skill bias theorists have argued that, as a matter of fact, the introduction of new technologies has increased the demand for educated labour, for the reasons that human capital theory predicts. Here, then, is a range of sophisticated theories that all view the education–economy relationship as crucial to social and economic progress.

In contrast to the consensus approach, conflict theorists have argued that education should be considered a site of struggle between groups, in which not only are economic development and social justice divorced, but the links between education and economic development are far more complex than consensus theorists assume. Perhaps for these reasons, most conflict theorists have focused on the inequalities in education in relation to social class, patriarchy and racist structures, and to state policies, rather than on the economic processes underlying them.

If we turn first to the issue of social justice, there is broad agreement across the two major conflict traditions, neo-Marxist and neo-Weberian, that education is a site of struggle, although the nature of the struggle is conceived in different ways. For the former, as represented most starkly in the correspondence principle of Bowles and Gintis (1976), education serves to discipline and socialise future workers into capitalist work and their social class station in life.

In doing so, it also reproduces the inequalities in life chances between working-class students and their wealthier counterparts from the executive and managerial ruling class. There is, therefore, a correspondence between the nature of a socially classed education system and the demands of capitalist work.

Neo-Weberian and related theorists have viewed education as a struggle for credentials between competing groups. They point to a range of strategies, intended and unintended, by which professional and managerial elites have loaded the competition for credentials in their favour (see, for example, Ball, 2003; Bourdieu and Passeron, 1977). But they can also explain why the connection between credentials and the labour market is also problematic in a way that consensus theorists cannot. For a start, they argue that any kind of direct relationship between education, productivity and economic growth is implausible because of the key role of credentials in linking education to the labour market. Credentials may not reflect the understandings and skills that workers have and they may not reflect the kinds of skill necessary for the workplace: they are a rather blunt instrument for the selection and sorting of workers (Livingstone, 1998). Most significantly, however, credentials are a positional good, which means that their value is socially determined (Brown, 2006; Hirsch, 1976). When there is an oversupply of a particular educational qualification, say a bachelor's degree, then it will lose its value in the marketplace, and students will have to gain a higher degree in order to restore their value as skilled workers; inevitably it is those students with access to the resources to pursue their studies that will gain, for example, those from professional middle-class backgrounds. Studies that have been undertaken of the degree to which the demand for a particular credential is driven by the associated inflation with positional competition, as opposed to the upskilling of jobs, suggest that both play a significant role in the level of credential that employers demand (Collins, 1979; Weedon, 2002).

Finally, we should note that these key elements in the relationship between education and nation-state capitalism are likely to be contradictory (Dale, 1989). In what follows, we will show how new forms of contradiction are clearly visible in the West, as capitalism has moved from being centred on the nation-state to economic globalisation. However, before examining the source of these contradictions, some comments on the limitations of both consensus and conflict approaches in the light of economic globalisation are appropriate.

One of the strengths of the consensus approach is that it has a theory of how education contributes to economic development through the impetus given by new and more sophisticated forms of technology. But it is a theory confined either to national boundaries (Baker, 2009; Goldin and Katz, 2008b; Heckman, 2008) or to a view of economic globalisation in which the superior education systems of America and Britain will enable graduates to win in the competition for high-skilled work (Reich, 1991; Rosecrance, 1999). However, the account of the global restructuring of work and the labour processes we present here suggests inadequacies in both consensus and conflict theories. While existing conflict theories have clear strengths in explaining why education gives advantage to professional and managerial elites at the expense of working-class students (the social justice question), they have little or no theoretical resources to explain the impact of economic globalisation on national education systems and job markets.

Changes in the global division of labour

In order to show why economic globalisation challenges both consensus and conflict theorists and to identify the trends that have led to the contradictions between higher education and the labour market in the West, we shall turn to an exposition of a study of the skill formation strategies of transnational companies (TNCs), because they have been at the heart of the changes in the global demand for skilled workers (Brown *et al.*, 2009; Lauder *et al.*, 2008).

There are three elements to the new phase of economic globalisation that we would identify from our study that challenge both consensus and conflict theories of the education–economy relationship, particularly in relation to higher education. These are: first, the advent of a global auction for high-skilled work, which in part has been made possible by large numbers of high-quality graduates from emerging economies, especially in the East; second, the development of digital Taylorism, which has the potential to routinise much of what was once considered knowledge work; and, third, the consequent new divisions within managerial and technical jobs. In turn, these changes have threatened many middle-class jobs while intensifying the positional competition for entry to elite universities, creating a significant mismatch between higher education and demand for 'knowledge' workers.

Higher education and the global auction for high-skilled jobs

The pace of expansion of higher education in China, India and Russia has contributed to the rapid increase in the global supply of high-skilled workers. Based on our analysis of enrolment figures for ninety-eight emerging and developed countries, we found that tertiary-level enrolments (undergraduate and postgraduate) virtually doubled within a decade, from 33.4 million in 1995 to 62.9 million in 2005.[1]

Figure 20.1 shows that, in 2006, China had almost six million more students than the United States and ten times as many students as Britain. But perhaps the most extraordinary statistic on education in China was enrolment to senior secondary schools, which has increased from 26 per cent to almost 60 per cent since 1990. To achieve this expansion, over 250 new teacher-training colleges were established, and qualified graduate teachers were offered better housing, remuneration and healthcare by the Ministry of Education.[2] Equally, participation in higher

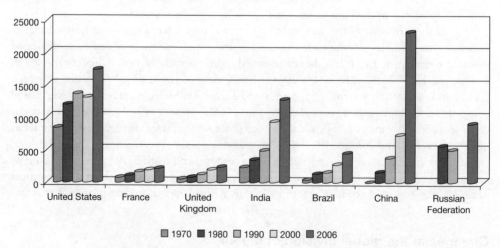

Figure 20.1 The expansion of tertiary education in selected emerging and developed economies (enrolments) (in thousands).

Source: Brown *et al.* (2008).

education increased from a little over 3 per cent in 1990 to 22 per cent in 2006.[3] These figures reflect a broader strategy presented in an official policy statement on employment prospects to 2020, which recognized the need to 'make efforts in improving education quality, so as to train millions of high-caliber workers, thousands of special talents and a large number of outstanding innovative talents for the socialist modernization drive'.[4]

While these data should be treated as indicative, and remembering that enrolment figures do not tell us how many actually enter the global job market on an annual basis, owing to high levels of drop-out in some countries, it is nevertheless salutory to consider that the expansion of higher education has not been limited to OECD member states or the BRIC nations of Brazil, Russia, India and China. Ukraine and Mexico have more people enrolled in higher education than the United Kingdom, with Poland and Turkey gaining rapid ground, doubling their participation rates between 1995 and 2005.

When we look at the subjects being studied, we can see a marked increase in numbers in Asia taking sciences and engineering (see Figure 20.2).

This supply of educated labour has enabled TNCs to create a new spatial division of labour for high-skilled activities, including research, innovation and product development. Whereas once it was assumed that the 'brain' work would be done in the West, especially the United States because of the high quality of higher education, while the 'body' work would be done in East Asia (Reich, 1991; Rosecrance, 1999), it is clear from the skill strategies of TNCs that this is no longer the case. In turn, this has led to the possibility of a global auction in which the same quality high-skilled work can be undertaken in East Asia for a fraction of the price of labour charged in the West. For example, a chip designer costs $300,000 per year in the United States, as against $28,000 in Shanghai (UNCTAD, 2005). This global auction, in which TNCs can choose where to locate high-skilled work, knowing that the quality of the work will be the same, whether it is performed in Shanghai, Los Angeles or Stuttgart, has profound implications for middle-class aspirations in America and Western Europe: middle-class students in these countries are no longer guaranteed the kind of work described by Drucker in which

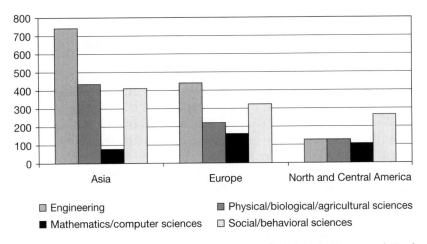

Figure 20.2 First university degrees in science and engineering fields in Asia, Europe and North America, by field: 2004 or more recent years (in thousands).

Note: Natural sciences include physical, biological, earth, atmospheric and ocean sciences.

Source: Science and Engineering Indicators 2008. Available online at www.nsf.gov/statistics/seind08/c2/fig02-34.xls.

graduates could expect high-paying, high-status jobs with a high degree of autonomy. But there are other processes at work that also undermine such expectations.

Digital Taylorism

One of the fundamental problems with the standard account of the knowledge economy and knowledge workers is that it is a-historical (Brint, 2001). Bursts of creativity are followed by the routinisation of work to enable profits to be made. In today's global competitive environment, knowledge workers are too expensive and difficult to control, so various attempts are now being made to codify, standardise and translate knowledge work into working knowledge. Rather than knowledge being locked into one person's head for which he/she can charge a premium, working knowledge is available to corporations in the form of software programmes and prescripts that can be utilised by lower-skilled workers. We call the routinisation of production platforms and processes in both offices and factories *digital Taylorism*, because innovations can be translated into sets of routines that might require some degree of education but not the kind of creativity and independence of judgement that is often associated with the rhetoric of the knowledge economy: the technical revolution in software that can translate knowledge work into working knowledge has been crucial to this process (Brown *et al.*, forthcoming).

Hence, when knowledge work has been standardised by software protocols, it is then possible for TNCs to ship work across the globe to where routinised knowledge work is cheapest. Where it once seemed impossible for high-skilled work to be codified, it is clear that even highly skilled jobs are being targeted in much the same way that craft knowledge was captured by companies in the development of Fordist assembly-line production. For example, law firms now send an increasing amount of their preparatory case work to places such as Manila.

This routinisation of knowledge work has contributed to a fundamental division within what were once considered high-skilled, middle-class jobs. But there are further sources of fracture within the middle classes created by the ideology of the 'war for talent'.

Divisions within managerial and technical occupations

Within the processes we have described above, the nature of skills and reward is fundamentally changing, creating significant divisions in what were once considered middle-class careers for graduates. Instead of a career ladder, it is clear that corporations are distinguishing between those they consider the 'talented', who are, typically, fast-tracked into senior managerial positions, and those who are considered worthy, loyal and committed, but who do not have the key ingredients for leadership positions. Beneath them are the workers who engage in routine knowledge work. The ideology of the 'war for talent' asserts that, despite mass higher education, there are only a few especially talented graduates who can take on leadership roles in large companies. It is claimed that global corporations now need a range of skills in leadership positions that were not in demand when companies were embedded in national economies (Brown and Hesketh, 2004). These new skill sets, which only the small minority of 'talented' are deemed to have, are therefore highly rewarded. In turn, this is exacerbating the positional competition for entry to elite universities around the globe.

Leading TNCs gravitate towards the global elite of universities because they are believed to have the best and brightest students. This view is actively promoted by universities, as higher education has become a global business. The branding of universities and faculty members is integral to the organisation of academic enquiry. Claims to world-class standards depend on attracting 'the best' academics and forming alliances with elite universities elsewhere in the world, while recruiting the 'right' kinds of student. Universities play the same reputational games as companies, because it is a logical consequence of global market competition between universities.

Social class and the intensification of positional competition

Both British and American higher education is differentiated by institution and social class. The advent of the global auction for high-skilled jobs has the effect of intensifying the competition for access to elite universities, because it is only those who gain entry to them (the 'talented') who can avoid a reverse (Dutch) auction for knowledge work. Recent figures for the socio-economic profile of British universities show that those from the upper end of the socio-economic scale dominate elite universities. For example, the university with the highest percentage of students from top socio-economic backgrounds (bands 1, 2 and 3) in 2006–2007 was Oxford, with 90.2 per cent, followed by Cambridge with 88.5 per cent (HESA, 2008).

A similar story applies in America. Bowen et al. (2005) have documented the inequalities in participation in higher education in the United States. There are several reasons for this, but they include the preferential treatment given to alumni of the elite universities, along with high costs. In 2000, the cost of a year at the big three universities, Harvard, Yale and Princeton, had reached $35,000, an amount that less than 10 per cent of American families could afford. By 2004, this had risen to $40,000. And while there was some assistance for less well-off students, the majority paid full fees. Even then, better-off families seemed to have captured the scholarships available. At Harvard, the majority of scholarship recipients had a family income of over $70,000, with a quarter having an income of over $100,000.[5] When this is translated into the share of family income that goes on tuition fees, even though there is a reduction for low-income families, the latter pay an estimated 49 per cent of family income. In contrast, the proportion of family income paid in tuition fees for unaided students, those that come from wealthy families, is 21 per cent.[6]

Not surprisingly, among the dominant classes in America there is over-representation in terms of degrees, especially from the elite universities. David Rothkopf (2008), writing of the new super-class, notes that, among the CEOs of America's leading corporations, 30 per cent attended one of only twenty elite universities, led by Stanford, Harvard and Chicago. He estimates that 91 per cent have an undergraduate degree, and 47 per cent a postgraduate degree, which makes them far better educated than the general population. He shows how these elite universities provide the basis for forging networks between students and alumni, listing the number of high-profile CEOs that graduated from the Harvard Business School Class of 1979.

Given that TNCs are seeking the most 'talented' from the elite universities, there is a clear difference in wages between those who have attended elite universities and those who have attended less prestigious institutions. In Britain, Hussain et al. (2008) calculate that those from elite universities earn double the wages of those from lower-ranked institutions, while in America Goldin and Katz (2008a) report that graduates from Harvard attract a massive premium with those, for example, entering finance occupations earning 195 per cent above other occupations.

Just as there are differences in the earnings of those attending elite universities when compared with those who do not, so not all graduates will have the same life chances in the labour market, nor will they have the same experience at university. Rather, it can be argued that there is a loose correspondence between social-class background, the type of university attended, extracurricula networking and labour market opportunities.

Naidoo and Jamieson have sought to examine the impact of consumerism on higher education, exploring both the field of higher education in Bourdieuian terms (Naidoo and Jamieson, 2006) and the impact on teaching and learning of where an institution is positioned within the higher-education field. They argue that lower-ranked universities are more likely to engage in pre-packaged learning materials, for example through e-learning type strategies, and forms of assessment and pedagogy that narrow the tasks that students need to accomplish. In turn, the knowledge that is 'transmitted' will be pre-packaged and divided into modular form. In other words, there appears to be a correspondence between the type of pedagogy and curriculum that lower-ranked universities offer and the creation of digital Taylorist work, because much of the latter is based on pre-packaged modular routines.

The opportunity trap

The analysis developed above suggests a scenario where the polarisation in professional middle-class jobs leads to an intensification of positional competition for access to universities. The consequence is that students will have to pay more in fees for less return in the labour market. This is a trap because, if students do not enter the higher-education game, they have even less chance of securing good work and reasonable pay (Brown, 2006). In the United States, male college graduates have seen a decline in their wages from the mid 1970s through to now, for all except those at the 90th percentile. Women have fared a little better, but their wages still lag behind those of men, as shown in Table 20.1 below (Mishel et al., 2007).

While graduates in the United States have not fared as well as the knowledge economy rhetoric suggests, the wages of non-college graduates have declined dramatically over the same forty-year period, so that, even if the wages of university graduates fall, they will still earn a premium over non-university or college graduates, which is why those who have the possibility of going to university are trapped.

In Britain, a similar story can be told: graduate wages flat-lined for all groups through 1991–2000, while the hours worked increased by half a day a week (Lauder et al., 2005). A more recent study has shown that a third of graduates, who started university in England at the

Table 20.1 Hourly wages for low, median and high earning college graduates: 1979–2005

	1979	1989	1995	2000	2005
Men					
High	38	39	41	45	48
Median	21	21	21	23	23
Low	11	10	10	11	11
Women					
High	23	28	31	35	36
Median	14	16	17	18	18
Low	8	8	8	9	9

Source: Mishel et al. (2007), Table 3.2, p. 160.

same time as student fees were introduced in 1998, are, by 2008, not repaying their fees.[7] In England, graduates only start to pay back their state-backed loans when they earn £15,000 or above before tax. This is not surprising, given the data on graduate incomes.

Moreover, the present economic crisis is unlikely to bring any respite to the majority of graduates. We are undergoing a financial crisis that will impact on the higher-education sector. In turn, there is a question as to whether the present participation target of 50 per cent of an age cohort attending university in the UK can be met. It may be that some universities will be closed because public debt is so high. In this case, positional competition will further intensify. On top of this, fees are likely to rise, especially in the elite universities. Even without the economic crisis, this will act as a deterrent to many middle-class, far less working-class students. Finally, governments will always support the elite universities, because their research is seen as a source of global competitive advantage, so again the positional competition to gain entry to elite universities will intensify.

The theoretical implications for changes in education and the global division of labour

The developments we have described in this paper raise fundamental problems for both consensus and conflict theorists. We identified a number of strands to the consensus theory tradition: Drucker's claim that knowledge workers would move to the centre of power; human capital theory, which assumes that graduate returns to education will be highly rewarded because of higher productivity; and skill bias theory, which has claimed that new technology is complementary to skills upgrading, because more highly skilled workers are required, especially in relation to ICT, to operate the new technology. But we can see immediately that the processes we have described have not given power to knowledge workers, quite the opposite: the fracturing of the middle classes has meant that the returns on an investment in higher education are variable and, with the loss of middle-class jobs overseas, are likely to fall. The process of digital Taylorism is what skill bias theorists call skill replacing, because much the knowledge and capability for independent decision-making and initiative have been taken away. Finally, when we look at recent research by human capital and skill bias theorists, it is clear that there has been no acknowledgement of the way the global division of labour for knowledge workers has impacted on national, in this case American, graduate prospects (Goldin and Katz, 2008; Heckman, 2008).

Turning to the conflict tradition, the focus has been on the social justice agenda, and, in particular, on the inequalities of resources, financial and cultural, that are created through social class, patriarchal and racist structures and that impact on children's education. Equally, on the way that the interests of the professional and managerial social classes interact with state policies (Apple, 2006; Ball, 2003) to produce the well-documented inequalities in life chances (Goldthorpe and Jackson, 2008).

One motivation for this agenda has been to mobilise debate about educational inequalities within nations and how they might be addressed. However, we would make two points in relation to the arguments presented here: first, social classes are structured through the labour market in interaction with nation-state policies, therefore, unless we understand the changing nature of the labour market, we cannot comprehend the changing relationship between class and education. Second, changes in the global division of labour are having a fundamental impact on the nature of the class struggle for credentials and, hence, on the issues of social justice,

237

which raise questions about the role of the nation–state and the focus of conflict theorists in seeking to redress inequalities in education.

Conclusion

We have had two aims in writing this paper: to argue that existing theories of the education–society relationship have been challenged by economic globalisation and to explain why this is so through an account of recent changes in the global division of labour. Here, we showed that these developments would lead to tensions, if not outright contradictions, between higher education and capitalism. There are two, related tensions that we have highlighted. The first concerns the opportunity trap: here, middle-class families will invest more heavily in higher education for less return in the labour market for their children. The second relates to the wages, lifestyles and opportunities that those in Britain and America can expect. A majority of Americans no longer believes that a good education and hard work are enough to find good jobs and financial security (Kusnet *et al.*, 2006). In turn, this breaks the basic contract between citizens and the state by which Americans, and arguably Britons, over the past thirty years have seen education as the key to opportunity and prosperity: a contract in which the state provided the educational opportunities to enable workers to become employable, so long as they were highly motivated and invested in their education. It is hard to tell precisely, at this time of economic depression, what the consequences of the breaking of this contract will be, but we believe they will be profound.

Notes

1   For details see Brown *et al.* (2008).
2   This represented a 41 per cent increase in the number of full-time teachers in secondary education since 1988. See China Education and Research Network (CERNET), available online at www.edu.cn/english_1369/index.shtml.
3   See Jack Chang (2008).
4   See Government White Paper (2004).
5   See Jerome Karabel (2005).
6   See Hill *et al.* (2003).
7   *The Guardian*, '1 in 3 graduates not repaying student loans', 3 October 2008.

References

Acemoglu, D. (2002) 'Technical change, inequality and the labour market', *Journal of Economic Literature* XL(March): 7–72.
Apple, M.W. (2006) *Educating the 'right' way: markets, standards, god and inequality*, 2nd edn, New York: Routledge.
Baker, D. (2009 forthcoming) 'The educational revolution and the transformation of work', *Journal of Education and Work*.
Ball, S. (2003) *Class strategies and the education market: the middle classes and social advantage*, London: Routledge Falmer.
Becker, G. (2006) 'The age of human capital', in H. Lauder, P. Brown, J.-A. Dillabough and A.H. Halsey (eds) *Education, globalization and social change*, Oxford: Oxford University Press.

Bell, D. (1973) *The coming of the post-industrial revolution*, New York: Basic Books.

Bourdieu, P. and Passeron, J.-L. (1977) *Reproduction in education, society and culture*, London: Sage.

Bowen, W., Kurzwell, M. and Tobin, E. (2005) *Equity and excellence in American higher education*, Charlottesville, VA: University of Virginia Press.

Bowles, S.and Gintis, H. (1976) *Schooling in capitalist America*, London: Routledge.

Brint, S. (2001) 'Professionals and the "knowledge economy": rethinking the theory of post industrial society', *Current Sociology* 49(4): 101–132.

Brown, P., (2006) 'The opportunity trap', in H. Lauder P. Brown J.-A. Dillabough and A.H. Halsey (eds) *Education, globalization and social change*, Oxford: Oxford University Press.

—— Lauder, H. and Ashton, D. (2010) *The global auction: the broken promises of education, jobs and rewards*, Oxford, New York: Oxford University Press.

—— and Hesketh, A. (2004) *The mismanagement of talent, employability and jobs in the knowledge economy*, Oxford: Oxford University Press.

—— and —— Lauder, H. and Tholen, G. (2008) *Towards a high-skilled, low-waged workforce? A review of global trends in education, employment and the labour market*, Monograph No.10, Centre on Skills, Knowledge and Organisational Performance, Cardiff and Oxford Universities. Available online at www.skope.ox.ac.uk/WorkingPapers/Monograph%2010.pdf.

Chang, J. (2008) 'Update in Chinese higher education developments', presentation to Asia-Pacific Association for International Education (APAIE), Waseda University, Japan. Available online at www.apaie.org/hoge2008piyo/final_ppt/1-2-1_Jack_CHENG.pdf

Collins, R. (1979) *The credential society: an historical sociology of education and stratification*, New York: Academic Press.

Dale, R. (1989) *The state and education*, Buckingham: Open University Press.

Drucker, P. (1993) *Post-capitalist society*, Oxford: Butterworth/Heinemann.

Goldin, C. and Katz, L. (2008a) 'Gender differences in careers, education and games: transitions: career and family life cycles', *American Economic Review* 98(2): 363–369.

—— and —— (2008b) *The race between education and technology*, Cambridge, MA: Harvard University Press.

Goldthorpe, J. and Jackson, M. (2008) 'Education based meritocracy: the barriers to its realization', in A. Lareau and D. Conley *Social class: how does it work?* New York: Russell Sage.

Government White Paper (2004) *China's employment situation and policies, Section VI. Employment prospects for the early part of the 21st century*, People's Republic of China, Beijing, April 2004. Available online at www.china.org.cn/e-white/20040426/6.htm.

Heckman, J. (2008) *Schools, skills and synapses*, Discussion Paper No. 3515, The Institute for the Study of Labour (IZA), PO Box 7240, 53072, Bonn, Germany.

Higher Education Statistics Agency (2008) *Higher Education Statistical Release*, Cheltenham, UK: HESA.

Hill, C., Winston, G. and Boyd, S. (2003) *Affordability: family incomes and net prices at highly selective private colleges and universities*, Williams Project on the Economics of Higher Education, Discussion paper No.66, October 2003.

Hirsch, F. (1976) *The social limits to growth*, Cambridge, MA: Harvard University Press.

Hussain, I., McNally, S. and Telhaj, S. (2008) *University quality and graduate wages in the UK*, London: Centre for Economic Performance, London School of Economics.

Karabel, J. (2005) *The chosen, the hidden history of admission and exclusion at Harvard, Yale and Princeton*, New York: Mariner Books.

Kerr, C., Dunlop, J., Harbinson, F. and Myers, C. (1973) *Industrialism and industrial man*, Harmondsworth: Penguin.

Kusnet, D., Mishel, L. and Teixeira, R. (2006) *Talking past each other: what everyday Americans really think (and elites don't get) about the economy*, Washington, DC: Economic Policy Institute.

Lauder, H., Brown, P. and Ashton, D. (2008) 'Globalisation, skill formation and the varieties of capitalism approach', *New Political Economy* 13(1): 19–35.

—— Egerton, M. and Brown, P. (2005) *A report on graduate earnings: theory and empirical analysis*, Report for the Independent Study into the Devolution of the Student Support System and Tuition Fee Regime, The Welsh Assembly, Cardiff.

239

Livingstone, D. (1998) *The education-jobs gap: underemployment or economic democracy*, Boulder, CO: Westview Press.

Mishel, L., Bernstein, J. and Allegretto, S. (2007) *The state of working America 2006/7*, Ithaca, NY: Economic Policy Institute/Cornell University.

Naidoo, R. and Jamieson, I. (2006) 'Empowering participants or corroding learning? Towards a research agenda on the impact of student consumerism in higher education', in H. Lauder, P. Brown, J.-A. Dillabough and A.H. Halsey (eds) *Education, globalization and social change*, Oxford: Oxford University Press.

Reich, R. (1991) *The work of nations*, London: Simon & Schuster.

Rothkopf, D. (2008) *Superclass: the global power elite and the world they are making*, New York: Little Brown.

Rosecrance, R. (1999) *The rise of the virtual state*, New York: Basic Books.

United Nations Conference on Trade and Development (UNCTAD) (2005) *World Investment Report 2005: Transnational corporations and the internationalization of R&D*. Available online at www.unctad.org/wir.

Weedon, K. (2002) 'Why do some occupations pay more than others? Social closure and earnings inequality in the United States', *American Journal of Sociology* 108(1): 55–101.

21

Education and the right to the city

The intersection of urban policies, education, and poverty

Pauline Lipman

In this chapter, I discuss the relationship of urban education and urban political economy. I focus on the intersection of education policy and globalized neoliberal political and economic processes that are reshaping cities. After a general overview of urban restructuring, I turn to a specific case. This case illustrates that education policy is not only shaped by neoliberal urbanism but may be productive of the intensified economic, social, and spatial inequalities that characterize cities in the global economy.

Neoliberal globalization and urban restructuring

Neoliberalism is the defining political and economic paradigm of our age (Apple, 2006). The neoliberal agenda extends the logic of the market to all corners of the earth and all spheres of social life, liberalizes trade, drives down the price of labor, and employs financialization as a principle strategy of capital accumulation. The result is a massive transfer of wealth upward, concentrated in the hands of a tiny global elite, and increased economic inequality on a world scale (Harvey, 2005; Jomo and Bodot, 2007). Cities across a range of economic contexts are concentrated expressions of these inequalities, with new geographies of centrality and marginality (Sassen, 2006). In economically "developing" countries, structural adjustment policies mandated by the World Bank and International Monetary Fund in the 1980s and the deregulation of international commodity markets have destabilized peasantry and further impoverished rural areas. As a result, cities have become meccas for millions of dispossessed and impoverished farmers and workers (Davis, 2006; Harvey, 2005).

As economic activity is reterritorialized at all spatial scales (Robertson and Dale, 2006), cities and large urbanized areas have become fundamental geographical units in the spatial reorganization of the new international division of labor and sites of a range of diverse political, economic, and cultural global connections. On one hand, "global cities," such as New York, London, Tokyo, and São Paulo, are command centers of the global economy, key nodes in global circuits of finance and production (Sassen, 2006). From this perspective, global cities are the pinnacle of an urban hierarchy that includes global niche cities, such as Miami; international cultural meccas such as Bilbao; small cities defined by capital accumulation typical of global cities; and declining, post-industrial cities such as Adelaide. On the other hand, post-colonial theorists (King, 1990; Rizvi, 2007; Robinson 2002; Smith, 2001) foreground transnational connections among "ordinary cities" in formerly colonized countries. They draw attention to multiple global urban functions, such as Manilla's role as hub of global circuits of low-paid migrant labor (Robinson, 2002). Extended urban areas in the global South have also emerged as the "production hearths" of the global economy (Smith, 2002). Global economic and political processes also intersect, in specific ways, with local and national institutions, ideologies, and relations of power, as well as with specific histories of colonialism, imperialism, post-colonialism, and socialism.

Yet there are common trends, with significant implications for those who live in cities and for urban education. In the following sections, I turn to some of these trends and their relationship to education in one kind of urban context—a "global city" in North America. My discussion is meant to be illustrative of an approach to understanding intersections of education and neoliberal urbanism.

Urbanization and inequality

The world is experiencing an unprecedented level of urbanization. Writing in 2006, Mike Davis noted that, for the first time, the urban population of the world would soon exceed the rural. (At the time of writing, in 2008, this milestone has probably been passed.) Virtually all the world's population increase will occur in cities, and 95 percent of the increase will be in urban areas of (economically) "developing" countries. Urban areas are also being reshaped as megacities of over 8 million (e.g. Jakarta and Delhi); extended hypercities of over 20 million (e.g. Mexico City and New York); conurbations of urban areas (e.g. the West African Gulf of Guinea, with Lagos as its center); extended urban networks and metropolitan regions (e.g. the Rio/São Paulo extended metropolitan region); and many more mid-sized cities are emerging (China is a key example) (Davis, 2006; Pastor et al., 2000; Scott et al., 2002; Simmonds and Hack, 2000).

Urban areas are concentrated expressions of the dynamics of extreme inequality, marginality, and centrality that characterize the global economy as a whole. While the new world order has spawned increased wealth and advantage for cities in the USA, its Western allies, and some Eastern Europe and Asian countries, most former European colonies have lost ground. Davis (2006) notes that, unlike urbanization fed by the growth of capitalism in Europe in the nineteenth century, cities in the developing world are low-wage labor intensive, rather than capital intensive. However, inequality has increased in both rich and poor states (Jomo and Baudot, 2007), with enclaves of hyper-affluence, transnational knowledge workers, and global elites juxtaposed with concentrations of low-wage and informal workers living in extreme poverty (Amin, 1997). This pattern is evident in cities as diverse as Mumbai, São Paulo, Beijing, and Los Angeles. In short, cities in the global North and global South are characterized by: accelerating urbanization; new patterns of social and spatial exclusion; increased inequalities and degradation of the quality of life for those living in poverty, which in many cities are the vast majority; informalization of labor and housing; and cultural mixes and transnational identities produced by migrations of labor and displacement of peasantry (Davis, 2006; Marcuse and Van Kempen, 2000; Sassen, 2006; Valle and Torres, 2000).

Urban education systems tend also to inequalities in educational provision, access, outcomes, and valorized languages, cultures, and identities (see Pink and Noblit 2008). Schools are certainly impacted by the economic and political processes and policies that are reshaping their contexts (Anyon, 1997; Thompson, 2002). But educational policies are also constitutive of these contexts as well as important sites of resistance.

The political economy of urban education

In *Social justice and the city*, Harvey (1973) argues the urban is "a vantage point from which to capture some salient features operating in society as a whole—it becomes as it were a mirror in which other aspects of society can be reflected" (p. 16). In particular, (Western) metropolitan cities are "the locus of the accumulated contradictions of a society." They concentrate major cultural, financial, social, and political institutions in close proximity with concentrations of low-income and marginalized populations that are excluded from these institutions (p. 203). This observation is even more prescient at the beginning of the twenty-first century, in the present social conjuncture of neoliberalism and resistance (Gill, 2003). In urban areas, this dialectic is unfolding in economic, political, and cultural struggles over what Henri Lefebvre (1996) famously framed as "the right to the city." Education is integral to these struggles.

In a germinal book on the critical study of urban education, Gerald Grace (1984) argued against the prevailing "policy science" approach to the study of urban education problems in the USA and UK. Drawing on C. Wright Mills' critique of "abstracted empiricism" in sociology, Grace rejected "technical and immediately realizable," within-the-system solutions to urban education problems abstracted from the urban context (p. 32). He called for "critical policy scholarship" that situates urban education theoretically and socially in the larger framework of the social, economic, political, and cultural contexts of society. Critical policy scholarship illuminates the material and cultural struggles in which schooling is located and is generative of social action towards social justice (p. 41). An underlying assumption is that policy is an expression of values arising out of specific interests and relations of power. Grace notes that this requires a multidisciplinary approach that draws on urban studies as well as urban sociology. In a somewhat analogous critique, Rury and Mirel (1997) argued that "educational researchers [in the USA] too often accept the urban environment as a given natural setting, rather than one that has itself been determined by larger economic and political processes" (p. 85). They proposed a political economy of US urban education that places at the center of the urban research agenda questions of power, particularly the role of capital and race in structuring urban space.

Building on these insights and extending Grace's multidisciplinary method, I bring in scholarship in urban studies, critical geography, and urban sociology to shed light on the role of education in restructuring urban space, materially and culturally, along multiple dimensions of power. The spatial restructuring of urban education and its relationship to urban development is illuminated by the work of critical geographers who see space as a constitutive aspect of capitalist accumulation (Harvey, 2005; Smith, 1996). This dynamic is located in what Harvey (2001) calls the "spatial fix." The territorial organization of capital—the physical location of production facilities, the built environment of cities, places of consumption—is destroyed and rebuilt elsewhere in order to establish a "new locational grid" for the accumulation of capital. Investment and disinvestment in schools, class and race-based school funding inequities, and policies that engineer student social mix are all implicated in this process. Cultural geographers also attend to ways power is reproduced (and contested) and daily life is regulated through socially produced meanings about specific places (Keith and Pile, 1993; Soja, 1999). Again, contested representations of urban schools are implicated in claims on the city.

243

Neoliberal urbanism

Beginning with the economic crisis of the 1970s, social democratic urban policies in the USA and UK were systematically eliminated. In ensuing decades, across a range of cities globally, capital employed neoliberal policies to ensure capital accumulation (Smith, 2002). "In this context, cities—including their suburban peripheries—have become increasingly important geographical targets and institutional laboratories for a variety of neoliberal policy experiments . . ." (Brenner and Theodore, 2002: 368). Despite neoliberal theory of reduced government, actually existing neoliberalism involves the intervention of the state on the side of capital, first to destroy existing institutional arrangements, and then to create a new infrastructure for capital accumulation. Discursively, urban governance has shifted from equity and redistribution to markets and entrepreneurship. In the global competition for investment, tourism, highly skilled "creative" workers, and production facilities, including the business services that drive globalization (Sassen, 2006), cities from Madrid to Beijing are engaged in place marketing.
     Neoliberal urban initiatives include:

* downtown mega-developments, "theme parks," and spectacles;
* gentrification of disinvested urban areas and working-class communities;
* demolition/renovation of public (social) housing and displacement of residents;
* privatization of public institutions and spaces;
* public–private partnerships and state subsidies to developers and corporations;
* governance by experts and corporate boards, with democratic "participation" relegated to citizen advisory groups;
* surveillance and policing of marginalized, racialized communities.

The role of education in these urban policy initiatives and the implications for equity and justice in the city are the subjects of the remainder of this chapter. I focus primarily on US urban policy, with Chicago as illustration.

Education and neoliberal urbanism

Urban school systems have been in the forefront of neoliberal education policy shifts in the USA. As in much of the world, public school policy is dominated by accountability, markets, and privatization in the service of "effectiveness" and global competition (Hursh, 2008). Under the banner of school choice, there is a turn towards greater differentiation and stratification of educational experiences and to militarization of schools serving low-income students of color (Lipman, 2004). Although contested, these policies and practices facilitate the production of neoliberal subjects through education (Demerath et al., 2008). What is less examined is their relationship to the neoliberal restructuring of cities.
     Chicago exemplifies this relationship. Over the past three decades it has morphed from industrial hub to center for global business services and finance, international tourism, downtown development, and gentrification. A contender for first-tier global city, Chicago has achieved this transformation largely through neoliberal policies, including a rich menu of incentives to real estate developers and corporate and banking interests, privatization of public institutions, marketing to the middle class and investors, and intensified policing and surveillance of communities of color (Lipman, 2004).

Chicago is also in the forefront of neoliberal education initiatives (Lipman, 2004; Lipman and Haines, 2007). Chicago's education accountability policies, begun with the "reform" of 1995, were a prototype for national policy. Accountability was coupled with a stratified system of school choice, with new selective enrolment speciality schools alongside public military schools, vocational high schools, and basic skills schools. In 2004, Chicago initiated Renaissance 2010, a plan to close "failing" public schools and replace them with schools of choice, most privately run but publicly financed charter and contract schools. Under the Obama administration, Chicago is a national model to be copied by other urban school systems. Although these initiatives reflect national and global trends, they also have specific consequences for the city.

The importance of education to interurban competitiveness can be gauged by the involvement of corporate and financial elites in urban school policy. Chicago is an exemplar. The Commercial Club of Chicago (CCC), an organization of leading CEOs and civic elites, takes a direct hand in school policy. Over the past twenty years, the CCC has issued a series of reports laying out an education agenda geared to global competitiveness. A 2003 report was the blueprint for Renaissance 2010 school closings, charter schools, and choice. The mayor announced the plan a year later at a CCC event. The CCC also created the Renaissance Schools Fund, a partnership with the public school system to oversee major aspects of the reform. There is also direct corporate governance though a mayoral appointed school board and administration comprised of corporate leaders, including a former vice president of Bank One and CEO of the Chicago Board of Trade, who took an unpaid position as chief administrative officer, overseeing seven departments. Mayoral control is now a national agenda.

Education policy and gentrification

In the neoliberal rollback of the early 1980s, the US federal government reduced funding for cities while devolving greater responsibility to city governments. To make up for shortfalls and driven by market ideologies, city governments adopted entrepreneurial measures. To address budgetary shortfalls, they looked to public–private ventures, privatization of public services, and revenue from real estate taxes repackaged as municipal bonds. As they became far more reliant on debt to finance public projects and ongoing functions, city bond ratings became more significant in determining policy than in the Keynesian period of more generous federal funding (Hackworth, 2007). In the USA, reliance on property tax revenues makes cities more dependent on, and active subsidizers of, the private real estate market, with developers benefiting from public giveaways of land through urban tax initiatives (Weber 2002). In turn, real estate development is a key form of speculative activity, with real estate properties essentially operating as financial instruments. This is a critical factor in the production of spatial inequality, displacement, homelessness, and racial containment. Facilitated by municipal governments, gentrification has become a pivotal sector in urban economies generally.

> Gentrification as a process has rapidly descended the urban hierarchy; it is evident not only in the largest cities but in more unlikely centers such as the previously industrial cities of Cleveland and Glasgow, smaller cities like Malmö or Grenada, and even small market towns such as Lancaster, Pennsylvania or Čveské Krumlov in the Czech Republic. At the same time, the process has diffused geographically as well, with reports of gentrification from Tokyo to Tenerife, São Paulo to Puebla, Mexico, Cape Town to the Caribbean, Shanghai to Seoul.
>
> (Smith, 2002: 439)

In this period, gentrification merges local, national, and transnational capital, lubricated by local government through re-zoning, diversion of tax dollars to infrastructure improvements, and the construction of public amenities such as parks, transit, and libraries (Smith, 2002). Moving beyond city centers, it transforms whole neighborhoods into gentrification "complexes" of consumption, recreation, cultural venues, and schools, as well as housing. In turn, increases in property taxes push out low-income and working-class renters and homeowners.

Selective public schools and choice are integral to this process. Good schools and choice within the public school system are important to market the city to middle-class home buyers and knowledge workers. They are also essential to attract investors to potential sites of gentrification and to subsequently market gentrified and gentrifying areas to new middle- and upper-middle-class residents. For the middle class, education is central to class formation and reproduction (Butler with Robson, 2003). Like new libraries, police stations, and streetscapes, new schools are infrastructure improvements, enhancing the real estate value of specific areas. "Education markets are now rivalling those in housing and employments as determinants of the nature, extent and stability of middle class gentrification of inner city localities" (Butler with Robson: 157). In Chicago, new selective schools opened through the 1995 and 2004 school reforms map onto patterns of gentrified and gentrifying neighborhoods, while basic skills, military, and vocational schools are all located in low-income communities of color (Greenlee et al., 2008; Lipman and Haines, 2007). The school district has closed schools in low-income African American and Latino communities undergoing gentrification and replaced them with selective public schools or charter schools, marketed to middle- and upper-middle-class families, which neighborhood children often cannot attend. Cucciara (2008) describes a similar strategy in Philadelphia.

In the USA, central cities experienced decades of public and private disinvestment (Anyon, 1997), opening them up as "soft spots" of neoliberal experimentation (Hackworth, 2007). The failure to adequately fund and support schools in these low-income African American and immigrant areas further devalued them and made them prime targets for a new round of investment. Education accountability served to index the schools as failures, then close and reopen them for the middle class or outsource them to private operators as charter schools. Closing schools and transferring students outside their neighborhoods, as has happened in Chicago, further contributes to the displacement of families, facilitating gentrification.

Thus, the policy serves capital accumulation and increases educational inequality. But it is also an intervention in the race- and class-inflected meaning of urban space (Leonardo and Hunter, 2008). Labeling "failing" schools in marginalized communities (e.g. low-income African American and Latino in the USA, Aboriginal in Sydney, Gulson, 2008) contributes to defining the communities as "dysfunctional" and "dangerous." Yet for those who live there, schools can be centers of historically rooted, culturally centered communities of sustenance and resistance against race and class oppression (Leonardo and Hunter, 2008). Dismantling them is part of dismantling the communities as a whole, materially and symbolically (Lipman and Haines, 2007). Conversely, reopening schools with middle-class inflected identities is part of symbolically reconstituting the city for the middle and upper-middle classes.

School policy and dismantling public housing

Throughout much of the English-speaking world, national and local governments have responded to the problem of neglected public (social) housing by demolishing or remodelling it as "mixed-income" developments, with considerable displacement of low-income tenants

(Lees, 2008). In the USA, the 1992 HOPE VI national housing law called for the demolition of distressed public housing units and their replacement with privately developed, mixed-income housing or vouchers for rentals in the private housing market. HOPE VI is a high-level, public–private partnership that provides millions of public dollars in subsidies to developers. A 1995 revision eliminated the one-to-one replacement requirement. At the same time, strict eligibility requirements exclude many public housing tenants from new developments, and only a fraction of the units are reserved for them. In Chicago, miles of dense, hi-rise public housing on the city's South Side have been razed and are being replaced by low-density mixed income developments, with fewer than one third of the units for public housing. This parallels other cities where the majority of original residents have been unable to return (e.g. Oakley *et al.*, 2008).

In the USA, most urban public housing residents are people of color—in Chicago, almost entirely African Americans. Public housing restructuring serves capital accumulation, while it is also a form of racialized exclusion. US cities have begun to resemble those in Western Europe, with the center claimed by the middle and upper classes (particularly whites), ringed by low-income suburbs (mainly people of colour). One cause is the state's failure to maintain public housing until it became uninhabitable, justifying its demolition and dispersal of the residents, some out of the city altogether. Chicago, where transformation of public housing and closing schools under Renaissance 2010 are coordinated, provides an example of the role education policy plays in the displacement of African American public housing residents through mixed-income development.

In Chicago and other US cities, razed public housing is being replaced by privately developed, mixed-income developments. (See also social mix strategies in the UK: Lupton and Turnstall, 2008). The strategic role of new, purposely designed, mixed-income schools with a middle-class majority was made explicit by the MacArthur Foundation, a major player in Chicago's transformation of public housing: "The city has made a commitment to improving the local schools, without which the success of the new mixed-income communities would be at great risk" (2005). Underlying this strategy is the deconcentration thesis: concentrations of poverty supposedly breed social isolation and social pathologies, which reproduce a cycle of poverty. Dismantling hi-rise public housing and creating socially mixed schools supposedly give low-income people access to middle-class values and resources to lift themselves out of poverty and improve academic achievement (Imbroscio, 2008; Kahlenberg 2001). This strategy has been critiqued for its normative assumptions that middle-class lifestyles are superior and lifestyles of low-income people of color are pathological. Moreover, mixed-income schools and housing exclude the majority of displaced residents, as redevelopment is primarily for the middle and upper-middle classes. In Chicago, about 20 percent of former public housing tenants are expected to relocate to the new developments (Wilen and Nyak, 2006).

Social mix is nonetheless a hegemonic legitimating discourse. Drawing on the neoliberal shift to individual responsibility and personal behavior as explanations for inequality, mixed-income solutions erase the structural roots of disinvestment in urban schools and inner-city communities and the state's responsibility to improve schools for the low-income students of color who live there. They also instantiate the idea that low-income people of color need cultural and social renovation, negating wider social processes of cultural differentiation and exclusion and ignoring strengths of public housing communities (Bauder, 2002). Public housing is iconic for racialized and pathologized representations of urban African Americans in particular. Mixed-income schools, like mixed-income housing solutions contribute to these representations and support the systematic displacement of public housing, even when initial gentrifiers are African American, as in Chicago's Midsouth (Smith and Stovall, 2008).

247

New urban governance—public–private partnerships, democratic deficits, and education markets

Quasi-private bodies that supersede the authority of elected government and democratic processes are a distinguishing feature of neoliberal urban governance. Large-scale European development projects have been used to establish new urbanist governance regimes defined by public–private partnerships, collaborations among networks of elites, lack of public accountability, and exclusion of real public participation. These regimes run "the public sector like a business," with the goal of enhancing the competitive advantage of cities and furthering neoliberal economic and social priorities (Swyngedouw *et al.*, 2004). Similar arrangements in the USA govern the planning and oversight of urban development projects, public housing, schools, and other public services (Bennett *et al.*, 2006; Lipman and Haines, 2007). HOPE VI, for example, creates partnerships of developers and public housing authorities to build and manage public housing and mixed-income projects with little genuine public voice (Bennett *et al.*, 2006). Typically, new urbanist governance disenfranchises public-housing residents, parents, workers, and community residents, reducing their civic participation to appointed advisory boards with no authority to make decisions.

Chicago's Renaissance 2010 is a high-level partnership of the Commercial Club and the public schools. The CCC's Renaissance Schools Fund typifies the increased corporate role in urban governance. Simultaneously, Renaissance 2010 eliminates democratically elected local school councils (LSCs) in all new Renaissance schools. LSCs, comprised primarily of parents and community residents with authority to select principals and approve the school improvement plan and budget, are the most radical democratic form of local school governance in the USA. Their elimination disenfranchises the mostly low-income parents of color whose children comprise 90 percent of public school students. Neoliberal governance also blurs lines between public and private goods, as municipal governments, strapped for funds and propelled by the logic of public inefficiency, sell off public assets and turn over public institutions to corporate management, e.g. sale or lease of bridges, highways, and airports to be run for profit. Market-oriented school policies—choice and quasi-privatization through charter schools—encourage the growth of an education industry and set a precedent for the marketization of urban public services generally. Charter and contract schools are run by private boards, and many are franchised out to corporate education management organizations. In Chicago, fifty-one of seventy-five schools created under Renaissance 2010, as of fall 2008, were charter or contract schools. Privatization of schools in New Orleans after the devastation of Hurricane Katrina in 2005 is the leading edge of neoliberal restructuring in that city. An influential report by the Urban Institute (Hill and Hannaway, 2006) hailed New Orleans as an opportunity for a grand experiment to decentralize and privatize the school system through vouchers and charter schools. Less than a month after Hurricane Katrina devastated New Orleans, the US Department of Education gave the state of Louisiana $20.9 million to reopen existing charter schools and open new ones, and nine months later the Department gave the state an additional $23.9 million for new charter schools, most in New Orleans. Prior to Katrina, there were only five charter schools in New Orleans. Of the fifty-five schools open in New Orleans in 2006–2007, thirty-one were public charter schools (Alexander, 2007).

Market-oriented school policies intensify polarization (Reay, 2007) and advance the middle-class conquest of the city (Smith, 2002). School choice provides an opportunity, not available through regular public school provision, for middle-class parents to strategically deploy multiple forms of capital to gain educational advantages for their children (Ball *et al.*, 1995; Butler with Robson, 2003). Thus choice, particularly options that appeal to the middle class, is a policy tool to attract the middle-class school consumer and home buyer. Governance of charter schools by private boards also advantages middle-class parents. Their political and economic power potentially gives them access and influence not enjoyed by working-class parents, who might otherwise hold public officials accountable and exercise collective influence through democratic processes such as elected LSCs in Chicago.

The Punitive State

Neoliberalism requires a strong enforcement state to suppress actual and potential dissent in the face of the disciplining of labor, growing inequality and impoverishment, and the redundancy of fractions of the working class (Gill, 2003) Thus, in Western Europe and the USA, there is a turn to increased state surveillance, constriction of civil liberties, and policing and incarceration of immigrants and, in the USA, African Americans and Latinos in particular (Wacquant, 2001). Aggressive urban policing to make the city "safe" for the middle class, made famous by New York Mayor Giuliani in the 1990s, has been exported globally (Fyfe, 2004). In the USA, the politics of race are central to the workings of the enforcement state, and schools are a strategic site. This logic is evident in the militarization of schooling in African American and Latino areas, where schools are characterized by lockdown conditions, electronic surveillance, metal detectors and police stations inside school buildings, and military programs. In this way, schools are implicated in racialized policies of containment and discipline as an aspect of political and cultural control of urban space.

Conclusion

Neoliberal economic and social policies are reshaping cities globally, producing greater social polarization and inequality and new urban geographies of exclusion and marginalization. It is impossible to fully examine the sociology of urban education without accounting for these global processes and their localization in specific cities. Taking this a step farther, education is also implicated in solidifying the neoliberal urban agenda, materially and discursively, through policies that support displacement and gentrification, privatization, democratic deficits, and the pathologization and policing of economically and racially marginalized inhabitants. Neoliberal education policies have important implications for the future of the city—politically, economically, culturally, and spatially. This makes it clear that education is an important site of contestation over the right to the city, that is, the need to restructure the power relations that underlie the production of urban space, fundamentally shifting control away from capital and the neoliberal state and towards the vast majority of urban inhabitants. It also makes clear the importance of multidisciplinary analyses that merge the insights of critical sociology of education with political and cultural geography, urban sociology, and urban studies. We also need a critical scholarship that documents and theorizes forms of urban resistance that connect struggles for equitable education with struggles for housing, jobs, cultural recognition, access to urban resources, and democratic participation.

References

Alexander, M. (2007) "Reinventing a broken wheel? The fight to reclaim public education in New Orleans," *Social Policy* 37: 18–23.

Amin, S. (1997) *Capitalism in the age of globalization*, London: Zed.

Anyon, J. (1997) *Ghetto schooling*, New York: Teachers College Press.

Apple, M.W. (2006) *Educating the "right" way*, 2nd edn, New York: Routledge.

Ball, S., Bowe, R. and Gewirtz, S. (1995) "Circuits of schooling: A sociological exploration of parental choice of school in social class contexts," *Sociological Review* 43: 52–78.

Bauder, H. (2002) "Neighbourhood effects and cultural exclusion," *Urban Studies* 39: 85–93.

Bennett L. Smith, J. and Wright, P.A. (2006) "Introduction," in L. Bennett, J.L. Smith, P.A. Wright (eds), *Where are poor people to live?*, Armonk, NJ: M.E. Sharpe.

Brenner, N. and Theodore, N. (2002) "Cities and the geographies of 'actually existing neoliberalism'," *Antipode*, 34(3): 349–379.

Butler, T. with Robson, G. (2003) *London calling: the middle classes and the re-making of Inner London*, Oxford: Berg.

Cucciara, M. (2008) "Re-branding urban schools: urban revitalization, social status, and marketing public schools to the upper middle class," *Journal of Education Policy* 23: 165–179.

Davis, M. (2006) *Planet of slums*, London: Verso.

Demerath, P., Lynch, J. and Davidson, M. (2008) "Dimensions of psychological capital in a US suburb and high school: identities for neoliberal times," *Anthropology and Education Quarterly* 39: 270–292.

Fyfe, N. (2004) "Zero tolerance, maximum surveillance? Deviance, difference and crime control in the late modern city," in L. Lees (ed.) *The emancipatory city? Paradoxes and possibilities*, London: Sage.

Gill, S. (2003) *Power and resistance in the new world order*, New York: Palgrave Macmillan.

Grace, G. (1984) "Urban education: policy science or critical scholarship," in G. Grace (ed.) *Education and the city: theory, history and contemporary practice*, London: Routledge & Kegan Paul.

Greenlee, A., Hudspeth, N., Lipman, P., Smith, D.A. and Smith, J. (2008, February) *Investing in neighborhoods Research Paper #1: Examining CPS' plan to close, consolidate, turn-around 18 schools*, Data and Democracy Project, University of Illinois-Chicago.

Gulson, K.N. (2008) "Urban accommodations: policy, education and a politics of space," *Journal of Education Policy* 23:153–163.

Hackworth, J. (2007) *The neoliberal city: governance, ideology, and development in American urbanism*, Ithaca, NY: Cornell University Press.

Harvey, D. (1973) *Social justice and the city*, Baltimore, MD: Johns Hopkins University Press.

—— (2001) *Spaces of capital: towards a critical geography*, London: Routledge.

—— (2005) *A brief history of neoliberalism*, London: Oxford.

Hill, P. and Hannaway, J. (2006) The future of public education in New Orleans, Urban Institute. Available online at www.urban.org/UploadedPDF/900913_public_education.pdf (accessed June 5, 2008).

Hursh, D. (2008) *High-stakes testing and the decline of teaching and learning*, Lanham, MD: Rowman & Littlefield.

Imbroscio, D. (2008) "'United and actuated by some common impulse of passion': challenging the dispersal consensus in American housing policy research," *Journal of Urban Affairs* 30: 111–130.

Kahlenberg, R.D. (2001) *All together now: the case for economic integration of the public schools*, Washington, DC: Brookings Institution Press.

Jomo, K.S. and Baudot, J. (2007) *Flat world, big gaps: economic liberalization, globalization, poverty and inequality*, New York: Zed Books in association with the United Nations.

Keith, M. and Pile, S. (1993) "The politics of place," in M. Keith and S. Pile (eds) *Place and the politics of identity*, London: Routledge.

King, A. (1990) *Urbanism, colonialism and the world-economy*, London: Routledge.

Lefebvre, H. (1996) *Writings on cities* (trans. and ed., E. Kofman and E. Labas), London: Blackwell.

Lees, L. (2008) "Gentrification and social mixing: towards an inclusive urban renaissance?" *Urban Studies* 45(12): 2449–2470.

Leonardo, Z. and Hunter, M. (2008) "Imagining the urban: the politics of race, class and schooling," in W.F. Pink and G.W. Noblit (eds) *International handbook of urban education*, Vol. 2, Dordrecht, Netherlands: Springer.

Lipman, P. (2004) *High stakes education: inequality, globalization, and urban school reform*, New York: RoutledgeFalmer.

—— and Haines, N. (2007) "From education accountability to privatization and African American exclusion—Chicago public schools' renaissance 2010," *Educational Policy* 21: 471–502.

Lupton, R. and Turnstall, R. (2008) "Neighbourhood regeneration through mixed conmmunities: a 'social justice dilemma'?" *Journal of Education Policy* 23: 105–117.

MacArthur Foundation (2005) "Revitalizing Bronzeville: mixed-income housing is key to community strength," *Newsletter*, Spring. Available online at www.macfound.org (accessed January 4, 2006).

Marcuse, P. and Van Kempen, R. (eds) (2000) *Globalizing cities: a new spatial order?*, Oxford: Blackwell.

Oakley, D., Ruel, E. and Wilson, G.E. (2008) *A choice with no options: Atlanta public housing residents' lived experiences in the face of relocation: a preliminary report*. Available online at urbanhealth.gsu.edu/files/gsu_public_housing_report1.pdf (accessed December 1, 2008).

Pastor, M. Jr., Dreier, P., Grigsby, J.E. III and Lopez-Garza, M. (2000) *Regions that work: how cities and suburbs can grow together*, Minneapolis, MN: University of Minnesota Press.

Pink, W.F. and Noblit, G.W. (eds) (2008) *International handbook of urban education*, Dordrecht, Netherlands: Springer.

Reay, D. (2007) "Unruly places: inner-city comprehensives, middle-class imaginaries and working-class children," *Urban Studies* 44(7): 1191–1201.

Rizvi, F. (2007) "Postcolonialism and globalization in education," *Cultural Studies _ Critical Methodologies* 7: 256–263.

Robertson, S. and Dale, R. (2006) "Changing geographies of power in education: the politics of rescaling and its contradictions," in D. Kassen, E. Mufti and J.Rrobinson (eds) *Education studies: issues and critical perspectives*, London: Open University Press.

Robinson, J. (2002) "Global and world cities: a view from off the map," *International Journal of Urban and Regional Research* 26: 531–54.

Rury, J.R. and Mirel, J.E. (1997) "The political economy of urban education," *Review of Research in Education* 22: 49–110.

Sassen, S. (2006) *Cities in a world economy*, 3rd edn, Thousand Oaks, CA: Pine Forge Press.

Scott, A.J., Agnew, J., Soja, E.W. and Storper, M. (2002) "Global city-regions," in A.J. Scott (ed.) *Global city-regions: trends, theory, policy*, Oxford: Oxford University Press.

Simmonds, R. and Hack, G. (2000) "Introduction," in R. Simmonds and G. Hack (eds) *Global city regions: their emerging forms*, London: Spon Press.

Smith, J. and Stovall, D. (2008) "'Coming home' to new homes and new schools: critical race theory and the new politics of containment," *Journal of Education Policy* 23: 135–152.

Smith, M.P. (2001) *Transnational urbanism*, Oxford: Blackwell.

Smith, N. (2002) "New globalism, new urbanism: gentrification as global urban strategy," *Antipode* 34: 427–450.

—— (1996) *The new urban frontier: gentrification and the revanchist city*, New York: Routledge.

Soja, E.W. (1999) "In different spaces: the cultural turn in urban and regional political economy," *European Planning Studies* 7: 65–75.

Swyngedouw, E., Moulaert, F. and Rodriguez, A. (2004) "Neoliberal urbanization in Europe: Large-scale urban development projects and the new urban policy," in N. Brenner and N. Theodore (eds) *Spaces of neoliberalism*, London: Blackwell.

Thompson, P. (2002) *Schooling the rustbelt kids*, Sydney: Allen & Unwin.

Valle, V.M. and Torres, R.D. (2000) *Latino metropolis*, Minneapolis, MN: University of Minnesota Press.

Wacquant, L. (2001) "The penalization of poverty and the rise of neo-liberalism," *European Journal of Criminal Policy and Research* 9: 401–412.

Weber, R. (2002) "Extracting value from the city: neoliberalism and urban redevelopment," *Antipode* 34: 519–540.

Wilen, W.P. and Nayak, R.D. (2006) "Relocating public housing residents have little hope of returning," in L. Bennett, J.L. Smith and P.A. Wright (eds) *Where are poor people to live?* Armonk, NY: M.E. Sharpe.

22

A revisited theme – middle classes and the school

Maria Alice Nogueira

In the early 1990s, I wrote an article about "Middle-class families and the school," humbly subtitled "Preliminary bases for an object in construction" (Nogueira, 1995). Two principles grounded that prudent gesture: (a) the heterodoxical nature of the object, which in a scientific context (international and national)—for acceptable, although sociologically insufficient reasons—prioritized (it still does today) the study of less favored social environments; and (b) the risks of stepping on uncertain terrain, beginning with the definition of "middle class," which is always controversial owing to its place on the social ladder and the heterogeneous nature of its internal composition. The first two sections showed my hesitation in going straight to the subject without first seeking the answers to two preliminary questions: "why study the middle class?" and "what is the 'middle class'"? These questions, idiosyncrasies aside, expressed the state of knowledge at the time.

Today, almost two decades later, I see this situation as partially altered. This is what this essay aims to outline, in general terms, namely, the change this issue has undergone in our day due to both new social dynamics and advances in the sociological mindset.

I will start by addressing the first question formulated initially (the "why") and argue that, today, it is certainly easier to defend a topic that has become more legitimate and carries less-negative connotations in terms of relevance.

As contemporary education sociologists admit, among the processes of theoretical–methodological reorientation the discipline has undergone from the 1980s onward to date, one stands out: the one that "shifts the glance of social disadvantage to the privileged" (Sirota, 2000: 166). Influenced by this movement, studies have appeared in different countries whose interests lie in investigating new modes of elite formation (Almeida and Nogueira, 2002; Fonseca, 2003; Wagner, 1998),[1] as well as the educational conduct of the middle class (Ball, 2003; Crozier *et al.*, 2008; Lareau, 2003; Power *et al.*, 2003; van Zanten, 2002, 2007).[2] I suppose this boom—and its fruitful results—weakened the suspicions of scientific futility around attempts to study the educational practices and strategies of these favored social groups.

Yet, this does not mean that this topic has completely lost its marginal status. In England, Power (2001) detects the continuing gap that Ball (2003) abhors when arguing for the fundamental role played by the middle class in the process of the permanent reconstitution of the inequalities in schools. In France, van Zanten (2002) encounters the same lacuna and suggests epistemological reasons as explanations:

> In fact, among the reasons suggested to explain the small number of studies on middle classes is the recurrent aversion of sociologists to carry out a self-analysis, since great is the proximity they have with the social strata they belong to.
>
> (van Zanten, 2002: 40)

As to the second question (what is the middle class?), it is worth keeping in mind that a definition remains problematic, even arbitrary, at least when it comes to the literature in Brazil, which could be compared to an arch going from the material to the symbolic pole, starting with the economist—who focuses on income level and consumption potential—then the anthropologist—who zooms in on the group's life styles and worldviews—and sociologists who give special attention to the group's place in the socio-occupational structure and access to material goods such as education, health, housing, etc. These are very different perspectives indeed.

However, it is worth noting that the reduction of any social group to a statistical income category may dissimulate important differences in lifestyle and patterns of thought, even when, in dealing with this population segment, both dimensions—the material and the symbolic—are strongly articulated. As Brazilian economists warn us, if the association of the middle class and consumption is so common in Brazilian literature, it is because this consumption above popular standards is key in the formation of identity of this class (Guerra *et al.*, 2006: 17).

Finally, as far as the internal heterogeneity of the middle class is concerned, everything indicates that the usual distinction established by social theory between the traditional fraction, composed of small owners and professionals (*petite bourgeoisie*), and the "new" middle class, composed of salary workers, makes even less sense for current educational research then it did in the time Bourdieu developed his analyses of the reproduction strategies of this group. Keep in mind that, for the French sociologist, the examination of the middle class–school relation should be carried out in the three levels into which he believed this group was divided: the *petite bourgeoisie traditionnelle* (in decline), the *petite bourgeoisie d'exécution*, and the *petite bourgeoisie nouvelle*, each one of them presenting certain attitudes towards culture and school.[3]

In contrast, more recent research resorts to forms of differentiation considered more efficient to deal with the complex system of relations established amongst the different segments within the middle class and the education of children in the present. For Power *et al.* (2003), guidelines and family attitudes towards school become more intelligible when three criteria (related to "employment sector," "field of production," and "parents' occupational resource basis") are taken into account:

1   the one that separates parents who work in the public sector and those who work in the private sector:

> The relevance of sector of employment is attributed to whether economic and ideological support is derived from the state or the market, competition between them for resources and legitimacy in the provision of services producing different positionings for those working in each.
>
> (p. 32)

2   the one (already present in Bernstein's classical analyses) that distinguishes parents whose occupation involves the production of material goods and those engaged in the production of symbolic goods:

> We have also analyzed our evidence in terms of the distinction between the 'old' middle class employed in the production and distribution of material goods and services, and the 'new' and rapidly expanding middle class engaged in the production, exploitation and distribution of symbolic knowledge.
>
> (p. 32)

3   the one that differentiates families according to the types of activity the parents are engaged in, classified by the authors as "professional," "managerial," and "entrepreneurial":

> The divide between managerial and professional occupations is seen as especially significant because it is those working in the latter who are likely to rely most on capital cultural to secure or enhance their children's social position.
>
> (p. 31)

Partially siding with the English authors, van Zanten (2007) makes the sector of employment the main divide among French middle-class families:

> The most important diversions are those occurring between parents who work in the public sector and have at their disposal a relatively high cultural capital . . . and the parents working in the private sector who have more economic capital.
>
> (p. 258)

According to her, significant distinctions between these two segments take place both at the level of the parents' views on the internal practices of schools and their attitudes towards the choice of educational institutions for the children. While parents in the private sector prioritize family interests (i.e. school competitiveness and the children's well-being), those in the public sector—although not without conflict—place more importance in the state and are prone to regard the school as a socially oriented institution.

The massification of education and its consequences

In general, researchers consider the contemporary changes—economical, political, ideological— as foundations for the current transformations at the educational level. They argue that economic restructuralization—derived from the globalization of the economy—raised uncertainties and risks in the marketplace, especially the instability and vulnerability of skilled jobs offer. They affirm that the political reforms in the 1980s and 1990s, which originated in the deregularization and shrinking of the state, led to reforms in the public services based on the market and free choice by the users. Furthermore, combined with these factors, changes in mentality exacerbated individualism by placing personal interests over collective values.

In the educational sphere, researchers highlight the phenomenon—triggered at the end of World War II—of elevation of general instruction level, which affected all social class groups, although not indistinctly.[4] The result of this process—they all agree—is the increase of competition in education and the contemporary demand for a longer educational trajectory.

As Dubet remarks (2007), school competition increases simply because there are more competitors, thereby bringing

> two important consequences teachers condemn, but which resulted from the very massification they supported: the formation of an education market on the very bosom of the public school, and the development of utilitarianism . . . with families seeking better school results.
>
> (pp. 54–55)

Here, Dubet is referring to the fact that, in a context of massification of the school system, families will "legitimately" demand for their children the type of education, the teaching premises, and, many times, the classrooms thought to be more efficient. The result is the formation of an education market at the very center of public school systems,[5] which become vulnerable to social demand and lose the power to impose norms on parents more and more transformed into "rational" users in search of the most profitable asset.

If Dubet calls our attention to the fact that, in all social class groups, the investment in education increases, other authors will deal, in particular, with its impact on the middle class by stressing how they have further intensified and refined their educational strategies to take advantage of the resources (cultural and economic) they have in favor of their children's education:

> I suggest a number of ways in which the context of class competition in education has changed and intensified in the past twenty years and the class perspectives and strategies of the middle classes have changed with them . . . The response of the middle classes to the increase in insecurity and risk involved in their established strategies of reproduction has been an intensification of positional competition.
>
> (Ball, 2003: 18–20)

These remarks echo Dubet's and Martuccelli's (1996: 119) earliest findings that "it is in the middle classes, more than in the upper ones, that the school is strongly integrated in a strategy of social reproduction."[6]

Yet, it is van Zanten (2007) who best outlines the scenario of the recent changes that produced a more *empowered class—conceptually and strategically—to face these new social and educational risks*. In fact, bearing in mind the middle class's intermediary situation (which allows it to move up or down the social ladder), its inner heterogeneity, and "close" relation to knowledge (highlighted by a greater openness to the divulgation and vulgarization by the media of scientific knowledge emerged mainly from education sociology and psychology) the author affirms that middle-class parents tend, more than others, to imagine themselves as

> masters of their own destiny, capable of fighting against social pressure and altering the course of their individual experiences. In the field of education, this results in stronger and more sophisticated educational involvement when preparing and following up their children's education, and, in general, in a process of planning, rationalization, and growing individuation of the child's cultural experience with the important intervention of knowledge produced by psychology and sociology.
>
> (van Zanten, 2007: 250–251)

In sum, after reaping the benefits—qualitatively—of the process of democratization of education, the middle class saw its "strategic capacity" increase, which resulted in the "sophistication" (that is, intensification and diversification) of its educational investments.

When it comes to intensification of investments, sociologists continue stressing "activism," "interventionism," and preventive attitudes; that is, "the enormous amounts of time and energy devoted to ensuring social reproduction. For the middle-class privilege requires continuous and intensive work" (Ball, 2003: 95).

This mobilization is manifested today at different levels. Here, I mention what scholars have discussed the most:

- practices of intense monitoring of school activities (including the activities of education professionals); help with homework; participation in the school's administration (Ball, 2008; Crozier *et al.*, 2008);
- attitudes when choosing schools that involve a variety of skills such as: access to information about the school system (including evaluation results and rankings); capacity to differentiate and interpret different educational establishments; power to deal with sectorization laws, be it to "colonize" public institutions with "mixed" clientele or influence recruiting and streaming policies, curriculum content, etc. (Power *et al.*, 2003; van Zanten, 2007);
- actions aiming to stimulate the cognitive development of their children. For this purpose, parents set up an intense schedule to structure out-of-class time (sports, arts class, foreign languages, etc.), which becomes an integral part in the logic of childrearing, called by Lareau (2003) *concerted cultivation*.

As for diversification of investments, the new trend seems to be the growing appeal of strategies of internationalization of children's education, even if with variations depending on the class segment and country of origin. If this is not a new phenomenon,[7] it presents, at least today, differences as to:

- change of scale, with a strong quantitative increase of mobility;
- extension to a new public, for it is no longer the privilege of upper-class youth;
- the range, which today encompasses all school levels. Although college level is still the most internationalized, there exists today early strategies of internationalization involving choice of pre-school, bilingual or multilingual primary and secondary school (Darchy-Koechlin, 2008);
- diversification of country of destiny, although a "tropism" towards developed English-speaking countries prevails (van Zanten and Darchy-Koechlin, 2005a).

This seems to be the reply of middle-class families to the demands of the globalization of different social spheres (economic, political, and cultural), so as to produce individuals with specific skills and international competence. Yet, this internationalization is not homogeneous for all countries and social class groups. It is stronger in less developed countries (culturally and economically) and in wealthier social groups.

However, even in countries whose dominant position, culturally and linguistically, make them more resistant to the advantages of internationalization, sociologists have noticed that in the middle class:

The parents are also trying to fashion new identities for their children as citizen of the multiethnic and multicultural twenty-first century, without which they fear they will not be able to cope adequately.

(Crozier *et al.*, 2008: 11)

257

Although the literature on this subject is still scarce, a few studies have already suggested the hypothesis that it is the process of accumulation or updating of capital, expressed in the idea that today "cosmopolitanism (cosmopolitan capital) is a form of social and cultural capital" (Weeninck, 2005) or that "multiculturalism is increasingly a source of cultural and social capital" (Reay et al., 2007). The latter observe:

> The white middle-class interest in difference and otherness can thus be also understood as describing a project of cultural capital through which these white middle-class families seek to display their liberal credentials and secure their class position . . . The ability to move in and out of spaces marked as "other" became part of the process through which this particular fraction of the white middle-classes comes to know themselves as both privileged and dominant.
>
> (Reay et al., 2007: 1046–1047)

In Brazil, researchers have noticed a growing expansion in the demand for this educational asset on the part of the middle class, which sees the international dimension of cultural capital as an indispensable component to expand and validate their cultural assets (Nogueira and Aguiar, 2008). Surveys on the impact of education abroad on students' educational trajectory as well as parents' expectations and motivations have revealed both instrumental goals, as a way to increase competitiveness, and identity objectives, targeting their children's enhancement and personal achievement. They try to develop in their offspring a group of attitudes (openness, autonomy, mobility willingness, tolerance to alterity, etc.), besides providing them with cultural (linguistic competence, general and specialized culture) and social (international contacts) capitals. Not to mention the fact that these strategies of internationalization also set a distinction between those who benefit from international capital and those who limit themselves to national resources (Nogueira et al., 2008: 371).

From meritocracy to parentocracy: a new problem arises

All of these groups of investments mentioned before illustrate, according to some sociologists, a contemporary transitional trend from meritocracy to a parentocracy (Ball, 2003, 2008; van Zanten and Darchy-Koechlin, 2005a).

To support such a claim, sociologists rely on P. Brown's (1990) article "The third wave: education and the ideology of parentocracy." In this text, Brown argues that the British school would be moving to a third "wave," after a first in the nineteenth century, characterized by the universalization of primary school (strongly permeated by social and gender factors), and a second that encompassed most of the twentieth century and placed individual merit as the main classification principle.[8] For him, the last decades of the twentieth century, thanks to neoliberal reforms—with free-market principles and *parental choice*—ended up weakening meritocracy by allowing

> the rise of the educational "parentocracy," where a child's education is increasingly dependent upon the wealth and wishes of parents, rather than the ability and efforts of pupils.
>
> (Brown, 1999: 66)

But Brown does not limit his rationale to the United Kingdom. He extends it to other Anglo-Saxon countries such as the United States, Australia, and New Zealand. In turn, van Zanten and Darchy-Koechlin (2005b) also believe in the pertinence of the model for countries as diverse as France, Japan, and Brazil. Elaborating on Brown's rationale, both authors affirm that two phenomena threaten meritocracy today: policies of positive discrimination, which suppress *financial, institutional, and pedagogical barriers*, and, with greater weight, the logic of markets to which families are subjected.

In sum, for these thinkers, a student's school results would be more and more dependent on his parents' financial resources and strategic capacity, and less and less on his or her own school merits:

> Parents try to re-direct the future determined by school results (through private lessons, for instance) and subject themselves less and less to the logics of the educational institution (they do their best to make sure their children attend the best school). This is parentocracy. It means the school competes with parents' strategies.
>
> (van Zanten and Darchy-Koechlin, 2005b: 18)

This multiplication of parental strategies to provide their children with the best opportunities for access and success in the noblest sectors of the school system has been Glasman's object of study (1994, 2005, 2008). He states that, in the last twenty-five years, a "school out of the school" has developed, namely, a current expansion of support mechanisms to provide aid to school actions, so as to prepare the student to face obstacles encountered in school. It is an arsenal constituted of para-school materials and outsourcing domestic help: private classes, psychopedagogy offices, specialized companies to follow up homework activities, etc. In a recently published article, the author summarizes:

> When we see these support devices flourishing in the school periphery, it seems something else besides the school is necessary for success. It seems that, more than ever, students and parents find it indispensable—to have better chances of success in an increasingly competitive school environment—to resort to external support as a complement to carry out activities or training.
>
> (Glasman, 2008: 631)

In sum, this new reality has led researchers to question whether the privilege of the cultural elite would not be undergoing erosion or, in other words, if their cultural advantages would not be losing power. If this hypothesis is taken, caution is necessary not to underestimate the importance of the cultural component, as a number of important sociological studies have demonstrated that families' cultural competences play a significant role when it comes to taking advantage of cultural investments. The studies of Gewirtz et al. (1995) stand out, in this sense, for drawing our attention to the power of intellectualized families when it comes to school choice, as they are capable of telling the difference between schools and the characteristics of each child, thereby allowing them to make adjustments and choose the "right" school for their children.

New sociological sensibilities: the individual's point-of-view

Among the transformations—originated in the very way of doing sociology—seen in recent literature on the relation between middle classes and school, one change stands out. If former

259

studies placed the emphasis on family practices and insisted on describing typical group patterns of investment behavior in school life, more recent studies have examined the phenomenon from another perspective: the meaning the actors place on these behaviors and how they live up to those ideas. By doing this, sociologists have done nothing more than echo the evolution taking place in sociology, namely, the question of individualization at the center of contemporary societies.

That is why van Zanten (2007), not disregarding "structural determinant" parental actions, is concerned with—inspired by authors such as A. Giddens and U. Beck—the reflexive capacity of parents, namely, their ability to employ the results divulged by scientific research (their perspectives being, evidently, different from those of the researcher) to analyze their current educational reality[9] and ponder the consequences of their acts (in particular, the choice of an educational institution):

> By reflexivity we understand the capacity of subjects to recognize, demonstrate and make visible the rational nature of their concrete practices, without implying an awareness or permanent attention to this dimension or, in Gidden's terms, the capacity of individuals as well as institutions and social systems to carry out continuous self-regulation through critical distance.
>
> (van Zanten, 2007: 247)

In sum, the author notices that the "middle and upper classes," more than the "bourgeoisie or low class," present a greater tendency to adopt a "distanced, informed, strategic and politically conscious position regarding their social experience" (p. 249). Yet, she will insist on the fact that all this strategic capacity produces, along with it, an "opposite effect," as these families are also more vulnerable to doubts and anxieties:

> These social class groups are also subject, more than the others, to doubts as to what is the best way of acting and their consequences—for example, what is the best school for each child. This leads to a great amount of anxiety and triggers an intense search of information which, in turn, increases anxiety.
>
> (van Zanten, 2007: 251)

Feeling, most of the time, ambivalent between prioritizing the child's interest or the collective good, or, in other words, between being a "good parent" or a "good citizen," these actors become victims of tension that will lead them to reason and act, as the author suggests, according to a logic of "cognitive dissonance," as, for instance:

> the cognitive dissonance these social classes experience between "social mixing" values, to which they adhere in different degrees, and their practices of avoiding socially heterogeneous schools.
>
> (van Zanten, 2002: 48)

In the Anglo-Saxon world, we find the same tendency to relativize the advantages of the middle class by focusing on the negative side represented by the "risks, uncertainties and fears" these families experience. Ball (2003) calls our attention to the fact that:

> The absence of complacency and the constant activity of distinction and status maintenance is the best and the worst of the middle class. They are in a sense their own worst enemies.

The commitment to individualism and "putting the family first," the defense of borders and strategies of social closure undermine both security and moral vision and encourage fearfulness.

(p. 179)

Reay *et al.* (2007)—in a study about White middle-class families that chose public schools with a high contingent of immigrant students, aiming to make them more tolerant and open to difference—noticed that these parents "feared" in particular: the pernicious influence of classmates from lower social class on their children; and the negative impact, on the children's school performance, of peers who do not value academic success.

Crozier *et al.* (2008), likewise, on investigating English White middle-class families that, despite possessing the financial means to afford a private school, opt—for ideological reasons— for a *comprehensive-school*, show that these parents

are thus caught in a web of moral ambiguity, dilemmas and ambivalence, trying to perform "the good/ethical self" while ensuring the "best" for their children.

(Crozier *et al.*, 2008: 261)

In my opinion, these authors have made the most progress in this matter, as they incorporate in their analysis the way parents deal with the anxiety they feel at placing their children along *with "the Other," with those "not like us."* Their texts account for the way families compensate for the supposed evils of a school environment seen as unsatisfactory from some perspectives. Through the use of several resources, they work to reduce the risks of a frustrating school experience by monitoring school activities, participating in the school administration, and incentivating out-of-school activities, trips, etc.

Final remarks

Based on a partial review of current sociological literature on middle-class family relations and the school system, this essay aimed at capturing the evolutionary trends social and educational reality have suffered and the theoretical-methodological treatment they have been given in recent decades. In this sense, the essay sees an effective renewal of the problem.

Bourdieu's analysis, which insisted on ascetic dispositions and attitudes of cultural goodwill to which middle-class families would tend to ascribe so as to compensate for their lack of capital, seems to give room now to an analytical emphasis on utilitarianism and the strategic capacity of the actors to utilize, for their own interest, their resources in favor of privileged school destinies.

However, in this final part of the essay, I would like to raise an issue that originates from the data and interpretation presented here, which, in my opinion, has not been properly researched yet. I refer to the growing protagonism of contemporary families—through choices and educational strategies—in the production and functioning of the school systems themselves. This means that focusing only on the state and limiting the analysis of educational policies are not sufficient to understand how the school system works. That is what the middle-class case teaches us.

While we perceive the family as a mere passive user suffering from the actions of the state, we will prevent ourselves from seeing its role as co-producer of educational reality and—

indirectly—of public educational policies. It is up to the sociologist to sharpen the data and arguments to show that families today represent "key actors in the course of educational acts" (van Zanten, 2002).

Notes

1   In French, the *Revue Internationale d'Éducation* (no. 39, September 2005) presents the dossier "*La formation des élites*;" and the periodical *Éducation et Sociétés* (no. 21, 2008/1) brings the dossier "*Former des élites dans un monde incertain.*"

2   The book *La montée de la parentocratie. Le choix éducatifs des classes moyennes* (Paris: PUF), by van Zanten, is in print.

3   I dealt with the middle class–school relations in Bourdieu's work, in Nogueira (1997).

4   van Zanten (2007: 250) distinguished between a process of "massification," which she defines as the "quantitative expansion" of access to high education on the part of working classes, and a true "democratization" reserved to middle and upper classes who have benefited from a "qualitative" increasing, that is, a "real and more extensive access to high levels of knowledge."

5   Scholars talk today of a "quasi-market" to account for the differences existing among public schools when referring to reputation and dispute for vacancies by families.

6   At this point, it is important to acknowledge that Bourdieu continues to be the conceptual reference to think about the middle class–education relationship. His thesis remains irrefutable that, if this social category is the one that most invests in school values, it is not only because it sees the diploma as the beginning of social success, but also because of the objective possibilities of success and mobility that are reasonable through it.

7   Student mobility around the globe has taken place since medieval Europe.

8   Brown (1990) reminds us, however, that the meritocracy never promised equality, only that inequalities would be distributed more fairly.

9   The author gives as an example "'short surveys' parents from middle and upper classes claim to make about the quality of schools near their homes, which the 'sectoring' system in France obliges them to sent their children to; also, the analysis they make of supposed cause of bad quality of some of these schools and the positive and negative consequences of the strategies they adopt to avoid them" (p. 249).

References

Almeida, A.M. and Nogueira, M.A. (eds) (2002) *A escolarização das elites—um panorama internacional da pesquisa*. Petrópolis: Vozes.

Ball, S. (2003) *Class strategies and the educational market: the middle classes and social advantage*, London: RoutledgeFalmer.

—— (2008) "Classes sociales," in van Zanten (ed.) *Dictionnaire de l'Éducation*, Paris: PUF.

Brown, P. (1990) "The third wave: education and the ideology of parentocracy," *British Journal of Sociology of Education* 11(1): 65–85.

Crozier, G., Reay, D., James, D., Jamieson, F., Beedell, P., Hollingworth, S. and Williams, K. (2008) "White middle class parents, identities, educational choice and the urban comprehensive school: dilemmas, ambivalence and moral ambiguity," *British Journal of Sociology of Education* 29(1): 261–272.

Darchy-Koechlin, B. (2008) "Internationalisation des formations," in van Zanten (ed.) *Dictionnaire de l'éducation*, Paris: PUF.

Dubet, F. (2007) "El declive y las mutaciones de la institución," *Revista de Antropología Social* 16: 39–66.

—— and Martuccelli, D. (1996) *À l'école: sociologie de l'expérience scolaire*, Paris: Seuil.

Fonseca, M.M. (2003) *Educar herdeiros—práticas educativas da classe dominante Lisboeta nas últimas décadas*, Lisboa: Fundação Gulbenkian.

Gewirtz, S., Ball, S. and Bowe, R. (1995) *Markets, choice and equity in education*, Buckingham/Philadelphia, PA: Open University Press.

Glasman, D. (1994) *Cours particuliers et construction sociale de la scolarite*, Paris: CNDP/FAS.

—— (2005) *Le travail des eleves pour l'ecole en dehors de l'ecole*, Chambery: Université de Savoie.

—— (2008) "Soutien hors école," in van Zanten (ed.) *Dictionnaire de l'éducation*, Paris: PUF.

Guerra, A., Pochmann, M., Amarim, R. and Silva, R. (eds) (2006) *Classe média—desenvolvimento e crise: atlas da nova estratificação social no Brasil*, vol. 1, São Paulo: Cortez.

Lareau, A. (2003) *Unequal childhoods—class, race and family life*, Los Angeles, CA: University of California Press.

Nogueira, M.A. (1995) "Famílias de camadas médias e a escola: bases preliminares para um objeto em construção," *Educação e Realidade* 2(20): 9–25.

—— (1997) "Convertidos e oblatos—um exame da relação classes médias-escola na obra de P. Bourdieu," *Educação, Sociedade & Culturas* 7: 109–129.

—— and Aguiar, A. (2008) "La formation des élites et l'internationalisation des études: peut-on parler d'une 'bonne volonté internationale'?," *Éducation et Sociétés* 21: 105–119.

——, —— and Ramos, V. (2008) "Fronteiras desafiadas: a internacionalização das experiências escolares," *Educação & Sociedade* 103(29): 355–376.

Power, S. (2001) "Missing: a sociology of education of the middle class," in J. Demaine (ed.) *Sociology of education today*, London: Palgrave Macmillan.

—— Edwards, T., Whitty, G. and Wigfall, V. (2003) *Education and middle class*, Buckingham and Philadelphia, PA: Open University Press.

Reay, D., Hollingworth, S, Williams, K., Crozier, G., Jamieson, F., James, D. and Beedell, P. (2007) "'A darker shade of pale?' Whiteness, the middle classes and multi-ethnic inner city schooling," *Sociology* 41(6): 1041–1060.

Sirota, R. (2000) "Le métier d'élève," in J.C. Forquin (ed.) *Sociologie de l'éducation: nouvelles approaches, nouveaux objets*, Paris: INRP.

van Zanten, A. (2002) "La mobilisation strategique et politique des savoirs sur le social: le cas des parents d'eleves des classes moyennes," *Éducation et Sociétés* 9(1): 39–52.

—— (2007) "Reflexividad y eleccion de la escuela por los padres de la clase media en Francia," *Revista de Antropología Social* 16: 245–278.

—— and Darchy-Koechlin, B.(2005a) "La formation des élites—introduction," *Revue Internationale d'Éducation* 39: 19–23.

—— and —— (2005b) "Parentocratie et marche contre meritocratie," *Le Monde de l'Éducation*: 340.

Wagner, A.C. (1998) *Les nouvelles élites de la mondialisation*, Paris: PUF.

Weenink, D. (2005) "Upper Dutch elite schools in an age of globalisation," unpublished thesis, School for Social Science Research, Amsterdam.

23

Governing without governing
The formation of a European educational space

António Nóvoa

Europe must be seen as a problematic entity. The concepts of European construction or integration cannot be taken for granted. The same applies for the European educational space. No member state will abdicate its right to govern its education. The very notion of 'Europeanization of education' causes concern in most countries, raising fears of homogenization and of loss of national identity. But, at the same time, it is undeniable that the European Union is increasingly intervening in the educational field, leading to orientations and guidelines that tend to organize a European educational space and even to configure a European educational policy.

The title of this chapter, 'Governing without governing', tries to address these tensions and ambiguities. At a formal level, there is no EU policy on education, but only cooperation and inter-governmental policy coordination. But after the Maastricht Treaty (1992), and especially after the Lisbon Strategy (2000), it is hard to understand the resistance to look at these coordination efforts as one of the most effective European policies.

The chapter is split into three sections:

*   In the first section I present a brief historical overview of the changes that have occurred in the Community action in education, since the Treaty of Rome that established the European Economic Community in 1957.
*   In the second section I focus especially on the current situation that is defined by an umbrella programme, called *Education and Training 2010*, which sets up the educational agenda of the European Union for the first decade of the twenty-first century.
*   In the third section I will explain the process of governing without governing, that is, of elaborating sophisticated ways of producing policies, in each member state and at the European level, but always pretending that no policy is being implemented.

My intention is to provide a critical perspective of the formation of a European education space that is, at the same time, a process of fabricating a European educational policy (Nóvoa and Lawn, 2002). It is obvious that this process is interconnected with globalization issues as well as with national policies. But the purpose of this chapter is to illuminate a layer of analysis – the role of the European Union – that is often neglected in the analysis of educational policies.[1]

Historical overview of the European educational policies (1957–2010)

Since its beginnings, in 1957, the European Economic Community has been reluctant to accept intervention regarding educational affairs at Community level. The fragile architecture of powers in the European space required that there were domains that remained under the exclusive responsibility of each member state. Even nowadays, after hundreds of EU texts and programmes that have led to profound changes in all the national education systems, the official discourse remains unchanged: 'Responsibility for education and training policy lies with Member States. Europe's role is to support the improvement of national systems trough complementary EU-level tools, mutual learning and exchange of good practice' (Commission of the European Communities (CEC), 2008a: 3).

The unionization process in the educational field cannot be viewed through the lens of traditional politics (Nóvoa and DeJong-Lambert, 2003). Of course, education has been one of the most contested arenas in Europe, not only owing to its symbolic value in national imaginaries but also because of public resistance to a 'common policy'. Yet, it is not difficult to establish the main phases of EU policy making in education, taking as turning points the Maastricht Treaty (1992) and the Lisbon Strategy (2000).

Some of the most emblematic programmes, such as Erasmus, launched in the 1980s, were characterized by a certain voluntarism and the need to abolish borders in Europe, between states and between people. At the same time, extending the concept of vocational training, it has been possible to include virtually all forms of education in the Community action. It led to a kind of *vocational bias* in the way educational policies were overcharged by a discourse related with human resources and workforce qualifications.

Quality as a pretext for a common educational policy (1992–2000)

An important turning point took place in 1992, with the inscription in the Maastricht Treaty of articles 126 and 127, creating the political and legal conditions for a more overt action of European entities in education and vocational training. Throughout the 1990s, a large body of literature was produced opening a space for future policies: 'Green Paper on the European dimension of education' (1993); 'White Paper on Growth, competitiveness, employment' (1993); 'Teaching and learning: towards the learning society' (1995); 'Accomplishing Europe through education and training' (1997); 'Towards a Europe of knowledge' (1997); 'Learning for active citizenship' (1998), etc.

It is possible to distinguish two different approaches, both contributing to build a European educational space. First, the emphasis on lifelong learning that is not only invoked with reference to education and schooling, but also to the problems of unemployment and preparation for the job market. Second, the idea of developing 'quality education', leading to the organization of data and statistics at European level. The invention of comparable indicators is not only an operation to describe reality; it is also a powerful way of constructing new ideas and practices in education.

The Lisbon Strategy as a turning point in the construction of a European educational space (2000–2010)

Since the very beginning of European cooperation in the field of education, ministers of education have underlined the diversity of their systems of education (Ertl, 2006). The Lisbon

265

European Council, in 2000, broke with this by asking the ministers to concentrate their reflection on what is common (European Council, 2000). The definition of a European educational space began to be clearly outlined, and, at its core, the educational policies influenced the set of national policies. It is difficult to imagine a member state that will not 'freely adhere' to this game, which is defined by *lifelong learning* as its overriding principle and by *quality* as its implementation method (i.e. appraising the performances of each member state).

The report from the Commission, *The concrete future objectives of the education systems* (CEC, 2001), expresses this shift. Throughout the document we are presented with a series of common concerns, methods for policy implementation and evaluation indicators. In 2002, the Barcelona European Council agreed upon the *Education and Training 2010* work programme, which serves as the basis for the European Union's political action in the field of education in the first decade of the twenty-first century (European Commission, 2009).

Education and Training 2010: the formation of a European educational space

The *Education and Training 2010* work programme clearly establishes a European educational space, taking into account 'that the development of education and training systems in a lifelong learning and in a worldwide perspective has increasingly been acknowledged as a crucial factor for the future of Europe in the knowledge era' (Council of the European Union (CEU), 2002: 4). The main purpose of the programme is to organize EU educational standards into a 'single comprehensive strategy'.

The document defines three strategic objectives, broken down into thirteen associated objectives:

- improving the quality and effectiveness of education and training systems in the EU;
- facilitating the access of all to education and training systems;
- opening up education and training systems to the wider world.

To pursue these objectives, the EU implemented the 'open method of coordination', that is a process of policy making based upon 'the identification of shared concerns and objectives, the spreading of good practice and the measurement of progress through agreed instruments, comparing achievements both between European countries and with the rest of the world' (CEU, 2002: 3).

Three strategic objectives: quality, access, openness

The *Education and Training 2010* work programme always comes back to the same topics, building a narrative that is intentionally circular and redundant. Two terms appear repeatedly, defined and redefined according to context: quality and lifelong learning. On the one hand, they define a strong tendency towards logics of evaluation, leading to rankings and classifications that consecrate as 'inevitable' a particular way of conceiving education and schooling. On the other hand, they introduce a new approach to educational matters, at both the personal and the social level.

'Improving quality and effectiveness' is the first strategic objective. The work programme focuses on key competencies for the so-called knowledge society. The attention is directed towards three key competencies: 'Learning to learn', an old pedagogical concept that is redefined by constructivism, but also by the economic world, in terms of lifelong learning; 'social skills', which relates to personal relations and networks, as well as to principles of self-responsibility and citizenship; and 'entrepreneurship', which underlines the importance of initiative, management and risk.

The intention to ensure and to monitor quality education leads to the evaluation of progress and achievement through comparable benchmarks and indicators. The intention is to move towards a more knowledge-based policy and practice, providing policymakers with reference points based on indicators and standards that are 'commonly' defined and 'freely' accepted. These benchmarks are governing principles that construct an educational policy lying in specific forms of knowledge and expertise.

The formulation of the second strategic objective – 'facilitating access for all' – intentionally emphasizes issues related to lifelong learning. On the one hand, it redefines 'employment' as a learning problem that should be solved by each individual. On the other hand, it creates the illusion that the 'crisis of schooling' will be solved if individuals simply continue to expose themselves to education and training throughout their entire lifetime. The Lisbon Strategy did invent the concept of employability in order to link employment to education, and to interpret unemployment as a problem of 'uneducated' people (CEU, 2008).

Active citizenship, entrepreneurial culture and lifelong learning are part of a process of reconfiguring the *self*. Thus, the responsibility for solving the crisis of the welfare state (and/or the European social model) shifts to citizens who are invited to become responsible for 'constantly updating their knowledge' in order to enhance employability and consolidate the process of unionization.

The goal of the third strategic objective – 'opening up education and training systems to the wider world' – is to create an open 'European area for education' and to promote the 'European dimension of teaching and training'. Mobility within the European space is described as not simply movement, but rather as a process that develops awareness of what it means to be a citizen of Europe.

The idea of experiencing Europe is concurrent with programmes of mobility and the project of reinforcing European citizenship. The politics of identity is formulated in terms of qualification and disqualification. Such a policy in effect exiles all those not endowed with the requisite attributes, as well as those simply unable to acquire them, producing at once new forms and new impediments to mobility.

Education and Training 2010 work programme: analysis and progresses

Between the Lisbon European Council (March 2000) and the Brussels European Council (March 2009), hundreds of documents have been issued by different European bodies. They all reveal a double meaning: on the one hand, the need to make up for lost time and improve education and training in Europe, as a whole; on the other hand, the need to accelerate 'the pace of reforms of education and training systems', whereby the European programmes 'should be duly taken into account in the formulation of national policies' (CEU, 2004: 6).

Adopting different structures and perspectives, these documents tend to focus on three main points. First, the need to concentrate reforms and investment on the key areas. There is a persistent call to channel more resources to the area of education, taking into account that 'most governments seem to recognize that the necessary reforms cannot be accomplished within the current levels and patterns of investment' (CEU, 2006: 2). Over the years, there has been a level of disappointment with the progress made in this field. At the end of 2008, it was pointed out that 'the current focus on the economic crisis must not divert attention from setting the right long-term, strategic education and training policies', because 'Europe has to address a number of educational shortfalls if it is to avoid falling behind globally' (CEC, 2008a: 16).

Second, the need to make lifelong learning a concrete reality. The intention is to equip 'all citizens with the key competencies they need'. The approval in 2007 of a very important document entitled *New skills for new jobs* again placed the issue in terms of employment and the job market (CEU, 2009). But also, here, there has been a degree of disappointment. The Council says that progress has been achieved in defining lifelong learning strategies, but implementation is far from being achieved satisfactorily (CEU, 2006: 3).

Third, the need finally to establish a Europe of education and training (Antunes, 2008). The Council of the European Union recognizes that many countries are establishing their own policies in relation 'to the reference levels of average European performance for education and training' (CEU, 2006: 2). But the European Commission explains, in a 2008 communication, that despite the impressive range of innovation and excellent policy practice in many countries, it is too often still locked behind national borders, and that is why 'Member States should cooperate to capitalise better on it' (CEC, 2008b: 12).

Progress towards the Lisbon objectives

The Commission publishes a detailed report annually analysing the progress made on an agreed set of statistical indicators and benchmarks in the framework of the *Education and Training 2010* work programme. It is impossible to analyse these lengthy reports in detail, which are justified due to the fact that 'educational policies and practices require a stronger evidence base' (CEC, 2007: 3).

Despite the frequent changes, a substantial proportion of the reports are based on five EU-level benchmarks set for 2010. By the end of 2008, it is obvious that most of these benchmarks will not be reached:

> The EU set itself the overall ambition of achieving 5 benchmarks by 2010, on literacy, reduction of early school-leaving, upper secondary attainment, maths, science and technology graduates and participation in adult learning. Only the benchmark on mathematics, science and technology graduates is likely to be exceeded. Indeed, low performance in reading literacy, which was benchmarked to decline by 20% by 2010, has actually increased by more than 10% between 2000 and 2006 and has reached 24.1%.
>
> (CEC, 2008c: 9)

The Commission's appraisal is especially critical with regard to the fact that too little progress has been made on those benchmarks related most closely to social inclusion. It is an important reference, when it becomes obvious that there is a need for a new generation of policies to respond to the economic and social crisis. The only indicator in which real progress has been made is in science and technology, an area that was given a big boost with the Lisbon Strategy. This perspective is coherent with the proposal for 'Energising Europe's knowledge triangle of research, education and innovation', which is finding its place into European policies.

The knowledge triangle is a strategy to attract more funds to research and innovation and to enhance the competitiveness of the economy. But the 2008/2009 economic crisis tends to lead people to underline the third dimension of the triangle: education. In March 2009, the Brussels European Council called for an improvement of member states' cooperation and an advancement in the member states' and the Union's methodological, analytical and mutual learning capacities for jobs and skills anticipation.

As the last year of the *Education and Training 2010* work programme approaches, one can note a critical feeling concerning its results. The response is, obviously, to strengthen European cooperation and take another step forwards towards concerted policies at European level: 'These challenges should be addressed in a joined-up policy across the systems as a whole (schools, higher education, vocational education and training and adult learning). Lifelong learning is therefore a fundamental perspective underpinning all the above challenges' (CEC, 2008a: 6).

The main objectives for the next phase (2010–2020) are not very different from the ones defined for the current decade, 2000–2010, even if they are defined with a new focus: (i) make lifelong learning and learner mobility a reality; (ii) improve the quality and efficiency of provision and outcomes; (iii) promote equity and active citizenship; (iv) enhance innovation and creativity, including entrepreneurship, at all levels of education and training (CEC, 2008a: 6). The way to achieve these aims is to deepen European cooperation, driving forward the dynamics of joint work: 'there is, more than ever, a need for an effective open method of coordination supporting the improvement of education and training policies' (CEC, 2008a: 16).

Governing without governing: fabricating educational policies at the European Union

The processes that we have just described are not specific to the European context. They are part of broader developments, which have been popularized by the imperfect concept of 'globalization'. But, inside the European Union, they are strengthened by a historic project that tends to integrate national states into a political union. And this fact gives them a different status, opening up new political possibilities. This is the main reason why this 'unidentified political object' known as the European Union is such an interesting object of study, both for comparative politics and for the socio-historical analysis of educational policies (Dale and Robertson, 2009).

The *Education and Training 2010* work programme emphasizes four verbs: identify, spread, measure and compare. To identify means to agree on shared objectives and guidelines for educational policies. To spread refers to the diffusion and transfer of the most successful practices from one country to another. To measure is to establish precise benchmarks and to evaluate the performance of each education system. To compare means to organize a way of assessing the progress made by each country. The goal of this process is described as 'to help Member States to develop their own policies progressively' (CEU, 2002: 5), but always in accordance with the objectives defined at European level.

To achieve this goal, an *open method of coordination* has been implemented in the framework of the Lisbon Strategy (Lange and Alexiadou, 2007). This method is built on the use of tools 'such as indicators and benchmarks as well as comparing best practice, periodic monitoring, evaluation and peer review etc. organized as mutual learning processes' (CEU, 2002: 5). Cohesion and configuration of policy are not achieved through sanctions, but through a much more sophisticated approach. Voluntary participation by each member state serves to legitimize these arguments. Yet it is hard to imagine how a member state could stand outside of this 'playing field'.

269

Comparison as a mode of governance

The issues that are being raised at the European Union do not direct our attention to a deepening of democratic decisions, but instead to a reinforcement of 'new means' (governance, benchmarking, good practices etc.) and 'new powers' (networks, informal groups, mass media etc.). The current approach to European affairs clearly reveals a strategy to shift the discussion away from matters of *government* (inhabited by citizens, elections, representation etc.) and place it in the more diffused level of *governance* (inhabited by networks, peer review, agreements etc.).

Policy is constructed through a logic of perpetual comparison, which is legitimized and put into action through 'new means' that are intended to find the most beneficial or efficient solutions. Benchmarking – and, for that matter, *comparability* – is seen as a solution that will become *the* policy. The last documents issued at European level are very precise in underlining the 'challenge of data and comparability':

> Mutual learning is a central element of the open method of coordination in education and training. It provides input for European policy initiatives and support to national policy development . . . For the future, the aim should be to strengthen peer learning in order to ensure that it fully respects the priority challenges identified above and to increase its impact at the political level.
>
> (CEC, 2008a: 12)

Thus, comparison can be understood as a mechanism to legitimize EU interference in national educational issues. The logic of comparison produces a vocabulary consisting of positive terms such as 'exchange', 'joint reflection' and 'agreement'. What is presented as a strategy to improve education should be understood as a mode of governance (Nóvoa and Yariv-Mashal, 2003).

Governing by data

Benchmarking practices are tied in with data and quality assurance. They are not only a technique or a method, but also one of the most successful tools for implementing governance policies. Therefore, it is obvious that these kinds of policy need data that can allow the establishment of aims and the monitoring of progress. It is not simply a matter of collecting and organizing data; rather, it is a process that constructs educational realities as much as it describes them. Through the arrangement of categories and classifications, a definition of the 'best system' is proposed. Each member state will act in accordance with these goals and ideals.

By the end of 2007, a very important working document asked for a stronger knowledge base for developing policy and practice at national and EU levels in order to improve the quality and governance of education systems: 'Member States and the EU institutions need to use evidence-based policy and practice, including robust evaluations instruments, to identify which reforms and practice are the most effective, and to implement them most successfully' (CEC, 2007: 3).

It is a very interesting document, based upon the idea that 'educational research currently appears to have a lower impact on policy and practice than research in other policy fields, such as social care or employment policy' (CEC, 2007: 25). The challenge of data and comparability has now been reworked from the point of view of knowledge and research (Ozga, 2008).

The new modes of governance are based on logics of contracting and networks, heavily backed up by data, assessments, impacts, benchmarking, best practices and mutual learning.

Research was the missing link for redefining policy formulation in the European Union. The reasoning is clear: on the one hand, the EU needs policies that are strongly oriented by research and knowledge; on the other hand, 'education and training are a prerequisite for a fully functioning knowledge triangle (education – research – innovation)' (CEC, 2007: 3). Along with this line of thought, one finds the rationale for the new phase of European education policies, in the 2010–2020 period.

Concluding comments

My argument is that Europe functions like a *regulatory ideal* that tends to influence, if not organize, national policies. It is obvious that no 'homogenization' will occur. Talk of the diversity of national education systems is almost a tautology. And, meanwhile, we continue to witness the development of tendencies towards defining common goals, similar strategies and, therefore, identical policies.

The example of the Bologna Process is extremely enlightening. On the one hand, it is a process that involves countries that do not belong to the European Union, and it is a process that cross-references trends that are expressed worldwide. But, on the other hand, it has gained an extremely relevant role in the EU policies, restructuring higher education and research. There is no legal obligation to take part in the Bologna Process, but it is unthinkable for any country to stay outside its dynamics, networks and connections, which are at the core of the modernization agenda of the universities. If one permits me the paradox, I would say that it is a 'compulsory option'.

The complexity of the debate calls for more theoretical tools and critical approaches. It is useless to reproduce distinctions and dichotomies that cannot raise new understandings. We must not look at this debate as a conflict between 'national states' and 'European institutions'. This is not a zero-sum game, where giving more power to 'Europe' will automatically lead to a weakening of the 'nation-state', or vice versa. An arithmetical conception of power is totally inaccurate.

New ways of governing without governing have proven to be extremely attractive. They are very sophisticated in naturalizing policies, in raising a sense of inevitability. It is as if they 'only' construct data, or identify good practices, or compare best methods, whereas, in truth, these data, practices and methods are in themselves powerful tools in the formation of a European educational space.

European policies should be understood as part of an expert discourse that is redefining educational issues globally. This movement of experts creates and circulates concepts and ideas without structural roots or social locations. We are faced with a strange 'worldwide bible' whose vocabulary, of unknown origin, is on the tip of every tongue. In this sense, the process of 'learning from one another' is a way of thinking and acting that establishes an educational policy without specifically formulating it.

The European educational space defines its own borders in the framework of this 'mutual learning', which brings, at the same time, a sense of increased competition on a global scale. The European Union seeks to attract students and academics from other world regions, aimed at turning European educational institutions into 'recognised worldwide centres of excellence' (CEU, 2002: 16). This objective is formulated against a background in which the United States of America and Asian countries are regarded as the main competitors in the world education market.

271

One of the main political undertakings of the European educational space is to build an internal identity among citizens and countries. According to the main driving force of the European construction, it is without surprise that employment and social cohesion are at the core of educational policies. That is why the European Union first adopted orientations strongly inspired by human capital theories and vocationalism, subsequently shifting to employability and lifelong learning.

The restructuring of the European educational space is related both to a new conception of the responsible citizen and the role of education for a new organization of the labour market. The former dictates that individuals should be able to 'manage their learning with self-discipline, working autonomously and collaboratively' (CEC, 2008b: 5). As regards the new organization of the labour market, this even involves a new way of looking at jobs, as well as personal and professional lives.

Notes

1   The European Union publishes hundreds of documents, every year, about education and training. Most of these documents have several versions, according to their status in the process of taking decisions at EU level. For this reason, I limited myself to documents issued by the Commission of the European Communities (CEC) and by the Council of the European Union (CEU) (See also Council of the European Communities, 1987–1993). The European Union provides extended versions of all documents online. I recommend the consultation of two sites:
   •   'European strategy and cooperation in education and training', available online at http://ec.europa.eu/education/lifelong-learning-policy/doc28_en.htm;
   •   'Education and Training 2010 – Main policy initiatives in education and training since the year 2000', available at http://ec.europa.eu/education/policies/2010/doc/compendium05_en.pdf.

References

Antunes, F. (2008) *A nova ordem educacional – Espaço Europeu de Educação e Aprendizagem ao Longo da Vida*, Coimbra: Almedina.

CEC (2001) *The concrete future objectives of education systems – Report from the Commission, Brussels*: document COM(2001) 59 final.

—— (2007) *Towards more knowledge-based policy and practice in education and training – Commission staff working document*, Brussels: document SEC(2007) 1098.

—— (2008a) *An updated strategic framework for European cooperation in education and training – Communication from the Commission to the European Parliament, the Council, the European Economic and Social Committee and the Committee of the Regions*, Brussels: document COM(2008) 865 final.

—— (2008b) *Improving competencies for the 21st century: An agenda for European cooperation on schools – Communication from the Commission to the European Parliament, the Council, the European Economic and Social Committee and the Committee of the Regions*, Brussels: document COM(2008) 425 final.

—— (2008c) *Progress towards the Lisbon objectives in education and training – Indicators and benchmarks 2008*, Brussels: Publication based on document SEC (2008) 2293.

CEU (2002) *Detailed work programme on the follow-up of the objectives of Education and training systems in Europe*, Brussels: document 2002/C 142/01.

—— (2004) *'Education & Training 2010': The success of the Lisbon Strategy hinges on urgent reforms – Joint interim report of the Council and the Commission on the implementation of the detailed work programme on the follow-up of the objectives of education and training systems in Europe*, Brussels: document 6905/04.

—— (2006) *Modernising education and training: a vital contribution to prosperity and social cohesion in Europe – Joint report of the Council and the Commission on progress under the 'Education & Training 2010' Work Programme*, Brussels: document 2006/C 79/01.

—— (2008) *Delivering lifelong learning for knowledge, creativity and innovation – 2008 Joint progress report of the Council and the Commission on the implementation of the 'Education & Training 2010 Work Programme'*, Brussels: document 5723/08.

—— (2009) *Council Conclusions on New Skills for New Jobs – Anticipating and matching labour market and skill needs*, Brussels: 2930th Employment, Social Policy, Health and Consumer Affairs Council meeting.

Council of the European Communities (1987–1993) *European Educational Policy Statements*, Luxembourg: Office for Official Publications of the European Communities, 3 vols.

Dale, R. and Robertson, S. (eds) (2009) *Globalisation & Europeanisation in education*, Oxford: Symposium Books.

Ertl, H. (2006) 'European Union policies in education and training: the Lisbon agenda as a turning point?', *Comparative Education* 42(1): 5–27.

European Commission (2009) *'Education & Training 2010' – Main policy initiatives and outputs in education and training since the year 2000*, Brussels: Directorate-General for Education and Culture.

European Council (2000) *Presidency conclusions – Lisbon European Council (23 and 24 March 2000)*.

Lange, B. and Alexiadou, N. (2007) 'New forms of European governance in the education sector? A preliminary analysis of the Open Method of Coordination', *European Educational Research Journal* 6(4): 321–335.

Nóvoa, A. and DeJong-Lambert, W. (2003) 'Educating Europe – an analysis of EU educational policies', in D. Phillips and H. Ertl (eds) *Implementing European Union education and training policy – a comparative study of issues in four member states*, Dordrecht: Kluwer Academic Publishers.

—— and Lawn, M. (eds) (2002) *Fabricating Europe – the formation of an education space*, Dordrecht: Kluwer Academic Publishers.

—— and Yariv-Mashal, T. (2003) 'Comparative research in education: a mode of governance or a historical journey?', *Comparative Education* 39(4): 423–438.

Ozga, J. (2008) 'Governing knowledge: research steering and research quality', *European Educational Research Journal* 7(3): 261–272.

24

The university in the twenty-first century
Toward a democratic and emancipatory university reform[1]

Boaventura de Sousa Santos

In an essay published fifteen years ago,[2] I identified three crises facing the university (Santos, 1994). First, the crisis of hegemony was the result of contradictions between the traditional functions of the university and those that had come to be attributed to it throughout the twentieth century. When it stopped being the only institution of higher education and research production, the university entered a crisis of hegemony. The second crisis was a crisis of legitimacy, provoked by the fact that the university ceased to be a consensual institution, in view of the contradiction between the hierarchization of specialized knowledge through restrictions of access and credentialing of competencies, on the one hand, and the social and political demands for a democratized university and equal opportunity for the children of the working class, on the other. Finally, the institutional crisis was the result of the contradiction between the demand for autonomy in the definition of the university's values and objectives and the growing pressure to hold it to the same criteria of efficiency, productivity, and social responsibility that private enterprises face.

What has happened since I wrote that essay? How can we characterize the situation in which we find ourselves? What are possible responses to the problems that the university faces today? In this chapter, I will try to provide answers to these three questions. In the first part, I will undertake an analysis of recent transformations in the system of higher education and their impact on the public university. In the second part, I will identify and justify some of the basic principles of a democratic and emancipatory reform of the public university, that is, a reform that allows the public university to respond creatively and efficiently to the challenges it faces at the outset of the twenty-first century.

Transformations in higher education

The last fifteen years

The predictions I made fifteen years ago have come to pass, beyond my expectations. Despite the fact that the three crises were intimately connected and could only be confronted jointly and by means of vast reform programs, generated both inside and outside the university, I predicted (and feared) that the institutional crisis would come to monopolize reformist agendas and proposals. This is in fact what happened. I also predicted that concentrating on the institutional crisis could lead to the false resolution of the two other crises, a resolution by default: the crisis of hegemony, by the university's increasing loss of specificity; the crisis of legitimacy, by the growing segmentation of the university system and the growing devaluation of university diplomas, in general. This has also happened.

Concentrating on the institutional crisis was fatal for the university and was due to a number of factors, some already evident at the beginning of the 1990s, while others gained enormous weight as the decade advanced. The institutional crisis is and has been, for at least two centuries, the weakest link of the public university, since its scientific and pedagogical autonomy is based on its financial dependency on the state. While the university and its services were an unequivocal public good that was up to the state to ensure, this dependency was not problematic, any more than that of the judicial system, for example, in which the independence of the courts is not lessened by the fact they are being financed by the state. However, contrary to the judicial system, the moment the state decided to reduce its political commitment to the universities and to education in general, converting education into a collective good that, however public, does not have to be exclusively supported by the state, an institutional crisis of the public university automatically followed. If it already existed, it deepened. It can be said that, for the last thirty years, the university's institutional crisis, in the great majority of countries, was provoked or induced by the loss of priority of the university as a public good and by the consequent financial drought and disinvestment in public universities. The causes and their sequence vary from country to country. In countries that lived under dictatorships for the previous four decades, there were two reasons for the onset of the institutional crisis: to reduce the university's autonomy to the level necessary for the elimination of the free production and diffusion of critical knowledge; and to put the university at the service of modernizing, authoritarian projects, opening the production of the university-as-public-good to the private sector and forcing the public university to compete under conditions of unfair competition in the emerging market for university services. In the democratic countries, the onset of the crisis was related to this latter reason, especially beginning in the 1980s, when neoliberalism was imposed as the global model of capitalism. In countries that made the transition from dictatorship to democracy in this period, the elimination of the former reason (political control of autonomy) was frequently invoked to justify the goodness of the latter (creation of a market for university services). In these countries, the affirmation of the universities' autonomy was on a par with the privatization of higher education and the deepening of the public universities' financial crisis. It was a precarious and deceiving autonomy, because it forced the universities to seek new dependencies much more burdensome than dependence on the state, and because the concession of autonomy was subject to remote controls finely calibrated by the ministries of finance and education. Consequently, in the passage from dictatorship to democracy, unsuspected continuities ran beneath the evident ruptures.

The onset of the institutional crisis by way of the financial crisis, accentuated in the last twenty years, is a structural phenomenon accompanying the public university's loss of priority among the public goods produced by the state. The fact that the financial crisis was the immediate motive of the institutional crisis does not mean that the causes of the latter can be reduced to the financial crisis. The analysis of the structural causes will reveal that the prevalence of the institutional crisis was the result of the impact upon it of the two other unsolved crises, the crises of hegemony and of legitimacy. And in this domain, there have been, in the last fifteen years, new developments in relation to the picture I described at the beginning of the 1990s.

The public university's loss of priority in the state's public policies was, first of all, the result of the general loss of priority of social policies (education, health, social security) induced by the model of economic development known as neoliberalism or neoliberal globalization, which was internationally imposed beginning in the 1980s. In the public university, it meant that its identified institutional weaknesses—and they were many—instead of serving as justification for a vast political-pedagogical reform program, were declared insurmountable and used to justify the generalized opening of the university-as-public-good to commercial exploitation. Despite political declarations to the contrary and some reformist gestures, underlying this first collision of the university with neoliberalism is the idea that the public university is not reformable (any more than the state) and that the true alternative lies in the creation of the university market. The savage and deregulated way in which this market emerged and was developed is proof that there was a deep option in its favor. And the same option explained the disinvestment in the public university and massive transferences of human resources that, at times, looked like a "primitive accumulation" on the part of the private university sector at the cost of the public sector.

The two defining processes of the decade—the state's disinvestment in the public university and the mercantile globalization of the university—are two sides of the same coin. They are the two pillars of a huge global project of university politics destined to profoundly change the way the university-as-a-public-good has been produced, transforming it into a vast and vastly profitable ground for educational capitalism. This mid- to long-range project includes different levels and forms of the mercantilization of the university. As for the levels, it is possible to distinguish two. The primary level consists in inducing the public university to overcome the financial crisis by generating its own resources, namely through partnerships with industrial capital. On this level, the public university maintains its autonomy and its institutional specificity, privatizing part of the services it renders. The second level consists of the biased elimination of the distinction between public and private universities, transforming the university as a whole into a business, an entity that not only produces for the market but which is itself produced as a market, as a market of university services as diverse as administration, teaching programs and materials, certification of degrees, teacher training, and teacher and student evaluation. If it will still make sense to speak of the university as a public good when this second level is attained is a rhetorical question.

The disinvestment of the public university

The crisis of the public university as a consequence of disinvestment is a global phenomenon, although its consequences are significantly different at the core, the periphery, and the semi-periphery of the world system. In the central countries, the situation is differentiated. In Europe, where, with the exception of England, the university system is almost totally public, the public university has had the power to reduce the extent of the disinvestment at the same time that it has developed the ability to generate its own income through the market. The success of this strategy depends in good measure on the power of the public university and its political allies to block the significant emergence of the private university market. For instance, in Spain, this strategy has so far been more successful than in Portugal. However, it is important to bear in mind that, throughout the decade, a private, non-university sector emerged in almost every European country, aimed at the professional job market. This fact led the universities to respond by structurally modifying their programs and by increasing their variety. In the United States, where private universities occupy the top of the hierarchy, public universities were motivated to seek alternative funding from foundations, in the market, and by raising tuition fees. Today, in some North American public universities, the state funding is no more than 50 percent of the total budget.

On the periphery, where the search for alternative income in the market is virtually impossible, the crisis attains catastrophic proportions. Obviously, the ills are long-standing, but they have been seriously aggravated in the past decade by the state's financial crisis and the structural adjustment programs. A UNESCO report from 1997 about the majority of African universities drew a dramatic picture of all sorts of shortages: the collapse of infrastructures, almost total lack of equipment, miserably remunerated, unmotivated, and easily corruptible teaching personnel, and little or no research investment. The World Bank diagnosed the situation in a similar way and, characteristically, declared it irreparable. Unable to include in its calculations the importance of the university in the building of national projects and the creation of long-term critical thinking, the Bank concluded that African universities do not generate sufficient "return" on their investment. As a consequence, the African countries were asked to stop investing in universities, concentrating their few resources on primary and secondary education and allowing the global market of higher education to resolve the problem of the university for them. This decision had a devastating effect on the universities of the African countries.

This is a global process and it is on this scale that it should be analyzed. The development of university instruction in the central countries, in the thirty or forty years after World War II, was based, on the one hand, on the successes of the social struggles for the right to education, translated into the demand for a more democratic access to the university and, on the other hand, on the imperatives of an economy that required a more highly qualified workforce in key industrial sectors. The situation changed significantly, starting with the economic crisis that peaked in the mid 1970s. Since then, there has been a growing contradiction between the reduction of public investment in higher education and the intensification of the international economic competition based on the search for technological innovation and, hence, on the techno–scientific knowledge that makes it possible, as well as on the training of a highly qualified workforce.

As for the demand of a qualified workforce, the 1990s revealed another contradiction: the growth of the qualified workforce required by an economy based on knowledge coexisted with the explosive growth of very low-skilled jobs. The neoliberal globalization of the economy has deepened the segmentation of the labor markets between countries and within countries. At the same time, it has allowed both the qualified worker and the unqualified worker *pools* to be recruited globally—the former, predominately through *brain drain* and *outsourcing* of technically advanced services, the latter, predominately through businesses delocalizing across the globe and (often clandestine) immigration. The global availability of skilled labor permits the central countries to lower the priority of their investment in public universities, making funding more dependent on market needs. Actually, there is another contradiction in this domain between the rigidity of university training and the volatility of the qualifications required by the market. This contradiction was shaped, on one hand, by the creation of modular, non–university, tertiary training systems and, on the other, by shortening the periods of university training and making the latter more flexible. Despite ad hoc solutions, these contradictions became enormously acute in the 1990s and had a disconcerting impact on higher education: the university was gradually transformed from a generator of conditions for competition and success in the market into an object of competition, that is, into a market of university services.

277

From university knowledge to pluriversity knowledge

The developments of the past decade presented the university with very demanding challenges, especially the public university. The situation is near collapse in many countries on the periphery, and it is difficult in the semi-peripheral countries. Although the expansion and transnationalization of the market for university services has contributed decisively to this situation in recent years, they are not the only cause. Something more profound occurred, and only this explains why the university, while still the institution par excellence of scientific knowledge, has lost its hegemony and has been transformed into an easy target for social criticism. I think that, in the past decade, the relations between knowledge and society began to change significantly, and these alterations promise to be profound to the point of transforming the way we conceive of knowledge and of society. As I said, the commercialization of scientific knowledge is the most visible side of these alterations. However, and despite their enormity, they are the tip of the iceberg, and the transformations now in progress have contradictory meanings and multiple implications, some of them epistemological.

University knowledge—that is, the scientific knowledge produced in universities, or institutions separate from the universities but that retain a similar university *ethos*—was, for the whole of the twentieth century, a predominantly disciplinary knowledge whose autonomy imposed a relatively decontextualized process of production in relation to the day-to-day pressures of the societies. According to the logic of this process, the researchers are the ones who determine what scientific problems to solve, define their relevance, and establish the methodologies and rhythms of research. It is a homogeneous and hierarchically organized knowledge insofar as the agents who participate in its production share the same goals of producing knowledge, have the same training and the same scientific culture, and do what they do according to well-defined organizational hierarchies. It is a knowledge based on the distinction between scientific research and technological development, and the autonomy of the researcher is translated as a kind of social irresponsibility as far as the results of the application of knowledge are concerned. Moreover, in the logic of this process of the production of university knowledge, the distinction between scientific knowledge and other kinds of knowledge is absolute, as is the relation between science and society. The university produces knowledge that the society does or does not apply, an alternative that, although socially relevant, is indifferent or irrelevant to the knowledge produced.

The university's organization and *ethos* were created by this kind of knowledge. It happens that, throughout the past decade, there were alterations that destabilized this model of knowledge and pointed to the emergence of another model. I designate this transition, which Gibbons *et al.* (1994) described as a transition from "type1 knowledge" to "type 2 knowledge," as the passage from *university knowledge to pluriversity knowledge*.

Contrary to the university knowledge described above, pluriversity knowledge is a contextual knowledge insofar as the organizing principle of its construction is its application. As this application is extramural, the initiative for formulating the problems to be solved and the determination of their criteria of relevance are the result of sharing among researchers and users. It is a transdisciplinary knowledge that, by its very contextualization, demands a dialogue or confrontation with other kinds of knowledge, which makes it more heterogeneous internally and allows it to be more adequately produced in less perennial and more open systems, organized less rigidly and hierarchically. All the distinctions upon which university knowledge is based are put in question by pluriversity knowledge but, most basically, it is the relation between science and society that is in question. Society ceases to be an object of scientific questioning and becomes itself a subject that questions science.

The tension between these two models of knowledge highlights the extremes of two ideal types. In reality, the kinds of knowledge produced occupy different places along the *continuum* between the two poles, some closer to the university model, others closer to the pluriversity model. This heterogeneity not only destabilizes the current institutional specificity of the university, it also questions its hegemony and legitimacy in such a way as to force it to evaluate itself by self-contradictory criteria.

Pluriversity knowledge has had its most consistent realization in university–industry partnerships in the form of mercantile knowledge. But, especially in the central and semi-peripheral countries, the context of application has been non-mercantile as well—cooperative and dependent on the solidarity created by partnerships among researchers and labor unions, NGOs, social movements, particularly vulnerable social groups (women, illegal immigrants, the unemployed, people with chronic illnesses, senior citizens, those afflicted with HIV/AIDS, etc.), working-class communities, and groups of critical and active citizens. There is a growing sector of civil society developing a new and more intense relationship with science and technology, demanding greater participation in their production and in the evaluation of their impact. In multi-ethnic and multinational countries, pluriversity knowledge begins to emerge from inside the university itself, when incoming students from ethnic and other minority groups understand that their inclusion is a form of exclusion. They are confronted with the *tabula rasa* that is made of their cultures and of the traditional knowledge of their communities. All of this leads scientific knowledge to confront other kinds of knowledge and demands a higher level of social responsibility from the institutions that produce it and, consequently, from the universities. As science becomes more ingrained in the society, the society becomes more a part of science. The university was created according to a model of unilateral relations with society, and it is this model that underlies its current institutionalism. Pluriversity knowledge supplants this unilateral notion with interactivity and interdependence, both processes enormously invigorated by the technological revolution of information and communication.

Democratic and emancipatory reform of the public university

What is to be done?

In the second part, I will try to identify some of the master-ideas that should preside over a creative, democratic, and emancipatory reform of the public university. Perhaps the first step is to identify the subjects of the actions that need to be undertaken efficiently to confront the challenges that face the public university. In the meantime, in order to identify the subjects, it is first necessary to define the political meaning of the response to such challenges. In light of the precedent, it becomes clear that, despite the fact that there are multiple causes of the university crisis and some of them are long standing, they are currently being reconfigured by neoliberal globalization, and the way they affect today's university reflects that project's intentions. As I have suggested for other areas of social life (Santos, 2004, 2005, 2006, 2007), I think the only efficient and emancipatory way to confront neoliberal globalization is to oppose it with an alternative, counter-hegemonic globalization. Counter-hegemonic globalization of the university-as-public-good means that the national reforms of the public university must reflect a country project centered on policy choices that consider the country's insertion in increasingly transnational contexts of knowledge production and distribution. These will become increasingly polarized between two contradictory processes of globalization: neoliberal globalization and counter-hegemonic globalization. This country project has to be the result of a broad political and social pact, consisting of different sectoral pacts, among them an educational pact in the terms of which the public university is conceived of as a collective good. The reform must be focused on responding positively to the social demands for the radical democratizing of the university, putting an end to the history of exclusion of social groups and their knowledges, for which the university has been responsible for a long time, starting long before the current phase of capitalist globalization. From now on, the national and transnational scales of the reform interpenetrate. Without global articulation, a national solution is impossible.

The current global context is strongly dominated by neoliberal globalization but is not reduced to it. There is space for national and global articulations based on reciprocity and on the mutual benefit that, in the case of the university, will reconstitute and broaden long-lasting forms of internationalism. Such articulations should be cooperative even when they contain mercantile components; that is, they should be constructed outside the regimes of international trade policy. This alternative transnationalization is made possible by the new information and communication technologies and is based on the establishment of national and global networks, within which new pedagogies, new processes of construction and diffusion of scientific and other knowledges, as well as new social (local, national, and global) commitments circulate. The goal is to resituate the role of the public university in the collective definition and resolution of social problems that are now insoluble unless considered globally. The new university pact starts from the premise that the university has a crucial role in the construction of its country's place in a world polarized by contradictory globalizations.

The counter-hegemonic globalization of the university-as-public-good is, thus, a demanding political project that, in order to be credible, must overcome two contradictory but equally rooted prejudices: on the one hand, that the university can only be reformed by the university community and, on the other, that the university will never reform itself. These are very powerful prejudices. A brief examination of the social forces potentially committed to confront them is in place. The first social force is the public university community itself; that is, those within it interested in an alternative globalization of the university. The public university today is a very fractured social field within which contradictory sectors and interests fight each other. In many countries, especially peripheral and semi-peripheral ones, such contradictions are still latent. Defensive positions that maintain the status quo and reject globalization, whether neoliberal or alternative, predominate. This is a conservative position, not just because it advocates the maintenance of the status quo, but mainly because, deprived of realistic alternatives, it will sooner or later surrender to plans for the neoliberal globalization of the university. University personnel who denounce this conservative position and, at the same time, reject the idea that there is no alternative to neoliberal globalization will be the protagonists of the progressive reform that I am proposing.

The second social force of such reform is the state itself, whenever it is successfully pressed to opt for the university's alternative globalization. Without this option, the national state ends up adopting, more or less unconditionally, or succumbing, more or less reluctantly, to the pressures of neoliberal globalization and, in either case, transforming itself into the enemy of the public university, regardless of any proclamation to the contrary. Given the close, love–hate relationship that the State carried on with the university for the whole of the twentieth century, the options tend to be dramatized.

Finally, the third social force to carry out the reform are citizens collectively organized in social groups, labor unions, social movements, non-governmental organizations and their networks, and local progressive governments interested in forming cooperative relationships

THE UNIVERSITY IN THE TWENTY-FIRST CENTURY

between the university and the social interests they represent. In contrast to the state, this third social force has had a historically distant and, at times, even hostile relationship with the university, precisely because of the latter's elitism and the distance it cultivated for a long time in relation to the so-called "uncultured" sectors of society. This is a social force that has to be won through a response to the question of legitimacy, that is, via non-classist, non-racist, non-sexist, and non-ethnocentric access to the university, and by a whole set of initiatives that deepen the university's social responsibility in line with the pluriversity knowledge mentioned above (more on this below).

Beyond these three social forces there is, in the semi-peripheral and peripheral countries, a fourth entity that may be loosely called national capitalism. Certainly, the most dynamic sectors of national capital are transnationalized and, consequently, part of the neoliberal globalization hostile to the emancipatory reform of the university. However, in peripheral and semi-peripheral countries, the process of transnational integration of these sectors is filled with tensions. Under certain conditions, such tensions may lead these sectors to see an interest in defending the project of the public university as a public good, especially in cases where there are no realistic alternatives to the public university for the production of the kind of technological knowledge needed to strengthen their insertion in the global economy.

Conclusion

The university in the twenty-first century will certainly be less hegemonic but no less necessary than it was in previous centuries. Its specificity as a public good resides in its being the institution that links the present to the medium and long term, through the kinds of knowledge and training it produces and by the privileged public space it establishes, dedicated to open and critical discussion. For these two reasons, it is a collective good without strong allies. Many people are not interested in the long term, and others have sufficient power to be wary of those who dare to suspect them or criticize their interests.

The public university is, thus, a permanently threatened public good, which is not to say that the threat comes only from the outside; it comes from the inside as well (I emphasized this aspect in previous work).

The conjunction between factors of internal threat and factors of external threat is quite obvious in evaluating the university's capacity for long-term thinking, perhaps its most distinctive characteristic. Those who work in today's university know that university tasks are predominately short term, dictated by budget emergencies, interdepartmental competition, professorial tenure, and so forth. The management of such emergencies allows for the flourishing of types of conduct and professional that would have little merit or relevance were it possible and urgent to focus on long-term questions. This emergency-ridden state of affairs, which is surely due to a plurality of factors, must also be seen as a sign that powerful outside social actors are influencing the university.

The proposal I have presented in this chapter is antipodal to this global and external logic and seeks to create conditions to prevent it from finding a welcoming plot for its local and internal appropriation. The university is a public good intimately connected to the country's project. The political and cultural meaning of this project and its viability depend on a nation's ability to negotiate, in a qualified way, its universities' insertion into the new transnational fields. In the case of the university and of education in general, this qualification is the condition necessary for not making the negotiation an act of surrender and thus marking the end of the university as we know it. The only way to avoid surrender is to create conditions for a cooperative university in solidarity with its own global role.

Notes

1   This chapter has been translated by Peter Lownds of the University of California, Los Angeles (UCLA). The first version of this text was presented in Brasilia, on April 5, 2004, in the context of the official calendar of debates about university reform organized by the Brazilian minister of education, Tarso Genro. A much larger version of this text was published in: Rhoads, R. and Torres, C.A. (eds) (2006) *The university, state and markets – the political economy of globalization in the Americas*, Stanford: Stanford University Press.
2   A chapter in the book *Pela Mão de Alice* (1994) Oporto: Afrontamento.

References

Gibbons, M., Limoges, C., Nowotny, H., Schwartzman, S., Scott, P. and Trow, M. (1994) *The new production of knowledge*, London: Sage.

Santos, Boaventura S. (1994) *Pela Mão de Alice*, Oporto: Afrontamento.

—— (2004) "A critique of lazy reason: against the waste of experience," *in* I. Wallerstein (ed.) *The modern world-system in the Longue Durée*, London: Paradigm Publishers, pp. 157–197.

—— (ed.) (2005) *Democratizing democracy. Beyond the liberal democratic canon*, London: Verso.

—— (ed.) (2006) *Another production is possible. Beyond the capitalist canon*, London: Verso.

—— (ed.) (2007) *Another knowledge is possible. Beyond northern epistemologies*, London: Verso.

Part 3
Inequalities and resistances

Part 5

Boundaries and resistances

25

The Indian middle classes and educational advantage

Family strategies and practices

Geetha B. Nambissan

Introduction

Disadvantage based on structural location, cultural marginalisation and institutional neglect is one side of the story of educational inequality in India that has received considerable scholarly attention. There is another, however, that is rarely brought centre stage in research and policy discourse. That is of social class and educational advantage. Few would contest that the middle class(es)[1] have reaped the major benefits from 'modern'/formal education in India, if one goes by their predominance in higher education, especially in elite institutions of professional and technical education, and disproportionate representation in 'high status' professions. A section of the Indian 'middle classes' is emerging in the global arena as a key player in the new economy and especially in sectors such as information technology, medicine, engineering and IT in the USA, UK and other West European countries. Despite their privileged position in education, these social classes have received negligible research attention.

In this chapter, I look at the middle classes in India to understand the 'micro practices of social reproduction' of these groups in relation to educational and social advantage (Ball, 2003: 3). I keep in mind that the middle class(es) is not a homogenous group and comprises class fractions that are likely to have responded differently to social and cultural changes and educational opportunities, including the process of globalisation. Scholars caution against generalising about the middle classes based on the projected 'success' of global Indians (Fernandes, 2007), who represent only a fraction of the Indian middle classes. I use Bourdieu's (1986, 1992) framework of capitals – economic, social, cultural and symbolic, and their 'fungibility' or convertibility to understand processes that underlie social/educational advantage, and attempt to do so specifically within the Indian context. The focus of the chapter will be on family strategies and educational privilege. I bring in Drury's (1993: 10) notion of 'family sponsorship', a term he uses to capture the diverse ways by which the family discharges its responsibilities towards ensuring that younger members are successful in life and uses all its resources to this end. 'The privileges of the older generation – family income, caste, education, father's occupation – are used to give the young the competitive advantage of a good education.' Like Ball (2003), I move beyond rational choice and 'culturalist' explanations of educational decision-making and look more closely at how choices and strategies are influenced by family and kin, social networks, identity and interests, within changing socio-economic contexts. I argue that the upper tiers of the middle classes have actively participated in the education system from a position of social and economic dominance that has allowed them to shape the system and define what 'good education' is, as well the desirable cultural resources for success. A relational view of social class suggests that it is important to see how educational practices of the upper/middle classes are linked to the changing practices of other middle-class fractions and the larger implications that emerge, especially in the era of globalisation. While using a socio-historical perspective, I locate this chapter in the period beginning around the mid 1980s, when economic reforms were being debated and subsequently implemented in India. It is also important to stress that globalisation is mediated through national systems, as well as local cultures and institutions that are historically rooted. This is true for India, where the historical experience of colonialism, the policies of the post-independence developmental state, the social structure, particularly the caste system of graded inequality, and plural cultures present diverse contexts where different social classes (and the castes, communities and genders that intersect with them) are reading and responding to globalisation through changing institutions in diverse ways.

Private schools and English education: constructing the 'good' in education

The key route to elite upper middle class status in India has been the exclusive English medium 'public' (private) schools, which followed in the tradition of the British public schools. These are among schools to which upper middle class Indians have always sent their children, thereby setting trends and laying down standards of the 'good' in education. They were among the first to access modern education and occupations in the colonial period and belonged to the socially privileged upper castes that had a literate tradition and were part of the colonial elite. Writing about the 'educated elite' in the mid 1970s, Kamat (1985: 192) refers to the 'super elite', who were products of the 'elitist channel of education of expensive English-medium schools and select prestigious institutions of higher learning'. They became technocrats, management personnel, bureaucrats and defence personnel, occupying 'strategic positions in the economy and state machine' as well as the 'best-paid professional positions' including in multinational organisations. He goes on to add that, 'Because of their crucial positions in the power structure, and their educational and social status, they also set the norm in social thinking and society life for the lesser educated elite below' (Kamat, 1985: 190–192). The privileged position of English-medium education in India can be seen in the fact that, even in the 1970s, the majority of the recruits to the prestigious Indian Administrative Service (IAS) had attended English-medium schools (Saxena, 1981: 19, cited in Potter, 1996: 233). The cultural capital that was sought in recruits and was in all probability emphasised in these institutions was 'pleasant manners, facility in English, an attractive appearance and dress (preferably English style) and an authoritative manner' (Taub, 1969: 38, cited in Potter, 1996: 233). Kumar (1987:35) concludes that 'the supply of elite civil servants is a "reproductive" process inasmuch as a few educational institutions account for a sizeable proportion of the total number recruited.'

The 'new rich', businessmen and farmers from the middle castes who had benefited from the early policies of the independent Indian state encouraging agriculture and industry, were quick to see the role of 'public schools' in linking economic, symbolic and social capital.

Upadhya's (1987) study of the *Kammas* (a rich peasant caste in the state of Andhra Pradesh) describes the strategies of families who had come into wealth with the 'green revolution' and looked to education for building cultural and social capital and raising their standing in society what Bourdieu calls 'reconversion strategies'. She says that they were keenly aware of the need to develop networks and to be accepted by those who were influential in government and business circles. 'To interact effectively in such social circles fluency in English and a good education . . . are necessary.' She goes on to observe that,

> Wealthy rural families often send their sons to private boarding schools from a very young age because that is the only way they can receive a good English medium education and hence the necessary 'cultural capital' to move into the urban upper middle class by joining white-collar executive occupations, the professions, or starting their own business.

Further, that 'wealth alone does not confer social status' but that 'social status can be acquired with wealth by giving a large dowry in marriage of daughters, sending sons to private engineering colleges . . .', including the establishing of private colleges (Upadhya, 1987: 68–69). Kumar (1987: 36) also points to similar strategies for social mobility and political dominance by the emerging rural elite in other states (Maharashtra and Karnataka), where 'private institutions on the "public school" model and professional colleges for medical and engineering education on a capitation fee basis' were being established. These studies only briefly capture some of the complex social processes linked to the strategies of the new upper middle classes that informed the demand for, and the rapid spread of, private educational schools and colleges as early as the 1960s.

The middle class, 'regional elite', educated in the 'middle-grade regional-medium high schools' and colleges, is Kamat's second tier of 'educational elite' in the 1970s. These were primarily state run/state supported, but also included privately managed institutions that offered better-quality education in the vernacular (regional languages). Those who accessed these schools, according to Kamat, were the not-so-affluent upper castes, 'with a literate tradition', who had to make do with middle-/lower-level salaried jobs. The other section was the relatively better off, newly educated middle/economically dominant lower castes in the cities and rural areas (1985: 193). For them, education was a path to middle-class jobs and social status. There were also those who graduated from 'low-grade, regional medium institutions' and came mainly from lower class/castes and who sought to 'acquire a smattering of education, and ultimately a degree, in the hope of landing some kind of white collar job or the other' (Kamat, 1985: 193).

Thus, until the late 1970s, apart from the upper middle classes (old and newly emerging), the middle classes were still enrolling their children in state schools or state-supported, privately managed schools. The middle class flight from state schools, a clear trend visible in urban India since the 1980s, was followed by the increasing desertion of these schools by the lower middle class in the next decade or so. Today, state schools are largely dominated by children from the poor, belonging mainly to 'lower' castes and minorities. This trend, beginning in the early 1980s, was pronounced in the 1990s, the period when policies of liberalisation were implemented in India, leading to the downsizing of the public sector and the coming of the new economy and insecure futures. Private schools are increasingly common in cities, small towns and the rural areas in response to the growing demand for good quality education, especially in English medium.[2] Behind the significant shift in enrolment from government to private schools lies the largely undocumented story of diverse strategies of middle/lower middle class families as they struggle and attempt to secure their children's future for a world very different from their own. In the section that follows, I discuss some of the strategies and practices of these families, especially in the changing context of globalisation.

Family strategies, educational aspirations and schooling

Family aspirations for education must be viewed in relation to their mobility strategies in the changing context of globalisation and the role that they see education (of specific kinds/qualities) playing in this process. Drury (1993: 8) notes that 'Folk theories of making it' (referred to by Ogbu, 1980) 'are crucial because they help to shape individual aspirations and family mobility strategies in general, and ideas about the value of education in particular'. The ways in which different fractions of the middle classes strategise, make choices and translate these into practice are likely to vary in relation to how they have engaged with the 'private' in education, as well as how they are able to mobilise economic, cultural and social resources. The following discussion is based on recent studies on different middle-class fractions based on research in specific sites in India.

Choosing the 'right' school

Waldrop's (2004) study 'among upper-caste, upper-middle class professional *Punjabis*' in metropolitan Delhi gives us a glimpse of what mobility strategies and 'choice' of schools mean for metropolitan upper middle class parents. The fathers were senior government officers, professionals or worked for 'big' Indian and foreign companies. Parents expected their children,

> boys and girls alike to pass through college, and preferably go for a university degree in England or the US. Because their English medium primary education in India is often combined with higher education abroad, they are global (meaning Western) and secular in their outlook, and travel abroad occasionally.
>
> (Waldrop, 2004: 205)

Scrase and Scrase (2009: 11) observe that, 'Increasingly, financial capital is being used to purchase an English-medium private education and to send a child abroad for university education, and so to build one's stock of cultural capital.'

All the parents in Waldrop's schools listed the same five prestigious private schools in the city as their 'first choices' of schools to enrol their children. While choosing a school, parents took into account the reputation of the school, including its philosophy, and the opinion of family and friends, including the 'old school tie' (Waldrop, 2004: 208). Waldrop's interviews with the principals of the five schools showed that the screening procedures adopted by the institutions factored in considerations that privilege upper middle class parents: preference was given to children of former students, as well as those who had siblings in the school. Schools were keen that parents were well educated, had at least a bachelor's degree and shared the values of the school. The knowledge of English was of course an important criterion for admission (Waldrop, 2004: 211–212). These are criteria that effectively exclude other middle-class fractions. Waldrop concludes that private schools are 'homogenous social arenas', which enable the building of social capital. 'Friendships form between children of the same elite class and, in India, where networking plays important economic and social roles, having gone to one of the prestigious private schools turns out to be an enormous social advantage in life' (Waldrop, 2004: 223).

Drury's study (1993) is located in the industrial city of Kanpur in the northern Indian state of Uttar Pradesh. In the early 1980s, Kanpur had a rapidly changing educational landscape characterised by '"educational upgrading": the flight from Parishad (state/municipal) schools into private unregulated schools among the lower middle class, and the intense competition for the better English medium schools among the more wealthy' (Drury, 1993: 58). Business-owning families whose lack of the requisite cultural capital may have been a major deterrent to their entry into private English-medium schools a few decades earlier (when noses were turned up at the 'new rich') find that they are able to convert economic capital into cultural and social capital. This is the section of the middle class that is increasingly and confidently entering old middle-class institutions, willing to engage private tutors and whatever it takes to provide cultural and other inputs that are required for school success and social status. They were giving their sons private English-medium education, not so much for the skills that it provided, but as a 'fall back option'. More importantly, they appeared to be evaluating the changing context of business and, consequently, the need to interact with administrative and other officials, as well as to exercise authority within their own firm. Drury notes that they were in fact looking at education as a long-term investment – out of character with what was traditionally expected of such families (Drury, 1993: 100–102).

'White collar' employees in the Kanpur study were a section of middle-class parents who realised that choosing a school was a critical decision that had long-term consequences for higher education and careers of their children. The most sought after schools were the English-medium schools, particularly the 'convent schools' run by missionaries. As these schools were limited in number, there was intense competition for school places. Parents were forced to use 'the full range of their material and social resources, deploying them within the legitimate admission channels of the schools, but also in temporary and informal channels of their own making' (Drury, 1993: 122). Drury observes that a result of the 'good schools scramble in Kanpur' was the 'rise of bribery, *jugarbazi* (using insider contacts) and other forms of backstage manoeuvring to gain admissions outside the normal channels' (Drury, 1993: 76–78).

Though some parents thought that the Hindi-medium schools were academically better, Drury says,

> It was the English language itself that counted most for these parents, for its prestige value as well as its practical usefulness. This held equally true for those who knew some English themselves and for the upwardly mobile parent who did not.

Parents say, 'English is the most portable language . . . With English you can impress people' (Drury, 1993: 76). They explore every opportunity to give their children the knowledge of the English language that they believe gives a child a crucial edge in school entry and success. More common are efforts to enrol children in private pre-schools (an expanding but unregulated sector) that admit children as early as age three. Parents say that they send children to pre-schools to get them 'used to the idea of school' and, more importantly, 'to prepare boys and girls for the "entrance examinations" to the kindergartens or first grade of good private schools'. Children are taught to take interviews/entrance examinations. Drury says 'Exam culture' begins at age three (1993: 90–91).

Donner's study (2005) focuses on the strategies of middle-class families in the metropolis of Calcutta in the context of the downsizing of the public sector and aspirations for opportunities in the new economy of IT-related industries that are yet to come to the city. Parents are well aware that professional careers and government service jobs that were the basis of their middle-class identity are no longer guaranteed for their children. Their generation was educated in regional-medium schools – 'the reputed Bengali medium neighbourhood school' that reinforced pride in the language and culture of the '*Bhadralok*' (the 'old' Bengali middle-class/upper-caste elite). However, they have switched to English-medium schooling for their children and are influenced by 'the powerful imagery of new global workplaces and competition' in their efforts to give their children an edge (Donner, 2005: 123).

As their children are the first generation to go to English-medium schools, parents in Donner's study have had to learn the ropes in getting their children into a 'good school' (vaguely identified as one that has a 'good reputation'/is 'English-medium') and ensuring success (2005: 125). Apart from standing in queues to get admission forms and filling them up, there are interviews to be faced by children for which knowledge of English is definitely advantageous. Unfamiliar with English and the requirements of schools, parents look to English-medium pre-schools/nurseries to prepare children for school interviews that they would face at age four. Once children secure admission to these schools, parents need to be familiar with school rhythms that include tests, examinations and other activities. Additional tutoring in school subjects, computer classes and other privately paid for inputs are becoming an essential part of the curriculum of school students (Donner, 2005: 125–129). The secondary stage of education is strategised with higher education/training in 'technology-oriented courses' in mind. Donner observes that 'parents judge successful secondary education largely in terms of the marks necessary to enter IT or science–related courses' (Donner, 2005: 125–129). What is most interesting in Donner's study is the manner in which family resources are mobilised towards children's success in school. This is dwelt upon in the next section.

Families in Calcutta and another city in West Bengal who were part of Scrase and Scrase's study (2009) were 'lower-ranking professionals, administrators, sales and service personnel' in the state and private sector. They are lower middle class (but upper and middle caste) families who have experienced downward mobility as a result of a number of factors and 'exacerbated by neoliberal reforms' (Scrase and Scrase, 2009: 11–12). Not surprisingly, they are extremely anxious about their children's future and see proficiency in English as crucial for mobility as well as for social status. The quotes of two of their respondents speak volumes about what the inability to speak English entails: 'English is not only important in getting a better job, it is everywhere in social interaction. If you can't speak it, then you are a nobody', and 'English is an international language. Your feel humiliated if you can't speak English. People think you are dumb'' (Scrase and Scrase, 2009: 131).

Scrase and Scrase's (2009) respondents differ from Donner's in that, among the former, 'Many had struggled through education to obtain secure employment in the public sector, but now they increasingly feel that they are being squeezed out' (Scrase and Scrase, 2009: 11). They appear to be less well educated and are financially more constrained, both of which are likely to make the educational pathways for their children far more difficult. Getting their children into the 'right school' is not an easy task, as there is need for familiarity with the English language as well as the increasingly complex school landscape. They feel that children must be first admitted in the 'right pre-schools' in order to be accepted by a good, regular English-medium school (Scrase and Scrase, 2009: 64).

The private English-medium schools and the numerous language coaching schools and tutoring centres that Scrase and Scrase observe in different neighbourhoods (mentioned by Donner as well) are emerging in response to the growing demand for proficiency in English.

However, the doubtful quality of these unregulated, privately run courses has been a major issue (2009: 141). This is of particular concern as families reported that they were cutting back on various kinds of expense but not on their children's education, which they felt was 'necessary expense' and one 'least likely to be rationed. It remains a high priority, and so families frequently forgo "luxuries" in order to ensure their educational needs are maintained' (2009: 64).

Benei's (2005) study in the town of Kohlapur in the state of Maharashtra suggests that decision-making in education among the middle classes is mediated by tensions between socio-economic interests (usually seen as based on 'rational choice') and identity (linguistic in this case). Although English education has 'traditionally' been availed of by the upper castes/upper middle classes, it cannot be assumed that middle-class parents will easily abandon instruction in the regional medium just because of globalisation and the opportunities that that are open to those with schooling in the English medium. She links the ambivalence that many of her respondents show towards English-medium education to the place of Marathi language in the identity of being 'Maharashtrian', 'regional patriotism' and nationalism. Thus, for instance, some parents may prefer that their children are enrolled in the state-supported private network of institutions (seen to be of better quality than state schools), where Marathi is the medium of instruction and English a subject of study. However, they would have no problem in encouraging their children to acquire computer skills, which they see as important (Benei, 2005: 151–153).

On the other hand, business communities were guided more by strategic economic interests. Thus, for instance, agri-business families who had made inroads into the global market well before the 1990s were already sending their children to English-medium schools (Benei, 2005: 144). I have already referred to Upadhya's (1987) study, which pointed to efforts by business families to convert economic capital into cultural and symbolic capital through elite private schooling. Benei also makes the point that, for minorities for whom socio-religious identity is dominant, the shift to English-medium instruction is far easier than for those for whom Marathi language is one of the defining elements of identity. It is here that strategic choices are being made by middle-class families. Lower castes and especially the Scheduled Castes (former 'untouchable' castes) see English-medium schools as the route to higher socio-economic status and an escape from stigmatised identities (Benei, 2005: 157). In Kanpur, there were lower middle class families who chose private Hindi-medium schools for their children. The reasons were pragmatic: lower costs than English-medium schools, better facilities than the municipal (*Parishad*) schools and so on. The child's gender also influenced the choice of school medium where it was observed that, 'sons should have English medium education if possible, but private Hindi or *Parishad* Schools are adequate for daughters' (Drury, 1993: 79).

Parenting practices and advantaged mothers

Parenting practices and especially the role of the mother are also linked to the social advantage that middle classes gain in education. This already finds mention in scholarship in Western societies, but in India, women's literacy and education have been emphasised, mainly in relation to improving children's education and health status. However, the fact that the educated mother, the norm in middle-class families, brings with her specific advantages for children and is seen as an important 'mobility' strategy especially in the period of globalisation, has received little attention.

For Bengali middle-class families, women's education was seen to have a crucial role in modernising the 'domestic sphere' as well as socialisation of children into the culture of the

Bhadralok in the colonial period. In the post-independence period, Donner observes that women's education received emphasis, not so much for careers and employment, but because of the role of the mother in the education and 'proper upbringing of children'. In the contemporary context of labour-market restructuring, she finds that education is seen as a 'precondition for marriage and motherhood', because in a 'more competitive and less regulated economy the schooling of children requires new parenting skills' (Donner, 2005: 121). This has become necessary with the new demands imposed on mothers by English-medium schools, to which many parents educated in the vernacular are now sending their children. Thus, we see that mothers plan their entire day around the school routine and requirements such as dropping their children to school (neighbourhood Bengali-medium schools are now no longer accessed), providing support for homework and organising private tutoring classes. Extracurricular activities such as computer classes and art and writing competitions are also planned, so as to give the children inputs that are seen as important for school success. Immediate and extended family support is mobilised, as women look to their mothers-in-law and mothers where possible for support. The older generation of women come in to help organise the home so that the daughter's/daughter-in-law's energies can be focused on school success. Donner suggests that, among educated upper middle class Bengali professionals who have migrated, shared parenting is likely be used as a crucial resource for children's education (2005: 130–134).

Mothers educated in English medium, usually graduates themselves, as in the case of upper middle/middle class families, are obviously at a greater advantage compared with those families where women are less educated and have had instruction in the regional medium/vernacular. Drury says that 'Biography is a resource often overlooked in educational research. A person's own experience with school affects not only the information he or she brings to bear on school decisions as a parent, but basic values and standards' (1993: 61). Hence, Kanpur middle-class respondents are able to recall wives'/mothers' greater involvement in their own or their children's school work. Drury rightly observes that higher levels of education among women in middle-class families today (compared with a generation ago) give them 'greater educational advantages than ever before', as

> mothers are now well qualified to act as academic coaches and not simply as disciplinarians, at least up to the high school level. They work regularly with the children in the first years of school, making sure that they learn the fundamentals of reading, writing and calculating. Though it can be a time-consuming task, few of these women work outside the home . . . Even those who do work there is usually the advantage of being able to afford domestic help full or part time.
>
> (Drury, 1993: 85–86)

Donner also draws attention to cultural and familial expectations of even highly educated women professionals. 'With the arrival of children . . . the privileged upper middle-class graduates who secure positions in teaching or as professionals are expected to leave or take up more flexible, part-time employment' (Donner, 2005: 122).

The 'mothering' role also includes 'creation of a favourable environment for study at home' defined as 'giving the children peace of mind' (Donner, 2005: 130). This is what lower middle class mothers, who are 'generally less well educated' and 'often feel that they cannot contribute a lot to English-medium schooling', focus their energies upon. They try and facilitate their children's study at home. 'Provide them with special meals, encourage them and remind them of their duties and organise their leisure time for them' (2005: 130). There are greater anxieties in such homes and this leads, as mentioned earlier, to the early search for pre-schools and language courses and the eventual spiral for private schools that such demands set in motion.

Thus, for business and other fractions of the middle class, the educated mother (with proficiency in English) is increasingly becoming critical for the 'appropriate parenting' that is being seen as necessary for school success. Drury (1993: 169) refers to the fact that the 'middle class [sic] are rapidly accumulating cultural capital in the form of values, standards and practical knowledge of the school system'. A key channel through which this capital is being circulated is what he calls the '"educational dowry" of brides, as families take greater care to select young women who can provide a good educational environment in the home'.

The middle classes and educational advantage: some concerns

The foregoing discussion has highlighted the complex educational strategies that middle classes in India are adopting to give their children an advantage in school and better life chances. While the location of families as middle-class fractions influences how they perceive linkages between schools and the labour (and marriage) market, as well as their ability to translate strategies into concrete practices, their decisions are also mediated by the institutional context of educational provision, socio-economic interests and diverse identities. What has emerged from the available studies is that middle-class fractions are differently advantaged in relation to children's education. For instance, while 'mothers' work' is increasingly factored into school success, social and educational advantage is likely to vary among middle-class families, depending upon the level of the mother's education and her proficiency in English.

The privileging of English-medium education and other inputs accessed from private schools and related markets in building what is seen as the required stock of cultural capital for school success has been highlighted. Fernandes (2007: 91–100) also points to new credentialising strategies by lower fractions of the middle classes in their attempts at upward mobility in the new economy, which include trying to acquire elements of the corporate culture, and 'symbolic capital' (manners, taste and style) being projected by 'hegemonic representations' of the metropolitan upper middle classes. These strategies and practices of middle-class fractions have led to the rapid growth of the unregulated private sector in education, which is exploiting the aspirations, anxieties and often helplessness of families belonging to the lower tiers of these classes.

The majority of Indian children continue to access elementary education in state schools. However, as mentioned, these are schools to which the middle-class and, increasingly, lower middle class families no longer send their children. Kumar notes that,

> The growth of private schools gradually siphoned off children of the better of sections of urban society from state schools, leaving them to look after the children of poorer parents, who lacked both the status and the means to exercise any kind of influence on the schools' functioning.
>
> (Kumar, 1996: 61)

What is of concern is that sections of the poorer/working classes are today seeking 'quality education' for their children in English-medium schools, and that the unregulated private sector sees this as a business opportunity. Advocacy networks for 'school choice' and 'private for-profit schools' for the poor are also making their presence felt in India (see Nambissan and Ball, forthcoming).

Policy and research in relation to educational inequality in India have been largely about addressing disadvantage and exclusion in education experienced by Scheduled Castes, Scheduled Tribes, socio-religious minorities, the poor and girls. However, educational dominance and advantage have received little attention. This chapter has sought to highlight the powerful influence that the middle classes (old upper middle class and more recently the new rich) have on the education system, particularly through their hold over elite, private, English-medium schooling. Equally important is the middle-class advantage that comes with cultural, economic and social capital acquired by families over generations, as well as the impact that 'representations' of the seemingly 'merit'-based success of the elite in the new economy have on the rising aspirations and demands of lower fractions of the middle classes. We know very little about the Indian middle classes, but their practices significantly impact the larger educational system and, hence, merit serious and urgent study.

Notes

1   Who are the middle classes? The much debated size and characteristics of this social group are matters beyond the scope of this chapter. It would suffice to say here that these are intermediate social groups that comprise a range of 'white-collar salaried occupations' from elite managerial and professional positions to lower-level, white-collar jobs and include technicians as well as owners of small business. (For debate/research on the Indian middle classes see Deshpande (2003), Fernandes (2007), Sridharan (2004) etc.)

2   According to recent statistics, 72.2 per cent of elementary school (Grades I–VIII)) enrolment is in state/government schools, and 27.6 per cent is in privately managed schools. Of the latter, 9.4 per cent is in schools run by private, aided (by the state) managements, while 18.2 per cent is in private, unaided schools (NUEPA, 2009: 1–2). There is a growing unregulated private-school sector, whose size is still to be estimated.

One of the main reasons for the shift from state-run to privately managed schools is the perception that the former provide education of poor quality. One of the key elements by which 'good quality' education is defined in popular perception is instruction in English. The policy in India has been to provide education in the regional medium in state schools and to bring in English as a subject of study around Grade V or later. More recently, some state governments have brought in the study of English in the early primary years in response to the growing demand for learning of the language.

References

Ball, S.J. (2003) *Class strategies and the education market. The middle classes and social advantage*, London and New York: RoutledgeFalmer, Taylor & Francis Group.

Benei, V. (2005) 'Of languages, passions and interests: education, regionalism and globalization in Maharashtra, 1800–2000', in J. Assayag and C.J. Fuller (eds) *Globalising India. Perspectives from below*, London: Anthem Press, pp. 141–162.

Bourdieu, P. (1986) 'The forms of capital', in J. Richardson (ed.) *Handbook of theory and research for the sociology of education*, New York: Greenwood Press, pp. 241–258.

—— (1992) *Language and symbolic power*, Cambridge: Polity Press.

Deshpande, S. (2003) *Contemporary India: a sociological view*, New Delhi: Penguin.

Donner, H. (2005) '"Children are capital, grandchildren are interest": changing educational strategies and parenting in Calcutta's middle-class families', in J. Assayag and C.J. Fuller (eds) *Globalizing India. Perspectives from below*, London: Anthem Press, pp. 119–139.

Drury, D. (1993) *The iron school master. Education, employment and the family in India*, New Delhi: Hindustan Book Company.

Fernandes, L. (2007) *India's new middle class. Democratic politics in an era of economic reform*, New Delhi: Oxford University Press (first published in 2006 by University of Minnesota Press, Minneapolis).

Kamat, A.R. (1985) *Education and social change in India*, Bombay: Somaiya Publications Private Limited.

Kumar, K. (1987) 'Reproduction or change? Education and elites in India', in G. Ratna and M. Zachariah *Education and the process of change*, New Delhi: Sage Publications Private Limited, pp. 27–41.

Kumar, K. (1996) *Learning from conflict*, New Delhi: Orient Longman.

Nambissan, G.B. and Ball, S.J. (forthcoming) 'Advocacy networks, choice and schooling of the poor in India' in M. Lall and G.B. Nambissan (eds) *Education and social justice in the era of globalisation: India and the UK.*

NUEPA (National University of Educational Planning and Administration) (2009) *Elementary education in India. Progress towards UEE*, New Delhi: NUEPA.

Ogbu, J.U. (1980) 'School ethnography: a multi-level approach', Paper prepared for the Fifth College of Education Symposium, *Ethnographic research in the schools*, University of Delaware, 23–24 May.

Potter, D.C. (1996) *India's political administrators. From ICS to IAS*, Delhi: Oxford University Press.

Saxena, N.C. (1981) 'The world of the IAS', *Administrator* xxvi (1): 16–17.

Scrase, R.-G. and Scrase, T.J. (2009) *Globalisation and the middle classes in India. The social and cultural impact of neoliberal reforms*, London and New York: Routledge, Taylor & Francis Group.

Sridharan, E. (2004) 'The growth and sectoral composition of India's middle class: its impact on the politics of economic liberalization', *India Review* 3(4): 405–428.

Taub, R. (1969) *Bureaucrats under stress: administrators and administration in an Indian state*, Berkley, CA: University of California Press.

Upadhya, C. (1987) 'Culture, class and entrepreneurship: a case study of coastal Andhra Pradesh, India', in M. Rutten and C. Upadhya (eds) *Small business entrepreneurs in Asia and Europe: towards a comparative perspective*, New Delhi: Sage Publications, pp. 47–80.

Waldrop, A. (2004) 'The meaning of the old school-tie: private schools, admission procedures and class segmentation in New Delhi', in A. Vaugier-Chatterjee (ed.) *Education and democracy in India*, New Delhi: Manohar and Centre De Sciences Humaines, pp. 203–228.

26

Equality and social justice
The university as a site of struggle

Kathleen Lynch, Margaret Crean and Marie Moran[1]

Introduction

Despite the proclaimed allegiance of most countries to principles of equality enshrined in the UN Declaration on Human Rights, inequality is a pervasive feature of the global order. Yet, it is important not to be overwhelmed by the scale of global injustice. In every country, there is resistance to power and privilege, with people working at many levels to create more equal societies.

In this chapter, we will summarise the reasons why we came to establish Equality Studies in University College Dublin (UCD) almost twenty years ago as one way of responding to injustices (for a more detailed discussion, see Lynch, 1995) and why, in 2005, we further institutionalised an academic space for this work by forming a School of Social Justice and a network of scholars from across the University, who are committed to research and teaching in social justice, to establish the Egalitarian World Initiative (EWI) network (www.ewi.ie). We begin by explaining why universities have a particular remit to challenge injustice and why it is important for them to retain that responsibility in a market-led era in higher education.

The public interest role of the university

Over the last decade, universities have been transformed increasingly into powerful consumer-oriented corporate networks, whose public interest values have been seriously challenged (Davies *et al.*, 2006; Rutherford, 2005). Commercialisation has been normalised and granted moral legitimacy (Giroux, 2002), and its operational values and purposes have been encoded in the systems of all types of university (Dill and Soo, 2005; Steier, 2003). Moreover, both the pace and intensity of commercialisation have been exacerbated (Bok, 2003; Henkel, 1997). Yet, universities are quintessentially public interest institutions (Harkavy, 2006).

This is not to deny that universities have often failed to honour their public interest inheritance. They have been embedded with professional interests, often doing little to challenge the evident social closure practices within powerful professional groups (Hanlon,

296

2000). In their internal operations, they have been both hierarchical and patriarchal (Morley, 1999; Reay, 2004; Saunderson, 2002). Certainly, it is hard to argue that universities were models of enlightened organisational practices, even prior to the endorsement of neo-liberal values. Although there have been critical voices in higher education, challenging its pedagogy and its exclusivity, it is also true that they have been minority voices, often working against the tide even in the pre-neo-liberal days. This has also been our own experience in trying to establish Equality Studies in UCD (Lynch, 1995).

Yet the university remains a site of social struggle; it is one of the few institutions in society where there is an opportunity for people to think critically and to document that critique in writing and in teaching. It is a space where one can exercise intellectual autonomy, no matter how circumscribed that might be in an age of market-led research funding. The freedom from necessity enjoyed by academics affords them the space to write and to teach, so there is a choice whether or not to use that freedom to act.

Why Equality Studies – the educational case

The setting up of Equality Studies (1990) and of the School of Social Justice (2005) was strongly influenced by the fact that, while many faculties and fields of scholarship address issues of equality and social justice, and there are some subjects that address specific group-related inequalities, including disability studies and Women's Studies, there are very few schools or centres that focus all their research and teaching on equality issues in a holistic way.

Clearly, working to promote equality is not a 'profession' in any traditional sense of that term, yet people within professions and occupations, who are fighting for social justice and equality, and especially those working in civil society organisations, but also in statutory and multilateral agencies, need research support and education. There was and is a need to create a scholarly space for equality activists. The university seemed an ideal place to do this, although there was, and still is, opposition to the ideal, first because some define the university as a place simply to educate the elite, while others see education about equality as peripheral to the education of a new generation of market-led professionals. The experience we have in Equality Studies shows, however, that the desire to create a better world for all of humanity is strong among university staff and students,[2] even though this is not culturally supported in an age of commercialised education.

Why Equality Studies – the academic case

Universities and higher education institutions are not neutral agents in the field of academic discourse. Like all educational institutions, they work either for 'domestication or for freedom' (Freire, 1972). They can indulge in banking education that controls and domesticates thinking in the practice of regurgitation and regulation, or they can engage in critical education that challenges both teacher and student to engage in praxis. Universities are also projects in the making, places in which academics can either become agents of history or docile subjects (Davies et al., 2006).

With the postmodernist turn and the rise of neo-liberal politics, it seemed intellectually vagrant and academically suicidal to establish a Centre for Equality Studies in University College Dublin in the late 1980s. Yet it was precisely these challenges that inspired us to act.

297

The normative intent of the word 'equality' sat very uneasily with the relativism of postmodern thinking. It smacked of that old authoritarianism that was associated with the certainties of grand narratives and with colonising cultural and political relations. Marxism's rejection of the normative approach to the analysis of oppression was a further disincentive to engage with normative questions. In establishing Equality Studies, we were mindful of these debates and of the binaries between the empirical and the normative embedded in social scientific analysis. We did not see the two as separate spheres and made a conscious decision to marry positivist research traditions with normative analysis in both the teaching and research of the Centre (Baker et al., 2004; Lynch, 1995).

While the scientific, including the sociological, must be distinguished from the political (Martinelli, 2008), there is a need to create spaces that allow more than professional sociology or policy sociology (or the professional and policy-led dimensions of any disciplines) to thrive. There is a need to make spaces for the subaltern within disciplines (Burawoy, 2005) and between disciplines. There must be a space for academic knowledge to learn from experiential knowledge, with its complex positive and normative dimensions, especially in the study of injustices.

Questioning the binary between positive/normative is also necessary because so much research in the social sciences and cognate areas, including law and education, is profoundly unitary in terms of the normative and the positive (Sayer, 2006). When scholars write of 'discrimination' in law, 'exploitation' in sociology or 'marginalisation' in education, they are not just describing a phenomenon, they are also naming it as undesirable because it undermines the well-being of particular groups of people. They are making a normative judgement, as well as an empirical statement, even if they do not explicitly name their normative position. Taking a 'critical' approach to scholarship promotes a particular normative position and set of values that make the very critique of oppression and, indeed, the enterprise of much academic work meaningful.

Even for those who do not subscribe to critical perspectives and lay claim to independence, the normative is encoded in every publication and every lecture. Although objectivity is vital for scientific analysis and for choosing the appropriate instruments for research investigation, there is an implicit normative dimension to the knowledge act because there is no view from nowhere.

In establishing Equality Studies, the goal was to do things differently in the university, not just by linking the positive and the normative, but by democratising the social relations of education and of research production and exchange. Inspired by the Freirean (1972) methods of dialogical teaching and learning, and by feminist and disability scholarship's challenge to employ emancipatory research methods (Harding, 1991; Oliver, 1992), we tried to open up new types of space for both doing research and for teaching (Baker et al., 2004; Lynch, 1999).

The rise of neo-liberal policies internationally in the post-1990 era, and the emergence of the so-called 'Celtic Tiger' in Ireland made social justice and equality issues appear anachronistic in an era glorifying choice and consumption. It remains a struggle academically and politically to survive, as the market model of funding bears down on our actions and planning. Yet the reality is there is no security for those who resist power, and in that sense the Equality Studies Centre will always be open to attack. The lessons of survival and resistance need to be relearned as university regimes change. There is no possibility of standing still.

Equality Studies and social justice – keeping a place in the university

Apple (2007: 168) claims that 'If you want to interrupt the right, study what they themselves did'. Indeed, the setting up of Equality Studies, and of the School of Social Justice, was inspired not only by a Gramscian-informed understanding of the role of culture and ideology in the realisation of change, and by the Freirean recognition of education's lack of neutrality, but also by lessons learned from the success of Thatcherism in the UK. One of the major achievements of the Thatcher era was that, not only did it change the terms of political discourse in the UK, but it also successfully institutionalised neo-liberal beliefs and values in law and public policy.

While writing and teaching are the tools of the academic who wants to act for global justice, there is a need, as Harkavy (2006: 7) has observed, for 'strategic organisational innovation'. There is a need to institutionalise ideals in the structures of organisations, not just in their language or written policies, no matter how essential the latter may be. One of the reasons inequalities are often difficult to challenge is because they are institutionalised in the categories of every day life (Tilly, 1998). By the same logic, if egalitarian changes are to be instituted, they need to be institutionalised in categories, positions, processes and systems that are built on egalitarian and social justice principles. And there is a need to promote the understanding of how to operationalise these principles over time. It was with the understanding that institutions tend to outlive their incumbents that we set out to institutionalise a physical and intellectual space to promote research and teaching on equality and social justice. While it was necessary to have programmes of education and research in the short term, in the medium to long term it was necessary to have institutional status.

Much of the struggle over the last twenty years has been about achieving institutional status and recognition. It began by creating spaces and titles that only got recognition after they were created: an 'Equality Studies Working Group' in 1986 and an Equality Studies Centre in 1990. The Centre was never given departmental status, despite repeated requests, but it was accepted as an operating academic unit within the Arts Faculty. However, it had to report annually on its achievements to the Academic Council, something not required of recognised departments, and it was and is in a constant state of struggle for funding.[3]

All centres were informed they would be abolished with restructuring in 2005; Equality Studies refused to accept this and insisted (using the market rhetoric of the new regime) that the Equality Studies Centre was a 'brand name' and necessary for survival. We were allowed to keep the name on our letter-head, on the Web and for advertising because of its market utility.[4]

Equality Studies led the movement to create the School of Social Justice in 2005, with the support of Women's Studies. Although the School of Social Justice is one of the thirty-five statutorily recognised schools within new structures of the University, this does not mean that Equality Studies and the School are institutionally unassailable. However, it is more difficult to disestablish a School and its units than a programme of studies, or an isolated Centre, not least because the School is listed in university statutes.

In realising change, there is a need to identify the interstices that Habermas noted, those places between spaces that allow for change and resistances to occur at different times. Times of transition within institutions are times that offer opportunities for resistance, for finding spaces to create new initiatives. While times of transition are also times of social closure, re-regulation and control, when those in power set out the terms of change and try to control its scope and impact, the transition itself creates instabilities. New orders are created, and spaces are opened up to establish new programmes and initiatives, if there are the resources to fight for these at the time. There is a very real sense in which these times of transition involve what Gramsci defined as 'wars of position'.

In establishing both Equality Studies in the late 1980s and the School of Social Justice and the EWI in the mid 2000s, we used the instability of transitions, in each case heralded by the

299

arrival of new executive presidents in UCD, to propose changes in courses, programmes and activities in the University.[5] In all cases, the proposals were met with oppositions and counter-resistances, not necessarily from central management, who were less concerned with their ideologies than with their likelihood of success, but by colleagues in other departments and schools, who mounted resistance on ideological grounds (dislike of all things critical or socially engaged) or for fear that the programmes we offered might jeopardise their own subject or department. There is a lengthy correspondence in our files and emails on these challenges, but being willing to stay the course and having a clear vision as to our role and purpose proved to be crucial.

The mind is a site of struggle, and control of the mind is central to all campaigns (Castells, 2000). It is not surprising therefore that managing conciousness has been a deliberate project of powerful capitalist interests over the last thirty years, both inside and outside the academy (Boltanski and Chiapello, 2007; Harvey, 2005). While academics can exercise some influence (more than they think) from within the academy in framing minds and public consciousness, the media remain a hugely powerful, ideological force outside the university, with the capacity to either undermine or support critical thinking. The media is also a space over which academics generally have little control.

Throughout the development of Equality Studies, we were aware of the political reality that truth is increasingly what the media define as true. The media is a space that academics who think critically and differently have to engage with in order to survive. By 2005, when the most recent wave of changes occurred, and the university moved into restructuring along neo-liberal lines, there was a sustained attempt to force Equality Studies to integrate with (in our view to be subsumed by) bigger departments in the College of Human Sciences. At this time, we had a well-established reputation, not only for research and teaching but also for engaging with civil society and statutory agencies, both nationally and internationally. Our alumni and supporters included a number of well-known activists and commentators. Both the alumni and others who believed in our work lent their support to our position on a number of occasions, both privately and in public. An unsolicited opinion piece in the leading Irish broadsheet, *The Irish Times*, praising our work was the clearest example of this in September 2005. The opinion writer pointed out in his column that he had been asked to come out against Equality Studies by a staff member from UCD; this undermined those who opposed us internally, as they appeared 'disloyal' to the university by writing secretly to the press about internal UCD matters. There was some negative media analysis as well in more conservative newspapers, although not in 2005 at the time of most restructuring. The *Irish Daily Mail* (11 August 2008) (a UK subsidiary) had a full-page piece referring to Equality Studies, Women's Studies and Sociology as 'Queer Studies'. It tried to demonise the subjects by feeding into public homophobia about Queer Studies.

Even though we did not have to mount a media campaign to retain Equality Studies per se in 2005, we were prepared to do this. As almost all of us had been engaged on issues at different times in the national media, this not only gave us social capital through media networks, but symbolic capital within the university; we were known to be media aware. Moreover, closing down the only Equality Studies Centre in the country would not look good for the University (so the fear of bad press was a motive to allow us continue), and, as we were a small centre by UCD standards, we were not a major target for mergers by the new administration.

Challenges – disciplinary issues

Equality Studies experienced the same difficulties that Women's Studies, Disability Studies and all interdisciplinary fields experience: it was and is not seen to be 'pure' scholarship; it is tainted by diversity[6] and tolerated on the boundaries of the academy. Although there is recognition internationally of the central importance of interdisciplinary and transdisciplinary research (Nowotny *et al.*, 2001), there is little status attached to such new areas of scholarship in most established universities.[7] Fields of study are indeed allowed to emerge, but the core activities of the university centre around 'established disciplines'. The history of our experience in this respect is salutary.

The established faculties of the university (which were assimilated into colleges in 2005) did not regard interdisciplinary programmes as 'pure' enough in academic terms to house them when they were first established, so Equality Studies (and other similar groups including Disability Studies) was faculty-homeless for several years, until an Interdisciplinary Faculty was established in 2003. In the autumn of 2004, a new president was appointed, and it was clear from the outset that he and his new 'team' were going to 'rationalise' (a euphemism for close down) a number of faculties and schools. Interdisciplinary Studies was closed, and Equality Studies was located within the College of Human Sciences. In all, over ninety departments in the University were reduced to thirty-five schools. There was considerable pressure on Equality Studies to join established departments at this time. Knowing that we would be minor players in large schools, we resisted this pressure and proposed to establish a School of Social Justice. This idea was accepted in principle after we made a strong written case to the president as to the importance of social justice in the history and future of the University and fought for the school at numerous boards. In addition, we used the University's own ideology to challenge our closure;[8] it was an exercise in legitimation (Thompson, 1990). However, Women's Studies was the only centre that agreed to join the new School of Social Justice. The Disability Studies Centre joined Pyschology, and the Development Studies Centre joined Politics, although we had asked them to join Social Justice.[9] In each case, the titles of the new schools did not reflect the merger. Politics was renamed as the School of Politics and International Relations, and Psychology retained its name, with no mention of Disability Studies.

In the neo-liberal age, fear plays a major role in controlling and regulating academic staff (Boden and Epstein, 2006). Moreover, because academics are preoccupied on a daily basis with anxieties about productivity within an intense system of surveillance, they disavow their own docility (Davies *et al.*, 2006). And fear was a major reason why academic staff did not want to join Social Justice, not just because it was seen to be a school without an 'established' disciplinary centre, but because colleagues believed that such a school would be closed down in time. However, fear was not the only motivation. Some of those we invited to join us made it clear that they did not wish to be part of a school based on the principle of social justice. The division between the normative and the positive was a priority value in the minds of many colleagues; Equality Studies and Social Justice had broken a taboo by aligning the normative and the positive, and this continued to be unacceptable.[10]

Challenges – academic capitalism

Although academic life has always been highly individualised and driven by personal interests and ambitions, it was not always as driven by academic capitalism as it is currently (Slaughter and Rhoades, 2004). Even not-for-profit higher education programmes have been forced to accommodate market activity in recent years. And under the globalised (and highly unscientific) league table regimes promoted by commercial interests, universities do not determine the conditions of their own appraisal (Marginson, 2006). Educational programmes that service low-income communities, or research that is of value at national level, do not feature on university

301

rankings. And as the experience of Cultural Studies in Birmingham (Rutherford, 2005) and multidisciplinary programmes and Women's Studies in many countries show, what is not counted can be closed. There is a serious threat to critical thought posed by marketised higher educational system (Webster, 2004); it is a challenge Equality Studies has to confront. However, history is there to be made; it is not pre-given. Being aware of the dangers and challenges facing the project is a key factor in survival and progression.

Facing up to regulation and counting

By definition, the Equality Studies Centre and the School of Social Justice have to be socially engaged. Their work has a public dimension in terms of research partnerships and in terms of researching with and educating those who work in social movements for social justice. Yet, if academic productivity is being measured by a narrowly construed bibliometric test, public service engagement is precluded. The devaluing of dialogue with persons and bodies other than academics effectively privatises learning among those who are paid-up members of the academic community, whether as students or academics. The lack of dialogue with publics, apart from one's peers, also forecloses the opportunity to have hypotheses tested or challenged from an experiential standpoint. It limits the opportunities for learning that occur when there is a dialogue between experiential and theoretical knowledge.

There is a strange irony in a narrowly framed peer review system focused on bibliometric measurement as it provides disincentives to challenge ill-informed absolutisms and orthodoxies. In effect, there is no incentive to publicly dissent or engage within the very institutions that are charged with the task of dissent and engagement. The reward system of academic life means that the 'good' academic is encouraged to become a locally silent academic in their own country, silent in the public sphere and silent by virtue of dialoguing only with academic peers outside one's own country. This silencing is also a product of the positive/normative split and the pressure on academics to eschew normative values if they are to demonstrate their credibility as legitimate scientists. Challenging the silencing is part of the struggle.

Conclusion

The intellectual independence of the university is always at risk, given its reliance on external funding. Yet the history of the university grants it the capability to reclaim its own independence (Delanty, 2001).

Rather than being bewildered and overwhelmed by neo-liberal rhetoric we need to re-envisage and re-invent the university as a place of scholarly work, grounded in the principles of democracy and equality that are at the heart of the public education tradition (Harkavy, 2006). And we need to re-emerge from the careerism and docility that are so much a feature of the neo-liberal university to do this (Davies *et al.*, 2006). All of this means that we must reassess our position as critical intellectuals and face up to the limitations of the positive–normative divide (Sayer, 2006), especially in the analysis of injustices.

We must also allow space for the subaltern to emerge, both across and within disciplines, so that the professional aspects of disciplines do not blind us to the need for engagement with the most significant issues of our time (Buroway, 2004). Creating space in the university for scholarship on equality and social justice demands that we learn through dialogue with experiential knowledge holders. Those with experiential knowledge of injustice have much to teach us as theorists and researchers, and through education and research the university can in turn re-resource activists. Engaging in a dialogue means democratising the social relations of teaching, learning and exchange. While the project is a long-term one, and the revolution is forever in process, it is worth the challenge.

Notes

1   This paper is really a collective effort. We would not have had the time to write it without the support and care of our colleagues in the Equality Studies Centre. Sincere thanks to John Baker, Sara Cantillon, Judy Walsh, Pauline Faughnan, Maureen Lyons, Elizabeth Hassell and Phyllis Murphy.

2   A call to colleagues in 2004 to create a university network committed to research and teaching on social justice led to a positive response from almost a hundred academics across all colleges of the university and the setting up of the EWI (www.ucd.ie/ewi). Since 2005, we have been offering undergraduate students across the University modules on various social justice themes, and all of these courses are well subscribed. We are planning to have a full undergraduate degree in Social Justice within the next 3–5 years.

3   While we are not as yet required to be entirely self-financing (although this is quite likely in the future, given marketisation) we are, and have been, subjected to constant financial monitoring. We have survived because our student intake has been good. One reason intake is good is because we do much of our teaching in the late afternoon and evening, to facilitate part-time Masters and PhD students. We also give a lot of attention to the quality of our teaching, engaging in regular dialogue with students. Our survival was also greatly enhanced by a bequest from a philanthropist, Atlantic Philanthropies, first in the late 1990s when they gave us funding to write *Equality: from theory to action* (Baker *et al.*, 2004), and secondly when they funded a chair in Equality Studies in 2003. This funding gave us legitimacy as well as money.

4   We had been quite successful in bringing in students and getting research funding; our marketability was part of our survival strategy.

5   We proposed new courses and programmes; first an M.Sc. and Graduate Diploma in Equality Studies, in the late 1980s and 1990, which naturally evolved to a Ph.D., a Certificate programme, in 1994, and most recently, in 2005, undergraduate optional courses available to all university students in Equality Studies, Women's Studies and Social Justice. We also established new structures (working groups in 1987, centres in 1990 and networks, the EWI in 2005).

6   There are 5.5 full-time permanent academics and researchers in Equality Studies, representing five different fields of study: economics, law, political philosophy, sociology and education. There is also a part-time permanent post held by the Outreach Co-ordinator and a range of Marie Curie Fellows, Researchers and Post-Doctoral Fellows whose positions are funded by research grants.

7   At a college meeting in spring 2008, the vice-president for research (who has a medical background) at UCD referred to the non-traditional subjects in the university as 'funny degrees'.

8   The UCD logo is '*Ad Astra Cothromh Féinne*', which means literally 'reaching for excellence (the stars) and working for the entire community'.

9   While a few individual staff from former centres and departments did want to join Social Justice, they were strongly encouraged by the university to accept the majority decision.

10 The place where this was forcibly articulated was at a meeting two colleagues and the first author were called to attend on 19 July 2005. The meeting was called on the pretext that it was to help us work out a framework for developing the EWI network within the College. It turned out to be an ad hoc meeting, chaired by the head of the College of Human Sciences and attended by three professors and some lecturers, all of whom made it clear they were opposed to the work in the EWI and the new School of Social Justice. We were informed that we were 'politicising the university' and 'bringing it into disrepute'. Those present had copies of letters in hand that they had sent to the senior management of the University, making formal complaints, but we were not allowed to see them.

References

Apple, M.W. (2007) 'Social movements and political practice in education', *Theory and Research in Education* 5(2): 161–171.

Baker, J., Lynch, K., Cantillon, S. and Walsh, J. (2004) *Equality: from theory to action*, London: Palgrave Macmillan.

Boden, R. and Epstein, D. (2006) 'Managing the research imagination? Globalisation and research in higher education', *Globalisation, Societies and Education* 4(2): 223–236.

Bok, D. (2003) *Universities in the marketplace: the commercialization of higher education*, Princeton, NJ: Princeton University Press.

Boltanski, L. and Chiapello, E. (2007) *The new spirit of capitalism*, London: Verso.

Burawoy, M. (2005) '2004 American Sociological Association Presidential Address: For public sociology', *The British Journal of Sociology* 56(2): 259–294.

Castells, M. (2000) *The rise of the network society*, 2nd edn, Williston, VT: Blackwell Publishing.

Davies, B., Gottsche, M. and Bansel, P. (2006) 'The rise and fall of the neo-liberal university', *European Journal of Education* 41(2): 305–319.

Delanty, G. (2001) 'The university in the knowledge society', *Organization* 8(2): 149–153.

Dill, David D. and Soo, M. (2005) 'Academic quality, league tables and public policy: a cross national analysis of university ranking systems', *Higher Education* 49: 495–533.

Freire, P. (1972) *Pedagogy of the oppressed*, London: Penguin.

Giroux, H. (2002) 'Neoliberalism, corporate culture and the promise of higher education: the university as a democratic public sphere', *Harvard Educational Review* 72(4): 1–31.

Hanlon, G. (2000) 'Sacking the New Jerusalem? The new right, social democracy and professional identities', *Sociological Research Online* 5(1). Available online at www.socresonline.org.uk/5/1/hanlon.html.

Harding, S. (1991) *Whose science? Whose knowledge?*, Milton Keynes: Open University Press.

Harkavy, I. (2006) 'The role of the universities in advancing citizenship and social justice in the 21st century', *Education, Citizenship and Social Justice* 5: 5–37.

Harvey, David (2005) *A brief history of neoliberalism*, Oxford: Oxford University Press.

Henkel, M. (1997) 'Academic values and the university as corporate enterprise', *Higher Education Quarterly* 51(2): 134–143.

Lynch, K. (1995) 'Equality and resistance in higher education', *International Studies in Sociology of Education* 5(1): 93–111.

—— (1999) 'Equality studies, the academy and the role of research in emancipatory social change', *The Economic and Social Review* 30(1): 41–69.

Marginson, S. (2006) 'Dynamics of global competition in higher education', *Higher Education* 52(1): 1–39.

Martinelli, A. (2008) 'Sociology in political practice and public discourse', *Current Sociology* 56(3): 361–370.

Morley, L. (1999) *Organising feminisms: the micropolitics of the academy*, Basingstoke: Macmillan.

Nowotny, H., Scott, P. and Gibbons, M. (2001) *Re-thinking science*, Cambridge: Polity Press.

Oliver, M. (1992) 'Changing the social relations of research production', *Disability and Society* 7(2): 101–114.

Reay, D. (2004) 'Cultural capitalists and academic habitus: classed and gendered labour in higher education, *Women's Studies International Forum* 27(1): 31–39.

Rutherford, J. (2005) 'Cultural studies in the corporate university', *Cultural Studies* 19(3): 297–317.

Saunderson, W. (2002) 'Women, academia and identity: constructions of equal opportunities in 'new managerialism', *Higher Education Quarterly* 56(4): 376–406.

Sayer, A. (2006) 'Language and significance or the importance of import', *Journal of Language and Politics* 5(3): 449–471.

Slaughter, S. and Rhoades, G. (2004) *Academic capitalism in the new economy*, Baltimore, MD: John Hopkins University Press.

Steier, F.S. (2003) 'The changing nexus: tertiary education institutions, the marketplace and the state, *Higher Education Quarterly* 57(2): 158–180.

Thompson, J.B. (1990) *Ideology and modern culture*, Cambridge: Polity.

Tilly, C. (1998) *Durable inequality*, Berkeley, CA: University of California Press.

Webster, F. (2004) 'Cultural studies and sociology at and after the closure of the Birmingham School', *Cultural Studies* 18(6): 847–862.

27

Educational organizations and gender in times of uncertainty

Jill Blackmore

In this chapter I identify and elaborate, from a feminist perspective, upon the theoretical shifts and key concepts that inform sociological analyses of gender and educational organizations.

> Gender inequalities are embedded in the multi-dimensional structure of relationships between women and men, which, as the modern sociology of gender shows, operates at every level of experience, from economic arrangements, culture and the state to inter-personal relationships and individual emotions.
>
> (Connell, 2005: 1801)

Even naming this a sociology of gender and organizations is problematic. Many sociologists consider gender as a key sociological concept, but not necessarily from a feminist perspective. Feminism is a multidisciplinary, transnational movement that 'focuses on the relationship between social movements, political action and social inequalities' (Arnot, 2002: 3) and on the everyday experiences of women and girls and how they translate into social and structural 'ruling relations' (Smith, 1988). Feminism takes on multiple trajectories and imperatives in different cultural contexts, although with familial resemblances, most particularly the shared objective of equality for women and girls. Education as a primary institution of individual and collective mobility and social change, but also social and economic reproduction, has long been a focus of feminist theory and activism. So a feminist sociology needs to address this complexity of feminist sociological 'encounters' with gender and organizations.

Gendering organizations

Within the field of sociology of education there are multiple perspectives about how gender is understood in relation to organizations, both informing but also informed by feminist theories and activism. Each perspective, itself a product of particular historical conditions, draws on particular notions of the relationships between structures, agency and social change.

Organizations as gender neutral

Sociologists regard education and the family as the primary socialization institutions. A dominant perspective embedded in sociology, characterized by large-scale statistical analyses, is that gender is a 'fixed category', one of multiple input or output factors such as class, race and ethnicity that can be 'controlled' statistically to determine their 'effects' in causal relationships; for example, controlling for class and race to measure the differential effects of gender on educational achievement. Within this frame, organizations such as schools and universities tend to be treated as culturally and gender neutral 'black boxes'. The pedagogical frame is developmental and psychological, premised upon the notion of the formation of the unitary individual who emerges fully formed. Power works through hierarchy and structures, and knowledge derives out of well-defined Enlightenment disciplines that privilege 'hard' science over the 'soft' humanities, with an implicit masculine/feminine binary.

Well into the twentieth century, organizations were seen to have functional relationships in relation to the wider economy and society, responding to external social, economic and political pressures. Human relations and marketing were marginal concerns of executives. Education remained a relatively distinctive field of policy, practice and professionalism, offering secure careers for men and later women. Schools and universities were viewed as discrete units, tightly or loosely coupled, respectively, to centralist and hierarchical government bureaucracies with a strong public service orientation. Wider socio-economic contexts tended to be either ignored or treated as backdrops. Class was equated to occupational status, and women's class was linked to a male relative. Within the reproductive framework of socialization into sex roles, the gender division of labour in educational organizations in which men lead and women teach is 'normalized' because it replicates the 'natural' gender division of labour within the family and society. Gender difference is either equated to biologically determined sex- and gender-specific psychological attributes, or gender is ignored altogether through the universalizing discourse of the neutered 'individual'. Such perspectives provide little capacity to understand social, organizational or gender change.

This notion of organizations as gender neutral meant gender emerged analytically as either an individual psychological attribute or a statistical variable explaining differential outcomes. It continues in much contemporary school effects, school improvement and school effectiveness literature. Gender neutrality is embedded in the corporate and human resource management literature of the new public administration, which penetrated public services during the 1990s, supported by human capital theory, which underpins contemporary education policy. Discourses of school choice and lifelong learning, for example, presume individuals are self-maximizing autonomous choosers, ignoring how 'human capital' is embodied and mobilized within unequal power relations (Leathwood and Francis, 2006). Women quickly find out in the workplace that they are less rewarded than men for equivalent if not greater educational achievement. Equal opportunity policies within this frame seek, through procedural justice, to gain for women and girls equal access to male-dominated organizations. The under-representation of women in leadership is treated as an issue of workplace planning and structural barriers, the lack of a pool of eligible women, or women's lack of skills or career aspirations. Upskilling women is the solution. The focus of this perspective is on problem solving from within the frame of the status quo of organizations, whether bureaucratic or corporate.

The sociocultural turn

The new sociology of education informed by and informing critical and feminist theory emerged from the social movements of the 1970s. Sociocultural perspectives argue that knowledge, organizations and gender are socially constructed. Gender identity is therefore not physically or epistemologically predetermined, thus moving beyond the biological determinism of sex role and socialization theory. From this perspective, gender, as race in critical race theory, is no longer 'fixed', but is constitutive of identity, wider societal relations and organizational life (Ladson Billings, 2004). Organizational structures, knowledges and practices, are socially constructed in ways that, because of historical power inequalities, disadvantage most women and advantage most men. This shift from individual and structural factors to sociocultural accounts of organizations focuses on culture, collective identity, values and the symbolic. Notions of organizational culture inform change theory and explain why policies do not produce the effects intended. But culture within conventional educational administration is presumed to be unitary and homogenous, encapsulated in the notion of 'the way we do things around here', something that could be measured, created, manipulated and managed by leaders and aligned with organizational ends (Blackmore, 1999). Gender, race and other forms of difference are ignored, marginalized or to be assimilated.

Feminist sociocultural theories of organization arose out of the 1980s' politics of identity, when marginalized groups sought recognition. Schools and universities are seen to be sites of collective and individual identity formation and contested cultural meaning, with dominant and subjugated knowledges. Earlier critiques link patriarchy to capitalism and analysed how bureaucracies subjugated women's knowledge and experience. Feminist standpoint theory (Smith, 1988) continues to analyse, from the position of women, the unequal 'ruling relations' of power/knowledge/gender embedded in organizational practices, texts and structures, as indicated by who does what work, how it is valued and who gets rewarded. This analytical focus on the sociocultural explains the ongoing resistance of men *and* of organizational practices to gender equity reform, because gender works through the relationships, symbols, values and artefacts of organizational life. It explains the real and symbolic power of masculinist cultures and images of leadership and the ongoing endurance of particular notions of leadership (Blackmore, 1999; Shakeshaft, 1987). The notion of dominant, marginalized or subordinate subcultures explains why women feel excluded, for example, from leadership, but also recognizes that there are spaces of resistance to the dominant by subcultures of students, women and ethnic/linguistic minorities.

Sociocultural accounts focus on the social relations of gender explicated by Connell (1987), who argues that, in each site, there are patterns of social relations, structures and practices that are gendered and 'systematically important' to organizations.

> Compact formal organizations like schools perhaps have particularly clear *gender regimes*, but others have them too. Diffuse institutions like markets, large and sprawling ones like the state, and informal milieux like street corner peer-group life also are structures in terms of gender and can be characterised by their gender regimes.
>
> (Connell, 1987: 120)

Thus different masculinities and femininities are constituted in relation to each other – hegemonic masculinities (managerial, working class) maintain their hegemonic power in particular organizational contexts by positioning as weaker and lesser other masculinities (homosexual) and all femininities (emphasized, butch . . .). Hegemonic masculinities are mobilized, for example, around notions of the rational, unemotional and strong leader, while depicting women leaders as irrational, emotional and lacking in the capacity to make hard decisions. This institutionalized gender regime within schools and universities is reinforced by the *gender order* of society and other institutional practices, including the family, religion and the state (Connell, 1987: 137–139).

Understanding organizations as contested cultures and products of the historical legacy of male heterosexual privilege provides more nuanced understandings about the failure of imposed organizational reforms, including gender equity. It explains how resistance to gender reform by many men and some women derives from their personal and collective investments in particular gender identities that provide a secure sense of self and that benefit from the existing gender regime. For example, men are usually advantaged in the workplace by women's part-time work in the caring professions and the devaluing of unpaid domestic labour. A sociocultural perspective recognizes that multiple versions of organizational life and subjugated knowledges exist that differ from the dominant corporate story and prescriptive gender scripts. Equity policies from this frame seek to make the cultures of educational organizations more inclusive, not only through greater representation of women but also by changing practices and values.

Postmodern organizational complexity and gender subjectivities

The context of educational organizations during the 1990s was one of rapid and radical change, restructuring, neo-liberal ideologies and a growing sense of precarious employment. The political and epistemological context was that of the politics of difference which highlighted the intersectionality of difference – gender, race, class and ethnicity – as Black feminists challenged White middle-class feminists' privileging of gender (Mirza, 1993). Post-structuralism posits the view that gender, as race and class, is part of a wider set of discursive relations that position individuals in particular ways within specific contexts. The self is here constituted as multiple subjectivities, in a constant state of being and becoming. Contradiction, dissonance and ambiguity are the norm both within oneself, but also within organizations and life in general. Notions of 'positionality' and 'subjectivity' foreground the complexity, for example, of being female, Black and an educational leader (Davies and Harré, 2000). The unitary developmental subject of modernist educational discourses is thus supplanted by forms of subjectivity that are fluid and hybrid, in a state of ongoing production through biography inflected by race, class, gender, culture and sexuality (McLeod and Yates, 2006).

Educational organizations are therefore seen to be part of a process of subjectification that provides both constraints and possibilities, as no outcomes are closed. Schools, universities and other educational organizations such as technical institutes and workplace training are sites where gender and other forms of difference are (re)constituted through multiple, often contradictory discourses (women are now equal but individual women do not feel that, girls' success and boys' underachievement) and texts (assessment, curriculum, promotion, equal opportunity policies) that mediate social relations (Skelton and Francis, 2004). Organizational life is seen to be open to flows of meaning, bringing a sense of ambiguity, ambivalence and uncertainty. How difference works in and through organizations is highly 'situated', with institutional and cross-sectoral differences. Gendered subjectivities are constantly remade through discourse that positions individuals differentially. Sometimes race, sometimes language and sometimes gender are foregrounded. Power works in organizations, from this perspective, in a decentred and diffuse manner through discourse, in ways that are both productive and oppressive of particular gendered subjectivities. Thus, women in leadership can feel simultaneously powerful and powerless. Post-structuralist perspectives see women and girls having agency owing to their capacity to mobilize particular discourses to their own benefit, while not ignoring their vulnerability and 'othering' due to wider power/knowledge relations. Here organizational change is depicted as unpredictable, chaotic and multifaceted. It also means that individual and group narratives of organizational life are always partial, as is the corporate meta-narrative produced through policy, strategic plans and mission statements.

Post-structuralist analyses of organizations also highlight the discursive and performative aspects of organizational life arising in the context of devolved modes of governance, marketization and managerialism (Blackmore and Sachs, 2007). They explore how the 'performative' is reworking the social relations of gender to (re)produce new entrepreneurial, transnational masculinities and self-managing worker-identities (Connell, 2005). Critical perspectives focus on the multiple representation of the body and how organizations are sites of competing sexualities, thus critiquing organizational theory for its dominant (white) hetereosexuality (Young and Sklra, 2003).

> Gendered organizations thus do not 'exist' as such; rather they are performed moment by moment through the communicative practices of their members. While such performances usually do not unfold capriciously, but rather, follow well-established scripts, it is still only in the doing – the performing – that such scripts are produced, reproduced, resisted, and transformed.
>
> (Aschraft and Mumby, 2004: 116)

Power is decentred and diffuse as it works through discourse. And feminists themselves can produce normative policy discourses that are counterproductive. For example, essentializing discourses about women's styles of leadership denies political, racial, ethnic or linguistic differences among women (Reay and Ball, 2000). Backlash discourses about recuperative masculinities meanwhile position women as advantaged (Lingard, 2003). Furthermore, studies of educational restructuring and organizational reform identify how embedded practices (redeployment, restructuring, outsourcing, downsizing) produce structural backlash (Blackmore, 1999). The message here is that 'gender inequalities can be subtle, elusive, and normalized via everyday practices such as networking and the construction of identities and opportunities' (Husu and Morley, 2000: 2).

Diversity and difference: hybridity and boundaryless organizations

Post-colonialism now troubles West-centric ways of thinking post 9/11. The global context is one of rapid flows of people, goods, ideas, money and images, producing greater cultural diversity in student populations, a diversity not represented in the dominant 'whiteness' of the education workforce and leadership. The context is of heightened uncertainty, high risk and low trust organizations, with schools and universities constantly restructuring to address market forces. Post-colonial theory views educational organizations within Western colonizing and settler nation-states (UK, USA, Australia, Canada and New Zealand) and post-colonial nation-states (e.g. India, Mexico) as sites reconstituting, through the processes of assimilation/ internationalization/entrepreneurialism, neo-colonial relations in ways that simultaneously protect/reinvent/destroy traditional cultures. Neo-colonialsm is also linked to the commodification of educational goods and services through the processes of westernization/internationalization, both desired and resisted in post-colonial states and by international students, such as the universalizing, seemingly neutral curriculum of the International Baccalaureate. Post-colonial theorists interrogate the Eurocentrism and whiteness embedded in organizational theory and promoted by transnational management experts in terms of theories of change, motivation and values. They unpack the discourses that view non-Whites as 'the other' (Prasad and Prasad, 2002). Meanwhile, diasporic communities in Western nation-states seek to transplant/reinvent/ negotiate traditional cultures locally, mobilizing through neo-liberal policies of privatization and school choice a trend towards institutionalizing difference (gender, class, religion, ethnicity) through schooling.

These processes of internationalization and entrepreneurialism are also gendered. On the one hand, sociologists focus on the hybridity of culture and cosmopolitan identities in the context of multiple organizational formations and public/private mixes, and in so doing frequently assume the gender-neutral subject (Stromquist and Monkman, 2000). On the other hand, women are seen to carry culture symbolically in their daily lives and transnationally, as well as within and between educational organizations (Mabokela, 2007). Protecting women is readily equated to protecting tradition and culture, as if gender and culture are fixed. Certainly, for many indigenous and ethnic minority women in White-dominated educational organizations, gender is less significant relative to race, ethnicity or religion (Optlaka and Hertz-Lazarowitz, 2006). Such women leading educational organizations are positioned within multiple contradictions: due to their lack of whiteness in White-dominated environments and the expectation that they represent traditional culture, or that they 'bridge' two cultures between White and 'the other', between school and community (Fitzgerald, 2006). Indigenous feminists point to how Western notions of leadership fail to address the mutuality of two-way learning or connectedness to land, and how organizational structures refuse to provide more than symbolic partnerships with community (Ah Nee-Benham, 2002; Battiste, 2005). Muslim feminists point to how religion and gender interplay to maintain traditional masculinities within diasporic communities, and highlight the complexities for women leaders in religious states, universities and schools where faith is central to education (Shah, 2006). For women in more traditional societies, gender dominates (Luke, 2001). For Western feminists, there is also a warning. The 'civilising overtones . . . selfless and disinterested project of Western (neo)colonialism' is seen to be about 'rescuing women from particular cultural practices' with an assumed moral and cultural superiority (Prasad and Prasad, 2002).

Post-colonialist approaches of organizations therefore unpack the intersecting and contradictory but changing social relations of religion, culture, gender, race and class and how they '(re)constitute the binaries of good/evil, black/white, active/passive, centre/margins, masculine/feminine, scientific/superstitious, and secular/religious' in patterned ways that produce gender inequality (Prasad, 2002: 124).

> Gender is constitutive of organization; it is omnipresent, defining feature of collective human activity, regardless of whether the activity appears to be about gender . . . the gendering of organization involves a struggle over meaning, identity and difference . . . [and] such struggles reproduce social realities that privilege certain interests.
>
> (Ashcraft and Mumby, 2004: xv)

Contemporary issues

Any analysis of educational organizations therefore needs to consider multiple dimensions to understand the interplay of the unequal social relations of power/knowledge that articulate through context, discourse and practice: the spatial (who gets to use what spaces), temporal (how time is used), material (distribution of resources), symbolic (representations of what is valued), semiotic (language and vocabulary mobilized), cultural (narratives about who we are), aesthetic (what constitutes beauty) and the technological (who benefits). But a feminist analysis foregrounds particular issues in any organizational analysis, as indicated below.

Dualisms

Feminist perspectives explore how Enlightenment dualisms between mind/body, rational/emotional, active/passive, science/humanities and masculine/feminine continue to be reinvented in contemporary organizations through the changing social relations of gender, despite shifts in discourses and theories of gender and organizations. Organizations embody social relations, producing gendered, racialized and sexualized distinctions. The body and discourse are inseparable, as the body incorporates the rules of organizations, in terms of how individuals dress, relate, use space and time and mobilize particular gender subjectivities. Leadership foregrounds the body in terms of its sexuality, the performative aspects of organizations, as well as self-presentation. The imagery of the well-groomed (White heterosexual) male (and now female) leader who 'fits' the organizational image remains the norm against which all contenders are measured. The body is therefore central to any analysis of the disciplinary power of organizations over individuals (e.g. lesbian leaders) and populations (disabled), and how such power produces particular institutionalized and performative practices.

Furthermore, feminists have long rejected any emotional/rational distinction, arguing that leadership and teaching demand emotions such as compassion in order for decision-makers and professionals to be fully human and indeed rational. Critical management and feminist organizational theory views organizations as emotional arenas, where rapid and radical change produces the full range of emotions: grief, anger, greed, envy, frustration, fear and anxiety (Fineman, 2000). Mainstream educational theory no longer treats emotions as pathologies, feminized and something to be eradicated, having recognized the reliance in knowledge-based economies on 'human' capital and on individual and collective emotional investment(s) and social relations that oil productivity. Marketing and human relations are central executive areas of control. Emotional literacy or intelligence is now presented as another skill for leaders to acquire. Now, emotional labour and educators' passion for teaching and research are being depoliticized (Boler, 1999) and co-opted through discourses of quality by management for organizational ends (Blackmore and Sachs, 2007; Morley, 2003). But gendered emotion scripts prescribe who does what types of emotional management and how emotional displays such as crying or anger are judged differently.

Finally, educational organizations are also historically constructed around knowledge hierarchies that privilege particular versions of science over the humanities and the social, whether in school subjects or research (Brooks and MacKinnon, 2001). These gendered knowledge hierarchies continue to be reinvented through the disciplinary technologies of accountability that determine what counts, what gets counted, what gets taught and assessed, and who benefits (Morley 2003).

Context

Gender has largely been addressed in mainstream sociologies of education as an individual or group characteristic rather than as a primary organizing principle of society and the economy and the relations of ruling at the global, international, national, regional, local and institutional level. Context shapes both organizational and leadership possibilities. The nature and purpose of education are fundamentally changing under the conditions of education capitalism; at the same time, wider structural relations of national economies and markets impact on the career possibilities and work conditions in gendered ways (Deem, 1996). In educational organizations, market discourses and practices now penetrate organizational structures, cultures and values, as well as priorities. Such contexts inform institutional discourses as leaders in middle management, many of them now women, mobilize discourses of survival to gain collegial consent, often becoming reluctantly complicit in the new work order. Responsiveness to international and local education markets requires significant institutional flexibility. Accumulating evidence is charting the feminization and casualization of academic and teachers' work arising from devolved systems of educational governance and deregulated international education markets (Brine, 1999).

These trends cannot be disentangled from how education professionalism is being redefined and judged through national and international professional-standards movements and escalating national and international accountability demands for comparison. The nature of educational organizations and leadership is also under revision. Discourses of lifelong learning have encouraged a seamlessness between educational sectors to facilitate smooth pathways for students. Educational organizations are part of a 'constellation of sites, spaces and opportunities for learning' (Arnot, 2002: 258), with multiple configurations locally (multi-site campuses and community and industry partnerships) and internationally (offshore campuses). So, as education as a field is increasingly subject to markets and the economy, the profession is losing autonomy. Global relations have shifted the locus of power upwards and outwards from educational organizations owing to externally driven demands for accountability and market forces.

Reconstituting the gender division of labour: public/private

The separation of public life (masculine domain) and the private lifeworld of family and community (female domain) was a premise of the modernist educational organization (David, 2003). Historically, teaching has been positioned as the naturalized extension of mothering and therefore women's work, with 'the importing through embodied social practice over time, of cultural metaphors of domesticity from a narrowly conceived private sphere into the apparently public world of work' (Acker and Dillabough, 2007: 298–299). Teaching is recognized as feminized, but not as White. This continues with institutionalizing policies exhorting parents (women) to be partners as quasi-literacy teachers, fundraisers or governors. Now self-managing schools and universities, public and private, seek to blur the public/private distinction in order to gain greater flexibility by transferring educational labour into the home through technologies or outsourcing educational work under contractualism. So, as educational organizations move into new public/private configurations, women are more vulnerable, as they are without the mobility and flexibility of their male counterparts.

Equity

Organizational texts (policies, mission statements, performance management protocols, perform-ance indicators, curriculum, assessment) are gendered in terms of their implications for workplace arrangements (time at work, continuity of employment) and which discourses get privileged (efficiency or equity). Devolved governance in education has meant policy is now the means by which governments and executives steer from a distance. Policy is one link in the cycle of

313

performativity arising from the accountability regimes focusing on outcomes. Meanwhile, contemporary individualizing discourses of diversity that have supplanted equal opportunity weaken claims of historical group, structural and cultural, gender inequality (Bacchi, 2000).

Critical feminist policy sociologists (Marshall, 1997) identify multiple tensions around how equity policies will work. Equity practitioners in organizations still rely on the state and executives for equity policies to provide legitimation for their activities, raise expectations for changes in behaviour and offer a language for action. Already, backlash discourses cite the existence of equity policies to argue that women and girls have equality or are advantaged in education. Recognition of one form of disadvantage (class, race) does not necessarily flow over to equality of gender. Each form of disadvantage has different legacies (slavery, colonialism) and power relations. Gender equity cuts across racial, ethnic and class difference because it challenges personal and power relationships at work and in the home.

Contemporary dilemmas for feminists

Coming from a focus on gender leads to different assumptions, questions and conclusions, but also produces ongoing dilemmas for sociologists of gender and educational organizations.

Category problem

Gender continues to be a problematic sociological concept in terms of what it supplants, such as a focus on women and girls, and what it ignores, in terms of sexuality. The feminist dilemma with regard to category has been that focusing on women as a sociological concept and policy strategy has positioned women as having to change or to initiate change, while essentializing women as a group (Bacchi, 2000). It thus diverts policy and sociologists' attention away from how the social relations of gender are embedded in the structures, cultures, identities and power configurations in educational organizations, on how leadership is understood and practised, how context and culture shape organizational practices and in turn how organizations (re)constitute gender, class and race and identities. At the same time, the focus on the social relations of gender and/or gendered subjectivities means attention reverts back to men as the 'dominant' or to the individual in ways that ignore structural and cultural factors. Both facilitate the appropriation by mainstream theory of those aspects of feminist research and discourse that do not undermine its normative frame.

The politics of gender research

With the focus on text, discourse and the rejection of modernist meta-narratives, post-modernist accounts of organizations localize the politics of gender, focusing on the processes of reflexivity and individualization that can be readily appropriated by neo-liberal discourses of the gender-neutral individual (Bauman, 2005). Materialist accounts consider this refusal to universalize endangers the feminist political project of social justice (Unterhalter, 2006). Post-structuralism's focus on situated gendered subjectivities, like the socio-cultural focus on women and leadership, has diverted attention away from the structural: that is, the reconstitution of gender relations occurring through the restructuring of educational organizations during the 1990s due to neo-liberal reforms of marketization and managerialism (Brine, 1999; Blackmore and Sachs, 2007).

A number of issues for inquiry arise from the above:

- How are shifts in educational governance from the bureaucratic to the corporate and now the networked organization impacting on women's capacity and/or desire to be leaders, policy actors or practitioners?
- How are the social relations of gender being reconstituted through the structures, processes, practices and cross-cultural relations of the networked organization, locally, nationally and transnationally?
- Are the global policy communities of the OECD, World Bank, UNESCO new sites for mobile transnational masculinities, while women remain as leaders of the domestic (national and local) in a reconfigured gender division of labour?
- Are men benefiting more from new public/private configurations, such as innovation centres in new knowledge economies and internationalization (Metcalfe and Slaughter, 2008)?
- How are neo-colonial masculinities in leadership – traditional and progressive – being reconstituted within different national contexts – religious nation-states, diasporic communities in Western nation-states?
- How to unpack and investigate the more 'subtle gender differentiation' that occurs in organizations and through discourses of individual choice and diversity?
- How to generalize across organizations owing to the complexities of articulation of gender, race, class and religion in specific institutional locations?
- As the role of the state changes with the emergence of regional polities and global policy communities, how will gender equity policy be mobilized, conceptualized and delivered in local educational organizations?
- What theoretical, ethical and methodological issues does this raise in terms of a feminist comparative sociology of organizations?

Conclusion

Discourses in Western societies are about post-feminism. Women and girls are disappearing as a sociological category of inequality in educational research and policy, with the focus on boys' underachievement and discourses of diversity. Yet women do not feel equal; either their progress into the executive level of organizations has stalled, or the locus of organizational power has moved beyond the organization. In developing nation-states, women and children are the losers owing to war, migration, unemployment, famine and global warming. Gender as a sociological category is increasingly complex in terms of how it relates to culture, context and educational organizations. So the question for feminist sociologists and policy activists is how to address this complexity of social and structural differentiation and patterned inequality.

References

Acker, S. and Dillabough, J. (2007) 'Women "learning to labour" in the "male emporium": exploring gendered work in teacher education', *Gender and Education* 19: 297–316.
Ah Nee-Benham, M. (2002) 'An alternative perspective of educational leadership for change: reflections on Native/indigenous ways of knowing', in K. Leithwood (ed.) *Second international handbook of educational leadership and administration*, Netherlands: Kluwer.

Arnot, M. (2002) *Reproducing Gender. Essays on educational theory and feminist politics*, Routledge: London.

Ashcraft, K. and Mumby, D. (2004) *Reworking gender: a feminist communicology of organization*, Thousand Oaks, CA: Sage.

Bacchi, C. (2000) 'The see-saw effect: down goes affirmative action, up comes workplace diversity', *Journal of Interdisciplinary Gender Studies* 5(2): 65–83.

Battiste, M. (2005) 'Leadership and aboriginal education in contemporary education: narratives of cognitive imperialism reconciling with decolonization', in J. Collard and C. Reynolds (eds) *Leadership, gender and culture in education. Male and female perspectives*, Buckingham: Open University Press.

Bauman, Z. (2005) 'Education in liquid modernity', *The Review of Education* 27: 303–317.

Blackmore, J. (1999) *Troubling women: feminism, leadership and educational change*, Buckingham: Open University Press.

—— and Sachs, J. (2007) *Performing and reforming leaders. Gender, educational restructuring and organizational change*, New York: SUNY Press

Boler, M. (1999) *Feeling power. Emotions and education*, London: Routledge.

Brine, J. (1999) *underEducating women: globalising inequality*, Buckingham: Open University Press.

Brooks, A. and McKinnon, A. (2001) *Gender and the restructured university*, Philadelphia, PA: Open University Press.

Connell, R.W. (1987) *Gender and power*, Sydney: Allen & Unwin.

—— (2005) 'Change among the gatekeepers: men masculinities and gender equity in the global arena', *Signs* 30: 1801–1825.

David, M. (2003) *Personal and political: feminisms, sociologies and family lives*, Stoke on Trent: Trentham.

Davies, B. and Harré, R. (1990) 'Positioning: the discursive production of selves', *Journal of the Theory of Social Behaviour* 20: 43–65.

Deem, R. (1996) 'Border territories: a journey through sociology, education and women's studies', *British Journal of Sociology of Education* 17(1): 5–20.

Fineman, S. (2000) *Emotions and organizations*, Thousand Oaks, CA: Sage.

Fitzgerald, T. (2006) 'Walking between two worlds: indigenous women and educational leadership', *Educational Management, Administration and Leadership* 34(2): 201–214.

Husu, L. and Morley, L. (2000) 'Academe and gender: what has and has not changed?', *Higher Education in Europe* 25(2): 2–4.

Ladson-Billings, G. (2004) 'Just what is critical race theory and what is it doing in a *nice* field like education?', in G. Ladson-Billings and D. Gillborn (eds) *The RoutledgeFalmer reader in multicultural education*, London: RoutledgeFalmer.

Leathwood, C. and Francis, B. (2006) *Gender and lifelong learning: critical feminist engagements*, London: Routledge.

Lingard, B. (2003) 'Where to in gender policy in education after recuperative masculinity politics?', *International Journal of Inclusive Education* 7(1): 33–56.

Luke, C. (2001) *Globalisation and women in academia: North/West-South/East*, Mahwah, NJ: Lawrence Erlbaum.

Mabokela, R. (ed.) (2007) *Soaring beyond boundaries: women breaking educational barriers in traditional societies*, Rotterdam: Sense Publishers.

McLeod, J. and Yates, L. (2006) *Making modern lives. Subjectivity, schooling and social change*, New York: SUNY Press.

Marshall, C. (1997) *Feminist critical policy analysis*, Vols. 1 and 2, London: Falmer Press.

Metcalfe, A. and Slaughter, S. (2008) 'The differential effects of academic capitalism on women in the academy', in J. Glazer-Raymo (ed.) *Unfinished agendas. New and continuing gender challenges in higher education*, Baltimore, MD: Johns Hopkins Press.

Mirza, H. (1993) 'The social construction of Black womanhood in British educational research: towards a new understanding', in M. Arnot and K. Weiler (eds) *Feminism and social justice*, London: Falmer Press.

Morley, L. (2003) *Quality and power in higher education*, Buckingham: Open University Press.

Optlaka, I. and Hertz-Lazarowitz, R. (eds) (2006) *Women principals in a multicultural society. New insights into feminist educational leadership*, Rotterdam: Sense Publishers.

Prasad, A. and Prasad, P. (2002) 'Otherness at large: identity and difference in the new globalised organizational landscape', in I. Aaltio and A. Mills (eds) *Gender, identity, and culture in organizations*, London: Routledge.

Reay, D. and Ball, S. (2000) 'Essentials of female management: women's ways of working in the education market place?', *Educational Management & Administration* 28(2): 145–159.

Shah, S. (2006) 'Educational leadership: an Islamic perspective', *British Educational Research Journal* 32(3): 347–363.

Shakeshaft, C. (1987) *Women in educational administration*, Newbury Park, CA: Sage.

Skelton, C. and Francis, B. (eds) (2004) *A feminist critique of education: 15 years of gender education*, London: Routledge.

Smith, D. (1988) *The everyday world as problematic. A feminist sociology*, New York: Open University Press.

Stromquist, N. and Monkman, K. (eds) (2000) *Globalisation and education. Integration and contestation across cultures*, New York: Rowman & Littlefield.

Unterhalter, E. (2006) *Gender, schooling and global social justice*, London: Routledge

Young, M. and Skrla L. (eds) (2003) *Reconsidering. Feminist research in educational leadership*, New York: SUNY Press

28

Bringing Bourdieu to 'widening participation' policies in higher education
A UK case analysis

Pat Thomson

This chapter examines an apparent 'policy failure'. It compares a statistically oriented policy narrative of increasing access to higher education with its representations in media. It then mobilizes the sociological approach of Pierre Bourdieu to sketch an alternative analysis of events. This analysis demonstrates how mobilizing Bourdieu's approach situates the case in a broad historical and social context, elaborates the connections between related events in different sectors of education, and makes clear what is at stake in polarized debates. And, while the context and data are drawn from the UK, and England in particular, this Bourdieuian framing suggests that, while the actual details of these events are specific in space/place/time, the 'logic of practice' at work is much more widely generalizable.

The case in point centres on struggles around access, entry and participation. Statistics on UK university entrance[1] are unequivocal: not only has the percentage of young people who go onto higher education (HE) remained relatively static, but those who gain entry are more often from middle-class and very wealthy families (Archer *et al.*, 2003; Galindo-Rueda *et al.*, 2004). Furthermore, the more elite universities have disproportionate numbers of already advantaged young people. Yet paradoxically, the percentage of young people getting 'good results' in school exams has increased.

In 1999, the UK government decided that 50 per cent of all young people would be enrolled in HE by 2010, an ambitious 11 per cent increase within a decade. This target was accompanied by a funding programme designed to help universities 'widen participation' by opening their doors to young people whose families did not have a tradition of university education. Named *Aimhigher*, the policy rhetorically designated the 'problem' of low participation to lack of aspiration among individual young people from homes assigned by government's statistics to 'lower socio-economic' categories (Thomas, 2001). The policy 'solution' was for universities to work together with schools with low participation rates to motivate students to become 'non-traditional' university entrants. The government also sought to increase the 'flow' into higher and further education by strongly encouraging schools to support the majority of young people to stay on until the end of formal schooling.

This agenda was only minimally successful. In 2008, official figures revealed that the HE participation rates among 17–30-year-olds had risen by just 0.6 per cent between 1999–2000 and 2006–2007, from 39.2 per cent to 39.8 per cent. The political opposition made much of this slow progress, suggesting that, at this rate, it would take to 2124 to achieve the stated target. Government ministers admitted the target was impossible, but argued that they never thought it was realistic and that their focus had recently shifted from the under 30s to the workforce as a whole.[2] Policy debates are now focused either on how to find the appropriate combination of carrots and sticks that will create further change, while moving away from the unreachable target (government), or blaming the very idea and the means by which it has been implemented (opposition).

Higher education access in the news

In the UK, summer is not just a time for holidays. It is also when exam results are anticipated and released, and, thus, there is typically more – and more polarized – public discussion about HE entry and the state of upper secondary education. Debates focus on both A levels, the 'gate-keeping qualifications' offered by schools, and the access and equity approaches taken by universities. I discuss each in turn, giving some examples of the kinds of media coverage that they warrant. These are taken from a corpus of UK print media reports collected between June and September 2008: items were selected because they are 'typical' of particular discursive positions (Thomas, 2006).

Debates about school qualifications

Media narratives suggest that concerns about school qualifications are extensive and include: the kinds of knowledge that are valued; 'problems' for universities in discriminating between the increasing number of young people with the same grades; and escalating efforts by schools – and young people themselves – to mark themselves out in the competition for university places and courses. This is somewhat different from the policy debate reported in the introduction. There are many 'takes' on these issues but three of the most prominent are:

1   Not everyone wants to go to university: In 2005 the government announced that it would introduce fourteen new vocational diplomas rather than replace A levels with a single new qualification that included both 'academic' and 'vocational' options.[3] Since then, there has been speculation about whether universities would accept the new qualifications as valid preparation for HE entrance, and whether this meant the 'end' of the A level as the 'gold standard' of quality. In August 2008,[4] the release of detailed government information about the new vocational diplomas brought accusations of vast exaggerations of the economic payoffs of undertaking vocational education (*Times Higher Education*, 7 August 2008) and a rejoinder from Education Secretary Ed Balls that A levels are 'not set in stone' (*Daily Telegraph*, 13 September 2008).

2   A levels are seriously flawed: At the same time, it was widely reported that increasing numbers of young people were achieving 'good' A levels, but this was not necessarily a cause for celebration. The *Education Guardian* (12 August 2008: 1) put it this way:

> Since 2000, the proportion of A levels awarded an A grade in England has shot up from 17.8% to 25.3%. It's been asked before, but let's ask it again: does this mean today's pupils are better prepared for summer exams or cleverer than they used to be? Or do markers perhaps expect less than they did in the past and mark more generously?

Newspapers made much of the alleged increase in the numbers of 'A' grades awarded, with accounts varying from one in seven, to one in ten and even 3 per cent (*Times Higher Education*, 21 August 2008: 5). Concerns about grade inflation were directed to three subjects in particular – drama, sociology and media studies. There were suggestions that 'easy' marking in these subjects allowed students to gain higher scores than their peers in science, technology and mathematics: students undertaking these courses had an 'unfair' advantage in the competition for access to university places.

There were also numerous reports about marking. While there was nothing like the spectacular failure of Educational Testing Services, the contractor who failed to deliver accurate and timely test results for the basic skills tests administered to pupils in the compulsory years of schooling,[5] there were reports that,

> some schools now routinely query a large proportion of their results in the hope of pushing up grades. Marsha Elms, headteacher of Kendrick girl's school in Reading, says the problem is not just with A levels: there is increasing concern about exam marking in general. And with new vocational qualifications about to come on stream, she fears the quality of markers may deteriorate further. 'I think the system is so stretched that we are beginning to lose faith – we are increasingly asking for remarks,' she says. 'But I do also think its to do with the clientele, wanting rechecks as it becomes more difficult to get into the universities – people want Cs turned into Bs and Bs turned into As.'
>
> (*Education Guardian*, 12 August 2008: 2)

While the formation of a new exams watchdog, OfQual, is intended to shore up trust in marking, the competition for places goes further than lack of faith in examinations.

3   Students and schools have lost faith in the system: Other news reports in the same period noted that many students are opting to take four rather than three A levels in the hope of getting an edge in the competition for elite university places and courses. But,

> Geoff Parks, director of admissions at Cambridge said . . . that he hoped the introduction of the new A* grade from 2010 would reverse the trend and persuade more students to take three because the key discriminator would be quality rather than quantity.
>
> (*The Times*, 15 August, 2008)

However, 150 UK schools announced that they would abandon A levels altogether in favour of a new Pre-U exam developed by Cambridge University (THE 31/7/2008, p. 5), while a US style aptitude test, proposed by government advisers as an alternative route for disadvantaged young people into university, was reported to 'favour white boys from grammar schools' (*Times Higher Education*, 18 September 2008: 5).

Debates about university access policies

All English universities are expected to achieve the widening participation targets. Media reports largely represent their problems in doing so as concerns about funding and administrative routines for HE entry. Among the most common stories are two that say:

1   Funding is the problem: The government recently announced that it would change fund-
    ing arrangements, so that young people from the most disadvantaged backgrounds would
    attract four times rather than twice the amount of HE funding. Universities with greater
    success in attracting such students welcomed the move as it would clearly direct more
    funding their way. But universities who were less successful countered, arguing that the
    funding ought to be on the basis of need, thus giving those with already large numbers of
    'non-traditional' entrants less.

2   Universities won't do as they are told: At the same time, the intervention programme
    Aimhigher,[6] which funds universities to work with schools and colleges, was critiqued for
    being directed to the wrong sector: some HE administrators argued that the money ought
    to go to disadvantaged schools to spend 'earlier' than the final year of schooling. Their
    argument – that better preparation in the middle years of schooling is the issue, not
    lack of motivation in the senior years – was not universally accepted (a two-page debate
    appeared in *Times Higher Education*, 24 July 2008: 6–7). Print media also carried reports
    that employers questioned the value of a HE degree because of concerns about marking
    variability across universities (*Times Higher Education*, 10 July 2008), and that many
    university students were finding it increasingly difficult to pay their way through university
    (*Times Higher Education*, 7 August 2008) and to accommodate the fees debt they accrued.
    Together, these reports hinted that some young people queried the point of a university
    education and would switch to the new vocational options.

The most vitriolic debates occurred around the failure of *Aimhigher* to achieve its policy
goals. These centred on the actions of the most elite universities. The polarized debates can be
seen in the two following newspaper columns.

Extract 1

Tom Kemp, admissions tutor at St John's College, Oxford, argued that elite universities are
not biased.

> As an admissions tutor I am perfectly aware than something is amiss in the huge
> imbalance between the proportion of students admitted to Oxford from the private
> schools and the proportion of the school population so educated . . . The simple starting
> fact is that Oxford wants the brightest, most academically committed kids as its
> undergraduates. It is completely immaterial to us what gender, colour, nationality they
> are, or what their family background, sexual orientation or anything else is . . . Given all
> such information we consider, and given the huge effort put into admissions (up to four
> interviews to about four times the number of candidates to the places available) no-one
> can reasonably accuse us of not working towards being fair to all, even if we have a good
> way to go.
>
> (*Education Guardian*, 12 August 2008: 4)

Kemp argues that entry to elite universities must be on academic 'merit' and 'performance',
and that while some compensations might be made, there are limits. To do too much would
be unfair to those who have done well in their exams. By implication, Kemp sheets the problem
home to schools: if they did a better job then more young people would be 'meritorious' and
deserving of a place.

Extract 2

The Observer columnist Barbara Ellen suggests that elite universities are just not trying hard enough, and this, she suspects, is because they want to protect their 'elite' brand.

> I suppose one has to be mature and resist the natural inclination of turning this into a 'Toffs versus Plebs' stand-off. A great shame, as in many ways it's asking for it. In 2008, are we meant to tug our forelocks and accept Cambridge professor Alison Richard opining: 'it's not our place to help the poor'? And with figures revealing that 40 percent of the Oxford and Cambridge intake is from fee paying schools, when the education private sector represents only 7 percent of the nation's children? It transpires that what Richard actually said was that educational institutions should not be turned into 'handmaidens of industry, implementers of the skills agenda, or indeed engines for promoting social justice'. Which seems to be a round about way of saying that dons are genuinely concerned about the shoehorning in of state students, with a less impressive record, at the expense of undermining the world-famous Oxbridge brand.[7] All fair points, until you ask the question – whose universities are they anyway?
>
> > (*The Observer*, 14 September 2008: 11)

Ellen clearly suspects that arguments about merit are a cover-up for underhanded actions that preserve the advantages of those who are wealthy and can afford to send their children to private schools.

How are we to understand these representations of problems with higher education access?

This selection of news items shows a range of issues coalescing around who gets into which university and which course, and by what means. If we are to believe these press items, then policy failure and students' distress are not attributable to flawed policy per se, but rather to the behaviour of universities, particularly those that have greatest market share and prestige.

In the remainder of this chapter, I want to re-read HE access and participation with the help of a French social scientist, the late Pierre Bourdieu, and to argue that what is at stake *is* a question of social, political and cultural privilege, but this is *not* a question of individual people or institutions being mean, bloody-minded or insincere. Rather, it is a complex matter of the way that social systems work (Zipin, 1999). The argument that I make is intended to complement empirical studies that focus on the 'habitus' of those young people making choices about which university to attend – or not (e.g. Ball *et al.*, 2000; Reay *et al.*, 2005).

There are two important ideas that underpin the argument I will make about HE access. These are, first, the reproductive practices of education and, second, the hierarchies that exist within education. I will briefly signpost each idea in turn and then bring them to a re-reading of the HE debates presented in the first part of the chapter.

Education and the reproduction of privilege

Research has consistently demonstrated that educational success is correlated with greater wealth, levels of education and social status (Teese, 2000; Feinstein *et al.*, 2008).

Bourdieu argued that education systems were heavily implicated in this production and reproduction of social and economic privilege and disadvantage (Bourdieu and Passeron, 1977, 1979; Bourdieu *et al.*, 1995). He demonstrated that some children come from families where the kinds of knowledge and behaviour that count in schooling already exist in abundance and they are thus at an advantage from the very first time they enter the school gates. Not only do they already possess 'capitals' that are important to school success, but they also feel comfortable in the school setting and are easily able to do what is required. This does not mean that some children come from 'good homes' whereas others come from 'bad' ones with low aspirations. Nor does it mean that some schools are failing or inadequate. Rather, Bourdieu suggests that the game of schooling is deeply discriminatory: those children who arrive at school without the 'right stuff' are behind at the outset and remain so throughout their schooling.

Over time, the school pedagogies, curriculum and assessment practices exacerbate initial differences (Anyon, 1980; Haberman, 1991; Thomson, 2002). By the time children have reached the part of schooling where they must decide whether to aim for university, their decisions are nearly made by virtue of their schooling success, or lack of it. This is not a case of some young people being possessed of merit, but rather a case of schooling as a game that is heavily rigged in favour of particular kinds of children and young people. The 'achievement gap' is the result of deeply embedded and embodied structural inequalities.

It is important to recognize that Bourdieu's argument about the reproductive effects of education does not mean that all children from so-called 'deprived'/'disadvantaged' homes do badly at school and therefore none of them gets to university. Some of them do very well at school, just as some young people from privileged homes do very badly. But it is only a comparatively small number who do so. Bourdieu is frank about his own origins: he was a 'scholarship' boy, selected through the workings of the school system to become upwardly socially mobile. But he demonstrated through his academic work how in his case, and in that of others like him, 'sorting and selecting' who was educationally successful occurred in a myriad of ways, from the more obvious promotion, setting and grouping practices, through to the language of the curriculum, and the kinds of knowledge considered to be of most value (Bourdieu, 2008). Thus, his theorization of (re)production allows for both change and for continuity.

Educational hierarchies and educational and socio-economic status

There are distinctive hierarchies of distinction within education (Bourdieu, 1984, 1988; Naidoo, 2004) around:

1   Qualifications: Qualifications are not simply valued for their age-related level, with a senior school certificate more valued than a junior. It is also the symbolic value of the qualifications that matters, that is, the uses to which they can be put to in employment and social networks. What is most commonly known as 'academic' knowledge is valued over 'vocational knowledge'. Thus, university degrees are 'better' than FE diplomas. This is because these qualifications are necessary for higher-status (although not always better remunerated) jobs (see disciplines below). School qualifications that act as gatekeepers for HE entrance are generally seen as 'better' than some FE qualifications, as they constitute the pathway to HE and thus to higher-status positions more generally.

2   Institutions: The schools that parents have to pay for have most status, and, within that group, those that are oldest and can boast large numbers of important people among their

alumni. HE too is hierarchically arranged, with the newest universities considered to be of lesser status than those that are older. In the UK, Oxford/Cambridge epitomize the high-status HE institution: because of their age, they have a vast tranche of important alumni going back centuries, various markers of distinction (heritage buildings, green spaces, museums, benefactors, large research grants, high on the league tables that signify 'quality') and they attract and are able to select those with the highest school qualifications. An 'Oxbridge' degree is often seen as 'better' by employers than that of a very recent university (redbrick, more vocationally oriented, less research-driven).

3 'Academic' disciplines (see Ladwig, 1996): Science, technology and mathematics (STEM) are the disciplines that are deemed to matter most to 'progress', but other disciplines such as economics, law and management are 'vital' to the management of civil society and government. Law and medicine also retain status because of their historical connections with classical learning. Some arts and humanities subjects have cultural cachet but do not dominate policies within HE institutions or elsewhere: this privilege is now afforded to STEM. In general, what are seen as the more vocational subjects – such as education and nursing – are of lower status than the older professional subjects such as medicine. The 'new professions' struggle for status.[8] The more recent branches of arts and humanities, such as drama, creative writing, cultural studies and media studies, are similarly low in the hierarchy and can be compared with new STEM subjects, such as nano and genetic sciences, which have acquired instant status (and large amounts of funding).

I will put these two concepts (the reproduction of hierarchies and the distinctions in HE) to work in re-reading the debates over HE access, which I will first put into a wider context.

Rising mass levels of education

Taking a long view shows that, over time, the mass level of education has been steadily rising. More and more people are staying at school for longer, and more and more people are entering HE and acquiring qualifications.[9] These changes are connected, although not in a simple cause and effect relationship, with changes in the economy and politics. I will briefly sketch some key events in the UK (see Jones (2003) and Whitty (2002) for more).

In the post-war period there were significant changes in the ways in which the economy functioned. Innovations developed within HE STEM disciplines meant that many jobs could be done by machines, rather than by human labour. At the same time, more women entered the workforce, and there were increasingly fewer jobs for young people. The government deregulated the economy in support of companies seeking expanding markets, but many of them also sought cheap labour and taxation advantages – they moved offshore. These economic shifts caused large numbers of people to lose their jobs, particularly in manufacturing and associated industries. But jobs also disappeared in agriculture and in declining resource-based industries such as coal mining. New industries and jobs have had to be developed, and these have largely been in the services sector and in a range of new 'knowledge-based' areas. Many new jobs require higher levels of specialized education.

Successive UK governments have had no choice but to attempt to manage the consequences of these often-abrupt shifts within the globalized economy. Education policy has been perceived to have a major role to play (Lauder et al., 2006). First of all, unemployed adults must be retrained. Second, the political creation of the European Union, combined with political upheaval in other parts of the world and the relative ease of global travel, has meant large numbers of new families of migrants and refugees who must be educated, housed and employed. Third, the potential costs of unemployed young people not gainfully occupied must be addressed: the general social belief in education and training as a 'good thing' provides the rationalization for raising school leaving ages. And finally, in order to provide partial solutions to the social consequences of economic shifts, education, which historically had a role to play in the 'civilizing' and 'nation-building' of the British state, is required to focus on:

- citizenship – to create social cohesion;
- well-being – to ensure basic health and welfare; and
- generic 'knowledge-economy' skills – to create a well-prepared workforce.

As well, schools, FE and HE must generally increase participation – in part to take the pressure off the youth labour market, leaving jobs for older workers.

The changes and pressures I have very briefly indicated have not been smooth and continuous, but rather have occurred in lurches. There have been – and are – particular times when education must make relatively rapid adjustments. This is one such time.

Struggles over expanding higher education

In reality, schools have, over the last sixty year period, been continually asked to cater for ever larger numbers of more diverse young people, and for longer. At the same time, they have been asked by governments worried about the labour market and the economy to educate students to higher levels and in new areas. There are also more and more young people staying at school long enough to gain the kinds of qualification that might allow them to gain entry to HE. In turn, governments require both higher and further education to increase the range and types of course on offer. These changes can be summed up as some demand and a lot of pressure for HE to expand *and* diversify at the same time.

This expand–diversify duality creates instability within the field of education and creates the occasion for intensified struggles over possible new hierarchies and (re)distributions. As seen earlier in the chapter, it has been the occasion for intense debates at the borders of HE and schooling and within HE itself. These struggles are around managing:

- flow – how many people can gain a basic university qualification without the award losing status in comparison and competition with an expanding range of higher-level vocational qualifications, and
- position – which institutions and disciplines will retain their position, that is, remain at the top of the relevant hierarchy by virtue of being the most selective of 'quality' (Morley, 2003), taken to mean offering the qualifications that are of highest status.

These struggles have occurred within an increasingly internationally oriented and marketized HE system, which places greater pressure on places and on the management of the *appearance* of academic distinction (Sidhu, 2006).

In the UK expand–diversify setting, changes to the gate-keeping A levels have become a crucible for various people and institutions to act out the positional struggles that are taking place. Students seeking to gain advantage take more A levels than are required. Universities who have lost faith in the capacity of A levels to sort and select in their interests set their own entrance exams and procedures. Institutions wary of having to take too many of the 'wrong sort' of young people argue that some disciplines (the newer, lower-status media studies and sociology for example) are 'easier' than STEM.

Paradoxically, widening participation policies both enhance and threaten the position of high-status universities. On the one hand, they must be seen to be accommodating, as elitism carries connotations that are no longer socially acceptable (as in Barbara Ellen's acerbic commentary earlier). On the other hand, they must maintain their elitism, as it is this that puts them at the 'top' of the HE tree. The rationale (doxa) that they adopt for this juggling act is one of merit (as in Tom Kemp's column). Students are said to advance through a neutral schooling system, regardless of their social, cultural or economic contexts. The ways in which schooling itself is implicated in the reproduction of privilege and of particular socio-economic groups are ignored. The qualification acts as an apparently neutral mechanism for sorting and selecting. And university interviews, where young people must perform as a particular kind of educated person, are argued to be 'additional effort' to be fair, rather than the exercise of additional selectivity, over and above that offered by the school qualification.

This rationale appears to be logical and natural, but, as Bourdieu suggests, what is at work is something profoundly social and structured (Bourdieu, 1990). The realities of (re)production are misrecognized.

Conclusion

The continued struggles over the (re)production of advantage are manifest in current struggles over HE entrance and the nature of the final school qualifications. Both government and media are powerful actors in the field of education, as are hierarchically organized universities and families and young people themselves. Their actions and words cannot be understood simply by looking at policy or by reading newspapers. Thinking about events through the lens of Bourdieu's sociology allows the phenomena to be understood not as a one-off or isolated series of events, but as part of a longer and wider struggle about the kind of education system, and world, we have – and that we want.

The media debates exemplified earlier are not predominantly moral debates about what is right. In essence, the widening participation debates are about the reproduction of relative positions and hierarchies. Differences over school qualifications cannot be separated from events in HE, as it is the nature of the gate-keeping afforded by the examinations that is at stake. An apparently 'scientific' argument about merit is mobilized, by the most powerful and highest-status agents, in order to bolster up traditional hierarchies and status and to justify greater selectivity. Self-interested arguments from new institutions and disciplines seeking to increase their standing and position focus on their importance in the new knowledge economy, even if they sometimes mount a case against elitism. The policies of government are also imbricated in these events: politicians too have significant interests and agendas. They seek to manage an economy, get (re)elected and to manage a rhetorical battle of 'spin'.

Reading these events with Bourdieu shows that inequitable differences are not produced by chance, but are a result of debates, contests and a myriad of actions and reactions. At some point, an uneasy and temporary settlement will be reached.

However, the outcomes of these struggles are not ruthlessly predetermined. While the history of this and similar struggles is strongly patterned by the need of various actors to preserve particular advantages, Bourdieu reminds us that the destiny effects of education do not preclude change. The reproduction of privilege is not inexorable, and it is clear from the different histories of different countries that social and economic inequities are fewer in some places than in others.

And, in the UK, there are signs that, under concerted pressure, even the most elite universities are opening their doors a crack.

Notes

1   See the various datasets on the Higher Education Statistics Agency (HESA) website, available online at www.hesa.ac.uk/index.php?option=com_datatables&Itemid=121 (accessed 20 September 2008).

2   'Labour concedes it won't deliver its 50% target on time', *Times Higher Education*. Available online at www.timeshigherducation.co.uk/story.asp?storyCode=401455&sectioncode=26 (accessed 12 July 2008).

3   A levels are public examinations whose aggregated scores are the basis for university entrance.

4   See http://yp.direct.gov.uk/diplomas/ for the video version (accessed 3 November 2008).

5   See www.timesonline.co.uk/tol/news/uk/education/article4538892.ece (accessed 13 September 2008).

6   See www.direct.gov.uk/en/EducationAndLearning/UniversityAndHigherEducation/DG_073697 (accessed 20 September 2008).

7   Oxbridge – an amalgamation of Oxford and Cambridge and common shorthand in the UK.

8   Lobbying for higher status, advocates for the field of education now make much of its integral connections with the knowledge economy, and those who are part of the 'cultural turn' in the arts and humanities argue the importance of the cultural industries to national economies and pervasiveness of multi-modal communication technologies.

9   But some qualifications no longer mean what they did. An ordinary degree is no longer 'worth' what it once was in terms of getting a job.

References

Anyon, J. (1980) 'Social class and the hidden curriculum of work', *Journal of Education* 162: 67–92.

Archer, L., Hutchings, M. and Ross, A. (2003) *Higher education and social class. Issues of exclusion and inclusion*, London: RoutledgeFalmer.

Ball, S., Maguire, M. and Macrae, S. (2000) *Choice, pathways and transitions post-16. New youth, new economies in the global city*, London: Falmer.

Bourdieu, P. (1984) *Distinction. A social critique of the judgment of taste*, Boston, MA: Harvard University Press.

—— (1988) *Homo academicus*, Stanford, CA: Stanford University Press.

—— (1990) *The logic of practice*, Stanford, CA: Stanford University Press.

—— (2008) *Sketch for a self analysis*, Oxford: Blackwell.

—— and Passeron, J.C. (1977) *Reproduction in society, education and culture*, London: Sage.

—— and —— (1979) *The inheritors, French students and their relation to culture*, Chicago, IL: The University of Chicago Press.

——, —— and de Saint Martin, M. (1995) *Academic discourse*, Stanford, CA: Stanford University Press.

Feinstein, L., Duckworth, F. and Sabates, R. (2008) *Education and the family. Passing success across generations*, London: Routledge.

Galindo-Rueda, F., Marcenaro-Guitierrez, O. and Vignoles, A. (2004) *The widening socio-economic gap in UK higher education*, London: Centre for the Economics of Education, London School of Economics.

Haberman, M. (1991) 'The pedagogy of poverty vs good teaching', *Phi Delta Kappan* 73: 290–294.

Jones, K. (2003) *Education in Britain: 1944 to the present*, Oxford: Polity Press.

Ladwig, J. (1996) *Academic distinctions. Theory and methodology in the sociology of school knowledge*, New York: Routledge.

Lauder, H., Brown, P., Dillabough, J. and Halsey, A. (eds) (2006) *Education, globalisation, and social change*, Oxford: Oxford University Press.

Morley, L. (2003) *Quality and power in higher education*, Buckingham: Open University Press.

Naidoo, R. (2004) 'Fields and institutional strategy: Bourdieu on the relationship between higher education, inequality and society', *British Journal of Sociology of Education* 25: 457–471.

Reay, D., David, M. and Ball, S. (2005) *Degrees of choice: social class, race and gender in higher education*, Stoke: Trentham Books.

Sidhu, R. (2006) *Universities and globalisation. To market, to market*, Mahwah, NJ: Lawrence Erlbaum.

Teese, R. (2000) *Academic success and social power*, Melbourne: Melbourne University Press.

Thomas, E. (2001) *Widening participation in post-compulsory education*, London: Continuum.

Thomas, S. (2006) *Education policy in the media: Public discourses on education*, Tenerife: Postpressed.

Thomson, P. (2002) *Schooling the rustbelt kids. Making the difference in changing times*, Sydney: Allen & Unwin (Trentham Books UK).

Whitty, G. (2002) *Making sense of education policy*, London: Paul Chapman Publishing.

Zipin, L. (1999) 'The suppression of ethical dispositions through managerial governmentality: a habitus crisis in Australian higher education', *Discourse* 20: 21–39.

29

The sociology of elite education

Agnès van Zanten

Research on elites (that is, on status groups that occupy dominant positions) is characterized by the lack of connection between studies that focus on elite recruitment and those that focus on the exercise of power by elites. As underlined by Giddens (1974), both types of approach are important and should complement each other in the analysis of mediations between the class structure, the organizational structure and the power structure in a given society. Giddens also insists on the need for recruitment studies to take account of two different dimensions: the types of channel that are privileged by elite groups to reproduce their social position, and the degree of social closure or openness of these channels to other groups (Parkin, 1974). This distinction is used to organize the present chapter, which focuses on a single channel that has come to play a crucial role in post-industrial societies, that is schools and, more precisely, upper-secondary and higher education institutions, and on their influence in three different national contexts: France, the United Kingdom and the United States. In the first section, the specific features of elite education are examined. The second section explores the extent and modes of institutional and social closure.

Socialization patterns in elite educational institutions

Elite schools as total institutions

Studies of elite education have underscored the common features of elite educational institutions that distinguish them from other institutions that look after young people from the same age cohorts. The interlocking character of these features allows elite institutions to be described as 'total institutions' that provide, through both formal and 'hidden' curricula, a strong secondary socialization model for students that will decisively influence their public and private adult life (Faguer, 1991). Two of the most visible ones are physical closure and small size, which contribute to distinctiveness as well as inclusiveness (Wakeford 1969). These two elements were important characteristics of boarding schools and of the most exclusive colleges in the UK and the US, until at least World War II. Because of the location of the French *classes préparatoires aux grandes écoles* in Paris and other big cities, physical closure was less marked, although most students, especially those coming from distant towns and rural areas, were boarders. In the *grandes écoles* themselves, boarding was the rule.[1] By relocating outside Paris in recent decades, moreover, some of them, such as the *Ecole Polytechnique* or the *Ecole des Hautes Etudes Commerciales* (HEC), have recreated to a certain extent the 'campus' atmosphere of their English and American counterparts, though on a much smaller scale. Internal cohesion has also been fostered and maintained over time in elite institutions by sophisticated rites marking entrance and departure, as well as important moments of the educational experience, by procedures concerning the allocation of boarding rooms and of various material tasks and by learning and social activities meant to develop a strong 'bonding' relationship among members and especially between 'established' students and new entrants, as well as between institutions and their alumni. These organizational forms have been strongly influenced by army and religious traditions and are frequently referred to through idiosyncratic terms that serve as social markers of membership.

Studies have also focused on the distinctive and exclusive character of the social culture prevailing in these institutions, notably on the prominent place occupied by sports and various games, some of which are practised only in elite boarding schools, and on the crucial socialization role played by fraternities, sororities, clubs and associations (Abraham, 2007; Cookson and Persell, 1985a). Elite institutions were also long characterized by a specific academic curriculum (Bernstein, 1977). This curriculum was distinctive in point of its content (with a key role attributed to Latin and the humanities and, in France, to mathematics), its pedagogy, which privileged individual modes of instruction (taking the form of 'tutorials' in British elite colleges or *'colles'* in French *classes préparatoires*, i.e. individual work sessions and evaluations by older students and professors), and its evaluation modes (the creation of specific college entrance examinations in England and the US and of *concours* for access to the *grandes écoles* in France). Academic distinctiveness has also been reinforced by the gender, educational and social profile of professors in these institutions – in particular, those of public school masters and Oxbridge 'dons' in England (Walford, 1984).

Educating the upper class

These dimensions of elite education are the outcome of explicit and implicit choices made by teachers and administrators and show the relative autonomy that these educational institutions enjoy by virtue of their symbolic, cultural, social and economic capital (Bourdieu, 1996). However, the ability of elite institutions to form their students is constrained by the expectations of dominant groups (Kamens, 1974). They work according to a social 'charter', that is a licence and mandate to produce specific educational subjects (Meyer, 1970), differing from those of institutions that cater to non-elite groups. This charter is subject to variations depending on the interests, values and ideas of the upper-class fractions that occupy or aspire to elite positions at a given time in each national context.

Although the expressive and moral dimensions mentioned above have been central elements of elite educational institutions in the three countries considered here, emphasis on sports and social life has been much more important in England than in France, owing to the prevalence of an educational model reflecting the aristocratic values and gentlemanly lifestyles of the nineteenth-century 'leisure class'. Elite schools were a key element in the dissemination of this model among other elite and middle-class groups during the first half of the twentieth century (Anderson, 2007). This model was also 'borrowed' by America's old money families when they sought to consolidate themselves and to build, through education in private prepatory schools and elite colleges, a 'class wall' separating old privileges from upstarts (Soares, 1999). On the other hand, the academic culture of elite educational institutions has been more distinctive in England and France than in the US, reflecting a historically constructed, 'high-brow', aristocratic and bourgeois culture (Cookson and Persell, 1985b), but it places a greater emphasis on the mastery of intellectual knowledge and skills in France than in England.

The charters of elite educational institutions in each country are nevertheless subject to changing external pressures resulting from status group struggles (Karabel, 1984). Historical analysis of the most prestigious American colleges (Yale, Princeton, Harvard) shows the transition from an emphasis on the non-academic side of campus life, which helped students master the subtleties of the dominant status culture and accumulate contacts crucial for success in large organizations and the political field in the early decades of the twentieth century, to a more academically oriented curriculum in the 1960s and 1970s. These changes reflect the difficulty of providing a common social model for a larger and increasingly heterogeneous upper class, with diverging interests, values and ideas, and show the growing influence of its most culturally endowed fractions. The influence of these fractions on the academic culture and social atmosphere of elite secondary schools and higher education institutions was also visible at the same period in England, although it was exerted indirectly, through the mediating action of the state. In France, the emphasis on academic culture was more precocious and more radical, as the French Revolution replaced the aristocratic ideal of the '*honnête homme*' with a bourgeois model emphasizing scholastic merit.

Preparing for political and economic power positions

It thus appears that, although upper-class groups have always tried to frame the charter of elite institutions, this charter is also subject to variations according to more general economic, social and political factors that might lead interest and political groups acting on behalf of elites, but also reflecting contradictions and struggles among established and new status groups, to encourage elite institutions to act as 'guardians' of national cultural models and stratification patterns, or as agents of innovation and diffusion of new cultural or social ideals. The role of the state as political mediator between conflicting status groups' interests is particularly visible in France, because it was the state that created or restructured the most prestigious *grandes écoles* after the French Revolution. Designed to serve state needs (those of the army and various technical corps and later on of public administrations), the *grandes écoles*' mandate has been to produce individuals endowed with strong scientific competence and capable of synthesizing large quantities of information, but also interested in practical matters and able to take decisions (Thoenig, 1973). In Alvin Gouldner's (1979) terms, these schools were expected to train the 'technical intelligentsia' more than the 'humanistic intellectuals'. Their culture was from the onset strongly distinct from the non-utilitarian university culture traditionally oriented towards teaching, scholarship and research, although some institutions, especially the *Ecole Normale Supérieure*, were clearly oriented towards the intellectual fractions of the upper class, whereas others, such as *l'Ecole Polytechnique*, have been characterized throughout their history by tensions between the divergent perspectives of scientists and engineers (Bourdieu, 1996; Belhoste *et al.*, 1994).

Strong state dependency has also influenced the non-academic activities and rites of these institutions, which were designed to instill respect for state hierarchies and loyalty to state institutions, at the same time that it has encouraged the development of 'organic links' between the *grandes écoles* and the state corps through recruitment processes directly linking valued positions in the most prestigious corps to class rank at graduation. However, since the 1970s, private firms and economic status groups have in various ways exerted a growing and more direct pressure on French elite institutions. The oldest is the practice known as *'pantouflage'* – that is, the departure of civil servants trained in the traditional state *grandes écoles* for work in the private sector (Suleiman, 1978). This movement coincided with the creation and growth in the 1970s of privately funded *grandes écoles* with a strong market orientation. In the 1990s, the state-funded *grandes écoles* began to follow suit, offering a larger number of courses and activities meant to prepare students for direct access to jobs in private sector management and finance (Lazuech, 1999). At the same time, in what can be seen as a kind of compensation for decreasing material and symbolic returns of state investments in these special schools, many of them have in the last ten years re-emphasized their social and political responsibility, especially by taking a prominent role on debates and policies concerning widening participation in higher education (van Zanten, 2008).

In England, public schools, as well as Oxford and, to a lesser extent, Cambridge, have traditionally maintained what have been called 'incestuous links of privilege and power' with the British establishment (Scott, 1990) and direct connections to the state and the professions. In the US, 'prep' schools and elite private universities were also directly linked to economic and political elite groups through their recruitment, funding and access to elite positions. The general expectations from these groups and the organizations that they control have led to a strong focus on leadership, 'character' and self-discipline (Cookson and Persell, 1985a). Nevertheless, after World War II, elite institutions in England became strongly dependent on the state for funding. Although the initial effect of state funds was to redirect education away from action and business and towards research, in the 1980s, the state began to put pressure on universities to become key elements in the global knowledge economy, orienting research towards industrial needs, especially high technology, and students' career choices towards high-paying jobs in the private sector (Brown and Hesketh, 2004). This latter tendency is particularly evident in elite American universities, which are extremely dependent on private endowments for their growth, which in turn determines their capacity to occupy the top places in international rankings of leading research institutions and to play an important role in global economic networks.

Social and institutional closure

The conditions of admission

Elite institutions have always enjoyed a large autonomy in setting their own conditions for admission (Douglass, 2007). However, although the admission criteria that they have devised reflect, above all, internal compromises between administrators and teachers and responses to competitive external pressures from similar organizations, they are also conditioned by changes in the distribution of power among status groups in the broader society (Bourdieu and Passeron, 1977; Karabel, 2005; Karen, 1990). In France, the state's early creation of a system of highly competitive examinations, ranking students according to a one-dimensional scale of merit for access to elite 'special schools', gave professors a high degree of latitude in the choice of future members of the elite vis-à-vis families and social or economic constituencies, while simultaneously endowing elites with a strong belief in their individual and social legitimacy as members of a 'state nobility' (Bourdieu 1996; Young, 1994). At the same time, the present extremely 'balkanized' system of competitive examinations for entrance to the *grandes écoles* is less the reflection of academic interests than a legacy of the powerful influence of the state corps that framed and have strongly controlled their functioning.

In the UK and in the US, the transition from 'ascriptive' criteria to an educational meritocracy was slower, and the notion of educational merit has been subjected to more diverse interpretations than in France. Entry at Oxford and Cambridge was, until World War II, based on a system of examinations in which merit was equated with the mastery of a traditional curriculum, though school and family connections also played an important role. The Oxbridge system of recruitment was formally realigned to that of other universities in the 1960s, following the increase in government funding and involvement. Nevertheless, recent investigation reveals the persistence of distinctive features. As in other universities, the results obtained by students in subject-specific, nationally standardized tests, that is GSCE grades (three A*, the highest grade, in the disciplines considered as the most relevant for the desired university subject are expected), and teachers' predictions of A level exam results (in 1983, 82.4 per cent of the Oxford entering class had top A level scores, the proportion has now reached almost 100 per cent) are the crucial elements in the first phase of admission. However, during the second phase, the various colleges take other elements into account. These are both meritocratic (results in specific language tests or qualities exhibited in the best two school essays and, more recently, as in the US, results on Scholastic Aptitude Tests (SATs)) and non-meritocratic, such as family and school background, which is assessed in closer examination of admission forms and interviews with tutors.[2]

Until the 1960s, students in the US mainly gained admission to four-year colleges by graduating with good grades from high school. However, elite private institutions, imitating Oxford and Cambridge, developed their own entry examinations in order to limit student numbers and increase their legitimacy. The SAT, introduced in the 1930s, progressively became an important component of the admission process, reinforcing the cognitive dimension of merit. However, when this system started to give a clear advantage to brilliant Jewish students, elite institutions and dominant groups once again reinforced the weight assigned to extra-academic criteria such as 'character' (determined on the basis of high school teacher recommendations), participation in extracurricular activities, autobiographical essays and interviews that could be used to legitimately exclude 'inassimilable' non-WASP students. Nevertheless, by the late 1950s, in an atmosphere of intense concern about 'talent loss', 'character' began to lose ground to the intellectually gifted applicant defined according to SAT scores, Grade Point Average (GPA) and class rank, as well as excellence in one or more extracurricular endeavours. A new turn was once again taken in the 1960s with the introduction of a new criterion: 'diversity'. Since its relationship to academic merit was not to be systematically defined, its adoption proved nevertheless highly controversial (Karabel, 2005; Soares, 2007).

Institutional routes

Institutional routes played an important role in the creation and consolidation of elite educational systems. The 'bonding' relationship between a small number of elite colleges and secondary schools was based on the 'chartering' process described above, that is on the monopolization of a mode of training and socialization required for admission to elite institutions of higher education, but also, especially in the US and the UK, on a 'bartering' process – that is, negotiations between school and college personnel concerning selection and admission (Persell and Cookson, 1985). However, this 'institutional sponsorship' was officially abandoned as the result of the expansion and of the increasing formal meritocratic dimension of educational systems (Turner, 1960). The most radical departure from this 'institutional sponsorship' has taken place in the US, where elite colleges have developed admission policies that severely hamper the effectiveness of 'bridging strategies' from secondary school feeders, except for a limited number of prep schools that still hold a special status because of their historical relationships with Harvard, Princeton or Yale (Le Tendre *et al.*, 2006). The importance attached to academic merit – and, in particular, class rank – has simultaneously allowed elite colleges to recruit excellent undergraduate students nationwide and led 'star schools' (schools that are particularly successful in getting students admitted to elite universities) to maximize the chances of their best students at the expense of those who have excellent test scores and high GPA earned in rigorous courses, but are not at the top of their class (Attewell, 2001). Despite this relative disadvantage, students in these schools – many, but not all, private – still benefit not only from a stronger focus on academic achievement by teachers and parents than students in other schools, but also from specific Honours and Advanced Placement courses that act as a 'signal' for college admissions staff (Falsey and Heyns, 1984) and from their 'brokering' strategies, that is from strong financial investment in and commitment to activities favouring the college-linking process, such as college visits, assistance with college and financial aid applications, and contacts with college representatives on behalf of the students (Hill, 2008; McDonough, 1997).

Institutional routes and sponsorship have also been weakened in England, but not to the same extent: a strong link remains between private secondary schools and elite higher education institutions. Privately schooled students are twice as likely to go to elite universities than state-schooled students and, although outnumbered by the latter in admissions (44.5 per cent versus 46.8 per cent in 2007 at Oxford), they are significantly overrepresented in relation to their total number in secondary schools. This overrepresentation is even more striking when one considers their share of the applicant pool and percentage among successful applicants. Given the expansion of the state sector and the strong meritocratic character of the admission procedures in elite universities, this overrepresentation is due less to explicit 'chartering' and 'bartering' than in the past. It is nevertheless important to note that, as in the US, students from private schools benefit from higher levels of advice and support on careers in higher education by internal staff and outside agencies working with the schools (Reay *et al.*, 2005), and that those from the so-called Clarendon Public Schools, in particular, frequently receive 'special notification' during the second phase of admissions at Oxford. However, the competitive advantage of private schools rests now to a larger extent on higher levels of educational achievement. These are the consequence of severe academic selection procedures as well as of the implementation over the course of the 1980s and 1990s of an Assisted Places Scheme (abolished by New Labour in 1997), intended to help 'able children from modest backgrounds' to enter independent schools of high academic reputation, but also of more marked 'school effects' linked to the concentration of academically and socially advantaged students (Halsey, 1995; Power *et al.*, 2003).

In France, on the contrary, the role of the state in elite education has given a competitive advantage to state *lycées* in admissions, with the evidence showing no clear advantage for upper-class students from private sector schools in terms of educational careers (Tavan, 2004). There are no official routes, but huge differences between *lycées* concerning their capacity to get students admitted into these classes. This result is strongly linked to provision, as those '*prépas*' that are most successful in getting students admitted to the top *grandes écoles* are all located in a limited number of old and prestigious *lycées* in Paris and other big cities, giving an advantage to students schooled at those *lycées*. In addition to that 'location effect', there is also some evidence that widening participation in secondary education has encouraged professors and administrators in the more selective *classes préparatoires* to weigh the grades, class rank and professional evaluations of candidates according to the supposed achievement level of their *lycée*.[3] Being accepted in these selective *classes préparatoires* is a key step for students who want to follow up their studies in the top *grandes écoles*, as there is a strong 'chartering' effect, both formal (teaching content, methods and evaluation are strongly conditioned by the explicit requirements of the *concours* of these *grandes écoles*, while less selective *classes préparatoires* prepare for less-selective examinations) and informal (use of knowledge of implicit requirements based on information provided by alumni, examiners, professors and managers at the *grandes écoles*). Students attending prestigious *lycées* and *classes préparatoires* also benefit from personalized counselling and assistance with applications.

Social advantage and parental strategies

In the three countries considered here, upper-class families strongly supported the initial institutional pathways that excluded other groups from access to elite higher education institutions. Although they have been able to resist and adapt to the development of meritocratic policies by these institutions, thanks to the competitive advantages provided by private schooling and selective public schools, and although in the US affluent upper-class parents, especially former alumni, have been able, much more so than in England or France, to continue to buy entrance for their children – not only because they can pay for tuition but also because they provide 'legacies' that contribute to university budgets – as a group, they have had to renounce collective admission privileges and accept that only some of their children with excellent academic results might be among the 'chosen' (Karabel, 2005). Moreover, members of this group now compete with larger proportions of members of the middle class. However, the respective advantages of middle-class families with high levels of cultural capital and those families with high incomes still have to be assessed carefully with respect both to the strategies available for parents and to the selection and channelling process in each educational system (Kerchoff *et al.*, 1997). In France, the intellectual fractions of the middle class have traditionally been advantaged by the formal and strongly scholastic meritocratic procedures of access to the state *grandes écoles*. However, changes in the educational context have forced them to develop, through 'colonization' of local schools, new, informal institutional pathways to maintain their position (Raveaud and van Zanten, 2007). Their advantages are also challenged, however, because, as in the UK and the US, families with higher incomes are able successfully to transform economic capital into cultural capital through residential and school choice, private tuition and private preparations for tests and competitive examinations (Ball, 2003; Johnson, 2006; van Zanten, 2003).

Another, even more important question concerns the extent to which this renewed 'class meritocracy' has closed off opportunities for other social and ethnic groups. Although meritocracy was initially conceived as serving the interests of hard-working students from dominated groups who could benefit from scholarships to go to elite universities, there has been a growing recognition of the existence of important inequalities of access. In response to strong social pressures, in the 1960s, elite US institutions developed ambitious 'affirmative action' policies giving an edge to Black, Hispanic and Native American candidates. This involved accepting candidates from 'tagged' groups with SAT scores a bit lower than other candidates yet still within the thresholds established by each university, as well as taking into account their capacity to succeed under 'adverse circumstances'. Such measures were needed because, for reasons linked to their family background and secondary school careers in poor and underperforming schools, candidates from these groups could not compete on an equal, 'meritocratic' basis. They nevertheless generated strong discontent, especially from the best-performing groups (Asians, in particular), in a context of 'college squeeze': a rise in the number of college-age students and a slow down of higher education expansion. In response to moves on the part of some states to make affirmative action illegal, some elite public universities (the University of Texas, the University of California) have adopted 'percentage plans' to recruit students from the largest possible number of high schools using class rank as the main indicator. While this measure has increased ethnic and social diversity in these universities, its success depends on the existence and maintenance of strong levels of segregation in high schools (Alon and Tienda, 2007). Elite private schools, on the other hand, count more on 'comprehensive reviews' of each proposal for achieving diversity. These reviews are more effective in detecting meritorious students from disadvantaged backgrounds without 'side effects', but they are very costly to implement.

In France efforts to increase social and ethnic diversity in elite higher education institutions have been much more modest. In 2001, Sciences Po developed a specific selection procedure for students from disadvantaged schools based on a specific academic exercise – a press summary – and interviews with a jury including scholars, administrators, public civil servants and managers from private firms (Sabbagh, 2002). Other less well-known institutions, such as the INSA (*Institut National des Sciences Appliquées*), have developed a selection procedure based, for half of the entrants, not on absolute results but on class rank. It is important to note that these two institutions recruit their students after the *lycée*, which allows them much more autonomy to set up original admission criteria than the *écoles*, which select their students after the *classes préparatoires*. They remain, in fact, isolated cases, and most institutions have only developed as elite universities in the UK outreach programmes providing information, assistance with the preparation of college applications and financial support for disadvantaged students. Although these programmes can be effective in limiting processes of self-exclusion due to institutional, cultural and economic factors when they are integrated into procedures including changes in the modes of selection, their impact seems limited when they are applied in isolation. It is also important to note that not all working-class and minority students are willing to submit to the cultural and social requirements of elite institutions, and that the kind of social capital they possess (strong bonding ties with members of their family and local community) not only constitutes a handicap for access but also prevents them profiting, to the same degree as middle- and upper-class students, from the social capital that these institutions provide (Allouch and van Zanten, 2008; Reay *et al.*, 2005).

Conclusion

This brief overview of elite education in the US, the UK and France has shown that, although elite institutions supported by established elite groups generally exhibit a strong reluctance to change, important transformations have taken place and are still at work in all three systems. The most important transformation, especially in the UK and US, took place after World War I, with the transition from an almost direct translation of social position into educational advantages, to the selection of talented individuals by educational institutions. Although this movement increased the autonomy and power of educational agents, it allowed only limited mobility opportunities for members of socially and ethnically dominated groups, as a new 'class meritocracy' emerged based on exclusionary processes exhibiting some differences between the three countries according to the relative importance of money, morals, manners or academic culture in class divisions (Lamont, 1992; Power *et al.*, 2003).

Also, although this article has mostly focused on changes in modes of social and institutional closure that have had significant consequences for educational and social inequalities, it is important to relate these to other changes linked to global transformations in the knowledge economy. These influences are creating new dividing lines between institutions, depending on their relationship to different economic sectors and their place in international networks and rankings, as well as between social groups, according to their capacity to integrate these new opportunities in their strategies of exclusion or usurpation (Brown and Hesketh, 2004; Wagner, 2007). These new divisions and their concomitant class strategies require specific attention from sociology of education research.

Notes

1   The largest part of the French elite is not trained, as elsewhere, in universities but at the *grandes écoles*, which are distinct institutions of higher education. To prepare for the competitive examinations allowing acess to these écoles, most students follow two- or three-year courses at *classes préparatoires*. Although these are more or less equivalent to undergraduate university studies, they are located in the *lycées*.
2   A. Allouch's personal communication based on ongoing Ph.D. research on English and French elite higher education institutions' admission procedures and outreach programmes.
3   Evidence on these processes is being collected and analysed in an ongoing project on elite education in France. For more details see van Zanten (2008).

References

Abraham, Y.M. (2007) 'Du souci scolaire au sérieux managérial ou comment devenir un "HEC"', *Revue française de sociologie* 48(1): 37–66.
Allouch, A. and van Zanten, A. (2008) 'Formateurs ou "grands frères"? Les tuteurs des programmes d'ouverture sociale des grandes écoles et des classes préparatoires', *Education et sociétés* 2: 49–65.
Alon, S. and Tienda, M. (2007) 'Diversity, opportunity and the shifting meritocracy in higher education', *American Sociological Review* 72: 487–511.
Anderson, R. (2007) 'Aristocratic values and elite education in Britain and France', in D. Lancien and M. de Saint-Martin (eds) *Anciennes et nouvelles aristocracies de 1880 à nos jours*, Paris: éditions de la Maison des Sciences de l'Homme.
Attewell, P. (2001) 'The winner take-all high school: organizational adaptations to educational stratification', *Sociology of education* 74: 267–295.
Ball, S.J. (2003) *Class strategies and the education market*, London: RoutledgeFalmer.
Belhoste, B., Dahan, N. Dalmedico, A. and Picon, A. (1994) *La formation polytechnicienne, 1794–1994*, Paris: Dunod.
Bernstein, B. (1977) *Class, codes and control*, Vol. 3, 2nd edn, London: Routledge & Kegan Paul,.
Bourdieu, P. (1996) *The state nobility: elite schools in the field of power*, Stanford: Stanford University Press.
—— and Passeron, J.C. (1977) *Reproduction in education, society and culture*, Beverly Hills, CA: Sage.
Brown, P. and Hesketh, A. (2004) *The mismanagement of talent. Employability and jobs in the knowledge economy*, Oxford: Oxford University Press.
Cookson, P.W. and Persell, C.H. (1985a) *Preparing for power*, New York: Basic Books.
—— and —— (1985b) 'English and American residential secondary schools: a comparative study of the reproduction of social elites', *Comparative Education Review* 29(3): 283–298.
Douglass, J.A. (2007) *The conditions for admission. Access, equity and the social contract of public universities*, Stanford, CA: Stanford University Press.

Faguer, J.-P. (1991) 'Les effets d'une éducation totale', *Actes de la recherche en sciences sociales* 86–87: 57–70.

Falsey, B. and Heyns, B. (1984) 'The college channel: private and public schools reconsidered', *Sociology of Education* 57(2): 111–122.

Giddens, A. (1974) 'Elites in the British class structure', in P. Stanworth and A. Giddens (eds) *Elites and power in British society*, Cambridge: Cambridge University Press.

Gouldner, A. (1979) *The future of intellectuals and the rise of the new class*, New York: The Seabury Press.

Halsey, A. (1995) *Change in British society*, 4th edn, Oxford: Oxford University Press.

Hill, L.D. (2008) 'School strategies and the college-linking process: reconsidering the effects of high schools on college enrollment', *Sociology of education* 81: 53–76.

Johnson, H.B. (2006) *The American Dream and the power of wealth. Choosing schools and inheriting inequality in the land of opportunity*, New York and London: Routledge.

Kamens, D. (1974) 'Colleges and elite formation: the case of prestigious American colleges', *Sociology of Education* 47(3): 354–378.

Karabel, J. (1984) 'Status-group struggle, organizational interests, and the limits of institutional autonomy: the transformation of Harvard, Yale and Princeton, 1918–1940', *Theory and Society* 13(1): 1–40.

—— (2005) *The chosen. The hidden history of admission and exclusion at Harvard, Yale and Princeton*, Boston, MA: Houghton Mifflin.

Karen, D. (1990) 'Toward a political-organizational model of gatekeeping: the case of elite colleges', *Sociology of Education* 63(4): 227–240.

Kerckoff, A.C., Fogelman, K. and Manlove, J. (1997) 'Staying ahead: the middle class and school reform in England and Wales', *Sociology of Education* 70(1): 19–35.

Lamont, M. (1992) *Money, morals, and manners. The culture of the French and the American upper middle-class*, Chicago, IL: The University of Chicago Press.

Lazuech, G. (1999) *L'exception française. Le modèle des grandes écoles à l'épreuve de la mondialisation*, Rennes: Presses Universitaires de Rennes.

LeTendre, G.K., Gonzalez, R.G. and Nomi, T. (2006) 'Feeding the elite: the evolution of elite pathways from star high schools to elite universities', *Higher Education Policy* 19: 7–30.

McDonough, P.M. (1997) *Choosing colleges: how social class and schools structure opportunity*, Albany, NY: SUNY.

Meyer, J. (1970) 'The charter: conditions of diffuse socialization in schools' in R. Scott (ed.) *Social processes and social structures: an introduction to sociology*, New York: Henry Holt Co.

Parkin, F. (1974) *The social analysis of class structure*, London: Tavistock Publications.

Persell, C.H. and Cookson, P.W. (1985) 'Chartering and bartering: elite education and social reproduction', *Social Problems* 33(2): 114–129.

Power, S., Edwards, T., Whitty, G. and Wigfall, V. (2003) *Education and the middle class*, Buckingham: Open University Press.

Raveaud, M. and van Zanten, A. (2007) 'Choosing the local school? Middle class parents' values and social and ethnic mix in London and Paris', *Journal of Education Policy* 22(1): 107–124.

Reay, D., David, M. and Ball, S.J. (2005) *Degrees of choice. Social class, race and gender in higher education*, London: Trentham Books.

Sabbagh, D. (2002) 'Affirmative action at Sciences Po', *French Politics, Culture & Society* 20(3): 52–64.

Soares, J.A. (1999) *The decline of privilege: the modernization of Oxford University*, Stanford, CA: Stanford University Press.

—— (2007) *The power of privilege: Yale and America's elite colleges*, Stanford, CA: Stanford University Press.

Scott, J. (ed.) (1990) *The sociology of elites. Vol. 1: The study of elites*, Aldershot: Edward Elgar Publishing Ltd.

Suleiman, E. (1978) *Elites in French society: the politics of survival*, Princeton, NJ: Princeton University Press.

Tavan, C. (2004) 'École publique, école privée: comparaison des trajectoires et de la réussite scolaire', *Revue Française de Sociologie* 45(1): 133–165.

Thoenig, J.C. (1973) *L'ère des technocrats*, Paris: editions de l'organisation.

Turner, R.H. (1960) 'Sponsored and contest mobility and the school system' *American Sociological Review* 25(6): 855–867.

van Zanten, A. (2003) 'Middle-class parents and social mix in French urban schools: reproduction and transformation of class relations in education', *International Studies in Sociology of Education* 13(2): 107–123.

—— (2008) 'Formation des élites', in A. van Zanten (ed.) *Dictionnaire de l'éducation*, Paris: Presses Universitaires de France.

Wagner, A.C. (2007) *Les classes sociales dans la mondialisation*, Paris: La Découverte.

Wakeford, J. (1969) *The cloistered elite*, London: Macmillan.

Walford, G. (1984) 'The changing professionalism of public school teachers', in G. Walford (ed.) *British public schools: policy & practice*, London and Philadelphia, PA: The Falmer Press.

Young, M. (1994) *The rise of the meritocracy*, 2nd edn, London: Transaction Publishers.

30

The dialogic sociology of the learning communities

Ramón Flecha

The role of egalitarian dialogue in transforming schools into learning communities

In Brazil, Chile and Spain, more than eighty schools have been transformed into learning communities through a process of making an egalitarian utopia real for thirty thousand children. This transformation process focuses on extending human rights to all children, without discriminating against anyone, and on building democratic schools (Apple and Beane, 2007), which includes providing the best possible education to every boy and every girl, especially to those who are traditionally the most excluded. The key to this transformation is egalitarian dialogue among all the actors involved. Contemporary sociological theories play a crucial role in building the conditions for this egalitarian dialogue, as described by relevant sociologists including Touraine and Wright.[1,2]

The first phase of this transformation consists of organizing an open and egalitarian dialogue among all the citizens who have a relationship with the school: students, teachers, students' families, administrators, school volunteers, trade union representatives, NGOs. In addition, these communities always ask researchers and members of other already active learning communities to participate in this dialogue. The basis for clarifying the roles that researchers and community members play in egalitarian dialogue is the current conception that society functions 'simultaneously as systems and lifeworlds' (Habermas, 1987: 118), as structures and subjects.

That means that researchers, as members of academic structures, have an ethical and scientific obligation to contribute to this dialogue: they can bring to it the knowledge that the scientific community has developed on each educational issue, and the activities that have been most effective in overcoming school failure and improving experiences of living together. Therefore, this dialogue is egalitarian in the Habermasian sense: arguments are appreciated for their own intrinsic value (validity claims) and not because of the power position of those promoting them (power claims). Because this kind of communication is so complex and unusual, the learning communities project draws from a wide theoretical framework on speech and communicative acts, which is presented in the next section.

Egalitarian dialogue represents a move beyond both the functionalist and subjectivist perspectives, because it grants importance to all the individuals who participate in all the school debates and decision-making processes. On the one hand, functionalism has served to legitimate a system in which educational structures determine the everyday situation in the classroom. Theories that consider only the structures do not need community dialogue: they are occupied with the analysis and decisions of academics and administrators. On the other hand, subjectivist perspectives (such as some projects in action research and participatory research) focus only on the subjects' contributions, without considering the knowledge that the educational structures have accumulated. The egalitarian dialogues that are held in learning communities integrate both the knowledge held by the scientific community and the experiences of the subjects; by considering the contributions of all parties, this more inclusive kind of community can reach agreements and make decisions that are more appropriate for all concerned.

Contrasting the researchers' scientific knowledge and the subjects' experiences, all the participants reach a mutual agreement about their own model of school. The participants can consider the best practices that research has assembled for overcoming school failure; they can discuss whether and how those findings are applicable to their own context, and whether to adapt them or try new approaches. They can also decide whether they want to go through the process of transforming themselves into a learning community. Once they conclude the process of decision-making, they notice that people start doing things differently in the school. In what follows, this transformation is illustrated through two examples that are also instances of egalitarian dialogue.

One result of this egalitarian dialogue in learning communities is that most of them decide, after discussion, to arrange their classrooms into *interactive groups* for as much time as possible. Interactive groups are small heterogeneous groups of students. In each group, there is one adult (a professional, a family member or a volunteer) who is responsible for encouraging interactions among students, so that everyone helps the others to complete all the planned activities. Thus egalitarian dialogue is present, not only during the community's debates on the main decisions regarding the school, but also in each and every learning space of the school.

Interactive groups are an example of deliberative democracy within the classroom: students from diverse backgrounds deliberate about their educational tasks, helping one another in a process that simultaneously generates solidarity and academic success. As Elster (1998) states, once people engage in deliberative democracy, they change their preferences through dialogue. A child whose goal was to be the first in his or her class shifts towards the goal of collaborating so that his or her peers can also succeed. Similar transformative processes are found among family members: those who previously wanted their children to be at the top of their class now want all the children in the classroom to succeed.

Additionally, interactive groups function better than earlier ways of organizing students and human resources, as they respond to the problems of mixture and streaming. When *mixture* (INCLUD-ED Consortium, 2006–2011) occurs, students in a heterogeneous group do not receive enough appropriate attention, because a single teacher cannot satisfactorily respond to all their diverse needs. They can get enough attention, however, when more adults are included, and they work to promote interactions among the students. Interactive groups are also an improvement on *streaming*, in which students are segregated by ability, thus missing the goal of high educational achievement for all.

A second example of educational practices that many learning communities have chosen and implemented through egalitarian dialogue is *family and community education*. This means that schools reach out to a wide range of family members and others in the community and extend educational opportunities to them. Such schools also stay open as many hours as possible throughout the week, and offer a coordinated blend of training and leisure activities. For instance,

341

many learning communities organize tutored libraries or dialogic literary gatherings, where parents and community members read classical literature. Egalitarian dialogue is at the centre of the *mixed committees*, where teachers, students, family members and other citizens use a process of deliberative democracy to implement the decisions they have made about the school. This process profoundly changes schools and the surrounding community.

The egalitarian dialogue makes it possible to offer all children a real utopia: academic success for everyone without discrimination. By engaging in this process, active citizens of the community reject the kind of research that promotes racism in education. For instance, the Spanish media reported one study that 'demonstrated' that when schools have more than three immigrants per classroom, the overall educational level declines (Izquierdo, 2005: 29). Later, the media rectified that incorrect statement: a major television news programme reported that, when schools that served mostly immigrants were transformed into learning communities, the academic level of all students improved. The programme showed an elementary school that had been transformed into a learning community: while the proportion of immigrant students had risen from 12 to 46 per cent, their achievement in the areas of language and reading had also risen significantly, from 17 to 85 per cent.[3]

Another similar example is found at the same school. Having been immersed in the mainstream public discourse, the English teacher believed that the arrival of immigrants from North Africa would lower the level of learning in the classrooms. Similarly, when some Muslim girls and mothers arrived wearing the hijab, the community generally believed that they would bring gender inequality back to Europe. When the school decided to transform itself into a learning community, however, the English teacher began to work in interactive groups in his class and he looked for volunteers in the neighbourhood. He found a Muslim mother wearing the veil, who was not highly literate and did not speak Spanish, but was fluent in English, having lived in Ireland for some years. When this Muslim mother started to volunteer in the English interactive groups, the teacher could see how the learning level of all students improved, along with the students' perception of Muslim women and gender equality. Transnational immigrants represent an important source of enrichment for European societies, so it is crucial that their talents be considered. For instance, many undocumented immigrants in Spain have higher levels of English knowledge than do Spaniards themselves.

Beyond the theory of communicative action: communicative acts

In the schools that have been transformed into learning communities, the dialogue occurs among all the citizens involved. It is not only a dialogue about pedagogical innovations between students and teachers in classrooms where other members of the community cannot step in. Instead, the dialogue is among people of very different status who may play quite different roles in schools and in society. Therefore, the main goal of this dialogue is not just to develop innovative teaching methods, but rather to move towards equality of results (beyond equal opportunity) by transforming schools, communities and society. Current sociological theories increasingly provide elements to develop descriptive analyses of those dialogues and offer normative criteria to make them more egalitarian.

As the social sciences and societies have turned dialogic, the analysis of dialogue has become a valued resource for either reproducing or transforming social reality. In turn, Jürgen Habermas (1984, 1987) built his theory of communicative action, taking John L. Austin's (1962) theory of speech acts as a starting point. Overcoming the traditional barrier between language and the world, Austin developed pragmatic linguistics with his concepts of locutionary, illocutionary and perlocutionary speech acts: 'The locutionary act has some meaning; the illocutionary act has a certain force in saying something; the perlocutionary act is the achieving of certain effects by saying something' (p. 121). For example, the utterance 'The administrator told us that "students learn more when they are organized in ability grouping"' is a locution, while 'We protested because most of the poor immigrants are placed in the lower ability groups' is an illocution for indicating a force (a protest), and 'The administrator discouraged us' is a perlocution because it includes the effect that this speech act had.

Habermas applies sociology to Austin's language theory by associating speech acts with actions. Because strategic action is oriented towards success, it is based on perlocutionary speech acts. Because communicative action is oriented to consensus, it is based on illocutionary speech acts. When a dialogue between a student, his/her teacher and his/her family members is a strategic action, at least one of them is using perlocutionary speech acts, oriented to succeed according to his or her power claims. Sometimes the expert teacher does not want to have the 'difficult' students in his/her classroom; s/he wants to see them moved to another classroom, often that of the newest teacher. He or she orients his/her conversation with the family members to convince them that this is good for the child. He or she may say, 'We want to put your daughter in the other classroom in order to accelerate her learning'. Because his/her goal is to get them to accept what he/she considers to be better for him/her, he/she uses perlocutionary acts based on power claims to hide his/her real intention. A mother may ask, 'Why are the "difficult children" who are excluded from regular classrooms almost always Roma, immigrant and poor children?' The teacher would then reinforce his/her opinion using a power claim based on his status, answering that he/she is the expert on education and the one who knows what is best for the children.

When a dialogue between a student, the teacher and a family member is a communicative action, they use illocutionary speech acts oriented to reach consensus about what will help the student to achieve the maximum of instrumental learning, values and emotional development. They will all say what they really think on the basis of validity claims, rather than power claims. For example, the expert teacher may explain to the family members that he/she finds it difficult to manage the classroom with so many different ability levels and with some students behaving badly. He/she even might propose putting the 'difficult ones' into a separate classroom with another teacher. Family members then can tell him/her that a citizens' assembly was analyzing the interactive groups at another school, which are one way of overcoming these difficulties without excluding any child. In communicative action, the teacher does not appeal to his/her status or use power claims; he/she only uses validity claims, as do the other members of the citizens' assembly.

In his theory of communicative action, Habermas (1984) elaborated on the work of John Searle (Searle and Soler, 2009). However, Searle criticized Habermas for not having understood the theories of both Austin and Searle as they apply to speech acts. We agree with this critique. Searle clarifies that Austin relates illocutionary speech acts to understanding, and Habermas wrongly includes in this notion of understanding an orientation to reaching consensus. According to Austin (1962), illocutionary speech acts allow the teacher and the family members to understand one another's positions, but this does not mean they are willing to reach consensus. As Habermas defines illocutionary speech acts, the teacher and the family members try to understand each other, but also aim to reach a consensus.

Although we agree with Searle that it is incorrect to attribute this normative dimension (reaching consensus) to Austin's illocutionary speech acts, we agree with Habermas that this dimension is important to the process of communication. We need the latter process, more than Austin's original concept, both to understand social actions today and to provide approaches to improve these actions. The Habermasian conception of illocutionary speech acts helps us to analyse the dialogues among all citizens about schools, as well as to provide perspectives for improving these dialogues in order to transform schools and educational systems today.

Post-structuralist critiques of Habermas have stated that he overlooks power. The theory of communicative action, however, differentiates between the use of power claims and validity claims. Foucault (1977) and Derrida (1967) consider that all relations are power based, including those that Habermas considers to be based on validity claims. Learning communities are not based on the thinking of these authors, because it is impossible to advance towards egalitarian educational transformations based on these post-structuralist stances. If all relations are based on power, why should we favour democratic schools that overcome segregation? And why should we work to transform authoritarian schools that segregate immigrants and poor students? Of course, Foucault and Derrida do not aim to provide a normative framework to help distinguish between what is democratic and egalitarian and what it is not. In fact, they have never pretended to do so.[4]

Still, it is true that Habermas has not developed elements that can be used to deeply analyse the power interactions that are present in communicative actions. His conception does not clarify that, in the real world, even the most dialogic relations include power interactions to some extent. When the experienced teacher talks to family members, even if his approach is totally dialogical, he cannot avoid the fact that he has a position of power in relation to poor students and families. Beyond Habermas' ideal conditions for communicative action, which are based on the speakers' intentions, egalitarian dialogue must consider those power interactions. Instead of being based on the ethics of intentions, learning communities are based on the Weberian ethics of responsibility, accounting for those interactions and therefore for the possible results of communication between teachers, students and family members. Those communities distinguish between dialogic relationships and power relationships. In dialogic relationships, dialogic interactions (not only validity claims) prevail over power interactions; in power relationships, power interactions (not only power claims) prevail over dialogic interactions.

In the learning communities, teachers, students, family members and other citizens have dialogic relationships. Their debates are grounded in arguments (dialogic interactions) and not in their unequal status in the social structures (power interactions); still, they are aware that those inequalities have an influence on their dialogues and on their consensus. In their dialogues they include the public awareness of this influence and the efforts they make to overcome it.

Another limitation of Austin's theory of speech acts for the present sociological analysis is that it implicitly reduces communication to speech. Communication is much more than words; it also includes looks, tones of voice, gestures and much more in the relationships among experienced teachers, family members and students. The theory of communicative acts, unlike the theory of speech acts, includes all those elements. Dialogic communicative acts are based, not only on arguments (words), but also on other elements of dialogic interactions, such as the practice of equally considering all the social actors who participate in them. Power communicative acts are based, not only on the words of those who place themselves in a superior category of knowledge and social structure, but also on elements such as their unequal and authoritarian attitudes.

The dialogic transformation of the school system

Through the egalitarian dialogue within the school context, citizens gain the strength to work to transform the school system. They gain this strength mainly from their arguments, which is the *force* that Austin attributes to the illocutionary speech acts and that learning communities attribute to the wider concept of illocutionary communicative acts.

These citizens bring into the public debate on education their practical and theoretical arguments in order to help overcome school failure and to improve everyone's experiences of living together. Of course, these public debates are based on dialogic communicative acts with dialogic interactions, but they also include many power interactions rooted in the school system and social structure. Policymakers and members of the upper and middle classes have many resources that allow them to impose their interests and objectives. However, in the public debate, it is the arguments that count the most. Thus, the learning communities have been built within a solid framework based on arguments that are not easy to dismiss publicly.

Learning communities succeed because they transform these public debates into dialogic communicative acts. They succeed because they place so much stress on arguments, so that the dialogic interactions have more force than the power interactions rooted in structuralist positions. Without public debates, it is possible for policymakers to impose their segregation policies on the most disadvantaged students in special classrooms. But when the learning community discusses the local children's school experiences, these policymakers must accept their arguments, especially if they reject these policies. These dialogic communicative acts demonstrate that the theories of reproduction are wrong when subjects challenge structures and transform them from their perspective as active citizens. These transformations resonate with what Wright (2008) calls *real utopias*.

Along similar lines, the collaboration between citizens and dialogic researchers has been very productive in social research. In the Framework Programs of Research (FPR) of the European Union, one instrument is commanding the most resources and high scientific recognition: the Integrated Projects. While the FPR have traditionally been dedicated to biochemistry, information technology and similar areas, for the first time an integrated project has been dedicated to analysing schooling: the INCLUD-ED. The European Union's purpose in launching these programmes was to generate new scientific knowledge that would better inform European policies. Thus, depending on their orientation, FPR projects have great potential to transform policies. In the social sciences, the programme's main objective is to promote social cohesion, which includes overcoming the social exclusion and inequalities that face the most disadvantaged groups. The final conference of the FPR project WORKALÓ (a transnational study about the Roma population in Europe) was held in the headquarters of the European Parliament. Members of the European Parliament (MEPs) were taking notes on the debates between researchers and subjects. A woman who introduced herself as an illiterate Roma grandmother presented the summary of the project's main conclusions (Beck-Gernsheim et al., 2003). One of the MEPs who attended brought these conclusions to the European Parliament; there they were included in a resolution that was later approved unanimously (European Parliament Resolution, 2005).

Similar resolutions were also passed at the level of EU member states. For instance, the Spanish parliament unanimously approved a resolution to recognize the Roma as one of the people of Spain (Congreso de los Diputados, 2005). As a consequence of this decision, the Spanish State Council of the Roma was created, and the state committed to consulting with this council on any policy that affects the Roma. This recognition is seen as a historically crucial change that has deeply transformed six centuries of relations between the Spanish state and the Roma. During the 1980s, some Roma warned about the potential negative consequences for their children, in terms of absenteeism and school failure, of the national school reform that was developed and finally approved in 1990.[5] But the experts and the policymakers dismissed their statements. After the transformation generated by the WORKALÓ project, today the state is obligated to listen to these voices. Dialogic sociology, as found in the WORKALÓ project, made real the objective of *public sociology* (Burawoy, 2005), by moving beyond the academy and engaging with wider audiences.

Citizens participating in the learning communities are very diverse in terms of gender, social class, ethnicity, age, sexual orientation, religion etc., as well as their ideological and political stands. Some citizens argue that if policymakers change their decisions through dialogic communicative acts in public debates, it is owing to a real change of attitudes: they see politicians as now assuming they must look for the best education for all children, including the under-privileged. Others argue that policymakers have not changed their attitudes but instead feel pressured by the public debate. Even if this is the case, this change represents important benefits for the egalitarian transformation of the school system. Elster (1999) explains this situation as the 'civilizing force of hypocrisy: If we take account of equity effects as well as efficiency effects, arguing in public is probably a superior form of collective decision making' compared to bargaining in private. But of course, 'this is not a statement for which proof can be offered' (p. 402).

Today, European Union officials are mainly preoccupied with efficiency and equity in the school outcomes of different social groups. Because statistics such the results on the PISA examinations have had such a strong impact in the media, most of the public debate focuses on the limited and biased data this survey provides. Some teachers and authors opposed these statistics; they defended their students' poor performance on the tests as a form of resistance and radicalism. In the learning communities, family members and other citizens criticize these authors and teachers as self-labelled 'radicals': they say they oppose the efforts made to obtain equal educational outcomes for all the students, including the most disadvantaged ones (efficiency and equity), while sending their own children to college (equity without efficiency for some, unequal efficiency for their own).

The activities of learning communities are oriented towards an egalitarian reform of the school system and society. They consider a wide range of dimensions. These schools are struggling with gender-based violence, racism and war. Instead of discussing values and emotions, these schools take action by restructuring all their spaces and dynamics on the basis of solidarity and emotional development. This process is part of the egalitarian transformation towards overcoming the current unequal results on mathematics, language and science along the lines of class, gender and race. The professionals and families participating in these schools are very aware that, if poor children fail an exam in mathematics, that does not mean that their school is more radical. What makes a school radical and transformative is that everything is done in solidarity, including the teaching of mathematics.

Learning communities demonstrate that egalitarian transformation is possible; they are aware that some actions support positive progress towards this aim and some do not. The FPR INCLUD-ED project is focused on clarifying the transformative strategies and their transposition into EU member states and regional governmental policies. There are many examples of this kind of transformation; we offer two of them below.

Having seen the success of the transformative actions that INCLUD-ED selected in twenty-six Basque schools, the Basque Country government developed a plan to extend this work to its entire school system. The minister of education said publicly that his dream is to transform the Basque Country into a learning community. This plan has not been developed by the Basque government itself, but through a very open and long dialogue among all kinds of citizen: trade union members, teachers, researchers, manual workers, members of social movements, families, students, women's organizations. This dialogue was conducted through illocutionary communicative acts.

A second example is found in the General Directorate of Education of the European Union, particularly in the cluster called 'Access and Social Inclusion in Lifelong Learning'. This body is composed of two representatives for each country: one from the government and one from the NGO sector. Members of the cluster have analysed the actions that INCLUD-ED selected, along with the theoretical developments and practical experiences of learning communities. They have done so by discussing them directly with the involved citizens in the communities. The cluster recommended that those activities be implemented in the various European member states.

Dialogic sociology has facilitated many of the transformations outlined here. These transformations are becoming relevant for many people, especially, but not only, the under-privileged. They are also important for those researchers who want to collaborate in a process of transforming the school systems and societies. In doing so, the authors in this approach are working along the lines of what Erik Wright (2008) calls the sociology of possibility and not of what he calls the sociology of impossibility. Just one day before this present chapter was completed, the European Union condemned segregated special classrooms for immigrants, arguing that they should not be separated from the rest of the children (Missé, 2009: 37). This resolution will transform the lives and the opportunities of many children. And this kind of transformation is the reason why an increasing number of sociologists are working on dialogic sociology.

Notes

1 'Sometimes, as Ramón Flecha here demonstrates, knowledge flows from the bottom up, when individuals with no degree or academic background "produce" and "invent" cultural analyses on the basis of their own experience, their thought, and the exchange with other inventors or their own culture' (Touraine, 2000).

2 'One site where this already occurs in some places is in education. In Barcelona, Spain, some public elementary schools have been turned into what they call "learning communities" in which the governance of the school is substantially shifted to parents, teachers and members of the community, and the function of the school shifts from narrowly teaching children to providing a broader range of learning activities for the community as a whole' (Wright, 2008: 20).

3 www.tv3.cat/videos/1009029/TN-migdia-2022009 (minute 31:22).

4 The learning communities project aims to transform schools by instituting dialogic relations instead of power relations. Learning communities represent a deep critique of the social and educational exclusion created by power and the lies associated with this exclusion. On the other hand, Foucault (1977) does not consider power to be negative in itself: 'We must cease once and for all to describe the effects of power in negative terms: it "excludes," it "represses," it "censors," it "abstracts," it "masks," it "conceals"' (p. 194). Along similar lines, Derrida (1967: 21) tries to deconstruct – to destroy – the signification of truth, while learning communities follow the opposite orientation, which Chomsky (1996: 56) describes: 'The responsibility of the writer as a moral agent is to try to bring the truth about matters of human significance to an audience that can do something about them.'

5   The school reform implemented at that time was LOGSE – Ley Orgánica de Ordenación General del Sistema Educativo de España.

References

Apple, M.W. and Beane, J.A. (eds) (2007) *Democratic schools: lessons in powerful education*, Portsmouth, NH: Heinemann.
Austin, J.L. (1962) *How to do things with words*, Cambridge, MA: Harvard University Press.
Beck-Gernsheim, E., Butler, J. and Puigvert, L. (2003) *Women and social transformation*, New York: Peter Lang.
Burawoy, M. (2005) 'American Sociological Association Presidential Address: for public sociology', *British Journal of Sociology* 56(2): 259–294.
Chomsky, N. (1996) *Powers & prospects*, Boston, MA: South End Press.
Congreso de los Diputados (2005) 162/000320 Proposición no de Ley presentada por el Grupo parlamentario de Esquerra Republicana (ERC), relativa al Reconocimiento de los Derechos del Pueblo Gitano, *Boletín Oficial De Las Cortes Generales* (186): 42–43.
Derrida, J. (1967) *De la grammatologie*, Paris: Les Éditions de Minuit.
Elster, J. (1998) *Deliberative democracy (Cambridge Studies in the Theory of Democracy)*, Cambridge: Cambridge University Press.
—— (1999) *Alchemies of the mind: rationality and the emotions*, Cambridge: Cambridge University Press.
European Parliament Resolution (2005) *Resolution of 28 April 2005 on the situation of the Roma in the European Union*, P6_TA-PROV(2005)0151. Available online at www.europarl.europa.eu/sides/getDoc.do?pubRef=-//EP//TEXT+TA+P6-TA-2008-0361+0+DOC+XML+V0//EN (accessed 6 April 2009).
Foucault, M. (1977) *Discipline and punishment: the birth of the prison*, New York: Pantheon Books.
Habermas, J. (1984) *The theory of communicative action*. Vol. 1. *Reason and the rationalization of society*, Boston, MA: Beacon Press.
—— (1987) *The theory of communicative action*. Vol. 2. *Lifeworld and system: a critique of functionalist reason*, Boston, MA: Beacon Press.
INCLUD-ED Consortium (2006–2011) *INCLUD-ED: strategies for inclusion and social cohesion in Europe from education*, FP6 028603–2. Sixth Framework Programme. Priority 7 Citizens and governance in a knowledge-based society, European Commission.
Izquierdo, L. (2005) 'Más de tres alumnos inmigrantes por aula dispara la media de suspensos de la clase', *La Vanguardia*, 20 July 2005.
Missé, A. (2009) 'La Eurocámara rechaza las clases especiales para niños inmigrantes', *El País*, 5 April 2009.
Searle, J. and Soler, M. (2009) *Lenguaje y ciencias sociales*, Barcelona: Hipatia.
Touraine, A. (2000) Commentary on back cover of R. Flecha (2000) *Sharing words: theory and practice of dialogic learning*, Lanham, MD: Rowman & Littlefield.
Wright, E. (2008) 'The socialist compass' in E. Wright (ed.) *Envisioning real Utopias*. Available online at www.ssc.wisc.edu/~wright/ERU.htm (accessed 6 April 2009).

31

The democratization of governance in the Citizen School project

Building a new notion of accountability in education

Luis Armando Gandin

Speaking at the World Social Forum in Belém, Brazil in January of 2009, David Harvey presented the concept of "the right to the city":

> I have been working for some time on the idea of the Right to the City. I take it that Right to the City means the right of all of us to create cities that meet human needs, our needs. . . . The right to the city is not simply the right to what already exists in the city but the right to make the city into something radically different.
>
> (Harvey, 2009: 5)

This concept summarizes what the experience of the Popular Administration (a coalition of leftist parties, led by the Workers Party) and its Citizen School project in Porto Alegre intended to create: rather than perpetuating the current narrow view of accountability in education, based on a market-centered worldview, the Popular Administration started implementing what Harvey describes. As Harvey says, people have a "right to construct different kinds of cities" and not only receive "crumbs from the rich man's table" (Harvey, 2009: 5). At the center of the Citizen School project was precisely the idea that the priority in public policy has to be, more than merely guaranteeing access to what the city already has to offer to its citizens (what, in the case of the *favela* dwellers, would certainly be already a step-up), changing the relationship between the communities and the state. The state has to be taught by the communities how to interact with them; the school has to change its structures and presuppositions and not simply demand students from the *favelas* to either adapt or leave, as traditional schools do. Being accountable to communities in this context is more than merely "doing what's best for the client"; it represents building up a relationship of commitment between state and communities; this is the kind of change in educational public policy that offers an alternative that is not only a distant reality but one that is being implemented in a large Brazilian city.

In previous publications (Gandin 2006, 2009a,b), I examined the experience of the Citizen School project implemented in the municipal schools of Porto Alegre. The conception of the Citizen School was implemented over a period of sixteen years (starting in 1989) by the Popular Administration, a coalition of leftist parties, led by the Workers Party. The Citizen School project evolved as a program, defined collectively by the actors involved, of democratization of access to schools, knowledge, and governance. In this chapter I will concentrate my analysis on the democratization of governance promoted inside the schools, in the relationship between the Municipal Secretariat of Education (SMED) and the schools, and between communities and the schools.

The democratization of governance in Porto Alegre's municipal schools

In the context of the Citizen School project, democratizing governance involved the democratization of the relationships inside schools, between the school and the community, and between the school and the SMED. The democratization of governance implied the creation of an institutional design that could generate the empowered participation of teachers, staff, parents, and administrators in the undertaking of decisions about education in Porto Alegre, as well as a system of monitoring that guaranteed that the collectively agreed-upon decisions were being implemented. The democratization of governance also gave the culture of the community a central role in the educational and administrative spheres of the school and school system; both the state agencies and the communities had to learn together how to construct new mechanisms that represented the will of the communities.

The decision-making and monitoring processes in the educational system of Porto Alegre occur at various levels: for example, the establishment of a broad city policy for education and its constant evaluation; deliberation about how to invest the money allocated by the central administration to the school; and the creation of an educational model that builds mechanisms of inclusion to struggle against a society that marginalizes the impoverished students and denies them valuable knowledge.

The Constituent Assembly of Education (held in 1995) was a core element of this process of democratization. Gathering more than 500 delegates (in a process that started with meetings in every school and extended for more than a year) from the school communities, the Assembly formulated the broad policy directives implemented by the SMED (Silva, 1999). This alone marks a significant departure from the traditional model, in which decisions are handed down from above while implementation is left to the schools. Through their elected delegates, schools and their communities were actively involved in the construction of the educational policy in Porto Alegre. This is a unique aspect of the Citizen School project. Fung, who studied the Local Schools Councils in Chicago (1999) and classified them as highly positive, nevertheless suggests that "centralized interventions, themselves formulated through deliberation, would then further enhance the deliberative, participatory, and empowered character of otherwise isolated local actions" (Fung, 1999: 26). This combination, suggested by Fung as ideal, seems to be exactly what has been achieved in Porto Alegre.

Another important element to emphasize is that the experience in Porto Alegre has been serving as a viable alternative to the neo-liberal market-based solutions for management and monitoring of the quality of public schools in other parts of Brazil. Involvement of the parents and of the students in important decisions and active monitoring in the school (not merely peripheral decisions) gives them a real sense of what "public" means in public school. At the same time, because the SMED has been able to involve teachers actively in the transformations— as well as to help improve their qualifications and salaries—instead of merely blaming them and their unions for the problems in education (common practice in the neo-liberal driven reforms), the Popular Administration has been able to include every segment of the schools in the collective project of constructing quality education in the impoverished neighborhoods where municipal schools are situated. Thus, instead of opting for a doctrine that merely treats parents as consumers of education (treated itself as a commodity), the Citizen School became an alternative that challenges this idea. Parents, students, teachers, staff, and administrators are responsible for working collectively, each contributing their knowledge and expertise, to create better education. In this way, the Citizen School has defined itself over and against the market logic that offers only competition and "exit" as solutions for parents.

The market logic, with "exit" as a solution to the problems of the disadvantaged groups in public schools, does not provide any mechanism for actively involving parents directly in improving the quality of the schools. As research has shown (Whitty *et al.*, 1998), "choice" schemes merely offer an individual option that does not contribute at all to the formation of networks of citizens interested in bettering, not only their schools, but also their communities. In the Citizen School, the active involvement of the community in the schools is a mechanism to guarantee the improved performance of the school and for holding teachers and administrators accountable to the parents and to the community. The school council, with its powers to deliberate, regulate, and monitor, together with the Constituent Assembly of Education, where principles were constructed, provides a mechanism that can generate schools that are open to assessment of quality by the community.

The Citizen School was a project for the excluded. Not only students, however, have been benefiting from the improved quality education they receive. Parents, students, and school staff, usually mere spectators of the processes of decision-making in the traditional school, are now part of the structure of governance inside the school council and bring their knowledge "to the table." In fact, the whole process challenges the cultural model that says that poor and "uneducated" people should not or cannot participate because they do not know how to do so.

It is true that lack of information can be a real deterrent for effective participation. The Popular Administration argued strongly that participation was a process that had to be nurtured; therefore, it launched, in the first years of the project, a program to provide training and information so that people could participate knowledgeably in the school councils and in other participatory structures such as the Participatory Budget (a mechanism that guarantees active popular participation and deliberation in the decision-making process for the allocation of resources for investment in the city; see Santos, 1998). Thus, the transfer of technical knowledge has been an important part of the process. In this sense, the Popular Administration and the SMED seem to have understood perfectly Offe's observation that the functional superiority of a new model of participation does not by itself solve all the problems involved in major democratic reforms (Offe, 1995: 125–126). The mechanisms of the Citizen School redefine the participants as subjects, as historical actors. Participants are not only implementing rules, but are part of an historical experiment of reconstructing the organization of the municipal state.

One problem that afflicts democratic governance structures such as the school councils is the possibility that participants who historically have held more power will continue to dominate them. This is a serious issue that needs to be addressed, given the experiences of similar experiments elsewhere. Some specific factors in the case of Porto Alegre, however, reduce the risk of this. First, the municipal schools are all situated in the most impoverished areas of Porto Alegre. Therefore, the classical examples of middle-class parents dominating the discussions (see McGrath and Kuriloff, 1999) are avoided because, as a rule, there are no middle-class parents in the regions where the schools are located. Two studies of the Participatory Budget (OP) in

Porto Alegre offer some indirect evidence (Abers, 1998; Santos, 1998), and one study offers direct empirical evidence (Baiocchi, 1999) that shows that there is no domination by powerful groups in the deliberative processes. In the OP, there is gender parity among the participants of the meetings, and the proportion of "less-educated" people corresponds to the city average (Baiocchi, 1999: 7). While it is true that there are more men and educated people speaking at the meetings, the research has also shown that the main factor determining who speaks is the number of years of participation. There is a learning curve that encourages people with more years of participation to speak. In fact "participation over time seems to increase participation parity" (Baiocchi, 1999: 10). This is a very encouraging conclusion, especially given the project's conscious pedagogical aims. Having said that, there are no data about the composition of the various mechanisms of the Citizen School itself, and therefore there is no evaluation of this potential problem in the schools of Porto Alegre.

The way financial resources are decentralized and transferred directly to the schools also brings about changes inside them. This requires principals, teachers, and the members of the school council to learn how to deal with public money. In contrast, the historical centralism of the educational system in Brazil instilled distrust and an inability to deal with the notion of public resources. The opportunity for those who take part in the Citizen School project is to learn, while doing it, how to create consensual democratic rules regarding how to allocate these public resources and how to create democratic ways of monitoring their use. In this sense it restores to the public the position that had been historically privatized by the interests of the dominant groups (Genro, 1999)—and it does so by including members of the community who recover their dignity by breaking with the dominant notion that, because they live in a *favela*, they are too miserable to be able to participate in a governance structure.

Baiocchi (1999), referring to the OP, says that there is a real empowerment of the poorer groups, because their demands now have a channel and their voices can be heard. This is also certainly true in the case of the Citizen School and its structures, as I showed above. In the Brazilian context, where citizenship has always represented merely a right to vote (actually a duty, because voting is compulsory in Brazil), the idea of being part of the real decisions concerning the life of the institution responsible for the education of their children is a tremendous achievement for those groups, something that organized social movements have been fighting for for decades. If we consider also the OP (and the close relation between the OP and the schools is itself a great democratic achievement), the consequences of the aggregated participation in essential spheres of their lives create a real change in the way impoverished communities organize themselves and relate to the state. Baiocchi (1999) shows how that participation in deliberative instances is not breaking down political interests into ever-smaller parochial issues, but promoting an increasingly active citizenry, attentive to the larger issues of the city and country. It is possible to conclude, therefore, that the Citizen School is helping to produce, together with the other initiatives of the Popular Administration, empowered citizens (all the segments of the school community), who not only deliberate about the best way of administering schools but have an active role in monitoring public institutions in order to generate effective state practices.

Yet another element of the democratization of governance is the radical democratization of the internal management of the schools. The election of principals was a long-time cause for teachers' unions in Brazil as part of the larger conception of democratic management. Direct elections for principals guarantee that the coordinator of the school is not a person chosen because she or he has a good relationship with the administration (something that happens in the majority of the public schools in Brazil). Any teacher can be a candidate, without needing a special degree—an important step towards challenging the idea that only those with a degree in school administration can manage effectively. By questioning this premise, the Citizen School project shows that the process that is occurring in the education of the students— problematization of what counts as knowledge—is also occurring at the administrative level. Having said that, the SMED is aware of the difficulties of a principal's task and therefore offers periodic training to those who wish to be candidates.

The process of direct election of principals by the whole educational community produces great voter turnout. Every election, thousands of people vote in the elections for principals; communities are involved in the election process. This is also an important part of the democratic learning process of the communities, especially because it triggers a debate about the proposals for management of the school. Prospective principals campaign in the school and in the community, where they must offer a proposal for their term of office with the ideas that they want to implement if elected.

Furthermore, in contrast to the traditional schools where curriculum is selected and constructed outside the school and only "implemented" by teachers (the ever-present separation between conception and execution in schools, analyzed by Apple, 1988), in the Citizen School the entire curriculum is developed by teachers inside each school. This alone is already an innovative governance structure of the SMED, which does not conceive the curriculum in the secretariat but urges each school to engage in a creative process of collective construction of the school curriculum. As a result, a totally new structure is created, one related to the management of curriculum development inside the school. The steps taken by the schools to create their curriculum, which involve research in the communities, guarantee that there are democratic spaces and that it is not only teachers who participate in the process of the con- struction of the curriculum. Community leaders, social movements (formal and informal), key cultural leadership, and so on, through the statements collected in the participatory research, also contribute to the final product.

In this sense, the school has a high degree of autonomy. Autonomy has come to mean several different things, especially after the neo-liberal rearticulation of this term, so it is important to develop a precise understanding of the autonomy to construct curriculum. Warde talks about a progressive and democratic definition of autonomy. According to her,

> School autonomy is the freedom to formulate and execute an educational project . . .
> It is only feasible when the school is involved in a radically new political project about democracy and its top-down structures and relations are destroyed.
>
> (Warde, 1992: 86)

This is the kind of autonomy that the municipal schools in Porto Alegre are constructing. By radically reconfiguring the "structures and relations," schools created spaces for the establishment of collective reasoning and the search for ever-better education, collectively developed by teachers. With the creation of spaces for critique and innovation, even if the administration were tempted to interfere in the schools, it would have to deal with this disposition for critique of top-down decisions and fixed structures. This is a significant indication of the success of the democratization of governance in the schools.

Finally, it is important to point out that, by building democratization of access to school, democratization of knowledge, and democratization of governance, the Citizen School project offers a concrete demonstration of its idea of citizenship. The project is producing citizens with access to quality education in schools where students construct knowledge in the dialogue between high culture and popular knowledge, with neither treated as ultimately superior to the other. Furthermore, these are citizens who can concretely understand that the solution to their economic difficulties is not individual escape; who view solidarity as a worthy goal; who both value the collective and respect differences. These citizens are much more than mere consumers, a category that reduces participation in society to exchanges in the marketplace. This is the notion of citizenship that the Citizen School is helping to construct.

The Citizen School project was able to provide a new social imaginary for all those involved in the progressive transformation of schools. By constructing a new model in the educational system of Porto Alegre, the Popular Administration and the SMED provided more than a new political language for progressive teachers, parents, and teachers' unions: they actually gave them a concrete working example that shows that it is possible to build a counter-hegemonic alternative. The Citizen School project offers not just a discursive anchor for the supporters of a school that aims at fighting exclusion and commoditization in education: it provides a reality, an example of success, a viable way of forging a counter-hegemonic movement in education, an alternative to the mainstream notion of accountability. This project is a reference that can always be pointed to as a working case of the principles of social justice in education. In a time where progressive experiences are attacked (correctly in some cases, maliciously in others) for not delivering what they promised,[1] the Citizen School project symbolizes the possibility of constructing counter-hegemonic reforms. Rather than affecting only the municipal schools of Porto Alegre, the Citizen School has an impact in the imagination of all who struggle for an education that deals at the same time with a redistribution of public goods and recognition of differences.

Final remarks

Analyzing the conservative reforms in education prevalent around the world, Smyth (2001) claims that there is a possible alternative to these reforms that, in the name of devolution, give schools all the "responsibilities and no power" (p. 73). As he states, this alternative should be "dramatically different" from the market-driven models and

> it is one in which schools are educationally vibrant places—where parents, teachers, students, and the community feel they are able to freely engage in discussion and debate about what is going on, why, and with what effect. There is also an absence of schools being bludgeoned into submission using crude and narrow economic agenda. There are genuine opportunities for dialogue, chances to understand one another's perspective outside coercion, and a greater tolerance, difference, and diversity in contrast to conformity and uniformity produced by some centrally determined market model.
>
> (Smyth 2001: 83)

In this chapter, I have sought to examine the capacity of the Citizen School project to convert itself into an alternative to the market-driven models in education. To a great extent, Smyth's description of what an alternative could look like matches what I found in the Citizen School project.

In fact, in my research I encountered schools that truly are "vibrant places," where there is an environment of creativity, participation, and dialogue, not only among teachers and between teachers and students, but also in the communities where the schools are situated. Even the critique of some of the practices and measures of the SMED is, in fact, evidence of the fertile terrain for discussion and dissent created inside the schools and of the effort that these schools make to search for better forms of constructing an education that really caters to the formerly excluded students.

The municipal schools in Porto Alegre are also clearly not subject to a "narrow economic agenda"; actually, they are explicit about their practices for avoiding this kind of subjection. In fact, the SMED acts as a protective shield, behind which schools can construct their curriculum and new ways to involve the communities in the educational process of the students, rather than responding to conservative attacks. The seriousness with which the SMED demands from the schools the precise implementation of what the educational laws mandate, the high priority it gives to creating schools that have excellent material conditions compared with the past, and the relatively high salaries it pays to its teachers, end up resulting in a great deal of legitimacy for its actions.

In the municipal schools of Porto Alegre, I have encountered teachers with a renewed hope in the possibility of constructing a radically different school from the one they attended. I witnessed teachers actively creating a curriculum for their school by interacting with the communities and meeting regularly at times especially allocated and institutionally guaranteed for dialogue about their methodology and their goals with the specific network of concepts they are developing with their students. Rather than being pressured for a kind of accountability that only looks at test results, these teachers are socially, politically, and culturally accountable. Quality in this context is not reduced to accumulation of information, nor even the ability to establish connections among concepts; it is also linked to the schools' capacity to generate a culturally embedded curriculum that engages students in creative thinking and, to a certain extent, in actions that could lead to social transformation in the future.

In fact, besides having the organizational aspects characterized by Smyth as central to any alternative project, the Citizen School has also challenged the dominant notion of what counts as valid knowledge. In the municipal schools, the curriculum creation is part of a larger process of questioning "official knowledge" and valuing the culture of the communities. In this sense, this is a project that is implementing the idea of a "culturally relevant pedagogy" (Ladson-Billings, 1994). Drawing from Ladson-Billings' conceptualizations, Fletcher (2000) talks about the kind of work that this pedagogy should be doing in schools:

> Instead of trying to convince students that the traditional curriculum will serve them, if only they can master it, a culturally relevant pedagogy offers students an active role in questioning the knowledge they encounter in school and attempts to give students a place to engage in their own critical reconstructions.
>
> (p. 177)

This is exactly what the Citizen School seems to be doing. It is constructing what Ladson-Billings (1994) would call "bridges or a scaffolding" that can help students to "be where they need to be to participate fully and meaningfully in the construction of knowledge" (p. 96). The Citizen School project is trying to invert the traditional linear conception of knowledge in schools. The notion of building "bridges or scaffolding" breaks away from this linear rationale and interprets knowledge construction as a process that must start with the culture of the students, but not stop there. It has to build what Santos (1989) calls a "double epistemological rupture," an undertaking that creates dialogue between common sense and scientific knowledge and, in this dialogic process, problematizes both of them. The fact that this goal exists in the project and has been actively pursued is promising in terms of forging this double rupture.

355

Yet another important aspect of the Citizen School project that makes it an alternative to mainstream models of accountability in education is the fact that it is not a voluntaristic experience, nor an experience that is restricted to the space of schools. Zeichner (1991) insists that one of the great problems with reforms in education is the fact that they are not linked to efforts of larger transformation in society. He states,

> advocating democratic educational projects without explicitly calling for general social reconstruction serves to strengthen the mistaken view—so successfully ingrained in the public consciousness in these times of conservative resurgence—that the schools are largely responsible for the whole host of rotten outcomes that confront so many of our children. Remaining silent on the need for broader social, economic, and political change only serves to create false expectations about what can be accomplished by educational reform alone. The position that I have supported here is that no school organizational plan or level of autonomy in school decision making for teachers or the community, by itself, will ever be sufficient for dealing with the institutional and structural inequalities in our society that underlie the educational problems in the schools.
>
> (Zeichner, 1991: paragraph 42)

What the case of Porto Alegre offers is educational reform that addresses the complex problems of exclusion and access, the issue of what is valued as knowledge, and the lack of democratic structures inside schools in a close relation with the larger project of the Popular Administration in Porto Alegre, which aims at redistribution and recognition (Fraser, 1998). Schools have an essential role in this larger project, especially because they educate citizens who will be better prepared to demand more and better democratic structures and to participate in the ones that are already in place. Nevertheless, as Zeichner points out, schools alone cannot perform the necessary social and political transformation necessary to construct social justice.

If constructing new school structures and culture is not sufficient to perform the kinds of necessary larger transformation that Zeichner calls for, without these new structures and culture, schools actually act as barriers for this larger project. That is why it was so important to break away from structures and a culture that perpetuates exclusion. This is something that the Citizen School project, despite the difficulties, has managed to achieve, by, among other things, its conception of democratization of governance.

Note

1   Diane Ravitch published a long book in which she, from a rightist perspective, criticizes the left and the progressives for not accomplishing in education what they promised (Ravitch, 2000). For a critical review of the book see Apple (2001). In this review, Apple argues that, in the book, Ravitch "misconstrues or ignores many of the most powerful dynamics that actually create the conditions that led to or prevented school reform, and . . . stereotypes thousands of committed educators who have devoted their lives to schooling" (Apple, 2001: 332).

References

Abers, R. (1998) "From clientelism to cooperation: local government, participatory policy and civic organizing in Porto Alegre, Brazil," *Politics & Society* 26(4): 511–537.

Apple, M.W. (1988) *Teachers and texts*, New York: Routledge.
—— (2001) "Standards, subject matter, and a romantic past," *Educational Policy* 15(2): 323–334.
Baiocchi, G. (1999) *Participation, activism, and politics: the Porto Alegre experiment and deliberative democratic theory*, Unpublished manuscript.
Fletcher, S. (2000) *Education and emancipation: theory and practice in a new constellation*, New York: Teachers College Press.
Fraser, N. (1998) "Social justice in the age of identity politics: redistribution, recognition, and participation," in *The Tanner Lectures on Human Values*, 19, University of Utah Press: 1–67.
Fung, A. (1999) "Deliberative democracy, Chicago style," unpublished manuscript.
Gandin, L.A. (2006) "Creating real alternatives to neoliberal policies in education: the Citizen School Project," in M.W. Apple and K. Buras *The subaltern speak*, New York: Routledge, pp. 217–241.
—— (2009a) "Creating local democracy, nurturing global alternatives: the case of the citizen school project in Porto Alegre, Brazil," in W. Ayers, T. Quinn and D. Stovall *Handbook of social justice in education*, New York: Routledge, pp. 576–585.
—— (2009b) "The citizen school project: implementing and recreating critical education in Porto Alegre, Brazil," in M.W. Apple, W. Au and L.A. Gandin *The Routledge international handbook of critical education*, New York: Routledge, pp. 341–353.
Genro, T. (1999) "Cidadania, emancipação e cidade," in L.H. Silva (ed.) *Escola cidadã: teoria e prática*, Petrópolis, Brazil: Vozes, pp. 7–11.
Harvey, D. (2009) Lecture at the World Social Forum 2009 in Belém, Brazil. Available online at www.ongcidade.org/site/arquivos/noticias/harveyfsm49906df97693e.pdf.
Ladson-Billings, G. (1994) *The dreamkeepers: successful teachers of African American children*, San Francisco, CA: Jossey-Bass Publishers.
McGrath, D.J. and Kuriloff, P.J. (1999) "They're going to tear the doors off this place: upper-middle-class parent school involvement and the educational opportunities of other people's children," *Educational Policy* 13(5): 603–629.
Offe, C. (1995) "Some skeptical considerations on the malleability of representative institutions," in J. Cohen and J. Rogers (eds) *Associations and democracy*, London: Verso, pp. 114–132.
Ravitch, D. (2000) *Left back: a century of failed school reforms*, New York: Simon & Schuster.
Santos, B.S. (1989) *Introdução a uma ciência pós-moderna*, Porto, Portugal: Afrontamento.
—— (1998) "Participatory budgeting in Porto Alegre: toward a distributive democracy," *Politics and Society* 26(4): 461–510.
Silva, L.H. (ed.) (1999) *Escola cidadã: teoria e prática*, Petrópolis, Brazil: Vozes.
Smyth, J. (2001) *Critical politics of teachers' work*, New York: Peter Lang.
Warde, M.J. (1992) "Considerações sobre a autonomia da escola," *Idéias* 15: 79–90.
Whitty, G., Power, S. and Halpin, D. (1998) *Devolution and choice in education: the school, the state and the market*, Buckingham, UK: Open University Press.
Zeichner, K. (1991) "Contradictions and tensions in the professionalization of teaching and the democratization of schools," *Teachers College Record* 92(3): 363–380. Available online from EBSCOhost database (Academic Search Elite): http://search.epnet.com (accessed 8 June 2002).

32

Syncretism and hybridity

Schooling, language, and race and students from non-dominant communities[1]

Kris D. Gutiérrez, Arshad Ali and Cecilia Henríquez

> Race is an issue that I believe this nation cannot afford to ignore right now . . . The fact
> is . . . the issues that have surfaced over the last few weeks reflect the complexities of
> race in this country that we've never really worked through—a part of our union we
> have yet to perfect. And if we walk away now, if we simply retreat into our respective
> corners, we will never be able to come together and solve [the challenges that face
> America today].
>
> (President Barack Obama, March 18, 2008,
> Philadelphia, PA; Scholars Roundtable)

The 2008 United States election exposed the ways racist ideologies and practices are deeply
implicated in US history and made visible the ways in which class alone cannot explain the
persistent inequities experienced by people from non-dominant communities.[2] President
Obama's historic speech on race, motivated by persistent racialized attacks throughout the
election, initiated an important discussion of race in the public sphere. Yet, despite attempts
to address key issues of race, as in President Obama's speech, the language of race relations too
often obfuscates the structural and historical basis of racial inequality (Steinberg, 2007). Similarly,
the discourses of schooling in the US veil the fundamental structural basis of racial and class
hierarchies and inequities.

This chapter uses the schooling experiences of non-dominant students in the US as a case
of a globalized phenomenon in which the significant backslide towards greater economic and
social inequality has heightened the educational disparities experienced by students from non-
dominant communities. It focuses on the ways the theoretical concept and social constructs of
race are implicitly and deeply connected to issues of culture and identity (Kubota and Lin, in
press). Further, it explores how language and literacies have become proxies for race that serve
as the means for instutionalizing curricular forms of segregation, marginalization, and othering.
Finally, it highlights the need for a theoretical explanation of the ways race, language, and literacy
constitute capital in schooling environments—and the need for a gendered and raced political
economy that emanates from the standpoints of non-dominant communities (Luke, in press).

Finally, it challenges approaches that rely on a reductive and essentializing mono-cultural and monolingual lens to define students' linguistic repertoires and to design their educational futures.

"Racing-language"[3]

The relationship between language, race, and culture has long been a topic of interest across disciplines and fields, such as anthropology and linguistic anthropology (Alim, 2009; Boas, 1940; Zentella, 1997), sociology (Bernstein, 1975), sociolinguistics (Baugh, 1988, 1997; Harris and Rampton, 2003; Lee, 1993; Smitherman, 1977), and education (Gutiérrez et al., 2001). However, the asymmetrical relations between language and language speakers have not been sufficiently addressed or explored intersectionally with class and race differences (Urciuoli, 1995: 533). For example, Urciuoli (1995) has addressed how language/power asymmetries, such as those between Spanish and English, emerge when "people have to negotiate across power relations" (p. 535) and public institutions; this is particularly poignant in school contexts where "class and race differences that are mapped onto language are reproduced in the practices and performances that make up students' experiences" (Foley, 1990, as cited in Urciuoli, 1995: 537). To change the way we theorize and examine these relationships, linguistic anthropologists suggest that a serious effort must be put into theorizing race to understand how the practices of language are tied to linguistic and racial inequality (Alim, 2009)—what Alim calls "race-ing language"; with simultaneous attention to "languaging race," that is, theorizing language to understand how race works.

Rethinking the constructs: syncretic and historicizing perspectives

These new theorizations notwithstanding, there has been insufficient attention to theorizing the relationship between race and language, and this has occurred across disciplinary boundaries, theoretical perspectives, and methods. Steinberg (2007), for example, has argued that sociology remains a "white sociology," even in discussions of racial inequality, where dominant perspectives and interests are maintained by focusing on the "victims" instead of those who perpetuate racial oppression and historical inequality. Steinberg proposes an inversion of normative practices so that the standpoints of those who are the object of racial oppression are privileged.

In the domain of education, researchers (Gutiérrez, 2006; Gutiérrez & Arzubiaga, 2008) petitioned scholars to examine how their own work helps to construct and sustain essentialist and deficit narratives of the educational potential of non-dominant students. The operant tasks of this project would center on locating the central constructs in researchers' work, naming the framework and field that give meaning to the constructs, as well as understanding their history of use vis-à-vis non-dominant communities. Identifying the ideological positions in the constructs and frameworks employed is fundamental to understanding whose interests have been served and how commonplace constructs such as "diverse," "at-risk," "limited-English-proficient," and "underachievement" have been naturalized in deficit discourses used to explain non-dominant students' performance in school (Rose, 1985).

Historically, language and naturalizing discourses of difference have not served the benign goal of identifying student needs, but rather have served as an insidious indicator of intelligence. The operant notion of culture here is based on its relation to genetics or deficit views that paint the practices of cultural communities as homogeneous, unchanging, and deviant from dominant, thus normative, practices. Further, the tendency to focus on explorations of language, language use, and practices, absent of their context of use, essentializes and dehistoricizes students' "linguistic repertoires of practice" (Gutiérrez and Rogoff, 2003). In misrepresenting and undervaluing students' linguistic toolkits, empirical work can serve to further exacerbate students' marginalization (Alim, 2005).

The work of critical race theorists (Gotanda, 2004) has highlighted the importance of historicizing racializing practices to theorize, to "re-mediate," and design new pathways, possibilities, and educational projects for students from non-dominant communities. In his work, Gotanda (2004) used the notion of *white innocence* as the analytic standpoint from which he examined racial ideology in *Brown v. Board of Education*, the US Supreme Court decision that ostensibly outlawed overt racial segregation in American schools. In his analysis, Gotanda argued that the US Court was engaged in the ideological project of defending and maintaining *white innocence*. Here, the racialized notion of *white innocence* does not refer to the racial category of whiteness, but rather to the dominant subject-position that preserves racial subordination and the differential benefits for the *innocents* who retain their own dominant position.

The practical logic of white innocence

In the 1954 *Brown* decision—a touchstone case for educational civil rights in the US—the US Supreme Court stated that overturning previous cases allowing segregated schools was based on scientific evidence previously unknown to the Court. New empirical research provided the basis for the Court to declare that racial segregation "generates a feeling of inferiority" among Blacks (347 US 483, 494), a fact previously unsubstantiated, according to the Court. By explaining that empirical evidence was absent during previous court decisions on racial segregation, the court created the space for the absolution of its own role in preserving the nation's history of racist practices (Gotanda, 2004; Gutiérrez and Jaramillo, 2006) and the reversal of a well-established legal precedent. As a consequence, there was no compelling moral obligation to make fundamental structural change in the legacy of cultural, social, and institutional racism in the United States or for the "innocent" to acknowledge and challenge the underlying logic of the inhumanity and inequity that fuels racism (Santos, 1992).

Drawing on Gotanda's (2004) work, we use the race-conscience construct of 'white innocence', later elaborated in educational domains (Gutiérrez, 2006), to illustrate how the practices of racism and inequity that orient educational policies and their discourses have a prevailing logic of practice. As Luke (in press) has argued,

> The practices of racism and marginalization have particular coherent *logics of practice*: explanatory schema, taxonomies, operating procedures, even sciences, that explain why, how and to what end particular tribes, communities and ethnicities count as less than fully human against an unmarked normative version of *Man*. But they also are characterised by degrees of volatility and unpredictability: human subjects tinker with, manipulate, bend and undermine rules in face-to-face exchanges.
>
> (p. 6)

Racism, then, is embedded within discourses, institutional arrangements, and structures of educational systems and activity, which can then be enacted in face-to-face interaction. Thus, rather than being fixed and predetermined, racial and ethnic identities are (re)created through continuous and repeated language use, and mediated by institutional practices and ideologies (Alim, 2009).

By extending the *white innocence* lens to the schooling of non-dominant students, we can begin to understand how educational institutions remain "innocent" through the use of "new" beginnings—i.e., new evidence, theories, methods, discourses, and policies that are detached from historical, moral, social, economic, and political ties to racialized practices and ideologies. Today, neoliberal educational reform efforts have reframed educational policies that threaten the possibility of a humanist agenda and a democratic education, and intellectual and social equity for large numbers of students. The principle mechanism has been to redesign the educational project using code words, phrases, and symbols that index racialized ideologies in ways that do not directly invoke race or racial/ethnic communities (Lipsitz, 1998). In doing so, the dominant subject-position is camouflaged as color-blind and becomes the uncontested baseline of educational reform.

Consider, for example, the organizing "sameness as fairness" principle at work in federal reforms such as No Child Left Behind (NCLB Act of 2001, 20 U.S.C. §1001), the largest educational reform in the history of the US (Crosland, 2004). The "sameness as fairness" principle orienting national educational policy flattens out differences that matter and employs an essentialism that makes it easier to mandate and monitor one-size-fits-all approaches, particularly in the delivery of language and literacy programs. Here, language becomes a proxy for race and ethnicity and serves as a tool for organizing schooling and sorting bodies without regard to the historical and present structures that gave rise to, and sustain, deeply rooted inequities. This form of essentialism, Luke (in press) argues, serves both "as a discourse strategy to massify, rule, and, in instances, eradicate whole communities and cultures" (Luke, in press: 17). For example, normalizing language has served as an object of the cultural wars in the US, especially around issues of immigration.

One strategy for leveling the community towards a "common culture" is to try to eradicate any vestiges of non-dominant communities' cultural past and the cultural artifacts that mediate everyday life; a form of erasure (Rampton, 1995a). Such practices are part of a larger process of "modernizing" non-western communities. In essence, through punishing speakers or prohibiting the use of non-dominant language, individuals and communities are "disciplined" into "appropriate" ways to engage and speak in "civilized" society (Heller, 2008). Thus, it is not only the use of English as the only acceptable form of speech, but a particular formation of English that precludes the use of non-dominant language repertoires. "Appropriate" or "true" English is not a reflection of sociocultural context, but rather a reflection of racialized economies of language.

Linguistic and social marginalization is predicated, in part, by essentialist views of cultural communities—views that assume that characteristics of cultural groups are located within individuals as "carriers" of culture. The tendency to conflate ethnicity, race, language preference, or national origin results in overly deterministic, static, weak, and uncomplicated understandings of both an individual's and a community's practices. Often, normative views of culture are employed in ways that appear benign, especially when they purport to focus on individual differences and indirectly on deficits in the individual and social groups. What is needed is a new language to talk and think about regularities across individuals' or cultural communities' ways of doing things; we also need to make progress in how we conceptualize regularities and variance observed in shared and dynamic practices of communities, as well as how participation in cultural practices contributes to individuals' learning and development, including their linguistic and social practices (Gutiérrez and Rogoff, 2003).

361

Reductive notions of culture and cultural communities are indexed in discourses of educational success and failure of students from non-dominant communities. Couched in the rhetoric of progress, accountability, and higher standards, the reforms purport to address the achievement or "underachievement" of non-dominant youth by "fixing" the language practices of Latino and other immigrant youth. These seemingly compassionate policy actions work to homogenize and "smooth out" variation in society, thus, normalizing linguistically and culturally different students, their curricular practices, as well as the educators who must implement them (Gutiérrez *et al.*, 2002).

Hybridity all the way down

The essentialism at work in language and literacy policies belies the hybridity of students' everyday lives, including their linguistic practices. Following Pavlenko and Blackledge (2004), increased transnational migration, new diasporic communities, and an explosion of technologies have resulted in a variety of intercultural activities in which a wide range of linguistic practices become available to members of non-dominant communities. The resulting "linguistic bricolage" creates a complex link between language and identity; in some contexts, languages function as markers of national and ethnic identities, as forms of symbolic capital, or as markers of intercultural competence (Pavlenko and Blackledge, 2004: 23). In yet other contexts, such as the English-only and anti-bilingual education movements, language can become a means of social control (Gutiérrez, 2008b). These contexts become the sites of struggle over which immigrant students' language practices are negotiated and shaped. In constructing and mediating multilayered identities, non-dominant students and communities face a national context where citizenship and national identity fall prey to economic utility. In such contexts, these communities must "find new ways of constituting themselves as regional markets of producers and consumers" (Heller, 2008: 513).

Sociolinguists have elaborated the idea of the inherent hybridity in today's youth, particularly immigrant, ethnic, and diasporic communities. In advancing the notion of "language-crossing" (1995a), Rampton suggests that language and sociological research has largely ignored what he calls the new plural ethnicities (p. 1), focusing primarily on bilingual in-groups. In studies of the language practices of adolescent youth in London, Rampton (1997) found that "language-crossing" is, in part, artful performance, intersecting everyday and local practices and media representations in complex and unpredictable ways. "Language crossing" involves using a language different from one's own, in which the speaker moves across social and ethnic boundaries. At the same time, to focus exclusively on conversation among participants could result in a form of analytical parochialism absent of the multilingualisms currently at work in the intersections between the local and global.

> With its eyes glued *only* to the properties of talk, research might end up waiving [*sic*] an antiquated banner of holistic coherence at precisely the moment when the crucial values became transition and hybridity.
>
> (Rampton, 1997: 15)

This movement, however, is not without consequence, as the speaker has to negotiate issues related to boundary-crossing, identity, resistance, and even ridicule, for example. To understand how youth navigate such border-crossing events requires theorizing the role of language in racialized schooling and learning practices, including the ways language-crossing opens up new learning and intercultural activity.

Sociolinguistics can play an important role in documenting the complexities involved in identity-negotiations that unfold in interaction, face-to-face, online, and across other media. Such forms of human activity cannot be reduced solely to statistical measures of social science, or even fully or accurately documented through interviews or questionnaires. Rampton (1997) suggests that sociolinguistics and similar methodological approaches are uniquely positioned to "illuminate the *innumerable* ways in which people are *incessantly* either reproducing, nuancing, or refusing established identities, and trying to create some space for new ones" (p. 11).

Linguistic communities, particularly immigrant communities, often have been studied with a focus on inter-group process, sustaining a reductive and essentialist analytical gaze on cultural communities (Hammers and Blanc, 2000; Pavlenko, 2002). From this perspective, the essential correlation is between language and identity and, hence, Pavlenko and Blackledge (2004) suggest that,

> the monolingual and monocultural bias . . . conceives of individuals as members of homogeneous, uniform, and bounded ethnolinguistic communities and obscures hybrid identities and complex linguistic repertoires of bi- and multilinguals living in a contemporary global world.
>
> (p. 5)

At the same time, extant theories of literacy often do not account for the multimodality of communication of the new media age and the complex and hybrid repertoires non-dominant students bring to schooling and learning experiences. "Language alone cannot give us meaning to the multimodally constituted message" (Kress, 2003: 35). As an example, long-term work with Latino, African-American, and Pacific Islander children in an after-school computer-mediated learning club in a port-of-entry elementary school in Los Angeles provides persistent evidence of the hybridity of language and social practices of the participants. In this setting "language-crossing" is a valued normative practice, and children consistently produce rich texts of high value and meaning to themselves and peers (Gutiérrez *et al.*, 2001; Nixon and Gutiérrez, 2007). These literacy events often entail students writing and talking about media events, television programs, and music that are highly valued practices in popular culture, even cross-cultural programs.

Las Redes (Networks) is a multilingual, multicultural space where multi-literacies are privileged; yet, it is a space largely dominated by Latino children whose first or home language is Spanish and who participate in a range of media practices, from World Wrestling Entertainment to Spanish language programs. One particularly popular program among the young Latinas is a Spanish language 'tween television program, *Rebelde*, which features a famous group of young Mexican singers who play a group of students forming a pop band. The young girls at *Las Redes* had become obsessed fans, talking and writing about the beautiful stars, their fashion sense, and their music, often importing *Rebelde* pictures into their digital stories. The normative practice in this intercultural space involved the production of texts in Spanish and English, or other hybrid varieties.

And because Latina youth were over-represented in this setting, as they were in the school, their language and social practices were salient and highly valued by peers. And it should have come as no surprise to find that young African-American girls, who knew little to no Spanish nor watched Spanish-language television, wrote about and included Spanish words and digital photos of *Rebelde* in their own productions as well (Nixon, 2008). Such language-crossing and intercultural activity were normative and often served as the basis for rich literacy production. At the same time, it also made visible the consequences of hegemonic language and cultural practices for under-represented groups and how race and gender are indexed and how identities are formed in recurring language practices (Alim, 2009). The ways racial and ethnic identities always intersect with class, gender, sexuality, (trans)national, and other social identities and are contested through language should highlight the need to focus attention on both (dis)identification and (dis)alignment among individuals and social groups. Further, the contradictions that emerge in schooling practices and among language groups should be the object of study and examination in multilingual and multicultural learning environments, including those attempting to promote democratic and robust forms of education.

The reality of the multiplicity and hybridity of the everyday lives of students from non-dominant communities and new theories promoting their understanding complicate traditional notions of race, racism, and cultural communities (Luke, in press). Historical racialized practices, Luke argues,

> were premised on two essentialist beliefs: (1) that there were inextricable phenotypical, genetic and structural isomorphisms between race and one's intrinsic human characteristics, virtues and value, and; (2) that race, culture, identity, affiliation and nation could be assembled by the state in homologous and singular correspondence.
>
> (Hall, 1993, as cited in Luke, in press, p. 17)

Ignoring the inherent hybridity in human activity has particular educational consequences for speakers of languages other than the dominant national language. Viewing students' language and literacy practices as static and bounded by culture belies the stable and improvisational nature of cultural practices. Today's students are much more adept in reading and talking about multimodal texts than conventional written texts. Their language and literacy practices are the product of the intercultural and hybrid practices of which they are a part. This hybridity can serve as a resource for expanding students' linguistic repertoires and for new learning if cultivated and not squelched.

Understanding the regularity and variance in an individual's sociohistorical life and the consequences of intercultural exchange can promote opportunities to engage students in literacy activities that build upon difference, rather than trying to ignore or eliminate it. However, the language practices of non-English speakers are rarely understood in social and institutional settings. Their linguistic toolkit has limited capital in reform pedagogies organized around autonomous forms of literacy (Street, 1984) delivered in English-only medium. Sociohistorical understandings of the language practices of non-English speakers could provide more accurate, robust, and useful descriptions of people's language practices, including their genesis and the sources of their mediation. From this perspective, educators and educational policymakers would focus less on students' linguistic "deficiencies" and instead would want to know more about students' history of involvement with language and literacy practices (Gutiérrez, 2008a).

The language practices of Latinos, and in this case Chicana/os, for example, exhibit the significant language contact they have experienced; their language practices the product of intercultural exchange (Santa Ana and Bayley, 2005). Sociolinguists (Santa Ana, personal communication, February 17, 2009) surmise that the linguistic features attributed to Chicano English in Los Angeles, California, actually originated as second-language learning features that

Euro-Americans made salient in the English/Spanish contact setting (p. 422). These stigmatized language markers were modified and reworked into some of the most distinctive elements of Chicano English phonology. As Santa Ana and Bayley's work has noted, this reworking reframed stigmatized linguistic features into a set of linguistic variables and discourse markers that instead affirmed ethnic solidarity,

> In the sociological sphere, it can render precise the human processes by which ethnic communities reformulate linguistic features of out-group markers of stigma into in-group solidarity features.
>
> (Santa Ana and Bayley, 2005: 432)

For example, in Los Angeles, California, between 1920 and the 1950s, Chicano English features, ridiculed and stigmatized by Anglo Angelinos, were actually part of a small set of phonological features of other second-language learner groups. These now salient features in Chicano English inverted the social valoration by using them to signal solidarity in the community, rather than avoiding their use because of their previous stigmatization (Santa Ana, personal communication, 2009).

In Canadian contexts for example, "ethnolinguistic difference has long been used to mask or legitimize class hierarchies" (Porter, 1965: 511). Historically, linguistic difference has served to maintain social hierarchy and dominance rather than valuing the sociocultural toolkit that individuals and cultural communities offer. Explanatory power based on linguistic difference engenders forms of "othering" and helps to sustain reductive and narrow views of students from non-dominant communities, their potential, and the expertise they bring to learning events. This focus necessarily centers on identifying and addressing the "deficits" in students' linguistic and literacy toolkit and gives support to one-size-fits all pedagogical approaches organized around weak forms of learning and marginalizing practices.

Developing powerful and syncretic literacies

The practices of nation, home, citizenship, that fundamentally undergird how we understand race, ethnicity, and culture are shifting in dramatic ways. With more than 125 million people living outside their country of origin, and another 2–4 million are added every year, traditional narrations of identity are necessarily challenged (Lipsitz, 2004). As Lipsitz (2004) has noted, "the new realities of our time have enacted a fundamental rupture in the relationships linking place, politics, and culture" (p. 3). This new world order requires an exploration of newer forms of public identities based on new iterations of social relations:

> These new times also require new strategies, new tactics, new ideas and identities, although our old identities have not disappeared. We still speak about race, class, gender, nation, and sexuality, but in different ways. Identities never exist in isolation; they are always intersectional, relational, and mutually constitutive. New times do not so much create new identities as much as they give new accents to old intersections, resulting in new associations, affinities, and equations of power.
>
> (Lipsitz, 2004: 7)

Another way to think about the language and literacy practices of non-dominant students, particularly new immigrant and diasporic communities, is to use the notion of syncretism to make sense of their hybrid and heteroglossic character (Hill, 2001). From this perspective, syncretic linguistic practices are best understood as,

> active and strategic efforts by speakers, who draw on their understandings of the historical associations of linguistic materials to control meaning and to produce new histories by variably suppressing and highlighting these histories through linguistic means.

> (Hill, 2001: 243)

Hill's work (2003) has documented the ways speakers both obscure and highlight their histories in talk and interaction. For Hill, one strategic step in the analysis of syncretic practices involves the identification of "relevant oppositions" (p. 241). From a cultural historical theoretical perspective of learning and development (Engeström, 1987), these contradictions can serve as the engines of change in expansive forms of learning (Gutiérrez and Larson, 2007).

Parallel views have emerged in the study of literacy and in the design of educational interventions (Gutiérrez, 2008a). In work with high school students from migrant farmworker backgrounds, robust forms of academic literacies, termed sociocritical literacies, where diversity, variance, and hybridity provided additive value, were advanced. Through a syncretic approach to literacy development, the hybrid character of migrant students' social and linguistic practices, most of whom were Mexican immigrant or first-generation students, served as a resource in the development of powerful literacies (Crowther et al., 2001) that far surpassed traditional instructional approaches. At the same time, a syncretic approach recognizes how intercultural exchange and the resulting "linguistic bricolage" both extend and suppress the practices of diasporic communities. This tension necessarily became an object of analysis and study in the curricular project with students and instructional staff.

In contrast to most approaches to academic literacy that dichotomize everyday and school-based literacy practices, the syncretic approach to literacy developed with migrant students brought together seemingly dissonant genres found in everyday and literary practices with academic genres and the conventions of academic writing to increase students' engagement with text, and new forms of discourse across reading and writing activity. Specifically, the strategy involved taking a language practice that was familiar in students' cultural communities and combining it with an academic genre to ground the everyday in new understandings and forms. For example, this syncretic approach integrated the *testimonio*—a cultural practice of testifying orally about one's life and witnessed by peers in an intimate and respectful community—and the extended definition, a writing genre essential to academic writing. Here, culturally familiar and valued forms of language and literacy were extended and elaborated with conventional writing tools, and academic literacy was made relevant, meaningful, and more authoritative with *testimonios* of migrant and immigrant life and accounts of border crossing. Using Spanish and English in various combinations, students produced powerful texts that were generalized subsequently to traditional literacy tasks and community organizing efforts. Such practices helped students develop insight into the organizational structures of written texts, including those most often employed in the academy, and provided a means to locate one's own experience in a sociohistorical context, both proximally and distally.

The cases of the complex linguistic and sociocultural practices of students from non-dominant communities presented in this chapter are intended to extend the ways we view the relationship of language, race/ethnicity, and culture in educational environments; to challenge reductive empirical and theoretical approaches that fail to capture the dynamism and hybridity of cultural communities and their cultural practices. Ignoring new understandings of the continually shifting linguistic demands of cultural communities functions to preserve the *white innocence* that has been employed historically in studies of non-dominant communities and in the design of educational arrangements for students from non-dominant communities in the US and globally.

Notes

1   We wish to thank Christine O'Keefe, Sandra Naranjo, Jessica Robles, Janet Rocha, and Anne Vo for their editorial assistance.
2   The term 'non-dominant' is used here to refer to students who have been historically marginalized in educational processes and to more accurately capture the collective historical circumstance of these students and issues of power relations in schools and other institutions.
3   The term and concept of "racing-language" is attributed to H.S. Alim (2009), who uses the term to emphasize the relationship between race and language.

References

Alim, H.S. (2005) "Critical language awareness in the United Sates: revisiting issues and revising pedagogies in a resegregated society," *Educational Researcher* 34: 23–31.
—— (2009) "Race-ing language, languaging race," Paper presented at CLIC 2009 Symposium on Race & Ethnicity in Language, Interaction, and Culture. UCLA.
Baugh, J. (1988) "Language and race: some implications for linguistic science," in F. Newmeyer (ed.) *Linguistics: the Cambridge survey, Vol. 4*, Cambridge: Cambridge University Press, pp. 64–74.
—— (1997) "Researching race and social class in language acquisition and use," in N. Hornberger and D. Corson (eds) *Research methods in language and education, Vol. 8, Encyclopedia of language and education*, The Netherlands: Kluwer Academic Publishers Group, pp. 111–124.
Bernstein, B. (1975) *Class codes and control: theoretical studies toward a sociology of language 3*, Unknown binding: Schocken Books.
Boas, F. (1940) *Race, language and culture*, Chicago, IL: University of Chicago Press.
Brown v. Board of Education of Topeka, 347 US 483, 493 (1954).
Crosland, K. (2004) "Color–blind desegregation: race neutral remedies as the new 'equal opportunity'," Paper presented at the Annual Meeting of the American Educational Research Association, San Diego, California.
Crowther, J., Hamilton, M. and Tett, L. (2001) *Powerful literacies*, Leicester: National Institute for Adult Continuing Education.
Engeström, Y. (1987) *Learning by expanding: an activity theoretical approach to developmental research*, Helsinki, Finland: Orienta Konsultit.
Foley D. (1990) *Learning capitalist culture deep in the heart of Tejas*, Philadelphia, PA: University Penn Press as cited in: Urciuoli B. (1995) "Language and borders," *Annual Review of Anthropology* 24: 525.
Gotanda, N. (2004) "Reflections on Korematsu, Brown and White innocence," *Temple Political and Civil Rights Law Review*, 13: 663.
Gutiérrez, K. (2006) "White innocence: a framework and methodology for rethinking educational discourse," *International Journal of Learning* 12: 1–11.
—— (2008a) "Developing a sociocritical literacy in the third space," *Reading Research Quarterly* 43(2): 148–164.
—— (2008b) "When non-dominant languages are unmarked," using students' paper presented at the Conference on Language, Interaction and Culture. May 24, 2008. UCLA.
—— and Arzubiaga, A. (2008) *Re-imagining community*, Unpublished Manuscript. University of California, Los Angeles.

—— Asato, J., Santos, M. and Gotanda, N. (2002) "Backlash pedagogy: language and culture and the politics of reform," *The Review of Education, Pedagogy, and Cultural Studies* 24(4): 335–351.

—— Baquedano-López, P. and Álvarez, H. (2001) "Literacy as hybridity: moving beyond bilingualism in urban classrooms," in M. de la Luz Reyes and J. Halcón (eds) *The best for our children: critical perspectives on literacy for Latino students*, New York: Teachers College Press, pp. 122–141.

—— and Jaramillo, N. (2006) "Looking for educational equity: the consequences of relying on Brown," in A. Ball (ed.) With more deliberate speed: achieving equity and excellence in education—realizing the full potential of Brown v. Board of Education," Yearbook of the National Society for the Study of Education 105(2): 173–189. Malden, MA: Blackwell Publishing.

—— and Larson, J. (2007) "Discussing expanded spaces for learning," *Language Arts* 85(1): 69–77.

—— and Rogoff, B. (2003) "Cultural ways of learning: individual traits or repertoires of practice," *Educational Researcher* 32(5): 19–25.

Hammers, J. and Blanc, M. (2000) *Bilinguality and bilingualism*, Cambridge: Cambridge University Press.

Harris, R. and Rampton, B. (2003) *The language, ethnicity and race reader*, New York: Routledge.

Heller, M. (2008) "Language and the nation-state: challenges to sociolinguistic theory and practice," *Journal of Sociolinguistics* 12(4): 504–524.

Hill, J. (2001) "Syncretism," in A. Duranti (ed.) *Key terms in language and culture*, Malden, MA: Blackwell Publishers, pp. 241–243.

—— (2003) "Hasta la vista, baby: Anglo Spanish in the American Southwest," *Critique of Anthropology* 13: 145–176.

Kress, G. (2003) *Literacy in the new media age (literacies)*, New York: Routledge.

Kubota, R. and Lin, A.M.Y. (eds) (in press) *Race, culture, and identities in second language education: exploring critically engaged practice*, New York: Routledge.

Lee, C.D. (1993) *Signifying as a scaffold for literary interpretation: the pedagogical implications of an African American discourse genre*, Urbana, IL: National Council of Teachers of English.

Lipsitz, G. (1998) *The possessive investments in whiteness: how White people profit from identity politics*, Philadelphia: Temple University Press.

—— (2004) "New times and new identities: solidarities of sameness and dynamics of difference," in G. Gonzalez, R. Fernandez, V. Price, D. Smith and L. Trinh Vo (eds) *Labor versus empire: race, gender and migration*, New York: Routledge, pp. 3–16.

Luke, A. (in press) "Race and language as capital in school: a sociological template for language education reform," in R. Kubota and A.M.Y. Lin (eds) *Race, culture, and identities in second language education: exploring critically engaged practice*, New York: Routledge.

Nixon, A.S. (2008) "From their own voices: understanding youth identity and literacy practices through digital storytelling," unpublished dissertation, University of California, Los Angeles.

—— and Gutiérrez, K. (2007) "Digital literacies for young English learners: productive pathways toward equity and robust learning," in C. Genishi and A.L. Goodwin (eds) *Diversities in early childhood education: rethinking and doing*, New York: Routledge/Falmer Press.

No Child Left Behind Act of 2001, 20 USC (2009)

Pavlenko, A. (2002) 'Bilingualism and emotions', *Multilingua* 21: 45–78.

—— and Blackledge, A. (eds) (2004) *Negotiation of identities in multilingual contexts*, Vol. 45, Clevedon, UK: Multilingual Matters.

Porter, J. (1965) *The vertical mosaic: an analysis of social class and power in Canada*, Toronto: University of Toronto Press.

Rampton, B. (1995a) *Crossing: language and ethnicity among adolescents*, London: Longman.

—— (1995b) "Language crossing and the problematisation of ethnicity and socialization," *Pragmatics* 5(4): 485–514.

—— (1997) "Language crossing and the redefinition of reality: implications or research on code-switching community, Paper 5," *Working Papers in Urban Language & Literacies*, Kings College, London.

Rose, M. (1985) "The language of exclusion: writing instruction at the university," *College English* 47(4): 341–359.

Santa Ana, O. (2009) Personal communication, February 17.

—— and Bayley, R. (2005) "Chicano English: phonology," in B. Kortmann and E. Schneider (eds) *A handbook of varieties of English: a multi-media reference tool*, Berlin/New York: Mouton de Gruyter Publishers, pp. 417–434.

Santos, M. (1992) "Demystifying affirmative action," Paper presented at the Annual Meeting of the American Association of Schools, Colleges, and Universities, Pomona, CA, October.

Smitherman, G. (1977) *Talkin and testifyin: the language of Black America*, Boston, MA: Houghton Mifflin.

Steinberg, S. (2007) *Race relations: a critique*, Palo Alto, CA: Stanford University Press.

Street, B. (1984) *Literacy in theory and practice*, Cambridge, UK: Cambridge University Press.

Urciuoli B. (1995) "Language and borders," *Annual Review of Anthropology* 24: 525–546.

Zentella, A. (1997) *Growing up bilingual: Puerto Rican children in New York*, Malden, MA: Blackwell Publishers.

33

Dilemmas of race-rememory buried alive
Popular education, nation, and diaspora in critical education

Grace Livingston

> Because so much in public and scholarly life forbids us to take seriously the milieu of buried stimuli, it is often extremely hard to seek out both the stimulus and its galaxy and to recognize their value when they arrive.
>
> (Toni Morrison, 1984: 185)

Critical knowing and remembering matters

Race and the hemispheric Americas remain intractably linked. In significant measure this is owing to the role and legacy of the transatlantic slave trade and enslavement in the Americas as grounding, generative, and globalizing projects of the Western Modern project itself. Race thus lives as a social problematic of the political that carries loaded narratives about difference, disparity, and distance and thus has been pivotal in (re)inventing and (re)instituting the hierarchical geo-political, economic, and social relations that shape our living, knowing, and remembering. Regarding the US region of the hemisphere, Plummer (2005) speaks to dimensions of the knowledge-producing labors of race as routed through the logic of White supremacy, which I suggest persist even in the face of the much-heralded November 2008 election of Senator Barack Obama to the US presidency. Plummer argues that, "blackness has not been dissolved and . . . remains a flashpoint in this society. Blackness continues to represent, for immigrants and others, the lowest common denominator, the absolute floor from which the only way is up" (p. 113).

Commenting on this racial logic in another part of the hemisphere, the Caribbean, Nettleford (1994) takes note of "the tenaciously held perceptions among Caribbean people that there exists a seemingly impregnable and lasting nexus between race and skin-colour on the one hand, and the deprivations of power, influence, authority, legitimacy and status on the other" (pp. 14–15). For example, the twenty-first-century steady upsurge in skin-bleaching (Brown-Glaude, 2007; Charles, 2003; Tafari-Ama, 2006) in Jamaica, among predominantly poor and lower-income urban people between the mid teens and mid thirties, despite health risks and mortality rates, bears witness to the entangled and contested endurance of this supremacist racial logic.

However, such visceral forms of knowing race are subject to structures of silencing and a "beleaguered status" (Livingston, 2006: 24, 26), even as we shall see, on the critical educational terrain. Amidst this silencing, the role of race in relating knowing to remembering as an act of "re-membering," "putting back together . . . what has been obscured, . . . forgotten, . . . [and] disappeared from view" (Scott, 1999: 80) does not relent. The racialized relationship between remembering or memory "as a social, political, and historical enterprise" (Said, 2000: 178) and the politics of knowledge production is the muse of this chapter. This relationship and its salience have been dramatized through several critical public and pedagogic moments or events in recent years that have had national, international, and Black diasporic traction and have also formed the social texts of formal classroom learning and teaching and that of other educational constituencies, including those of which I am part.

For example, this relationship was palpably at work in evoking the internationally broadcast, race-related memory, or what I call race-memory,[1] expressions of joy and disbelief, along with those of criticism, indignation, and dismay, which met Barack Obama's election as US president. This interaction between memory and knowledge also routed the historical race-memory undergirding the differential readings of "Americans of different races" (Harris-Lacewell, 2007: 28) regarding the US government's response to the breaking of the levees in New Orleans in the wake of hurricane Katrina in 2005, with "Black Americans [feeling] abandoned in their grief" (p. 41) and visited by the memory of another disaster, the 1927 Mississippi flood.

Critical events such as these serve as "primal scenes" for the "discovery" and performance of race-memory and the production of further "memory" "associations."[2] The focus of this chapter is on probing and problematizing the race-memory knowledge produced by the interplay of the logic of selectively visiting or remembering and forgetting particular moments or events, especially when such race-memory enacts a form of silencing on the political knowledge that race carries. In order to do this, I also engage a particular conceptual inflection of the term memory, called "rememory," and turn geopolitically to the Caribbean, specifically Jamaica. In this part of the Americas, I look at a critical educational practice within civil society, one that is linked to the project of nation formation. I examine the practice of popular education, one with which I worked for almost a decade, so as to gather and interrogate primal scenes of race-memory. In order to do this, I must say some crucial things about memory and rememory in general.

Connecting memory and rememory to critical education in the Caribbean

Rememory, arguably a signal infusion into the lexicon of the terms of critical inquiry into memory, has been made available to the multidisciplinary deliberations on memory by novelist and literary scholar Toni Morrison. It grows out of Morrison's own work which "depend[s] heavily on the ruse of memory" (Morrison, 1984: 386) as a "form of willed creation" (p. 385), "ignit[ing] some process of invention" (p. 386), and is particularly vital due to the untrust-worthiness of mainstream "literature" and "sociology" as regards "the truth" of Black diaspora "cultural sources" (p. 386). Morrison's work with memory predated what is recognized as the "scholarly boom" (Klien, 2000: 127) in the turn to memory during the 1980s threshold of the crisis over what counts as historical knowledge, the distances between academic and popular historical knowledge, and methods of accessing and knowing the past.

Toni Morrison's approach to the two terms of memory and rememory emboldens them with discernable political and epistemological properties. Rememory, coined and demonstrated most fulsomely in Morrison's 1987 novel, *Beloved*, rivets her sense of the importance of memory as "dwell[ing] on the way" an event or any other social formation is recollected, "the way it appeared and why it appeared in that particular way" (Morrison, 1984: 385) on a new register. The rememory register is attentive and brings significance to the revisitation of a particular appearance or recollection and why it gets revisited and repeatedly so. This new register allows us to ask why a particular appearance or memory related to issues of race is repeatedly visited, operating then not only as a race-memory but as a race-rememory. The matter of what is at stake politically and epistemologically in this revisitation of race-memory or race-rememory surfaces as crucial. In a conversation between Sethe and Denver, mother and youngest daughter in *Beloved*, which takes place, like several encounters in the novel, in the haunting of Sethe's killing of her first daughter, Beloved, at two years old, so that she would not have to be sold away from her into enslavement, Sethe speaks of rememory in this way.

> Some things go. Pass on. Some things just stay. I used to think it was my rememory. You know. Some things you forget. Other things you never do. But it's not . . . [T]he picture of it . . . stays, and not just in my rememory, but out there, in the world.
>
> (pp. 35–36)

Turning to the Caribbean, specifically Jamaica, and diachronically to two significant ideological and institutional waves in the formation of popular education and new forms of Jamaican nationhood,[3] I probe a particular historical rememory of race or a particular revisiting and "staying" of memory regarding race. This race-rememory is one that I argue enacts a specific form of silencing on the political knowledge that race carries, framed as a triumphalist and an exceptionalist relation to race, especially as it relates to the positioning and figuring of Blackness and Black life. The Caribbean, "the Other America" (Glissant, 1989a: 4), is an apt site for probing silencing dilemmas in patterns of race-rememory and the national, international, and diasporic forces that condition them. On one hand, the Caribbean persists in the commonsensical political imaginary, particularly, though not solely outside of its borders, as a territory of "Caribbean beaches waiting to be visited, invested in, and exploited" (Mignolo, 2005: 96). On another, it is simultaneously grounded as a signal part of the unsettling "'preface' to the American continent" (Glissant, 1989b: 561), a site of colonial "encounter" and "complicity" (p. 561) and "a product of [the] globalization" (Hall, 1997: 29) instantiated by the transatlantic slave trade and slavery, both as part of its "back end" (p. 29) and "leading edge" (p. 29).

Popular education—with its deliberate commitments to critical nation building through a community development ethos as a basis for "popular participation," "popular sovereignty," fostering "views alternative to those in the dominant State," "protest action," and reputation as a "lively, at times turbulent 'space'"[4]—serves as a vivid and sobering site on which to stage the paradoxes of race-rememory. While bearing important ideological distinctions, popular education of both waves, as it battled within twentieth-century post-(slave) emancipation, colonial and neo-colonial Modern Jamaica, has sought to bring and fashion the circumstances of the social fray as social texts for educational processes in the name of exploring socio-political possibilities. This proximity of the social and the educational is done in a way that brings educational sensibilities to incite and facilitate skill capacity development, social action, and political struggle through consciousness-raising activity across local communities and constituencies of interest.

In discussing the connections between race-rememory and popular education, I draw on particular moments or events related to both waves as primal scenes of race-memory and rememory, starting with the second wave—the wave of my involvement in the 1980s and 1990s. The second wave emerged in the late 1960s and early 1970s through Non-Government Organizations (NGOs), called Development NGOs (DNGOs) and Community Based Organizations (CBOs), with an investment in shaping an anti-colonial, independent nation. The first wave arose in the 1930s through NGOs mostly known as Private Voluntary Organizations (PVOs), with a commitment to securing a decolonized nation. The moments or events related to both critical educational and nation practices to which I draw attention serve as "point[s] of entanglement" (Glissant, 1989a: 26) for critical educational practioners, thinkers, and researchers, to which we "must return" (p. 26). Such a return is crucial because "our problems lay in wait for us" there (p. 25) concerning how race is remembered, especially accumulated recollection tendencies that effect a race-rememory pattern that inflicts modes of silencing on race. My interest is in uprooting historical and ideological moments or events and their national, international, and Black diasporic tugs, which serve as primal scenes and "buried stimuli" (Morrison 1984: 385) that I propose are attached to the production of the troubling form of race-rememory—a triumphalist and an exceptionalist relation to race. Further, I suggest that such scenes have been mis-recognized, "disremembered," "buried alive"[5] and "unaccounted for"[6] in critical educational and national practices.

Primal scenes of race-rememory trouble in critical education and nation

Jamaica 1994: recoiling from embattled Blackness

The instigating primal scene that served as a sign of trouble in race-rememory made its appearance in a moment of reflection on praxis in 1994. Around September 1994, there was a particular gust of tension in the air within one of the second-wave DNGOs and affiliated CBOs that had been working in both rural and urban Jamaica for, at the time, over thirty-five years. A 1994 follow-up evaluation (to one done in 1991) focused on the following program components: "animation, consciousness raising and skills training; economic and housing projects; and community organizing and mobilization" (Heron, 1994: i).[7] Its completion was marked by a notably disturbing set of findings. The findings that sparked the climate of unease stated that 53 percent of the community respondents across CBOs in a particular parish[8] in which the DNGO and CBOs worked said that the notion that "Black people can't run tings" (p. 36) was as a significant contributing factor to the economic problems at the community and national levels. Only 33 percent were definitive that this was not a factor at all, with the responses of the remaining 14 percent placed in the category, "don't know" (p. 36).

"Run things" is a much beloved and used idiomatic phrase in modern urban Jamaican vernacular language, most often articulated as "a wi run things." It could be understood as the defiant capacity to formulate and execute a task exemplarily, with almost bravado expertise and style. The nuance of defiance in its meaning figures at a racially inflected decibel that denotes the will and ability to do better than expected and out-do in a context of structural and psychic odds set up by elite and supremacist power relations. "Black people can't run things" thus meant that respondents were indicating that this was not a faculty of Black people, or a dubious one at best. "[R]espondents were asked to give their opinion on the factors which may or may not contribute to Jamaica's economic problems" (Heron, 1994: 36). This kind of inquiry was pursued, at least in part, to get a sense of what was happening and what issues were being "covered in the educational sessions" of popular education (p. 36).

The inquiry also served as a broader investigation of the key "indicators of social change in the community organizations."[9] Many did raise and link factors such as the International Monetary Fund (IMF) and World Bank, national "corruption," "mis-management" and lack of (national) self-reliance.[10] However, that such a significant number articulated and indexed "Black people can't run things" as a strong factor said that there was a relationship or an "attribut[ion]" being made between socio-economic problems of society and "their blackness."[11]

As if to exacerbate the conditions of reception of this kind of finding, the evaluation also exposed that, in trying to ascertain the "social profile" of the communities under investigation, there was a notable resistance from some respondents when it came to placing their social identities in relation to race. While the process of getting responses about "gender," "occupation and employment," and "age" went relatively seamlessly, the process of getting racial "identity," "heritage," or "classification" responses from the 93 percent of the community group members who eventually affiliated or placed themselves as of "African descent," involved significant moments of "unwillingness" and "difficulty."[12] "It should be noted" the evaluation said, "that . . . Chinese and Indians who were covered in the survey were not reported as having a problem in acknowledging their racial identity" (Heron, 1994: 33).

This was the DNGO and related CBOs with which I was working at the time in community mobilization, popular education, and administrative roles. This 1994 moment has persisted in returning to me through the years as a primal scene for working through the politics of race-memory and race-rememory, as I have moved and worked across critical educational sites of learning–teaching, non-formal and formal. I recall that verbal and non-verbal expressions of disappointment and anger, and disavowal and disbelief were intense and marked the hesitant and spontaneous discussions and interactions that came in the wake of these findings from the evaluation. There was a sense of incredulity that "Black people can't run things" as a statement of an embattled and a shameful relation to Blackness could feature (still) so pronouncedly in the social belief systems and actions of Jamaicans, given that the nation was then over three decades into its formal independent status. Also, there was a sense that the prominence of such a belief system contradicted the influence of the radical political practice of "development-oriented,"[13] second-wave popular education, with its conceptual and ideological frameworks including liberation theology, Marxism, or "some form of socialism to meet the manifestly oppressive conditions of the poorer classes in the country"[14] and Freirian conscientization.[15] This mood of incredulity concerning race and the figure of Blackness came into more pivotal focus, given that this conception was at work in and among social actors who were at the forefront of community mobilization work at the grassroots and were creative and resilient participants in popular education and consciousness raising processes in some of the most challenging circumstances, particularly in the traditional (slave) sugar plantation areas of Jamaica.

Emerging further as part of this mood came paths of questioning and commentary that made it more clear that there was a troubling silencing of the social problematic of race being wrestled over. The questioning and commentary amplified the tangle of possible Black diasporic, national, and international routes contouring the production of this silencing, particularly with regards to the triumphalist and exceptionalist relation to race. Perhaps the report from the evaluation merely gave a melodramatic[16] representation or perverse sampling[17] of a lingering relic and now aberration of modern Jamaican life, was the flavor of some conjectures. Black enslavement in the Americas ended (*de jure*) too long ago for "Black people can't run things" to be (still) rearing its head this pronouncedly, was the tone of other interjections. After all, Jamaica has earned and worn the reputation as an imprimateur of exemplary and resilient "Black consciousness," which has influenced those beyond its shores. Such consciousness has been carried through the cherished Black diasporic race-memory agency of Jamaica's legendary slave rebellions; fierce-fighting and relatively autonomous Maroon communities; Crown colonial uprisings; national heroes, notably Paul Bogle, Sam Sharpe, and Nanny of the Maroons; cultural, spiritual, and ideological forces of Garveyism, Rastafari, Reggae; and a Jamaican inflection of democratic socialist state governance.[18] Additionally, from the mood shaped by the evaluation report came versions of the ever so (in)famous and almost commonsensical sorts of assertion that surface often in Jamaican life, particularly in times of crisis, when social predicaments and antagonisms that spin from the axis of race and power come to the fore. Such assertions may be placed in this manner: "But after all, are we not a majority Black independent nation?" and, in tandem, the barely screened bravado and exceptionalist kind of utterance, "After all, this is or we are not the US."

This 1994 moment and the issues of race that give it weight have yet remained unremarkable, unnamed, and thus disremembered in the albeit small body of descriptive and analytic scholarly literature and published reports on Jamaican NGO mobilizational and educational work.[19] In order to help make sense of this 1994 primal scene of race-memory, which enacts a simultaneous recoiling from a struggling and debased Blackness and preferential attachment to a triumphant and an exceptional one, I move to a buried stimulus found in an earlier critical moment within the breaking of second-wave popular education in 1968 to which this 1994 moment triggers attention. The 1968 moment, which played a key role in constituting the font of social texts conditioning the late 1960s emergence of the second wave yet still begs analysis as a "usable past"[20] in the production of the history of popular education, works as another primal scene of race-memory. It allows 1994 to be viewed as representing a particular pattern in the way race-memory is visited and renders the attachment to a triumphalist and an exceptionalist relation to race a significant dilemma of race-rememory.

Jamaica 1968: soiling special Blackness

Grounding this 1968 primal scene is the presence of Walter Rodney in Jamaica and his banning and denouncement as *"persona non grata"* (Gray, 1991: 157) by the government on October 15, 1968. In January 1968, Walter Rodney, an Afro-Guyanese, arrived in Jamaica to work as a lecturer in African history at the University of the West Indies (UWI), Mona campus, Jamaica, after teaching in Africa for approximately a year and a half and, prior to that, having pursued doctoral studies between 1963 and 1966 in London at the School of Oriental and African Studies. Rodney's coming to Jamaica was actually "a return," given that he was a student at the UWI, Mona, between 1960 and 1963. At the time of Rodney's second coming, the UWI was still deeply attached to the colonial impetus of the "university's civilising role"[21] even amidst the momentum of national independence formalized in 1962. The University was a site where it was greeted as anomalous and revolutionary when a Black Jamaican faculty member referenced and differentiated his national identity in the midst of an academic presentation as being "one of those Jamaicans of the color of the black in flag [of independence]" (Brodber, 1997: 70).

Rodney not only set about to teach his assigned classes in African history. Within weeks of his arrival on the campus, he had begun to give public campus lectures on African civilization, committed to "filling the emotive and cognitive gap" (Lewis, 1998: 14) that he had recognized in himself as an undergraduate and one that was particularly endemic to much of the formally schooled of the British colonies up until that time. Along with focusing on Africa's past, Rodney's talks were distinguished by tying a "reexamination of African history . . . directly to the scrutiny of the black experience in Jamaica" (Gray, 1991: 152) and "an appraisal of the current condition" (p. 152). Additionally, very soon after beginning the public campus lectures, Rodney moved to taking his lectures beyond the University to constituencies that would come to be key participants and sites of second-wave popular education work. He could be found "discussing aspects of African history in working-class districts in Kingston" (p. 152), notably, Western and Eastern Kingston, and "at workers' sports clubs and among the unemployed in the ghettos of West Kingston" (p. 152). Crucially, Rodney did recognize that, especially with respect to Rastafari, Garveyism, and Rudie or Rude-boy culture,[22] he was not bringing in "brand new" (Sunshine, 1988: 59) ideas, noting Rastafari as "the leading force of [the] expression of Black consciousness" (p. 59) on the Jamaican terrain.

The growing critical, political, and educational momentum and alliances highlighted and generated by Rodney's type of activism and scholarship "frightened the daylights out of . . . the government" (Abrahams, 2000: 251), triggering the head of the Ministry of Home Affairs (now known as the Ministry of National Security) to declare "I have never come across a man who offers a greater threat to the security of this land than does Walter Rodney" (Lewis, 1998: 113). In mid August of 1968, the government "summoned the vice-chancellor of the university to protest Rodney's activities" (Gray, 1991: 157). However, their meeting did not end with "assurances that the university would put a stop to Rodney's activism" (p. 157). By mid October, still unable to build a secure legal case against Rodney, the government tried to press the University into withdrawing his contract in a specially convened "extra-ordinary meeting of the national cabinet" (p. 157). With these efforts yielding no definitive agreement from the University, the government seized the opportunity of Rodney being out of the country attending a Black writer's conference in Montreal, Canada, and prevented him from disembarking on his return to Jamaica, October 15, serving him, when his plane landed, with expulsion papers. In response, protests emerged.

Enacted in the then prime minister's commentary on the events surrounding Rodney's expulsion from Jamaica was a silencing on race matters within the nation in a way that expressed a triumphalist and an exceptionalist relation to race similar to the silencing relation in motion, yet buried alive, in the 1994 critical event in the life of popular education and primal scene of race-memory. Such an enactment of silencing was arguably not unaffected by the tugs of cold war circumstances that confronted newly de-colonizing, "less developed" countries with insinuations and coercions about alignments with one of the "great powers."[23] Consonant with the racialized signal sent by the government's banning, earlier in 1968, of publications related to Black diaspora activism coming out of the US, such as those by Stokely Carmichael, Elijah Muhammad, and Malcolm X, and "The Crusader" by Robert Williams,[24] the prime minister's articulations placed matters at the nexus of race and power outside of the independent Jamaican experience.

The prime minister accused "people from other islands" (Gray, 1991: 161), "'foreigners' and 'non-Jamaicans' at the university, . . . [of] fomenting dissidence among 'our sons and daughters'" (p. 162). Prominent spokespersons for the labor union constituency—one that would become an important site and ally in second-wave popular education—represented and positioned this constituency as colluding in the production of this triumphalist and exceptionalist form of silencing race. The leader of the Bustamante Industrial Trade Union (BITU) pronounced:

People in the world have come to point at Jamaica as a leading example—as a small country where reason, law and order are fundamental to the country and our people, and where races work and live in harmony with ever increasing respect for each other.

(Gray, 1991: 54)

In racial silencing tandem, from the leader of National Workers Union (NWU) came the following words:

Ugly forces are rising in our country. All over the land people have begun to preach race hatred—colour against colour, race against race. Movements are being formed dedicated to the destruction of the very idea of inter-racial harmony. [They are] a dangerous throw back into the past.

(Gray, 1991: 56)

Importantly, Gray (1991) does not allow for the significance of political knowledge production of this critical 1968 moment, especially in relation to race, to pass by unnamed. Gray characterizes the knowledge produced in a way that uncovers conundrums of nation, diaspora, and the international that route the production of a triumphal and an exceptional race-memory. He perceptively, if in too discretely nationalist terms, calls it "Jamaican Exceptionalism" (p. 54), a "defensive political ideology" (p. 54) formed out of the pressure of the "Rastafarian challenge" (p. 53) and as "a counter-ideology meant to stem challenges to class inequalities posed by expanding race consciousness, and . . . a means to secure the moral-ideological framework for the country's development strategy" (p. 54). It "sought to purge the antagonistic elements from the ideology of the urban unemployed by hailing the subordinate classes as exemplary racial neuters" and to "appeal to the overwhelming black population was that they were a special people in the world" (p. 82).

This 1968 primal scene, while undoubtedly significant, does not illustrate the primary momentum of the appearance and visitation of a triumphalist and an exceptionalist relation to race in modern Jamaica, as Gray's (1991) position on Jamaican exceptionalism as a "novel ideological invention, designed to address the dilemmas of the incipient independent state" (p. 54) suggests. Earlier critical moments during the first wave of popular education, which live hidden and unrelated, disclose stimuli producing this silencing relation that resonate with the national, diasporic, and international patterns shaping its 1968 and 1994 second-wave manifestations and thicken the basis for its consideration as a crucial, if buried, rememory matrix underwriting popular education and the modern Jamaican nation. Turning to this earlier history deepens my arguments about race-rememory.

Jamaica 1938: combustible Blackness staining show-window Blackness

At the time of the birth of the initiative that marks the emergence of the first wave of popular education, the Jamaica Welfare Limited (JWL), in June 1937, Jamaican life "very much reflected the island's two main historically formative experiences . . . chattel slavery and Crown Colony oligarchy" (Munroe, 1972: 1), "split into 'Black,' 'Brown' and 'White' sections" (p. 5) functioning as "a system of social and economic apartheid based on skin colour" (Birbalsingh, 1970: 29). Also a time of "tremendous intellectual and social ferment" (Levy, 1995: 349), that very year of the JWL's birth saw "the whole country rumbl[ing] with huge marches and strikes" (Williams, 1970: 446). Activities such as the "blocking of roads, cutting of telephone wires, breaking down of bridges, burning of [sugar] cane, destroying [of] banana trees and, on several occasions, the ambushing [of] armed police with nothing but sticks and stones" (Post, 1969: 376) were increasingly visible across the Crown Colony Jamaican landscape.

Less than a year later, in May 1938, rural and urban upheavals, significantly stirred by the strike actions of workers at "the largest sugar [plantation] estate in the country" (Sunshine, 1988: 38), reached to the scale and sound of rebellions that served as "a symbol of region-wide upheaval" (p. 38). "East and West, North and South, on Properties and Roads, Labour Demand[ed] More Pay" read the headlines of the *Jamaica Daily Gleaner* (Brown, 1979: 93). "Street cleaners, power station workers, pumping station employees and municipal workers joined the throng of people who surged through the street. Traffic was halted, business places closed. Shops were invaded. Passing cars were stoned . . . the military moved in" (Sunshine, 1988: 39). "Police Fire To Drive Back Mob," "Sugar Workers Mown Down By Police Fire," "Labour Leader . . . Arrested and Held Without Bail," and "Another Hectic Day and Night in the City" reflect the tenor of additional newspaper headlines" (p. 39).

These events and the interpretation of them played a centripetal role in charting the ideological and institutional direction of the national decolonization commitment of first-wave popular education. As understood through the JWL's founding chairperson and prime mover, Norman Washington Manley, this vision of decolonization also connected with the nationalist and later Fabian socialist orientation of the People's National Party (PNP), launched after the rebellions with Manley's leadership. This vision carried tenets of "self government," "collectivisation," "egalitarianism,"[25] and "support[ing] the progressive forces of this country . . . to raise the living standard of life of the common people" (Nettleford, 1971a: 13) and was expressed through a program strategy of integrated community development. This strategy included such features as: establishing contacts with key people in the community; social surveys conducted with the help of local leaders in order to learn or verify demographic information and community priorities; identifying existing groups and leaders through house to house visits; strengthening and expanding existing village organizations; engaging indigenous culture; and developing local leadership (Francis, 1969; Girvan, 1993; Levy, 1995).

However, amidst this critical educational praxis, a silencing of race ensued that illustrated the deeper historical tracks of the problematic triumphalist and exceptionalist relation to race and how this problematic feeds a buried-alive dilemma of race-rememory. Rastafari, which was coming into being during the 1930s, along with some resurgence of Garveyite ideas and practices among rural and urban low-income groups who participated in the 1938 rebellions, did not form an integral part of the mobilizational and educational approaches deployed by the JWL. Though Garveyites and Rastafari were engaged in community education, organizing, and economic activity, the first wave did not turn to such social texts for their work of learning–teaching, consciousness raising, and building alliances. Even in the dimensions of the JWL's work that engaged in facilitating the expression of cultural–religious forms, the musical genres associated with such African-inspired spiritual and cultural ways of life as Pocomani and Revival Baptists were deflected. Rhythmic forms more closely resembling British Christian Protestant hymns were more often incorporated, as if in attempt to stay away from the deemed "vulgar"[26] and uncivilized bodily moves and vocal sounds of Black Jamaican life.[27]

As found in the 1968 primal scene of race-memory during the emergence of the second wave of popular education, there was an emphasis in the first wave on interpellating Jamaicans as a people-in-common and a people apart, setting up the social problematic of race as belonging to an unusable past, a past over which there had already been triumph and thus outside, and an interruption of a decolonization vision for the nation. Tantamount to missing from even the critical historiography of popular education is that while, for instance, Manley "understood the implications and indulged the Rastafarians in their quite valid demands for recognition and status" (Nettleford, 1971b: lxviii), his caution about them resembled a position that surfaced in the second wave. Manley was weary of "a recrudescence of race-consciousness in the assertive stance of groups like Rastafari and in the revival of UNIA [United Negro Improvement Association] enclaves against the persistent force of slave heritage *viz* the correlation of blackness with poverty and deprivation" (p. lxviii; italics in original).

Such a position was echoed in the lament of foundation JWL staff person, D.T.M. Girvan, who noted that with the rise of "Rastafarianism . . . [as] a national phenomenon" and also "race feeling and class antagonism," there was a "breakdown of national consensus and togetherness" (Girvan, 1993: 18). Additionally, casting race in a strident political position was viewed by Manley as precluding any "reconcil[iation] of black nationalism with plural democratic nationalism" (Nettleford, 1971b: lxvii), as race spoke to a "sectional identity" (p. lxvii). Matters of race and color were considered ones of "cultural identity" (p. lxvi), through which the core subjectivity of decolonized Jamaican nationhood could be articulated in exceptionalizing terms as an "African-European creolized fusion" (p. lxvi) capable of facilitating "the emergence of a class of colour indifferent persons" (p. lxx).

Further, in pursuit of unearthing the tracks of the triumphalist and exceptionalist race-rememory dilemma, such first-wave positions and practices regarding race may be understood as folding into and complicit with other silencing strategies coming from the international ground in the wake of the 1938 rebellions. Britain was "especially worried" (Johnson, 1977: 66), in the light of "possible repercussions of the strikes and disturbances" (p. 66), about the opinion of the US with regards to race relations in the British empire, and more so, the treatment of Black people who were viewed by "the white population of Jamaica" as "combustible blacks" (Bryan, 1991/2001: ix) capable of rendering the Jamaican colony "as volatile, potentially unstable, subject to incendiary and insurrectionary action"(p. ix). There was worry about the "American tendency to judge British colonial administration by the West Indian colonies" (Johnson, 1977: 66). The contents of a 1938 memo by a British cabinet member reveal the role of international entanglements in co-scripting an exceptionalist racial gaze on Jamaica that is reminiscent of that which faced the first wave:

> One sees signs of a growing interest in the administration of these territories [the British colonies] on the part of Americans, reflected in the American magazines. The W. Indies, are to some extent, the British show-window for the USA. I am afraid it is not a very striking exhibit. For the moment, "the differentness" and the picturesque aspect, predominate; but criticism is already there; and it will I think grow.
>
> (Johnson, 1977: 66)

Conclusion

The triumphalist and exceptionalist relation to race that inhabits the rememory logic of modern Jamaican life is pernicious, even as its harmful silencing lives buried in an often benign and normative bravado disposition. Such a silencing rememory habit continues to position Jamaican phenomenology at an exoticized distance from contemporary analyses of the layered brutalities of race and power in the broader Americas; it obscures and misrecognizes the constitution of some of the challenges facing the nation, especially matters of the political that operate at the nexus of race and power; and it renders usable pasts irrelevant. Critical educational practice faces the imperative of helping to "generat[e] and sustain a public culture of memory" (Scott, 1999: 81) regarding this rememory dilemma and the buried stimuli complicit in its production and re-articulation.

Acknowledgements

I am thankful to Michael Apple for the invitation to write this chapter and for the opportunity to process these ideas that it has afforded me. I am also appreciative of the valuable reviewer and editorial feedback. For responding to my writing, and for crucial spaces of listening and conversation, in different measures and at important times, Jay Hammond Cradle, Dexter Gordon, Suzanne Livingston and Hannah Tavares have my thanks.

Notes

1   The idea of historical memory routes is developed and discussed in Grace Livingston (forthcoming) "Historical memory and the foundations of the critical categories of justice in education."
2   See Rushdy's (1990: 303) discussions.
3   See, for example, Girvan (1993), Hart (1993), and Nettleford (1971a, 1971b, 1989) for references to transforming Jamaican nationhood as building a "new" Jamaica.
4   See Baker (1983), Brown (2000: xii–xiii), and Levy (1994: 1–2, 2000: 101).
5   "Buried alive" is developed and discussed in Grace Livingston (under journal review) "Silencing habits: race-memory routes of the production of the political in critical educational research."
6   See Morrison (1987: 274) for the use of the terms "disremembered" and "unaccounted for."
7   These program areas under evaluation are also mentioned at different points throughout Heron (1994).
8   Jamaica is organized into fourteen main geographical spaces, known as parishes.
9   See Heron (1994: Chap. 4).
10 See Heron (1994: Chap. 4, 34–36), for instance.
11 See Heron (1994: 36)
12 See Heron (1994: 33–34) for the social profile terminology and broader discussion of findings.
13 See Levy (1994, 1995) for the ideological significance of a development orientation to popular education of the second wave, in contrast with the more "welfare" approach of first-wave work.
14 See Levy (2000: 102–103, 113) about the role of these ideological frameworks.
15 See Hope and Timmel (1984) for examples of the role of Freirian conscientizaton and also versions of Marxism and liberation theologies.
16 See Dash (1989) for the use of "melodrama" in a comment on race in the modern Caribbean. Dash's commentary for me is exemplary of a type of Caribbean thinking that tends to use such terms to deflect and deride harsh representations of racial problematics.
17 I adapt this phrase from Soyinka (1982: 10).
18 See for example Thomas's (2005) commentary on some of these features as constitutive of modern Jamaican Blackness.
19 For example, I think of this absence in Levy's (2000) contribution to investigations of Caribbean NGO work through his valuable study of the DNGO Social Action Center that I have been discussing here.

20   See Hershatter's (1997: 34, 393) use of the notion of a "usable past" and the related idea of when pasts "enter into the historical record."

21   This notion appears throughout Mathurin-Mair (1969).

22   Rudie or Rude-boy refers to a cultural form and social disposition of protest that emerged among Black, urban, male life in western, central and eastern Kingston around the late 1950s and early 1960s. See, for example, Lewis (1997, 1998).

23   Mills (1989), for instance, places independence movements and other transitions happening in British colonies in the context of cold war pressures.

24   See, for instance, Abrahams (2000: Chap. 10) and Lewis (1998: 112–113) for discussion of these bannings.

25   These principles are discussed throughout Nettleford (1971a).

26   See Cooper's (1993) use of this term.

27   See Girvan (1993) and Hart (1993) for this tendency in the JWL's work.

References

Abrahams, P. (2000) *The Coyaba chronicles: reflections on the Black experience in the 20th century*, Kingston, Jamaica: Ian Randle Publishers.

Baker, P.L. (1983) "The people and the development process: themes and strategies in the evolution of popular participation," unpublished thesis, University of Sussex, United Kingdom.

Birbalsingh, F.M. (1970) "'Escapism' in the novels of John Hearne," *Caribbean Quarterly* 16(1): 28–38.

Brodber, E. (1997) "Re-engineering Blackspace," *Caribbean Quarterly* 43(1&2): 70–81.

Brown, A. (1979) *Color, class and politics in Jamaica*, New Brunswick, NJ: Transaction Books.

Brown, S.F. (2000) *Spitting in the wind: lessons in empowerment from the Caribbean*, Kingston, Jamaica: Ian Randle Publishers in association with The Commonwealth Foundation.

Brown-Glaude, W. (2007) "The fact of blackness: the bleached body in contemporary Jamaica," *Small Axe* 24(October): 34–51.

Bryan, P. (1991/2000) *The Jamaican people, 1880–1902: race, class and social control*, Kingston, Jamaica: The University of the West Indies Press.

Cooper, C. (1993) *Noises in the blood: orality, gender and the 'vulgar' body of Jamaican popular culture*, London: Macmillan.

Charles, C.A.D. (2003) "Skin bleaching, self-hate, and black identity in Jamaica," *Journal of Black Studies* 33(6): 711–728.

Dash, Michael J. (1989, originally 1981) "Introduction," in E. Glissant (ed.) *Caribbean discourse: selected essays* (trans. J.M. Dash), Charlottesville, VA: University Press of Virginia, pp. xi–xlv.

Francis, S. (1969) "The evolution of community development in Jamaica (1937–1962)," *Caribbean Quarterly* 15(2/3): 40–58.

Girvan, N. (ed.) (1993) *Working together for development: D.T.M. Girvan on cooperatives and community development, 1939–1968*, Kingston, Jamaica: Institute of Publications Limited.

Glissant, E. (1989a, originally 1981) *Caribbean discourse: selected essays* (trans. J.M. Dash), Charlottesville, VA: University Press of Virginia.

—— (1989b) "Beyond Babel," *World Literature Today* 63(4): 561–563.

Gray, O. (1991) *Radicalism and social change in Jamaica, 1960–1972*, Knoxville, TN: University of Tennessee Press.

Hall, S. (1997) "Caribbean culture: future trends," *Caribbean Quarterly* 43(1/2): 25–33.

Hart, P.R. (1993) "Norman Manley: out to build a new Jamaica," *Jamaica Journal* 25(1): 29–37.

Harris-Lacewell, M. (2007) "Do you know what it means: mapping emotion in the aftermath of Katrina," *Souls* 9(1): 28–44.

Heron, A.B. (1994) *Social action centre (SAC): follow-up evaluation of SAC and CBOs in Westmoreland and Clarendon*, Kingston, Jamaica: Social Action Centre.

Hershatter, G. (1997) *Dangerous pleasures: prostitution and modernity in twentieth-century Shanghai*, California: University of California Press.

Hope, A. and Timmel, S. (1984) *Training for transformation: a handbook for community workers*, Vols. 1–3, Gweru, Zimbabwe: Mambo Press.

Johnson, H. (1977) "The West Indies and the conversion of the British colonial classes to the development idea," *The Journal of Commonwealth & Comparative Politics* 15(1): 55–83.

Klien, K.L. (2000) "On the emergence of memory in historical discourse," *Representations* 69 (Winter): 127–150.

Lewis, R. (1997) "Learning to blow the Abeng: a critical look at anti-establishment movements of the 1960s," *Small Axe* (1): 5–17.

—— (1998) *Walter Rodney's intellectual and political thought*, Detroit, MI: Wayne State University Press.

Levy, H. (1994) "The new actors—civil society organizations: the case of Jamaica," unpublished paper, Kingston, Jamaica: Association of Development Centre & Social Action Centre.

—— (1995) "Notes and comments: Jamaica Welfare, growth and decline," *Social and Economic Studies* 44(2/3): 349–364.

—— (2000) "The Social Action Centre story, 1958–1998," in S.F. Brown (ed.) *Spitting in the wind: lessons in empowerment from the Caribbean*, Kingston, Jamaica: Ian Randle Publishers in association with The Commonwealth Foundation, pp. 100–148.

Livingston, G. (2006) "Race and the habits of scholarship of critical social thought: probing the archaeology of Nancy Fraser's justice interruptus," *The International Journal of the Humanities* 3(10): 15–30.

—— (forthcoming) "Foundations of critical categories of justice in education," in S. Tozer, A. Henry, B. Gallegos, M.B. Greiner and P.G. Price (eds) *Handbook of research on the social foundations of education*, New York: Routledge.

—— (under journal review) "Silencing habits: race-memory routes of the production of the political in critical educational research."

Mathurin-Mair, L. (1969) "The student and the university's civilising role," *Caribbean Quarterly* 15(2/3): 8–19.

Mignolo, W.D. (2005) *The idea of Latin America*, United Kingdom: Blackwell Publishing.

Mills, D. (1989) "Jamaica's international relations in independence," in R. Nettleford (ed.) *Jamaica in independence: essays on the early years*, Kingston, Jamaica: Heinemann Publishers (Caribbean), pp. 131–171.

Morrison, T. (1984) "Memory, creation and writing," *Thought* 59(235): 385–390.

—— (1987) *Beloved*, New York: Knopf.

Munroe, T. (1972) *The politics of constitutional decolonization: Jamaica 1944–62*, Kingston, Jamaica: Institute of Social and Economic Research.

Nettleford, R. (ed.) (1971a) *Manley and the new Jamaica: selected speeches & writings 1938–1968*, New York: Africana Publishing Corporation.

—— (1971b) "General introduction: N.W. Manley and the politics of Jamaica: towards an analysis of political change in Jamaica 1938–1968," in R. Nettleford (ed.) *Manley and the new Jamaica: selected speeches & writings 1938–1968*, New York: Africana Publishing Corporation, pp. xi–xciv.

—— (ed.) (1989) *Jamaica in independence: essays on the early years*, Kingston, Jamaica: Heinemann Publishers (Caribbean) Ltd.

—— (1994) *Emancipation – the lessons and the legacy: challenge to the church*, Kingston, Jamaica: Emancipation Commemoration Committee, Webster Memorial United Church.

Plummer, B.G. (2005) "On Cedric Robinson and Black Marxism: a view from the academy," *Race and Class* 47(2): 111–114.

Post, K. (1969) "The politics of protest in Jamaica, 1938: some problems of analysis and conceptualization," *Social and Economic Studies* 18(4): 374–390.

Rushdy, A.H.A. (1990) "'Rememory': primal scenes and constructions in Toni Morrison's novels," *Contemporary Literature* 31(3): 300–323.

Said, E.W. (2000) "Invention, memory, and place," *Critical Inquiry* 26(2): 175–192.

Scott, D. (1999) "The archaeology of Black memory: an interview with Robert Hill," *Small Axe: A Journal of Criticism* 3(1): 80–150.

Soyinka, W. (1982) *The critic and society: Barthes, leftocracy and other mythologies* (Inaugural Lecture Series 49), Ibadan, Nigeria: University of IFE Press.

Sunshine, Catherine A. (1988) *The Caribbean: survival, struggle and sovereignty*, Washington, DC: EPICA.

Tafari-Ama, I. (2006) *Setting the skin tone* (audio-visual production), Kingston, Jamaica: A Digital Images Production.

Thomas, D.A. (2005) "The emergence of modern Blackness in Jamaica," *North American Congress on Latin America (NACLA) Report on the Americas* 39(3): 30–36.

Williams, E. (1970) *From Columbus to Castro: the history of the Caribbean, 1492–1969*, New York: Harper & Row Publishers.

34

Momentum and melancholia
Women in higher education internationally

Louise Morley

The melancholia of missing women

Women have become highly visible as students, or consumers of higher education, while simultaneously remaining invisible or partially visible as leaders and knowledge producers. Hence, there is a curious two-step of recognition and misrecognition that threatens to confuse and confound debates on gender in the academy. Women's under-representation in leadership is international and multi-sectoral (Davidson and Burke, 2004). Some women have been allowed into higher education, embassy style, as micro-level representatives of a wider diverse community. However, women continue to be benchmarked in relation to masculinist norms, entering a matrix of declared and hidden rules. Organisational environments can create and regulate subjectivities and identities. Inclusion and exclusion both appear to produce dangers and opportunities. Women are simultaneously constructed as winners and losers. Winners because they are gaining access, as students, in significant numbers, but losers because of their lack of entitlement to leadership and prestigious disciplines. In this chapter, I will attempt to discuss these topics in a global context.

It would be easy to rehearse yet another pessimistic repertoire of challenges for gender equity in the academy. Gender and melancholy are often deeply connected (Butler, 2002), with a sense of loss, hurt and grief often underpinning studies of gender and power in higher education. Desire, as well as loss, needs to be considered. Indeed, writing on gender equality means that we have to refer to something that does not yet exist. The tendency therefore is to critique, rather than to engage in futurology. Questions about the desired morphology of the university of the future seem to be eclipsed by pressing concerns in the present. The melancholia, however, has been productive! There have been multiple questions about the obduracy of gender inequalities in the face of equality interventions, and recognition of how gender is formed and reformed in the spatial and temporal context of higher education. Studies have been conducted on gender (in)sensitive pedagogy (Sandler *et al.*, 1996; Welch, 2006); sexual harassment (Townsley and Geist, 2000); gendered curricula and subject choices (Lapping, 2005); gendered micropolitics (Morley, 1999); women's access (Kwesiga, 2002), and how differing spatial and temporal modalities impact on women's engagement with higher education (Moss, 2006).

Employment, representation and exclusion have been explored in relation to women's limited opportunities for promotion and professional development (Knights and Richards, 2003; Morley et al, 2006); the under-representation of women in senior academic and administrative positions (Blackmore and Sachs, 2001; Husu, 2000), or in high-status disciplines (Bebbington, 2002), and prestigious institutions (Dyhouse, 2003). Women's relation to knowledge itself has been theorised in terms of the way in which gender structures relations of production and reproduction and is linked to knowledge construction, research opportunities and dissemination (Mama, 1996; Spivak, 1999; Stanley, 1997). Studies have revealed how liberal and strategic interventions for change, such as equality policies (Bagilhole, 2002; Deem et al., 2005), and gender mainstreaming, are poorly conceptualised, understood and implemented (Charlesworth, 2005; Morley, 2007a). All reasons to be cheerful indeed, raising questions about what it takes to challenge the irrational mayhem of gender inequalities.

Marginson (2006) reminds us about global connectivities and how higher education is becoming a single, worldwide arrangement. Without wishing to advocate an economy of sameness for women in different national locations, it seems that some gender inequalities are also globalised (Morley et al., 2005). For example, there is consistently low representation of women in positions of seniority in a range of countries in divergent cultural and geopolitical contexts (Brooks, 1997; Morley et al., 2006; Singh, 2002, 2008). Curiously, in a culture of measurement and audit in higher education, women's representation in leadership is not always perceived as sufficiently important to measure, monitor or map. International data on gender equity among heads of universities are noticeably uneven. Since 1998, the Association of Commonwealth Universities (ACU) has attempted to address this lack of data with five yearly analytical reports of data (Lund 1998; Singh, 2002, 2008). Its most recent publication (Singh, 2008) reports that in twenty-three of the thirty-five countries in the Commonwealth from which the ACU receives gender disaggregated data, *all* universities are led by men (Singh, 2008: 12). The organisation notes 'the depressing reality . . . of a still relatively stable hierarchical pyramid in which there are fewer and fewer women the higher up the ladder of seniority one looks' (Garland, 2008: 4). As Figure 34.1 on page 386 shows, women's participation in leadership of universities in the Commonwealth has remained stable over the past decade. Throughout this period, only one in ten vice chancellors or presidents of Commonwealth universities has been a woman (Singh, 2008: 12).

While patterns of representation among women have remained largely unchanged in leadership, women are faring slightly better in some academic positions (Singh, 2008). Women's participation as professors and associate professors has increased slightly since 1997, as Figure 34.1 shows. However, women still only comprise 15.3 per cent of professors, and 29.1 per cent of associate professors, readers and senior lecturers across the Commonwealth.

Among Commonwealth countries, women's participation in management and academic leadership tends to be higher than average in high-income countries such as Australia, Canada and the United Kingdom. Very few women are appointed as head of administration in South Asian or African Countries (Singh, 2008).

At this stage of the argument, it might seem as if patterns of gender and leadership directly map on to economic contexts, and that women's under-representation in senior positions in higher education correlates, or indeed is caused by, poverty and under-development. So, it is worth shifting the focus to another geopolitical area.

The European Union examines systematic evidence of gender imbalances among scientists and researchers and maps progress towards gender equity through the *She Figures* series launched in 2003 (European Commission, 2006). *She Figures 2006* provided gender disaggregated data

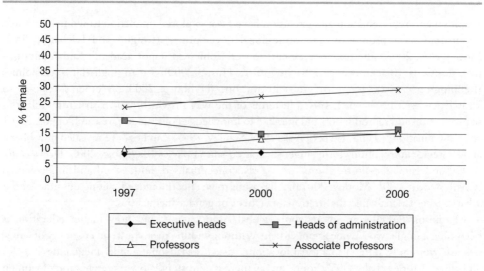

Figure 34.1 Whispers of change? Women's participation in the leadership[a] of Commonwealth universities between 1997 and 2006.

Source: Singh, 2008: 45.

[a] Executive heads defined as vice chancellors, presidents, rectors. Heads of administration defined as registrars, secretaries. Professors defined as full professors only. Associate professors defined as associate professors, readers, principal lecturers and senior lecturers.

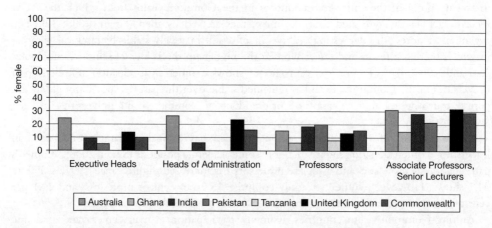

Figure 34.2 Women's participation in management and academic leadership in selected Commonwealth countries, 2006.

Source: Singh, 2008: 11-33.

for the twenty-five member states of the enlarged European Union and seven countries associated with the 6th Framework Programme, namely Bulgaria, Switzerland, Iceland, Israel, Norway, Romania and Turkey. The European Commission revealed that only 15 per cent of those at the highest academic grade (Grade A[1]) in higher education in the European Union were women (European Commission, 2006). This can be seen in UK figures. In 2006/7, women

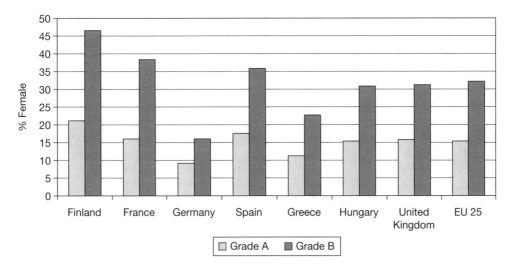

Figure 34.3 Proportion of female academic staff by grade[a] in the European Union, 2004.

Source: European Commission, 2006: 57.

[a] Grade A: highest grade or post at which research conducted, professor. Grade B: researchers not as senior as top position but more senior than newly qualified Ph.D. holder, e.g. associate professor, senior lecturer, senior researcher.

comprised 42.3 per cent of academics, but only 17.5 per cent of professors in higher education institutions in the UK (*Guardian*, 28 February 2008: 1).

The disappearance of women in the higher grades is evocative of Sen's construct of 'missing women' (Martin, 2008; Sen, 2003). Women disappear when power, resources and influence increase. So a question to consider is whether gendered opportunity structures only relate to women staff, as women students appear to be flourishing?

The momentum of women's increased participation

One major success is the increased numbers of women entering higher education as under-graduate students. If we consider that women were barred in the UK until the late nineteenth century (Dyhouse, 1995), this represents quantitative progress. Indeed, there is a morality to the whole widening participation debate that suggests that a democratising state intervention is promoting meritocratic equalisation and redistributing an unquestioned 'good' (Morley and Lugg, 2009). Whatever the sociopolitical drivers, it is worth noting that, in the UK in 1995, there were two and a half times more women in the system than in 1970–1971 (Abbott and Wallace, 1997). Participation rates for women in higher education have increased between 1999 and 2005 in all regions of the world, with a global gender parity index of 1.05, suggesting that there are now more undergraduate women than men in higher education (UNESCO, 2007:132). However, the increase in women's participation has been unevenly distributed across national and disciplinary boundaries. Women's participation rates are higher than those of men in North America and Europe, but lower in regions such as East Asia and the Pacific, South and West Asia and Sub-Saharan Africa.

Globally, women students are concentrated in non-science subjects. There is still a sense of what constitutes a gender-appropriate discipline in many high- and low-income countries, with worldwide concern about the under-representation of women in the science, technology, engineering and mathematics (STEM) subjects. Men predominate in subjects related to engineering, manufacturing and construction, and maths and computer science (OECD, 2007). In many countries, two thirds to three quarters of graduates in the fields of health, welfare and education are women (UNESCO, 2006). Thus, women continue to be concentrated in subjects associated with low-wage sectors of the economy, in particular health and welfare, humanities, arts and education.

What do all these facts about women's increased participation or exclusion add up to in terms of how women experience the academy? I have conducted studies on the micropolitics of academic life and frequently find that the gendered relays of power that cause the most distress and discomfort are the everyday transactions and relations (Morley, 1999; 2006). Blending quantitative 'facts' with interview data helps to reveal both the scale and the lived complexities that structure women's participation in higher education, as students and staff. Focusing on everyday micro-level incidents can provide important information about more macro-focused challenges for gender equality. The personal is political, or to use more contemporary vocabulary, the self can become an object of reflexive knowledge (Beck and Beck-Gernsheim, 2002; Hey and Leathwood, 2007). The following sections will attempt to relate some of these concerns to a global feminist polity.

The feminisation hysteria

An equity paradox seems to have arisen. Instead of celebrating the fact that some women have succeeded in entering the academy in certain disciplinary and organisational locations, a moral panic over the feminisation of higher education has emerged. Happily, some Western feminist scholars are taking issue with popularist beliefs that women are taking over the academy and that their newly found professional and economic independence is responsible for societal destabilisation and a crisis in masculinity (Evans, 2008; Leathwood and Read, 2008; Quinn, 2003). The feminisation debate itself is partial and exclusionary. First, it does not include consideration of leadership in higher education and only seems to relate to female participation at undergraduate level in some programmes and in some geopolitical regions. Second, it is debatable as to whether quantitative change has allowed more (or perversely less) discursive space for gender? Third, it fails to intersect gender with other structures of inequality, including social class; and, fourth, it silences advocacy for gender equality.

Issues of silence, voice and participation have long been a concern of feminist theorists (Gatenby and Humphries, 1999). Speaking as a woman can mean speaking as a gendered self that is often at odds with the putative ungendered or gender-neutral representations and assumptions of academia (Evans, 2008). However, voice is not just about women speaking, but about the inclusion of gender equality in policy, pedagogy and planning. In the UK, gender is a disqualified discourse in higher education policy. Quantitative change seems to imply to policymakers that gender is no longer an issue in a post-feminist era (Morley, 2007b). For example, the former minister for higher education in the UK – John Denham – made a speech about priorities for the next fifteen years, and these all relate to innovation and wealth creation, rather than to wealth distribution, inclusion and equalities. Gender equality was not mentioned once (Denham, 2008).

Transnational challenges

A criticism of much of the scholarship on academic women is that it focuses on the experiences and voices of socio-economically privileged white women in high-income countries (Twombly, 1999). Theorising links between differently located practices can produce a sense of the patterns and scale of gender challenges. I would like to draw, first, upon some research findings from Morley et al. (2006). This study explored gender equity in higher education in five Commonwealth countries. It aimed to go behind the statistics and explore women's everyday experiences of higher education in Nigeria, South Africa, Sri Lanka, Tanzania and Uganda. Identifying key sites of gender-differentiated experiences of the academy was a purpose of the research. The countries were selected for their varying national policies on gender equity and their commitment to international policies to end discrimination against women. There were 209 interviews held with students, academic staff and managers. Observation of classrooms and boardrooms was conducted, and statistics and policies were analysed. A noticeable finding was how gender inequalities appear to be globalised. While transnational feminism is problematic in terms of the diversity of women's oppressions (Mills and Ssewakiryanga, 2002), observations from women in low-income countries can sound remarkably similar to women's voices in the west.

In the study, a strong sense of a hidden curriculum emerged (Margolis, 2001). The overt and the hidden curricula are not mutually exclusive but form a complex mechanism of production and reproduction (Apple, 1980). The hidden curriculum is irrational and contradictory. Negative attitudes to women's academic abilities do not correlate with their actual achievements. One aspect of the hidden curriculum relates to the conjunction between gender and academic ability and authority. Studies have reported how discrimination against women can involve not taking them seriously and doubting their ability and motivation (Seymour and Hewitt, 1997). Discrimination due to perceived incompetence is based on descriptive gender stereotypes (Rudman and Glick, 2001). Difference is frequently expressed in terms of deficit and located within particular bodies rather than in the 'invisible values and assumptions structuring curriculum and pedagogy' (Abu El-Haj, 2003: 411).

Femaleness is repeatedly perceived as irreconcilable with intellectual authority (Shah, 2001). In many cultures, the higher-educated woman is in antagonistic relationship to other discursive practices. In Morley et al. (2006), there was widespread reporting of negating women's academic abilities and hostility from male students and staff, as a South African student illustrates:

I have also noticed how we've had maybe two or three female lecturers and how the guys in our class just do not listen to them, they do not respect them. And I mean these women are really good, they are brilliant, they know their stuff they worked hard they have their PhDs, but guys laugh at them, ridicule them.

In an observation evocative of Spender's early work in the UK (1982), and Brooks' early work in the USA (1982), the Sri Lankan team relate how their classroom observations revealed male students receiving more pedagogical attention:

Towards the end of the lecture when the lecturer was relating real-life examples to the theory he had been teaching, he mentioned a project the female student was involved in and briefly asked her a question related to it but he did not give her any time to answer, smiled and moved on to the next question very swiftly.

389

The Sri Lankan team also note how, generally, male students were invited to comment and question more than females. Consequently, male students became more confident, more assertive and relaxed than their female counterparts. This gendered interaction did not go unnoticed by students. A Sri Lankan student describes discriminatory behaviour from some male lecturers:

> There are some who try to put the women down by asking a question and then laughing at us when we can't answer it, or ask something just to put us down.

The gendering of pedagogical interactions poses questions about the full meaning of the concept of women's participation.

Women students in Morley *et al.* (2006) were also perceived as impeded by internalised oppression, i.e. their interior worlds or psychic narratives that constantly played recordings of inferiority. Women's academic self-worth was often presented as fragile and unstable. A Ugandan student states:

> The problem most girls have is lack of confidence.

A Sri Lankan policymaker in Morley *et al.* (2006) also attributed the low level of women in management to women's reluctance to apply for the posts:

> Managerial posts are not held by women in large numbers. In universities, if you take generally speaking how many heads of departments are females . . . no not even 20 per cent are held by the females . . . That is because they don't come forward. That is the reason.

The problem with affective explanations and attributing problems to psychic narratives, such as lack of self-confidence, is that they suggest that women are in deficit and lacking the personal attributes to succeed. Cognitive, rather than organisational, restructuring is seen as the solution. Problems that are largely collective and social are individuated. It represents the privatisation of the public. The myth of meritocracy is reinforced. As Knights and Richards (2003: 218) suggest:

> Meritocracy has the power to pass the responsibility for unequal outcomes back onto the individual and therefore to stigmatize the unsuccessful as incompetent or incapable.

The power relations that create structures and barriers and, indeed, that undermine women's confidence in their abilities, are overlooked. By offering very conventional indicators of professional success, it also marks out women as losers who prefer not to occupy managerial roles.

The gendering of academic ability has been a theme that has emerged in my recent study on widening participation in higher education in Ghana and Tanzania (Morley *et al.*, 2009).[2] This study utilises statistical data, life history interviews with 200 students and semi-structured interviews with 200 staff in two public and two private universities. It focuses on how gender and socio-economic status intersect and constrain or facilitate participation in higher education. The interview data so far suggest that any activity that is perceived as difficult is seen to be inappropriate for women. A Tanzanian female student describes how female students frequently believe that they need to be academically rescued by male students:

You know that for example this question is tough and only boys can tackle it . . . and a girl cannot, and we have to look for a boy, who we think can tackle it.

Success criteria for gender equality frequently relate to women's increased participation in male-dominated areas. It is almost if, by working and studying with men, there will be disidentification with the inferior world of women and a type of positive contagion of male values and behaviours. Success is constructed as crossing a gendered threshold to become more like a man, rather than removing the gendered code from the activity.

Hegemonic codes of femininity and masculinity continue to influence subject choice (Lapping, 2005). Women are constructed as poor choosers when it comes to academic disciplines. Their entry into 'non-traditional' disciplines is seen as a form of empowerment and, hence, a cause for celebration. In Tanzania especially, where affirmative action interventions have created access or pre-entry programmes for women to enter science, quantitative change is widely acknowledged as success. Women's academic identities are frequently constructed in terms of remediation or absence. A Tanzanian Dean of a Science Faculty discusses women's under-representation in high-status disciplines:

When it comes to gender, I think it's the girls who are not well represented particularly in some disciplines. Sciences is less than fifteen percent . . . When it comes to Physics, Mathematics, Geology there is huge imbalance between the girls and boys . . . In Mathematics it could be up to . . . you know between eighty and twenty percent. Even in Geology you know twenty percent girls, eighty percent boys.

Under-representation usually features in relation to certain high-status STEM subject areas. Men's under-representation in female-dominated disciplines is rarely mentioned in policy terms.

The question of what and where women are accessing can also be related to the type of higher education institution (HEI). In Ghana, women comprise 35 per cent of the overall university population (NCTE, 2006a,b), although they make up 41 per cent of the students in private higher education (NCTE, 2006b). In Tanzania, 33 per cent of the overall undergraduate population is female, with women comprising 38 per cent of students in private higher education (Ministry of Higher Education, Science and Technology (MHEST), 2006). If rates of participation for women are higher in lower-status private higher education, this poses questions about core and periphery provision. Socially disadvantaged groups could be getting diverted into peripheral higher education, thus reinforcing stratification of the sector and social differentiation. In this analysis, widening participation in higher education can be conceptualised as a process of diversion, i.e. a rerouting of members of socially disadvantaged groups into lower-status institutions in order to reserve the higher-status universities for the elite (David, 2007). 'Buying an education becomes a substitute for getting an education' (Kenway et al., 1993: 116).

Policy evaporation

An ongoing source of grief and melancholy for many feminist scholars is the way in which policy commitments to gender can evaporate during implementation (Goetz, 1997; Longwe, 1995). In the UK, gender is no longer included in higher education policy. Elsewhere, there are gender policies that fail to be implemented. In Ghana, an academic relates how gender remains at the level of policy text, with no strategic implementation plans:

They are all making any noises about tertiary education. All they said was they recommended 50–50 and that was it, that was it . . . The only one I can think of is with regard to women, it's a little bit more of lip service, if anything.

These observations about the implementation gap are evocative of findings from a UK-based study that I conducted with Rosemary Deem and Anwar Tlili (Deem *et al.*, 2005: Deem, 2008). The research involved six case studies of higher education institutions across England, Scotland and Wales. The project's aims included exploring staff experiences of equity issues and institutional equity policies. A central finding was that, although all six institutions studied had equal opportunities policies in place, not all the policies were comprehensive, completely up to date or easy to understand. Policies were often communicated to staff via email, which may not reach those with email overload or staff with no computer access at work. Some policies gave the impression of often having been reactively rather than proactively constructed and with an eye to compliance with legislation rather than empowerment of the work force and enhancement of their working conditions. Staff were wary of utilising grievance procedures for fear of recrimination and professional suicide. The policies were not integrated into strategic management, and there was little action planning or pro-activity. The problem of senior and middle management inactivity was observed by an academic trade union representative from one university, who felt that, for some, it was sufficient simply to note the numbers rather than take any action to rectify under-representation:

> Now on sex equality last year there was a round of promotions to principal lecturer and, it was noted that I think the proportion of women who applied, as compared to the proportion of women employed, and the proportion of women I think, was one out of six appointees. And the personnel office simply in their report, noted the numbers. But we tried to push them to think about what might they do about it but they were quite content to just note the disparity between the number of women employed in the academic role and the outcome of this round.

Many of the staff that we interviewed frequently noted how policies existed at a textual level – often to meet the requirements of audit and funding bodies – rather than building momentum at the grassroots level of day-to-day work.

Conclusion

Women's exclusion from higher education is a historical injustice sometimes framed today in terms of a human rights violation. Today, women are participating, in increasing numbers, in higher education, in a range of national locations. Yet, women's academic identities are often forged in otherness, as strangers in opposition to (privileged) men's belonging and entitlement. This means that gender in higher education is often encoded in a range of formal and informal signs, practices and networks. The gender debates are full of contradictions. Quantitative targets to let more women into higher education can fail, or be meaningless, while femaleness continues to be socially constructed as second-class citizenship. Women are positioned as holding back as a consequence of low confidence and self-esteem, while simultaneously threatening to take over or feminise (and, hence, devalue) the sacred space of academe. A further contradiction between policy as text and as lived experience is a noticeable feature of gender architecture.

Policy interventions, including gender mainstreaming and gender equality, suggest that now gender sensitivity and strategic actions should be everywhere – including the curriculum, management and resourcing of academic life – yet informants in my studies report that it is nowhere!

Feminist scholars and researchers will continue to critique, theorise, audit and grieve power and privilege in higher education, as it is a major site of cultural practice, identity formation and symbolic control. Whereas the former UK minister for higher education (Denham, 2008) has a wish list for the next fifteen years that includes the expansion of technology, innovation and research-based wealth creation, we also need to build on the momentum of women's increased participation and imagine or re-imagine a different future.

Notes

1   Grade A as a marker of seniority corresponds to 'full professor' of the highest grade/post at which research is normally conducted (European Commission, 2006: 50).
2   For further information, see www.sussex.ac.uk/education/wideningparticipation.

References

Abbott, P. and Wallace, C. (1997) *An introduction to sociology: feminist perspectives*, 2nd edn, London: Routledge.
Abu El-Haj, T. (2003) 'Challenging the inevitability of difference: young women and discourses about gender equity in the classroom, *Curriculum Inquiry* 33(4): 401–425.
Apple, M.W. (1980) 'The other side of the hidden curriculum: correspondence theories and the labor process', *Journal of Education* 162: 47–66.
Bagilhole, B. (2002) 'Challenging equal opportunities: changing and adapting male hegemony in academia', *British Journal of Sociology of Education* 23(1): 19–33.
Bebbington, D. (2002). 'Women in science, engineering and technology: a review of the issues', *Higher Education Quarterly* 56(4): 360–375.
Beck, U. and Beck-Gernsheim, E. (2002) *Individualization*, Thousand Oaks, CA: Sage.
Blackmore, J. and Sachs, J. (2001) 'Women leaders in the restructured and internationalised university', in A. Brooks and McKinnon, A. (eds) *Gender and the restructured university*, Buckingham: Open University Press.
Brooks, A. (1997) *Academic women*, Buckingham: Open University Press.
Brooks, V. (1982) 'Sex differences in student dominance in female and male professors' classrooms', *Sex Roles* 8: 683–690.
Butler, J. (2002) 'Melancholy gender-refused identification', in M. Dimen and V. Goldner (eds) *Gender in psychoanalytic space: between clinic and culture*, New York: Other Press.
Charlesworth, H. (2005) 'Not waving but drowning: gender mainstreaming and human rights in the United Nations', *Harvard Human Rights Journal* 18: 1–18.
David, M. (2007) 'Equity and diversity: towards a sociology of higher education for the 21st century?', *British Journal of Sociology of Education* 28(5): 675–690.
Davidson, M.J. and Burke, R.J. (eds) (2004) *Women in management worldwide: facts, figures and analysis*, London: Ashgate.
Deem, R. (2008) 'Managing a meritocracy or an equitable organisation? Senior managers' and employees' views about equal opportunities policies in UK universities', *Journal of Education Policy* 22(6): 615–636.
—— Morley, L. and Tlili, A. (2005) *Negotiating equity in UK universities*, London: HEFCE.

Denham, J. (2008) 'Check against delivery', Speech given at the Wellcome Collection Conference Centre, London, 29 February 2008. Available online at www.dius.gov.uk/speeches/denham_hespeech_290208.html.

Dyhouse, C. (1995) *No distinction of sex? Women in British universities 1870–1939*, London, UCL Press.

—— (2003) 'Troubled identities: gender and status in the history of the mixed colleges in English universities since 1945', *Women's History Review* 12(2): 169–194.

European Commission (2006) *She figures 2006: women and science statistics and indicators*, Brussels: European Commission. Available online at http://ec.euorpa.eu/research/science-society (accessed 12 June 2008).

Evans, M. (2008) 'The silence of the girls', Paper presented at the Centre for Higher Education and Equity Research (CHEER) Seminar, University of Sussex, 21 January. Available online at www.sussex.ac.uk/education/documents/cheer_seminar_papers__the silence of the girls.pdf.

Garland, D. (2008) 'Where are all the women?' *ACU Bulletin* no. 163 February 2008. Available online at www.acu.ac.uk (accessed 30 April 2008).

Gatenby, B. and Humphries, M. (1999) Exploring gender, management education and careers: speaking in the silences, *Gender and Education* 11(3): 281–294.

Goetz, A. (ed.) (1997) *Getting institutions right for women*, London: Zed Press.

Hey, V. and Leathwood, C. (2007) 'Gender/ed discourses and emotional sub-texts in UK higher education: governing the demo(cra)tic self', Paper presented at the SRHE Conference, Brighton, UK.

Husu, L. (2000) 'Gender discrimination in the promised land of gender equality', *Higher Education in Europe* XXV(2): 221–228.

Kenway, J., Bigum, C. and Fitzclarence, L. (1993) 'Marketing education in the post-modern age', *Journal of Education Policy* 8(2): 105–122.

Knights, D. and Richards, W. (2003) 'Sex discrimination in UK academia', *Gender, Work & Organisation* 10(2): 213–238.

Kwesiga, J. (2002) *Women's access to higher education in Africa: Uganda's experience*, Kampala: Fountain Series in Gender Studies.

Lapping, C. (2005) 'Antagonism and overdetermination: the production of student positions in contrasting undergraduate disciplines and institutions in the UK', *British Journal of Sociology of Education* 26: 657–671.

Leathwood, C. and Read, B. (2008) *Gender and the changing face of higher education: a feminised future?*, Maidenhead: McGraw-Hill/Open University Press.

Longwe, S.H. (1995) *The evaporation of policies for women's advancement, in a commitment to the world's women: perspectives on development for Beijing and beyond*, New York: United Nations Development Fund for Women (UNIFEM).

Lund, H. (1998) *A single sex profession? Female staff numbers in commonwealth universities*. London: CHEMS.

Mama, A. (1996) *Women's studies and studies of women in Africa during the 1990s*, CODESRIA Working Paper Series 5/96.

Marginson, S. (2006) 'Dynamics of national and global competition in higher education', *Higher Education* 52: 1–39.

Margolis, E. (2001) *The hidden curriculum in higher education*, London: Routledge.

Martin, J. (2008) 'The missing women in higher education: a case study of culture crossing', in A.M. May (ed.) *The 'woman question' and higher education: perspectives on gender and knowledge production in America*, Cheltenham, UK and Northampton, MA: Edward Elgar, pp. 77–92.

Mills, D. and Ssewakiryanga, R. (2002) '"That Beijing thing": challenging transnational feminisms in Kampala', *Gender, Place & Culture* 9(4): 385–398.

Ministry of Higher Education, Science and Technology (MHEST) (2006) *Basic statistics on higher education, science and technology 2001/2002–2005/2006*, Dar es Salaam: MHEST.

Morley, L. (1999) *Organising feminisms: the micropolitics of the academy*, London: Macmillan.

—— (2006) 'Hidden transcripts: the micropolitics of gender in Commonwealth universities', *Women's Studies International Forum* 29(6): 543–551.

—— (2007a) 'Sister-matic: gender mainstreaming in higher education', *Teaching in Higher Education* 12(5/6): 607–620.

—— (2007b) 'Gender and UK higher education: post-feminism in a market economy', in M. Danowitz Sagaria (ed.) *Women, universities and change: gender equality in the European Union and the United States*, New York: Palgrave Macmillan, pp. 133–144.

——, Gunawardena, C., Kwesiga, J., Lihamba, A., Odejide, A., Shacketon, L. and Sorhaindo, A. (2006) *Gender equity in selected Commonwealth universities*, Research Report No. 65 to the Department of International Development. London: DFID.

——, Leach, F. and Lugg, R. (2009) 'Democratising higher education in Ghana and Tanzania: opportunity structures and social inequalities', *International Journal of Educational Development* 29: 56–64.

—— and Lugg, R. (2009, in press) 'Mapping meritocracy: intersecting gender, poverty and higher educational opportunity structures', *Higher Education Policy* 22(2).

——, Sorhaindo, A. and Burke, P. (2005) *Researching women: an annotated bibliography on gender equity in Commonwealth higher education*, London: Institute of Education.

Moss, D. (2006) Gender, space and time: women and higher education, Lanham, MD: Lexington Books.

NCTE (2006a) *Statistical digest of universities and IPS 2005/6*, Accra: NCTE Ghana Records.

NCTE (2006b) *Student enrolments for private tertiary institutions from 1999 to 2006*, Accra: NCTE Ghana Records.

OECD (2007) *Women and men in OECD countries*, Paris: OECD. Available online at http://oecd.org/gender (accessed June 2007).

Quinn, J. (2003) *Powerful subjects: are women really taking over the university?* Stoke-on-Trent: Trentham.

Rudman, L. and Glick, P. (2001) 'Prescriptive gender stereotypes and backlash toward agentic women', *Journal of Social Issues* 57(4): 743–762.

Sandler, B.R., Silverberg, L.A. and Hall, R.M. (1996) *The chilly classroom climate: a guide to improve the education of women*, Washington, DC: National Association for Women in Education.

Sen, A. (2003) 'Missing women-revisited', *British Medical Journal* 327 (7427) 6 December: 1297–1298.

Seymour, E. and Hewitt, N.M. (1997) *Talking about leaving: why undergraduates leave the sciences*, Oxford: Westview Press.

Shah, S. (2001) 'Tertiary colleges in Pakistan: gender and equality', *The School Field* X11(3/4): 49–70.

Singh, J.K.S. (2002) *Still a single sex profession? Female staff numbers in Commonwealth Universities*, London: Association of Commonwealth Universities.

—— (2008) *Whispers of change. Female staff numbers in Commonwealth universities*, London: Association of Commonwealth Universities.

Spender, D. (1982) *Invisible women: the schooling scandal*, London: Writers and Readers Co-operative.

Spivak, G. (1999) *A critique of postcolonial reason*, London: Harvard University Press.

Stanley, L. (ed.) (1997) *Knowing feminisms*, London: Sage.

Townsley, N. and Geist, P. (2000) 'The discursive enactment of hegemony: sexual harassment and academic organizing', *Western Journal of Communication* 64(2): 190–217.

Twombly, S. (1999) 'Review essay new scholarship on academic women: beyond "women's ways"', *The Review of Higher Education* 22(4): 441–454.

UNESCO (2006) *Global education digest 2006: comparing education statistics across the world*, Montreal: UNESCO Institute of Statistics.

—— (2007) *Global education digest 2007: comparing education statistics across the world*, Montreal: UNESCO Institute of Statistics. Available online at http://stats.uis.unesco.org/unesco/ (accessed 22 November 2007).

Welch, P. (2006) 'Feminist pedagogy revisited', LATISS – *Learning and Teaching in the Social Sciences*, 3(3): 171–199.

35

Sociology, social class and education

Diane Reay

Introduction

The relationship between the educational system and social class inequalities is one of the most fundamental issues in the sociology of education. Schools have been held up as both the means of achieving equality in society but also as centrally implicated in the reproduction of inequalities. So we are confronted with a conundrum. How is schooling to be understood in relation to social class? Is it a source of social mobility or even emancipation for the working classes or does it remain a means of controlling the lower orders and maintaining upper- and middle-class advantage? What is clear is that sociology has struggled to understand the complexities of, let alone provide solutions for, social class inequalities in education.

A variety of causes for educational inequalities, together with possible ways of addressing them, have been posited over the last seventy years. These can be divided into three main approaches. The first focuses on internal school factors, exemplified most recently in the school effectiveness and improvement movement (Hallinger and Heck, 1998). Enshrined in this internalist perspective is the view that schools can and do make a difference to social class inequalities, that a focus on improving practice at the micro level of school and classroom is enough. However, this approach, which was at its most popular in the 1990s, is on the wane, as increasingly research states that the effectiveness of schooling in addressing social class inequalities is relatively small. Olive Banks' conclusion in 1955, repeated in 1970 by Basil Bernstein, that schools have limited capacity to compensate for economic and social inequalities is being borne out in contemporary research across the globe (Cassen and Kingdon, 2007; Freeman-Moir and Scott, 2003; Gamoran, 2007; McLeod and Yates, 2006). Furthermore, the worrying tendency has been for such approaches, especially in their interpretation by media and politicians, to degenerate into blaming teachers, without any recognition of the impact of wider external influences. There remains a lack of consensus about the extent of the role schools play in social class inequalities. However, what is now generally agreed is that internal educational processes are not in themselves sufficient to explain class inequalities in education.

As Gamoran (2007) succinctly points out in relation to the US, differences in school performance are rooted in inequalities that lie outside the school, and, as long as wider social inequalities persist, so will educational inequalities. More influential within sociology have been factors that are seen to be external to schooling, ranging from the labour market to working-class culture. However, here too a blame culture has often been in evidence. Within this externalist perspective, the working–class family is often positioned as the villain. With depressing frequency, the media, politicians and even academics have tended to focus on interpretations that view the working classes in terms of a range of cultural deficits that are then portrayed as the reasons for working-class underachievement. Most position the working classes as either victims or deficient in one way or another, and nearly all focus on the home as the locus of class practices.

In both the two approaches outlined above, states shift the blame for educational inequalities from themselves onto individual schools, parents and children (Apple, 2003). The third approach, which spans internal and external causes, concentrates on educational policy as key to remediating social class inequalities. However, here sociological understandings come up against the fluctuating presence of class in educational policy, a case of 'now you see it, now you don't'. Too often within political elites, a commonsense view of social class, namely that we are all classless now, is espoused. Across the globe, class inequalities become overlaid, and partially masked, by dominant discourses, for example of race in the US and rurality in China and Latin America. This other terminology works to bury class as a key marker of educational inequality. The consequence is that all too often social class does not count within education. So, in different countries at different times, in some policies but not in others, social class is recognised as a problem to be addressed in educational policy. Currently, the main discourse within education is one that uses the language of social exclusion, yet another way of avoiding social class. As a result, within educational policy the main division is seen to lie between deprived minorities on the one hand and a large mainstream on the other.

However, even when policymakers and politicians recognise the importance of social class in education, there is often contestation, primarily between policymakers and academics, as to whether educational policy can make a difference to social class inequalities in education. While politicians and policymakers are increasingly preoccupied with targeting policies to address class inequalities, research over the last half century indicates that 'in most places at most times, educational policy has contributed relatively little, if anything, to reducing social inequalities' (Paterson and Iannelli, 2007: 330). In fact, depressingly, much of the research evidence indicates that current policy initiatives are worsening rather than improving social class inequalities. So research focusing on policies that impact on internal aspects of schooling, such as assessment (Reay and Wiliam, 1999) and tracking, setting and streaming (Gillborn and Youdell, 2000; Kelly, 2007; Oakes, 1985), illustrate the ways in which school processes of testing, tracking and streaming result in inequitable outcomes for students that remain strongly related to social class. Similarly, research on marketisation and selection policies reveals polarised educational systems, with the high-achieving, well-resourced, popular schools with largely middle-class intakes at the top of school league tables, while less successful, unpopular schools with mainly working-class students are clustered at, or near, the bottom (Ball, 2003; Brantlinger, 2004).

In this brief overview, I have separated out these three approaches, but they are also to a degree overlapping. So some key educational policies such as No Child Left Behind in the US and Sure Start in the UK specifically target the working-class home and are premised on a cultural deficit view of working-class families, while there is a fuzziness between school level and wider systemic educational policies. In the next section I attempt to bridge internalist, externalist and policy-centred approaches through a focus on social class experiences of education that centres dimensions of the relationship that are often muted in contemporary accounts. I want to argue that we cannot begin to make adequate sense of contemporary class relationships to schooling until we include notions of temporality, spatiality and relationality.

The past in the present: a brief history of social class in education

In relation to temporality, class relationships to education constitute a significant continuation of the past in the present (Teese *et al.*, 2007). Freeman-Moir and Scott's (2003: 10) retrospective analysis of the last half of the twentieth century concluded that, under the most favourable possible conditions, even the most liberal of capitalist societies still operated with educational systems that restricted access and achievement for working-class children in myriad ways. In relation to social class mobility, education across the globe is still about social reproduction and reinforcing the status quo. The reasons are of course partly economic: it remains a question of the level of resources, material as well as cultural, that families can bring to their relationship with schooling. But there remain issues of representation and othering that both feed into and are fed by social and economic inequalities. Any notion of education as liberatory has always been undermined by ruling elites' instrumental view of education as a form of control of the working classes.

A focus on temporality centres not only collective class trajectories but also family histories. The working classes bring to their experience of schooling family memories of educational subordination and marginalisation. Children negotiate schooling not only directly through their own experiences but also through the sedimented experiences of parents and even grandparents. Ruth Lupton's (2004) research in the UK and Annette Lareau's (2003) in the US found that working-class families' expectations of social mobility through education are often minimal, conditioned by their own experiences over several generations.

Specificities of historical time are also critical in understanding class relationships to education. Paul Willis's (1977) lads were leaving school in the late 1960s and early 1970s, at a time when there was a buoyant labour market with an abundance of male manual jobs in the UK. Their oppositional rejection of schooling was, in part, made possible by the opportunities awaiting them in the labour market. The American working-class young men in Lois Weis's (1990) *Working class without work* were dealing with very different economic conditions. Their more positive attitudes to schooling and desires for credentials were, in part, a response to the lack of working-class male jobs in the US economy of the 1980s. And economic conditions have also changed dramatically in the UK and much of Europe over the last forty years. While the working classes in the global South remain outsiders in education, across the global North (Connell, 2007), they often resemble Bourdieu's 'outcasts on the inside'. The current global economic recession and changing labour market demographics leave them trapped in schooling, and increasingly further and higher education, because there is no longer sufficient non-degree employment.

Middle-class relationships to education, while maintaining many common features with the past, have also evolved in response to an increasingly competitive globalised labour market (Ball, 2003; Raveaud and van Zanten, 2007). The middle classes have had to engage in more and more academic, practical and emotional work in order to ensure their social advantage (Lareau, 2003; Reay, 1998). Middle-class relationships to schooling, particularly in the inner cities, have become characterised by high levels of anxiety. Here, as with the working classes, relationships to education have changed along with economic conditions. In particular, the premium put on educational credentials has grown as graduate jobs have diminished relative to the number of graduates.

While economic circumstances change, the negativity with which the working classes are viewed within education does not. It is this historical legacy of being the inferior 'other' within education that resonates in the present. Deference always has been, and still is, expected of the working classes (McDowell, 2007). In fact, what is surprising is that some of the working classes still make enormous efforts to succeed educationally in educational systems that hold little prospect of a positive academic outcome. The working classes across the globe continue to have access to relatively low levels of the kind of material, cultural and psychological resources that aid educational success. Most can neither afford the private tuition and the enriching cultural activities that many middle-class parents invest in for their children, nor do they have the same degree of confidence and sense of entitlement that the middle classes possess in their interactions with schooling. So the negative representations and othering that characterised the past continue in the present. This lack of positive images of the working classes contributes to them being disqualified and inadequately supported educationally. Just as the tendency has been to locate behavioural problems in minority ethnic rather than white students, so the working class across ethnicity has become the universal repository of educational failure. But educational success and failure are necessarily relational. Those who succeed do so at the expense of others' failure. In the next section I examine relationality and its contribution to class experiences of schooling.

Schooling: a classed culture of winners and losers

In place of 'the usual suspects', namely either working-class culture or 'failing' schools that invariably have predominantly working-class intakes as key to working-class failure, a focus on relational aspects of educational achievement reveals the crucial role of power within education. And, as Wilkinson and Pickett (2009) point out, educational failure becomes more prevalent as societies become more unequal. Under the new educational hegemony, we have all become personally responsible for our own educational success and social mobility. Within the highly individualised and competitive cultures that characterise the global North (Connell, 2007), large sections of the working classes are pathologised as unmotivated, unambitious and underachieving. The irony is that the rhetoric of social mobility and equal opportunities within education has increased in volume and intensity as both have become less possible in practice. The objective of many middle-class parents is to ensure that their children are educational winners, but not all children can be winners, and the provision of systems that cater for winners also helps reinforce the position of losers (Butler and Hamnett, 2007: 1166). We cannot all succeed academically. If we did, what counts now as educational success would lose its value. Neither is there any glimmer of recognition that the middle classes' intense and increasingly anxious preoccupation with educational achievement can be as damaging as working-class underachievement. Numerous studies indicate that one of the key lessons middle-class children learn is that failure is intolerable, unwanted and belongs somewhere else. We can glimpse this in what white middle-class Camilla says about class differences in her multi-ethnic London state secondary school:

> I had everything that the working-class kids didn't have. You know everything that my mum and dad had given me and I was more intelligent than they were and there was more going for me than there was for them. And I think also because my mum and dad had achieved so much I think I probably felt quite second rate to them and being friends

399

with these people made me feel like the one you know who was achieving you know and was superior to them.

(Camilla)

Here we are presented with the pervasive middle-class sense of intellectual superiority. Camilla was part of the sample in an ESRC project on the white middle classes sending their children to urban comprehensives in England. In the 250 transcripts, there were 574 allusions to 'being bright', all references to white middle-class students and their friends. This monopolising of 'brightness' by the middle classes within schooling yet again positions the working classes across ethnicity as the 'lesser other' within educational systems.

I am going to draw briefly on a number of empirical research projects, in order to further highlight relationality and the ways in which students experience a zero sum game in which one child's educational success too often means another child's sense of educational failure. They also illustrate what I have called the psychosocial dimension of class in education (Reay, 2005, 2008). The two quotes below, both from working-class students, one in the US and the others in the UK, are infused with a potent sense of unfairness and unequal treatment:

> Girl: What I don't like about my school is how they treat us like animals, like they cage us up and like they keep putting more gates and more locks and stuff though they expect us to act like humans.
>
> (US quote from Fine *et al.*, 2007: 229)

And:

> Martin: Teachers look down on you.
> David: Yeah, like they think you're dumb.
> David: We don't expect them to treat us like their own children? They're not. But we are still kids. I'd say to them 'you've got kids. You treat them with love but you don't need to love us. All you need to do is treat us like humans.
>
> (UK quote from Reay, 2006: 297)

In both quotes we can see powerfully how the system of value that produces the middle classes as valuable, academic stars simultaneously generates a working class that is represented as incapable of having a self with value (Skeggs, 2004). While entitlement and access to resources for making a self with value are central to how the middle classes are formed within education, the consequence is too often a residualised, valueless working class. Class destinies in the twenty-first century remain tied to academic achievement. Furthermore, class has entered psychological categories as a way of socially regulating normativity and pathology within the educational field. However, although children expressed anxieties about school achievement across class differences, in the studies on which I am drawing it was not the white middle-class boys panicking about being exposed as no good through school tracking, testing and assessment procedures. Rather, it was the black and white working-class girls agonising that they would be 'a nothing' (Reay and Wiliam, 1999). Working-class students, such as the girl in Michelle Fine and her colleagues' study, and the two boys in my UK study with Madeleine Arnot (Reay, 2006), inhabit a psychic economy of class defined by fear, anxiety and unease, where failure looms large, and success is elusive, a space where they are positioned, and see themselves as losers in the intense competition that education has become.

Relationality raises issues not only pertaining to the relationships between classes but also of how different aspects of identity co-exist within class. At the most basic level, class is always gendered and raced. This is evident in the extent to which girls across class express higher levels of anxiety about educational performance than boys (Arnot *et al.*, 1999). Of course there are an array of intersectionalities that cross-cut class. Social classes are striated not only by gender, ethnicity, sexuality and (dis)ability but also by differing class fractions. Relations differ widely in terms of how different groupings within the same class position themselves and are positioned by others, and in terms of how their relationships to education have evolved. So to take one example, the white working class have a different relationship to education to many minority ethnic working–class groups. While the white working classes, as we have seen in the earlier section on temporality, often bring a collective memory of educational subordination and marginalization to schooling, some minority ethnic groups in the global North bring histories of educational achievement in their countries of origin, although migration has often brought economic impoverishment and downward mobility. Others, despite a lack of educational credentials, bring a strong conviction that a fresh start in a new educational system will provide crucial opportunities for educational advancement that were denied to their parents. Yet other ME groups, such as the African Caribbean in the UK, have, like their white working-class peers, learnt to live with educational failure, compounded, in their case, by racism. And these different ethnic groups are viewed very differently within the white middle-class imaginary, with the white working class regularly ethnicised as too white and labelled as white trash (Wray and Newitz, 1997), while some minority ethnic groups, such as the Chinese and Indians, are singled out as the acceptable face of working classness (Archer and Francis, 2006) – the so-called 'model minorities' (Leonardo, 2004).

Geographies of schooling: classed places and spaces

Finally we need to examine the extent to which place and space generate unequal classed relationships to schooling. Spatial protection and insulation have become a key strategy of the white middle classes in protecting their children, and their academic achievement, from classed others. For example, the private school system in the UK has historically been an effective mechanism for the affluent middle classes to separate their children off from polluting differences. But spatial separations are increasingly operating within a range of educational systems that criss-cross the globe (see, for example, Gulson (2007) in relation to the Australian educational system and Thrupp (2007) in relation to New Zealand). As Beverley Skeggs points out (2004: 15), in the twenty first century 'geographical referencing is one of the contemporary shorthand ways of speaking class'. This geographical referencing is particularly visible in schooling. The emergence of predominantly working-class schools as deprived, failing and disadvantaged and so needing either remediation or closing down has become a pervasive feature of educational debates, particularly in the US, Australia and the UK.

Recent research (Narodowski and Nores, 2002) provides many examples of educational spacialisation as schools are represented as either 'good' or 'bad' places by the media, the general public and school students themselves. As Brantlinger (2004) points out in the US context, increased emphasis on parental choice and diversity of school provision has allowed middle-class parents and schools to choose one another, leaving the working classes stranded in an increasingly segregated system mediated in many cases by housing costs and the ability to move house.

Over and above processes of increasing segregation and polarisation, education markets have an everyday spatial–temporal quality that varies between classes (Ball *et al.*, 1995). A rich body of research reveals relationships to both time (Reay *et al.*, 2005; Vincent and Ball, 2006) and space (Butler and Robson, 2003; Gewirtz *et al.*, 1995; Reay *et al.*, 2007) vary both across, and within, the working and middle classes. The middle classes are future-oriented. As Ball (2003: 163) argues, 'middle-class ontologies are founded upon incompleteness, they are about becoming, about the developmental self, about making something of yourself, realising yourself, realising your potential'. This encapsulates the middle-class relationship to schooling. It is about 'the making of the middle-class self'. In contrast, we could argue that schooling is about 'the unmaking of the working classes'. The working classes often lack the resources and requisite confidence for the futurity that characterises the middle classes. Time richness and poverty are also key, with the working classes relatively constrained in terms of how much time they can devote to their children's education. Different class groupings also have very different relationships to the local. While working-class groups are more likely to envisage their children's careers developing within a familiar locality and in familiar ways, the middle classes tend to have a more cosmopolitan orientation, characterised by an investment in children moving beyond the local into unfamiliar spheres and possibilities (Moore, 2004).

Such class relationships to educational places and spaces are all part of the ways in which, across the globe, economic inequalities become internalised, embodied in both those advantaged by the economic and social status quo and those who are disadvantaged. This lived experience of class varies across time and place, so class is experienced in different ways in different national contexts. The rural poor in China and the urban working class in the UK have very different classed relationships to education but share 'injuries of class' (Sennett and Cobb, 1970) that come from being educational outcasts (Bourdieu, 1999). Despite a continuing pervasive denial of class, it lies at the core of individuals' relationships to education, and a key sociological task is to uncover and understand its many varied manifestations. Only then can the gross educational inequalities class generates begin to be addressed.

Conclusion

History, geography and the relationships between social classes, as well as within them, are key to understanding not only social class inequalities in education but also the substance and texture of those inequalities; how they are enacted and experienced on an everyday basis in different cultural and national contexts. The history of educational systems (see, for example, Green, 1990) focuses our attention on the continuities, the ways in which social class inequalities are perpetuated despite changing economic conditions, and very different educational systems to those of a hundred, fifty, even twenty years ago.

A focus on spatiality emphasises the differences both within social classes as well as between them, revealing the differing forms of class inequalities across educational spaces and places. Clearly, class takes on a very different form and texture in Croatia to, say, Chile. And within different national contexts, the experience of educational inequalities of a working-class child in a predominantly working-class school is qualitatively different to that of the working-class child in a predominantly middle-class school. Geography increasingly matters within educational systems as diversity within schooling proliferates (Tomlinson, 2005) and segregation and polarisation increase (Söderström and Uusitalo, 2005; Webber and Butler, 2007). However, we also need to focus on class relationships within schooling in order to grasp the part education plays in social class inequalities. Increasingly, educational systems across the globe enshrine an educational competition premised on middle-class levels of resources and defined by rules that advantage the middle classes. As I have argued earlier, too often, for too long and across too many educational spaces, education has been about the making of one class at the cost of the unmaking of another.

References

Apple, M.W. (2003) 'Creating difference: neo-liberalism, neo-conservatism and the politics of educational reform', in J. Freeman-Moir and A. Scott (2003) *Yesterday's dreams: international and critical perspectives on education and social class*, Christchurch, NZ: Canterbury University Press.

Archer, L. and Francis, B. (2006) *Understanding minority ethnic achievement: the role of race, class, gender and 'success'*, London: Routledge.

Arnot, M., David, M. and Weiner, G. (1999) *Closing the gender gap: postwar education and social change*, Cambridge: Polity Press.

Ball, S. (2003) *Class strategies and the educational market: the middle-classes and social advantage*, London: RoutledgeFalmer.

—— Bowe, R. and Gewirtz, S. (1995) 'Circuits of schooling: a sociological exploration of parental choice of school in social class contexts', *Sociological Review* 43(1): 52–78.

Banks, O. (1955) *Parity and prestige in English secondary education: a study in educational sociology*, London: Routledge & Kegan Paul.

Bourdieu, P. (1999) 'The order of things', in P. Bourdieu, A. Accardo, G. Balazs, S. Beaud, F. Bonvin, E. Bourdieu, P. Bourgois, S. Broccolichi, P. Champagne, R. Christin, J.-P. Faguer, S. Garcia, R. Lenoir, F. Oeuvrard, M. Pialoux, L. Pinto, D. Podalydes, A. Sayad, C. Soulié and L.J.D. Wacquant *Weight of the world: social suffering in contemporary society*, Cambridge: Polity Press.

Brantlinger, E. (2004) *Dividing classes: how the middle class negotiates and rationalizes school choice*, New York: RoutledgeFalmer.

Butler, T. and Hamnett, C. (2007) 'The geography of education: introduction', *Urban Studies* 44(7): 1161–1174.

—— and Robson, G. (2003) *London calling: the middle classes and the re-making of Inner London*, London: Berg.

Cassen, R. and Kingdon, G. (2007) *Tackling low educational achievement*, York: Joseph Rowntree.

Connell, R. (2007) *Southern theory: the global dynamics of knowledge in social science*, Cambridge: Polity.

Fine, M., Burns, A., Torre, M. and Payne, Y. (2007) 'How class matters: the geography of educational desire and despair in schools and courts', in L Weis (ed.) *The way class works*, New York: Routledge.

Freeman-Moir, J. and Scott, A. (2003) *Yesterday's dreams: international and critical perspectives on education and social class*, Christchurch, NZ: Canterbury University Press.

Gamoran, A. (2007) 'Persisting social class inequality in US education', in L. Weis (ed.) *The way class works*, New York: Routledge.

Gewirtz, S., Ball, S. and Bowe, R. (1995) *Markets, choice and equity in education education*, Buckingham: Open University Press.

Gillborn, D. and Youdell, P. (2000) *Rationing education*, Buckingham: Open University Press.

Green, A. (1990) *Education and state formation: the rise of education systems in England, France and the USA*, Basingstoke: Macmillan Press.

Gulson, K. (2007) 'Repositioning schooling in Inner Sydney: urban renewal, an education market and the 'absent presence' of the middle classes', *Urban Studies* 44(7): 1377–1392.

Hallinger, P. and Heck, R. (1998) 'Exploring the school principal's contribution to school efectiveness 1980–1995', *School Effectiveness and School Improvement* 9(2): 157–191.

Kelly, S. (2007) 'Social class and tracking within schools', in L. Weis (ed.) *The way class works*, New York: Routledge.

Lareau, A. (2003) *Unequal childhoods*, Berkeley, CA: University of California Press.

Leonardo, Z. (2004) 'The souls of white folks', in D.Gillborn and G. Ladson-Billings (eds) *Multicultural education*, London and New York: RoutledgeFalmer.

Lupton, R. (2004) *Schools in disadvantaged areas: recognising context and raising quality*, CASE paper 76. London: CASE.

McDowell, L. (2007) 'Respect, deference, respectability and place: what is the problem with/for working-class boys?', *Geoforum* 38: 276–286.

McCleod, J. and Yates, L. (2006) *Making modern lives: subjectivity, schooling and social change*, Albany, NY: State University of NY Press.

Moore, R. (2004) *Education and society*, Cambridge: Polity Press.

Narodowski, M. and Nores, M. (2002) 'Socio-economic segregation with (without) competitive education policies: a comparative analysis of Argentina and Chile', *Comparative Education* 38(4): 429–451.

Paterson, L. and Iannelli, C. (2007) 'Social class and educational attainment: a comparative study of England, Wales and Scotland', *Sociology of Education* 80: 330–358.

Oakes, J. (1985) *Keeping track: how schools structure inequality*, New Haven, CT: Yale University Press.

Raveaud, M. and van Zanten, A. (2007) 'Choosing the local school: middle class parents' values and social and ethnic mix in London and Paris', *Journal of Education Policy* 22(1): 107–124.

Reay, D. (1998) Class work: mothers' involvement in their children's primary schooling, London: University College Press.

—— (2005) 'Beyond consciousness?: the psychic landscape of social class', *Sociology special issue on social class* 39(5): 911–928.

—— (2006) 'The zombie stalking English schools: social class and educational inequality', *British Journal of Educational Studies special issue on social justice* 54(3): 288–307.

—— (2008) 'Psycho-social aspects of white middle-class identities: desiring and defending against the class and ethnic 'other' in urban multiethnic schooling', *Sociology* 42(6): 1072–1088.

—— David, M.E. and Ball, S. (2005) Degrees of choice: social class, race and gender in higher education, Stoke-on-Trent: Trentham Books.

—— Hollingworth, S., Williams, K., Crozier, G., Jamieson, F., James, D. and Beedell, P. (2007) 'A darker shade of pale: whiteness, the middle-classes and multi-ethnic inner city schooling', *Sociology* 41(6): 1041–1060.

—— and Wiliam, D. (1999) '"I'll be a nothing": structure, agency and the construction of identity through assessment', *British Educational Research Journal* 25(3): 343–354.

Sennett, R. and Cobb, J. (1970) *The hidden injuries of class*.

Skeggs, B. (2004) *Class, self, culture*, London: Routledge.

Söderström, M. and Uusitalo, R. (2005) *School choice and segregation: evidence from an admission reform*, Working Paper 7, Uppsala, Sweden: IFAU (Institute for Labour Market Policy Evaluation).

Teese, R., Lamb, S. and Duru-Bellat, M. (eds) (2007) *International studies in educational inequality, theory and policy. Vol 1: Educational inequality: persistance and change*, The Netherlands: Springer.

Thrupp, M. (2007) 'School admissions and the segregation of school intakes in New Zealand cities, *Urban Studies* 44(7): 1393–1403.

Tomlinson, S. (2005) *Education in a post-welfare society*, Buckingham: Open University Press.

Vincent, C. and Ball, S. (2006) *Childcare choice and class practices: middle-class parents and their children*, London: Routledge.

Webber, R. and Butler, T. (2007) 'Classifying pupils by where they live: how well does this predict variations in their GCSE results', *Urban Studies* 44(7): 1229–1254.

Weis, L. (1990) *Working class without work: high school students in a de-industrialising economy*, New York: Routledge.

Wilkinson, R. and Pickett, K. (2009 forthcoming) *Inequality*, London: Penguin.

Willis, P. (1977) *Learning to labour*, Farnborough: Saxon House.

Wray, M. and Newirtz, A. (eds) (1997) *White trash: race and class in America*, New York: Routledge.

36

Interfaces between the sociology of education and the studies about youth in Brazil

Marília Pontes Sposito
Translation: Jessé Rebello de Souza Junior and Sophia Marzouk

The birth of sociology in Brazil and the studies about education have clustered, since the mid twentieth century, around several centers of research, many of which were dismantled by the authoritarian regime of the 1960s. Part of that tradition, which will be examined in this text, refers to a heuristic and suggestive way of articulating the interfaces between the sociology of education and the studies on youth that must be considered these days. It is not a case, therefore, of carrying out an appraisal of the vast sociological production about education in Brazil developed in recent years, but of problematizing important perspectives that have been guiding the development of this discipline in this country.[1]

In the 1950s, the budding sociological reflection, particularly that practiced in São Paulo under the guidance of Florestan Fernandes, considered that the specific domains of sociology—education, labor, culture, among others—should not imply excessive segmentation and specialization:

> As in any science, the sociological methods can be applied to the investigation and explanation of any particular social phenomenon without, for that reason, making it necessary to admit the existence of a special discipline with its own object and problems! ... In other aspects the more or less free usage of such expressions facilitates the identification of the content of the contributions, thereby simplifying the relations of the author to the public. This seems to be sufficient to justify their usage, once the intention of indefinitely subdividing the fields of Sociology lacks logical sense.
>
> (Fernandes, 1960: 29–30)

At that time, those guidelines were intended to understand the Brazilian society from the perspective of its historical singularity, an attitude that demanded a position of critical dialogue in the incorporation of the theories produced abroad. The sociologists of the so-called São Paulo School of Sociology were concerned with the issue of underdevelopment and consequently with questions related to development, but they defended a breakaway from the predominant dualist view that saw social change as part of a continuum that moved from underdevelopment to modernization. Thus, Brazil was seen as a *peculiar form of realization of the*

405

capitalist system where the economic vitality did not exclude, but rather associated with, the archaic elements of organization of the society and the persistent forms of inequality. The tensions were therefore not conceived as anomie, but as constitutive elements of society.

History and totality were the hallmarks of these theoretical–methodological guidelines, that is, it was necessary to understand the historical specificity of the Brazilian society in its multiple dimensions (political, economic, and cultural) (Bastos, 2002; Martins, 1998).

From this spectrum of orientations emerge the first works about the school institution, which takes center stage in the reflections of the sociology of education practiced in Brazil. However, these studies limited their concerns to the scenario of the recent processes of migration, industrialization, and urbanization, which brought to the school life a series of tensions that required analysis (Pereira, 1967, 1971, 1976).

At that time, an important text for research about the school, put forward in 1953 by Antonio Candido, already disclosed Durkheim's pedagogical illusion, which in its formulation defined the educational act as the unilateral action of the adult generation upon the immature, considered as a "clean slate" (Durkheim, 1970). It examined, and this may be the pioneering and most stimulating aspect of Candido's analyses, the conflictive potential and the tensions that were to exist in the relations between the adult generations and those under education, the latter offering resistance to the educational work carried out by the former.

Candido proposed study of the sociability inherent in the group of students and investigation of their expectations, which were not exhausted by the formal relationships predicted by the institution, and limited to the processes of teaching–learning. There is already at that point an analytical opening to the examination of aspects of school life that related to forms of student sociability that could be interfering with the life of the institution. He proposed an analytical perspective sufficiently open to less institutionalized and visible dimensions of school life, which were recovered by the sociology of education only after the 1970s, with the crises of explanations of purely structural slant within the context of theories about the school.[2]

The same theoretical and methodological inspiration—the historical singularity of Brazilian society and the totality of social processes—was present in the first studies about youths in Brazil. One of the central ideas of this perspective, which clearly produced a way of constructing the research problems, lay on the premise that, from the periphery and margins, one would better understand the movement of society as a whole, making it possible to inspect the principles that structure it (Bastos, 2002: 184). By situating youth as a social category, inspired by Karl Mannheim (Mannheim, 1968, 1973), Marialice Foracchi examined in her works the relative marginality of youngsters before the social structure and centers of power. Along these lines, her research positioned Brazilian university students as emerging actors in a dependent society who became protagonists of the political radicalism of the student movement of the 1960s (Foracchi, 1965, 1972).

The theme of juvenile radicalism was also investigated by Octavio Ianni in the 1960s, when he proposed the strong interrelation between the history of the capitalist regime and the history of the political awakening of the youth (Ianni, 1968). Thus, for these authors, the singularity of youth as a social category would contain the omissions, benefits, and tensions of a social configuration, because youth would represent the social category upon which "the crisis of the system falls in a particular way" (Foracchi, 1972).

Based on such framing of the historical problems and of the totality of the conditions that constitute the cultural and social specificities of Brazil, the interfaces between the sociology of education and youth are made clear, taking this theoretical–methodological assumption as a point of departure. These orientations refused an inadequate specialization of the sociological studies that were then being initiated both in the sociology of education and in the sociology of youth.

In the 1970s, when graduate studies were being structured in Brazil, the sociology of education reappears, albeit with significant difficulties to establish itself as a field of study (Cunha, 1981, 1992, 1994; Gouveia, 1989). Several studies were already pointing out these limitations, because some of the dilemmas experienced by academic research were due to difficulties in understanding the singularities of Brazilian society and of its system of education, in addition to the lack of deeper discussion about the theoretical frameworks, often born abroad, which founded the investigations. At any rate, the research centered around the processes of school inequalities, although the sociology of education could cover an extremely wide field beyond the school format, for "the mechanisms through which a society transmits to its members the knowledges, the know-how, and the know-how-to-be that it regards as necessary to its reproduction are of infinite variety" (Duru-Bellat and van Zanten, 1992: 1).[3]

With the birth of the new sociology of education in England after the studies about curriculum and language developed by Michel Young (1971) and Basil Bernstein (1975) in the early 1970s, and with the theoretical diversification of the 1980s through the incorporation of interactionist and ethnographic perspectives, the interest in the school institution persists. However, the research and analyses shift to the processes internal to the institution, attempting to understand how the routines, practices, modes of teaching and learning, the selection of contents, and the interactions in the classroom between teachers and pupils constitute elements of control, establish power relations, and engender inequalities, not just related to social classes, but also of ethnical and gender origin (Zago et al., 2003).

In Brazil, the emphases on the micro social situations favored by these researches renewed the sociological studies about the school, albeit with quite uneven results. The widening of theoretical frameworks also raised criticisms due to the clear difficulties in articulating the perspectives around a careful study of the school institution with the wider processes of a structural nature, as stated by Zaia Brandão in the field of educational research in Brazil (Brandão, 2002).

At any rate, the expanded theoretical arch and the new studies developed alongside the movement for the democratization of the country, reincorporating into the public debate the relevance of school education as a democratic right and the need to investigate and propose deep changes in school practices, thereby preventing the more perverse elements of the school system in what concerns the reproduction of inequalities.

The majority of studies about the school developed by the sociology of education in Brazil for some decades have not offered elements for the study of an important part of the school educational processes: the pupil. In its development, the sociological research about the school has increasingly been faced with the elements that constitute the school practices and in them the pupil's situation, obscured or absent in most analyses. In this period, an intense process of expansion of opportunities of access to schooling takes place, alongside the recognition of the crises in efficacy of the socializing action of the school institution, that is, aspects of the cultural and social domination and reproduction would be affected by the current school organization and its new public.[4] Somehow, the students became a problem for the practices and processes of cultural and social reproduction, and demanded a new perspective in the field of research.[5]

In this way, the studies that constituted the school reality as an object of analysis gradually turned to the examination of the pupil, reinforcing that set of possibilities proposed by Candido in the 1950s. As observed by Duru-Bellat and Agnes van Zanten, the situation of being a pupil must be a problematic object of investigation in the context of the sociological study of the school: one is not *born* a pupil; one *becomes* a pupil (1992). In order to consider such a perspective, at least three assumptions are needed: the dissociation between teaching and learning, which gives rise to the notion of school work to be carried out by children and youngsters; the recognition that this work by the pupil is not limited to respond to the explicit demands inscribed in the official programs and regulations, but to the implicit expectations of the institution and teachers. In this case, it is important to integrate the perceptions elaborated by the student in his/her extra-school socialization in the family and others spheres, with emphasis on the orientations that derive, not just from their social or ethnical origin, but from the fact of having been born male or female. Finally, the third assumption is *"the need to recognize that the pupil is also expression of* a peculiar form of his/her insertion in the life cycle—*the childhood and youth— specific categories endowed with relative autonomy in society and in the sociological literature"* (Duru-Bellat and Van Zanten, 1992: 179; our emphasis).

Around the investigation of the situation of the pupil (Perrenoud, 1994; Sacristan, 2005) and of the multiple agencies that constitute nowadays his/her process of socialization, some investigations are thus resumed about the youth in Brazil, particularly in the field of education. It aims therefore at thinking beyond the pupil, about the juvenile experience as a social condition built and rebuilt from vectors inscribed in social, gender, and ethnic-racial inequalities of contemporary society.

Partly owing to the loss of the monopoly of the process of educating new generations, as already observed, and also because of the internal characteristics of the current school systems, which are incapable of responding to the new challenges posed by their expansion, reflection about the school has been accompanied by a certain diagnostic of its crisis in which violence would be one of its main expressions (Sposito, 1998, 2001).[6]

The new public attending schools, mainly adolescents and youngsters, constitute an ever more autonomous universe of interactions within these, removed from the institutional references and bringing again in its specificity the need of a non-school perspective in the study of the school, what Barrère and Martuccelli (2000) call the non-school path. According to these authors, the autonomization of an adolescent sub-culture engenders for the pupils of mass education a reticence or opposition to the action of the normative school universe, which is itself in crisis. The school gradually ceases to be molded only by the criteria of adult sociability and witnesses the diffusion of the adolescent criteria of sociability, which demand a peculiar way of understanding and investigation (Barrère and Martuccelli, 2000: 256).

A consolidated idea in the studies of youth regards the fact that the modern juvenile condition would follow from the effects of the expansion of schooling and from the gradual withdrawal of children and youngsters from the world of labor, in such way that some authors state that "schooling creates youth" (Fanfani, 2006; Parsons, 1974). However, since the expansion of schooling in Brazil is recent, considering that in the last fifty years a significant fraction of the Brazilian youth remained outside school or had access only to the initial level of the school system, we should problematize some of these classical statements that attribute the modern constitution of youth to the school mediation. In other words, looking beyond the pupil, we need to understand that these agents experience today the juvenile condition in non-school spaces, and that they come into the institution with these practices and ways of life already consolidated, because they have sociability alternatives that they certainly want to preserve. Those who do not find, outside the school space, possibilities of rich interactions within their peer groups, either in leisure activities or in cultural consumption or production, share this symbolic universe filled with expectations, and thus hope to realize them as students. They certainly constitute these demands from the moment they leave childhood, because school is not the only agency that offers them cultural models for the experience of being young. We cannot fail to consider that styles, habits, and ways of life are also shaped by other agencies, which brings us to the idea of the multiple socializing spaces or ways of life that inscribe interactions and practices that go beyond the school boundaries and family life; that is, they pose the challenge of understanding how a stage of life—youth—and the insertion of subjects into the social structure are articulated in unequal and heterogeneous societies such as the Brazilian one.

Knowledge of the sociability, of the forms of solidarity, and of its conflicts and practices has been the incipient object of a sociology of youth in Brazil fairly articulated to the studies of the sociology of education.

Despite constituting important interfaces with the sociology of education, the studies of youngsters in Brazil embrace theoretical sources that derive from contributions from other domains of sociology.

A first outlook is related to the importance of the constitution of a specific field that appears in the sociology of the life stages or cycles, conceived as socio-historical constructions, that is to say, the constitution of sociological studies of childhood, youth, and old age.

Under this perspective, not just the specificities of each moment, but also the relationships between generations—adults and youth—are again studied, and characterized more by a certain notion of crisis than by the traditional idea of generation conflict (Barrère and Martuccelli, 2000; Dubet, 1987).

Sirota points out that within the sociological studies about childhood there can be observed a movement that goes from a sociology of schooling towards a sociology of socialization, in an attempt of "de-schooling" the approach to the child (2006, 2001: 27).

The studies about youth in Brazil, although still under consolidation, have opened up paths for the understanding of the condition of youngsters beyond the school universe. By centering on the young subjects and their dilemmas in the outlines of a society, which until recent years had increased the levels of social inequality, and faced with profound changes the world of labor, the sociology of youth has also dedicated itself to examining the conditions of insertion and maintenance of youngsters in a labor market in sharp evolution, interacting with several of the studies that have occupied the fields of interest of sociology in the world of labor and unemployment (Corrochano, 2001, 2008; Guimarães, 2005; Nakano, 2004).

Incorporating the issue of the multiple spaces of the circulation of urban youngsters,[7] several studies offer important clues for the understanding of the bonding elements of juvenile life through style groups and the so-called juvenile cultures (Abramo, 1994; Caiaffa, 1985; Carrano, 2002; Costa, 2003; Dayrell, 2005; Herschmann, 1997, 2000; Magnani and Mantese, 2007; Pais and Blass, 2004; Sposito, 1994; Tella, 2000; Vianna, 1987, 1997).

However, most of these studies have sought to break away from the classical models for the study of juvenile groups, which were anchored in the tradition of functionalism that privileged deviance and anomie as categories of analysis. A relative influence of the studies of the juvenile sub-cultures developed by the researchers of cultural studies from Birmingham, England, could be observed. The contributions from the sociology of the Portuguese youth made by José Machado Pais (1993, 2004) were also very important, as were the anthropological studies developed by Carles Feixa (1998, 2004), which examined this sociability based on the idea of juvenile cultures (somehow overcoming the assumption of sub-culture). More recently, the studies of urban anthropology conducted by José Guilherme Magnani (2007) about the juvenile circuits and trajectories in the city have also widened the perspective of analysis of the juvenile groups.

Similarly to the reflection carried out during the 1950s and 1960s, the research into youth in Brazil seeks to understand the outlines and practices that build youngsters as political actors. Some of the studies still devote their efforts to the analysis of the forms of student militancy, but have enlarged the spectrum of subjects investigated beyond the universe of higher education. Thus, the study of new formats and young collective actors that express new modalities of presence in the public sphere, both through cultural and artistic expressions and within movements that have marked the social struggles of the Brazilian society in the last years, as well as the movement of the agrarian society and the struggles of blacks against discrimination and racism has constituted an important challenge. The analysis of the presence of youngsters in collective actions draws from the theoretical tradition of the sociology of the social movement, of collective action, and of political participation (Sposito, 2000), preserving to some extent the perspectives of analysis that emerged in the 1950s.

The density of the field of studies about the youth under a sociological perspective resides in the challenge to articulate the analysis of the domains regarded as classical to sociology, namely, labor, culture, political action, and social movements. The studies of Brazilian youngsters in their diversity of modes of circulation, of practices, and of orientations derived from social, gender, and race conditions cannot be confined as a domain of analysis constituting a specialty refused in Brazil by the sociological tradition examined in this article.

The trajectories analyzed here illustrate a possible path for the interaction between the sociology of education and the studies about youth that reinforces theoretical–methodological orientations of the 1950s/1960s in Brazil. By seeking support in the sociological studies of the school institution within historical and cultural processes that constitute the singularities of Brazilian society, we reinforce the practice of sociology of education not restricted to a strictly school perspective of the domain of study. Inscribing the sociology of youth in the processes that give shape to contemporary Brazilian society, both from the point of view of the transformations of the world of labor, and under the optics of the sociology of collective action, social movements, and cultural practices, we rescue a theoretical–methodological point of view focused on the understanding of the singularities that constitute Brazil in its constant dialogue with international production. By examining the interfaces and specificities of this field of investigation, such a perspective refuses to inscribe the sociology of education or the sociology of youth into the segmented mode of the special sociologies. On the contrary, the basic assumption rests on the idea of a theoretical domain—the sociology—that tries to understand how the conflicts and tensions around the social reproduction, and the socialization and individualization processes take place from some privileged protagonists—the youngsters—in the condition of iceberg tips of contemporary social dilemmas (Melucci, 1997).

Notes

1   In another article—*Uma perspectiva não escolar no estudo sociológico da escola* [A non-school perspective in the sociological study of school]—I have analyzed the fruitfulness of that perspective for the analyses of social struggles somehow affected by the place that the school has acquired in contemporary society (Sposito, 2007).

2   The North American and European studies about the school establishments offer important contributions to the study of school life in its less visible and formalized aspects. An assessment of these orientations and their impacts on the sociology of education in Brazil can be found in the article by Leila Mafra (2003).

3   A promising example of inflexion in the field of sociological studies on education in Brazil can be seen in the studies about families and their relations to schooling developed since the 1990s by researchers such as Marialice Nogueira, Zaia Brandão, Nadir Zago, and Geraldo Romanelli, amongst others (Nogueira *et al.*, 2000).

4   Since the 1980s, an important group of sociological studies about education tried to understand the perverse consequences of the expansion of schooling out of precarious conditions, fostering an intense debate about the quality of the public education offered in Brazil. Education in conservative times has been the object of analysis in recent works that examined the neoliberal inclinations in educational policies (Haddad, 2008; Hypólito and Gandin, 2000).

5   When examining the emergence of the sociology of childhood, Sirota affirms that, in the context of the sociology of family or sociology of education, the child was a ghost character, almost invisible (Sirota, 2006). The same could be said about the young students in the works about school developed until recently within the context of the sociology of education in Brazil (Dayrell, 2002).

6   The studies conducted by François Dubet about the crisis of the socializing action of the school have inspired some of the works developed in Brazil about the relationships between youngsters and the school (Dubet, 1991, 1994, 1998, 2002).

7   One of the fragilities of the research about youth in Brazil is the little emphasis given to the study of rural youngsters.

References

Abramo, H. (1994) *Cenas juvenis: punks e darks no espetáculo urbano*, São Paulo: Escrita.

Barrère, A. and Martuccelli, D. (2000) "La fabrication des individus à l'école," in A. van Zanten (ed.) *L'école, L' état des savoirs*, Paris: Éditions la découverte.

Bastos, E.R. (2002) "Pensamento social da Escola Sociológica Paulista' in *O que ler na ciência social brasileira 1970–2002*, São Paulo: Ed. Sumaré.

Bernstein, B. (1975) *Langage et classes sociales*, Paris: Minuit.

Brandão, Z. (2002) *Pesquisa em Educação: conversas com pós-graduandos*, Rio de Janeiro: PUC/Loyola.

Caiafa, J. (1985) *Movimento punk na cidade: a invasão dos bandos sub*, Rio de Janeiro: Zahar.

Carrano, P.C.R (2002) *Os jovens e a cidade*, Rio de Janeiro: Relume Dumará.

Corrochano, M.C. (2001) "Jovens olhares sobre o trabalho: um estudo dos jovens operários e operárias de São Bernardo do Campo," Dissertação de Mestrado, FEUSP.

—— (2008) "O trabalho e a sua ausência: narrativas de jovens do Programa Bolsa Trabalho no município de São Paulo," Tese de Doutorado, FEUSP.

Costa, M.R. (1993) *Os carecas de subúrbio: caminhos de um nomadismo moderno*, Petrópolis: Vozes.

Cunha, L.A. (1981) "Educação e sociedade no Brasil," in *Boletim Informativo e Bibliográfico de Ciências Sociais, BIB*, Rio de Janeiro: Anpocs, no. 11.

—— (1992) "A educação na Sociologia: um objeto rejeitado?" in *Cadernos CEDES*, 27, Campinas: Papirus.

—— (1992) "Reflexões sobre as condições sociais de produção da sociologia da educação: primeiras aproximações," in *Tempo Social, Revista de Sociologia da USP*. São Paulo: Departamento de Sociologia, 4(1–2) (edited in 1994).

Dayrell, J. (2002) "Juventude e Escola," in M.P. Sposito (coord.) *Juventude e escolarização (1980/1998)* Série Estado do conhecimento, número 7, Brasília: MEC/INEP, Comped.

—— (2005) *A música entra em cena: o rap e o funk na socialização da juventude*, Belo Horizonte: Humanitas.

Dubet, F. (1987) *La galére: jeunes en survie*, Paris: Fayard.

—— (1991) *Les lycéens*, Paris: Seuil.

—— (1994) *Sociologie de l'expérience*, Paris: Seuil.

—— (1998) *Dans quelle société vivons-nous?* Paris: Seuil.

—— (2002) *Le déclin de l'institution*, Paris, Seuil.

411

Durkheim, E. (1970) *Sociologia e Filosofia*, Rio de Janeiro: Editora Forense.

Duru-Bellat, M. and van Zanten, A. (1992) *Sociologie de l'école*, Paris: Armand Colin.

Fanfani, E. (2006) 'Culturas juvenles y cultura escolaro', in *SNTE, IV Congresso Nacional de Educação, documento de discussion*, Tomo I., México.

Feixa, C. (1998) *De jóvenes, bandas y tribus: antropologia de la juventud*, Barcelona: Ariel.

—— (2004) "Los estúdios sobre culturas juveniles en España—1960–2004," in *Revista de Estudios de Juventud*, Madrid, no.64.

Fernandes, F. (1960) *Ensaios de sociologia geral e aplicada*, São Paulo: Pioneira.

Foracchi, M.M. (1965) *O estudante e a transformação da sociedade brasileira*, São Paulo: Nacional.

—— (1972) *A juventude na sociedade moderna*, São Paulo: Pioneira.

Gouveia, A.J. (1989) "As ciências sociais e a pesquisa sobre educação," in *Tempo Social, Revista de Sociologia da USP*, SP: 1(1).

Guimarães, N.A. (2005) "Trabalho: uma categoria-chave no imaginário juvenil?" in H. Abramo and P.P. Branco (eds) *Retratos da juventude brasileira. Análises de uma pesquisa nacional*, São Paulo: Instituto da Cidadania/Fundação Perseu Abramo.

Haddad, S. (ed.) (2008) *Banco Mundial, Omc e FMI: o impacto nas políticas educacionais*, vol. 1, São Paulo: Cortez.

Herschmann, M. (ed.) (1997) *Abalando os anos 90: funk e hip hop, globalização, violência e estilo cultural*, Rio de Janeiro: Rocco.

—— (2000) *O funk e o hip hop invadem a cena*, Rio de Janeiro: Editora UFRJ.

Hypolito A.M. and Gandin, L.A. (eds) (2000) *Educação em tempos de incerteza*, Belo Horizonte: Autêntica.

Ianni, O. (1968) "O jovem radical," in S. Britto (ed.) *Sociologia da Juventude I*, Rio de Janeiro: Zahar.

Mafra, L.A. (2003) "A Sociologia dos estabelecimentos escolares: passado e presente de um campo e pesquisa em re-construção," in N. Zago, M.P. Carvalho and R.A.T. Vilela (eds) *Itinerários de pesquisa, Perspectivas qualitativas em Sociologia da Educação*, Rio de Janeiro: DP&A editora.

Magnani, J.G. and Mantese, B. (eds) (2007) *Jovens na metrópole, Etnografias de circuitos de lazer, encontro e sociabilidade*, São Paulo: Terceiro Nome.

Mannheim, K. (1968) "O problema da juventude na sociedade moderna," in *Sociologia da Juventude I*, vol. 1, Rio de Janeiro: Zahar.

—— (1973) "Funções das gerações novas," in M.M. Foracchi and L. Pereira, *Educação e Sociedade*, São Paulo: Cia Editora Nacional.

Martins, J.S. (1998) *Florestan. Sociologia e Consciência Social no Brasil*, São Paulo, EDUSP/FAPESP.

Melucci, A. (1997) "Juventude, tempo e movimentos sociais," in *Juventude e contemporaneidade, Revista Brasileira de Educação*, São Paulo: ANPED, números 5/6.

Nakano, M. (2004) "Jovens no encontro de gerações: democracia e laços solidários no mundo do trabalho," Tese de doutorado, FEUSP.

Nogueira, M. and Romanelli, G. and Zago, N. (eds) (2000) *Família & Escola: trajetórias de escolarização em camadas médias e populares*, Rio de Janeiro: Vozes.

Pais, J.M. (1993) *Culturas juvenis*, Lisboa: Imprensa Nacional/Casa da Moeda.

—— and Blass, L.M.S. (eds) (2004) *Tribos urbanas: produção artística e identidades*, São Paulo: Annablume.

Parsons, T. (1974) "La classe en tant que système social: quelques-unes de ses fonctions dans la société américaine," in A. Gras, A *Sociologie de l'éducation. Textes fondamentaux*, Paris: Larousse Université.

Pereira, J.B. (1976) *A escola secundária numa sociedade em mudança*, 2nd edn, São Paulo: Pioneira.

Pereira, L. (1967) *A escola numa área metropolitan*, São Paulo: Pioneira.

—— (1971) "Rendimentos e deficiências do ensino primário brasileiro," in L. Pereira *Estudos sobre o Brasil contemporâneo*, São Paulo: Pioneira.

Perrenoud, P. (1994) *Le métier d'élève et le sens du travail scolaire*, Paris: ESSE.

Sacristan, J.G. (2005) *O aluno como invenção*, Porto Alegre: Artmed.

Sirota, H. (2001) "Emergência de uma sociologia da Infância: evolução do objeto e do olhar" in *Cadernos de Pesquisa*, São Paulo: Fundação Carlos Chagas, no. 112.

—— (2006) *Élements pour une sociologie de l'enfance*, Paris: PUF.

Sposito, M.P. (1994) "A sociabilidade juvenil e a rua: novos conflitos e ação coletiva na cidade," in *Tempo Social, Revista de Sociologia da USP*, São Paulo: Departamento de Sociologia, FFLCH/USP, 5(1–2).

—— (1998) "A instituição escolar e a violência," in *Cadernos de Pesquisa*, Fundação Carlos Chagas, 104.

—— (2000) "Algumas hipóteses sobre as relações entre juventude, educação e movimentos sociais," in *Revista Brasileira de Educação*, São Paulo: ANPED número 13, Jan/April: 73–94.

—— (2001) "Um breve balanço da pesquisa sobre violência escolar no Brasil," in *Educação e Pesquisa*, São Paulo: FEUSP, 27(1).

—— (2007) "Uma perspectiva não-escolar no estudo sociológico da escola," in L. Paixão and N. Zago (eds) *Sociologia da Educação, Pesquisa e realidade brasileira*, Rio de Janeiro: Vozes.

Tella, M.A.P. (2000) *Atitude, arte, cultura e autoconhecimento: o rap como voz da periferia*, São Paulo: Departamento de Ciências Sociais da PUC-SP (Dissertação, Mestrado).

Vianna, H. (1987) *O mundo funk carioca*, Rio de Janeiro: Jorge Zahar.

—— (ed.) (1997) *Galeras cariocas: territórios de conflitos e encontros culturais*, Rio de Janeiro: Editora da UFRJ.

Young, M. (1971) *Knowledge and control*, London: Collier Macmillan.

Zago, N., Carvalho, M. and Vilela, R. (eds) (2003) *Itinerários de pesquisa: perspectivas qualitativas em sociologia da educação*, Rio de Janeiro: DP&A Editora.

37

Social class and schooling

Lois Weis

Researchers have long argued that school outcomes, whether achievement or attainment, are linked in large part to social class background (Coleman *et al.*, 1966; Gamoran, 2001, 2008; Gamoran and Long, 2007). In the United States, what is particularly stunning, perhaps, is that in spite of the massification of the US system of education during the twentieth century, differences by class have persisted at largely consistent levels. Campbell *et al.*, (2000), for example, suggest persistent relative class differences in achievement related outcomes (as linked to NAEP data over three decades), while Hout *et al.*, (1993) indicate that class differences in attainment have remained relatively constant over the course of the twentieth century.[1]

Raftery and Hout's (1993) theory of "maximally maintained inequality" helps explain such persistence. Under the theory of "maximally maintained inequality," as the privileged classes are generally better positioned to grasp new opportunities than their non-privileged counterparts, it is only when a level of attainment is saturated for the privileged group that members of the less privileged classes have the opportunity to catch up. Under conditions of massification, then, "maximally maintained inequality" demands that educational allocation must be understood "as an expanding pie: each group's piece of the pie becomes larger, but the relative differences among pieces are preserved" (Gamoran, 2008: 170). Lucas (2001) tweaks this theory by suggesting that, even as quantitative distinctions fade in access to the overall educational system, inequality will be "effectively maintained" through increased differentiation within particular strata (Gamoran, 2008; Shavit *et al.*, 2007), a phenomenon empirically documented in the US and elsewhere.

With careful attention to empirical trends, Gamoran (2001, 2008) predicts that educational outcomes as related to social class background will continue "largely unabated throughout the twenty-first century despite much rhetoric and a few policies directed against it" (2001: 135). While there is ample evidence to suggest that this is the case, such research fails to address the mechanisms through which parents and schools are actively linked to the reproduction of social class inequalities. Close attention to empirical work on such "enabling mechanisms" both allows us to chronicle the ways in which class is produced via the concrete, everyday practices of parents and schools, and simultaneously opens up possibilities for intervention.

Here I outline the ways in which parents and schools contribute actively to the reproduction of inequalities of social class; in other words, the ways in which parents and schools embody class-related practices while simultaneously producing class-linked economic and social outcomes. While not intended to be a comprehensive review of the literature on this set of issues, I highlight work in three key areas: official knowledge and its distribution; valued parental capital and the ways in which such capital is linked to schools; and the production of youth social identities.[2] Although these issues must be explored in contexts other than first-wave industrialized nations, examples here are drawn largely from the US and UK. I will raise the question of class production in an increasingly globalized context at the end of the essay.

Social class has been defined in a variety of ways and, as Erik Olin Wright notes, "the concept of class is one of the most contested within sociology." (2008: 25). While class must be understood and theorized primarily in relation to the economy, we must additionally recognize that class rests fundamentally in the "lived" realm in that it organizes the social, cultural, and material world in exceptionally powerful ways. The books we read, or if we read at all; our travel destinations and mode of travel; the clothes we wear; the foods we eat; whether we have orthodontically straightened teeth; where (and if) our children go to school, with whom, and under what staff expectations and treatment; the "look" and "feel" of home- and school-based interventions if our children "fail"; where we feel most comfortable and with whom; where we live and the nature of our housing; and, specifically in the United States, whether we have health insurance and, if so, what kind and with what coverage, are all profoundly classed experiences, rooted not only in material realities but in culturally based expectations and practices. Given massive shifts in the global economy and accompanying neoliberal policies and practices, which produce deepening inequalities both within and between nations (Aron-Dine and Shapiro, 2006; Piketty and Saez, 2003; Reich, 1991, 2001), a recognition of the structuring effects of social class has never been more pressing.

This is not to deny the ongoing and partially independent effects of race in relation to the production of class, a point that is particularly salient in the United States, yet increasingly important in the UK, France, Germany, and Canada, where large immigrant populations of color have significantly altered the social and economic landscape. Rather it is to suggest that class is a *fundamental organizer* of social experience, both "objective" and subjective," an organizer that has been largely eclipsed over the past twenty years by other forms of social interrogation and analyses. As Cameron McCarthy (1990) reminds us, however, the experiences and subjectivities of racially subordinated groups cannot be read entirely off class. I now turn to research on three specific drivers of social class formation as linked to families and schools.

Official knowledge and its distribution

Spurred by calls in England in the 1970s for a "new sociology of education," scholars address questions related to what constitutes "official" knowledge and the ways in which such knowledge is differentially distributed through schools .The theoretical starting point for most of these analyses is articulated by Michael F.D. Young (1971), who argues that there is a "dialectical relationship between access to power and the opportunity to legitimate dominant categories, and the processes by which the availability of such categories to some groups enable them to assert power and control over others" (p. 31). Young (1971), Bernstein (1977), Anyon (1979), Bourdieu (1977), Apple (1979/2004), Whitty (1985) and others argue that the organization of knowledge, the forms of its transmission, and the assessment of its acquisition are factors in the production of class and class relations in advanced capitalist societies.

415

As Geoff Whitty (1985) makes clear, and as Weis *et al.* argue elsewhere (2006), mainstream sociologists often assume that the most important school-related question is that of "access" to a range of educational institutions—who has it; what blocks it; and what might encourage it. While not an unimportant set of questions, the assumption in most such research is that simple access to schooling will ameliorate the apparent handicaps associated with a working class and/or poor background. In sharp distinction to this research genre, scholars began to focus on the nature of knowledge itself and the ways in which "legitimate" knowledge works for some and not others. Young (1971), for example, discusses the ways in which particular kinds of knowledge are validated in the academy—knowledge that is "pure," "general," and "academic." In contrast, knowledge that is "applied," "specific," and "vocational" is marginalized. Although this distinction is arbitrary, it powerfully serves to keep particular (elite and relatively elite) groups in control of the official school curriculum and, by extension, tightly linked occupational and economic outcomes (Weis *et al.*, 2006).

Important research has also been done on the ways in which knowledge is distributed across groups. Jean Anyon (1980, 1981) offers a compelling set of essays related to the ways in which knowledge is differentially distributed across student social class background in the US. Working-class students, for example, are offered knowledge as rote memorization and a series of structured tasks, while knowledge distributed to students in executive elite public (state-supported in the US parlance) schools is far more challenging. Students in these latter schools are socialized into an academic culture of excellence, while working-class students are socialized into a culture of rote memorization.

The school-based practice of tracking (placing low- and high-achieving students in instructional environments tailored to their current level of academic achievement) is heavily implicated in the reproduction of social class. Although the assumption is that all students benefit from such an arrangement, Sean Kelly (2008) argues that four decades of empirical research lead to the conclusion that "low-track classrooms do not offer as rich an educational environment as high-track classrooms" and that "high track students benefit the most from the practice of tracking," with low-track students being left far behind (Kelly, 2008: 211). Significantly, track placement is a strong, independent predictor of college entrance patterns (Erigha and Carbonaro, 2006; Rosenbaum, 1976), with social class being a consistently strong and independent predictor of track placement (Kelly, 2004, 2008; Oakes, 1985).

Given massive changes in the global economy and accompanying class reconfiguration in countries all over the world, it is important to broaden research on the official curriculum (both nature of and distribution of), with particular attention to the ways in which certain groups are creating class through the instantiation of a newly forged (or re-affirmed) selective tradition, one that works to the benefit of some and not others. The hegemonic role of English as the language of science, technology, and the academy is key here, as some groups are better positioned to access and function in this now indisputable language of power. While some such work has been done over the years, we have remarkably little scholarship that tracks and theorizes social class in relation to schooling under new global conditions. In sum, then, we need to take seriously the emerging stratification map as related to contested notions of "official" knowledge and its distribution globally.

Valued parental capital

Large-scale studies attest to the importance of family background in children's academic achievement, academic attainment (how far children go in school), occupational status and income. Given this uniformly strong finding, it is important to probe what it is about the family and the family's relationship to the school that produces outcomes of interest.

Engaging in extensive ethnographic work, and employing Pierre Bourdieu's (1977, 1984) theoretical insights, Annette Lareau (1987) argues that middle-class parents, in contrast to working-class parents, have the cultural capital necessary to actualize positive ties with schools, in that they have more information about schooling, as well as the social capital to connect with other parents. More recently (2003), she turns her attention to class habitus, specifically the ethnographically informed cultural logic of child rearing, arguing that middle-class parents across race (African American and White in the United States) engage in a process of "concerted cultivation," which results in a "robust sense of entitlement" among middle-class youth (2003: 2), a sense of entitlement that "plays an especially important role in institutional settings, where middle-class children learn to question adults and address them as relative equals" (p. 2). Working-class and poor children, in contrast, are raised under strictures more closely approximating the "accomplishment of natural growth" (p. 30). While working-class and poor parents may similarly love their children, "the cultural logic of child rearing at home is out of synch with the standards of institutions" (p. 3), wherein schools, for example, value child-rearing practices associated with concerted cultivation, suggestive of the fact that middle-class children, simply by virtue of parenting practices, will always have an edge in school.

Drawing on follow-up data, Lareau and Weininger (2008) find remarkably consistent behavior with regard to decisions about college choice:

> Class-specific cultural orientations to child rearing retain their purchase on family behavior—at least in the area of relations to institutions—approximately ten years after the original data collection took place. Thus the behavior of middle class parents in managing their children's high school career and transition into college can be viewed straightforwardly as an extension of the same "concerted cultivation" child rearing strategy they practiced earlier. Similarly, the propensity of working class and poor parents to assume that their children's education is the responsibility of professional educators constitutes an extension of the "accomplishment of natural growth" approach.
>
> (pp. 142–143)

Ellen Brantlinger (2003) further directs our attention to the role of parents in processes of class-based stratification. Her ethnographic study of professional middle-class parents suggests that members of the educated middle class generate bifurcated notions of students: those that win based upon merit and those that lose based upon their own deficiencies. More specifically, "losers," students unfamiliar with the dominant, middle-class system of values and codes (appropriate language, ways of behaving, and so forth), are deemed culturally and intellectually deficient and therefore deserving of less; "winners," on the other hand, those familiar with the moral, linguistic, and behavioral codes privy to the middle class, are both rewarded for their hard work and academic success, and discursively constructed as deserving of their privileged status. Brantlinger's research suggests that middle-class parents actively maintain and simultaneously ideologically neutralize class-based stratification through schools.

Important work in the UK by Diane Reay indicates that, even when middle-class parents intentionally send their children to mixed urban state schools, thereby being seen as "acting against [class] self-interest educationally" (Reay, 2008: 88), they end up constructing themselves and their children as privileged in such multi-ethnic, working-class settings. Paralleling Brantlinger's research, middle-class white parents increasingly work towards their own class interest, as both parents and children begin to define themselves as morally and educationally superior to their working-class counterparts, although they send their children to working-class schools with the opposite intent. The intractable nature of class as acted upon and transmitted by parents is clearly apparent in this study.

Carol Vincent and Stephen Ball extend this discussion in their exploration of choices related to childcare and class practices in the UK (2006). Based on an intense ethnographic investigation of middle-class parenting choices and practices, Vincent and Ball indicate that, while such families are highly dependent upon the involvement of these women/mothers in careers and highly paid jobs as part of being middle class, they nevertheless practice "professional mothering," wherein they juggle intense work and family commitments in order to position their children for comparable adult class status. Such juggling lies firmly in the gendered realm, where

> women's employment and mothering histories can be plotted on an "investment continuum," where women move between time-investments in their children or in their paid work, in most cases trying to manage the two to the detriment of neither, and being trailed by varying amounts of guilt, responsibility and anxiety.

(p. 164)

Adding a critically important gendered component to work in this area, Vincent and Ball's research extends the literature on the way class works through parenting choices, practices, and linkages to schools.

Active production of identities

In the above sections, I focus on the ways in which schools and families directly shape and produce class and class inequalities. This ignores the fact that students produce class on their own located, cultural level, albeit in relation to parents, communities, schools, and the economy. Paul Willis (1977) breaks important theoretical ground in this regard by focusing our attention on students themselves in the process of class production and reproduction. In his now classic *Learning to labour* (1977), Willis focuses on a group of working-class boys in the UK Midlands as they proceed through the last two years of secondary school and into the work force. Rather than passively accept the socialization messages embedded in the school, the "lads" actively differentiate themselves from the "ear'oles" (so named because they simply sit and listen) and school meanings in general, categorizing both as effeminate and unrelated to the "real" masculine world of work, thereby reproducing at their own cultural level key elements of social structure. As Willis notes, "The difficult thing to explain about how middle class kids get middle class jobs is why others let them. The difficult thing to explain about how working class kids get working class jobs is why they let themselves" (p. 1). Breaking new theoretical ground, Willis probes the ways in which the semi-autonomous level of culture is implicated in the sustainment of social structure.

Taking up the challenge afforded by Willis, we have excellent studies of class (and class linked specifically to race) (re)production that theorize around the role of students as they engage processes of identity construction in school (Foley, 1990; Lee, 2005; Solomon, 1992; Weis, 1990; Wexler, 1992). Most such studies have, however, been done in the industrialized West, and it is important that we broaden our research to include studies of cultural production in a range of national contexts. In addition, while acting back on school meanings appears to constitute a key element of identity work among specific groups of disenfranchised youth across national contexts, scholars have yet to address, in a sustained fashion, the consequences of such "resistance" over time, and in relation to new economic circumstances. While Willis suggests that working class student "resistance" is tied to class-linked labor market possibilities, while simultaneously limiting the intensification of demands for production on the shop floor, what we do not know is where such resistance "sits" as youth grow older, particularly in shifting economic times. Although this genre of study—and specifically the body of work known as "resistance theory"—offers a great deal with respect to what we know about students and schools, serving ultimately to invert understandings as to the absolute power of educational institutions and their ability to "name" others, we must theoretically situate such studies within massively changing economic context.

In *Class reunion* (Weis, 2004), a fifteen-year follow-up study of white working-class males and females who originally appear in *Working class without work* (Weis, 1990), I take up this challenge. Rather than growing up to be part of any kind of romantic collective that capitalizes upon and engages oppositional behavior within the walls of the factory, the (1985–1986) secondary school male resistors are, at the age of 30–31, almost uniformly bouncing between the homes of their mother and current girlfriend, earning very little money, and having no steady job to speak of. Given male wage-earning capacity under the former industrial economy, in earlier decades they would, in all likelihood, have begun and sustained a family of their own, cashing in on both the capital–labor accord and the secret guarantees of earning the family wage: sacrifice, reward, and dignity. Now in their early thirties, the high school "resistors" are almost uniformly marginally employed and bereft of collective, except that which is aimed at the consumption of alcohol, drugs, car races, dirt bikes, and the like. This suggests that the shift in the global economy demands that our entire notion of cultural resistance—what it is and where it deposits as youth grow up—must be challenged.

Kathleen Nolan and Jean Anyon (2004) affirm this point, arguing that oppositional identity as produced and enacted by black urban youth in high-poverty contexts "does not lead to the shop floor. Rather, in this postindustrial era of mass incarceration, oppositional behavior by working-class youth of color in educational institutions often leads them directly into the criminal justice system" (p. 133).

Conclusion

This essay traverses territory on social class and schooling. I argue that research strongly indicates that "official" knowledge and its distribution; parental capital and ways in which such capital is linked to schools; and youth located cultures/identities as produced inside educational institutions contribute in important ways to the reproduction of social class. Although this essay is based primarily on quantitative and qualitative research rooted in the United States, and, secondarily, the UK, issues highlighted here inevitably play out in a wide variety of countries, although in specific national and local parlance. A variety of jobs—whether those for working-class or middle-class individuals—are increasingly exported from highly industrialized countries such as the United States, United Kingdom, and Japan to places where multinational companies can hire both unskilled and highly skilled/well-educated laborers at lower pay and without benefits. In the US, for example, we are witnessing decreasing economic opportunities for the working class and poor who live in particular gender and racial/ethnic relational forms, as well as intensified and pressure-packed expectations directed towards the privileged. This evolving

419

set of international economic and human–resource relations affects the educational aspirations and apathies of younger generations in a variety of countries, wherein the push and pull dynamics of globalization (in the sense of pushing certain kinds of job outside the borders of first-wave industrialized nations, while simultaneously pulling such jobs to nations such as China and India) exert particular class-linked forms of pressure on schools, families, and youth.

In addition, the movement of peoples across national borders, including those who possess "flexible citizenship" by virtue of possession of high-status knowledge—for example, high-powered intellectuals, engineers and medical professionals who are seduced to work in economically powerful nations—bring new demands to school systems in economically powerful nations. By way of example, upper middle class Hong Kong Chinese parents in Vancouver have little use for what they see as the "soft" curriculum associated with North American schooling (Li, 2005). Given class-linked cultural and economic capital, such privileged world citizens are demanding more strongly framed knowledge and less of the "fluff" that they associate with Western, particularly North American, schooling, even though they currently reside in Canada. This scene is being played out in schools up and down the Pacific North American coast, where a new form of "white flight" is taking place as white parents are removing their children from schools heavily populated by Asians, a phenomenon linked both to what white parents often see as the inappropriate demand for more strongly framed and intensified knowledge on the part of Asian parents, as well as the indisputable fact that their children are not, overall, performing as well (see Lee, 2009, however, on the myth of the model minority). Such intensifying transnational migration patterns have implications for class formation in the US and elsewhere, as class is now being produced and re-aligned in relation to large numbers of recent immigrants, whether those who possess "flexible citizenship" or those who enter economically powerful nations with little more than the clothes on their back, a proportion of whom do relatively well in school (Centrie, 2004; Rumbaut and Portes, 2001).

This means that class and class relations must be studied and theorized in relation to the increasingly interconnected world (Crespo Sancho, 2009; Li, 2008; Weis, 2004, 2008). Given shared international press in relation to the flight of jobs from first-wave industrialized nations, as well as the movement of both unskilled and professional workers *to* such job-exporting nations (at one and the same moment as a greater number and variety of jobs are being *exported* to nations such as China and India), we must consider the ways in which class is constitutive of newly articulated and lived out race/ethnic and gender dynamics in an international context (for an important example, see Zhao, 2008). The movement of peoples and accompanying processes of transnationalization wherein people live "here and there" (Crespo Sancho, 2009) have deep implications for class formation, particularly in first-wave industrialized nations that are increasingly host to new immigrants. As migrants position and reposition themselves inside new global circumstances, the nature of class relations inevitably changes, ushering in a new era of race/class relations.

The bottom line here is that our worldwide economic and social context is shifting dramatically, demanding both increased attention to the production of class *and* new ways of understanding such production in a wide variety of nations. In light of the review offered in this chapter, we need to focus specifically on the ways in which parents and children of varying social class background and across race/ethnicity/nation experience and interact with educational institutions from pre-K through post-graduate school, as well as the ways in which educational institutions themselves change in response to new global circumstances. This all must be tilted towards understanding the production of broader class relations and outcomes. Updating and extending earlier important work on knowledge and its distribution; parental capital and its "effects"; and the production of youth culture and identities will enable us to make great strides towards understanding schooling and social class in the twenty-first century.

Notes

1   Adam Gamoran (2001, 2008) powerfully highlights notions of "maximally" and "effectively maintained" inequality in two recent essays.

2   It is not my intent to discuss all ways that families and schools are linked to the production of class inequalities. High stakes testing, for example, is not covered in this essay, although there is ample research that suggests that such testing is linked to such production.

References

Anyon, J. (1979) "Ideology and United States history textbooks," *Harvard Educational Review* 49(3): 361–386.

—— (1980) "Social class and the hidden curriculum of work," *Journal of Education* 162(1): 67–92.

—— (1981) "Social class and school knowledge," *Curriculum Inquiry* 11(1): 3–42.

Apple, M.W. (1979/2004) *Ideology and curriculum*, Boston, MA and New York: Routledge.

Aron-Dine, A. and Shapiro, I. (2006) *New data show extraordinary jump in income concentration in 2004*, Washington, DC: Center on Budget and Policy Priorities. Available online at www.cbpp.org/7–10–06inc.pdf (accessed March 31, 2007).

Bernstein, B. (1977) "Social class, language, and socialization," in J. Karabel and A.H. Halsey (eds) *Power and ideology in education*, New York: Oxford University Press.

Bourdieu, P. (1977) "Symbolic power," in D. Gleeson (ed.) *Identity and structure: Issues in the sociology of education*, Driffield: Nafferton Books.

—— (1984) *Distinction: a social critique of the judgment of taste* (trans. R. Nice), Cambridge, MA: Harvard University Press.

Brantlinger, E. (2003) *Dividing classes: how the middle class negotiates and rationalizes school advantage*, New York: Routledge.

Campbell, J.R., Hombo, C.M. and Mazzeo, J. (2000) *NAEP trends in academic progress: three decades of school performance*, NCES document no. 2000–469. Washington, DC: US Department of Education.

Centrie, C. (2004) *New lives, new freedoms: the identity formation of Vietnamese immigrant youth in an American high school*, New York: LJB Scholarly Press.

Coleman, J., Campbell, E., Hobson, C., McPartland, J., Weinfeld, F. and York, R. (1966) *Equality of educational opportunity*, Washington, DC: US Government Printing Office.

Crespo Sancho, C. (2009) "Migration in the age of globalization: transnationalism, identity, social class and education of Latino families," unpublished Ph.d. dissertation, University at Buffalo, State University of New York.

Erigha, M. and Carbonaro, W. (2006) "Who goes to college? Linking tracking to post-secondary enrollment," Unpublished manuscript, Center for Research on Educational Opportunity.

Foley, D. (1990) *Learning capitalist culture: deep in the heart of Texas*, Philadelphia, PA: University of Pennsylvania Press.

Gamoran, A. (2001) "American schooling and educational inequality: a forecast for the 21st century," *Sociology of education, Special Issue, Current of thought: sociology of education in the dawn of the 21st century*, 74: 135–153.

—— (2008) "Persisting social class inequality in U.S. education," in L. Weis (ed.) *The way class works: readings on school, family, and the economy*, New York and London: Routledge.

—— and Long, D.A. (2007) "Equality of educational opportunity: a 40–year retrospective," in R. Teese, S. Lamb and M. Duru-Bellat (eds) *International studies in educational inequality: theory and policy*, Vol. 1, New York: Springer Press.

Hout, M., Raftery, A. and Bell, E.O. (1993) "Making the grade: educational stratification in the United States, 1925–1989," in Y. Shavit and H.-P. Blossfeld (eds) *Persistent inequality: changing educational attainment in thirteen countries*, Boulder, CO: Westview Press, pp. 25–49.

Kelly, S. (2004) "Do increased levels of parental involvement account for the social class difference in track placement?" *Social Science Research* 33: 626–659.

—— (2008) "Social class and tracking within schools," in L. Weis (ed.) *The way class works: readings on school, family and the economy*, New York: Routledge, pp. 210–224.

Lareau, A. (1987) "Social class differences in family–school relationships: the importance of cultural capital," *Sociology of Education* 60: 73–85.

—— (2003) *Unequal childhoods: class, race and family life*, Berkeley, CA: University of California Press.

—— and Weininger, E. (2008) "Class and the transition to adulthood," in A. Lareau and D. Conley (eds) *Social class: how does it work*, New York: Russell Sage Foundation, pp. 119–151.

Lee, S. (2005) *Up against whiteness: race, school, and immigrant youth*, New York: Teachers College Press.

—— (2009) *Unraveling the "model minority" stereotype: listening to Asian American youth* (revised edn), New York: Teachers College Press.

Li, G. (2005) *Culturally contested pedagogy: battles of literacy and schooling between mainstream teachers and Asian immigrant parents*, Albany, NY: State University of New York Press.

—— (2008) "Parenting practices and schooling: the way class works for new immigrant groups," in L. Weis (ed.) *The way class works: readings on school, family and the economy*, New York: Routledge, pp. 149–166.

Lucas, S. (2001) "Effectively maintained inequality: education transitions, track mobility, and social background effects," *American Journal of Sociology* 106: 1642–1690.

McCarthy, C. (1990) *Race and curriculum*, Philadelphia, PA: Falmer Press.

Nolan, K. and Anyon, J. (2004) "Learning to do time; Willis's model of cultural reproduction in an era of postindustrialism, globalization and mass incarceration," in N. Dolby and G. Dimitriadis (eds) *Learning to labor in new times*, New York: Routledge, pp. 133–150.

Oakes, J. (1985) *Keeping track: how schools structure inequality*, New Haven, CT: Yale University Press.

Piketty, T. and Saez, E. (2003) "Income inequality in the US, 1913–1998," *Quarterly Journal of Economics* 118(1): 1–39.

Raftery, A.E. and Hout, M. (1993) "Maximally maintained inequality: expansion, reform, and opportunity in Irish education, 1921–1975," *Sociology of Education* 66: 22–39.

Reay, D. (2008) "Class out of place: the white middle classes and intersectionalities of class and 'race' in urban state schooling in England," in L. Weis (ed.) *The way class works: readings on school, family and the economy*, New York: Routledge, pp. 87–99.

Reich, R. (1991) *The work of nations: preparing ourselves for 21st-century capitalism*, New York: Alfred A. Knopf.

—— (2001) *The future of success*, New York: Alfred A. Knopf.

Rosenbaum, J. (1976) *Making inequality: the hidden curriculum of high school tracking*, New York: John Wiley & Sons.

Rumbaut, R.G. and Portes, A. (eds) (2001) *Ethnicities: children of immigrants in America*, Berkeley, CA: University of California Press; New York: Russell Sage Foundation.

Shavit, Y., Arum, R. and Gamoran, A. (eds) (2007) *Stratification in higher education: a comparative study*, Palo Alto, CA: Stanford University Press.

Solomon, P. (1992) *Black resistence in high school*, Albany, NY: State University of New York Press.

Vincent, C. and Ball, S. (2006) *Childcare, choice and class practices: middle-class parents and their children*, New York: Routledge.

Weis, L. (1990) *Working class without work: high school students in a de-industrializing economy*, New York: Routledge.

—— (2004) *Class reunion: the remaking of the American white working class*, New York: Routledge.

—— (2008) *The way class works: readings on school, family, and the economy*, New York and London: Routledge.

—— Dimitriadis, G. and McCarthy, C. (eds) (2006) *Ideology, curruculum and the new sociology of education: revisiting the work of Michael Apple*, New York: Routledge.

Wexler, P. (1992) *Becoming somebody: toward a social psychology of school*, London: Routledge.

Whitty, G. (1985) *Sociology and school knowledge*, London: Methuen.

Willis, P. (1977) *Learning to labour: how working class kids get working class jobs*, Westmead, England: Saxon House Press.

Wright, E.O. (2008) "The continuing importance of class analaysis," in L. Weis, (ed.) *The way class works: readings on school, family and the economy*, New York: Routledge, pp. 25–43.

Young, M. (ed.) (1971) *Knowledge and control: new directions for the sociology of education*, London: Collier-Macmillan.

Zhao, Y. (2008) "Positioning and positioned in globalizing socialist China: higher education choices, experiences and career aspirations among Chinese college students," unpublished Ph.D. dissertation, University at Buffalo, State University of New York.

Routledge International Handbooks of Education Series

The Routledge International Handbook of Critical Education

Edited by **Michael W. Apple,**
Wayne Au and
Luis Armando Gandin

The Routledge International Handbook of Critical Education is the first authoritative reference work to provide an international analysis of the relationship between power, knowledge, education, and schooling. Rather than focusing solely on questions of how we teach efficiently and effectively, contributors to this volume push further to also think critically about education's relationship to economic, political, and cultural power. The various sections of this book integrate into their analyses the conceptual, political, pedagogic, and practical histories, tensions, and resources that have established critical education as one of the most vital and growing movements within the field of education, including topics such as:

- Social Movements and Pedagogic Work
- Critical Research Methods for Critical Education
- The Politics of Practice and the Recreation of Theory
- The Freirian Legacy

With a comprehensive introduction by Michael W. Apple, Wayne Au, and Luis Armando Gandin, along with thirty five newly commissioned pieces by some of the most prestigious education scholars in the world, this *Handbook* provides the definitive statement on the state of critical education and on its possibilities for the future.

Feb 2009: 246x174: 512pp
Hb: 978-0-415-95861-5

To Order:
Call (Credit Cards): +44 (0) 1235 400524
Internet: www.routledge.com/education
Email: education@routledge.com

Also Available by Stephen J. Ball

Education plc

Understanding Private Sector Participation in Public Sector Education

Stephen J. Ball

Is the privatisation of state education defendable? Did the public sector ever provide a fair education for all learners?

In *Education plc*, Stephen Ball provides a comprehensive, analytic and empirical account of the privatisation of education. He questions the kind of future we want for education and what role privatisation and the private sector may have in that future. Using policy sociology to describe and critically analyse changes in policy, policy technologies and policy regimes, he looks at the ethical and democratic impacts of these changes and raises the following questions:

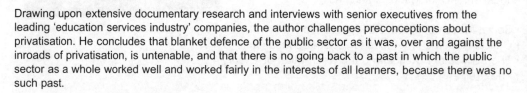

• Is there a legitimacy for privatisation based on the convergence of interests between business and the 'third way' state?
• Is the extent and value of private participation in public education misunderstood?
• How is the selling of private company services linked to the remodelling of schools?
• Why have the technical and political issues of privatisation been considered but ethical issues almost totally neglected?
• What is happening here, beyond mere technical changes in the form of public service delivery?
• Is education policy being spoken by new voices?

Drawing upon extensive documentary research and interviews with senior executives from the leading 'education services industry' companies, the author challenges preconceptions about privatisation. He concludes that blanket defence of the public sector as it was, over and against the inroads of privatisation, is untenable, and that there is no going back to a past in which the public sector as a whole worked well and worked fairly in the interests of all learners, because there was no such past.

This book breaks new ground and builds on Stephen Ball's previous work on education policy. It should appeal to those researching and studying in the fields of social policy, policy analysis, sociology of education, education research and social economics.

2007: 234x156: 232pp
Hb: 978-0-415-39940-1
Pb: 978-0-415-39941-8

To Order:
Call (Credit Cards): +44 (0) 1235 400524
Internet: www.routledge.com/education
Email: education@routledge.com

Also Available by Michael W. Apple

Global Crises, Social Justice, and Education

Edited by Michael W. Apple

Education cannot be understood today without recognizing that nearly all educational policies and practices are strongly influenced by an increasingly integrated international economy. Reforms in one country have significant effects in others, just as immigration and population tides from one area to another have tremendous impacts on what counts as official knowledge and responsive and effective education. But what are the realities of these global crises that so many people are experiencing and how do their effects on education resonate throughout the world?

Global Crises, Social Justice, and Education looks into the ways we understand globalization and education by getting specific about what committed educators can do to counter the relations of dominance and subordination around the world. From some of the world's leading critical educators and activists, this timely new collection provides thorough and detailed analyses of four specific centers of global crisis: the United States, Japan, Israel/Palestine, and Mexico. Each chapter engages in a powerful and critical analysis of what exactly is occurring in these regions and counters with an equally compelling critical portrayal of the educational work being done to interrupt global dominance and subordination. Without settling for vague ideas or romantic slogans of hope, *Global Crises, Social Justice, and Education* offers real, concrete examples and strategies that will contribute to ongoing movements and counter-hegemonic struggles already active in education today.

December 2009: 234x156: 224pp

Hb: 978-0-415-99596-2

Pb: 978-0-415-99597-9

To Order:
Call (Credit Cards): +44 (0) 1235 400524
Internet: www.routledge.com/education
Email: education@routledge.com

Routledge International
Handbooks of Education Series

The Routledge International
Companion to
Multicultural Education

Edited by James A . Banks

This volume is the first authoritative reference work to
provide a truly comprehensive international description
and analysis of multicultural education around the
world. It is organized around key concepts and uses
case studies from various nations in different parts of
the world to exemplify and illustrate the concepts.
Case studies are from many nations, including the
United States, the United Kingdom, Canada,
Australia, France, Germany, Spain, Norway, Bulgaria,
Russia, South Africa, Japan, China, India, New
Zealand, Malaysia, Singapore, Indonesia, Brazil, and
Mexico. Two chapters focus on regions - Latin
America and the French-speaking nations in Africa.
The book is divided into ten sections, covering
theory and research pertaining to curriculum reform,
immigration and citizenship, language, religion, and
the education of ethnic and cultural minority groups
among other topics.

The Routledge International
Companion to Multicultural
Education

Edited by James A. Banks

With 40 newly commissioned pieces written by a prestigious group of internationally
renowned scholars, *The Routledge International Companion to Multicultural Education*
provides the definitive statement on the state of multicultural education and on its
possibilities for the future.

Mar 2009: 246x174: 592pp

Hb: 978-0-415-96230-8

To Order:
Call (Credit Cards): +44 (0) 1235 400524
Internet: www.routledge.com/education
Email: education@routledge.com